THE LIFE OF A
SOUTH AFRICAN TRIBE

THE LIFE OF
A
SOUTH
AFRICAN
TRIBE

BY HENRI A. JUNOD

II. MENTAL LIFE

UNIVERSITY BOOKS INC. NEW HYDE PARK, NEW YORK

First Printing August 1962
Second Printing March 1966

FOURTH PART

AGRICULTURAL AND INDUSTRIAL LIFE

In the first volume of this work, I have tried to give a description of the Social Life of the tribe by depicting its customs in relation to the individual, communal and national life. In the second volume I shall consider its Mental and Spiritual Life, its Literature and Music, its Religion, Magic and Morality. The Agricultural and Industrial Life will afford a transition from the one to the other of these subjects ; this belongs primarily to the social manifestations of the tribal life, but the imagination displayed by sculptors, weavers, potters (or rather "potteresses") brings it also into relation with the mental. I do not however pretend to draw a sharp line of distinction between these two domains, as the mental life is reflected in the social customs, and the social idea strongly dominates the mental life of the tribe.

CHAPTER I

AGRICULTURAL LIFE

A. THE LAND AND THE NATIVE SYSTEM OF LAND TENURE.

I. *The nature of the soil.*

Considering that the Thongas dwell in the South of Africa, a part of the world which is generally rocky and sterile, Nature has favoured them to no inconsiderable extent as regards the soil of their country.

The coast belt is an ancient ocean-bed, and consists of dunes of white or reddish-brown sand, extending from the South-West to the North-East; between these dunes are basin-shaped hollows, at the bottom of which are ponds of stagnant water.

The pond in the hollow.

The hillocks rarely reach a greater elevation than 150 feet above the sea level (120 feet above the level of the lakes). The sand on the dunes is naturally quite unproductive, but the vegetation which has managed to develop there during past centuries, and the forests, which are fairly dense in certain spots, have gradually deposited a thin layer of soil, and this, when mixed with the sand and watered in due season by the rains, is capable of producing abundant crops. The hollows *(nhlangwa, mu-mi)* (1) are hardly more fertile than the dunes, although their continuous moisture

(1) For linguists, I indicate the class to which Native nouns belong. See the explanation of classes or genders, Part V. Chap. I. *Mu-mi* are the prefixes of the singular

2

is favourable to the growth of certain plants. But by the side of the sand *(pfunye)* and the hillocks *(shitshunga)*, here and there, is found a sort of black earth, containing a large proportion of vegetable detritus, in which maize, sweet potatoes, sugar cane, etc. thrive splendidly. *Ñyaka* is the name given to this black soil : it is found at the foot of the hills which run from Lourenço Marques in the direction of Morakwen, and extends for a distance of some fourteen to eighteen miles. Several small springs rise at the bottom of this gentle slope, and tend to form a curious marsh, covered with beautiful tropical growths, of which gigantic palms *(mimale)* are the most striking. These are found in forests covering hundreds of acres, with an impenetrable undergrowth of ferns, enormous rushes and evergreen shrubs : magnificent palm groves, where apes, wild boars and large storks find a safe retreat.

Between this marsh of primitive mud and the hills extends the arable tract of nyaka. There the fields are lovely ; maize can be grown all the year round. In other places the nyaka is parched and dry, as in the valley of the Lower Nkomati, from the point where it leaves the Lebombo hills to the elbow of Magule. Here the annual overflow of the river deposits on the low-lying plains a fertilising slime, as is the case in Egypt. It is strange to see, during the winter, tufts of grass which were carried down by the stream, months before, caught in the branches of the trees and suspended some 15 to 20 feet above the ground!

The sand of the coast belt is replaced in the hinterland of Matjolo, in the low level between the Nkomati and the Bila plain, etc. by another kind of soil called *hundjusi*. This is a reddish earth containing much sand, but much finer and more fertile than the sand proper.

On leaving the coast belt we reach the Lebombo and Longwe hills, which are composed of a hard reddish porphyraceous stone. Further West, a broad plain extends from the Lebombo to the Drakensberg Mountains, in some places consisting of a greyish or brownish clay, in other regions very dry and stony. The foot

and plural of Cl. II. When a noun begins with *shi*, it belongs to Cl. shi-psi, with *li* to Cl. li-tin, with *bu* to the Class bu-ma. As a rule nouns will be given in their singular form.

Phot. P. Berthoud.
Mimale palmtrees in the marshes near Lourenço Marques.

of the Drakensberg is very fertile, as water flows abundantly from the mountain gorges. Some rivers, however, on reaching the Low Country, dry up entirely, at least during the winter time.

4

The soil of Spelonken is of a similar nature and very well watered. So the Thongas, who settled in Zoutpansberg, found there a soil which was, in certain respects, more favourable to agriculture than their sandy dunes or their hundjusi on the Coast.

Such is Mother Earth for the Thongas. They call it *misaba*, the plural form of nsaba, grains of sand. This word plainly shows that they come from sandy regions. For them the earth is a collection of grains of sand.

II. *Native System of Land Tenure.*

The Native population, taken as a whole, is a very sparse one. Let us consider the Ronga territory, for instance : 100,000 in a territory which may be estimated at 5000 square miles ; this gives a population of only 20 per square mile. The country is, however, very unequally peopled. Natives will only settle in spots where water is found, and, the sand dunes to which I have previously referred being exceedingly dry, they mainly inhabit the slopes of the hills and the immediate neighbourhood of the marshes already described.

To confine myself, amongst the Rongas, to the region in which I have principally travelled, that is to say the neighbourhood of Rikatla, the villages of Nondwane, which extend along a somewhat narrow strip (800 yards wide by 5 miles in length), stretching from the border of Mabota as far as Morakwen, contained in 1880 a population which I should estimate at about 1100 (1). This gives over 350 inhabitants to the square mile. Taking everything therefore into consideration, it may be confidently asserted that the country can easily support its population ; in fact it could support one three or four times as large.

It is important to bear all these circumstances in mind in order to be able properly to appreciate the Ba-Ronga laws relating to landed property.

(1) This population has very much diminished since the Ronga Portuguese war in 1894.

By law the soil belongs to the Chief, but only that, through him, it may be, become general property. No one can buy land. It is gratuitously assigned to any and all who wish to settle in the country. The mere fact of *kondza*, viz., making submission to the chief (Vol. I, p. 433), entitles the Native to as much land as may be necessary for his subsistence.

It will be readily understood, however, that the supreme Chief, however small his territory may be, can hardly assume the duty of marking out the various small allotments for his subjects. In ordinary practice this is done by the headmen of the villages (numzane), the important men of the country, (I will call them A), who obtain the grant of considerable tracts of land, which they apportion amongst those under their jurisdiction. They and their near relatives cultivate the most fertile parts of these tracts, or districts, and when any one (say B) wishes to settle on their reserve, they "cut the bush" for him, "tjemela nhoba," to use the technical expression ; they accompany the would-be-settler to an uncultivated piece of land and together they fix the boundaries of a plot of ground which is then assigned to him. A tree, the corner of a lake, a well, or an anthill, may be used as landmarks in this primitive surveying operation. The new-comer will clear as much of the land as he can, till it, and the fields, together with the trees they contain, will become thenceforth his property. Should any of his relatives wish to settle near him, he will, in his turn, assign to them a portion of his land, which they may clear and cultivate ; and so the distribution continues. Supposing B is not satisfied with his allotment, or is unable to live on neighbourly terms with A, and builds his hut in some other spot, he cannot sell or otherwise dispose of his land, as it must revert to A, the original owner. On the other hand, should B die, his wife would inherit his gardens. Should father or mother die, the property would naturally pass to the sons, who would divide the fields between their wives. Thus we see that real estate is hereditary, but cannot be sold. A similar state of affairs would result should A, the numzane, who ranks almost as a petty chief, leave the country : all his rights in connection with the tract that he may have occupied for the last fifty years will cease with his departure.

It might be supposed that the title to real estate being gratuitously given, was not very secure. Quite the contrary! Once
having assigned a plot of ground to B, A has no further
interest in it ; B is the absolute master of his land and of all that
it produces. I recollect one day, at Rikatla, being almost dumb-
founded when our own petty chief, Muzila, came to me and
humbly asked permission to pick up some of the nkanye fruit,
which I had left to rot on the ground! The land at the station
(about 5 acres in extent) was granted to us by Maphunga, chief
of Nondwane, and here was his relative and representative
coming to me, requesting permission to make use of the produce
of a tree which was useless to me! And he would, moreover,
have made a like polite request to the meanest of his subjects,
had he been desirous of making use of anything growing in
that man's fields. I must admit that I have often admired the
practical character of the Native law in this connection, and,
still more so, the respect paid by the original proprietor to the
individual to whom he has voluntarily assigned a portion of his
land. It is, of course, entirely to the interest of the numzane
to keep his protégé on his land, for he adds considerably to its
value by cultivating an otherwise useless bush (nhoba). He also
helps to people his protector's tract of country, and thus to
increase his strength ; finally he makes certain payments in kind
or rather in labour. The Chief gladly welcomes new-comers,
as they will assist in the tilling of his fields each year, and the
more labourers he has, the better for him !   As for the headman
of the village, the possessor of a "small country" (tikwana, dji-ma),
his protégés will be always ready to do him a good turn on occasion,
and he is therefore quite content to assign to them portions of his
domain. Human nature is, however, much the same everywhere,
and this system, which appears so perfect at first sight, has also
its drawbacks. A numzane, or even a Chief, will give to his
favourites the best pieces of land. A clever flatterer, or one
knowing how to regale the great man with beer in due season, and
thus gain his good graces, will be apt to receive an allotment of
good, fertile forest land, while a less fortunate individual, out of
favour at Court, will only get a piece of barren hill-side which has

7

already been tilled and abandoned as exhausted. I noticed this at Rikatla. Muzila favoured his pagan subjects, who joined him in his drinking bouts, and invited him to orgies in their villages, at the expense of the Christians who no longer brew the byala beer. Thus interest at Court works here as elsewhere, although it be based on nothing nobler than pots of beer!

The difficulties of this system also become apparent in the more thickly populated parts of the country, where all the land has been assigned and taken up. The women look round for fresh arable land and may, wittingly or unwittingly, encroach on the ground of another numzane. There is, indeed, a neutral zone, vaguely defined, of which no one has as yet taken possession, as it has not been needed : the wild fruits growing there are common property ; any one who likes can gather them. When the population increases, the inhabitants of the more congested districts go and appropriate this land without any kind of formality. Such was the case when the people of Libombo, dwelling on the edge of the palm-marsh, (to the East of Rikatla), sent their women to the hill-side to clear a piece of land which Muzila considered to be his property. This petty chief sent remonstrances to Nkolele, his colleague, headman of the village of Libombo ; but they were not heeded. Then the men of Rikatla hid themselves in the bushes surrounding the spot in question, and, when the women commenced to hoe the ground, rushed out upon them, seized their hoes, and drove them off. This was the "fait patent," the actionable proceeding, which was necessary in order to have the matter brought before the Chief's tribunal. This incident doubtless led the parties interested to define their respective boundaries more carefully.

To go and till another's land would be quite impossible, even taboo, between people of different clans. In the present case, the Rikatla and Libombo men belonged to the same Nondwane country. There was a good understanding between them. The Rikatla men would not have dared to plough a field without permission on Mabota's ground, the boundary of which was on the other side of the big water-tree (muhlu).

As regards *boundary marks* between the different clans, they consist of natural objects such as rivers, big trees, etc. To define the boundaries of their gardens, Natives dig an ordinary ditch (ndjilekana, mu-mi) round the field, of about one foot in depth, which can be plainly traced even after the lapse of several years, when the field may have become fallow land and overgrown with vegetation.

The question of *roads* is a somewhat difficult, and often thorny one to settle. Where has one the right to go ? And if, after having used a certain path for years, you suddenly find it blocked by some individual whose field it skirts, and who has taken a fancy to hoe it up, what is to be done ? To try to come to some friendly agreement is always the most practical course. How often have we not experienced this difficulty with our cart ! The agriculturists were the more annoyed because we required a road three or four yards wide, while the Native footpaths are only little tracks of 15 to 20 inches in width. Being the only "carriage folk" in the district, we often had to ask permission to be allowed to pass, and have rarely met with any kind of refusal, for the Black is a reasonable being and quite appreciates the fact that roads are a necessity. If they see that a road is "ripening" (wupfile), viz., that it is more and more frequently used, they bow before the facts ; here, as everywhere else, custom makes the law.

At the present moment matters have been made much more simple as the Portuguese Government has constructed wide highways in all the more frequented parts of the country.

B. PRODUCTS OF THE SOIL.

I. *Cereals.*

"Hosi ya psone i *psithjama*" — "Their king is the *maize*," says Mboza. This cereal is indeed the most widely cultivated in Thongaland. It is called *psifake* in Djonga. In the more fertile regions of the North, the size of the cobs and of the grains (nhleke, yin-tin) is much larger than on the sandy dunes of the Ba-Ronga. So the people of Khosen make fun of the Ba-Ronga and compare their mealies with the small pimples of their tattooing (tinhleke ta Ba-Ronga). If maize is the most appreciated cereal, it is certainly not the most ancient known to the tribe. Owing to its modernity, no doubt, it is not subject to any taboo. It is sown and harvested without any rite. At Christmas time, when the first cobs are edible, people joyfully feast on the new crop. They cook some of them in the ashes, but they allow the rest to ripen and dry upon the stalks. Although no taboo prevents any owner of a field from eating the first mealies whenever it suits him, Mboza asserts that people who have obtained green mealies before the other inhabitants of the village, do not precede them in the enjoyment of this much appreciated food : "It would cause jealousy amongst them." This reason is perhaps at the bottom of the luma taboo (I, p. 394). Moreover they fear lest they might have to share their good luck with all their friends !

. Next in importance comes the *mabele*, plur. of bele, dji-ma (Ro.), ñwahuba (Dj.), the *millet* or *Kafir corn*. This is the well-known millet which we give to birds in cages, small, round, blackish grains which grow on a stem 3 to 5 feet high, in elongated cylindrical ears. Kafir corn is pounded, or ground, and may be eaten in the form of flour. But its main use is to provide the yeast for the Kafir beer. As already pointed out (I. p. 42) the mabele is one of the oldest cereals known to the Thongas. It is the ritual cereal, that used for the "shimhimbi," the dish offered to the confined mother or prepared for the luma ceremony. Its seeds undergo a certain treatment before being sown : the sub-chief blows upon them after having taken a small piece of a certain root in his mouth ; this root obtained from a kind of juncus found in the mountains, is supposed to have the power of keeping the ants away from the seeds. He distributes the seeds thus treated amongst his people, and every one mixes some of them with his own supply. Men of the reigning family alone possess this root. Later on, when the time for sowing has come, it is taboo for subjects to precede their chiefs or sub-chiefs in sowing mabele. The bones are consulted. Should the "madjuma" fall showing their mouths (see Part VI), it is the answer of the gods. They say: "Yes! this is the proper time! The mabele will do well!"

10

The horoscope is all the more satisfactory if the astragalus of the sheep is in the positive position, showing that the chiefs are happy and prosperous. At harvest time, Kafir corn is subject to the luma taboo, as explained in detail in a preceding chapter. All these rites prove the antiquity of the cereal.

The *sorghum*, (*maphila*, plur. of phila, dji-ma), is also extensively cultivated all through Thongaland. There are many kinds of sorghum : the *phila* proper, with reddish and white grains, the *timba*, whose stem has a sweet taste and is enjoyed almost as much as sugar cane, the *shikombe*, whose ears are curved, the *ntjyaka*, with a particularly elongated ear and the *djabana* with white seeds. The last has a somewhat bitter taste and is consequently spared by the birds, which are so fond of the other kinds of cereals that people have to stay in their gardens for months together to scare them away.

Rice (*mpunga*, mu-mi) is met with in a few districts only, notably on the Lower Nkomati, where the tide provides a natural irrigation, and in some depressions of the coast belt, especially near Rikatla. I could not say when it was introduced amongst the Thongas. In Shiluvane, its cultivation was entirely unknown in 1890, when it was brought thither by Lourenço Marques Natives. However a storekeeper told me that rice had been extensively cultivated in the country between 1870 and 1880. As it is subject to certain taboos (see later on) it may be that it is older than one would at first suspect.

In some places another cereal is cultivated, the *likoro* (probably Eleusine indica).

II. *Vegetables.*

Three Leguminosae play a considerable part in the feeding of the tribe : the ground nut, Kafir pea and Kafir bean.

a) The ground-nut, (Arachis hypogea), (rumane plur. marumane or tinumane (1) (Ro.), timanga (Dj.), is extensively cultivated,

(1) Rumane (cl, dji-ma) can form its plural either by prefixing *ma* which is the regular way, or by prefixing *tin*, which is exceptional. In the second case, the *n* of the prefix causes the initial *r* to permute into *n*.

being of every day use in the Thonga culinary art, in which it provides the fatty principles. This curious Papillonacea, after having blossomed, elongates the peduncle of the flower, which enters the ground, and the seed grows in the soil, well protected against the rays of the sun. Its taste is delicious, either prepared as a sauce to season mealie flour, or roasted. When there are no nuts inside the shells, which often happens, Thongas call the empty shells *mabvobo*. They say : "The ground nuts have refused" — "Ma yalile marumane." But this is a euphemism. They mean that the *baloyi*, the wizards, have refused to let them grow or, rather, have stolen them from their shells during the night (See Part VI).

b) Another Leguminosa frequently cultivated is the *nyume* (yi-tin (Ro.), *ndlowu*, yi-tin, (Dj.), the *Kafir pea*. This also grows in the earth, like the ground nut. It is much coarser than the European pea, but is twice or three times as large and very nourishing. This vegetable is subject to very curious taboos amongst the Rongas. Whilst all other seeds are sown in one and the same garden, this must be planted in a separate patch, and the tinyume field must be shut off from the others by a fence of thorns. Men are allowed to plant them, but, as soon as they have grown a little, only women can enter the field. Should a man imprudently do so, he would transgress a severe taboo. The danger is twofold : firstly the man himself would be punished ; he would get a hydrocele. But the owners of the field would also suffer : the crops would fail. They would reproach the transgressor with these words : "You have taken away (hungula) the strength of our peas !" In order to prevent any such mischance, the husband of the woman who owns the field goes and treats (daha) it in the following manner : he throws his assagay across the field, in the direction of the four cardinal points. Then the danger is removed and men can pass through the plot. It might be supposed that this taboo was of the same kind as that which rested on bananas, for instance, when they were still new in the country and feared on that account. But it would not seem that the Kafir pea is a recent innovation in Thonga agriculture. It has been known for a long time. Another taboo in connection with Kafir peas is this :

during the first year of her married life a woman is not allowed to plant them.

Amongst the Ba-Pedi of the Transvaal the planting of Kafir peas is taboo. They are said to prevent rain and to cause intense and injurious heat.

c) The Kafir bean, mbawen, yi-tin, (Ro.), nyawa, yi-tin, (Dj.), is a small round brownish seed, with a pleasant flavour, eaten either green or dry. I do not know of any taboo in regard to it.

Vegetables of other families also contribute to the food of the Thongas.

Sweet potatoes (nhlata, mu-mi) cultivated either in the sand of the hills or in the richer nyaka of the marshes, are a great resource, especially when they are farinaceous and not too watery. Their leaves (matsimbo) are also used as a vegetable.

Pumpkins also constitute one of the chief articles of diet of the Blacks, from one end of Africa to the other. They are of several kinds : the *ranga* (dji-ma) and *gawana* (dji-ma) of medium size, the *shilutana*, small, sometimes pear-shaped, the *khalabatla* (djima), huge water melons, with white or pink pulp and black pips, which are eaten both cooked and uncooked. Pumpkins are not grown for their fruit alone, as the leaves of certain kinds, especially the ranga, are excellent eating, and make a very good substitute for spinach. The flowers also are greatly appreciated by the Natives. Some kinds of pumpkins are used to make gourds and calabashes. (See I. p. 50.)

There are some taboos to be mentioned in connection with the *ranga*, which seems to be the oldest kind of pumpkin known to the Bantus (1). We have seen (I. p. 184) that girls are not allowed to walk amongst the leaves and must take special precautions when plucking them. It is taboo to plant any kind of pumpkin before the Chief and the sub-chief. They are subject to the law of hierarchy in the same way as Kafir corn. The prohibition is so conscientiously observed that, should an old man keep the people waiting and be too slow in planting his

(1) See in Meinhof, *Grundriss einer Lautlehre der Bantusprachen*, p. 183, the different forms of this word, which was *tanga* in Ur-Bantu. Compare Torrend, *Comparative Grammar of the South African Languages, p. 89*.

pumpkins, another will go to the field and plant some seeds in it without the old man's knowledge ; then people will venture to plant in their own gardens. Transgression of this taboo is said to be punished by lumbago.

There are, besides, many wild plants which the housewives collect and of which they make excellent dishes : the *tjeke*, a kind of Chenopodiacea, which is also used as a medicine to induce forgetfulness ; the *nkakana*, a pretty plant of the Cucurbitaceae family, which climbs up the dried stems of maize after the harvest, and of which they eat the leaves and also the pretty little oval pointed fruit.

Tomatoes (shimati) are also found growing round the villages, where they propagate themselves, and seem to prosper the better the less they are cared for : the Natives take them to Lourenço Marques for sale in very original baskets made of a single palm leaf, with the follicles artistically twisted. I am unable to say when they were introduced. There is a agreeable kind of small tomato which grows wild in Khosen, about the size of a cherry.

Natives also cultivate a kind of *onion* (nyala, yi-tin), smaller than the European varieties, which they very much appreciate in their sauces.

The sugar cane (moba, mu-mi) is never grown in large plantations, but you find it on the Coast, as well as in Zoutpansberg, cultivated on a small scale, either for eating, or for preparing the strong *shiwayawaya* drink, which I shall describe later on.

The *pine-apple* (lalasi, dji-ma) has spread as far as the Bilene country and must be of ancient date ; it differs considerably from the Natal pine-apple, being longer, coarser and not so sweet. In many villages large plantations are to be seen.

Tobacco (fole, dji-ma) is also wide-spread and seems to have been cultivated for a long time. A curious fact is that its cultivation is the business of the men, and women have nothing to do with it. Amongst the Ba-Ronga it is sown first in a damp spot in the marsh, in a special little garden called *shibibi*, and, when it has grown a little, is planted out (simeka) on the hill, near the villages. When nearly ripe the lower leaves are first cut, dried and ground "ku djinga," as a foretaste! Then the other leaves are cut, covered with nkuhlu foliage and left for three days to mature (ku pfundja) ; a string is then passed through them and they are hung to a tree to dry. Before they have become brittle, they are rolled up together so as to form the "mfunge," a bunch of tobacco leaves which is sometimes three or four feet long by 4 to 6 inches thick. This bunch is exposed to the sun on the roof for one day. When the process of drying is finished, the leaves are put once more outside in the evening so as to get a little damp, and are then finally rolled up together. The bunch of tobacco is kept inside the house and often used for barter.

The *manioc* (ntjumbulu, mu-mi) is extensively cultivated both in the sand of the hills and near the marshes. The root, dried, and eaten either whole or ground, is very good food, but some plants have a bitter taste. But manioc can hardly be called a vegetable and borders on the domain of trees.

III. *Trees and fruits.*

Fruits play an important part in the diet of the Thongas. but wild fruits alone, the fruit with which Mother Earth presents them. They neither plant nor cultivate the trees ; when clearing the ground, they simply spare the fruit-bearing kinds which grow naturally. It may be that a man will sow some seeds of a particularly good *nkuhlu*, or *nkanye*, in his garden, if that garden happens to be devoid of trees : this is all they do to improve the quality of the fruit. It is no wonder, after all, that tree cultivation is almost entirely absent in Thonga agriculture : villages move so frequently, owing to contamination by death, accusations of witchcraft, or exhaustion of the soil, that nobody takes the trouble to plant trees which he will not be able to carry away with him to his new residence.

As regards the indigenous fruits, they are varied and numerous. Natives systematically spare every fruit tree when clearing their fields and, thanks to this wise precaution, the fructiferous growths have increased enormously ; and wherever the land is cultivated it presents the appearance of a huge orchard.

One of the best of the Native fruits is the *sala* (dji-ma), which

The nsala tree bearing the sala fruits.   *Phot. A.*

takes a leading place in the diet of the Ba-Ronga ; it is a large shining, green ball, taking on a yellowish tint when ripening, and consists of a thin shell, easily broken, containing some twenty flat oval stones, covered with a yellowish coloured pulp, very sweet and delicate in flavour, but a little nauseating to the European taste.   The sala is very invigorating and is a great and precious resource in times of shortage of crops.

Its first cousin, the *kwakwa* (dji-ma), is of the same shape and size, but, when ripening, becomes quite an orange yellow ; it is never eaten uncooked. The pulp surrounding the stones is prepared in a certain way and made into strips (nhasa, yi-tin), which are hung on the trees to dry or over the fire to be smoked ; this is what is called *nfuma*. Once the *nfuma* is dried, it can be pounded and made into a flour much valued when the storehouses are empty, and the new season has not yet begun.

The sala and the kwakwa are two species of the genus Strychnos (Strychnos spinosa and ungasha) which furnishes chemists and poisoners with the well-known drug strychnine. Does the fruit contain any proportion of this substance ? I do not know. It has never been known to kill any one, although it may be the cause of many intestinal troubles which naturally result when the Natives, having no more maize or sweet potatoes, live on nothing but this particular fruit. Strange to say, the kwakwa stones are credited with the power of attracting lightning ; the old women say that, when making *nfuma*, these large white stones must never be allowed to lie in a heap in the open air : lightning would surely strike the village were any such imprudence committed. It is a taboo.

I have already described the *nkanye* (mu-mi), (Sclerocarya caffra, Kafir plum), which is certainly the most highly valued of all the trees in Thongaland (I. p. 398). The fruit is used primarily and essentially for the brewing of bukanye, by pressing the pulp, but the kernels of the stones of the nkanye are also much appreciated ; they are very oleaginous and a modicum of oil may be obtained by merely squeezing them between the fingers! They are called *mongo*, and the saying is that they are food for kings, for the stones are very hard, the kernels very small and it is hard work to obtain even a small quantity! Not that there is any lack of stones! Heaps, which have been thrown away at the time of the famous bukanye brewing, are to be found in the vicinity of all villages, but the cracking is the difficulty. For this a stone must be sought, far and wide, and small hollows must be made in it of a size to fit the circular nkanye stones ; these are then inserted in the sockets and cracked by a sharp skilful blow with another stone,

17

great care being taken to avoid crushing the small tender kernel, the royal delicacy ! In times of famine the *mongo* is in great request, in spite of the trouble involved in obtaining it.

Another very valuable tree is the *nkuhlu* (mu-mi) (Trichilia emetica I. p. 395) whose nuts are the *tihuhlu* (yin-tin) (1) the mafureira. This is a curious fruit, the nut itself being of a greenish black colour, bitter and very oily ; on this grows white pulp (bululu), covered with a beautiful skin of a bright orange, which, however, only covers about three quarters of the central black nut. The Natives pick this fruit in November and December, and stuff their cheeks with it ; the saliva softens the pulp, which melts gradually in the mouth, affording them a prolonged enjoyment of its exquisite flavour. One sees children, and also folks of mature age, with their cheeks puffed out as if they were badly swollen and throats contracted with the effort of sucking down the delicious pulp ; when nothing remains but the black nut which is called nkampfi, viz., the product of suction, it is carefully put aside and will be used for making vegetable fat ; or it will be sold to the Whites, who export them to Marseilles where, it appears, they are used for making really good oil. Let us hope these nuts, thus sucked clean by the Blacks, have never supplied any portion of our salad dressing! But there is no occasion to be alarmed, as they are only used for making machine oil. The Blacks themselves do not use the tihuhlu oil for culinary purposes but for outward application only.

The *bululu* can also be made into an edible fat by the following process : whole fruits of nkuhlu are first dried, then softened in water ; when quite soft, they are pressed between the fingers so as to separate the white pulp, which is then called *munyantsi*, from the black nuts (nkampfi). This munyantsi is cooked and the fat is skimmed off (wungula) with spoons as it melts and comes to the surface. This edible fat, as well as that used for smearing the body, is preserved either in calabashes or in sala shells (shikutja). The preparation of nkampfi fat takes place as

(1) A certain number of fruits instead of belonging to the dji-ma class, as is the rule, are incorporated with the yin-tin class, the tihuhlu, the tihlu (fruit of the muhlu tree), the tindjole (fruit of the ndjole), etc.

follows : the nuts are thoroughly dried (womisa), and slightly pounded in a mortar so as to remove the thin peel which covers them ; they are then winnowed, and ground into a kind of flour ; this flour is put into a pot with a little water and cooked ; the fat is then collected in a big shell of Achatina and kept for external use. The residue is called *bubindje*.

I do not mention all the other fruits, more or less succulent, which serve the Natives for food. One must be terribly famished to enjoy them. I may just specify the *pfilu* (dji-ma), Vangueria infausta, a kind of insipid medlar ; the *tjhopfa* (dji-ma), fruit of the *ntjhopfa* tree, which I could never muster courage enough to taste, and the *bungu* (dji-ma) sometimes dignified with the title of the Kafir orange. This latter is the fruit of one of the varieties of the india-rubber tree, which grows along the shores of Delagoa Bay. (Landolphia Kirkii.) In the Morakwen forest grow the ntjhole shrubs from which the *tintjole* berries are picked during the summer.

The *muhlu* or water tree bears a berry called *tihlu*, which has an agreeable taste. The *mphimbi* bears the *mahimbi*, a large round fruit similar in form to an apricot with a double stone. Both these fruits are used to prepare a drink, and we shall mention them when treating of Thonga drinks.

*

* *

There are a few taboos to mention in connection with trees.

It is considered dangerous to cut the trunk of any large tree. Should you wish to make a mortar of a nkanye, first smear some of the bark with certain drugs and also burn them at the foot of the tree before cutting it down. Should you want to cut down a nkwenga or a mahogany-tree, nhlapfuta (Ro.), shene (Dj.), to make a canoe, the master of the forest must first offer a sacrifice to the spirits of his ancestors who have been buried there. If you omit this precaution, you will be unable to find again the tree you have chosen.

C. AGRICULTURAL CUSTOMS.

I. *The Agricultural Year.*

At the season which is called *shimumu*, the little heat, that is to say in July, when the warm weather begins, the nkuhlu puts forth new shoots. Though rain is still far off, the mahogany and sala trees become covered with leaves of a wonderfully delicate green. A kind of Composita (the Helychrisum parviflorum, shirimbyati), which is wide-spread on the sandy dunes, blossoms all over the country ; a beautiful lily (Crinum Forbesii) will expand its splendid white and pink flowers : the *winter* (bushika) has passed away : soon the *hlobo* (summer) will come.

When the Ronga woman notices these signs, she picks up her hoe (shikomo) and starts for the hills, or for the marshes. Her husband has already repaired the implement for her, at home. If the handle was worn out, he has cut a branch of nkonono, (Terminalia sericea), which is the wood invariably used for the purpose, and has shaped it so that one end is thicker than the other ; in this thick end a hole is bored, while the iron hoe head is heated in the fire : the head has, at its base, a long iron point which is inserted nearly red-hot into the hole, burning its way in, and thus solidly fixing the two parts together. This method of fixing on the handle is called ku lumela shikomo. The Ronga hoe has a very short handle, sometimes not more than two feet in length. The Transvaal Thongas use handles three to four feet long. The woman has now nothing to do but to work hard, her lord and master having duly accomplished his share of the labour.

It is the end of August. Two or three months must still elapse before the rainy season sets in. This period of the year is devoted to a two-fold work : the clearing of fresh land and the cultivation of marshes.

The *clearing of fresh land*, ku tlhaba lisindje (Ro.), ku khatsha

(Dj.), in the bush which has never yet been cultivated, or has been lying fallow for a long time, is very hard work indeed! Beginning in the early morning the woman cuts down the small trees with her axe (khaula, dji-ma) ; if the stems are too large she lights a fire at their base and leaves them to burn until they fall. Natives have not the slightest idea of the value of trees, if

Tilling the fields near Makulane (Maputju country). *Phot. D. Lenoir.*

these trees do not bear edible fruit, and destroy whole forests without any compunction. As previously mentioned, the labourer spares only the nkanye, mphimbi, nkuhlu, etc., and sometimes the mimosa parasol (gowane, Albizzia fastigiata) which provides a beneficial shade for the maize. Then she breaks the soil with her hoe and piles up in heaps the weeds (bibi, dji-ma) and bushes which she has uprooted, leaving them to dry before burning them. This is a long job and requires great patience. The old adage says very truly :

U nga bone bibi u ku ndji rimele. (Don't waste your time in looking at your heaps of rubbish, and fancying that your work is done !)

21

This work continues all through the months of August, September and October.

Cultivation of Marshes (tjhobo, dji-ma). If the woman has already tilled plenty of ground on the hill, during the previous years, she will devote these three spring months to the cultivation of the wet hollows near the lakes, between the dunes. The gardens in the marsh are called *shiramba* or *mashamba* and are very different from those on the hills called *masimo* (1).

I will now describe those which I saw in the Rikatla depression. The middle of the hollow is a marsh filled with long Papyrus (bungu), slender Typha (papala, dji-ma) or reeds (lihlanga). They are cut, uprooted ; small canals are dug, in which the water collects. The roots and stems are piled in heaps, some three feet high, called *psibibi*, but they are not burnt. They are left to decay, and shilutane pumpkin seeds are sown in them, high enough to avoid putrefaction in the water. The soil is a wet black mud very favourable to the cultivation of rice. So a small plot a few square feet is sown, a *shingubya*, and, when the seeds have sprouted, they will be planted out all round. It seems that planting out has been known and practised for a long time by the Makaneta people who have large plantations of rice. Mealies are also sown in this region, in the spots where it is somewhat less wet : they will ripen one month earlier than those on the hill. The great pity is 'that the papyrus marsh is full of small birds called *nkapa* (mu-mi), which pluck out the tiny sprouts of mealies as soon as they appear and eat the half rotted grain at the roots. So children and women must scare away these marsh birds during these months, as they will the sparrows of the hills later on.

On the raised edge of the canals sweet potatoes are planted, not the tuber, but growing stems, which will bear fruit much earlier than those on the hill. Where water has entirely disappeared, manioc is also planted in the hollows and seems to prosper well. In early November the pumpkins of the *psibibi* will be fully developed and their leaves will provide the mistress

(1) Nsimu, cl, yi-tin, becomes in the plural masimu, cl.dji-ma ; it is one of the few exceptions met with in Thonga grammar.

of the garden with a good vegetable until the first-fruits themselves ripen and furnish a more substantial food.

When the rains commence, sometimes as early as September, but generally later, it is *time to begin the regular sowing*. Everybody then starts for himself, because, although the fields tilled by the mother are the largest, every member of the family has tilled his own : the husband has his *mpashu* (I. p. 337) and each girl has her plot.

The Native idea is that every owner of a field must sow all principal cereals and vegetables in his garden, except peas, on account of their taboo. So, in a line on the border, are planted sweet potatoes and manioc. Mealie seeds are sown at a given distance from each other, alternating with Kafir corn and sorghum, and in between are planted ground nuts and beans. Watch how the mistress of the field proceeds to sow her maize : she walks along with short steps, at each one digging up a shovelful of well tilled earth, and planting in the holes three or four grains of maize, which she carefully covers over. The work is done in haste so as to take advantage of the last rains. The *lisindje* is first sown ; then begins the hasty tilling of the old fallow fields (pula, dji-ma). The crop is not likely to be so plentiful as that obtained from virgin soil, but the same fields can be used for three or four consecutive years before they become exhausted.

Natives have no idea of *fertilising the ground* in any way whatever ; at the most they may take advantage of the manure which has accumulated in some disused oxen kraal, to plant thereon a few gourds or some tobacco.

The operation of hastily tilling the fallow fields is often carried on by a *djimo* (dji-ma). Knowing that her fallows are very large and that she can hardly cope with them by herself, the owner calls all her neighbours to a djimo, viz., a working party, having wisely prepared a number of large jugs of beer. Neighbours will certainly accept the invitation as they may have to ask for similar help later on. So they come in the morning, and attack the fields with energy, singing and shouting all the time. There are special djimo songs, in particular amongst the Ba-Sutho. One may see them, some fifty black bodies toiling vigorously,

23

making the sand fly, their hoes working with marvellous rapidity! What excitement, what strenuous work, each one urging the other to still greater exertion and all hurrying to finish the job! They know that, there in the hut, ten big jars of beer brewed to a nicety wait for them, and that they will have a good time at midday, when the heat will be unbearable and the work done.

The maize grows and the weeds grow with it ; after the tilling comes the *weeding* ; this is the work for November, December and January.

It is done twice or thrice for the mealies. The first weeding is called *tjutja*, and is done when the mealie stems have reached a height of about one foot. The second is called *hlakula*. By this time the ground nuts and beans have grown, and this weeding is intended to be for their benefit also.

In January it is the *nwebo*, the time for the first ears of maize to ripen : it is also at that time that the fields of maize are apt to be ravaged by a species of coleoptera, called the *nunu*, of which I shall have more to say when treating of the superstitions of the tribe.

In January also the sorghum and millet attain their full growth, and the grain begins to form. *Sparrows, finches*, and other chattering birds take up their residence in the fields and begin to plunder them. Then women and children camp out from morning to night, in their plantations, and spend three whole months shouting, yelling and making a most infernal hullabaloo, with tin cans and other musical instruments, in their endeavour to scare the thieves. This is what they call *psaya* or *rindja tinyanyana*. The flocks of sparrows, etc., move on at a single flight to the acacias or mimosas, close by, whence they.make a descent on the fields of the next neighbour. This proprietress is also on guard, and, in her turn, drives off the birds with a frightful uproar ; thus the duel between birds and human beings goes on for weeks. The mother and children prevail upon the father to build them a little hut (ntjonga, mu-mi) right in the middle of the field, to enable them to protect their sorghum against the feathered enemy, and there they take up their quarters until the cereals have ripened and are ready

to be harvested. Poor cereals ! Many grains are wanting !
Those mischievous sparrows have taken more than a tithe ! In
the marshy lands of Lebombo I noticed the people scaring
the birds in a somewhat original manner. A cord was stretched
right across the field, for a distance of at least thirty or forty
yards, supported at intervals by poles, and on it were strung
large snail shells (Achatina lamarkiana) as big as one's fist ; when
the watchers heard the sparrows chirping on the other side of
the field, instead of getting up and running after them, yelling
and shouting to scare them away, they merely pulled the cord,
which made the shells jingle against one another, the movement
and noise frightening the birds and sending them off to attack
the crops of some less ingenious neighbour ! I have also seen
scarecrows set up in some places, the ordinary stuffed figure.
During these months of bird scaring it is impossible to get the
caretakers to do anything but guard their plantations ! The
little maidservants scamper away to join in the work and the
Christian girls no longer come to school ! I can well imagine
that the husbands often find empty larders at home !

The attraction of the plantation does not however hinder the
labourers from doing full justice to the national beer, the bukanye,
which is consumed from the middle of January to the end of
February ! Besides, it is principally after the bukanye that
it is necessary to protect the sorghum from the beaks of these
winged destroyers.

The agricultural year ends with the *harvest*. Every one
harvests his own fields and keeps, as far as possible, his product
separate in his own store house. The ears of maize which
have been left to dry on the stalks are broken off (tshobela)
and are carefully piled in conical baskets in such a manner as
to make them hold large quantities. The precious burden is
at once deposited in the storehouse. After this the beans are
picked (khaya) : these do not ripen much before May, after all
the other produce, at a season which is called "the time of beans"
(nkama wa timbawen). The ground-nuts are unearthed by
pounding on the ground all round the stem, and pulling up the
whole plant by the roots. It is curious to see the stalks coming

25

out of the earth with their well filled double pods attached to their extremities.

The men then construct *drying floors* (tjala, dji-ma) : a mat made of reeds, or of the wood of the palm-tree, is placed in the middle of the field, and supported by four poles ; and on it are

The storehouses of Sokis (Rikatla). *Phot. H. A. Junod.*

laid (yaneka) ground-nuts, and peas, to remain there exposed to the sun until they are completely dried.

The next operation is the *threshing*, or separating the grain from the ears (hula). This is done with sorghum and Kafir corn, but not with maize, of which the cobs are generally kept entire in the storehouse until wanted. The *hula* is done on a specially prepared threshing floor in the middle of the field. The floor has been hardened by means of nkanye stones, and smeared over with clay. The sorghum and corn stems are brought thither, and the ears are beaten with small sticks. Or the ears are cut, placed in mortars and slightly pounded to liberate the grains. The best have been preserved for seed. When the threshing is finished, the grains are collected (wolela or hlakula) in the *lihlelo* basket and winnowed (hehera). Kafir corn and sorghum are then stored in the big *ngula* basket (1). As regards maize, it is kept in the storehouses proper (shitlanta),

Dula storehuts in the Shiluvane village   *Phot. H. A. Junod.*
(The man sitting on the right is Viguet, my faithful informant).

little huts built of reeds with a moveable roof and raised on piles. All the shitlanta belong to the husband, though most of the tilling and all the weeding has been done by the wife, as already explained (I. p. 337). In the Transvaal, beans, peas and ground nuts are packed in the *dula* (dji-ma), which are smeared outside with clay,

---

(1) It is taboo to weave the *ngula* before harvest, just as it is to prepare the ntehe before the birth of the baby. Before harvest Kafir corn is still *nyimba*, viz., a child not yet born. Who knows if the hail or the locusts will not destroy it ? Wait till you have harvested, then you will see what size your basket must be !

or in small storehouses hung to the branches of trees (mfunge). When the harvest has been plentiful and all the storehouses have been filled, then begins the happy time of winter, of beer drinking, *bunanga* playing, (I. p. 431) paying visits, etc.

II. *Agricultural taboos.*

The first category of agricultural taboos are those previously mentioned, which spring from the idea of *hierarchy* : the prohibition to sow pumpkin seeds before the elder members of the family, the prohibition to enjoy the first-fruits (Kafir corn, bukanye, etc.) before the gods, the chief, the headman, and the elder brothers have *luma* (I, p. 394). Others belong to the *special feminine taboos,* (girls not allowed to walk amongst the pumpkins, to pluck their fruit or to pick their leaves without certain precautions, I. p. 184). Another category is that of *shimusi*. Certain days are proclaimed by the chief, or fixed by custom, as sabbath days, on which no one is allowed to till the soil. In Ñwamba, when there has been a little rain, it is taboo for the people of the clan to work in the fields ; they must remain at home. Amongst the Nkunas the day on which the new moon appears is also shimusi. The moon must be left to "become firm" (tiyela, hola) ; to cut roots while it is still "soft" is taboo : it would cause strong winds and hail. Complete rest is also customary in Khosen the day following the birth of twins. (See Part VI. Chap. II). Some other taboos are due to the fear of *wizards* : it is forbidden to whistle in the fields after having sown or until the mealies are grown. This would call the "baloyi" and endanger the harvest.

It is a taboo for a woman to remain in a standing position when she borrows a living ember (woka) from people cooking their food in their gardens ; she must sit down when she takes the ember. Should she break this law, it would cause the mealies of the owners of that garden to be burnt (psha) ; the women has "crossed their gardens" (tjemakanya). If however she does this, they will call her on the day they begin to sow, and she will have to sow the first seed ; thus she will prevent all the seeds from "burning."

But the most stringent taboos are connected with the *threshing of the cereals*. This work is exclusively done by women, and it is taboo for the men to approach the threshing floor. The Makanetas, who cultivate rice extensively, cut the ears and pile them into heaps in their own huts and not on the threshing floor. When the grain is dry, they thresh it by trampling on it. Should any woman pass by, it is taboo to speak to her. If she enters the hut and helps for a little while with the work, then the taboo is removed and you, the owners of the rice, can talk to her. — "Should you do so without that condition being fulfilled, this person would *take your rice* and leave you nothing but the husks (mataha). Should a relative, dwelling in the neighbouring district, come and see you whilst you are threshing rice, don't give her any part of your harvest : let her crush it in the mortar and take it away husked, lest you lose all your grain and keep the husks only ! The husks of the rice which you give to your relative must remain with you." (Mboza). The same applies to Kafir corn. To allow a relative from outside to pluck ears from your garden, to thresh them and take them home means to "spoil your corn" (onha mabele). When you are threshing Kafir corn, let the visitor first take the pestle and help you before you speak to her.

As regards *tree culture*, it was formerly considered a taboo to plant foreign kinds, such as bananas, oranges, etc. When Mboza planted the first mango trees in Morakwen, people told him : "You will die! You have called misfortune on yourself (u tihlolele), and other people will eat your fruit!" I heard this taboo explained in Shiluvane as follows. When a man has been obliged to move, and leaves trees planted by him in his old village, people passing near the ruins shake their heads and say : "Look at those trees! They have chased away the master of the village." These two testimonies are interesting, and fitly illustrate the origin of a taboo. The desolation of a ruin has been connected with the presence of new trees, as they have often been noticed together. Hence the idea that the trees are

29

the cause of the desolation. Planting new trees is consequently a taboo! Nowadays however, this superstition has died out, and one may see a great number of mango, orange, lemon (1), and pho-pho trees in Thonga fields, on the Coast as well as in Zoutpansberg.

Natives do not generally fence their gardens. Stealing is therefore very easy and it is no wonder that they have recourse to . magical means to protect themselves. Here are some of them ; they are characteristic instances of Bantu magic.

The *rihehlo*. This consists of a kind of mysterious influence exerted on the thief by throwing a magical powder into his footprints or by taking a little of the earth found in these foot-prints and treating it with the drugs. The inhabitants of the village where the thief lives will be seized by disease ; this will induce them to come to the owners of the garden to confess their fault and pay a fine. Then the magician who had furnished the drug will give them a counter-drug and they will be healed! Amongst the Pedis, the magician anoints with his drugs the stem from which a cob has been stolen. Then the thief will feel intolerable suffering in his little finger and come to the village of the people whom he has robbed crying : "I have stolen!" He pays the fine, receives in exchange the counter-drug and the pain ceases! (Spelonken)

The tinhlamalala. This is the name of the central nervules of the leaves of the Hyphaene palm tree. They are like little snakes, very slender, and flexible. To make the resemblance still greater, the owner of a field makes a knot at the extremity of the rod : this represents the head of the snake. Then he looks for the dried skin which has been cast off by a real snake ; he reduces this to ashes, makes a powder with these ashes and anoints the rods. He weaves the rods together to form a kind of crown and places it on one of the mealies stems in his garden. When the thief

(1) The lemon tree is called mbomu (mu-mi). This seems to be a Native word and the tree also may be indigenous in the country. It grows wild on the banks of the Lower Nkomati to such an extent that there is an island in the river, some distance above Morakwen, which is called Ilha dos Limões, Lemon Island. The lemons are of large size and their rind resembles that of the orange.

enters the field, the tinhlamalala at once transform themselves into small snakes which also bear the name of tinhlamalala. (Notice the correspondence of names: a curious instance of verbal magic.) These snakes rush towards the thief, who runs away, seized with terror. Should he take the stolen cobs with him instead of throwing them on to the ground, the tinhlamalala would follow him to his village! This dreadful powder was prepared by a Nkuna named Ñwadjokwane and the people of his village used to inoculate themselves with the drug ; in this way they had nothing to fear from the snakes.

*

*   *

Answers to some of Professor Frazer's questions on Agriculture.

There are no special ceremonies at the clearance of land for cultivation ; no grafting, nor artificial fertilisation of fruit trees is practised. (They think that trees fecundate each other by means of their roots. See, later on, paragraph on Thonga Botany). They do not believe that a deity animates the crops, only that baloyi (wizards) can increase or diminish the product of the fields (See Part VI). As regards the rite of driving away the vermin from the fields, we shall describe it in Part VI. There are no superstitions about the last corn cut, and no special ceremony practised on the harvest field. Except the rule of silence which must be kept by women threshing rice and Kafir corn, there are no special regulations for persons engaged in agricultural operations, and no sexual taboos. The plough, the hoe, the pestle and the winnowing basket are not used in ceremonial purifications or to avoid dangers.

*

*   *

As regards Agriculture, it cannot be said that the Thonga tribe is in a very backward stage. Thongas, as well as most of the South African Natives, are essentially agriculturists, and they succeed in obtaining their food in abundance from the soil, although it is not very rich. The variety of their cereals is indeed remarkable, but they have never developed their cultivation to any great extent, because they did not wish to harvest more than was necessary for their immediate needs : there would have been no market for a surplus. Moreover they have never invented the plough, or thought of the use of irrigation, or of manure, those three great means of intensive production which civilised people have so long possessed. As regards irrigation, the Makaneta people made use of the tide, which drives back the waters of the Nkomati River, to water their rice plantations, but they never dug channels for the purpose.

Civilisation having brought these means of progress within their reach, they show themselves, however, quite ready to take advantage of them. Ploughs are wide-spread amongst Transvaal Thongas, where missionaries have taught them their use. There is no doubt that, having been initiated into civilised methods of cultivation, South African Natives, who have such a strong natural taste for agriculture, will in future considerably develop the resources of their soil.

But two conditions are necessary for this :

1) European Agencies who have at heart the welfare of the Natives, Colonial Governments, or Missionary Societies, must help them to acquire some technical knowledge, and better seeds and implements.

2) The laws of the country must be amended in such a way that the Natives will be encouraged to buy land. As long as they are only tenants of big Land Companies, or provisional occupants, squatters on Crown land, always threatened with the possibility of their gardens being turned into farms, and sold to White people without any compensation, how can they be expected to devote much time and interest to the betterment of the soil ? Individual land tenure will be the best incentive to agricultural progress.

D. PREPARATION OF FOOD AND DRINK.

Bantus of South Africa being mostly agriculturists are also vegetarians, not however vegetarians on principle, as they eat meat as often as they have the opportunity ; but these opportunities are rare, so that, as a matter of fact, their diet is essentially vegetable. I shall later on describe the two ways in which they procure meat, viz., cattle-breeding and hunting. Having seen what are the products of their fields, we can confidently proceed to the study of their kitchen, as meat seldom makes its appearance in the "pots on the fireplace!"

I. *Fire and salt.*

Thongas do not remember a time when they did not possess these two most important elements of the culinary art.

As regards *fire* (ndjilo, mu-mi), the Hoñwanas knew it before the XVth or XVIth century. The traditions reported I. p. 24 show that some clans believe that there was a time when food was not cooked.

There are four trees used to produce fire by friction (tsika) :

1) The *bulolo*, a kind of Hibiscus growing in the estuary of the Nkomati, in the region regularly watered by the tide, is the best *ntsiko* or wooden flint. It is a very light and soft wood and is still used near the Coast, though matches are now to be found everywhere.

2) The *mpahla* (mu-mi), a bush of the Compositae family, whose wood is very hard and used to make handles for hoes. It grows all over Thongaland, in the plains as well as in mountainous regions.

3) The *nkuwa* (mu-mi), the large wild fig-tree, which covers the banks of the Nkomati and the Maputju rivers, and is common in the low lands.

4) The *ntjopfa* (mu-mi), the wild custard tree, employed to light the sacred fire of nyokwekulu (I. p. 388). It is taboo to use it for ordinary purposes, or to warm oneself at its embers. Medicine-men alone are allowed to make ntjopfa fire, having drugs to prevent the disease caused by its use.

Dealing with fire taboos, I may add that it is taboo to use branches of a tree which has been struck by lightning ; taboo also to keep alight the fire of a deceased person after the conclusion of the great mourning. It must be ritually extinguished (I. p. 135). In case of misfortune also (khombo), if the bones order it, the old fire must be put out and a new fire be lighted on the central fire-place of the first wife by means of the wooden flint. Each woman will go and take an ember from it and start her own fire again. These laws show that in the eyes of the Bantus there is an intimate connection between fire and the life of the village. When death or misfortune contaminates the community, fire is affected also, and it must be destroyed if the village is to resume its normal life.

Gungunyana used to levy a tax on fire : he ordered all the fires of his kingdom to be extinguished at a certain time, and sent messengers to relight them by means of embers procured from the royal kraal. Each village had to pay a tax for the new fire. It seems that this kind of royal right was exercised in the old times by the famous Monomotapa king. Nothing of the kind is met with amongst the more modest Thonga chiefs.

The manner of producing fire with the wooden flint is as follows. A dry branch of the tree is secured, from half an inch to an inch thick, and cut into two pieces, each of about 18 inches in length ; one half is called the wife (nsati), the other half, the husband (nuna). The first piece, the female, is laid on the ground and a notch is made in it with a knife ; the notch is cut in two movements : first on the upper part of the wood, secondly on the side of it. The male is then somewhat rounded, inserted perpendicularly in the notch, held firmly between the palms of the hands and made to revolve by a rapid motion of the hands from top to bottom. The operator having reached the bottom of

the male at once starts again from the top; thus the friction continues without an interval. The motion widens the notch in the
female to such an extent that the male penetrates and begins to
burn it : the ashes find their way out by the lateral notch ; a little
dry grass has been placed there and soon begins to smoulder. An
expert obtains fire after six or seven consecutive frictions, especially
when using bulolo.

Embers are kept burning as far as possible the whole night
in the fire-place. Should they however have been allowed to
go out, the mistress of the kitchen will send her daughter to
the neighbouring hut or village to fetch a glowing cinder. This
is called *ku woka* (1). The ember will be carefully carried in a
sala shell or occasionally in a big snail shell. There is a characteristic rule to be observed in the woka operation. It must generally
always be performed by the same person. If two women go to
fetch an ember the same day from two different villages, the first
must spit upon the ember of the second and extinguish it, because
it is a taboo to have in the same village two fires obtained from two
different sources. The act of spitting on one of the embers will
"remove misfortune (susa khombo)."

Salt, also an object of primary necessity in culinary art, has always
been known to the Thongas, as far back as can be remembered ;
the name *munyu* (mu-mi) is a genuine Bantu word. Natives
can procure it in three different ways : by gathering dried
salt on the lagoons near the sea (wolela sole), and in the pans
(salt pans) on the mountains (Zoutpansberg), or, when salt is not
deposited on the soil, they take salted earth, put it into a conical
basket and slowly pour water upon it : this percolates through into
a pot, carrying the salt with it, and the solution thus obtained is
evaporated. See the adjoining reproduction of a photograph,
taken in the extreme North East of the Transvaal, by the Rev.
P. Rosset. A third way of obtaining salt is from a certain
Composita plant which is wide-spread in the plains of the Low
Country ; it is burnt and its ashes washed in order to extract the

(1) *Woka*, from the same root as *wora*, to warm oneself at the fire and *wosha*,
to roast meat.

small amount of salt it contains! This is a long process attended with very unsatisfactorily results. During the Anglo-Boer war, Natives round Leydsdorp reverted to it, as all the stores were closed and no salt was procurable.

Salt manufacture, Northern Transvaal. *Phot. P. Rosset.*

Nowadays Native manufacture of salt has entirely ceased. The beautiful glistening white article has advantageously replaced the greyish, blackish mixture of former times.

II. *Food.*

It is not an exaggeration to speak of a culinary art amongst the Thongas. They give great attention to cooking. Of a woman who knows how to cook well, it is said : "Awa hisa" "she burns ;" not that she lets the sauce burn, but this expression corresponds to the French "cordon bleu." A girl who "hisa" will have more chance of being "lobola" than another.

This importance given to cooking explains the great richness of the culinary vocabulary. Every variety of dish or of culinary process has its particular name, and to master all these terms a special apprenticeship ought to be served to one of the queens of the kitchen. I cannot boast of having gone as far as that!

As a rule women cook only once a day, towards the end of the afternoon. The big meal is eaten in the evening when everybody is expected to eat till satisfied (shura), and what remains of it is generally finished the next day in the morning (fihlula). This evening meal consists of two component parts : the cooked cereals, and the sauces seasoning them. But the menu can be greatly varied. In most cases the cereals are prepared as *bupsa* (flour), or *mapa*, and the sauce, *muru* (Ro.), *sheshebo* (Dj.), is made of monkey nuts, ground and boiled in water, vegetables, India-pepper, tomatoes, shrimps, etc. Or the cereals, maize, millet or sorghum, may be only husked (tlhokola) and cooked whole ; they are then called *tihobe* (plur. of hobe, the central part of the grain), and the monkey nut sauce is often replaced by beans or peas cooked together with the tihobe. All these dishes are very tasty and many White people readily eat the Thonga food, which seems to me superior to the Sutho.

However, I never very much appreciated the *bupsa* which the Thongas consider superior to the tihobe and which takes a longer time to prepare. The grains must first be soaked for several hours in water (lobeka) to soften them ; they are then crushed, the husks being carefully removed by the winnowing process (hehera) in the *lihlelo* basket, which is spasmodically shaken by sudden jerky movements ; the interior of the grain is then pounded until it forms a very fine flour, as light as the best Australian flour ; the small round particles remaining are called *buse*, and eaten as tihobe, as the bupsa must be perfectly homogeneous. When it boils in the pot, the cook stirs it the whole time with a stick provided at the bottom with small cross bars, two to three inches in length ; she twirls the stick with her hands in the same way as a man lighting a fire with the wooden flint, and this operation prevents the flour from forming lumps. The lobeka process gives a somewhat nauseating taste to the bupsa ; that is why Europeans do not care for it, but Natives like it precisely for that reason. The preparation of *tihobe* is not so complicated, as no preliminary softening is necessary. It is a somewhat coarse food which, however, answers admirably to the wants and capacities of the Native stomach! When the bupsa of the previous day has undergone too much fermentation during the night, it is given to the dogs. A small supplementary meal is often cooked at midday : a plate of vegetables, for instance. Or, if the pangs of hunger are too keenly felt, a little nfuma meal (p. 17) is eaten with honey. Any addition of this kind to the ordinary every day fare is welcome!

There are a few other preparations made from cereals : the *mbila*, raw meal mixed with water, the *ntlatu*, a lighter kind of maize flour used for invalids, the *shimhimbi* made of Kafir corn which is the special dish for women who are more or less fasting during the confinement period (I. p. 42).

Thongas also know how to cook by steaming. They put a large plate (mbenga, mu-mi) on top of the pot and hermetically seal it with ox dung. This prevents the steam from escaping. Dung is a thing by no means to be avoided in the culinary art. They look upon it as quite clean (1).

Men have now become accustomed to ordinary ground mealie meal *(mugayo)* which Europeans use extensively as porridge in South Africa. They eat it in the mines and in the schools ; but women do not touch it and think it vastly inferior to their own *bupsa*.

As regards the husks they are called *budangwana*, a word which may mean : "that which is eaten by the dogs." They are given to the dogs, the pigs, and the fowls.

We shall see in the next paragraph how milk and meat are dealt with.

III. *Drink*.

Natives are fond of the fresh clear water (mati) running in the spruits of the Transvaal, but they also make use of the

---

(1) I remember on one of the Transvaal roads, meeting two converts of a German colleague returning from an evangelisation tour. I offered them a piece of bread, for which they were very thankful and they moved on some distance to eat it by themselves. I was much struck to see them, after having said grace, pick up a large piece of dried ox dung which was lying there and place their bread upon it before eating : they evidently thought it was much cleaner than the bare ground !

whitish, greyish mixture found in the pools, in the midst of the sandy hollows, or in the neighbourhood of the lakes, in the Delagoa plain. To drink from a pot, or from a river, lying on your belly, or kneeling down, is *ku nwa*. But there is another word, *ku kapitela*, which describes the manner of drinking adopted in olden times by the warriors of Gideon, and of which the Thongas have not lost the secret. The Book of Judges tells the story of the 500 "who lapped, putting their hands to their mouths" (VII, 6). When crossing a spruit, you will often see Thongas drinking by throwing water into their mouths with a rapid upward motion of the hand. I had never properly understood Gideon's story until I saw a Thonga drinking by *kapitela*.

But the Thonga kitchen provides the tribe with many other drinks. They can be divided into 3 categories : drinks made from cereals, from fruits or from other ingredients. From cereals are made the buputju, madleko, byala and mpheka ; from fruits, the bukanye, buhimbi ; the busura, made from the sap of the palm tree, also belongs to this group. In the third category, I may mention the shiwayawaya and shikokiyane.

1) *Drinks made from cereals.* Under the name of *Kafir beer* are generally comprised all the varieties of intoxicating drinks prepared from mealies, millet, sorghum. But these varieties differ greatly, according to the proportion of alcohol they contain. There is a light beer called buputju and madleko and a strong beer, the byala proper, and mpheka.

The *buputju* (corresponding to the Sutho *leting*) is brewed in the following manner : a little bupsa of mealies is cooked and ground (sila) in a plate together with Kafir corn yeast. Water is poured on the mixture and fermentation soon sets in. After one day it can be consumed ; its taste is agreeable and it is hardly intoxicating (Mboza). This was the old-fashioned way of preparing buputju, and it is probably what the Ba-Ronga called *madleko*. Maize madleko looks like a thick oatmeal soup. The recipe in Shiluvane is somewhat different : mealie flour is placed in a pot, with cold water, and stirred. This mixture is poured into another pot of hot water and boiled. It is then left to cool and some Kafir corn yeast is mixed with it in the evening. Next day it is sufficiently fermented to be drunk. It must be finished the same day for it would become sour, if kept longer, not having been boiled long enough to keep for any length of time. Nowadays the craving for alcohol having greatly increased, Natives do not content themselves with the original madleko. They follow more or less the Shiluvane recipe, but obtain more alcohol by mixing yeast twice with the flour, before and after boiling.

The brewing (yenga) of *byala* (Ro.), *byalwa* (Dj.), is much more complicated. It lasts nine days (I. p. 108) and this is the order of procedure amongst the Nkunas. The five first days are devoted to the preparation of the yeast ; Kafir corn is soaked in water, and left to soften for one day in a pot. On the second day, the breweress pours away (minya) the water, and covers the Kafir corn with leaves to keep it moist (pfhimba) ; this favours the growth (mila) of the germs which are left to sprout on the third, fourth and fifth day. On the sixth day the yeast (handjelo (Ro.), tshomela (Dj.) so obtained is dried and ground. Mealies are then threshed in great quantities and soaked in water ; in the evening all the women and their relatives pound them in the mortars and make flour, but they do not remove the husks. Next day they fetch water in jars and boil it ; their mealie flour is placed in other pots with a handful of yeast added to each of them ; boiling water is then poured over it and stirred so as to mix it well with the flour. When this has cooled down, they add a little yeast (kandjela). On the eighth day, at dawn, they put all these pots on the fire : the beer must be kept boiling for a long time. In the afternoon, they remove the pots from the fire (phula) and pour the beer into other jars to let it cool down. Afterwards they add all the yeast which remains. During the night, the beer must ferment (kukumuka, literally "swell"). If they find it in this condition on the morning of the ninth day, it shows that the time has come to strain it off (hluta) which is done by means of a Native sieve. (See illustration in next chapter.) All the husks floating in it are thus removed and the beer is poured into the best pots to await the guests of the beer party. In the hut it keeps its flavour for two days, after which it loses both strength and taste, and turns into vinegar (ntjubi).

Amongst the Ba-Ronga a very similar process is followed. They call *mbila* the flour and yeast on which boiling water has been poured on the seventh day, the name of the operation being *ku bandjekela mbila*. They let it remain in a cask for three days before boiling it, collecting in the meantime all the necessary fuel for the cooking. After the boiling, it is called *phiriho*. Empty wine barrels being everywhere available, beer can be brewed in greater quantities than was formerly the case.

When they took refuge in Bilen, during the war of 1894-96, the Ba-Ronga there learned to boil the beer a second time : the flour is cooked twice with the yeast and this greatly increases the strength of the byala, which is then called *mpheka*. From the innocent madleko, full of husks, which are as much food as drink, up to the very strong mpheka, passing through the different kinds of buputju and byala, all the different percentages of alcohol are met with. The quantity of yeast mixed with the flour and the length of the boiling are the two main elements to be considered, and it is very difficult to say where buputju ends and where byala begins! However the following rule may be adopted to differentiate them : beer is *byala* when yeast has been added more than once, when the boiling has been prolonged, when the liquid has been strained and when the amount of alcohol it contains is sufficient to keep it in good condition for more than one day.

2) Drinks made with fruits or other tree products. The *bukanye* is the most famous, being the great drink at the national feast (I. p. 399). But another very strong and much appreciated drink of this category is the *buhimbi*. The tree *mphimbi* (Ro.), *mbimbi* (Dj.), has an impenetrable mass of branches on which grows a very agreeable fruit of an orange colour with a double stone inside, externally very much like an apricot. When ripe in December, it is very juicy and sweet and produces a very alcoholic beverage. The fruit is pressed between the hands (phamasa) ; the liquid thus obtained is mixed with water and boiled. Any scum rising to the surface is removed (wungula) and the drink left to ferment for five days. It is so alcoholic that it will keep in good condition for a year and is said to be more intoxicating than wine. The mphimbi tree is found all over the Delagoa dunes.

There is an exotic tree, the Anacardium occidentale, called *nkadju* in Ronga which has been introduced and is widely cultivated in the neighbourhood of Lourenço Marques. It bears

Milala palm trees.

very juicy fruit which the Natives use to prepare a pretty strong alcoholic drink, the *bukadju*. At the season of bukadju there is an enormous amount of drunkenness round the town.

The *milala* or palm tree, from which is made palm wine, *busura*, grows in forests at various places, especially in Nwamba, the North of Nondwane, Maluleke, etc. and in some regions Natives devote considerable time to its brewing. The people of Phesen (Pessene Station on the Komati Poort Railway) are said even to neglect their agricultural duties and to indulge in busura to a great excess. The preparation of palm wine is done according to rule. The forest is divided by the chief amongst the headmen, in the same way as the ordinary bush. Each headman exploits the milala of the region which has been apportioned to him and which is called *fashi*. He may take partners from other villages. The stem of the palm tree is cut to a point (batla) at its upper extremity, where the top shoot

Collecting the palm wine.   *Phot. A. Borel.*

is growing. After four days this extremity is cut on the slant and a sala shell is tied on with a string and placed in a position to receive the exudation which oozes from the cut. This shell (shikutja) is soon filled up; the owner of the tree unties it, pours the liquid into his calabash and drinks it at home. When there is plenty of it, it is stored in a big pot called *gandjelo*, which is hidden somewhere in the bush. Gandjelo means altar, the utensil in which offerings are placed for the ancestor-gods. (Part VI.) But the busura gandjelo does not seem to have any religious meaning. If a traveller happens to find it, it is good luck ; he will say : "My god has blessed me and shown me this gandjelo," and he is quite welcome to help himself to the wine. On the other hand, it is prohibited to touch the shell and to drink from it. It is taboo. A stranger doing so would be addressed as follows : "Are you a bee, are you a butterfly to go and help yourself from a shikutja, which does not belong to you?" He would be tied up, arms and legs, and left to sleep in the open for the whole night. On leaving him they will taunt him, saying : "Go and drink from the shikutja." He may even be condemned to pay a fine, a goat, or a hoe. This palm wine has a very sweet and agreeable taste.

According to the Native idea, *honey* (bulombe) is also a drink! The prefix *bu* classifies this product amongst liquids. It is very much appreciated and Natives readily submit to be stung in order to collect it (hakula) from the holes in old trees or rocks. They generally burn some grass which they hold in one hand, keeping the bees away with the smoke and the flame, and gathering the honey combs into a pot with the other hand. Thongas frequently secure honey in an artificial way by placing a broken pot upside-down in the bush. Bees are attracted and a swarm will occasionally make its home in the pot. In the Ñwambukota region (near Morakwen) I saw a Ronga who even had bee hives of his own invention and succeeded in securing plenty of honey. Native honey is of a brownish, blackish hue. When eating it, Thongas do not at all despise the larvae : are they not meat?

3) *The Shiwayawaya and Shikokiyane drinks.* The various kinds of beer and drinks made from fruit were not, however, enough for the Thongas. They saw that White people used sugar-cane to distil rum and they attempted to do the same. The result of their attempt is called *Shiwayawaya*. Inhambane Natives seem to have been the first to brew it ; their kinsmen of the Lourenço Marques district soon followed their example. They crush the sugar-cane in a mortar, after having poured some water into it ; they then collect the crushed cane in a sack, press it, and extract all the liquid they can in one or two barrels. During the night a fire is lighted in a hut, near the barrels, to

warm them, and someone must keep watch all night, removing the scum and preventing the liquid from rising or overflowing. It then ferments and becomes very alcoholic. Where shiwaya-waya is drunk, quarrels and blows are sure to follow. The accompanying plate from a photograph, taken near Antioka (Khosen), shows a primitive Native press used for the preparation

Sugar-cane press, Magule (Khosen country). *Phot. A. Clerc.*

of sugar-cane drink. The crushing operation takes place in the large hollowed trunk of a tree and the liquid flows out, through a pipe fixed in its lower extremity, into a pot.

The *shikokiyane* is prepared from Golden Syrup bought from the stores. A large quantity of tins of this harmless "missionary jam," as it is called in South Africa, imported into Johannesburg, are used not by missionaries but by Natives of the Compounds who brew shikokiyane in big empty oil cans. Some of the more civilised do quite a trade in this strong drink, selling it illicitly on Sundays to their unsophisticated brethren, who thus attain to the happy state of drunkenness in which they so much delight, and which is not allowed by the regulations of the Compounds.

A number of other drinks have been invented by the South African Natives, but the foregoing are the principal.

See in the Practical Conclusions, I, at the end of the Volume, my remarks on "Alcoholism and the South African Tribe."

E. LIVE STOCK BREEDING.

I. *Oxen.*

Oxen were plentiful in Thongaland before the Zulu invasion ; the Ba-Ngoni warriors stole and killed them wholesale. They have never been so numerous since then, and in 1910 they were fewer than ever, owing to cattle plague and to Texas Fever, which has destroyed the herds in the Transvaal and in the greater part of the Lourenço Marques district. Oxen are not the property of chiefs only. Any *numzane* can possess a kraal, *ranga* dji-ma (Ro.), *shibaya* (Dj.), where he keeps not only his own cattle but those entrusted to his care. Having plenty of boys to herd them, he readily accepts the cows which his neighbours ask him to look after, all the more so as the milk will be his, and he will be given one of the calves, according to custom (I. p. 440). Much care is taken of the welfare of the cattle : the herding-boys are expected to lead them to pasture in the morning, when the dew is still on the grass ; during the five or six winter months hardly any rain falls, but heavy morning dew replaces it, moistening the grass, and Natives firmly believe that it makes the cattle fat. So it is said that the oxen must go out early and "eat the dew." (Compare the tale of Piti, *Chants et Contes des Ba-Ronga*, p. 156.) Moreover the best kinds of grass, those which are the most nourishing, are well known, and the boys are sent to the places where they grow. Parts of the bush are also burnt as soon as the grass dries up, so as to obtain fresh grass as early as possible in the spring. In autumn, after the harvest, oxen are allowed to wander about in the gardens, where they eat the mealies and millet and sorghum stems, and find better grass.

The Thongas castrate most of their bulls ; however they keep one or two in each herd for breeding purposes. Strange to say, these beasts are generally very tame ; they are hardly any wilder than the castrated oxen. However, the boys sharpen their horns and excite the bulls of different herds to fight. They pour live ants on their foreheads to irritate them. They give them names ; e. g. Makonyama, the one who threatens on both sides, — Mombomakhele, the one who has curly hair on his head, the terrible one, — Ntlhontlha-ba-tsha, shisa-sha-munga, the one who beats the fire... people are burnt by the sparks as by embers of the mimosa tree, — Mabala-ya-tilo, the "stripes of heaven," — Mabata-bata, the one with many spots, etc. Many of these names are suggested by the colouring of the animals (1). I never heard songs in praise of the cattle similar to those found amongst the Ba-Sutho for instance. It does not seem that oxen have at any time played such an important part in the tribal life of the Thongas as is the case amongst Zulus or Suthos.

Women, especially those of childbearing age and having sexual relations, are not allowed to take care of oxen. It is taboo. When they require dung to smear the huts, they send little children or girls whose menses have not yet begun or who are at any rate unmarried, to fetch it from the oxen kraal. When oxen are sick, they are entrusted to the care of little girls, who must sometimes stay with them as long as two months without returning home. We have already met with these feminine taboos concerning oxen (I. p. 184) and seen that these prohibitions are based on the idea that the menstrual blood is as dangerous for oxen as for

(1) Native cattle are by no means of pure breed. There are many races which have been crossed : a small race with short horns and another with large lyre-shaped horns, probably brought from the Transvaal to the coast of Delagoa Bay. Madagascar oxen, with their strange prominence on the back, resembling zebus, have also been imported in great numbers into Lourenço Marques for butcher's purposes. Possibly some have been used for breeding.

men having relations with women during menstruation (I. p. 187). Should a drop of it fall in the cattle kraal, this would endanger the health of the whole herd. Women are even prohibited from passing through a herd of oxen ; they must go round it, because otherwise the death of the calves would ensue. Amongst the Ba-Ngoni this taboo is so strong that a woman guilty of having transgressed against it was put to death (1).

The object of oxen-breeding is not milk but the acquisition of *wealth* ; oxen mean wealth to the Native, a means of purchasing girls and of thus increasing his family. Oxen are also bred for food, the meat being highly appreciated and divided amongst all the members of the family according to the strict rules previously explained (I. p. 329). The slaughtering is done by piercing the heart with an assagai, a painful and sometimes very protracted operation. This occurs at marriage feasts, at other family and national gatherings, at the sacrifice for rain (Part VI), and on special occasions, once a year for instance, when a headman wishes to feast his people. All, even neighbours who are not relatives and travellers, are welcome to the feast. Natives have wonderful olfactory powers. They seem to smell out the *lisuna*, viz., the peculiar odour of the meat, a mile off, and when an ox has been killed you see them emerging from the bush on all sides!

As regards *milk*, it certainly plays a part in the food of villages which are fortunate enough to possess a well-filled oxen kraal. The *milking* of the cows presents difficulties unknown in Europe! African cows have not yet learned to submit tamely to this operation! The calf must always be allowed to suck a few mouthfuls, then a boy pulls it away from the teat and the cow consents to be milked. Should a cow be too wild, they pass a string through its

(1) We meet here with an interesting instance of a superstition having no scientific basis whatever, which is nevertheless productive of good results. Women must keep apart from oxen. Since the plough was introduced amongst South African Natives, they have been quick to notice that it is a very useful instrument, and have adopted it in many places. The plough has to be drawn by oxen and men alone are allowed to drive them. Thus women are relieved of the heavy work of tilling the fields which had been allotted to them by immemorial custom. It is probable that further knowledge will free the Natives from their old fear and from the taboo which resulted from it ; yet the idea that everything connected with oxen belongs to the domain of man will remain and thus real social progress will have been obtained through an absurd superstition !

48

nostrils and so keep it quiet during the whole operation. The milk is generally taken in a large wooden bowl. It is very seldom consumed as a liquid, but is *eaten* when thickened by coagulation. The fresh milk is poured into a calabash with an opening at the bottom closed by a cork : a certain quantity of whey has been kept in the calabash and this causes the fresh milk to curdle at once. When curdled but not yet set, it is called *shitjubi* and is eaten with spoons by men and women. But it is left to decompose : the whey *(mulaza)* soon separates from the thick part, which becomes entirely solid and is then called *ntjhwamba*. The cork at the bottom of the calabash is removed, the *mulaza* flows out freely and is drunk by the men and herd boys. The *ntjhwamba* is put into a plate and each man or woman, not having her *tihweti* (I. p 187), approaches and takes a spoonful of it. A woman during menstruation must never drink milk, nor during her confinement or until her child has been presented to the moon (I. p. 52).

The milk of the first week after a cow has calved is taboo. It must not be mixed with other cows' milk, because the umbilical cord of the calf has not yet fallen off. It can, however, be boiled and consumed by children, as they do not count! After that milk is never boiled : not that there is any taboo to fear, but it is not customary. Natives do not give any clear reason for these milk taboos. They have no objection to selling their milk to strangers ; on the contrary, they are so eager to make money out of it that they often add water to it, and any European having had dealings with them in milk matters would have his story to tell!

Goat's milk is left for the herd boys ; men do not touch it.

II. *Other domestic animals.*

Besides oxen, the Ba-Ronga breed *goats* (mbuti, yin-tin), the care of which is relegated to the small boys (I. p. 62). Practically every one possesses one or more goats, whilst oxen are much more rarely met with.

49

Native goats are very small and frequently attacked by a disease called ndlwabane which decimates whole herds. They are not tended with sufficient care, although a special hut (mhala) is sometimes built to protect them from the rain.

Goats are killed by piercing the heart : this is at any rate the ritual way of killing them (I. p. 158). The officiating person stands on the right of the animal and stabs it in the left side, holding the left leg. The animal suffers acutely ; goats are however often slaughtered by cutting the throat, not from any feelings of compassion, but in order to prevent them crying too long, as "this would surely bring many people on the spot and you would have to share the meat with them!" (Mboza.)

If the ox plays an important part in *social life*, the goat seems to be specially reserved for sacrifices, that is to say for *religious usages*. This ritual use entitles us to suppose that, as millet seems to be the oldest cereal, the goat is the most ancient domestic animal amongst the Thongas, and, no doubt, amongst all South African Bantus.

The gall bladder, the astragalus, the half digested grass found in its intestines, strips made of its skin, all play a special part in the ceremonies and superstitious practices of the tribe previously mentioned. The gall bladder (nyongwa) is fixed in the hair of the person in whose honour the goat was slaughtered. The astragalus (nhlolo) is fastened to the wrist, the ankle or the waist as a means of protection. The *psanyi* (half digested grass) is taken from the shihlakahla stomach, and is used in connection with the invocation of the gods in the sacrifices. (See Part VI, Compare also I. p. 111, 160-162.)

Sheep, hamba, yin-tin, (Ro.) nyimpfu, yin-tin, (Dj.) are scarce in our tribe, and are mostly without wool. The wool sheep is called *shitlapu*. It is not taboo for subjects to possess sheep, but this animal is connected in a special manner with the chiefs. Its astragalus designates royal personages in the set of divinatory bones. It is used in the national sacrifices, those offered to the chief's ancestors at the capital. (See Part VI.) Let us remind the reader that its skin is used to carry a child in case of *bovumba* (I. p. 194).

The *pig*, as previously mentioned, is a new comer in the Bantu village. Its name, *nguluve*, means the wild pig. Most villages, however, possess one or two. They are never slaughtered in connection with sacrifices.

Poultry (tihuku) is the most common of all live stock. Not a village is without its fowl house (shihahlu) ; these are generally fashioned like a small hut and perched on piles to protect the poultry during the night from snakes. (See illustration I. p. 312.)

When a hen and her brood of young chickens have to be cared for, a much smaller hut is built on the ground, but the utmost precaution is taken to keep it almost hermetically sealed, as the mhamba (a long green snake, very venomous) and the shipyahla (Echnida arietans, a large viper resembling the puff-adder) do great execution amongst fowls! As cows are not bred for milking purposes, neither are chickens raised for the sake of their eggs. In fact Thongas consider it a sheer waste to eat eggs and always allow the hens to hatch them out. Hens are wilder than they are with us and often make their nests in the open country, returning some fine day with a flourishing young family. The breed is of very small size and the eggs are tiny : it would require at least two to equal the weight of one ordinary egg such as are for sale in the European markets ; it is therefore evidently more advantageous to hatch eggs than to eat them! If, by any chance, a hen dies on the nest from the bite of a snake, the Natives will willingly devour the half hatched or three quarters addled eggs ; the more developed the chicken, the greater their appreciation of the delicacy, for, says the Thonga, "i nyama!" — "this is meat!" Fowls are extensively used as timhamba, viz., sacrificial offerings. The throat is cut ; a little of the down plucked off the neck is dipped into the blood, and brought close to the mouth for the performance of the *tsu* rite, one of the smaller feathers of the wing (shihluwa), one of the claws, and the beak are tied together and fastened to the wrist, ankle or neck of the person for the sake of whom the offering has been made. (Part VI.)

Thongas assert that they have always possessed fowls. "They

made their appearance together with men" — "ti tumbulukile ni banhu," they say. But we know that the critical sense is absent from their minds, so we cannot rely on any such absolute dictum. "The Hoñwanas had them" they add ; and this we may believe, as the Hoñwanas have always kept more or less apart from the invaders of the XVth or XVIth century (I. p. 357) and may have preserved their traditions. This shows that poultry was known in Delagoa Bay 300 or 400 years ago. Not having seen the Portuguese chronicles of 1550-1600, I cannot say whether they make any allusion to the presence of fowls at that date (1).

F. HUNTING AND FISHING.

Whatever may be the antiquity of cattle breeding amongst South African Natives, there was a time when they had no domestic animals at all. Then, however, there were plenty of antelopes, elephants, and hippopotami in the country and they satisfied their craving for meat by hunting. Hunting was undoubtedly more developed in those remote times than now, and it was accompanied by customs and rites which are still to be found in some places, though rapidly disappearing, and in which are embodied some of the most curious animistic ideas of the tribe. Moreover, in their primitive state, Bantus only possessed very simple and inadequate weapons. It was hardly possible for an isolated member of the tribe to attack and kill big animals alone. The collaboration of his fellow clansmen was indispensable Hunting therefore was not an individual affair, but a collective concern. This gave rise to social rites, as generally happens when collective acts are performed. These ani-

(1) As regards the Pedi-Suthos of Zoutpansberg, the introduction of fowls amongst them is quite modern and they admit that they owe them to the Ma-Lemba who brought them into the country about 150 years ago. See my paper in *Folklore* Sept. 1908.

mistic and social rites connected with hunting constitute an elaborate system which forms a most interesting study.

The interest of this study has been further enhanced by the discoveries made in the caves of France and Spain regarding our forefathers of the paleolithic age. They also were great hunters, and the rites of the Bantus, who are to-day in a state of civilisation very similar to that of the Mousterian and Magdalenian periods, are capable of throwing much light on the customs of primitive humanity. The cave-dwellers of those remote times used to depict wild animals on the walls of their caves and on some of these artistically drawn figures may be noticed characteristic spots ; these would seem to represent the wounds which the hunters intended to inflict on the animals in the course of their next hunting expeditions. This was probably a magical method of achieving success in the chase. Bantus of the present day do not possess this wonderful pictorial art. Their magic is different, but it rests on the same principles, and who can say whether the description of their hunting rites may not help us to understand some of the discoveries already made or still to be made in the deposits of prehistoric times, just as the position given by them to the corpse in the grave explains why in the Mousterian skeletons the legs and forearms are bent towards the sternum.

I. *Big Game Hunting.*

Big game is plentiful in Thonga territory, more so of course in the remote places (mananga) than in the populated areas. Elephants are still found in the desert, in Hlengweland and Maputju ; hippopotami swarm in the Nkomati and Limpopo ; antelopes of subtropical Africa still abound north of Khosen and in the low plains of Zoutpansberg : the sable antelope, (mhalamhala), water buck (mhetlwa), koedoe, gnu (hongonyi), reed buck (nhlangu), etc. The duiker (mhunti) is met with everywhere. The smaller antelopes are the shipeya, mangulwe, etc. The giraffe (nhutlwa) and the buffalo (nyari) are still found north of Khosen, but are decreasing in number.

Let me first mention some of the *social rites* connected with hunting.

When a man finds *a dead animal* in the bush, if it is not too heavy, he can hoist it on his shoulders and take it home to eat. We know that Natives are not afraid of eating dead meat and enjoy an extraordinary immunity from its dangers. But if it is an elephant, for instance, the man who has found it, perhaps by following the vultures which gather round the dead body, will first carefully examine the soil all round the beast to be sure that nobody has seen it before him. If no footprints are to be seen, he cuts a piece of meat, places it on a fire and eats to his heart's content. Then he cuts off the tail (tjoba) of the animal and runs home to call his fellow-clansmen. The tail is his "means of notification" (bika) ; they all rush to the spot, cut off the limbs and carry them to the village. Should the animal have fallen in a country which is not that of the finder, the latter will give the owners of the land one of the limbs and the ribs which were in contact with the ground (1).

To find a dead animal is not a common occurrence. Generally the hunter meets with *living game*. He at once sets off in pursuit with his dogs. He may pursue the animal for hours, or even days. My friend Spoon (I. p. 7), though suffering from asthma, often succeeded in killing an antelope which had been overcome with fatigue and was found by him lying asleep. But he may often have to start without having seen anything. *The study of footprints* is then of paramount importance. In the sandy plains

(1) The Nkumba clan, 10 Kil. north of Lourenço Marques, lost its independance on account of a dead elephant under the following circumstances. One of the men of this clan had found a dead elephant. He at once cut off the tail and went to the village of the chief to " bika." Whilst he was away a troup of men of the Libombo clan, settled some kilometers further north, came to the spot. They put an axe into the animal's rectum, and when the Nkumbas arrived they said to them : "This beast is ours ! You have cut off the tail, but we had put our axe into its rectum long before." And a big warrior took the axe out triumphantly. The Nkumbas said "goo," i. e. they were greatly embarrassed and answered : "You lie ! We had cut off the tail before you came !" — "Not at all," answered the Libombos ! "Our method of appropriating a dead animal is to put an axe into its rectum." This led to a fight in which the Nkumbas were defeated, and later on, one of them having died and been buried in their sacred wood (ntiñwen), the Libombos dug up the corpse and threw it away. The poor Nkumbas were obliged to bury it in another place : they had lost their country !

of the coast, antelopes leave well marked traces in the soil. A hunter starts at 8 a. m. and notices that the footprint is of a dark colour ; this shows that the morning dew has fallen into it ; therefore the footprint was made during the night, some hours before. If the edges of the print are sharply cut, this means that the animal passed in the early morning, when the sand was still a little wet and firm, whilst if the edges are irregular or have crumbled down, it is a sign that the print was made at noon, when the sand is quite dry and loose. The Rev. A. Aubert living in the Maputju country, who often questioned hunters on the subject, told me that these men had wonderful skill in drawing their conclusions at a glance, apparently without any reasoning process. It is evident that the reasoning process must have taken place at some period, but it has become almost instinctive : the sight of the footprint immediately gives the hunter the information required. They are even able, when on the track of two antelopes of the same kind, to state which are the footprints of the male and which those of the female, the latter being generally somewhat smaller.

When the soil is hard, or clayish, there may be more difficulty. The hunter will observe the depth of the footprint ; if it is deeply marked, this shows that the earth was wet and soft when the animal passed ; therefore it was in the early morning, just after the fall of the dew. Or he may notice that a stone has been displaced and turned upside down by the antelope's hoofs ; should the upper side of this stone be wet, the displacement took place before the dew fell. On the contrary, should it be dry, the stone has just been moved and the animal is not far off. The Rev. P. Rosset, who was once led in an eland hunt by an experienced "phisa", told me that the man was all the time muttering volubly, talking to himself in a low voice, interpreting to himself all the signs he observed and drawing his conclusions without taking any heed of his white companion (1).

---

(1) Native children begin very early to learn the science of footprints. They notice the peculiar aspect of the footprint of all the inmates of the village and are soon able to recognize them. They even connect them with their respective ways of walking, which is indicated by the footprints being turned more or less outwards.

When the hunter has chosen, amongst all the prints, those which seem to him the freshest, he follows them up with his dogs, and there is some chance of his being able to overtake the antelope. Should he succeed in killing the animal without having received help from others he can appropriate it without rewarding anybody. Only if it is too heavy to carry home, he will shout loudly, on a high, piercing note : "Hoooooyiooo..." perhaps after having climbed up a tree so as to make himself heard a long way off. Or he will cut off the tail, cover the beast with branches to prevent vultures from damaging it, plant his assegay in the ground to show his right to the possession of his victim and go home to fetch his companions. When they have helped him to carry the animal, he will give each of them a good piece of meat.

But if the hunter who discovered the antelope sees that he will not be able to come up with it, he will blow his trumpet (lihlanga) to call for help. When the men arrive on the spot, he will cry : "Nkuna yowee!.." if he is a Nkuna, and all will repeat after him : "Nkuna yowee!.." to acknowledge his right. He may abandon the pursuit, but his right has been proclaimed and will be remembered. The second hunter who stabs the antelope will do the same ; he will shout "Mabota yowee!.." if he is of the Mabota clan, and so on till the animal has been killed. Then the meat will be distributed amongst the killers in the following way. The first will receive the body, the second one leg, the third the foreleg and the fourth the throat, a portion being reserved for the chief, the owner of the soil on which the antelope has fallen. This manner of pursuing an animal, in which helpers are summoned by means of the trumpet, is called ku nyikanana, i. e. to surrender to each other.

If the hunter has killed a very big animal and wants his clansmen alone to help him, he has recourse to another method of calling them. Each clan possesses its own rallying cry, and this he shouts loudly. This is intended to exclude men of other clans and to prevent fighting or any dispute about the possession of the animal. For the Ba-Nkuna this cry is : *Nyandlaleyo*! For the Tsungus : *Hi nhlanga*! For the Manukosi clan : *Muyamba ngwenya ya nambu wa tingwenya*! (Crocodile of the river of

crocodiles.) For the Mavundjas : *Kahlamba ntjhaba yo nonoha!*
(The big mountain, difficult to climb.) (1)

I have already described the part of a slain animal which is to
be given to the chief, when speaking of the prerogatives of the
master of the country (I. p. 406). Here are some supplementary
details : The general idea is that he must receive that part of the
body which was in contact with the soil, because the chief is the
owner of the soil. In the case of smaller antelopes however he
does not claim anything. For the eland he requires, in addition
to the ordinary tribute, half of the *bofu* i. e. of the paunch of fat
which is found round the heart of this animal and which is believed
to possess precious medicinal properties (especially for new-born
children born with a
membrane round the
head). As regards
buffaloes and other
big animals, should
they be killed far
away from home,
their meat is cut
into strips (misha-
katsu) and two bun-

Buffalo hunter with his victim.

dles are brought back to the chief ; it is also the rule that the head
of any beast of great size should be eaten on the bandla, the
meeting-place of the men in the capital.

So far I have described hunting with assegais, sticks and dogs.
But Thongas possess another method of killing big animals, a
method which is perhaps more ancient and which has sometimes
proved very useful. This is the *marindji trap*, i. e. a large pit dug
in the earth, covered with branches and full of pointed stakes upon
which the animal falls and impales itself. These stakes are made

---

(1) The Pedis have the same custom. · The Ba-Khaha cry: " Haratsha ! Mugoni!
We" ! This expression comes from the verb *ratsha*, to cross a river on a tree trunk,
as the Khaha clan is said to have been held back in its ancient migrations by a swollen
river and to have *ratsha* it successfully. The remembrance of this feat of their
ancestors has remained and has given rise to this rallying cry. Other Pedis say :
'Sivandja khomo," viz., " the killer will be given an ox for his reward."

of the very hard wood of the ntjenga tree, a sort of mimosa shrub, and are anointed with a powder called *tjulu*. This is a deadly poison ; it is obtained from a shrub which has very pretty flowers and grows abundantly in the forests near the sea, the Strophanthus petersianus. Should an elephant fall into the game pit and succeed in escaping, it will soon die from the poisoned wound.

The marindji trap was already known to the Honwanas, three or four centuries ago, before they possessed any iron weapon. They used to kill elephants in this way and, being unable to dismember them, they made a fire all round the beast to cook it on the spot!

In order "to make the game forget," viz., to circumvent its wariness (djibata), certain magical charms are used in connection with the trap. The fence which surrounds it is smeared over with a powder made from a human placenta. A hunter's wife carefully preserves the afterbirth of her child ; she bakes it on the evening of the day of delivery, hides it during the following day, dries it the next evening, puts it between two pieces of a broken pot, and hangs it from the roof. When the father returns from his hunting trip, he makes a powder of it, mixes it with other drugs, and uses it to smear the fence of the trap, also his arrows, or his gun. Should an antelope be wounded by a projectile covered with this drug, it is sure to fall at once! This powerful medicine is called *ndzedzena* and is deemed so important that a hunter's wife who loses the afterbirth must pay a fine of one hoe ; the hunter will try to obtain the placenta of another woman ; it is therefore not necessary that the afterbirth be that of his own wife (Viguet).

Game pits are not common in Thongaland ; they were still used some years ago in the South of the Maputju country and in the Hlengwe territory, but I never came across any myself. At a more remote period they were employed for the most profitable collective hunting the Thongas ever attempted. All the members of the clan were summoned ; they built a strong fence as much as two kilometers in length, leaving about ten openings at equal distances ; at each of these gates was dug a game pit. In the afternoon the men assembled and prepared torches which they lighted in the evening ; and with loud shouts they chased the game towards the fence into the pits. My informant asserts that the result was sometimes marvellous ; the pits were soon full and the animals coming behind ran over their comrades and escaped ; the men followed closely and stabbed the antelopes in the neck. But this of course meant the wholesale destruction of game. Happily a stop has been put to this kind of hunting.

Nowadays Natives use *iron traps* which they buy in the European stores, some of which are quite sufficiently strong to catch a duiker or a wild pig. They smear them with another charm, the *buriba*, a kind of brownish moss growing on the roots of a tree called shivumbunkanye. It also is said to have the power of "making the game forget."

I have described some other traps when dealing with boys' games.

Everybody was allowed to hunt in the good old times when the White authorities had not yet introduced so many restrictive regulations. Ordinary hunters are called bahloti or bazingeli (Zulu term). But there were others who had made a kind of trade of hunting, regular, professional hunters, who were called *phisa* (pl. maphisa). They were not satisfied to kill an occasional antelope near their village, but they undertook big expeditions to the great deserts of the Hlengwe country where game was plentiful and where the most precious of all, i. e., elephants, abounded. It cannot be said that the maphisa formed a definite class in the tribe like the bone-throwers, for instance. I never heard of a true initiation taking place prior to their becoming maphisa. Yet they were known and recognized as a kind of superior caste and were very proud of their name of maphisa. They claimed a special power over big game owing to the mysterious rites which they practised ; thus they partook more or less of the nature of magicians. I have come across some of them and heard marvellous stories about others. Old Madyashikulu of the Nhlongo clan, whom I met in the Ntimane country, near Antioka, boasted that he could pick out an elephant in a herd and force it to come and fall down at the foot of the tree up which he had climbed. He had then only to stab it from his retreat, and kill it ; after which he came down from the tree to dance over the carcase of his victim! Another was Mubandane, a relation of Mboza, who lived in Nondwana. As is customary with many Natives of the neighbourhood of Lourenço Marques, he hunted elephants for a Portuguese trader, named Fonseca, who provided him with guns and powder. When ready to undertake his hunting trip to the north of Gazaland (Mosapa), he had to undergo a purification (hlambo). His medicine-man cooked a pot full of his drugs, washed him with the froth and poured the contents of the pot on the roof, over the entrance of the hunter's hut. Mubandane had then to stoop and enter his hut, the water leaking through the grass and falling on his shoulders. These words were pronounced by the medicine-man, during this ritual entry into the hut : "Go and be happy! Though the rain fall on you, though the dew make you wet, when you sleep, you will be everywhere as in a hut ; everywhere it will be like home (kaya). You will have taken your hut with you, you will enter it in a wet state!"

Other maphisa were the hippopotamus hunters settled on the banks of the Nkomati river, whose customs I shall describe later on.

In connection with their *hunting trips*, these professional hunters are subject to many taboos. As we have just seen, they must undergo a purification before starting, and also be inoculated in the wrists with special drugs, the most important being those of the tintebe (I. p. 479) the same which are used by the slayers of enemies in battle. Another favourite medicine for hunters is made from the piece of meat which is found between the heart and the lungs of big animals. In some cases they have to prepare themselves for their expedition by daily ablutions and by absolute continence for a certain number of days. The sacrifice of a fowl is also sometimes made before starting. It is taboo for adults to eat the meat of this fowl ; it might endanger the success of the expedition. Little children may eat it : "they are quiet" (i. e. they have no sexual relations), and so the hunting will not be spoilt. When all these preparations are finished, the hunters start with their rattles, singing special songs, the songs of the hunters (Part V).

The trip itself may last for months, and constitutes a kind of marginal period during which the maphisa must use protective medicines against the dangers of the bush, and keep certain rules.

As a protection they carry their charms, especially the *ndjao*, the root of a certain juncus which is used on many other occasions. As regards the taboos which they must observe, I will first mention those applying to travellers in general, especially the *salt taboo* (I. p. 339). Should they take salt with them, this would "precede them" (rangela), and they would kill no game. It will be soon enough to look for salt when they have killed. But the great taboo of these hunting trips is the *sexual taboo*. This was already imposed before starting and it must be observed Phroughout the expedition. The necessity of avoiding anything connected with sexual relations is so great that maphisa will take with them to cook their food little boys under marriageable age. What is the reason of this prohibition? I have explained it in dealing with the Thonga idea of sexual relations (I. p. 189). If the hunters transgress the law, the big animals will be so wild that it will be impossible to approach them ; they will furiously attack the men who have sinned, because they know them, and woe upon them! So much so that if the hunters see an elephant or a hippopotamus in obstinate pursuit of one of their number, they will begin to insult him for having spoilt the whole trip by his misbehaviour, and send him home.

The law of continence is also binding on *the hunters' wives* at home. It is true that when the absence of their husbands is prolonged for a very long time they may become unfaithful to them and the men, on their return, will find babies waiting for them which are not their true children. This will cause them no unhappiness, as these babies none the less belong to them, their wives having been duly bought, and the time for fear is now passed, as they have returned home safely. The fact that these men welcome the children born during their absence caused me to think that hunters' wives were not subject to the sexual taboo as their husbands are. But further inquiry has shown that this is not true. Old Makhani assured me that incontinence on the part of the wife at home would have as a consequence that the husband would be attacked and killed by wild beasts far away in the desert.

61

These women must moreover observe certain rules in their everyday life. They must smear the floor of their huts only early in the morning or late in the evening, viz. at that time of day when their husbands are not busy hunting ; then all will go well with them. Thus the behaviour of the wife has its effect on her husband's fate. Sometimes she will take a plate, fill it with attractive food, call her children and distribute it to them in order that the husband, when passing through the villages in the far-distant country may be well treated by the inhabitants of the land. Should a death occur in the hunter's village during his absence, it is very dangerous for him! It was for this reason that Makhani was attacked by a buffalo which injured his skull! Those at home must expose themselves to vapour baths (mahungulo, I. p. 145) in the early morning and late in the evening, as in the case of smearing the hut.

The aim of these practices is in the first place to protect the hunter against the fury of wild animals ; but it is also to make him a man of the bush through and through. Mboza said : "The hunter must forget everything about home. Were he to have relations with women, his charms would get heated, whilst they must remain cool (titimeta). He must himself become a man of the bush (wa nhoba), similar to the animals which are found there. In this way, they will not fear him, nor will he fear them. If he sees a lion devouring an antelope, he will dare to approach it, kneel before it, clasp his hands and say : 'You, lion! give me some meat, that I may eat ; I am hungry!' The lion goes slowly away and leaves the antelope to him!" When they have killed enough game, the maphisa cut the meat into strips, which they take home. When they return they stop at the main entrance of the village. The headman comes to them, greets them and offers a hen in sacrifice on their behalf, to thank his ancestor-gods for having saved them from death. Should one of them have died during the journey, they fire a volley on arrival and are not allowed to enter before having undergone the purification rites.

Hunters must not give meat to eat to people "who are bad" (la'ba bihiki), i. e. to their wife just after a birth, to women during menstruation, to persons in a state of defilement. This would "spoil their gun." When they go to attend the burial of a relative, they fire a shot upon reaching the mortuary village. Thus the ball which was in the gun at the time of the relative's death will be expelled ; was it not contaminated? Moreover the hunter will wash his gun ; without these precautions the weapon would not kill anything in future.

These maphisa are very jealous of each other. Some of them try to destroy the power of a rival by securing a part of an animal killed by him ; they subject the meat to a treatment which was not explained to me ; they then bury for instance a bone thus smeared ; after which they are convinced that their rival will no longer be able to dispute game with them. Therefore when a hunter distributes meat to other people, he keeps for himself a little piece of each limb in order to prevent a possible enemy from "going away with his meat."

Let me now pass in review the *more important kinds of big game,* and I will reproduce as literally as possible the information gathered from Thongas of all parts of the country with regard to each of them. Some of my readers, upon reading these extraordinary statements, will no doubt exclaim: "What does all this mean? Are these actual facts or pure imagination or folklore?" All three elements are certainly represented in these stories, but I think it would be useless to take much trouble to distinguish between the three. My endeavour is not to produce a scientific zoological treatise but to find in these accounts a means of penetrating more deeply into Bantu mentality ; and there is no doubt that the study of hunting rites has a great deal to teach us on this subject.

The *eland* (*mhofu,* Oreas canna) is a splendid beast, highly coveted but dangerous to kill. Viguet says : "It possesses the *nuru.* When you kill it, it is taboo to walk round its body. Go straight to its head, and there, in the hair of the forehead, you will find a louse ; take it. Then dig in the earth where the head has fallen : you will find a root tehre ; cut it off and bring it home together with the louse. Then you are safe!" (—Other people add : "Remove its eye before cutting it open, if you wish to escape the

63

danger of nuru.")— "Having reached home, you ask the medicine-man to prepare a charm with the root and the louse : he will *lurulula* you, viz., free you from the *nuru*. Should you omit this treatment you may lose your senses, be unable to find the way home or, when you are back, you may forget everything about your hunting trip. People will say to you : 'U ni nyanyunyu', — 'you are cracked' ; you act as if you had killed an eland and had not been *lurulula*, delivered from its nuru!"

Hunters assert that there is not the slightest doubt about the presence of this root into which the nuru has entered. Even if no tree grows near the spot where the eland has fallen, the root will still be there and the hunter will find it, at least if it is really he who killed the animal. Should another hunter falsely pretend to have killed it and try to claim it, he will never find the root, even if he should dig all over the ground for ten days!

Another rule in connection with the eland is this ; should one of these animals have been killed whilst you were bringing your wife home, you must cut off a piece of its skin and make a bracelet of it, which you tie round your wrist. Then you can eat your meal with your wife. To-morrow go with her to an ant-hill and fix this piece of skin to it with two wooden pegs, one on either side. In the middle between the two pegs, set fire to the skin by means of a burning brand. You are then saved. You have *lurulula* yourselves. If you do not take this precaution, your child will be miserable : it will dry up, viz., be so thin that all its tendons will become visible. — Never let your children eat eland's meat until they have been inoculated with a preventive drug! The danger associated with the eland for the hunter's family is so great that people say : "Married people ought to abstain from killing it and leave it to bachelors." In fact everything connected with this beast is dangerous. When you follow its tracks, if you see that it is tired and that saliva has fallen from its mouth, take care not to tread on it. It is taboo : you will be seized by an irresistible sleep. The reason of these dangers is that the eland has a pouch of fat round its heart called *bufu* (same root as mhofu, the name of the eland). This fat, to which I have already alluded, is a very remarkable substance! Hence all these rules!

On the other hand, should an eland be found dead, transfixed, no nuru need be feared.

We have already met with the *ndakazi antelope* taboos. Amongst the Nkunas (I. p. 366) this ndakazi, or shidyanaman, must not be killed intentionally lest the hunter and his whole family should shortly die. We have seen how the danger can be avoided when the antelope has been unintentionally killed. The hunter must place his head between his hands, as if in despair, and shout : "Ho! mamana! ndji ta dya na man" i. e. "Alack! my mother! With whom shall I eat it?" By this cry the nuru can be overcome and the possession of the meat assured. Otherwise if a hunter neglects this precaution and comes home with the tail to summon people to help him to carry the eland's meat, they will find that the body of the animal has disappeared.

Clever hunters know a second way of attaining the same end ; it is to dig in the soil near the nose (the same as in the case of the eland) and cut off the root you find there : "This root has received the nuru of the animal. When you have finished cutting off the limbs of the ndakazi, you dispose of the dung (psanyi) found in the bowels, handling it with this root. In former times hunters used to throw the limbs in all directions : this would 'spread' (hangalasa) the nuru" (Mankhelu). Amongst the Hlabis, the ndakazi is called *hingakaya*, viz., closing the way home. It is not taboo to kill it, but the hunter must shout, when throwing the assagai : "Kaya! Mawako!" i. e. "May I return home!" If the antelope is swifter than the man and runs away (with a sound like kha!) the hunter will be lost in the bush : the animal will have *hinga kaya* viz., closed the way home. It will be necessary to *lurulula* the hunter, whether he has killed the antelope or not.

A third big antelope concerning which tales abound is the *kodoe* (*gantla*, Strepsiceros kudu), which is not uncommon in the Maputju country where I gathered the following information. The man who told me these stories, Movumbi, had a great admiration for the kodoe, whom he called the elephant's brother ; he said that the old males had between their horns a green snake which dwells there and warns them when there is any danger threatening them. This snake is their shikwembu (protective genius ?) It is taboo to kill one of these old males : the hunter who committed this fault would never kill another kodoe. It is taboo also to kill a young one first ; one must begin with a female ; later on the hunter may try for a male. He must not, however, kill it at once but only wound it ; the kodoe must not fall on the spot ; it must run away and the hunter must follow it for a long time, perhaps two days : "two days, it is all right." Should he find it resting on the ground, he must not shoot it in that position, but whistle in order to make it stand up; then only he may shoot. The nuru of the kodoe enters a root, as in the case of the eland and the ndakazi. The protective medicine prepared from this root, powdered and mixed with fat, is employed as an ointment beneath the eyes, and behind the ears and the knees in order to "strengthen the bones." This is the lurulula rite in the case of the kodoe. There is also a *luma*, rite of the first mouthful (see later on). It is performed by eating ritually a piece of the muscle which lies between the heart and the lungs, and which is the chief hunters' medicine (p. 60).

There do not seem to be any special laws in regard to the other antelopes except the *duiker* (*mhunti* Cephalophus grimmi). The first duiker killed by a hunter must not be eaten by him ; it must be left for his parents. Should he transgress this rule, "his heart would be disgusted" and he would lose any further interest in hunting: When a duiker falls first into a game pit it is necessary to "blow over it" (huhutela) ; if this precaution is neglected, the pit will not catch anything in future. According to Madyashikulu the operation is performed as follows. The hunter chews a little of the magic root of the kind of juncus called *ndjao* which, as we have already stated, plays a great part in Thonga ritual, and blows pieces of it over the duiker all round its body on both sides, ending with the head ; the aim of the operation would seem to be in some way to collect the nuru which is distributed over the whole body, and to convey it into the head in order to let it come out through the nostrils. If the rite is properly accomplished the game pit will succeed in catching any number of buffaloes, gnus, antelopes, etc., whilst if the precaution is neglected no other animal will be obtained henceforth. In this case the "huhutela" is performed not so much to prevent an attack of insanity as to guarantee further success in hunting. Should the hunter have killed a duiker after a long pursuit, the dog which started the chase must also be lurulula. The hunter cuts off one of the hoofs of the duiker, makes a notch in the cleft of the hoof and blows the ndjao into it : then he buries the hoof, calls the dog and shows it the place where it has been buried. The dog will then scratch, find the hoof and run away with it. This lurulula will help both the hunter and the dog to become greater adepts in hunting, the dog learning to follow the trail and the hunter identifying himself so much with bush life and bush animals that these will not be afraid of him and he will be able to approach them.

We now pass to the three largest animals of the country, those which could hardly be killed except by the collaboration of a considerable body of men ; they are also the three beasts which are "climbed" i. e. on the carcase of which the hunter climbs to perform the lurulula rite; these are the hippopotamus, the elephant and the rhinoceros.

There are a certain number of herds of *hippopotami* (mpfubu) in the lower part of the Nkomati river, from the Khosen country down to the sea. Natives have noticed that these herds consist of eight to ten females with a single male. When a female is just about to give birth to a young one she emigrates to some lonely creek ; if the young one is a female, she returns with it to the herd ; if it is a male, she leaves it in the creek and joins the herd alone, but comes every day to feed her offspring. Should she take it to the herd at once, the old male would kill it immediately, as the master of a herd is terribly jealous and tolerates no other male near him. The young male grows alone ; when he feels himself strong enough to attempt the venture, he goes to the herd and engages his father in battle ; he will probably be chased away, mauled, half killed ; but he will come again the following years till he succeeds in overcoming the old bull, who will in his turn fly with one of his old faithful females and found a new herd, or perhaps die miserably. These herds always keep to the same region. When a canoe passes through these dangerous spots, the backs of the hippopotami are seen from far off emerging from the

67

water, and Natives point to them saying : "The mapseko!" *Pseko* is the name given to old pots employed in connection with the cooking operations (to cook, ku pseka); they are turned upside down in the fire-place and the pots containing the food are placed on top of them. The backs of the hippopotami are like these inverted old black pots and that is why these animals are called after them. It would be dangerous to call them by their own name ; they might become angry if they knew that they had been noticed...

I owe to Mboza a graphic description of the rules of hippopotamus hunting. There are a few villages, near the Nkomati or other rivers, whose inhabitants are regular hippopotamus hunters, and possess the special science, or art, called *butimba* ; the hunters themselves are called *batimba*. This science is hereditary : it is taught by the father to his sons. These men possess a peculiar drug, the *mbangulwa* ; when the hunter is inoculated with this, he acquires a special power over the hippopotami : should he wound one of them, the beast will not be able to go very far, and it will be possible to follow it and quickly find it. But this inoculation makes the man very dangerous to his fellows : should he beat any one, that person will be at once seized by a disease which will prevent his passing water or stools.

This is the manner in which these batimba hunt. During the day, the hunter fishes, watching the movements of the hippopotami all the time. When he sees that the propitious moment has come and is ready to undertake hunting operations lasting a month, he first calls his own daughter to his hut and has sexual relations with her. This incestuous act, which is strongly taboo in ordinary life, has made him into a "murderer": he has killed something at home ; he has acquired the courage necessary for doing great deeds on the river! Henceforth he will have no sexual relations with his wives during the whole campaign.

Before starting he calls his principal wife, the one to whose care the butimba magic drug is committed, and both expose their bodies to the smoke of a medicinal pill. On the same night, immediately after these acts, he sets off with his sons ; they close the drift where the beasts leave the river by placing a canoe across the track. The hippopotami are in the neighbouring forest, busy feeding, and perhaps ravaging the fields. When they return to the river, they stop in front of the canoe which obstructs their retreat : the first assagai is then thrown at them. It has been smeared over with the Strophantus powder. The animal rushes into the water ; when it reappears on the other side, it is pierced by a second assagai. These assagais are arranged in such a way that the blade, which is provided with hooks at the sides, is not firmly fixed to the handle ; moreover a long string is twined round the handle connecting it with the blade. So, when the hippopotamus enters the river, the assagai which is planted in its skin is separated from the handle, which remains floating and acts as a buoy ; the string unwinds and the handle follows the animal as it retreats, showing in which direction it has gone.

As soon as the assagai is thrown, somebody runs to the hunter's village to inform his wife. The woman must at once shut herself up in the hut and remain perfectly quiet. She lights a fire and keeps it burning the whole time. A little child brings her her pipe (old Ronga women are great pipe smokers). She must neither eat nor drink ; or, if she is very thirsty, the child will bring her some water. In any case she must not crush her mealies; she must not go out of the hut except to satisfy her natural wants. Why ? Because if she were to move to and fro in the village, this would induce the hippopotamus to rush wildly upon her husband and possibly kill him. Moreover the fact that she remains confined within the circular walls of the hut will have as a consequence that the wild beast will be in some sort imprisoned in a small space ; it will not be able to run far away and escape.

We find here a characteristic instance of the two kinds of magic which we shall explain later on : the communionist magic according to which the different parts of a whole act and react on each other (the great wife, whose life is in close connection with her husband's life, saves him by her quiet demeanour) and the imitative magic according to which like acts on like or produces like (the confinement of the woman within the walls of the hut prevents the hippopotamus from escaping from the circle formed by the canoes on the river. (Similar customs are found amongst many primitive peoples. See Part VI. Ch. I.)

Then all the hunters of the village are called ; they enter the canoe and follow the beast. To facilitate the pursuit, they replace the floating handle of the assagai by a *male*, viz., the big nervule of the leaf of the mimale palm tree, resembling a pole of 30 feet in length. As soon as this species of pole is fixed, somebody informs the woman at home that she can come out of the hut. But let her be prudent, as victory is not yet won. The hippopotamus will come to the surface to breathe : an assagai will be thrown into its nostrils and later a second ; it will be no longer able to close its nose when plunging and will be drowned. But it may attack the hunters furiously, instigated by the spirits of baloyi (wizards) which are riding on it "just as men ride on a horse!" The fight will perhaps last a long time!

When the hippopotamus has at last been killed, songs of rejoicing burst out on all sides ; the hunters bring their canoes together and row in the direction of the village, singing the whole time special songs which are called *nyangamela*. The peculiar cries of the women are heard on the hill, their "mikulungwana." They come to the shore to meet the men. The great wife, having now been entirely set free, comes dancing and singing. The carcase is left on the sand till low tide (the tide is perceptible for a long distance in the Lower Nkomati river). Then all the hunters assemble to proceed to the two great hunters' rites, the lurulula and the luma.

First the *lurulula*. I have obtained a more precise description of this rite from two new informants. The beast is laid on its back, and its forelegs are pulled out on both sides, so as to separate them from each other. The hunter who has killed the beast takes his *ndjao* root, chews it, together with the butimba medicine, blows pieces of it into his hands, closes his eyes and introduces himself, creeping on his belly, between the forelegs ; he then creeps along the side of the hippopotamus, anointing it with the medicine which is in his hands. When he reaches the hindleg, he squeezes it with both hands, does the same to the other hindleg, creeps along the other side and at last reaches the head, muttering the following words : "A ti fe! A ti bole" i. e. "Let them die! Let them rot." Then he prays to his ancestor-gods, asking them to give him many more such beasts. He opens his eyes, and this is the end of the ceremony.

As a rule two persons must perform the lurulula rite, first the hunter who has killed the hippopotamus and after him the headman of the batimba village.

The lurulula is the great hunters'rite. There is, however, a second rite to be performed before they can enjoy the flesh of their victim, the *luma*. The luma is the removal of a food taboo by a rite which must accompany the first mouthful taken. It is obligatory for the first fruits, for the food left by a deceased person, etc. (I. p. 146, 394.) This precaution is also necessary in the case of game. The hunter who transfixed the hippopotamus is the first to luma. He takes the diaphragm of the animal (mapfalo), and puts a piece of it into his mouth ; he then plunges into the river, and eats this meat while under water, "as if he were a fish." Having accomplished this feat, he emerges triumphant. His sons and the inmates of his village *luma* after him. They take a portion of the flesh of the neck, called shipelo, from that part of the hippopotamus which pushes the mud in front of it, and which is supposed to be the seat of its strength. This they mix with the mbangulwa medicine and, standing in a line, they all eat a little of it, men, women, and children. All the neighbours assemble : they have smelled out the meat! The portion for the chief is put aside (I. p. 406), as the hippopotamus is very heavily taxed, and must even be cut open by the men of the capital. Then every one receives a piece of the flesh, and luma, either by smearing the sole of the foot with it, or by taking a small live ember and mixing it with the meat. The object of the luma rite is to remove the danger of eating meat to which you are not accustomed : it might "hate you (benga)" and cause colic. The taboo is not very strict, as there is only danger of colic and not of death. (Luma is necessary for elephants, when eating the meat for the first time, but not for lions or panthers. For elephants it is performed by smearing the soles of the feet with the meat.)

The reader must certainly have noticed the curious connection established by Mboza between hippopotami and wizards. As we shall see when studying the witchcraft theory, wizards are supposed to have the power of *sending* wild animals to kill their victims. Here the idea is somewhat different. In the three stories which I have collected and of which I give a literal translation, the wizards have become the masters of the hippopotami and ride upon them during the night : they are the maleficent agents who induce these animals to play havoc in the gardens of the people. Two of the stories are supposed to have taken place in the Khosen country, the other lower down on the river, at a spot called Shihahlu. Let us begin with this one.

First story. "The wizards put a bit into the mouth of the hippopotamus and climb upon it. You cannot get the animal unless you first get its master. The 'phisa' knows the wizard because he possesses drugs more powerful than those of the wizard. At Shihahlu there was a hippopotamus which ventured to come out of the river even in daylight ; it came on to the road and frightened the women passing there who had gone to buy food on account of the famine. They threw away their baskets in fear. The beast used also to go and plunder the fields. The chiefs called a very clever hunter and showed him where the hippopotamus used to come out of the river. This man, who was from Sihhahlu, swallowed his medicine and put on a great many amulets (timfisa) made of varan skin ; he also took his tail, the tail of a young hippopotamus, went during the night to that spot and saw the beast ; there was fire on its back ; this fire belongs to the wizard. (Where do these lights come from ? I do not know. Perhaps it is the work of the Devil !) The hunter returned home. Another day he went again and heard a noise in the water ; the hippopotamus came out of the river and the hunter saw rings round its ears and bracelets round its legs. He shot it and it died. Then he went to tell the chiefs. They came, and sure enough they found four bracelets on each leg and six rings on each ear. I saw them myself. It had put on all its ornaments ; but it was very thin because it was made to work hard for its master. We went to eat the meat of the hippopotamus which was thus adorned (longile)... During the night cries of mourning were heard on the Lombye rivulet. It was the masters of the hippopotamus who were mourning over it, and the next morning we found pieces of the blue cotton print which is used by mourners hanging on the reeds where the hippopotamus had been cut open. These people had put them there to mourn their hippopotamus. As regards the hunter, he was given a reward of £ 6."

Second story. "A phisa called Shitjobeke from Matlotlo was called and shown where the hippopotamus used to emerge from the river. He went there during the night and saw its master on its back. He told him : 'So it is your hippopotamus which ravages the gardens. Hold it firm! I am going to kill it.' The wizard answered : 'I beseech you, Khosa, do not kill it ; I will not come any more to spoil the mealies!' The hunter let him go and went away. Next evening the animal came out again, its master on its back. The hunter possessed a drug by which he could kindle the lights on the back of the hippopotamus. He saw the wizard and said : 'My friend, now hold it fast. I am firing! If you do not hold it I will kill you.' He fired and the master went away. The hunter remained on the spot fearing that the wizard might come back and ressuscitate it. Next day he told the chiefs to come and cut it open. He performed the lurulula ; he blew his ndjao over the legs, the belly, the chest, and the ears ; then they turned the beast over on the other side, and he did the same thing. They cut off the tail and gave it to him : the hunter uses this as a medicine ; he will mix it with other drugs and this will help him against the wizards ; they will no longer be able to come to him during the night and make him dream of hippopotami ; it will also give him the power of killing other hippopotami. Then they cooked the meat of the chest, which is a tit-bit. The divinatory bones showed who was to roast it and eat the first mouthful and then distribute their portions to the others. The bones often say also : 'If it is the meat of a male hippopotamus do not eat it in the village, eat it at such and such a place...'"

Third story. "There was another hunter, Mundjindji, of the Nyoka clan. His father had been killed by Heaven (lightning), because he possessed charms which he had got from the Ba-Sutho. This man used to dig up the corpses of the dead ; he dissected the skin of their foreheads and killed, (with the drugs thus obtained,) the boys who came back from the mines (magaisa). The Commandant (Portuguese Administrator) arrested him, and he was imprisoned in Lourenço Marques. He said : 'They are telling lies about me,' and he was released. However he killed some more people and was imprisoned for one month. Even now he is still doing it. He is a 'phisa.' They called him in to get rid of a hippopotamus which was annoying them. It was the Commandant who called him. He went to hunt it. For many days he did not see it, but one day, at sunset, he took his canoe and went on to the river. He took a red piece of cotton ; this was reflected at the bottom of the river. The hippopotamus saw it there and came up to see what was the matter. The hunter fired at it ; he fired a second time. And lo! there on its back was the one who rides upon it! One of the balls pierced him whilst the other pierced the hippopotamus. The animal rushed towards the hunter, but he fired a third time and killed it. Next morning they found the hippopotamus floating on the water, dead. In the village also a man had died during the night, and they were mourning there. The hunter had said to the people : 'I have killed a man who was on the hippopotamus.' And on one side of the river people were eating meat whilst on the other side people were crying. But they did not lodge a complaint against him ; no action can be taken in such a case."

As regards *the elephant (ndlopfu)* it was the favourite object of the chase, because killing one of these large beasts meant not only abundance of meat but also wealth on account of the ivory. Madyashikulu used to bring the tusks to Manukosi (Gungunyana's grandfather) who returned some of them to him, and with the money thus obtained the hunter could buy a wife. There are different systems of lurulula in the case of the elephant. The hunter takes a little of the tintebe powder (the charm of the slayers) pierces the eye of the beast, mixes the vitreum with the powder, adds drugs prepared from the end of the trunk and the tail and uses this mixture to overcome the nuru. A phisa of the Maputju country employed another method. He cut a piece of meat from the foreleg, cooked it, anointed it with powder from the calabash of the slayers, chewed it and began to blow it over the animal after having "climbed it." He then crept over the elephant in the same way as described above in the case of the hippopotamus, holding his gun in his hand the whole time. His comrades used to anoint him with a white medicine round both eyes. When he had returned home the treatment was continued by the administration of two vapour baths (mahungulo). He had to expose his body to the steam produced first by a decoction of various twigs, secondly by another decoction prepared from medicinal roots mixed with pieces of meat taken from a goat and from the elephant itself. Afterwards he had to drink the broth and eat the meat. The aim of the treatment was to enable him to kill more elephants. In the case of the elephant as well as of the hippopotamus the chief of the country has to perform the lurulula as well as the hunter "because he is the chief of all the animals of the country and he would be unable to govern it successfully if he did not do this."

The *rhinoceros (shibetshana)* is not common in Thongaland ; a few of these animals are found in the extreme south of the Maputju country. The same rules were observed when the hunters had succeeded in killing one ; but this is no easy task because, as Muvumbi said, the rhinoceros is terribly wild, as it has no "mapfalo." The mapfalo is a piece of cartilage which is found in all animals between the ribs, beneath the sternum ; it is the diaphragm ; it is also the seat of fear or of the conscience. It is this particular cartilage which throbs in the case of great fear. The rhinoceros has no mapfalo ; therefore it fears nothing and rushes savagely upon the hunter. Its meat is so delicious that when a man has tasted it he no longer wishes to drink water!

I never heard mention of the lurulula in connection with the *lion (nghala* (Djo.), *ndjau* (Ro.). To avoid being mauled by lions the hunters put into their mouths a little of every kind of food mixed with their powerful drugs and spit it out to the four winds in order to appease the ancestor-gods of the country. Then if they meet with a lion, the wild beast, instead of rushing upon them, will look at them quietly, its saliva dropping from its mouth, and will do them no harm.

Strange to say the *buffalo* (nyari) has no nuru, and when I asked why this was, my Maputju informant told me : "The buffalo is an ox." This answer may perhaps help us to understand something more about the nuru idea.

The statement regarding the *zebra* (mhangwa) is more curious still. "Mhangwa a yi lubiwi! Yi ni mabala ; i nala ; a yi ngeni hosin" viz. "No tax is paid for the zebra ; it is an animal with many colours (stripes) ; it is an enemy ; it must not enter the village of the chief." We have met with the same prohibition in connection with the village of the parents-in-law (I. p. 250).

As regards the *crocodile (ngwenya)* also called *shiwutlani-*

75

mintjeko, the one who seizes even the calabashes (he is not satisfied with seizing the woman who goes to the river to draw water, but takes her calabashes also), I heard of a medicine-man in the Rikotjo country who knew the manner of blowing over it (huhutela). There are a number of stories told of crocodiles, for instance the story of a man who was caught by one of these terrible saurians and dragged into a creek where the crocodile intended to eat him later on. The half-dead man came to his senses, saw the sky through the dense reeds in which he had been left by his captor and eventually managed to escape!

There is still a great deal of picturesque Bantu lore to be gathered by listening to hunters telling their stories round the fire when travelling with them through the desert. I will add only two in connection with two smaller animals.

The *honey-eater, shinwabulombane* (Mellivora ratel) is a kind of badger which lives on wild honey. It is said to proceed in the following way. It collects the honey from the hollow trunk where the bees have built their hive and takes it to a little distance. Should you have noticed it preparing its store, do not take the honey at once, but wait till it has finished its work. Then attack it ; this is however very dangerous, because the honey-eater has a special method of defending itself ; it rushes upon its enemy and tries to seize his testicles and tear them out with its claws. The honey-eater does not fear to attack even buffaloes by creeping under their body and serving them in this evil fashion ; afterwards it carefully buries the testicles... The hunter takes a branch of a very hard and thorny mimosa (the nkaya), and so keeps the animal at a distance and pierces it with his assagai. But the honey-eater has the faculty of swelling up and hardening its skin so much that it is very difficult to thrust an assagai through it. When the hunter has succeeded in killing it, the skin must go to the chief.

The *ant-eater (mpandana or sambane)* digs large holes in the ground. This is the method used by hunters to kill it. They send their dog into the hole, which is horizontal. The animal is inside, sleeping behind a protective wall of earth ; the dog pierces this wall and attacks it in its retreat. In the mean time the hunter digs a hole from above, some distance in front of the spot where the ant-eater was sleeping. Attacked by the dog, the sambana begins to burrow deeper into the earth; it reaches the spot where the hunter has dug his hole and tries to escape through this ; but seeing that a man is waiting for it there, it suddenly turns back and returns to the opening of its burrow, where it is easily killed, notwithstanding the hard scales which cover its body.

Conclusion on the nuru idea and the lurulula rite.

I once asked old Makhani, the hunter who had suffered from an attack of insanity because he had slain an enemy : "What is the nuru?" He burst out laughing, and this was the only answer I could get from him. I suppose an uneducated peasant of any European country would do the same if he were abruptly asked : "What is the soul?" An ethnologist, however, cannot rest satisfied with this avowal of ignorance or this utter want of interest. He must try to find an explanation, and some sort of an explanation is always likely to be found when we are dealing with beliefs which are not purely individual but which belong to a community.

The *nuru* (pl. miluru)—to sum up all the above accounts (see also I. p. 478)—is a peculiar power possessed by man and by several wild animals in virtue of which they avenge themselves on the person who has killed them. This power resides in their body and appears to pass out of it through their nostrils with their last breath. The fact of having killed a person or an animal *possessing the nuru* places the slayer in a state of dangerous contamination. It would sometimes appear as if the nuru had entered into him and remained sleeping in him, ready to awake in certain circumstances (I. p. 400). The danger connected with the nuru must be overcome by a special treatment ; if this is not done, the nuru will cause an attack of madness and may even do great harm to the family of the slayer or hunter.

Let us try to go a step further in our analysis by putting the following question : What is the relation between the *nuru* and the *shikwembu*, first in relation to man, and secondly, as regards animals?

As regards man, we know that, for the Bantus, every human being at his death turns into a *shikwembu* and becomes an ancestor-god for his descendants and a hostile spirit as regards his former enemies. The shikwembu, roughly speaking, is the ghost of a deceased person. This

77

notion is clearly animistic. The shikwembu, as we shall see in the VIth. Part, is a personal spirit to which prayers are addressed and offerings presented. The *nuru* is not personal. It is a power, an influence, a force of Nature. This is not a distinctly animistic idea. It belongs rather to the domain of Dynamism (See Part VI, Chapter I). Moreover any deceased person becomes a shikwembu, whilst the term nuru is used only in the case of a slain enemy, or in relation to strangers who died in a foreign country and were not properly buried. It is consequently clear that these two words nuru and shikwembu have not the same meaning ; they cannot be employed one for the other.

On the other hand there is a resemblance between the two ideas. Thongas believe that any shikwembu of a hostile tribe, and not only the shikwembu of an enemy slain in battle, can take possession of a man of their tribe and cause a disease very similar to that of the nuru at the outset (although it develops into something very different later on). This disease is a possession in the full sense of the word, and must be treated by exorcism, as we shall see in the Chapter on Possessions. Thus it is also clear that there is a similarity between the action of the nuru and of a hostile shikwembu. In the story told concerning slayers (I. p. 481, Note) we met with a typical case of nuru, ending in a sacrifice offered to the slain enemy. Undoubtedly the two ideas are connected, though not identical.

As regards wild beasts, the question does not arise, at least amongst the Thongas. Despite the green snake found between the horns of the Kodoe, which my Maputju informant called its shikwembu, animals do not turn into shikwembu. They have only the nuru.

It would be interesting to know what the ideas of other Bantu tribes on the subject are, and I would urge students of African anthropology to inquire if the root *luru* exists in other Bantu languages and what its significance is. In his book on the *Ila-speaking people*, the Rev. Ed. W. Smith does not mention the exact corresponding term ; but he describes hunting rites which bear a close analogy to those we have met amongst the Thongas. I may mention specially the two following facts (Compare his Vol. I, p. 167 and II, p. 136). 1) When a hunter has killed an elephant and has "climbed" its body, a prayer is addressed to Leza, the Supreme Being, to the ancestral spirits (mizhimo) and to the ghost (muzhimo) of the deceased elephant. These are the words of this last prayer : "O spirit, have you no brothers and fathers who will come to be killed? Go and fetch them!" Here we meet with a tribe which definitely believes that the animal becomes a shikwembu (muzhimu). 2) When a person commits a murder, the ghost of the deceased takes possession of the murderer, at least temporarily. Possession, amongst the Ba-Ila, is thus directly connected with murder. So far for the Ba-Ila. It is to be hoped that information as to other tribes will throw further light on the problem of the relation between nuru and ghost.

Considering the question only as it involves the Thongas I come to the following provisional conclusion: The nuru idea is no doubt very ancient, dating perhaps from a time when Animism was not yet clearly distinguished from Dynamism, and when man was not even greatly differenciated from the animal. It originated in the instinctive fear which primitive man felt after shedding the blood of his fellow men and of certain particularly redoutable wild animals. This blood must be avenged (Compare the old saying of Genesis IV, 10 : The voice of thy brother's blood cries unto me from the ground. The vendetta custom which is so wide-spread is a further consequence of this natural feeling). Hence a peculiar remorse and the conviction that purification is necessary to remove the contamination involved or the malediction incurred. This remorse is absent in the case of domestic animals. For this reason the buffalo has no nuru ; as my informant said : "The buffalo is an ox." Why does the shedding of ox-blood cause no fear? Probably because oxen are considered as the lawful property of their owner, who has the right of killing them, whilst the men of another tribe and the animals of the bush do not belong to him.

The *lurulula rite* above all is a *protective* rite aimed at the removal of this dangerous nuru. This is proved etymologically by the fact that this verb is a doubly reversive derivative. It comes from the root *luru* to which is added twice the reversive suffix *ula* which means to remove, to take away (Compare my Shangaan Grammar § 208). The blowing over (huhutela), which is a part of the rite, means the same thing. It is a magical proceeding which is often employed in order to combat hostile spirits or influences. But the lurulula has still another meaning for the professional hunters who so eagerly practise it : It is *a means of identification of the hunter with the animal world*, so that he will be able to live in its midst without being noticed and so kill more game. As my Ronga informant says : "By this operation the hunter takes upon himself the defilement of the animal (its smell, its nature) so that the other hippopotami, when they see him, mistake him for one of themselves ; this man will therefore have great courage and will not run away when

79

they come to him," For this reason hunters strongly assert that should he neglect to perform the rite he will have no success in his future hunting expeditions. A third aim, at least in the case of hippopotamus-hunting, is to overcome the charms of the wizards who ride upon them.

When studying these old hunting rites I had the impression of living for some hours in close contact with primitive humanity, at a time when man, owing to the elementary character of the weapons at his disposal, was almost on the same level as the wild beast and was obliged to display an enormous amount of courage, skill and endurance in order to assert his domination over the animal world and to make it serve his purposes. Since the discovery of gun powder and modern weapons a new era has set in for the hunter. Did not old Viguet assert that now, when an elephant is killed by means of a gun, the nuru is no longer to be feared? Hunting has become for the Bantu of to-day an amusing sport, more profitable indeed but by no means so interesting!

II. *Psinyama-nyamana. The flesh of small animals.*

This word which comes from the well-known Bantu word nyama, meat, is a triple diminutive, obtained by the reduplication of the stem, the prefix *psi*, and the suffix *ana*. It means all kinds of food derived from animals of small size, of which the Thongas are very fond.

Anything in any way resembling meat is welcome to them. Amongst Mammalia they specially enjoy certain kinds of rodents, not the domestic rats, but field mice called maphephe and mabuti which boys catch in their traps. Civet cats (nsimba, yi-tin) and wild cats (goya, dji-ma) are not frequently seen near the villages.

As regards birds, they eat them all with the few exceptions which I shall shortly mention, from the tiniest sparrow to ducks and Guinea fowls, which they manage to snare. They have no aversion to the lower types of animal : they collect the *matomane*, large caterpillars belonging to a species of Saturnidae called Cirina similis (Dist), which are found in families on the nkanye tree, during October. By the exercise of a gentle pressure on the hideous creatures, the inside is squeezed out, and the rest is thrown into a saucepan and boiled, resulting in an indescribable broth of a blackish colour. To see it is quite sufficient... and they enjoy it! Several other kinds of Saturnidae also figure at their feasts : the matomane of nyamari (Bunaea Caffraria), others of a brick red colour (Melanocera Menippe), those of the nhlangula shrub (Gonimbrasia Zambezina), etc. When the cooks go out to split the trunks of old half decayed nkanye trees, from which they get their kindling woòd, they are most careful to put on one side the big white larvae of two large Cerambycidae coleoptera (Mallodon Downesii and Plocoederus frenatus, etc.). These enormous white worms (shipungu) will be fried in their own fat, and served up as a tit-bit for the ladies on their return to the village.

The insect world does great injury to the gardens through the agency of its winged members, the *locusts*, and Natives avenge themselves by eating them wholesale. When a swarm of these destructive creatures has alighted somewhere in the evening, and is benumbed by the cool air of the night, the villagers go and collect them in bags or baskets in great quantities. The heads, wings and legs are torn off and the bodies roasted on the embers, or boiled and used as seasoning. When plentiful, the locusts are dried and crushed in mortars to make a much appreciated flour. To our taste, locusts are simply nauseating.

Another favourite dish, the secret of which the Nkunas learnt from their Pedi neighbours, is provided by *the winged imagos of white ants*. At Christmas time, these insects emerge by thousands from the ant-hills of that region. Some are of small size ; the boys introduce grasses, smeared with glue, into the holes from which they come and catch a large number of them by this kind of fishing. They eat the head, which can be heard cracking between their teeth, and throw the bodies into a calabash to season the evening meal. But there is a larger kind which is even more appreciated. The body is whitish, as large as an almond. A hole in the ant-hill, three feet wide by two feet deep, is dug at the spot where the insects are most likely to emerge. An old pot is placed in the clay of the ant-hill at the bottom of this hole. The hole itself is covered with green branches. These curious winged termites, as soon as they have emerged from their retreat,

81

try to fly ; but they soon fall to the ground and you see them running towards each other and shedding their slender transparent wings, so that they remain on the spot, like worms, creeping slowly along, unable to defend themselves, an easy prey for the birds and the *shinana* toads, which have a grand feast on the happy day when winged termites appear! Those which happen to emerge where the hole has been dug, try to escape by flying, but are prevented from doing so by the covering of leaves. They at once fall heavily to the bottom and roll into the pot, which may become quite full in a few hours. The owner of the trap then comes and makes a splendid sauce with its contents! This kind of termite is not met with on the Coast.

I cannot enter into details as to all these more or less questionable foods. (See I, p. 65, the mention of the Shitambela beetle.)

Although the caterpillars, coleoptera, larvae, and locusts are universally appreciated, there are other "meats" which appeal to certain individuals or clans, but are disdainfully eschewed by others. For instance the boa is eaten with great gusto by the Rongas and disliked by the Nkunas. The same is true of the big varan lizard. The tortoise is generally eaten, but the Mpfumu boys, who esteem themselves more civilised, reject it. On inquiring why some persons or clans exclude certain kinds of meats which other persons or clans consider delectable, we find that there are two different reasons for this, between which it is important to differentiate. The exclusion is due either to a *nyenya*, viz., disgust, or to a *yila*, viz., a taboo.

1) Owing to *disgust*, some people refuse to eat *pork* : "their hearts fear it," probably because pigs are modern and some people are not yet accustomed to eat their flesh. Zulus reject every kind of fish (nhlampfi) from the same feeling of disgust. Snails are despised by all the Thongas ; it is true that the snail of the country (Natica Wesseliana) is not very tempting, its shell being of a transparent green and its flesh reddish ; moreover it is said to "singita," viz., to bring bad luck to any one meeting with it on the way.

But the flesh of some other animals is abstained from, even dreaded, because they *yila*, they are taboo. Thongas have no

82

totems, and do not exclude certain meats from their diet on account of totemic fears. But they proclaim as taboo some animals : amongst them four kinds of birds, the hawk, the vulture, the crow and the stork, because they are used by magicians to prepare powerful charms ; the toad, because when teased its "urine" (murundju) oozes out and is dangerous, causing itch, as is generally believed ; a kind of Tenebrionida beetle (Psammodes Bertoloni), called *shifufunu sha paripari*, because it strikes the ground with its abdomen, making a noise represented by the word *baribarr*. I could not discover the particular danger feared by the Natives in connection with this beetle, but there must be one ; hence the yila. We have already met with the special feminine taboos as regards food (I. p. 183). Women abstain from certain animals, or parts of animals, fearing an evil effect on parturition. Amongst the Nkunas, women are also afraid of the meat of the leopard, the civet-cat, of any animal with paws (psa marubo) ; they only eat animals which have hoofs (psa masondjo). "The former are wild beasts, things of the hubo (I. p. 311), with a bad smell, food for men" (Mankhelu).

The comparison of *nyenya* and *yila* is interesting, as it may help to explain the origin of certain taboos, which is a very important subject indeed. The nyenya is the feeling of disgust which induces a person to abstain from a given food ; in the yila there is, in addition, the dread of a supposed danger connected with the consumption of this food. Thus there is a great difference between the two : the idea of danger does not exist in the nyenya. However, it is quite possible that what was merely a nyenya has evolved, in the course of time, into a real yila or taboo, in which the disgust is no longer the mere individual repulsion for a distasteful food, but has become a social matter, a characteristic custom of a clan, or of a group.

Let me quote two instances which came under my personal notice. Amongst my servants was a young man belonging to the Ngoni clan. The Ba-Ngoni, being of Zulu origin, do not eat fish. Sometimes the cook put shrimps into the ground nut sauce : this was a treat to all the boys, as they are very fond of shrimps and the addition greatly improved the flavour of the dish. But our Ngoni boy, having smelt the "lisuna," used to inquire about the sauce, and if he heard that there were shrimps in it, he disdainfully refused to take his share. — "We are Ba-Ngoni! We do not eat fish," he said with disgust. First, shrimps are not fish ; he was "plus royaliste que le roi!" Second, he did not abstain from the sauce because it had an unpleasant flavour ; it was more tasty than ever! But the *social idea* dictated his attitude. He boasted of belonging to a superior race. He was not like these wretched Ba-Thonga who eat fish! It would be lowering himself to partake of such a meal, so he preferred to fast.

I witnessed the same scene when we were distributing cakes to our school children in Lourenço Marques. One of the girls was the daughter of a pure Ronga woman and an Indian Mussulman. She inquired if the cakes had been cooked with lard. The cakes were excellent, and she found them so, nevertheless she refused to eat them if they contained lard, because her father was not allowed to eat pork. It is evident that there is but one step from this clan repulsion, which is still a nyenya, to a definite taboo. Let the boy or girl *fear* that some evil will happen to them, because they have transgressed a sacred rule, and the nyenya will become a yila. Let it be admitted by them that the transgression of the rule may bring death to the family or the clan, and the primitive individual feeling of disgust will be transformed into the most severe collective taboo. I can quote no instance in proof of this evolution, as we have no knowledge of the past history of the taboos. From the psychological point of view, however, this process is quite within the range of possibility.

III. *Fishing.*

There are no particular restrictions to fishing so long as it is carried on by *hooks*. Any one can go with his boat on the river, the lake, or the sea, and throw his line into the water. The fisherman will then say : "Thu! (not the sacramental tsu, but only an onomatopœia describing the fall of the hook into the water). You! my hook! they eat to their heart's content, people who dwell yonder, where they pound their mealies kneeling down (bugimamusi), there where the khwekhwe and the mhulu are, etc. (names of different kinds of fish)." Afterwards the fisher throws a pinch of tobacco on the spot where his hook fell, not as an offering to the gods, but in order to help his hook to see (hanyanyisa), to awaken it and "give it eyes to catch." This sentence referring to the place "where people pound their mealies standing, or kneeling down," is an allusion to a curious cosmographic notion, which we shall explain later on (Part VI. Chap. I). Seeing the sky reflected in the water, the fisherman thinks of the ends of the earth, where heaven rests on the ground, and where women are obliged to kneel down when crushing their mealies, lest their pestles hit the sky!

There are three other principal methods of fishing, and, as they are more or less of a collective nature, they are regulated by laws and attended with taboos : the nhangu, the shibaba and the tjeba.

The *nhangu* is a triangular enclosure made of sticks stuck in the sand on the seashore. This enclosure has an opening looking seaward. The tide covers the nhangu, bringing with it all kinds of denizens of the sea, big lobsters, shrimps of all sizes, fish, etc ; when it retires, all these creatures are imprisoned in the nhangu, and try to find their way out through the opening ; this however is closed, and the fishers collect their catch, which is sometimes considerable. A man who wishes to build a nhangu must pay a tax to the chief of the country. During the operation he must observe the law of silence ; if anyone should speak to him, he must not answer. When the nhangu is ready he goes straight to his hut, and washes his hands, and then he can speak again. Should he transgress this taboo, the fish will rush about wildly in the trap and he will be unable to catch it. This is not a *kunga* proper (I. p. 124) but only another application of the rule imposed for example on the wife of the hippopotamus-hunter (II. p. 69). On the day of inauguration, (khangula), all the inhabitants have the right to come and partake of the result of the first fishing. This is a *luma*, the luma of the nhangu. The owner of the trap is not allowed to take a single fish home that day. Everything must be consumed on the spot.

The *shibaba* is another kind of trap, made of woven reeds, which is placed on the banks of a river, of the Nkomati, for instance, near the sea, within the tidal reach ; when the tide is

low, the fish is imprisoned between the reeds and the bank.
The construction of this trap is governed by strict laws : no
sexual relation is allowed during the five or six weeks of the
fishing. The owner of the shibaba must cut the first reed.
Women must not approach the spot. On the day of inauguration
there is also a luma ceremony similar to that for the nhangu.

But the most curious fishing custom is the *tjeba*. "Ku tjeba"
means to kill fish in company in lakes which are drying up.
At the end of the winter most of the small lakes scattered all
over Thongaland, get smaller on account of the drought, and the
fish they contain, consisting mostly of carp and barbel, are obliged
to congregate in much smaller spaces. Natives take advantage
of this and the whole country-side is summoned to go and tjeba,
on a certain day, as it is important to be as numerous as possible
in order to ensure success. The chief orders all his men to make
shiranga, a kind of conical basket, a foot and a half high, whose
upper end is open and wide enough to admit the hand. The
shiranga must be very strong ; the tree used for the purpose is
called ntjangari. When the shiranga are ready, a messenger is
sent to all the villages, crying :

> Kho ! Khoooo ! Hobe ! Hobeee ! U yala nsateeee ! Na nsati a randja
> nyamooo ! A randja mihlubeee ! Kho ! Hobe !
> You hate your wife ! Your wife also is fond of flesh food ! She is
> fond of the flesh of the tail of fishes !

Every male member of the tribe must answer to this summons
by going to the shore. Should he refuse the call, he is blamed and
despised, and his companions will sing to him a mocking song :

> U yala ku tjeba, nyañhwaku !
> You refuse to fish, nyañhwaku (1).

In the evening his wife will scold him, on seeing that he brings
no fish home ! She will punish him by giving him mealie pap
without any sauce !

Before the throng enters the lake, someone must *make an
offering* ; he must be a descendant of the inhabitants of the country,

(1) Nyañhwaku is a formula of insult (I. p. 445).

not necessarily a member of the reigning family. He does not perform the full sacramental *tsu* ; he merely spits without having put anything into his mouth, and says : "Let fish abound! Let them not hide in the mud! Let there be enough of them to satisfy every one." Then all the men, quite naked, throw themselves into the lake, which is only one or two feet deep ; they put their shiranga into the water and hold it firmly down on the bottom ; a fish has perhaps been caught ; it is heard flapping

The tjeba fishing.   *Phot. A. Borel*

about inside the basket. The lucky fisherman seizes it through the opening. He carries a wooden pin to which a string is attached ; this string is called by the technical name of *ntjungwa*. He passes the pin through the gills of the fish and ties it on his string. Then he goes on fishing. All his companions do the same. The frightened fish scatter in all directions : but on all sides the shiranga fall over them, and the men have soon made a good haul. When they have reached the extremity of the lake, they come back shouting the following words : "Phindu-na-ye!" —"Come back, following them!" They are allowed when tired to come out of the water and rest in the rays of the sun. The more pertinacious, however, remain in as long as they like. When

87

the fishing is finished, they all sit down and compare their catches. Perhaps an enormous barbel has been caught, "the king of the lake," as these fish sometimes attain a very large size. "Woo! a dle ñhwakwe!" — "Oh! he has killed his mother," say the men, making fun of the fortunate fisherman! But the chief sends an induna who levies the tax. Each fisherman unties one fish from his string and gives it to him.

The tjeba fishing is practised all over Thongaland, in Ronga territory, where such ponds are numerous in the sandy hollows, amongst the Hlabis, and in the neighbourhood of rivers where there are lagoons which dry up, as far as the Maluleke country. Should there be crocodiles in the pond, which may very well happen when the lake is connected with the Limpopo or the Nkomati, the religious ceremony is more important on account of the danger incurred. Then the bones are thrown and declare who must make the offering in order to secure adequate protection from the ancestor-gods. The officiator enters the lake first, and, plunging his shiranga into the water, says : "If you are here, crocodile, go away! you hyena, do not bite." Amongst the Maluleke, a man of the Ba-Nyai tribe must perform the religious ceremony, as the Ba-Nyai were in the country before the Thongas. He must go first and catch a fish, bring it out alive, and then, surrounded by his fellow Ba-Nyai, offer it to his ancestor-gods. Then he throws it back into the water. The Thonga chief, having ordered his men to keep silence, then makes the following proclamation in a loud voice : "Let the fish abound, and kill them all, but do not bewitch each other!"

The Hlengwes have a very curious custom which I have already explained when discussing the Bantu notion of sexual relations (I. p. 189). When they tjeba they take a little boy and a little girl, and lay them down together under a lion's skin, as if they were husband and wife, during all the time that they are fishing. The children keep quiet, — so the fish will also keep quiet and not swim away. When the fishing is concluded, these children are "awakened," and are given a part of the catch : they are praised and thanked, as they are supposed to have secured the fish by their action... or rather by their inaction! This very significant

88

rite may explain why sexual relations are prohibited during all important hunting and fishing operations. With their magic conception of Nature, Bantus do not separate the domain of man from the animal world ; human actions have their immediate effect amongst animals. So if men and women keep strict control over themselves, hippopotami, fish or elephants will not be so wild, and hunters will have more success!

*
*   *

Meat is either boiled (pseka), or roasted (wosha). When boiled, the broth is called *muru*, (Ro.) or *sheshebo*, (Dj.) the same name that is given to monkey nut sauce or any other seasoning. When roasted, it is either placed on the embers, or skewered on sticks (lihanga) and exposed to the heat of the fire.

The blood of animals (bubendje) is also eaten by most men. However, many fear it (tshaba), not on account of a yila, as if it were taboo, but rather from individual loathing. There are no special laws to be observed as regards bones. The meat of sacrifices, offered in the funeral rites, must be eaten *on the road*, not in the mortuary nor in the guests' villages, as we have already seen.

Meat is welcome, and eagerly sought after in time of famine (ndlala). Should the October rains fail, or the crops be destroyed by grasshoppers, as has been, alas, frequently the case since the first appearance of these pests in August 1894 (1), the Natives are bereft of every resource (2). They dig up all the edges of the

(1) Just at the commencement of the war between the Natives and the Portuguese, grasshoppers arrived in thick clouds in the district of Lourenço Marques. They had not been seen for a great number of years : old folk only recollected having seen them in bygone times. Since then the scourge has never entirely disappeared. The coincidence of their coming and the beginning of hostilities struck the Blacks very forcibly ; they often said, at the sight of the grasshoppers : "They announce the armies of Gungunyana."

(2) Here is a pretty couplet with reference to famine :
Nkondjo wa nhlengana shipopokwana ?
— Lembe ra ndlala a he ngume kusuhe !
The traces of the little antelope (nhlengana) (which one sees in the desert a long way from its lair) recall the year of famine, when one does not stay near home ; (one must go a long way to search for food). See also the several allusions to the year of famine in *Les Chants et Contes des Ba-Ronga*, p. 158, 160 et seq.

lakes, to find the tubers of the nenuphars (Nymphea stellata), and cook these indigestible roots (matibu). They have also gone so far as to make flour of the pith of the palm trees (mimale). They disinter the bodies of dead animals, or cram themselves with *masala*, which often engenders serious vomiting. Some eat big Copris beetles.

Such famines were frequent in former times, and special years are still known as having been years of *ndlala*. So, in the chronology of Shinangana (Part IV) the year 1875 (?) was called "the year of the Magadingele famine." On the Coast the Goñhwen famine is still remembered (1). The proximity of a seaport which is easily provisioned, and the possibility of earning money wherewith to buy rice and maize constitute a real advantage which Natives are the first to recognise. In this respect civilisation has rendered signal service to the Thonga commissariat!

(1) It does not appear that starvation ever induced Thongas to practise cannibalism on any considerable scale. Cases are known of this happening as when, during the war of 1895, a Ronga killed a man and ate his lungs and kidneys quite raw. He was prosecuted and deported to Mozambique. In the mountains, the Ba-Pedi and Ba-Sutho began to consume human flesh after the raids of Chaka and his generals. They first ate the corpses ; then, having acquired a taste for this food, they began to attack travellers, springing out from the caves in the mountains, where they were hiding ; they even made organised expeditions in search of men to devour. These cannibals are known by the name of Makhema and caused the Queen of the Bokhaha, Male, to change her residence (I. p. 477).

CHAPTER II

INDUSTRY OF THE THONGAS.

Industry, in the human race, is born of necessity. Man feels the need of protection and shelter from wind and weather ; this need leads him to make some sort of a covering (clothing) and to build a dwelling (habitation). The necessity of procuring food, of preparing it, of keeping it, suggests to him the idea of fashioning weapons for killing game, and utensils of various kinds for tillage, and for cooking the products of the soil.

But Nature must also provide the wherewithal to be turned to account by man's intelligence. The development of human industry depends therefore on a variety of circumstances. We shall now study the inventions of the Thongas, what they have been able to evolve in the matter of clothing, habitation and utensils : we shall also consider their wood-carvings, and their exceedingly primitive commerce, and shall endeavour to find a solution of the several questions which will naturally be suggested by the extremely slow industrial development of these tribes.

A. CLOTHING AND ORNAMENTS.

I. *The Evolution of Costume.*

As regards *women*, Mboza asserts that, in remote times, Ronga women wore well tanned and softened skins, to which they hung pieces of brass, as the Pedi women still do. At present, amongst the Rongas, they are all clothed with pieces of unshaped material, which they call *ḳapulane* ; this piece of stuff is fastened round the

91

waist, whence it falls down to form a skirt. With this most women in the interior are satisfied ; they do not cover the upper part of the body. The undergarment, covering the genitalia, is

Phot. P. Berthoud.
Camilla, a Lourenço Marques woman.

called *ntlhomo* in front, (a word which is taboo), and *mphela* at the back, (this term is less taboo than the first).

In the Transvaal, Thonga or Shangaan women have also from time immemorial adopted European materials, of which they make double pleated skirts adorned with beads, as seen in the illustration I. p. 195. This is the typical heathen costume. The Pedi or Sutho women are at once distinguishable from their Ronga sisters by the fact that they have preserved their ancient skin dress. In the neighbourhood of Lourenço Marques, a further development has taken place, as women there wear a large plaid which they knot over the breast and. which hangs down behind as far as their heels, a costume by no means lacking in the picturesque. They cover their breast and shoulders with a bodice (kimao), generally very close-fitting, especially in the sleeves.

Phot. J. Bennett.

Christian girls of the Training Institution of Lemana (Northern Transvaal).

The pattern is said to have been borrowed from India. (See on the opposite page the portrait of Camilla, an old resident of Lourenço Marques, wearing the costume adopted by the women in the town and suburbs.)

Ordinary frocks are preferred by Christian converts, and so the European fashion tends to supplant the Indian, or the heathen.

As regards *men's costume* among the Ba-Ronga it was little more than the traditional smile. It consisted, in fact, of a small article made of narrow strips of palm leaf, plaited together, and could hardly be termed "clothing." This was called *mbaya* and bears a great resemblance to the "libyan sheath" which is seen on the old Egyptian monuments (1). The last mbaya were seen in the neighbourhood of Rikatla, when the war of 1894 broke out. In the Northern clans they were still commonly used by the generation which preceded Viguet, by the Nkunas who fled before Manukosi in 1835. (See Introduction to the *Grammaire Ronga*, page 17). The Kafirs of Cape Colony were still in 1903, at this stage of dress... or rather undress, and the Pedis of the Transvaal, with their *musindu* (a mere piece of skin protecting the genitalia), are not much in advance of the mbaya stage even now. This state of affairs arose in the first place from the fact that, as yet, the sentiment of modesty had hardly been conceived. It must not be supposed, however, that morals were the more depraved for that reason ; on the contrary, they were much purer, and innocence far more general, judging from the reports of those who remember those days.

But a second fact which allowed the Thongas to go about without clothing, 'in puris naturalibus,' or nearly so, is the warmth of the climate ; the temperature rarely drops below 44° Fahrenheit and frequently rises to 113° F., the annual mean near Lourenço Marques being about 74° F. according to our observations extending over seven years. It is thus easy to dispense with a coat in that part of the world, and it is by no means a rare occurrence to see children in the interior absolutely naked (2).

This very primitive article of attire has, however, been supplanted by one designed by the Zulus, and worn by men up to

(1) The "phallic sheath" of the earliest Egyptian statuettes, which is also to be noticed on the engravings of the XIXth dynasty, as belonging to African populations, is not of quite the same pattern as the Thonga mbaya or the Sutho musindu. However there is a real similarity between all these primitive costumes ; many of the customs of the Bantus of to-day seem to have existed amongst the early Egyptians, and this fact shows that the origin of Egyptian civilisation is partially African.

(2) The Chopi tribe, which is very industrious, dwelling in the neighbourhood of the Thongas N. E. of the mouth of the Limpopo, has succeeded in obtaining a very superior kind of dress by beating the bark of the *mphama*, a kind of fig-tree which is wide-spread in the country, and which the Ba-Chopi even planted for this purpose. The pieces of bark become very soft and can be strung together. They are called *ntjalu*. Several samples of this curious stuff can be seen in the Neuchâtel Museum. Thongas used to buy the article from their Chopi neighbours, but never knew how to manufacture it.

Zulu costume.   *Phot. Natal.*

a recent date from one end to the other of the Thonga tribe
(except, I am told, in some remote spots in the Hlengwe country).
It consists of a belt to which are hung tails of animals, or strips of

95

skin (djobo, dji-ma), covered with hair or fur, or even the entire
skin of a civet cat, or antelope. The nsimba skins are in great
demand, but are rather expensive, and the majority of the Ba-
Ronga men wear merely two pieces of ox hide (mabebe), one in
front and the other behind. Small boys often content themselves
with one in front only. The young men prefer to wear them
rather full, something like a petticoat! The *shifado* (Vol. I.
Annotatio I) is worn with the belt of tails. This "sphaerula" is
made either of carved wood or plaited milala leaves, or of a
small calabash just the size required. When it is fixed in place,
raw Natives consider that they have satisfied all the exigences of
decency. Although much more decent than the *mbaya*, this
garment of tails, or pieces of skin, is still a trifle incomplete...

Sandals of ox hide (tintango) are also an old article of dress ;
they were used by hunters and travellers. They belong to the
bush and it is taboo to bring them into the hubo (I. p. 355).

At the present time European costume is tending to supplant
the belt of tails. The first step consists in adopting the *ladula*, a
piece of stuff hanging down from the loins as far as the knees.
This style of garment was still worn in 1910 by most of the young
heathen round Lourenço Marques ; it was sometimes combined
with the madjobo, which were still in use. But men, and
especially youngsters, soon aspire to something better : trousers
and jackets! (1). However ungainly the Native may appear when
duly arrayed in coat and trousers, there is nothing he covets
more than these garments. As they cannot all afford complete
suits, they often have to be satisfied with such odds and ends as
they can get from the Banyans, or pick up from their European
masters. One sees them gravely walking about in worn-out long
frock coats, the trousers being conspicuous by their absence.
Others think themselves very fortunate if they can manage to get
hold of a very much patched waistcoat with which to adorn

---

(1) The taste for European fabrics is said by thoughtful Natives to have been the
cause of the loss of their independence. They support this somewhat surprising theory
by the following argument : "Without this," said one of them to me, pulling the flap of
my coat, "the Whites would never have conquered us ! In our wars with them there
have always been some of us who would not give up these stuffs, and so made alliance
with the Europeans. We were divided, and thus our power of resistance was broken."

themselves, the rest of the body remaining stark naked... except, of course, for the indispensable belt of tails. One day a Rikatla lad came to see me with an eye-glass fixed triumphantly on his forehead, and when I asked him what was the use of that article he replied, really meaning what he said : "Ndji yambalile" — "I have dressed." He intended to do me honour. The same lad came, on another occasion, wearing coquettishly on his head a lady's black lace hat, which he seemed to consider very "chic." I much preferred the get-up of an individual, by name Glas, who put a red lily in his tightly-curled hair, and made a chin strap of a flexible reed which he passed through the holes in his ears on either sides, so that it formed a sort of frame to his face. Every Thonga has already learned to know a *buluku* (trousers), a *djansi* (jacket), a *fascikoti* (apron, a corruption of the word waistcoat), a *hembe* (shirt), *masokisi* and *memeya* (stockings) and *shilembe* (hat). The majority of these words have doubtless come from the Boer dialect, and have changed somewhat in passing into the language of the Natives.

The "civilised" attain the height of bliss when they are able to procure an irreproachable suit of clothes, and it is a sight to behold these young men returning direct from Johannesburg, dressed in the latest style, with a white starched shirt, a silk cummerbund, and jacket and trousers to match. They think themselves handsome, but we do not share their illusion! How often have we not longed to see them adopt some costume suited to their colour, their customs, their occupations, and their climate! But they want to be like us, so what is to be done ? (1) Their idea of costume is evidently different from ours : they consider it as an adornment rather than as an actual protection against cold or heat. If it rains, or if it is cold, they much prefer to wrap

(1) I have heard it asserted that the adoption of European clothing by the Blacks tends to enfeeble them, even to the extent of rendering them liable to new diseases. I was assured that the introduction of tuberculosis amongst them is due to their clothes. This assertion is at least very much exaggerated. However it is certain that the exposure of their skin to the rays of the sun was extremely healthy. On the other hand, they do not know that wet clothing must be changed (they may have no second suit to put on), so they catch cold, and pneumonia or pleurisy sets in... I have also heard it stated that the second-hand, cast-off garments which traders sell them often infect them with syphilis (especially after circumcision), or other poisons.

themselves in the big rug (ngubo, mpisi-mpisi), which they all buy to sleep under at night. The end of the process of evolution will certainly be that they will adopt exactly the same dress as their European masters : a complete suit for the men, frocks, hats and boots for the women ; as soon as the majority of them obtain enough money to buy these, they will do so, and seeing how particular most of them are as regards their external appearance, it may be safely anticipated that Bantu beauties will submit to the tyranny of the London or Paris fashions as readily as our European élégantes!

It is easy to see the evolution of dress in the Bantu tribe by comparing the illustration of the South African woman (a Sutho, I. p. 46) representing the first stage, those of the Thonga women (I. p. 179 and 195) representing the second, Camilla, depicting a third stage (p. 92), and the ordinary European frock forming the fourth (1).

As for men, I unfortunately possess no picture of the primitive *mbaya*. But the following stages are illustrated by the two Zulu boys (p. 95) by the habitué of the Nkuna Court (I. p. 435), and by Tobane (I. p. 4) and Muhlaba (I. p. 426).

II. *Ornaments.*

The taste for decoration, for ornament, is innate with the Black. Ages ago, before he took to fixing a flower in his hair, he used to tatoo himself. We have already described (I. p. 178) the various patterns of *tattooing* of men and women, and have pointed

---

(1) I must however mention a piece of information which was given to me by two trustworthy authorities, according to which Thongas of the Northern clans possessed in former times a kind of primitive *textile industry*. The Rev. Calvin Maphophe, who belongs to the Hlengwe group, asserted that Natives of the Tshobane clan, near the Sabie river, knew how to weave threads of cotton in order to form a kind of cloth called shombe, and another man of the Bilen plain told me that this cloth was worn by women at a time when men were satisfied with the mbayi. This industry has long since disappeared ; European cloth probably killed it as soon as it became procurable. The presence of subspontaneous plants of cotton in various parts of the country is in favour of this assertion. Where and when did these ancient Thongas obtain the precious textile plant and who taught them to use it ? This is an interesting historical point which I am afraid will never be elucidated.

out that this custom probably had a social significance in former times, though at present it is practised as an adornment.

As regards *hair* (nsisi, mu-mi), women often cut it, men less

Maputju women with "tingoya."   *Photo P. Aubert.*

frequently. A man only cuts his hair when his wife dies, as a sign of mourning : it is a taboo (I. p. 146). In former times they never shaved their beards. People made fun of those who did so, saying : "Are you an Angolese ?" (The Angolese, who are numerous in the neighbourhood of Lourenço-Marques,

99

used to shave their beards). Young men sometimes let two or three of their curls grow on their forehead like horns! Others stretch out their curls and smear them with a gluey substance obtained from the nkanye tree. This is called *ku hoba misisi*. As regards women, those who are nursing babies regularly turn their hair into an ornament : the small curls are stretched out, smeared with fat and made to fall on the temples and on the occiput ; they are then covered with ochre. This operation is called *ku hora misisi*, and the rats'tails thus produced are the *tingoya* ; they are the characteristic ornament of women during the nursing period. Nursing women undoubtedly think the tingoya improve their appearance. "Look! She has *hora misisi*! How well it suits her!" people will say of a woman who has succeeded in altering her coiffure in this way. But this custom has also a ritual value (1).

Nursing women cover their whole body, their clothing, and their *ntehe* (I. p. 46) with *ochre*. The habit of anointing (tota) or smearing with ochre (tshumane) goes hand in hand with that of tingoya. This rather disgusting custom marks them as nursing, and is a protection (shisibelo) against the husband ; so long as a woman covers herself with ochre, it is a sign that she will not cohabit with him. They say also that ochre prevents the bad smell resulting from childrens' unclean habits, and that it softens the ntehe and makes the baby grow (2). The skin of children is also covered with a coating of this pigment ; some say it is done not so much with the object of beautifying the child as of hiding the dirt which the mothers are too lazy to remove! No wonder that, in these conditions, it has been found that this smearing with ochre fosters conjunctivitis and other diseases!

(1) The Ngoni taught the Northern Thongas another and more elaborate way of curling the hair : the queens, wives of Gungunyana, transform their "thatch" into regular cylindrical chignons (shifoko), standing up like towers (I. p. 416). The Ba-Ronga have not adopted this custom, except, in some cases, the chiefs. (I. p. 386).

(2) It is very curious to observe that these two feminine modes of adornment, the tingoya and the ochre, have been adopted by the magicians, those who pretend to possess supernatural power in smelling out witches and treating possessed people (Part VI). They like to assume the appearance of women. People suffering from the Ba-Ndjao possession especially use ochre. Their spirits order them to do so : they would torment their victims should the latter not obey.

Ornaments, calabashes, pottery.

The use of ochre is, however, not restricted to nursing mothers or magicians : it is the special province of young marriageable girls, wishing to attract attention : their brilliant skin shines like a mirror, setting off to perfection the white of their eyes and the black of their hair, which is sometimes made flossy by means of antimony or ground charcoal. A quaint saying puts it thus :

Shindzingeri pundjene ? -Banhwanyana tolan !...
What says the pretty bird with the coral neck that sings in the grass ?
It says : Girls, anoint yourselves with ochre ! (if you wish to be as beautiful as it is).

Another ornament, of ancient date, is the *bracelet*. There are several kinds : 1) the big heavy copper rings, called *masindana*, which greatly resemble those of the lake-dwellers, having a similar rather oval shape with an opening for slipping them over the wrist ; 2) the modern bracelets, called *busenga*, which the Rongas first bought in Natal, and which the Ma-Lemba introduced in the Northern clans ; they are made of iron wire twined round a ring of hide ; 3) the *mafowa* are more ancient, being made of seeds strung on thongs of skin, and are wound several times round the leg. This is an ornament for either dance or war. The mafowa are sometimes made of the silvery cocoons of Argema Mimosae, the Queen Moth, which are found on nkanye trees, emptied of the chrysalis which is inside and filled with grains of millet which rattle when dancing!

Beads (nkarara) are evidently of later date ; they were introduced by the Whites in the XVIth century, when the Portuguese were already in regular communication with Delagoa Bay and trafficked with the Natives, exchanging glassware for gold and ivory. Glass fascinated the Blacks : its brightness and transparency pleased them immensely. An old song echoes their simple transports of delight :

E! Bashabi! Batatana ba shabile; ba buya ni shintshirimana sha balu-ngoooo !..
Hi! Here come the buyers ! Our fathers return with their purchases ; they bring back with them the beautiful glittering things which the Whites sell !...

"A few years ago an ordinary glass bottle was thought a wonder by the people in the interior," said Timoteo Mandlati to me.

(He was a Nkuna from Shiluvane.) It is not strange therefore that they became enamoured of beads. They give them special names, according to colour and size, and succeed in turning them to very good account. The chief ornament the women make, (beadwork is exclusively done by the women), is the *mugangu* (No. 2), used in love-making (gangisa) ; it is a kind of crown of blue beads with red chevrons, worn by girls when they wish to beautify themselves. Some are wide and some narrow ; the beads are strung on threads which are crossed and knotted as the work proceeds : no canvas foundation is used. The bead necklace is called *shihekisana*. Bead bracelets on the wrist are *shibolisa*, and on the ankles *maluwada*. Beads are also used in making large and heavy belts (mugadzi), weighing one to two pounds, and very much appreciated as an ornament when dancing. In the same way calabashes (No. 5) are covered with beads, bags made of hide (No. 4), bottles and even baskets. This bead work calls for a good deal of patience. One of the things which the Ronga most dearly loves to have decorated with beads is his tobacco pouch, (ngulana, No. 3), which is for him not only a means of satisfying his passion for taking snuff, but also one of his most prized ornaments. I do not now refer to the carved ebony tobacco box, worn *en bandoulière*, but to the article consisting of eight or nine large seeds, hollowed out, in which is kept the powder which stimulates the brain. Each of these seeds (which come from another country) is closed with a small piece of reed ; when one is walking they rattle against each other, producing a most delightful sound! The first thing a man will say to a friend on meeting him, will be : "Fole?" — "Tobacco?" and before anything further is said, each will indulge in a pinch. The same act of politeness is essential before beginning any discussion. The Thonga does not smoke the calumet of peace, but uses for a like purpose the many receptacled tobacco pouch, decorated with beads, which hangs from the belt at his hip. He takes from it a pinch of snuff, which he offers to his opponent ; the latter takes another pinch and proceedings then commence under the happiest auspices. Hearts are not far from concord... when noses have already fraternised!

103

Beads are merely an ornament and have no ritual value, except the large white ones used by people possessed by the Ba-Ndjao spirits. (Part VI.)

B. HABITATION.

While there has been such a rapid change in Thonga customs regarding dress, — so rapid that in these last fifty years they have changed more in that respect than during the fifty preceding centuries —, in the field of architecture the tribe appears to have stood still ; their huts are built precisely as they were in ancient times. It is true that it is easier to put on a jacket and trousers than to alter the style of one's house : besides it must be admitted that the Thonga hut possesses several advantages. It is comparatively easy to construct, cool in the hot weather, perfectly watertight in the rainy season and is fairly ingeniously contrived.

That which is called *yindlu* (yin-tin) properly speaking, is more especially the *roof* of the hut (lwango, dji-ma) ; for it is the roof which is the most troublesome to make. A strange fact too, and one which appears paradoxical, is that, in the construction (ku yaka) of the house, they begin with the roof!

The Thonga architect — and every man is his own in that country — gathers together a few hundred straight sticks, one to one and a half inches in width and from three to ten feet in length. He digs a hole in the ground, a yard and a half in diameter and 16 inches deep, in which he arranges his sticks in a circle, points downwards, at the bottom of the hole, and supported in such a manner that they lie at an angle of 45 degrees with the ground. Any one of these sticks will thus be at about a right angle with the opposite one, and all together they form, as it were, a huge conical basket with its point in the hole. To fasten all the sticks together, he ties them to round hoops (something like cask hoops) made of bent branches. These hoops (balelo, dji-ma) are concentric, very small at the bottom, and getting gradually larger as the work progresses. Any spaces which remain between the sticks first arranged are filled up, one after the other, with shorter sticks, which are pushed in here and there as the building proceeds, and the architect ends by obtaining a sort of enormous, pointed hat lying on its apex, all the branches and sticks composing it being solidly tied together with strips of a very resistant bark, that of the bulolo Hibiscus (p. 33) or of other trees. It is now only necessary to turn the big cone over, and place it on a wall, and there you have the typical Thonga hut.

The *wall* is built with stakes, about four feet in length above the ground, planted at intervals along the circumference of a circle which the architect traces with wonderful accuracy in the sand. He then takes two flexible branches and fastens them to the stakes, at a height of one foot above the ground, the whole way round the wall, one on the inside, the other on the outside. Between these branches and in the spaces from stake to stake are inserted reeds of the same height, completing the wall : the reeds are firmly fastened to the supporting branches by a band passing alternately over and underneath them. The same operation is repeated half way up the wall (two feet above the ground), and again at three quarters of the height (three feet). The wall is now ready to put on its large conical hat, which will fit it perfectly : a cone on a cylinder!

Placing the roof in position (ku tlakula yindlu), the next procedure, requires the display of considerable muscular energy. All the men of the village are convened for the job : their strong arms raise the monumental basket and place it triumphantly on the wall. Beer is then given to the helpers, and a little jollification ensues ; the equivalent of the "fête du petit sapin enrubanné" which the carpenters celebrate in Switzerland when they have completed the roof of a house.

The roof must now be *covered* (fulela) *with a thatch* (byanyi) to make it impermeable to the heavy rains of the wet season, and it is here that considerable ingenuity is displayed in the method adopted. The Thonga pulls up by the roots, in the low lands on the borders of the lakes, a kind of very wide grass (luhlwa), which attains a height of one and a half to two feet : this he separates into small bunches which he lays side by side on the ground and ties together, one by one, with his string made of bark, fastening them with a special knot. The result is a series of hundreds of contiguous bunches seemingly sewn together with a regular seam, at about 6 inches above the roots. This can be rolled up like a mat, forming a beautiful sheaf, and carried away on the workman's shoulder to be placed on the roof. Once there, it is unrolled and fastened to the hoop of branches forming the outer circle at the base of the cone. One man runs a huge needle, threaded with a long string, through the thatch, taking care to do so just above the seam which unites the bunches of grass ; another man, who is inside the hut, receives the needle and pushes it back again through the thatch, but, in his case, just underneath the seam : the two thus continue sewing the thatch, with long stitches, all round, so that the seam itself is securely fixed to the outer hoop at the base of the roof. When they have completed the circle and provided the hut with a first belt of thatch, they fetch another sheaf of grass and unroll it on the next hoop above. Now a certain proportion is to be observed between the distance separating the two hoops (A B) and that of the seam from the roots of the grass (C D) ; that is to say if, for instance, the space between the concentric hoops is five inches, the seam will be six inches above the roots ; whence the following result : the roots of the thatch fixed to the lower hoop (A E) reach as far as the second hoop (B F) and even overlap slightly. The fresh sheaf which will be sewn on to the second hoop will thus overlap the first sheaf in such a way that its seam will be fastened practically on the top of the roots of the lower sheaf. On the second hoop there will therefore be a double thickness of thatch (at point G) all round the hut. As the *luhlwa* is about 24 inches in length, it follows that the third and fourth sheaves or layers of thatch will also cover the second hoop ; the thickness of the thatch at this point will thus be fourfold, as also all over the hut. A well built roof of this description is perfectly rain-proof. As the work goes on, progress becomes more and more rapid, as the hoops diminish in size and the apex is reached almost unexpectedly.

On the top of the cone is fastened a *circular crown* (shihlungwa) of very carefully plaited grass ; the architect doubtless had a double object in view in thus crowning the huts : first to keep the rain from percolating through at the top, and secondly to impart to the building, by means of this highly ornamental addition, a degree of finish, an air of beauty, ease and opulence which it certainly would never have possessed had it terminated in an ordinary point. It is, no doubt, owing to the fact that the crown is the glory of the house that it is removed as soon as the occupant dies!

There are still two more operations to be performed before the hut is finished : *the plastering* (bama (Ro.), phama (Dj.) and the making of the *door*. But these two jobs can be undertaken at the same time for the very good reason that plastering is the work of the wives, while making the door is that of the husband. Accompanied by other women of the village, the future mistress of the hut starts out for the marshes to collect some black clay

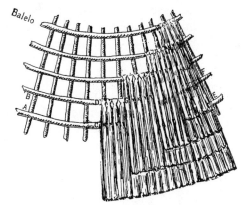

Construction of the Thonga roof.

(bompfi). If the marshes are too far off, she will content herself with digging in one of the ants'nests on the hillside. These terrible ants, which destroy everything, collect large quantities of hard earth, with which to build their nests, and this differs largely from the sand of the surroundings. (It may perhaps be simply sand hardened and changed by the acid secretions of the termites.) The shirundju, the conical basket which women carry on their heads, will be used to take home clods of red or black clay, and, using the same baskets, they will fetch from the cattle kraal some fresh dung which they mix with the clay, inside the new hut, pouring water on the mixture to reduce it to the proper consistency. They tread the unsavoury mud with their feet, and, with this semi-liquid mortar, plaster the wall on the inside, introducing the mud between the reeds and spreading it out with the palms of their hands until it forms a smooth layer all over the interior. Not a ray of light can now enter the hut, except through some small open spaces to be seen, here and there, between the roof and the top of the wall. The air circulates more or less through these small vents, which, however, were not included in the original plan of the hut. The remainder of the clay makes a hard even flooring which will be re-covered from time to time with a fresh coating of black plaster (I. p. 187).

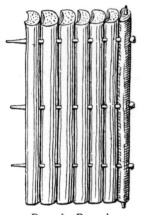

Door of a Ronga hut.

As regards the *door*, the Ba-Ronga in the country round Rikatla generally make it of the wood of the mimale palm (Raphia vinifera, see p. 4). They cut down one or two of the giant leaves of this tree, which grows in the marshes. The leaf itself is one enormous central stalk with narrow folioles on either side ; these are cut off and the nerve remains : a sort of gigantic switch, twenty to thirty feet in length, about four to six inches wide at the base and tapering gradually to its point, convex on one side, and concave on the other. Once dried, it turns a grey colour. The interior is a fibrous pith, of extraordinarily light weight, whilst the exterior bark is very thin, hard and shiny as though it had been varnished with copal. It is impossible to imagine a lighter wood. Comfortably established under the shady trees of the square, our joiner cuts the nerve into several pieces of a given length (say about four feet, the height of the wall). This is not difficult, for it is only necessary to cut through the thin outer bark, when the knife slips through the inner pith, like so much butter! These lengths are then bored through from front to back in three places, say at one, two and three feet from the bottom, and three stout sticks are passed through the holes, firmly holding the several pieces of the nerve together : this makes the door. The ends of the transverse sticks are fixed into a pole which is pointed top and bottom, thus forming pivots or hinges.

The *sill* consists simply of a piece of wood (ntjandja wa shipfalo) laid flat on the ground, with one edge raised so that the door cannot be opened outwards. It must always open inwards, doubtless with a view to facilitate the exclusion of unwelcome visitors by the simple expedient of sitting with one's back against it. The threshold is not attended with taboos, excepting that of the principal hut of the master of the village, beneath which

The Thonga hut.   *Phot. A. Borel.*

protective drugs have been placed at the foundation of his village. It is taboo to sit on it (this may cause disease), but not to tread on it. Most huts are now fitted with padlocks which are, of course, of European origin. The palm wood doors are only seen in the districts where the mimale palm grows.

A number of small sticks are stuck in the straw crown at the top of the hut, and certainly add to the picturesque appearance of these constructions. It would seem that they are put there to hinder birds from perching on the huts, and more especially to avoid any chance visit during the night from screech-owls (ma-kuñhunu) and other nocturnal fowl, which might alight on

109

the hut and terrify the occupants by their lugubrious cries.

I may mention another advantage of the Thonga hut. Between the sticks and the hoops of the roof small interstices, of a few square inches, are left when the thatch is in place ; in these small lockers all kinds of things are stowed away : ears of sorghum, or of millet, kept for seed, sticks, spoons or knives ; baskets can be hung up, by hitching the string by which they are usually carried across

The Native tin town near Pretoria Station. *Phot. A. Borel.*

the shoulder on to the handle of a spoon which is sticking out of the thatch. On entering a hut the roof looks like a regular museum ; it is useful as a cupboard or hanging wardrobe!

The Thonga hut, formed of two distinct parts, wall and roof, is far superior to that of the Zulus, which looks like a bee hive, and consists only of a semi-circular roof. Thongas know how to build this kind of huts, but they are generally made quite small (six feet in diameter) and used as shelters for the boys who look after the goats. They are called *mitjhonga*. The Ba-Ngoni adopted their system of building from the Thongas of the plain, and Gungunyana's people constructed huge conical huts, but the

110

entrances were still smaller than those of the Ba-Ronga. To get in, it was necessary to wriggle, or at least to go on all fours (1).

As I am dealing here only with the architectural side of the subject, and do not touch on its social side, let me merely state that the hut is divided into two parts, the right half belonging to the husband and the left to the wife (I. p. 138, 187), that it is contaminated by the death of its owner, and, being looked on as a *rumbi*, a ruin, must be pierced through (I. p. 138), deprived of its crown (I. p. 145), and ritually crushed down (I. p. 157) or closed (I. p. 162, 163).

Nobody will deny that the conical roofed Thonga hut is a charming thing to see, and is wonderfully in keeping with the African scenery. To judge how "Civilisation" improves the condition of things for the Natives of South Africa, let my readers contemplate the Native village as it was a few years ago, in the vicinity of Pretoria Station. Boys working on the Railway had built a horrible mass of tiny sheds of old paraffin tins, cut and flattened for the purpose. There is no lack of imagination in these constructions, but they are a perfect illustration of what the raw Native becomes when plunged suddenly into our XXth century civilisation and attempting in his poverty and ignorance to adapt himself to it. I am glad to say that, on the Missionary Stations, where Native Christians are directed by their missionaries, they build much better houses, having learnt to mould clay into bricks, and to build ovens (I. p. 536). Some of them are good masons and know the use of the level and of the square. There has been also a considerable improvement in the type of buildings erected in Town Locations during recent years.

(1) I have previously described the *shitlanta*, storehouses of various sizes, made for storing maize and other field produce, and have given (p. 26) an illustration of two of them, especially interesting as they contain the food of Sokis, who died from a sudden attack of pulmonary tuberculosis (lifuba). The provisions which are in the large storehouse must be sold as they are contaminated and dangerous to members of his family ; the small one contains mealies bought from other people for his widows, who are not allowed to consume the food of the deceased, whilst strangers have nothing to fear from it. (See for the notions of contagion, Part VI.)

C. UTENSILS.

Nature, which has provided the Ba-Ronga with skins of animals for clothing, and with poles, reeds, grasses and fibrous barks for their habitations, has also favoured them with several exceedingly useful trees of which they have not been slow to take advantage. Of these the most valuable is the *milala* palm, *(Hyphaene crinita)* used for nearly all basket-work ; next comes the *nkuhlu (Trichilia emetica)* whose wood is particularly serviceable for all descriptions of carving. She has also deposited in their plains beds of clay, of more or less desirable quality, which they use for making pottery. I shall begin with the latter.

I. *Pottery.*

An excellent clay is to be found at Shibindji, in the neighbourhood of Lourenço Marques, a district close to Morakwen, and the people of this place — they are the same who abstain from eating any animal liver (I. p. 364) — are the potters who supply the whole country. They are said to be the masters (benyi) of the art. But clay is found in many other places, in Shifukundju, Mpatshiki, etc. It is said that the clay of Muweri, near Lemon Island, on the Lower Nkomati, is even better than that of Shibindji. So the art of the potter does not belong to a single family, and is not hereditary. Any one may learn it and practise it. Pottery amongst the Thongas is essentially woman's province. Is this because earthenware utensils are principally used in the kitchen, where woman's sway is paramount and indisputed? Possibly ; in any case it is so.

Let us suppose then that the mother of a family wishes to renew, or to add to her stocks of pots, large and small. She starts out for the marshes, picks up in the well-known hollow several clods of clay and returns to the village carrying them on her head. No one salutes her : everyone pretends not to see her, doubtless to avoid bringing any ill luck to the venture! She buries the clay at the foot of a tree to keep it moist, and only takes it out of its hiding-place on the day on which she has decided to start the work.

Let us see by means of some photographs, taken by the greatly regretted A. Borel, how Meta, a Shibindji girl, married in Rikatla, proceeds in her work. Placing a broken piece of an old pot in the

Fashioning the pots. *Phot. A. Borel.*

mortar, she pounds it until it is reduced to small fragments, the size of a grain of maize : these she mixes with her clay, adding water and sand, and kneads the whole together until she has made it into a very soft ball. She makes a hole in this, a wide opening which she enlarges by degrees, hollowing it out more and more and gradually giving it the shape she wishes. I have already alluded to the clever way in which the Blacks trace the circumference of a circle on the ground (I. p. 126) ; the same natural instinct enables them to model perfect spheres. It is astonishing to see the beautiful symmetry of these utensils, although these pots are fashioned without the aid of a wheel or measuring instrument of any kind.

The jar, still soft and wet, is put on one side. Now is the time to decorate it with very simple designs, generally triangular, after which the industrious worker leaves it to dry for a few hours, taking care to cover the opening with a thin piece of wood to prevent the wind from spoiling the shape. As soon as she dares to lift it without danger, she turns it over, smooths the bottom (tshaku), which will harden in its turn, and places the

Constructing the furnace.   *Phot. A. Borel.*

pot in a hut where it continues to dry in the shade. On the day she chooses for the firing, she digs a hole in the sand, arranges the various pieces of pottery in it and covers them with a heap of small pieces of wood or with palm pith ; this she sets alight, and keeps a quick clear fire burning until she considers the firing is finished, when she leaves her red and glowing utensils to cool down (hola). The cooling accomplished, she begins to inspect the result of her work. This is the psychological moment! How many have cracked, how many have withstood the testing? The worthless ones are smashed, and the perfect ones reserved to be painted a brilliant brown, which is done with a decoction of the bark of the mangrove (nkapa) and of the nkanye, boiled with a kind of creeper (mahlehlwa), which has a sticky sap. Such is the primitive method followed in the manufacture of all Native pottery.

The process of firing being often unsuccessful, taboos are plentiful in the manufacture. When women collect the clay,

The furnace ready. *Phot. A. Borel.*

only one of them digs and gives it to the others ; should each make haste to dig for herself, this would bring mishap : the pots would break. If no accident happens and the firing is successful, these women will say : "She who dug the other day has a lucky hand (a ni boko dja hombe). Let her dig again another time." When the clay has been hidden in the ground, at the foot of a tree, it is also taboo to tread on the spot, when walking through the village. When the heap of wood is ready, the potteress will call a little child, an innocent creature, to set fire to the furnace. She shows it where to place the glowing ember, and, if the result of the firing is good, she will always call the same child on future occasions (1).

If all these precautions prove useless, and the woman sees that she is not succeeding, she will go so far as to consult the bones, and, if they so order, she will make an offering to her gods, gods of the father, gods of the mother, or possessing gods (Part VI), if she is a spirit-possessed woman, as the bones may

Result of the firing.   *Phot. A. Borel.*

declare. People will say to her : "You manufacture pots and sell them and do not give anything to your gods : that will not do!" So she will offer a piece of clothing, a coin, etc., at the altar (*gandjelo*).

(1) Meta, the Rikatla potteress has entirely given up the manufacture of pottery of late years. All her pots cracked, because, she said, she was the only woman practising this art in the country. In her former home, everybody made pots and in this way the potteresses "strengthened each other (tiyisana)." Moreover when a pot was heard cracking in the furnace, somebody ran to the hut and collected a little of the dust on the floor and threw it into the other pots, and this prevented them from being spoiled. It was too far for Meta to run to her former home to get the dust—so she gave up her trade ! The case of poor Meta is a good illustration of the collective character of industrial pursuits amongst primitive peoples.

Another taboo in connection with the making of a pot is this : when a pot has been fired, it must still be *tested* ; this operation is called *ku khangula*, or *kwangula*, and is performed in the following way. A little water is poured into it, and the potteress washes it thoroughly ; then some grains of maize are cooked in it and thrown away. This is to remove the *nkwangu*, or *nkhangu*, viz., the danger attending the use of an untested, unpurified pot : people using such an implement would suffer from an eruption on the arms, and even on the whole body. To give any one food to eat from a pot which has not been *khangula* is looked on as an act of hatred.

The pot, or boiler, used for cooking is called *nhlambeto* (yintin, Ro.) or *mbita* (yin-tin Dj.) ; it has a very wide opening. Smaller boilers are also made , even quite diminutive ones called *shihlembetwana* or *shimbitana*. The beer jar (khuwana, dji-ma), illustrated on page 101,

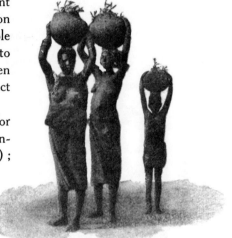

Phot. D. Lenoir.

Pots used to draw water.

No. 13, is of the same size as the boiler, but can be easily recognised by its straighter neck. Enormous beer jars are sometimes manufactured, perfect amphoras (hotjo, yin-tin), but they rarely stand the firing and are therefore scarce and expensive, fetching as much as ten shillings each : they may be two feet high ; the ordinary cooking pot does not cost more than sixpence. The porringers, or large plates, are called *mbenga* (mu,-mi; No. 12) (1).

Shibindji clay is also used for making very short *pipes* (shipana), prettily shaped, probably in imitation of the European cutty. Smoking does not seem to be an indigenous habit ; in the interior

(1) No. 11, on page 101, shows a small vase modelled by a young Native girl, an invalid from Natal (Station of Inanda).

one rarely sees a Native with a pipe in his mouth, tobacco being almost exclusively used in the form of snuff. The only smokers in the country are the old women of Lourenço Marques, and the youthful dandies who try to imitate the Transvaal Boers!

Clay modelling is perhaps the art for which South Africans are best gifted. In all the tribes children amuse themselves by

A young Spelonken artist and his work.   *Phot. J. Dentan.*

modelling oxen, human beings, wheels, even waggons, sometimes very cleverly. I knew a boy in Shiluvane who was a true artist and could copy anything he saw, for instance a white lady with her hat on (1). The accompanying plate shows one of these young artists, from Spelonken, with his handiwork.

(1) The same boy, without having received any special training, could cut out a frock, and used to make the dresses of all the brides of the congregation. He had a wonderful eye for form and would have made his mark, had he received a professional training. But he died from consumption contracted in the towns!

II. *Basket-work.*

The milala palm, whose sap supplies the tipplers of Pessene with their famous busura (II. p. 42), is a very valuable tree to the Ba-Ronga, as it is of its leaves that the greater part of the baskets in use by this tribe are made. The basket-maker gathers the most perfect leaves. These are not like the mimale folioles, growing opposite one another on a central nerve. The *milala* (plur. of nala) are true palms, the leaves consisting of folioles from half an inch to an inch in width radiating from a common centre, which itself grows on the end of a long peduncle.

These trees are found in the woods of Mabota, Nondwane, Tembe, on the Coast, and in the low plains of the North Eastern Zoutpansberg, etc., sometimes in large numbers. Returning home, the workman (here we employ the masculine, basket-making being essentially man's work) spreads out the leaves in the sun to dry, having previously straightened the folioles somewhat, separating (hangela) them one from the other ; when they dry, they turn a light grey colour with a shining polished surface, and are then hung up in the hut where they will be sheltered from the dew and ready for use. When the work is to be started, the folioles are torn (phatlula) from their peduncle, and, with a sharp pointed instrument, are split longitudinally into strips or straws of 1/8 or 2/8 of an inch wide, the ribs of the leaves (nhlamalala, yin-tin) being carefully kept ; these delicate wands have their special use.

The Ronga basket makers are very fond of decorating their baskets with *designs in black*. These triangular and square patterns are produced by artistically plaiting dark and light coloured straws, and are not painted on after the baskets are manufactured. The straw is dyed black in the following manner : it is soaked in the black ooze (ntjhaka) of the marshes for two weeks, and then laid out to dry, which gives it a reddish-brownish colour. This hue is deepened by a second treatment. The leaves of a shrub called *mpsabutimu* are gathered and placed in a pot with the red brown milala in alternate layers, until the utensil is full : water is then poured over them and the whole put on to boil ; very soon the straw becomes a brilliant black. The basket-maker has now only to pull up some of the grass growing in the hollow near the lake, dry it, and he is ready to commence work.

In the accompanying plates illustrations will be found of the principal specimens of this art, stereotyped shapes which have passed on from generation to generation, doubtless from

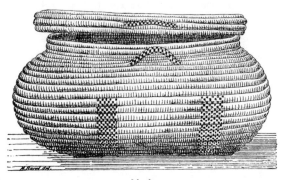

Ngula.

prehistoric times, and are called respectively : *ngula*, *hwama*, *shihundju*, *lihlelo* and *nhluto*.

The *ngula* (yin-tin) (p. 27) takes the place of honour, and is the most prized of all the Ronga baskets. It requires days or even weeks of continuous work to make one, but the result is worthy of the time and labour bestowed upon it ; I brought with me to Europe several *ngula* of various sizes. The particular one shown below, is oval and measures six feet two inches in circumference ; but there are many much larger, both spheroid and ovoid. This is how they make or, to use the technical Native term, "tlhaba" — "pierce" this basket. The workman takes his dried grass and plaits it, lengthening the plait according to requirements, as he goes along : this plait is bound round, and entirely hidden, by a special binding of palm leaf straw, thus forming a thickish cord of about half an inch in diameter ; the cord is soon doubled back upon itself, and forms a centre, around which

are fixed several concentric rings ; each inner ring is pierced with
a kind of awl and the straw of the outer ring pushed into the hole,
thus fixing them securely together. Hence the expression *thlaba
ngula*, to pierce a ngula. The bottom is soon finished, and
differs but little in appearance from an ordinary straw-mat, such as

Manufacturing a ngula in Spelonken.   *Phot. P. Rosset.*

is used to prevent hot dishes spoiling the polish of the European
dining table. The sides are made in the same manner by
superposing rings of the straw cord, giving the basket a well
rounded convex shape, after which two or three rings are super-
imposed perpendicularly, to form the opening, the mouth of the
chef d'œuvre. The cover, made in the same way, must fit exactly
over the mouth of the basket ; in fact it should require to be
slightly forced over it : the fastening will then hold better. On
the upper part of the basket, as also on the cover, the manufacturer
has carefully plaited four handles, two corresponding pairs, those

121

on the basket pointing upward while those on the cover point downward, so that they meet. Two rings are also plaited, and passed round through each pair of handles, forming simple but solid hinges on which the cover can turn without ever being separated from the basket, of which it is henceforward an integral part. A well-made ngula is absolutely impermeable, and not the smallest hole can be found in it. I think it would even hold water. Such a basket is surely a work of art!

The ngula is the Native's Savings Bank. In it he keeps all his riches, the best grains of maize, or the best grown monkey nuts, reserved for seed at the next rainy season ; also the material with which the women will deck themselves on grand occasions, etc. The enormous basket reposes at the far end of the hut, on a low table (buhiri) specially designed for the purpose. The ngula of the northern clans, where palm leaves are not to be found, is more rounded and the palm straw replaced by solid dry grass. (See the adjoining illustration, p. 121.)

While the ngula is enthroned in the hut, and is never moved out of it, the *hwama* (yin-tin, Ro.) or *funeko* (Dj.) (p. 124 No. 4 and 6), on the contrary, is the wallet of the traveller. It is a square bag made of plaited palm straw. The cover is about as large as the bag itself and, so that it may not be lost (which might easily happen while travelling), it is secured by the string used as a shoulder strap to carry the *hwama*, this being passed through it. The bag can thus be opened by sliding the cover right along the string, but it cannot be entirely separated from it. These bags are of different sizes, some more ornamental than others. A round variety is also made by a certain basket-maker of Masana. He makes three or four projecting horns to his hwama, which then takes a cylindrical shape, and has the advantage of being able to stand upright when placed on the ground. This bag or basket, is called *shiraba* or *baki* (No. 2) ; it is the kind used by the magicians for carrying their medicines, and bones.

The third classic shape of Ronga basket-ware (No. 3) is the *shihundju* (Ro.) *shirundju* (Dj.), the conical basket employed by the women for transporting maize, clay and manure. (It is by no means certain that the shihundju is cleaned out between these several loads!) It is made in much the same way as the roof of a hut, point downwards, ribs of folioles taking the place of sticks. This basket may be said to be the special property of the women (1) : they are very clever at balancing it on their heads ; it is very rarely that a woman, old or young, lets her shihundju fall. When empty it is turned upside down and serves as a hat. It is a really pretty sight to see the young girls starting out for the fields with their conical baskets standing straight up on their fuzzy locks. When they are travelling and arrive at a friendly village, they hold themselves perfectly upright, shooting glances here and there without stooping or turning their heads, till their friends rush out to meet them, seize their shihundju and place them on the ground, in small holes which they hastily make in the sand. This is the first duty of hospitality amongst women!

The *lihlelo* (No. 8) is used by cooks for winnowing the maize. Palm leaves not being sufficiently strong for this purpose, the lihlelo is made of the roots, of a tree called *nukanhlelo* (a kind of mimosa), cut into strips, and is coated with a reddish brown varnish prepared from mangrove bark. It is the lihlelo, or rather a smaller basket of the same sort called *ndjewane*, that the house-wife takes with her when picking the small wild cucumbers, or gathering the various herbs which serve for the supplementary noontide luncheon.

In the northern clans one often meets with a spherical basket made of the same material as the winnowing basket and covered with an ordinary lihlelo.

Besides the foregoing, the Ba-Ronga have two or three baskets which are not in such general use : the *nhlaba*, a kind of plaited bag with interstices between the palm straws, for carrying fish, the *ntjaba*, etc.

Another article, which might, at first sight, be taken for a basket, but which serves quite a different purpose, is the *nhluto*, the strainer. (No. 1.) This unusually shaped strainer is a sort of long bag of plaited straw into which is poured the beer made

(1) The male members of the family are called "ba matlhari, those of the assagai" and the female "ba-shihundju, those of the basket," as these objects are characteristic of each sex.

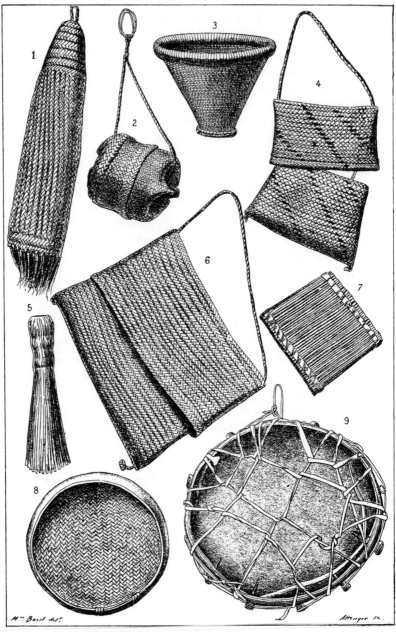

Thonga basket work.
(One sixth of the natural size.)

124

from maize : the particles floating in this liquor are caught by the straws overlapping the top, or accumulate at the bottom, whilst the liquid filters through the interstices of the plait. The thick sediment remaining in the strainer can then be squeezed so as to extract all the beer. This straining and squeezing has the effect of rendering the drink much more alcoholic (p. 40).

The art of basket-making is by no means commonplace. Practised by men only, it is, in certain families, in certain villages,

Phot. A. Borel.

Carrying lihlelo baskets, grinding and pounding mealies.

handed down from father to son. Children with a natural taste for this sort of work are initiated into its mysteries by their parents. But no young man is ever forced to take up the profession of a basket-maker. His heart (mbilu) must be in it! Amongst primitive peoples art, and even industry, always remains a matter of individual genius. It never becomes a mechanical output, as is the case in the factories of the civilised world : for this reason it retains a character of individuality, sincerity and natural beauty, not always to be met with in the products of XXth century European industry!

125

In the environs of Lourenço Marques, in our sub-station of Masana, lived the family of Tumbene, famous for its ngula. One of the sons inherited the father's talent. He was an evangelist in our Mission, and, when he was but a lad, people came to him from far and wide, to have their old baskets or broken lihlelo repaired.

Although basket-making is confined to certain families who more or less monopolise the business, without, however, preventing any one from practising the art, the manufacture of *straw mats*, or matting (*likuku*, li-tin (Ro.), *rikuku* (Dj.), is very wide-spread. Many men know how to "tlhaba likuku" — "pierce a mat." For this the Ba-Ronga collect a quantity of solid rushes of at least 3 feet in length, (myriads of them grow in the plains), and pierce holes through them, all along the rush, at intervals of 3 inches, passing strings through the holes. A net-work of string, half an inch wide, is run down the two sides at the edges to prevent fraying. When new, these mats are of a beautiful golden yellow, but the smoke in the huts soon turns them brown. Every Native possesses his own mat, on which he sleeps rolled up in his rug. Women possess two, an old one, used during menstruation, and a better one on which they usually sleep (I. p. 187).

The *string* (ngoti, yin-tin) used for these mats is made as follows : the leaves of the nala palm are picked when very young and tender (nshunya) : a knife is passed all along the folioles, in order to remove the green fleshy covering ; the parenchyma, composed of very light but tough fibres, (nkwampa), then remains. The workman takes two small bundles of these fibres and rolls them (yahliya) together with the palm of his hand along his thigh, twisting, intertwining, firmly uniting them, continually adding fresh fibres as he goes along : in this way he can make a string as long and as thick as he likes.

The following are the technical expressions employed for different kinds of basket-work.

Luka (plaiting) for ntjaba, shihundju, lihlelo, ndjewana, hwama nhalaba, tjala (drying floor), shitlanta (store house).

Tlhaba (piercing) for ngula and likuku.

Betsha (tying) for the small *brooms* also made of palm straws (mpsayelo, No. 5), and the reed walls (khumbi, dji-ma).

Bangela (making) for the *bunana*, a sort of hammock, made of plaited milala which is hung to the branches of the trees and sometimes in summer used for sleeping in, to escape the mosquitoes which swarm inside the huts.

Runga (sewing) for the boats (byatsho, dji-ma). The ancient Native boats built before the appearance of nails, hammers and saws, were made of pieces of wood securely tied together. Some of these antiquated craft are still to be seen on the Maputju river.

On the rivers up country, boats are frequently made of a large piece of curved bark, bent on both sides, which will hold two or three persons. I crossed the great Letaba in a boat of this description. Such boats are also used for storing water. Where mimale branches (or nervules) are procurable, they are tied together so as to form a raft called *shikhakhafu*. These are used on the Nkomati River, and on the lakes in Ronga territory. Big rafts made of trunks of trees fastened together, and called *magudhlwana*, were used in former times on the sea, when going to meet the White men, the Ba-Godji. (See later.) They are now no longer used and there is scarcely one to be found. In the neighbourhood of Lourenço Marques the Natives now build their boats on the European model. The fishermen cut down forked branches, which serve as ribs, to which they nail planks. They are wonderfully clever at this work ; one man, Sam Matlombe, nicknamed the "King of the Bay," was particularly expert at it.

The sewn boats of olden times might well be included under the heading of basket-ware. Those of to-day belong definitely to another branch of industry, and will afford us a natural point of transition from basket work to wooden articles.

III. *Wood-carving.*

It is the *nkuhlu*, mafureira tree, Trichilia emetica, as we have already seen, that is used by the Natives of these parts for their wood-carving. If the name of this tree is very hard to pronounce, its wood is, to an equal degree, soft and possesses the great

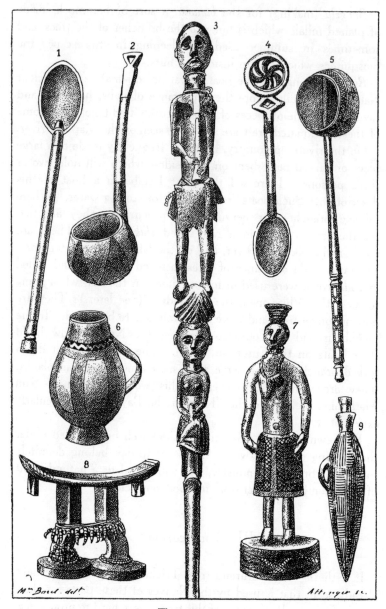

Thonga carvings.

(One seventh of the natural size.)

advantage of not easily splitting or cracking when being dried. If Nature had not bestowed on the Thongas this excellent tree, who knows if they would have ever thought of executing the works of art which are depicted in the accompanying illustration!

However before thinking of art, they began by cutting, or fashioning, with their small knives, articles of every day use: *spoons* (nkombe, mu mi) for instance, (see illustrations of carvings, No. 1), made in several sizes ; the big one is used for serving out the potful of maize amongst the rightful claimants, and the small one for conveying food to the mouth when the hands are ritually soiled (I. p. 193). One often finds really well carved spoons. I give drawings of two which are particularly interesting ; the first shows a sort

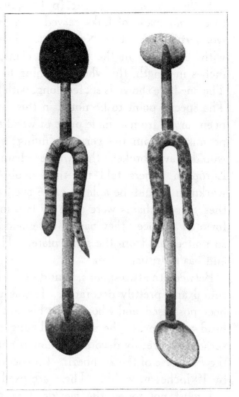

Carved spoon from Maputju country.

of spiral, or catherine-wheel decoration at the top of the handle (No. 4) ; the other, brought by Dr. Audeoud from the Maputju country, has a carved snake as an ornamental motive. Spoons are all ornamented, even the plainest, with designs in black, burnt into the wood with a red-hot iron. For beer, ladles are used, made of a single piece of wood ; these are generally decorated with large black triangles (No. 2). In Inhambane and Quelimane, the Natives make them of cocoa nut shells, on which they carve curious geometrical figures (No. 5). *Goblets* (ntcheko, mu-mi) are generally made with a handle. (No. 6).

In the accompanying plate, (p. 131), two spoons are seen hanging to a *chain* made of links carved from nkuhlu wood. This is a wonderful product of Native art. These chains are often met with, especially in the Northern clans, some with links of six inches in length, the whole attaining to a length of many yards. The one here shown is six feet long, with links of only three inches. The special point to be noted in this "objet d'art" is that it has been carved from a single piece of wood and the artist had to make no mistake from the very beginning; a single slip of the knife would have broken the whole chain and made it useless. European joiners told me they doubted whether an ordinary workman would be able to carve such a chain. I was told that these spoon-chains were used by two individuals who wished to form an alliance ; they passed the chain over their shoulders and, so united, ate from the same plate. This, however, is mere play and has no ritual value.

Between the two spoons, a kind of *bowl* is seen, almost perfectly round and prettily decorated. It was used by a man who had been possessed, and who washed his face in it every day to cool his head and appease the spirits. Thongas also carve large dishes, sometimes prettily decorated, though not so attractive as those of the Ba-Rotse of the Zambezi. I possess one of two feet in length by 10 inches in width. These are used for serving meat.

I must not forget the *mortars* (tshuri, dji-ma) usually made of mahogany, or of nkanye, and the pestles (musi, mu-mi) made of nkonono. The former are often adorned with triangular carvings.

The same style of decoration is to be seen on the *calabashes* which Natives use as bottles. The calabash, as every one knows, is a sort of gourd composed of two spheres of unequal size with a narrow connection between them. By an ingenious system of supports, placed under the gourd during its growth, Natives succeed in imparting to the upper sphere the shape of an elongated neck. There are many varieties of calabash, some small, furnished

with a long projection and used for drawing the bukanye from the
large jars. They are specially kept for this purpose! (See p. 101,
No. 7, and also I, p. 400). In Vol. I. p. 50, I have given an

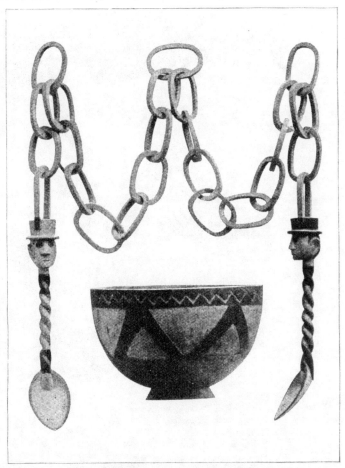

Carved chain and bowl, (Neighbourhood of Lourenço Marques).
(One fifth of the natural size.)

illustration of these bukanye calabashes, called *ntjeko* (mu-mi),
very prettily decorated by a Tembe artist. The black designs are
burnt in and represent huts, birds, palm trees and, last but not
least, two warriors fighting! The white dots are beads inserted

Phot. H. Gros.

Thonga kitchen ware.

in the soft bark of the calabash. The largest calabash on this plate measures 21 inches in length and 7 in width.

Some plainer calabashes are Nos. 8 and 9 of the illustration of ornaments. Others are simply shells of sala (shikutja), (p. 16), with a good-sized hole cut in them for an opening (Nos. 6 and 10) ; a circular piece, say one third the size of the other, makes a capital cover ; a string passes through the bottom of the calabash and the middle of the cover, fastening the two together. When this is knotted on top of the latter the *lard tin* is securely closed. This kind of calabash is generally thus designated, for it is in these round balls that the mafureira grease is kept, to which I have previously referred (p. 18). They are hung up in the roof of the hut where they ·swing to and fro in the smoke and become well browned. The young folks amuse themselves by carving designs on these shells.

Mankhelu's stick.

The artistic element is still more striking in the *snuff boxes* (ngulana, yin-tin), carved in ebony, which the chiefs are fond of carrying ; the one depicted (p. 128, No. 9) came to me from Mavabaze who was, for a time, chief of the Khosa clan. It is also conspicuous in the strange *pillows* (shidamu) on which the Ba-Ronga rest their heads at night. Let us contemplate this article (No. 8) with the respect it deserves ! It is probably on this description of pillow that primitive humanity in all parts of the world has dreamed its dreams ! We see it sculptured on the Egyptian monuments, above or by the side of princely couches. We find also among the relics of the lake-dwellers stone objects of a similar shape, which were doubtless used for the same purpose. The Bantu has adhered to this piece of prehistoric furniture all through the ages. The specimen in the illustration was bought from a young man, a traveller, on the road ; the bird's claws, beads and other articles tied all round it, doubtless hunting trophies, are plainly to be seen. He had the advantage of literally

Thonga statuettes.
(One third of the natural size.)

resting on his laurels, and naively believed they would bring him good luck while sleeping.

The Thonga artist has even dared to portray the *human form*, and the result of his audacity, however grotesque, is not without originality, and even a certain characteristic style, which may be recognised in all their statuettes. More often they content themselves with carving a man's head, with his crown, on the top of their walking sticks. I here give an illustration of Mankhelu's stick, which was a very old one, dating from 1850, at least, and shows the primitive style without any European influence. Sometimes they carve the whole body from head to foot ; (as grapes do not grow in their country the use of the classic vine-leaf is quite unknown). No. 3 represents a stick with a man and a woman, the one standing on the other's head, the stronger sex treading the weaker under foot! Large statuettes, of at least one and a half to two feet in height and broad in proportion, are to be seen in the Neuchâtel Ethnographical Museum, which without doubt contains the largest collection of Thonga implements in the world, having been plentifully provided with them by the mission-

A panther devouring an Englishman.
(One twelfth of the natural size.)

aries of French Switzerland. No. 7 is smaller, and represents a woman having on her head the typical conical basket, the pride of the workers in the fields, and of the cooks. The five small figures on the accompanying plate are very amusing indeed. They were carved by an artist of Movumbi (near Rikatla), who asserted that the man on the right was a Banyan. The other figures are Natives, men with their wax crowns, and the ladula garment (p. 96) adorned with beads ; one is a woman carrying a child!

The finest specimen of Native art that I ever saw is the carving of a *huge panther* about to devour a human being, the work of Muhlati, a sculptor living in the neighbourhood of Lourenço Marques. This artist, who was very proud of his work, and asked a tolerably high price for it, claimed to be able to carve anything and everything : birds, four-footed beasts, or men. He was famous throughout the land for his talent. Nothing more quaint

could be imagined than this large spotted creature, (the spots being
obtained as usual by burning with a hot iron), planting his claws
in the flesh of a man, (an Englishman, I was told by the inspired
author of this group!), and glaring at him with two great round
eyes, not very symmetrical! With touching forethought, this
modern Phidias has made the posterior half of the tail quite
independent of the rest of the animal. A tenon and circular

Thonga canoe. *Phot. A. Borel.*

socket allow the caudal appendage to be so neatly adjusted that
the joint is hardly visible! Muhlati told me how the idea of a
removable tail had occurred to him. He thought that if ever his
masterpiece had to be packed up and cross the ocean, it would
thus be more easily cased. This can hardly be called the idea of
a savage! Besides, the work itself would never have been
accomplished had there been no Whites in the country. Evidently
the sculptor, indolent like all his race, would not have worked day
in and day out at carving such an animal as a play-thing for his
children. He concluded that his talent might well bring him in
some money ; it was mercenary considerations that urged him on
to the execution of the work, and no mere love of art ; nevertheless

136

I do not believe any foreign influence was exercised in the conception of the idea. His group is absolutely original, and, as such, shows us to what lengths the sculptural talent of the Ba-Ronga can go. This group is now in the Neuchâtel Museum.

While statuettes are the most elaborate products of Native sculpture, *canoes* (shene (Dj.) are the largest. I have already mentioned the taboos connected with the cutting of the mahogany and nkwenga trees when used for this purpose (p. 19). Other trees, the mpfubu and the muhlu, can be cut without these precautions being taken.

IV. *Metallurgy*.

When and how did iron reach the Ba-Ronga ? Probably we shall never be able to ascertain. Tradition has it that the primitive inhabitants of Nondwane, the Honwana, who cooked elephants in order to tear them in pieces, had no iron implements. Some authorities tell us that the hoe in use in olden times was of an exceedingly hard wood, wrenched I know not how from a species of teak tree called *ntjhiba*. The Natives of these parts must have passed directly from the age of wood to that of iron. There was certainly a stone age, comparable to that of the lake dwellers, in Cape Colony, where a great quantity of silex and of polished stones have been found. I never heard of any such implements having been used by the Thongas, nor found within their territory. As regards the bronze age, they have known the use of copper for a long time, but it cannot be proved that they knew it before iron.

Iron and other metals seem to have been first introduced in Delagoa Bay by the "Godji" traders and whale fishers, of whom I shall shortly speak ; they are the first White visitors whom the Natives now remember. The Ba-Ronga used to exchange fowls and other domestic animals for hoes, brass bracelets, and copper brought by the strangers, and they had found out how to make copper wire by forging (fula) the pieces bought from the "Godji."

Later on wrecked boats provided Native smiths with iron to make hoes, axes, etc. In certain villages there were regular forges, (Matlharin, near Mbengelen Island, Matjolo etc.). The hoes were in the well-known form of an ace of spades and were fixed into a wooden handle, as are also the axes, and battle axes (I. p. 453). But the principal supply of iron came from the Transvaal Mountains, especially from the Northern Zoutpansberg, where the Bveshas have practised the art of mining iron ore for an unknown period. These Sutho hoes have played a great part in the history of the Thonga tribe, having been extensively used as currency for lobolo purposes.

These Bveshas — the word is said to be a Thonga corruption of Venda — built their furnaces in ant-hills, as shown in the accompanying illustration supplied by M. H. Gros, near Iron Mountain, East of the Spelonken district. They excavated three holes under the furnace, and blew into them by means of bellows made of a skin, the air being expelled through an antelope horn. The ore, broken in small pieces and mixed with charcoal, was smelted, crushed, smelted a second time, crushed again and made into hoes and axes, etc. Who had taught the Vendas this art ? Did they learn it from the Ma-Lemba, that curious tribe, half Semitic in its customs, which invaded the Northern Transvaal during the XVIIIth century ? Nobody knows for certain. I am under the impression that this art is older than that, as the Lebombo Natives, who invaded the Nondwane in the XVIth century, seem to have possessed iron weapons. The origin of iron and the date of its introduction into South Africa is still a mystery.

Among the ornaments illustrated will be found a very pretty belt (No. 1). It is the work of a young man named Philemon, living in the outskirts of Lourenço Marques, who employed his leisure moments in making objects of this description with twisted wires of iron, brass and copper, bent in festoons and fastened with small tongues of metal. European influence is doubtless very marked in these belts, but still they possess a certain cachet of their own. Amongst the Zulus as in our tribe, large cups of various descriptions, including egg-cups, are

Phot. H. Gros.

Native Ironfoundry in Zoutpansberg.

139

manufactured, and it is evident that, in this branch, Native art is capable of considerable development. Their method of fastening the blades of assagais to the handles with iron wire is also very ingenious. Sometimes they cover their ebony sticks from top to bottom with a delicate network of steel and brass wire. A Native expert in wire work once mended the stock of my sporting gun, which was broken, and made a wonderful job of it. This wire, so extensively used for bracelets, was formerly made by Native blacksmiths, but now they buy it at Lourenço Marques or from the Hindu traders.

D. COMMERCE.

Thongas have an inborn inclination for trade and have always been addicted to it. Before there was question of any currency, when hoes were not yet procurable, or the *ritlatla* bracelet brought by the Whites (I. p. 385), or the copper stick called *lirale* (1) melted by the Palaora Ba-Sutho, they knew how to buy (shaba) and to sell (shabisa), viz., to exchange their primitive produce. A mat was bartered for a fowl and the thrifty savage thought : "This is good business ; the hen will lay eggs and hatch chickens and this will bring me a profit (bindjula)." A shihundju basket was also exchanged for a hen. Another way of buying was adopted when dealing with pots ; the pot was filled with mealies by the buyer and the contents left to the potter as corresponding to the value of the pot. For monkey-nuts, not husked, the pot had to be filled twice ; for more precious products, such as sorghum and Kafir corn, half of it only was measured out. I have myself witnessed some transactions of this kind amongst the Nkunas. If the pot broke when first used, the potter had to give another in its place.

But this primitive trade became much more extensive when the Whites made their appearance. Delagoa Bay was one of the

(1) Compare my article in *Folklore*, 24 June 1903.

first spots visited and occupied by Europeans in South Africa, and a considerable Native trade developed there in the XVIth century, according to Portuguese documents. These Portuguese records show that, as far back as 1545, Lourenço Marques and Antonio Caldeira made a commercial exploration of the Bay and tried to establish regular exchanges with the Natives. These relations were not continuous, but in 1650 there were five factories in the vicinity of Delagoa, on the island of Inyak, at Sheffin, on the Nkomati (Manhisa) and on both sides of the Bay. In 1721 the Dutch settled there and remained for fourteen years. The Austrians also stationed a garrison on Inyak Island in 1781, but this stronghold was destroyed by a Portuguese frigate. Since the beginning of the XIXth century the Portuguese occupation has been more continuous. The only reason for Whites settling at Delagoa was, of course, the opportunity of traffic with the Natives, and the presence of foreigners doubtless stimulated a certain commercial development among the Ba-Ronga and the tribes of the interior. This is, at any rate, asserted by a Portuguese who visited Lourenço Marques at the end of the XVIIIth century, and wrote an account of his impressions to Don F. Amaro de San Thomé, Prelate of Mozambique. His description may appear somewhat highly coloured to those who know the localities, but I quote the following passages which bear upon our subject :

"On the Southern shore of the Bay resides King Capella (a surname bestowed by the Portuguese on the royal family of Tembe) who is now known as Antonio, (perhaps the Muhari of the Natives). He is very powerful, and has always with him a merchant who trades in ivory... To the North of the river is our factory, where we have a fort and as many as 170 soldiers. The King of Matolla (Matjolo) is very powerful, and well supplied with all necessaries. His village consists of over 400 huts. (This probably means all the villages of the country collectively). It is here that the inhabitants of the mountains bring for sale gold and copper and ivory, for which they have to pay dues. This Monarch owns a province called Cherinda (Shirindja). He obtains from it quantities of ivory... I saw in the house of the King of Maouote (Mabota) two large chests full of amber. About thirty or forty days' journey up the river (Nkomati) dwells the

Grand Caxa (Cacha, doubtless Khosa, in the country of Khosene), who is a kind of emperor. It is here that all trading vessels come (1). He dispenses hospitality to all the merchants who wish to buy ivory, gold, rhinoceros horns, hippopotamus' teeth, or copper, articles which they obtain particularly cheaply. A great number of negroes from the kingdom of Quitève (not far from Beira) come down from the mountains to this village for purposes of barter. They bring a large quantity of gold... The Grand Caxa and his people are in continuous relations with the Imperialists (the Austrians who occupied the Bay in 1781), who make large profits out of them. Every month two or three vessels, laden with black clothing and glass ware, arrive here for traffic with the Natives. These two rivers (the Maputju and the Nkomati) can supply each year, from my observation, sufficient ivory, gold, rhinoceros horns and hippopotamus' teeth to load more than twelve ships... The whole shore of the Bay is thickly inhabited with people who transact a large business in amber, and go to sell it to the King Matolla, Maouote and the Grand Caxa."

This description, though perhaps somewhat extravagant, proves that in the XVIIIth century the Ba-Ronga were doing a considerable trade.

It is interesting, in view of these White records, to note what Natives themselves remember regarding their trade in former times. According to them, the first White people they dealt with did not dare come on shore. They were whalefishers and gave the Makaneta people whale flesh to eat. The Ba-Ronga used to go and meet them in the Bay, on rafts made of stems of trees tied together (p. 127). They said : "We go to Godji ;" *Godji* meant that kind of trade. Blacks and Whites could not understand each other. However, the trade was not " silent trade," as has been the case in other quarters. They managed to communicate by gestures, and the Natives obtained mainly metals from these sailors, the brass ritlatla, iron hoes, pieces of copper which they made into wire, etc. Who were these strangers? The Natives cannot say for certain, but think that they were Englishmen, as the

(1) These ships, it must be understood, were in all probability very small craft carrying at the most about five tons of merchandise. During the greater part of the year it is impossible to ascend the Nkomati higher than Magule (where the river forms an elbow) with anything drawing two feet of water.

name *Ba-Godji* is still commonly applied by them to English people. After these Whites, the Natives remember the arrival of the Moslems, who came with their "vessels with an elevated tail," (even to-day Arab dhows have a raised stern answering this description), called *mapangayi* and were the first to land and to undertake a regular commercial exploitation of the country. They soon learnt to speak with the Natives, and to make use of them in their trade, sending them far away into the interior to barter ivory and skins against hoes, beads, clothing, and, later on, powder and bullets.

Whatever may have been the order of arrival of these strangers, one fact is certain : the Ba-Ronga of Delagoa Bay have acted as intermediaries between the Whites and the tribes in the interior for a considerable time, the Mpfumo, Nondwane, Mabota and Hlanganu (1) Natives being particularly engaged in this trade, and going as far as Mosapa (Ba-Ndjao country) and Bvesha (Ba-Venda country), to exchange goods.

The *commercial journeyings*, though they are now a thing of the past, are well remembered by the old people, with all the particular customs accompanying them. The Ba-Sutho called these travellers *Makwapa* (Thonga pronunciation of *Magwamba*), perhaps from the name of a Thonga chief who dwelt on the Oliphant (see *Grammaire Ronga*, p. 21), or near Inhambane. The company, called *mpfhumba*, was generally led by a *ndjilashi*, viz, "the master of the expedition," to whom the Banyan entrusted goods for barter. This man had to find a certain number of carriers, who would share in the profits of the venture. The Banyans estimated the value of the goods in pounds sterling. Should the whole be worth £ 60, for instance, he put 60 mealie cobs into a trunk and the ndjilashi did the same in his own hut ; on reaching home again, he had to deliver to the Banyan money or skins or whatever he had sold the goods for, to the value of

(1) The people of Hlanganu, neighbours of Nwamba, were renowned as commercial travellers. Hence their nickname : "Ba ku hlomula fumo ba tlhaba misaba." — "Those who take the assagai and pierce the earth." They used their weapon not for fighting but for pacific purposes : the assagai served as a walking stick in their commercial journeyings. Another version is this : "Ba shaba ndlela," — "they buy the road," they do not fight, they would rather pay to be allowed to pass (I. p. 362).

£ 60 ; and, in case of disagreement, the 60 cobs were counted again in corroboration of the contract made.   If he brought an elephant's tusk, the Banyan gave him the value of a full lobolo.   Carriers received two pieces of calico as reward.

After having visited Kimberley, in 1870, some Thongas, having begun to understand better the advantages of trading, attempted to undertake such expeditions on their own account.   But they soon gave up the experiment as the Ngonis of Muzila often robbed them of all their goods.   When they were working for White men, the Ngonis were afraid to pillage the company ; on the other hand, if by chance there was a loss, it concerned the White merchant.   So they preferred the system of trading for the White men.

These travelling companies had to observe many taboos in order to succeed in their expeditions, in particular the *travellers' taboos*, which have been explained I. p. 339.

There are several popular songs which the traders used to sing on the road, or which were sung about them.   One of these has already been quoted (p. 102).   Here is another in which the tired carriers ask their leader to allow them to return home :

> Hoho ! hoho ! maringele wa mamano !
> Hoho ! hoho ! dla nkambana hi muka !
> Hulukati ya ndlopfu yi nga siyi ñwana !

> Oho ! Oho ! Thou who leadest us as a mother !
> Oho ! Oho ! Break the platter and let us go home !
> The female-elephant never forsakes her young !

The company generally consisted of men only.   The allusion to the female elephant, however, may mean that there were sometimes also women amongst them.   They address the leader of the expedition, asking him to destroy the platter so that no utensils shall be left in which to prepare food, thus necessitating a return home.   They are thinking besides of their little ones left behind in the village, from whom it is unnatural for them to be separated so long.   The mother elephant never forsakes her little one !

On their way back, they had carefully to watch a certain bird called *hwati*, fish-eater ; if this bird flew in the right direction, homeward, it was a hopeful sign. If it emitted its cry *kwekweru-kweru*, (kweru means at home), or if it settled on the crown of a hut, then the travellers were happy and shouted their joyful *mikulungwane*. On the contrary, if any member of the company had died on the road, another bird, the *magu-djwana*, would come and perch on the crown, with a tired air and drooping head... Then there were tears instead of shouts of joy!

These great commercial expeditions were superseded later on by the *trade in skins* which the Ba-Ronga conducted, bartering them in the interior for powder or other European produce. I knew one Native who organised regular expeditions to Bilene, where he bought the skins of civet-cats with which the Zulu warriors delight to deck themselves. Thence he went into the hill country of the Swazis, or Zulus, to sell his merchandise. It was reported that he obtained scores of oxen in exchange for his precious nsimba skins. The last time, however, the venture did not turn out well, and it has not been attempted again.

Native trade, fifty years ago, consisted also in selling *wax*, and *rubber*, and tons of *nkampfi* (mafureira almonds) to the business houses at Delagoa, (the supply of ivory was exhausted years ago), but this trade has fallen off almost entirely. My impression is that Native commerce has greatly diminished during the last fifty years. So the fact is evident that civilisation, which at first gave a decided stimulus to the commercial spirit of the Thongas, has latterly almost entirely destroyed their trade. How has this been done?

One reason for this decrease in Native commerce may be found in the advent of a large number of Asiatics, Banyans from Goa and Bombay, who are past masters in the art of shopkeeping, and who set up in business wherever they consider there is a sufficient population to warrant the venture. Living very cheaply (rice and curry are their staple food), in any kind of shanty, selling at enormous profits, keen at making bargains, these people monopolise the retail trade throughout the country, and the Natives are quite unable to meet this competition ; they have consequently almost entirely given up all their earlier attempts at business transactions ! (1)

A second reason why the trade of former days has almost entirely disappeared is to be found in the *great economic changes* resulting from the fact that Lourenço Marques has become an important seaport, in close relation with the miners of Johannesburg who receive their supplies via Delagoa Bay. Thousands of Natives are employed in discharging the large steamers which arrive by hundreds in the roadstead. At this work a Native can earn fifteen shillings a week or more ; in a short time he has made ample provision for the wants of his family and no longer finds it necessary to go to Bilene, to Zululand or Swaziland to make a living. The women too can make money by selling tomatoes and sweet potatoes to an ever increasing White population. All this is much easier

(1) On one occasion, in 1892, I made a list of various articles displayed for sale in and around a Banyan shop, in the district of Mahazule (to the North of Nondwane). This is what Mr. Nala, a Hindu from Goa established for many years amongst the Rongas, offered to the Natives living in the neighbourhood of his primitive store.
Stuffs. These are sold by measurement taken on the individual ; say, by the *shikumba,* length of one arm, or by the *nkumba* or *bemba* (two arms), or by the *peça,* the entire piece, the equivalent of two bemba. The materials most in demand are called ; *tingidaò* (white), *mashita* (black with white stripes), *sh landana* (all red), *shinwakana* (red and black), *mempana* (a special red stuff worn as mourning) and *malopa* (a navy blue material still more frenquently worn as mourning). Besides these are *handkerchiefs* (minturu) of various colours, principally red, a large proportion coming from the manufacturers of East Switzerland ; white *blankets (gampongo,* meaning snow), for three or four shillings ; coloured blankets, thicker, varying from five to seven shillings ; towels, called *thawula* (an adaptation of the English word) and even some articles of ready-made clothing such as *djansi* (overcoats) at fifteen shillings ! Amongst the stuffs I would more particularly note the *gangisa ntombi,* that is "for use when courting the girls", dark blue with a pattern of white flowers.
Beads. There are at least a dozen kinds to be found at Nala's ; djiridja (black) mbanda (white), shingazana, shimuzana, nkankana, habo, matshimbarole, bafa, tshambo.
Sundries. Rings, fish-hooks, buttons (masowa), thread, needles, snuff boxes to be worn in the ears (tinhlanga), knives, spoons, balls of string, padlocks (makandjate) with key attached ; little chains, to be hung from the belt, which tinkle when walking ; bracelets (busenga, ten for a shilling) ; wooden spoons, combs, coils of fine iron wire ; skins ; a large trap for catching hyenas or other wild animals ; small brass petroleum lamps ; sardines at sixpence a tin, English biscuits, and last but not least, a cask of German brandy diluted (tempora) with 50 % of water ! This would now be replaced by three casks of Vinho colonial, one of white wine, one of red wine and one of I do not know what colour !

than collecting mafureira or wax, or tapping trees for rubber (1).

Moreover the fashion of going to the *Transvaal mines*, to earn money, has become so universal that a Thonga would think he had in some sort failed if he had not made a stay in town (shilungu). There, in Johannesburg, they earn £ 3 in the mines, or £ 4—£ 5 monthly as kitchen boys ; so they despise the old primitive trading expeditions which brought less money and were attended with more danger.

These new economic conditions not only discourage Natives from trading on their own account, reducing them more and more to the condition of mere hired labourers, but are rapidly destroying their picturesque and interesting industry. For a few shillings they can buy European utensils. Their attractively carved spoons are replaced by ugly tin ones ; their wooden tumblers by less artistic enamelled ones, their primitive plates by European ware decorated in doubtful taste. Instead of the piece of reed which they wore in their ears as a snuff box, they now buy brass cartridges, and the Thonga beauties, discarding the *tihuhlu* fat, now anoint themselves with a scented oil imported from Europe. There may be certain advantages in these changes, but the picturesqueness of Bantu life promptly disappears, together with the incentive to develop their Native arts and crafts!

E. GENERAL OBSERVATIONS ON NATIVE INDUSTRY.

It is a strange destiny, that of these African races amongst whom the civilisation of the XIXth century has appeared, effecting the most radical changes in the minds and manners of people who, for centuries, perhaps for tens of centuries, have remained in the same primitive condition, marking time, so to speak, on the same spot, or, at most,

(1) There are at least two species of shrubs whose sap, when hardened, produces excellent rubber. These are fairly wide-spread and M. Dewèvre, a Belgian botanist, who has made a special study of rubber plants, and to whom I sent leaves and fruits of the trees, has classified them amongst the Landolphia. One is said to be a Landolphia Petersiana, and the other a variety of the Landolphia Kirki (Dyer) called by others Landolphia Monteiroi. Natives make an incision in the bark of the tree, and a milky sap exudes, which soon thickens and the somewhat sticky filaments are then wound

progressing almost imperceptibly. The transformation would seem to be as rapid as the previous immobility was fixed.

Let us try to discover the causes which may account for this extraordinary stagnation.

All are agreed in bearing witness to the fact that the state of civilisation in which Europeans found the Bantu tribes of South Africa is of an extremely ancient date. It is true that we have but little historical data to go upon as regards the development of these people, but, nevertheless, it seems to me highly probable that the shape of their ngula, their hwama, their shirundju, their pillows, the construction of their huts, dates from a very remote antiquity, and has been handed down unchanged from generation to generation. How are we to account for this lack of development, whilst the Indo-European races, starting probably from similar, primitive conditions, have advanced to so high a degree of civilisation as that of the Greeks and Romans, and ultimately to that of modern times?

The reply given by many casual observers to this question is that *the Bantu races are incapable of progress*. They are condemned, by reason of their mental and spiritual constitution, to vegetate in perpetual barbarism or to make themselves ridiculous by a servile imitation of the superior races. This view is not justified by the facts of the case. We recognise a relative mental inferiority in the Thongas, as in their congeners the Bantus, but their minds, nevertheless, possess in a more or less rudimentary state, all those faculties of which we are wont to boast. During the several years I have passed in close contact with these intellects, supposedly so limited, I have been more often struck with the points of analogy between the Africans and ourselves than by the differences which separate us. Besides, it is an error to assert that they have not progressed. Their inventive genius is fully proved by the various ways in which the several tribes have taken advantage of the materials with which Nature has supplied them. The Ba-Ronga do not make their baskets in the same way as the Zulus, or the Ba-Sutho. Again, in many separate instances, we can note a distinct forward movement in their industry ; the arrival of glass beads,

round small sticks. A good yield of rubber could undoubtedly be obtained in this country if the trees were cultivated and tapped in an intelligent manner.

(With regard to the name of the rubber tree, compare *Delagoa Bay, its Natives and Natural History*, London, Philip and Son, 1891, written by Mrs Monteiro, an Englishwoman who spent several years in Lourenço Marques and published interesting observations on the country. Without claiming any great scientific accuracy, this volume affords much interesting information.)

one or two hundred years ago, gave birth to an entirely new and original decorative art ; during the last century, the contest with a tribe better clothed than themselves led them to adopt a different and more decent costume. (Compare "Introduction à la Grammaire ronga" § XXXI.) When copper and brass wire became procurable, they not only made pretty bracelets, but invented quite a new art, the weaving of belts,

Phot. Dentan.

Manual work at the Lemana Training School (Northern Transvaal).

(p. 101 No. 1), egg-cups, and cups of various forms very different from those of European make.

The ability of the Native to progress in industry cannot be doubted when one sees the results of the industrial teaching they receive in many Missionary Institutions. The Swiss Romande Missionaries have introduced, in their schools, the manufacture of baskets and mats with the materials found in the country, and the results of the experiment have been altogether in favour of the intelligence of the Natives, as shown in the accompanying illustration. One of the pupils of Shiluvane even invented a new form of basket, made with a single leaf of a big palm tree (mpfuñwana) growing in the Leydsdorp plain. In those institutions

149

where carpentering and waggon building are scientifically taught,
the results are very satisfactory, and I myself saw at Lovedale a splendid
American desk which had been made entirely by a Native, and was
as perfect as if it had been manufactured by a European craftsman.
So the industrial stagnation of the South African tribes must not be
put down to an innate incapacity for progress. I think we must look
elsewhere for its causes, and, without claiming to exhaust the question,
I will proceed to enumerate the factors, which, to my mind, explain the
exceedingly slow development of these tribes.

Their *political system, social and religious,* is one of the chief causes
of this state of things. The deceased chiefs are the gods of the nation.
Whatever they did should be done now ; their lives are the supreme
examples to be followed ; the traditions handed down by their ancestors
are the only religious and moral guides which these people possess.
Customs which have come down from prehistoric times are law.
No one would think of abandoning them. To do otherwise than
others do, *psa yila,* is forbidden. It would be a denial of the divine
authority of the ancestors, and a danger to the tribe. This principle
is most strictly maintained in such tribes as are the freest from foreign
admixture and the least exposed to outside influences. In the Khosen
country, for example, when an evangelist trained in Spelonken, Yosefa,
wanted to build a square house, he was prevented from doing so. It
was against the law. How could he expect to live in a hut of a different
shape from those his forefathers had inhabited ? Had there been no
Whites in the country, Yosefa would have found it impossible to build a
house to his liking! This is a typical case of the immobility of Native
industry (1).

But in advancing as a reason for this immobility the all-powerful sway
of custom, supported and maintained by the national authorities, we
have only pushed the difficulty further back. How has it been possible
to maintain such a system of oppression ? How is it that no stronger
minded individuals have arisen to throw off this yoke and gain liberty
of action, stirring up the tribe, in spite of itself, from the lethargy in
which it is plunged, like an organism with its blood congealed !

---

(1) The lack of imagination in these races seems specially noticeable in mechanics,
and it has been remarked that South African Natives have not yet invented a single
machine. This may be true. However, I heard it attested by a Johannesburg technician
that the Thongas have a real aptitude for running engines and a real bent for mechanics.
As not one of them has ever studied advanced mathematics, no wonder they have not
invented new machines.

Amongst our own races, men of genius, great thinkers, have, from the earliest times, been able to impress their new ideas upon the masses, and lead them eventually, however recalcitrant, upon the march of progress. We shall have to content ourselves with two considerations which may help to solve the problem.

Our civilisation is the result of a combination of millions of minds and hundreds of peoples. The lake-dweller, of the stone-age, was not much more developed than the present-day Black of South Africa: in some respects he was less so. But he inhabited Europe, and, to the South of that Continent, stretches an inland sea, the Mediterranean, which spreads out its many arms in gulfs and bays reaching to the very heart of the countries on its shores, and thus facilitates access between nation and nation. Every new discovery by one soon became the property of its neighbour. Rome inherited from Greece, and Greece from Egypt and Abyssinia, and these international relations, favoured by the geographical conditions of the Old World, explain the development, *the arithmetical progression* shall we call it, of our Indo-European civilisation. In Africa, nothing of the sort exists. Few, if any, gulfs or bays are to be found in this Continent, whose coasts are hopelessly unbroken and inhospitable. Many a long stretch of river, otherwise navigable, is closed to navigation by impassable cataracts. Deserts of burning sand separate the tribes from one another, and sometimes they are isolated by veritable ramparts of lofty mountains. Communication is almost impossible, and the Black tribe, left to its own resources, amidst natural surroundings of an enervating description, remains stationary and content with the elementary industry to which it has attained. *Outside influence is wanting* to stimulate the intellectual energy, the inventive faculty of which they possess the germs.

In addition to all this a second factor is noticeable in the course of human development, and this, while all in favour of the Indo-European races, accentuates still more forcibly the differences between the several branches of the human family. Through the centuries the Egyptian hieroglyphs slowly evolved into ideographic signs, which eventually gave place to the phonetic alphabet of the Phoenicians. This *alphabet* goes forth to conquer the world, and to give a fresh aspect to things in general. These twenty to thirty letters of which the Blacks had not the slightest notion, these signs, thanks to which stone, wood and paper have been made to speak, will henceforward allow great minds to transmit their thoughts direct to their fellow-men. The knowledge of one epoch will then be passed on intact to following generations, whilst, formerly, ideas were frequently lost or distorted by popular tradition ; progression will henceforth be not merely *arithmetical* but *geometrical*. The *book* will be the accumulator in which the intellectual forces of the race will be stored for future transmission, without wastage, prolific of light and stimulus to every sphere of human activity. The Blacks of South Africa have never invented any system of writing. The idea of representing an object, a number, a thought, or a sound by any conventional sign, seems never to have occurred to them. Makhani, Muzila's old counsellor, did not know his own age. He probably thought, in common with many of his contemporaries, that he was at least ten years old. One day I said to him : "Why didn't you go each year, when the leaves begin to appear on the trees, and make some kind of a mark on the bark of a nkuhlu? Then, to-day, you could have counted all the marks and you would know how old you are!" He laughed and considered the idea futile, absurd! The absence of any system of writing is, doubtless, the proof of a certain intellectual inferiority, but environment may easily account for the illiterate condition of the Natives. In fact it is environment which is the chief cause of their centuries-long stagnation.

It would, however, be doing a wrong to these people, were we to judge them solely by the absence of industrial progress. Mental activity is not manifested only in the manufacture of machinery or in the transactions of high finance. Man is a being endowed with thought and speech. Speech and literature, which reflect thought, are phases of human activity more essential than industrial undertakings. The Thongas, in common with their neighbours the Ba-Sutho and the Zulus, do most certainly possess a literature, although they have no system of writing and may be classed as illiterates ; of this fact I shall furnish abundant proof when treating of their *literary and artistic life*.

FIFTH PART

LITERARY AND ARTISTIC LIFE

Ethnography does not consist merely in the description of customs and rites. Beneath the manifold manifestations of the Life of the Tribe, the ethnographer tries to discover its soul... The further we proceed in our study, the nearer we approach to the mystery of its mental life.

The mental life reveals itself in two great sets of spiritual facts, those relating to the intellectual and those relating to the religious and moral side of life ; in other words, the mind of a nation may be considered under two different aspects : the intellectual, and the moral and religious. We have not yet gone far enough to come to any conclusion as regards the Religion and Morality of the Native, but we can now attempt to describe the main characteristics of the Native intellect.

CHAPTER I

CHARACTERISTICS OF THE BANTU INTELLECT.

I intend to give here, briefly, the results of a study of the language, the language of a nation being one of the most trustworthy and complete manifestations of its mind.

I have been bold enough to speak of the *Bantu,* and not merely of the *Thonga* intellect, because the grammatical features of all

153

the Bantu languages are so similar that conclusions drawn from one of them apply to most of the tribes, *mutatis mutandis*. At any rate Sutho, Zulu, Chopi, Venda, and Thonga are very much akin, as regards their structure, forming as they do the South Eastern group of Bantu languages ; and, though the Central or Western groups differ on certain points, it may be asserted that the Bantu dialects present a remarkable uniformity.

My aim is not, by any means, to enter upon a grammatical study. This has been done for most of our South African languages, and the linguist who wishes to learn Thonga can use the Grammaire Ronga, or the Elementary Thonga-Shangaan Grammar already referred to. Leaving aside all technicalities, I shall now only attempt to show what the language reveals as regards the Bantu intellect. Let us, on this important question, take the testimony of the Noun, the Verb, the Conjunction and the Adverb.

A. THE NOUN AND THE POWER OF CLASSIFICATION.

The Bantu system of Nouns shows that the Bantu intellect possesses the *Power of classification*. All nouns are divided into a certain number of classes or genders, seven or eight in the South Eastern group,᾽ as many as ten in the Central groups ; these classes are known by their singular and plural prefixes, which are very similar in all dialects. What is the system of classification which these Genders denote? The Indo-Germanic languages divide natural objects into two categories, male and female, and, in most cases, add a third category, the neuter. They are *sex-denoting* languages, as Bleek used to call them. Nothing of this kind is met with amongst the Bantus (1). They follow an entirely different

(1) The Thongas, however, possesses a feminine suffix *ati* (eti, etsi) corresponding to a feminine prefix *mi* (I. p. 36). This suffix is found in nsati, wife, rarakati, paternal aunt, hulukati, female elephant, hweti, moon, nyeleti, star, mati (?) water, etc. It appears in many names of rivers : Nkomati, Ñwebeti, Ñwanetsi, Selati, Nfoloti, Shingwedzi, etc. Other names of rivers belong to the li-tin or ri-tin class : Limbelule (Oliphant) Limpopo, Lisuthu, Letsitele (Ritshindjele), Ritabi (Great Tabie), etc.

system. As a matter of fact, it is very difficult to understand it fully. These languages have already undergone a long process of evolution, and, just as it is impossible to state why a French word like *"chemin"* is masculine and another word like *route* is feminine, so the reason why such and such a noun belongs to such and such a class is not always apparent. However, as a whole, the Bantu system of classification is much more rational than the Indo-Germanic. I shall not study it etymologically, viz., by searching for the original meaning of the prefixes, a very difficult task which has been accomplished by Prof. Meinhof, who had at his disposal an enormous quantity of material for comparison. I shall only consider it in its broad features, as it now presents itself in the living language, and I assert that it reveals a true power of classification.

The Bantu mind divides natural objects into seven or eight categories :

1) *Personal beings*, which are classified by prefixing *mu* (n) in the singular and *ba* in the plural, thus forming the first class, the class *mu-ba* ; munhu, man, nuna, husband, nsati, wife, etc. This class is so clearly defined in the Bantu mind that new objects bearing a personal character are immediately incorporated into it : e. g. mulungu, White man, muhanu, White woman (from an Indian word). Animals which behave like rational beings in folk tales are also removed from their class into the mu-ba class by prefixing *Ñwa* to their names, and innumerable verbal nouns are formed by prefixing *mu* to the verbal stem, if they designate persons (e. g. ku fa, to die, mufi, the dead man).

2) The second class, *mu-mi*, designates *trees* ; almost all trees belong to it (I. p. 397), and those recently introduced into the country have been named according to this rule, e. g. manga, mimanga, the mango tree. It is true that we find a number of other things with the prefix of the tree-class : the wind (moya), and similar objects (mumu, heat, ndjilo, fire, mpfuka, space, nkari, time), the body (miri) and some of its organs (nomo, the lip, nenge, the leg). But trees are the characteristic element of this class.

3) The third class, *yin-tin* (Zulu in-izin, Sutho (n)-li) is evidently that of *animals*. Ninety per cent of these belong to it ; and

though a number of other objects have these prefixes (different degrees of affinity for instance : namu, ndjisana, etc., I. p. 223), this is definitely the animal class.

4) The fourth class (*dji-ma* (Ro.), *ri-ma* (Dj.), Zulu : ili-ama, Sutho : le-ma) is that of *fruits*, and new fruits are constantly incorporated into it (e. g. malalandji, oranges). Many other categories of objects are found in this class : natural objects, hard, shining (pala, skull ; rambu, bone ; fumu, thlari, assagai ; dambu, sun) and things grouped together. It may be that the prefix *ma* originally applied to objects conveying the idea of duality (mahlo, eyes ; mabele, breasts ; maboko, arms ; mahahla, twins) ; but in the present state of the language fruits seem to me to be the characteristic feature of this class.

5) The fifth class (*li-tin* (Ro.), *ri-tin* (Dj.), ulu-izi (Zulu) is most difficult to define and seems to be tending to become obsolete : it is wanting in Sutho, and nearly so in Djonga. I call it the class of *organs*, at any rate of organs of an elongated form (lidjimi, tongue ; libambo, rib ; likhongotlo, spine, etc.). The primitive idea may be that of length.

6.7.8) The sixth, seventh and eighth classes bear a strongly neuter character : the sixth (*bu-ma*, Zulu ubu-ama, Sutho bo-ma) designates *abstract notions* derived from adjectives or verbs (bukulu, greatness), the seventh (*shi-psi*, Zulu isi-izi, Sutho se-li) *instruments* and the eighth (*ku*, Zulu uku, Sutho hu) *actions*. This is the verbal class, the infinitive of the verb, ku famba, meaning the march as well as to march.

The class bu-ma may also be called the class of *liquids*, as most liquids belong to it (bukanyi, buputju, etc. See I. p. 397).

Considering the principal meaning of these eight classes, we can state that, whatever may be the origin of the prefixes, the present-day Bantus, at any rate the Thongas, classify natural objects as : personal beings, trees, animals, fruits, organs, liquids, abstract notions, instruments, actions, other objects being incorporated into one or other of these classes in a more or less arbitrary way.

That this is a true classificatory system, every one speaking one of these languages will be able to testify ; instinctively one incorporates new objects into the fitting class, or one uses the prefixes in the formation of new words according to their classifying value. The power of classification of the Bantu mind is certainly not inferior to that of Aryans.

B. THE VERB AND THE POWER OF COMBINATION.

The Bantu verb has no inflexion ; Bantu languages belong to the agglutinative type, viz., they express the various tenses and moods of the verb not by a change of the root, but by the addition of verbal elements, either prefixes or suffixes. But these additions are so varied, and can express such subtle ideas, that the student of Bantu languages stands amazed at the powers of combination which they reveal. It is impossible here to prove this assertion by technical examples, but I can assert that any one conversant with the use of these verbal principles is able to express all the ideas which are conveyed by the conjugation of inflective verbs and a good many more. It is no exaggeration to speak of the thousands of combinations of the Bantu conjugation.

To illustrate the power of combination of the Bantu mind, I need only refer the linguist to the wonderful set of verbal derivatives which are to be found. Take the simple form *ku bona*, to see. We may derive from it the passive *boniwa*, to be seen ; two qualificatives, *boneka* and *bonakala*, to be visible ; the applicative *bonela*, to see for somebody else, to take care of ; the causative, *bonisa*, to cause somebody to see ; the intensive, *bonisisa*, to see perfectly well ; the reciprocal, *bonana*, to see each other ; the reflexive; *tibona*, to see oneself. The reversive is still to be mentioned, as *pakula*, to unload (from pakela, to load). All these various derivations may be combined according to given laws, each adding its own meaning to the others. So, from *ku tira*, to work, can be formed *tirelana*, the applicative reciprocal, to serve each other, *tireriwa*, applicative passive, to be served, *tirisiwa*, to be made to work, etc. An endless number of combinations is thus rendered possible.

C. CONJUNCTIONS AND THE POWER OF ARGUMENT.

Thonga conjunctions co-ordinate ideas rather than subordinate them to each other and this may certainly be regarded as a proof that the language has reached a less advanced stage of development than our modern Indo-European languages.

The conjunction which answers to our "that" and "in order to" is *lepsaku*. This word comes from the demonstrative pronoun *lepsi*, followed by the genitive particle *a* and by the verb *ku*, to say. It therefore means etymologically "that is to say," Let me give two examples : "I believe that he has gone : Ndja kholwa lepsaku a fambile." The exact translation would be : I believe that is to say he has gone. "I eat in order to find strength : Ndja dya lepsaku ndji kuma matimba," literally : I eat that is to say I find strength. The two ideas are presented as parallel, co-ordinate, not as subordinated one to the other. In the Ronga dialect however "in order that" is rather expressed by *akuba* i. e. to be or to become, which implies more or less the idea of an aim ; but this conjunction is not followed by a conjunctive form of the verb.

A similar deficiency consists in the fact that *when* and *if* are not differentiated from each other, both these ideas being expressed by the conjunction *loko* which is merely the demonstrative pronoun of the neutral class *ku* employed in a wider sense ; I never succeeded in finding a true word to express the abstract notion of *condition*.

We ought not, however, to conclude from these facts that the Bantu mind is still in the "prelogic stage" which the sociological school attributes to primitive mentality. There exist in the language a number of other conjunctions which show that the Native method of reasoning is not very different from our own. *Because* is rendered by *hikusa* or *hikuba*, lit. by to be ; *therefore, then* (French donc) by *hi-lepso* or *hi-lepso-ke*, lit. by this, and this little word *ke* is sometimes pronounced with a peculiar movement of the index finger which proves that the speaker has as much pleasure in asserting his conclusion as Cicero when he reached the end of his argument and uttered a victorious *ergo*! The syllogism is not unknown to the Bantus though they may not have clearly thought out all its rules. It is true that logical reasoning is often interfered with amongst these primitive peoples by the mystic associations which Mr. Lévy-Brühl describes in his books on *Les Fonctions Mentales dans les Sociétés Inférieures* and *La Mentalité Primitive*, interfered with also by emotional factors or by the intervention of the will ; this unfortunately happens in non-primitive races also. But as regards the mechanism of reasoning, I do not think there is any great difference between the Bantu mind and the mind of more civilized peoples.

At any rate the power of co-ordination disclosed in the Bantu languages is extremely large and gives these languages a remarkable clearness. Its main feature is this : the prefix of the noun is used to form all the adjectives and pronouns connected with it, as will be clearly seen from the following sentence :

Tindlopfu	letinyingi	ta	tiko	ti	khalutile :	hi tone
The elephants	numerous	of	the land	they	have passed :	It is they,

hi toleti,	le'ti	bonekaka	mutjwen	wa	tone.
it is these	which	are visible	in the forest	of	them.

This is what grammarians have called the Euphonic Concord. It is certainly *euphonic*, bringing about frequent alliterations which are pleasing to the ear, and at any rate prevent misunderstanding, as they help us to realise, at once, to which noun the pronouns and adjectives refer.

D. ADVERBS AND THE POWER OF DESCRIPTION.

The Adverbs of place, manner, time, etc., form a very interesting study ; they show the presence of remnants of the three locative classes, *pa*, *mu* and *ku*, which still flourish in Central African languages, and have become obsolete in those of South Africa (*h*andle, outside ; *h*ansi, on the ground ; *h*ase, on the other border ; *mu*ndjuku, to morrow ; *k*aya, at home ; etc.) and this seems to prove that our dialects represent a further development of the old Bantu languages. But I am here considering especially what I have called the *Descriptive Adverbs*, a category of very curious words which have not been sufficiently noticed and which show a wonderful power of description in the Thonga mind.

These words, hundreds of which are employed by the Natives, consist of monosyllables or polysyllables, often repeated twice or thrice, and generally following the verb *ku*. This verb *ku*, which is also one of the curious features of Thonga grammar, a very primitive verb (1), designates any manifestation of self, either in action, speech, or thought, and can be translated accordingly by to do, to say, or to think. Now, for the wonderfully acute senses of the sons of the bush, everything — man, beasts, objects of Nature — speaks and thinks, and these adverbs attempt to express in picturesque words these actions, this language of things, sounds as well as movements, attitudes, feelings, etc.

Let us begin by the *sound*. The Hare, in one of the Thonga tales, is represented as sleeping, when it suddenly awakens on hearing a sala, the fruit of the nsala tree (p. 16), fall from the branch and *say* : katla-katla, katla-katla, be! Katla-katla evidently translates the noise made by the hard shell of the fruit knocking against the branches on its way down until it reaches the ground and abruptly ends its journey, the termination of which is rendered by the short monosyllable *be!*.. The Hare, frightened by the noise, runs away and arouses all the beasts of the bush, one after the other, saying : "I have heard a noise of *katla-katla, katla-katla, be*" or, — here he changes the word, probably to avoid a tiresome repetition : "*ngaya-ngaya, ngaya-ngaya, be!*" This may be called an *onomatopoeia* and is met with in a great many languages. A certain number of the adverbs descriptive of sound are universally known and used. Birds say : *pse! tswi! tsiri!* The wind says : *wotshyu-wotshyu...* A man says *go-go-go*, he knocks at the door ; *mpfaaa*, he tears a cloth ; *pfotlo*, he breaks a stick, etc. There are hundreds of these in Thonga, and any one with enough

(1) It may be that *ku* is an abbreviated or simplified form of *ku ri* which corresponds to the Kafir *ukuti*. At any rate *ku* is employed as the past narrative tense of the verb ku *ri*.

imagination can further invent new ones · I remember hearing a Native describe a waggon rolling along a stony road : you could recognise the sound of the wheels, of the chain, of the frame, grinding, rattling, creaking!

Sometimes the descriptive adverb is very different from the sound it is intended to imitate : thus, when the dog is said to say : *ndo-ndo-ndo*, the mouse : *tlulu-tlulu*, the duyker : *rurururu*, the hare : *tlwa-tlwa-tlwa*, the character of the movement, or of the gait, is described as well as the sound. We find indeed that a considerable number of these adverbs are *descriptive of movements*, viz., of phenomena perceived by the eyes, and not by the ear. They translate the impression made on the brain by objects, motions *seen* and not heard, *phenomena of vision*.

Movements of all kinds, of animate or inanimate beings, are vividly reproduced by the descriptive adverbs. Movements of the whole body : a man says *gaa*, he falls on his back ; *dlomu, nyupe,* he plunges into the water ; *retemuku*, he slips ; *ngiri-ngiri-ngiri*, he walks down ; *khaga*, he climbs ; *bvumbuluku*, he rises briskly. Movements of one limb : *ume*, he lifts an arm to threaten ; *ntshuki*, he shakes his head to deny ; *kutje*, he nods in assent ; *tjope-tjope*, his eyes twinkle. Movements which entail definite actions : *ntswi, mpsi*, he ties ; *nkwaa*, he opens a door ; *petlu*, he breaks something ; *dli*, he pierces ; *bvonyu*, he spoils ; etc., etc.

The various *kinds of gait* can also be described in this primitive way : *ntu-ntu-ntu*, the elephant, a bulky thing, advancing slowly ; *kwanyi-kwanyi*, the lion walking heavily ; *pha-pha-pha*, the jerky flight of the butterfly ; *kwe-kwe*, a man walking with difficulty : *tsere-tsere*, walking deliberately ; *kwiti*, limping ; *gutsele-gutsele*, a lame man ; *nyantsa-nyantsa*, spying out. The frog jumping on the ground, and later on into the water says : *nwe... nwe...nwe... djiama!* (this last word describing the plunge into the water). A man running slowly says *wahle* ; with small steps : *nyakwi-nyakwi* ; with rapidity : *phene-mene-mene*, or *nyu-nyu*, or *kwaru-kwaru* ; sprinting, *nana-nana*, or *nwana-nwana*.

The various *attitudes* are expressed by words, sometimes in a very amusing way : a man says *phavava*, or *nhabalala*, or *bara-tjatja*, he lies on his belly ; he says *wololoko*, he stands erect ;

khempfa, he sits down very tired ; *yinti*, he stands listening attentively, etc.

The *facial expressions* are minutely described by a great wealth of such words : a man says : *langu*, he looks at something ; *lori*, with attention ; *dloto*, intently, and for a long time ; *pari*, with anger ; *dlanya*, with kindness.

Let us take another step forward and we shall find another category describing the *state of mind*, the feelings of the heart, which are also phenomena of vision in as far as they correspond to given attitudes of the body or to certain expressions of the features. A man says *gee*, he is happy ; *kono*, he fears ; *nkwi-nkwisi*, he is in a bad humour ; *doko-doko*, he covets ; *punavuna*, he has pity.

By means of such adverbs *phenomena of Nature* and even *abstract ideas* can be described. Heaven says, *mphu*, it becomes dark ; *dzunu*, the day breaks ; the smoke says *tobi-tobi*, it ascends to heaven ; the water, or the rays of the sun, say *lululu*, they begin to feel warm ; the fire says *lasi-lasi*, it is seen flickering far away.

Abstract ideas. Men say *bi* or *kutlu*, they are all killed, to the last one (total destruction) ; somebody says *kwemetelo*, he does not attain his end, etc.

The list of descriptive adverbs which I have collected comprises more than 250 of them. Most of these were obtained in the following way. When teaching my pupils the Bukhaneli, viz., the Grammar of their own language — which I always found a very interesting and useful subject of study for them — I asked each of them to write down at once 50 of these strange words. Without hesitation they complied with my demand, one of them writing as many as 70. Almost all of them were different. This shows the extreme wealth of the language in this respect. It is no exaggeration to say that, in Thonga, there are ten, perhaps twenty times as many descriptive adverbs as those quoted by my pupils. In dealing with the characteristics of the Thonga or Bantu mind, I think they are worthy of close consideration. These thousands of words, instinctively formed to express the impression made on the brain by any kind of phenomena, prove the existence of a wonderful power of description. The Bantu mind is extraordinarily sensitive to any shock from without, and it finds a way of expressing this sensitiveness by picturesque words which give an extraordinary interest and colour to speech. Bantus are far superior to us in this respect, and that is why so few Europeans can really learn to use these descriptive adverbs properly (not to mention those who look upon them with contempt!) And this is one of the signs of what I do not hesitate to call the literary sense of the Bantu mind!

In the first edition I asked the question : Are these descriptive adverbs confined to the Thongas or are they to be found in other Bantu languages? The knowledge which I possessed in 1910 gave me reason to suppose that they were indeed to be met with in at least a great number of these. Torrend in his *Comparative Grammar* quotes some of them from Kafir and Senna and refers to a whole list compiled by the Rev. A. Hetherwick in his *Yao Grammar* and by Rebmann in the *Kinyassa Dictionary*. Torrend calls them onomatopoetic substantives. Colenso gives a good many of them in his *Zulu-English Dictionary*. Grout only briefly mentions five of them in his Chapter on Zulu interjections. Endemann, in the first edition of his *Sotho Grammatik* recognizes their existence (p. 170) and classes them also as interjections, but adds : "Most of the interjections of this kind do not belong to the written language." Since then the Rev. R. Godfrey has published the second edition of the Kropf *Kafir-English* Dictionary (1915) and in his remarkable Introduction has shown the immense part these expressions play in Kafir. He calls them Primary or Strong Stems. Prof. Westerman in his *Grammatik der Ewesprache* has also shown their importance in the languages of the tribes of Western Africa. It may thus be asserted that this linguistic phenomenon is met with all through primitive Africa and the conclusions which I draw from the presence of these descriptive adverbs with regard to Thonga mentality equally apply to all Africans.

As regards the name given to them, I would object to the term *interjection*. While some of them can be used as such, i. e. "thrown amongst" other words without syntactic connection, they generally follow the verb *ku ku* (or *li* or *ti*) just as "yes" or "no" follow the verb to say. So they are rather adverbs than interjections. Nor can I approve of the term employed by Torrend : *onomatopoetic substantives*. Substantives they certainly are not, as they pertain to none of the eight classes and have nothing of the nature of nouns. On the other hand, only a

163

certain number of them are real onomatopoeiae, i. e. words resembling
the sound made by the thing of which they are the names. The term
adopted by the Rev. R. Godfrey, Primary or Strong Stems, has been
severely criticised by the Rev. W. Bourquin (see Christian Express,
August and September 1916) and it would seem that this expression
Primary must at any rate not be taken to mean that these words necessarily belong to the oldest elements of the language. A considerable
proportion of the Kafir descriptive adverbs (60-70 %) bear the trace of a
Hottentot or Bushman origin. It would however be an error to
conclude from this fact that these words, amongst the Bantus, have
been borrowed from the non-Bantu races. They abound in Thonga
and Thonga has not been in any way influenced by the Bushmen and the
Hottentots. But there is still another fact which proves that the
descriptive adverbs have not been inherited from the *Ur-Bantu* ; as far
as I am able to judge, the Kafir descriptive adverbs are totally different
from those of the Thongas (1). There ought on the other hand to be
many common to both languages (which have a great number of
common roots as regards nouns, adjectives and verbs) if the present
descriptive adverbs had really been used in the mother tongue. For
all these reasons the term Descriptive Adverbs seems to me the best and
should professional grammarians not wish to adopt it, I would suggest
that they should be considered as words having no true equivalents in
our more polished European languages and therefore as forming a new
category, a new species to be added to the classical eight parts of speech!
After all, language is not made for Grammar, but Grammar for
language ! And we Europeans cannot claim to have found all the
forms of expression of which the human mind is capable. If the Bantus
have discovered another class of words which render them great service,
why should we proclaim them as unworthy of consideration and exclude
them from the written language?

For linguists, I add a few particulars concerning the grammatical
nature of these words and the importance they may have had in the
evolution of human speech. The intonation, the gesture, accompanying
these adverbs of course greatly assist in understanding their meaning.
Sometimes the word is *short*, ends sharply, as *gi*, a blow on a pole to
drive it into the earth ; or it is *prolonged* as *ra-a-a*, the unrolling of a

(1) It is not possible to pronounce a definite judgment on this question as the lists
of Kafir and Thonga descriptive adverbs which we possess are far from being complete.
Full lists of these interesting particles in all the languages ought to be compiled by
Bantu grammarians as soon as possible for purposes of comparison.

mat which drags along the ground ; or *repeated* many times, when the action consists in a series of repeated motions : *ngiri-ngiri-ngiri,* walking down to the spruit.   From the etymological point of view, some adverbs may be termed *primitive* and others *derivative.*   Amongst the primitive are, for instance, *dzi,* the act of planting (hence the verb ku dzima), *nyupe,* the act of plunging (hence ku nyupela), etc.   But others are distinctly derivative, for instance : *humelelo,* the impression caused by somebody who suddenly appears.   This is certainly derived from the verb ku humelela, which is itself the double applicative derivative of ku huma, to come out ; ku humelela means, according to the law of verbal derivation, to be produced, to happen, to arrive, to appear.   Hence the descriptive adverb.   Other instances of such derivations are : *retemuku, rendjeleku, tlheriso, woloko, khabutelo.*   They are generally long words (though all the long ones are by no means derivatives).   A regular means of derivation even seems to consist in the addition of the suffix *iyani* to the infinitive of the verb ; so a man "says" *yetleliyani,* he sleeps, (from ku yetlela, to sleep) ; *yimisiyani,* he stands erect (from ku yima, to 'stand).   It would seem as if people had found so much pleasure in expressing their ideas by this picturesque method that they even convert regular verbs into descriptive adverbs !

I must further mention that some of these adverbs, placed between the verb *ku* and the adverb, as shown in the following examples, have a true transitive nature and may be preceded by a direct object, especially those which express actions.   Ex.: A ku *shi* wuyuwuyu, he throws *that* away ; a ku *mu* mpsi, he makes *him* mpsi, he binds him ; even the verbal reflective prefix *ti* (which is a kind of invariable pronoun) can be used in this connexion.   Ex.: A ku *ti* mpsi, he ties himself.   Some are at the same time transitive and intransitive, according to the sense.   Ex.: A ku *kwe-kwe,* he drags his leg ; (a way of walking) ; a ku yi kwe, he drags it (the pole) ; (a transitive action).

In Kafir these particles are capable of modifying their meaning considerably owing to the fact that the auxiliary *ukuti* to which they are appended can adopt the derivative verbal forms called by Godfrey the reciprocal, the relative, the stative and the reflexive.   This is not possible with the Thonga auxiliary ku ; I have only met with the reflexive ti, and this was not prefixed to the auxiliary as in Kafir but to the adverb itself.

In Kafir as in Thonga many of these words give rise to regular verbs. This fact, which is one more proof of their importance and is highly interesting, would alone substantiate my contention that they should be carefully studied. They correspond to a phase of human development when language is still living and creating new expressions, enriching itself by means of vocables invented on all sides. Let me remind the reader of what I said in Vol. I, Appendix II about *nxoko*. This expression was invented by an old Thonga of Rikatla, a blind man of 70 or 80, who expressed by this exclamation his satisfaction at finding himself in good company. The word seemed so much to the point that it became famous. The inventor was surnamed Nxoko and created the verb ku *nxoka*, to be happy, even to *nxokela*, the relative derivative, to be happy in a certain place. Certainly such linguistic phenomena can do much to explain the origin of language. Even lofty spiritual terms have been derived from these exclamations, springing from the childish mind of the Natives. So *phati-phati*, the shining of a fat ox, has given rise to *ku phatima* and *kwetsi-kwetsi*, the brilliancy of a bottle, to *ku kwetsima*, both verbs which were chosen as best expressing the idea of sanctity or purity (in its positive sense). Did not Max Muller conjecture that the root of *Deus*, a word which has played such a great part in the evolution of mankind, originally came from the exclamation *Devar* to which our Aryan forefathers gave vent when contemplating the sky? Devar was probably nothing but a descriptive adverb.

It is to be feared that books and book language will destroy this most interesting mode of speech, so much used by those Natives who are true Bantus, and the genius of the race will certainly suffer from this loss. Let Europeans, in this as in so many other domains, try to *understand* the Native in order not to spoil him !

E. THE NUMERALS, AND THE WANT OF AN ARITHMETICAL SENSE.

Compared to the thousands of descriptive adverbs, Numerals make a poor show indeed in the Thonga Grammar! The Thongas possess only seven : ñwe, one ; *biri*, two ; *raru*, three ; which are declined like adjectives ; *mune*, four ; *ntlhanu*, five, *khume*, ten ; *dzana*, a hundred, which are nouns. With these seven words they must express all numbers. The process is very complicated indeed. Nine hundred and eighty seven will have to be rendered as follows : five hundred, and four hundred, and five tens, and three tens, and five, and two. This system of numeration is clearly decimal, and is in direct relation with the ten fingers of the hands ; this is proved by the fact that, when counting, Natives generally use their fingers. They start with the little finger of the left hand, *one* ; then the little finger and the third finger, *two* ; these two and the second, *three* ; these three and the index, *four* ; these four and the thumb, *five* ; they then add the fingers of the right hand, beginning with the thumb : five plus one, five plus two, five plus three, five plus four. *Ten* is shown by clapping both hands ; notice that five, the left hand with the thumb separated from the four other fingers, imitates the Roman sign of V, and ten, the two hands joined, with the fingers crossing each other, make an X, the Roman sign for 10 ! This shows that our system of numbers, of which we are justly proud, probably began in the same way as amongst most of the Bantu tribes !

On the other hand it must be said that, if this system has not reached a higher development, the cause lies in the fact that Thongas do not wish, or do not *take the trouble* to deal with high figures. They very soon declare that a number is : "tjandja-bahlayi (Dj.) or hlulabakonti (Ro.)" viz., "the one which passes the capacity of reckoners." When Gungunyana made a raid into the Ntimane district and stole the oxen there, his men tried to count the cattle, but, having experienced much difficulty in the operation, they said to their king : "It is tjandjabahlayi !" — "They are innumerable !" There were a few hundreds of them (1).

More than that ! Bantus have not attained to *any precision* in counting the hours of the day, for instance, because there was no necessity for doing so in the primitive state. Consider how greatly our habit of always consulting our watches has contributed to create a sense of precision in us and to introduce it into our lives. For the Bantus, the sun is the only watch, and that great time-keeper is all sufficient for them. Do they wish to make an appointment for the following day ? They point to a place in the

---

(1) As regards *counting men,* in former times this was positively prohibited. If any one, seeing a throng assembled on the hubo, wanted to know the number of people present, they would say to him : " What ! You are counting us ? Whom do you want to do away with ? " (Shana wa hi nkonta, u ta hi pumba na ?)

sky, and say : "We shall meet when the sun has reached that spot." It may be in the morning, at the time "when the rays of the sun begin to pierce" (tlhaba-sana) ; at noon, nhlekanhin "when the sun is in the middle of its course ;" in the afternoon, *hi mfenya*, say the Rongas "when the sea breeze comes up", as is the case almost every day ; or "when the sun is going down" (ndjenga) (1). It must be added that the sun is rarely hidden in these lands of light.

As regards the counting of days, they have special names for to-morrow (mundjuku), the day after to-morrow (mundlwana), and the three following days ; for the third day, pambari ; the fourth, wo dlankambane, viz., the one when the travellers going on a business journey break the plate in order to be obliged to come home (p. 144) ; for the fifth, wa tiki- tiki. Tolo, is yesterday ; tolwen, the day before yesterday ; tolwen wa hase, the day preceding the day before yesterday ; ñanwaka, this year ; hashau, next year ; nweshemu, last year ; ñwaka lowo, the year before last. One hardly counts days, or years, beyond this point (2).

One occasion on which arithmetical skill, or at least the faculty of addition, is specially required, is the counting of the lobolo, when this consists of hoes. Then the tens are carefully piled up separately, the whole family witnessing the operation, but this can hardly be called a mathematical achievement.

So, on the whole, opportunities of using the arithmetical

---

(1) If this use of the sun as a means of fixing the time inevitably leads to a want of precision, it has on the other hand, created a wonderful sense of direction amongst the Natives. They never lose sight of the North, they always know where the sun rises and sets, and this is no doubt the secret of their instinct. When travelling with them, it is not necessary to consult the compass; I would rather put my fate in their hands, knowing that they will not make any mistakes as regards direction (they will certainly make many as regards distance), as they say their *hearts* (timbilu, the same word employed for genius and instinct), viz., their subconscious powers, help them better than our instruments in the midst of the African bush ; not to mention their knowledge of native paths. These powers have been cultivated by the constant observation of the sun.

(2) In my Grammaire Ronga, another list of names of the days following to-day is given, containing as many as 7. This seems to be the Ronga version, whilst that here given is the Djonga. However, in neither case is the list in constant and common use. It is known only to certain individuals who look on it more or less as a curiosity. To count days further than the day after to-morrow is quite unusual.

faculty are very rare in primitive Native life, and we ought not to be astonished that this faculty has remained undeveloped. To pretend however that it is altogether wanting would be erroneous. I can give many proofs that it exists, and sometimes manifests itself in an interesting way.

First, in the game called *nyengeli-nyengeli mune.* The players place a number of fruit stones on the ground two by two. One turns his back, and the other player, pointing to the first group of two, asks : "Nyengeli nyengeli mune?" i.e : "How many stones are there?" The one whose back is turned replies : "Take one away and place it elsewhere," specifying where. The same thing is done with the second, and so on. Certain groups have eventually more stones than others. When a group is entirely scattered, the guesser says : "Makua ntsikitane," meaning "There are no more." The questioner then passes rapidly from group to group, over and over again, and the guesser must state how many stones each group contains. The game requires a considerable effort of memory.

Second proof : Shinangana! Shinangana is a man living in Spelonken, near Elim Station, a raw Native who is ignorant of the art of reading and writing, and who never went to school, but who has created a *chronology* embracing the past 70 years. He knows what has happened in each year since 1859, and has arrived unaided at the conception of an era. His era starts from the emigration of the Thonga tribes into the Transvaal, when they fled before Manukosi, on the return of the Ngoni chief from the Mosapa or Gaza country (I. p. 28). The Nkunas, Mavundjas, Tsungus and other Hlabi clans were obliged at that time to take refuge in Spelonken, and this is the beginning of the era. Most of the years after that great event have their special designation. I had the good fortune to have an interview with Shinangana in 1905 and was able to note the details of his chronology, as he dictated them to me. After having enumerated all these years, he concluded in a triumphant tone with the exclamation : "All these years since the return of Manukosi make five hundred, and three hundred, and four months!" This is a most curious piece of Native historiography, I think quite unique in the whole Thonga tribe.

169

Having a remarkable bent for this work, he developed his gift, acquired fame, and was consulted by all those who wished to know their age, or the date of some event. This increased his powers. He took a great delight in these consultations and, working at his subject every day, aided by his wonderful memory he could recite the whole chronology without the slightest hesitation. I give it in Appendix I, and it is worthy of publication, not only as a proof of the possibility of a development in arithmetic amongst raw Natives, but also for its contents, as a contribution to the history of the Northern Transvaal.

We come to the same conclusion when teaching our pupils arithmetic in our missionary schools. This is certainly the branch of study in which they are the least proficient, and their teachers will all confess to having sometimes despaired of their mathematical faculty. However, when taught European numeration, English or Portuguese, most of them learn the four rules, and many attain to the Weights and Measures, and the Rule of Three. I saw a class of young Natives successfully studying Algebra in Lovedale, and they are not altogether incapable of Arithmetic. However they succeed better when the effort is one of memory, and this explains why they are much more at their ease when learning the English Weights and Measures, entailing complicated operations of reduction, than when put to the metric system which seems so much more simple and rational. The English system requires a perfect committal to memory of the relation between the various measures, yards, feet and inches, gallons, pints, gills, pounds, ounces and grains, and, these being once mastered, all the work becomes purely mechanical. This is what Natives like, whilst in the metric system there is one idea pervading the whole and a certain minimum of reasoning is necessary for its use : the necessity for this minimum explains the unpopularity of the metric system amongst the Native pupils, and the difficulty increases ten times when they come to problems, and have to solve them without having been told whether addition or substraction is necessary! So arithmetic, when workable by means of the memory, seems to them an easy and agreeable study ; when it requires reasoning, it is a painful occupation. If

Shinangana had been trained, would he have been a genius in that kind of mathematics where the power of reasoning is needed? It is impossible to say, but it may be noticed that all his achievements were, after all, but masterpieces of memory, and that reasoning had very little to do with them.

The conclusion of our observations is then as follows : in the Bantu mind the literary sense is infinitely more developed than the mathematical. This is probably the case in all uncivilised or half civilised races, but amongst the South Africans it is strikingly apparent.

F. THE LITERARY SENSE OF THE THONGAS.

Let us look more closely into this literary faculty which the Thonga grammar has already revealed to us. It not only consists in the possession of a well constructed language, denoting powers of classification, combination, co-ordination and graphic description, but also shows itself in the poetic expression of their feelings, in a remarkable power of comparison, and in a rich folklore.

The *facility of expression*, amongst the Thongas, is very great. Any one, man or woman, is at any time ready to speak, and speaks correctly with the greatest ease. In this respect, the race is perhaps more advanced than many civilised peoples. There is nothing like the timidity you so often meet with amongst the peasants or workmen of our own lands, who, though they have had a full course of primary education, would be totally unable to deliver an address. A Native can always stand up and say what he thinks on any given question. Even if he has not thought much about it, he can speak! Finding words is no difficulty to him. Knowledge will perhaps be lacking, but fluency of speech never! This ease of elocution has evidently been acquired through a long experience in the discussion of public affairs on the *hubo*, where, as we saw (I, p. 436), every one has the right of expressing his opinion. This habit has developed literary ability, and the Bantus, as a whole, deserve the compliment once paid to the pupils of the Lovedale Institute by the Rev. J. Henderson, when he said to them : "Your race has certainly received the gift of eloquence!" (1)

As regards the subject matter of their speeches, it does not always show much reflection, or many new ideas. Nor is there much order or sequence in their discourses. This would require proportion, measure, forethought, and all these virtues belong rather to the arithmetical sense which is so sadly deficient in the Bantu mind. What makes a Bantu address especially interesting is rather the *power of comparison* exhibited by Bantu speakers. They excel in discovering spiritual truths in material facts, or rather in perceiving the relations between the spiritual and the external world. This is one of the characteristics of the poetical faculty, and these so-called savages certainly have some sense of poetry in their minds. Most of the antithetic riddles, which will be quoted shortly, are instances of this power of comparison. When developed by proper training, this faculty will certainly become productive of valuable work.

So far, the training of Natives has been mostly in religious subjects, and I beg to give my readers some examples of their mode of comparison which I noted while listening to the preaching of evangelists, examples which bear the strong impress of the Bantu character. Sometimes the imagination is so subtle that the result is almost incoherent. They are satisfied even if the point which the two things compared have in common, that which grammarians call the " tertium comparationis," is almost infinitesimal.

---

(1) This power of elocution is very useful in Mission work, when evangelising the heathen villages all over Thongaland, the converts being always willing to make a speech or deliver an exhortation. They generally do this with great animation, and although the thinking is often poor, and does not show much sequence, they at least are never at a loss for words. I only once witnessed such a sad occurence ! One of my pupils had prepared a sermon and was delivering it, when suddenly he stopped and could not proceed. He had lost the thread. Then a good natured smile appeared on his features and all his companions laughed heartily. This was the first time they had seen one of their countrymen in this predicament ! The student had prepared a plan for his address, and had forgotten it ! In former times plans were entirely absent and consequently there were no threads to lose !

172

For instance a Tembe Christian exhorting his hearers to fight against evil, says :

Let us, in this fight, take the shield which has been made from the skin of this ox slaughtered for our sake, Jesus Christ.

A moment of reflection is required to find the logical sequence which unites all these images. The Bantu shield being made of ox-hide, the scriptural image of the slaughtered lamb had to be transformed into that of an ox, for the sake of comparison!

Another evangelist, whose discourses were specially interesting because he was a master in this art, one day spoke for more than half an hour on the text "Charity which is the bond of perfection." In Thonga, bond, string, or rope is expressed by the same word (ngoti). So he showed how a string could be compared to charity by a great number of images, of which I remember at least the two following :

This rope, charity, is the rope which fastens the donkey to the trunk of a tree. In the evening you tie up the donkey ; it can graze the whole night all round the tree without any fear of being lost. So when we remain in connection with our Saviour, who is the tree, then we are happy and protected against all danger.

He evidently remembered the words of Christ : I am the vine. And he added :

Charity is the string, the string which ties up a parcel. You have many precious things in your parcel... But if you possess no string to tie up all these things, they will be lost on the way, one after the other, and you will reach the end of your journey (or of your life) having kept none of your spiritual advantages, etc.

This is how Simeon Gana tried to explain what conscience is :

Conscience resembles two companions who have made an arrangement to plunder, with impunity, another man's field of sweet potatoes. One of them climbs a tree, the other takes the hoe and digs up the potatoes. As soon as the owner of the field appears, the one on the tree whistles and the other promptly runs away, so that he is never

173

caught. But one day, the climber ran a thorn into his foot and he was obliged to sit down and extract it, as he could not climb to his post of observation in that condition. In the meantime his companion was stealing the potatoes in perfect tranquillity, thinking that his comrade was on guard. The owner arrived on the scene and caught him. Now you see clearly that conscience is the man who climbed up the tree. As long as he was doing his duty, success attended their plan. As soon as he fails to work, the man falls into disgrace. So let our conscience always be awake and warning us !

We Europeans would never have dreamt of such a simile. Conscience represented by a thief helping another to steal! But the Bantu audience was perfectly satisfied...

Here is another comparison bearing on a similar subject :

The words of God are powerful and stir up the heart. They are like intestinal worms (manyokwana) which for a long time remain quiet in the body. But one fine night they awake and man cries out from pain, saying : "I am ill !" For years the man mocked the word of God, but that day he felt its power !

Hundreds of such comparisons, not always denoting a very refined taste, but always picturesque, might be collected from the addresses of Native Christians. I will only add this, which is deeper and more significant than many others, and which occurred to the imagination of one of my pupils :

We, preachers of the Gospel, are messengers of mourning. We have been sent to inform people of the great mourning of Jesus Christ by which He saved the world. Let us not resemble that messenger who had to go to another country to deliver his errand. On the way he passed a village where people were drinking beer. He heard the songs, looked on at the dance, entered and did not deliver his message. Such would we be, if distracted by worldly amusements, we were to neglect our sacred duty of preaching the cross.

Besides this undeniable power of comparison, Native addresses often reveal another curious feature ; the Native tendency to present ideas in a round-about manner. This is called ku pamba. Beneath expressions apparently simple they hide other meanings in a manner so ingenious and subtle that some of their hearers

174

often fail to understand them. This literary device is often apparent in their riddles, or proverbs.

The literary gifts of the Natives, finally, manifest themselves in the very interesting and rich folklore which will form the subject of our second chapter.

*

*   *

Is it possible after this rapid study of the Thonga language to fix with greater accuracy the place which the Bantu languages occupy in the historic development of human speech? Languages which are regarded as the most primitive are characterised by a linguistic phenomenon which is called holophrase, viz. a single word means not only a single action, but an action accomplished under a number of peculiar circumstances. Mr. Marett in his excellent little book entitled *Anthropology* (p. 140) quotes some very curious examples of holophrase borrowed from the American languages, especially from the Fuegian. A single expression is said to mean : "to look at each other hoping that either will offer to do something which both parties are unwilling to do." I have found in Thonga only one instance in which traces of the holophrase system might be found, and this is by no means so wonderful. The demonstrative adjectives are met with in three forms, which indicate not only the object referred to, but its place as regards distance and in relation to the person speaking. Tihomu *leti*, means these oxen, near at hand, near me ; tihomu *leto*, these oxen, somewhat further off, near you, my interlocutor ; tihomu *letiya*, those oxen, far away and near a third person. The more the final a is prolonged, the further off are the oxen. Moreover these demonstrative adjectives indicate not only the situation of the oxen in space but also in time ; *leti* are the oxen of to-day, *leto* those of a near past and *letiya* those of which we were speaking a long time ago. But this is an isolated case. In Thonga ideas are differenciated almost as completely as in our Indo-European languages. The language has evolved from the holophrastic to the analytic. My conclusion is therefore that the Bantu languages, though they belong to the agglutinate variety, have reached a high degree of development ; they reveal the existence of intellectual powers not essentially different from those of civilized races. They certainly constitute the greatest achievement of Bantu mental activity and the most precious treasure inherited by the Bantus of to-day from their forefathers.

175

CHAPTER II

Thonga folklore.

Thonga folklore may be said to exhibit three different styles : *didactic* and sometimes *sententious* poetry, in its proverbs and riddles, *narrative* poetry in its manifold tales, and *lyric* poetry in its songs. The two first may be called to a certain extent *collective* or *traditional* : all the riddles or tales are ancient products of the literary activity of the tribe, handed down to the Thongas of to-day by oral tradition. On the other hand, new songs are continually being composed, and bear a much more *personal* or *individual* character. I have given a great many examples of tales and songs, in my "Chants et Contes des Ba-Ronga" (324 p.), as well as in "Les Ba-Ronga" (p. 253-363).

My present object is not to compile all the available material, which would be far too long a process, but to give a general idea of Thonga folklore, and to complete my previous study by the publication of some new tales and riddles chosen from those collected since the two preceding works were published. The source is almost inexhaustible, and would suffice for the compilation of two or three volumes. The examples here given will be representative enough to convey a true idea of this rich folklore, and I refer the reader to the two books previously cited if he wishes for more information.

A. PROVERBIAL SAYINGS AND RIDDLES.

Riddles certainly furnish us with a very precious means of gaining an insight into the secret workings of the Native mind, as they form doubtless the quaintest part of their literature, and

176

that which bears the least resemblance to any portion of our own! I have already quoted some examples of riddles in my first volume, and the obscurity of these sayings has been sufficiently obvious. Without special explanation it would be difficult indeed to discover their meaning.

I. *Proverbial sayings.*

As regards *proverbs*, the Ba-Ronga possess a few containing a single statement, as for example :

1) Mumiti wa nhengele a dumba nkolo wa kwe.
   He who swallows a large stone has confidence in the size of his throat !

This might be said in any country and will be recognised, at once, as applying to bumptious and pretentious folk!

2) U nga hlaule matjhuna ya mhangela.
   One must not point out the male of the guinea-fowl.

Guinea fowls are all alike, male and female. So do not point to one and say : "This is a male." You would be liable to make a mistake, and to be made fun of! This proverb is said to a young husband who might be tempted to prepare the *ntehe* before the birth of his child, which is taboo. (I. p. 46.) Compare this with the proverb : Don't count your chickens before they are hatched.

3) Tinhlange ta le ntjhaku ti tibyiwa hi mutlhabi.
   The tattooing marks made on the back are known to the tattooer (not to the tattooed !).

You do not know what may happen when you have turned your back. This warning was given by one of the Church elders, of Lourenço Marques, to a missionary who was leaving on furlough!

4) Matimba ya ngwenya i mati.
   The strength of the crocodile is water.

When you are in your own domain you can succeed ; do not try to fight outside it. You would be like "a fish out of water..

5) U nga nwe mati, u seletela nhlobo ; mundjuku u ta nwa kwini ?
   Do not fill up the well after having drunk. Where would you drink to-morrow ?

Here the sense is at once apparent.

6) Mbuti ya shihaha a yi belekeli ntlhambin.
A good goat does not bring forth in the midst of the flock.

I heard this proverb in one of our Synods. One of the Native members wished to exhort his co-delegates to abstain from giving their advice, and voting precipitately on a certain subject : let us rather go outside, and discuss amongst ourselves, and when we have come to an understanding we will come back and vote as one man !

This last example shows how such proverbs are used... They are sometimes quoted in a low voice, so as to be heard only by those whom it is desired to warn. It is an instance of the *phamba* just referred to.

Compare also the proverb quoted (p. 21) in connection with tilling the fields :

Do not look at the weeds and think : Now ! I have tilled a large field !

Do not be satisfied by mere external appearances ! Weeds may be plentiful, yet the field be small !

Hundreds of such sayings might be collected (1), though I do not think they are so extensively used as, for instance, in the Sutho tribe, where M. Jacottet told me he collected a thousand of them. The Thongas replace them by riddles, which seem to be more developed amongst this people than in the neighbouring tribes.

II. *Riddles.*

I have already described (I. p. 350) the part riddles play in the games of the Thonga village. The riddle, *mhumhana*, consists first in divining where the piece of charcoal is hidden, and in that

(1) We might also regard as proverbs, and include under this heading, the figurative terminology used to express the principles of right and justice, which are, as it were, a primitive codification of the common law, and to which I have previously referred — as for instance the curious sentence : A cow which has calved is not used for payin a debt. (I. p. 217).

case it is merely a matter of guess work. But it may have a more literary character, when it consists in a more or less witty question requiring a given reply. The answer is here contained in one word ; so these riddles may be called *riddles in one sentence*.

> Leshi u nga khandjiyiki nsinya ya shone, n'shini? — Hi ndjulu.
> What is the thing up the trunk of which one cannot climb? It is the juncus.
> Leshi nhaka nenge wa shone u nga rwali hi ku bindja u ya tlhasa shilungwin, n'shini ? — Hi nsuna.
> What is the animal whose leg is so heavy that you could not carry it to Lourenço Marques ? — The mosquito (which is so very light !)
> Leshi shi nga heta hubo ya ka Machakene, shi ndjundja, shi kwala hubyen?
> — Hi nhwala!
> What is it that is all over the square at Machakene, that creeps and crawls about on it ? It is the louse !

This last is full of malice! The village of Machakene, formerly in the immediate vicinity of Lourenço Marques, where the fashionable European quarter is now situated, was the place where men arriving from the interior to find work at the seaport usually passed the night. They appear to have been somewhat annoyed with unwelcome attentions! Hence the riddle.

Here is a rather more difficult one :

> Tiban leshi, nambi mamana wa ñwana a ku mu randja ngopfu, loko a tlhasa kaya a nga hluleka ka ku mu yamukela? — Hi nyimba.
> Guess what it is that a mother loves dearly but which could not run to meet her on her return home? — It is the unborn babe in her womb.

Another riddle of the same kind is this :

> Tiba leshi, nambi shi shongile, afaka u nga ti wopsana na ye ? — Hi makwenu.
> Do you know the person to whom you would not make an improper proposal, however handsome she may be? — It is your sister.
> Leshi nsinya ya shone yi nga bonekiki, ntshini ? — Yendje-yendje.
> The thing of which the stem is invisible, what is it ? — The cuscuta.

This plant is a cause of wonder to Natives, because its root and stem are so rarely seen. It is known that it grows from a root, but when it has developed, the stem dies and the plant lives on as a parasite.

> Leshi nambi wa ba, ntjonsi wa kone wu nga boneki ? — I mati.
> The thing which you can beat without leaving a scar ? — Water.

Here is one more which has a more philosophical character and which may be of later origin.

Leshi nga hamba Tilo ni Misaba, hi tshini ? — Ntumbuluko!
The thing which made Heaven and Earth, what is it ? — Nature !

Ntumbuluko comes from ku tumbuluka, to be created, to appear, and is well translated by the word Nature (See Part VI, Chapter I).

The Thongas possess a plentiful supply of *riddles containing two statements*, which they call *psitekatekisana* and of which I have collected about a hundred. I could easily have found ten times as many. One of our female neighbours (Lishanyi) knew a great number of these and could pour them forth without stopping well on into the night.

Whoever is most expert at asking questions takes the lead, and commences with a kind of invocation of which I have not been able to discover the meaning : Nwanyanga mintjuti, lit. son of the moon, shadows. Then addressing one of the other players, and speaking very rapidly, he (or she) will say : "Teka, teka, teka (take, guess) heeee...!" following this up with the question to be asked, which forms the first part of the riddle ; the person addressed must immediately reply with the phrase forming the second part. If he is unable to answer, or gives a wrong reply, the questioner says : "Psi ku hlulile" — "you are beaten," and passes on to another player, again beginning with "teka, teka, teka" and asking the same question until some one is able to give the correct rejoinder. Hence the name of this game, psiteka-tekisana, i. e. things which you make others guess.

It will be seen that we are not here dealing with riddles in the true sense of the word, with solutions only to be arrived at by keenness of thought and reflection ; the answers to these must be learnt by heart, and it only requires a good memory to become an adept at the game. The ancestors, however, who composed the riddles, and handed them down to posterity, were by no means lacking in wit and ingenuity. The examples given below I owe mostly to Timotheo Mandlati, a Nkuna of Shiluvane, who wrote them down for me in the dialect of his own tribe ; some of them are in Hlengwe. I also obtained a good many from my Ronga informants, Spoon and Galu of Libombo, Titus, and Shilati, a blind man who thought himself very learned in the "riddling art," but understood very little of what he was talking about, and, in any case, was quite unable to give any explanation of his riddles. Some are the common property of both Ba-Ronga and Ba-Nkuna ; they seem to be very popular throughout the Thonga tribe.

To begin with, here are some examples of which *the inner meaning is not difficult to discover* :

Teka-teka-teka-he ! Tiba ro pshya hi matlhelo ? — Ndlopfu yi fa hi tshembeti.
The lake dries up at the edges ? — The elephant is killed by a small arrow.

A great result (the drying up of a lake, the death of an elephant) is often produced by a very small cause (the gradual evaporation of water at the edges, a little arrow). The idea is similar to that expressed in the proverb : "Il ne faut pas mépriser les petits commencements," or "small beginnings make great endings."

Ndja ha batla mpalala ? — Ndja ha hleketela...
I am still carving an iron wood stick ? — I am still thinking about it.

An undecided man might reply thus to those urging him to immediate action. The wood of the *mpalala* is extremely hard. "It is a long business to carve a figure of this wood" says the cunning fellow ; "I am not going to make up my mind about it in a hurry!"

Ndji pfumala tshati ; nha ndji ya tjhema nhonga ?
— Ndji pfumala ntlhambi ; nha ndji ya lobola munhu lweyo.
I have no axe, or I would go and cut a stick ?
— I have no oxen, or I would go and lobola this girl.

This is the sigh of the impecunious lover. In the first sentence he laments the want of an ordinary every-day object (an axe) which prevents his obtaining something he wishes for (a stick) ; he lets it be understood that a much more precious article is lacking (oxen, money, a lobolo) which would enable him to obtain something infinitely more to be desired (the girl he loves).

Ndji tshukumetele kwakwa, dji ya wa ngolongolo ?
— Ndji yamukele psikomo psi pfa ni Ba-Nhlabi.
I have thrown away my kwakwa ; it has rolled away to the ends of the earth
(into distant lands) ?
I have accepted the hoes which come from the Ba-Hlabi.

I have sold my daughter in marriage to the people of Hlabi
(on the other side of the Limpopo, further up than Bilene, in
Gaza) ; by so doing I have lost my child for ever. She has
disappeared like a round fruit (kwakwa) which, when thrown
a long distance, rolls and rolls away until it can never again be
found.— Moral : Don't let your girls marry foreigners (Compare I,
p. 260).

Shiyindlwana mpfontsho ?   — Mundjuku milandju.
The little hut falls down ?   — To morrow, debts.

If you don't keep your house in good order, you will soon
find yourself in difficulties. A disorderly life leads to debt.

In other riddles the meaning is not so self-evident as in the
preceding examples. There are some which are simply *a
comparison of two objects* or of an object and an idea which
resembles it in some one particular. With the rapidity of
perception characteristic of the Native mind, some clever
individual has been struck by this resemblance, and has thereupon
composed a riddle the obscurity of which is in direct proportion to
its conciseness.

Rihondjo ra ndlopfu ku mpfara ? — Munhu wa ndlala tihanyi ?
The sound of a cracked elephant-tusk ?   — The anger of a hungry man.

Both have a false ring.

This Nkuna riddle is met with amongst the Rongas, in the
following form :

Litimbo la phila ku mbvetshe ?   — Amunhu wa ndlala mahlundju.
The creaking of the dried sorghum stalk ?   — The anger of a hungry man.

Sikisiki dja mbangwe ?   — Longoloko dja Ba-Tschwa.
The stem of hemp ?   — The Zulu formation (when on the march, in single file).

In the way the leaves grow on the hemp stalks, there is a
suggestion of the formation, or rather of the forest of plumes
of Zulu warriors on the march...

Ntshiba ukulu wa mpfafati ?   — Ndjeko yikulu ya balungu.
The tall ntshiba?   — The long tumblers of the Whites.

The ntshiba is the tallest tree on the Ronga hills, and casts a grateful shade. The long tumblers used by the Whites answer the same purpose ; both conduce to the refreshment of the weary !

Tihuku ta ka Manyisa ta ka nhingena he psisuka ?
— Bañwhanyana ba ka Manyisa ba ku kandja ba khisamile.
The fowls of Manyisa enter the fowl-house tails first ?
— The Manyisa girls pound maize sitting down.

This is probably a sly hit at the girls of the Manyisa country who are reported to sit down when crushing maize ; everywhere else this operation is performed standing up. They don't do things like other people. — Chickens also sometimes do things the wrong way !

Riddles which refer to some *historical event* may be classed in a third category. The best known is that concerning Tembe and his sons. (See I, p. 23.) — Here is another :

Ndji fambi nhlangwa lokulu ndji heketa Mimaleyane ?
— Ndji djimi nsimo leyikulu, ndji byala ndlowu yiñwe.
I walked right across a big plain to accompany Memaleyane ?
— I hoed a large field and only planted a single pea.

This is doubtless the story of a rejected lover who thus wittily relates his discomfiture. He took all the trouble to accompany Mimaleyane a long way, right to her home, and received no reward for his gallantry. As well hoe a whole field and only plant one pea ! A great deal of trouble for nothing !

A fourth category of riddles comprises those in which no real similarity of ideas would seem to exist, but merely a *similitude in sound*, a sort of graceful alliteration which is pleasing to the ear. The two following examples are very popular and very pretty from the point of view of euphony :

He kumi nkuhlu, u wupfa, ka ku sala huhlu yiñwe ?
— He kumi mulungu, a wondja-wondja, ka ku sala ndjepfu yiñwe.
We found a *nkuhlu* which ripens, which ripens ; only one nut is left ?
— We found a White man who gets thinner, thinner : nothing left but a hair of his beard.

The comparison of ideas is not difficult to perceive, but what conclusion or moral can the author mean to convey? None!

He has been merely led away by the musical charm of the words.

Lastly I would class in a final category *the riddles which are altogether incomprehensible*, of which there are quite a large number.

> Be khumbi ?   — Mayo !   Ku fa.
> The people against the wall ?   — Ah ! if only I were to die !

Zebedea, a very intelligent man, who gave me this riddle, could not tell me what it meant. Possibly the words may have been altered in the course of transmission from generation to generation. I am unable to say. In any case we are discouraged from expending our energy in trying to discover meanings in the *psitekatekisana* when they are too obscure by the fact that several of these questions, or primary phrases, can be answered in different ways ; the answer, or second phrase, varies with the informant. Suppose for instance, that the following question be put :

> Makhoi ya nyari yinga-yinga ?
> The horns of the buffalo wander hither and thither ?

The answer may be the well-known proverb (p. 21).

> U nga bone bibi u ku ndji rimele.
> Do not contemplate the heaps of weeds saying to thyself : I have finished hoeing.

Or it may be :

> Barara ba bambe ndji nabela.
> I covet the fathers of other girls.

It may be that, in the parlour game previously described, when some one fails to give the right answer, he quotes the second sentence of another riddle on the spur of the moment, and so false connections are established between sentences which have no common meaning.

Are these *psitekatekisana* peculiar to our tribe, or are they to be met with elsewhere ? I cannot be certain on this point, but I have not heard anything like them quoted from other places. Some bear a strong resemblance to the antithetic proverbs of Solomon. But it must be confessed that they are entirely lacking in the deep religious or moral meaning of most of the Jewish proverbs !

B. THONGA SONGS.

I. *Thonga poetry and Thonga poets.*

Bantu poetry differs widely from our own! So do Bantu poets from our "literary men." I had the good fortune to make the acquaintance of one of them on the same day that I witnessed the crushing down of Mayibane's hut (I, p. 156). Attracted by the big gathering, and knowing that he would have plenty of hearers, and meat to his heart's content, this poet had come to grace the occasion with his presence. He was on a literary tour, going from one village to another, singing his songs and dancing from one end of the land to the other. Tall, his face absolutely clean shaven, his eyes having a kind of absent, semi-conscious look, he at the same time appeared most contemptuous and remained in a state of olympic calm, as if he were a very superior kind of being. He was a man of the Manyisa clan, and all seemed to show him much consideration. When those officiating at the sacrifice were busy cutting open the victim, he appeared in the circle formed by the spectators (see illustration I. p. 159, No. 7), and began his performance. He had put on a skirt of *milala* palm-leaves and imitated a lame man, assuming an air of intense suffering. Suddenly, with wonderful strength, he began to trample the ground with his feet. He had an assagai in his hand, and feigned to pierce his own side, and his thigh. Then, lifting the weapon, he cast an authoritative look on the throng and those who had been laughing stopped and kept perfectly quiet. He remained immovable, regarding them with an air of supreme contempt, impassible... And then he commenced his song (suma).

(Chorus) Oho! Oho! (Soloist) Where are you going, mother (See tune No. 1 in the collection of Thonga tunes.)

The throng joined with him in the chorus, which was really very effective. The women clapped their hands in cadence

A Thonga minstrel.

Phot. A. Borel.

(wombela) to encourage him. Judging that they did not do this with sufficient vigour, he scooped up a handful of sand and threatened to throw it into their eyes. They clapped with renewed ardour. One of them, the tall, light-coloured one who had sung the obscene songs referred to I. p. 159, came, and with a peculiar smile wrapped a yellow piece of cloth round his loins. He sang other songs, again trampling furiously on the ground, until the sacrificers had finished their work ; then he was made to stop, and the prayer to Manyibane began.

This performance was indeed, wonderful, and its interest was in no wise inferior to the funeral ceremonies themselves. It is a typical example of Thonga poetry, where three elements are generally present : the music, the dance and the words, which are more or less poetical.

This Manyisa bard is by no means a unique specimen. I remember having heard, many years ago, a poet of exactly the same type, from Bilene, who visited the Ronga clans, singing everywhere and asking for old rags as his reward. There are professional poets who earn their living by their art. There are also a number of occasional poets, who compose new songs and perform them in their own villages, not aspiring to a world-wide fame. If their tunes are pleasing, they are spoken of by others, and so become known throughout the land, on the strength of their own merit. In this way songs become popular and a great number of them are constantly sung at beer-parties, after harvest, at the feasts, some gradually falling into oblivion and being replaced by new ones each season (1).

In this chapter I shall not treat of the musical character of the

---

(1) I met later a blind minstrel, Mungomana, who earned his living in the neighbourhood of Lourenço Marques by giving concerts in the yard of an important Native woman named Ñwalanga, at which a number of boys from Inhambane and Chopiland used to stop before leaving for Johannesburg. He accompanied their dances with his timbila (xylophone) and was payed 4.800 reis per month. He told me his story. When quite young he showed a quite unusual gift for music and dancing. He went everywhere where a feast was taking place and boys were trying to outdo each other in dancing and singing, and was always proclaimed first. A woman impressed by his wonderful art, asked him to marry her, but he declined on the plea that he was still too young. Once as he was passing along a field where this woman was at work, she said to him: " If you do not marry me, you shall not live." Frightened by this

songs ; that will be considered in the next chapter, in which I intend to publish the forty-one tunes of my collection. Here I shall only consider them as literary products, and in trying to classify them, I have noticed that, though most of them cannot be said to be very elaborate compositions, they pertain to many different styles, lyric, elegiac, epic, dramatic, etc. and, in addition, there are those which are sung while at work, as well as the incantations to animals and spirits. I will give some examples of each of these categories.

II. *Lyric poetry.*

Thongas, like most human beings, have felt the need of chanting their joys and sorrows, joining words to music in order the better to express their feelings. These feelings are not as a rule very deep, and their lyrics are rather play than a painful cry of the heart. Here for instance is *the complaint of the childless woman,* who longs ardently for a baby. She has been to other people and asked them to lend her one. But they have refused and only consented to lend her a mortar and a plate. She then sings to a charming melody (Tune 7).

> A ba boleki ñwana ! — Ba boleka tshuri ni nkambana !
> Ngi ndji mangatlu ! — Ngi ndji shimungwe ! — Ngi n'ta ku utla !
> They won't lend me a baby ! — They lend me but a mortar and a plate !
> Were I an eagle ! — Were I a bird of prey ! — I would carry thee away !

The thousands of young Thongas *who go to the mines of Johannesburg,* to extract the precious auriferous quartz, seem to be quite contented with their fate. They, however, chant their

threat he fled to another country, but soon one of his eyes began to swell. His elder brother told him : "You have been bewitched by that woman," and his paternal aunt tried to heal him. She covered him with a piece of cloth, and made him expose his eye to the steam of a certain drug boiled in a pot below. She claimed to have succeeded, having found an ox-tail hair at the bottom of the pot when she poured out the water. This was however a lie. The eye complaint became worse, till he entirely lost his sight. He then devoted his life to music, and composed many songs to accompany the dances of the magayisa (boys going to work.) These songs became popular ; if a boy wished for one of them, his favourite, to be executed, he would willingly pay 200 reis ! — Mungomana is the only Thonga I heard of who used music in his religious rites. I shall give the words of his canticle in Part VI.

misfortunes to a very melodious tune (No. 8) which I once heard in Rikatla repeated a dozen times by children's voices along the bushy paths. The words were in Zulu and were said to mean :

> Stones are very hard to break
> Far from home, in a foreign land.

The tune is so catching that it has become quite popular even in French Switzerland, where I have had the opportunity of singing it on many occasions.

Once when I was walking after sunset in the neighbourhood of a miserable village of two or three huts in Rikatla, I was attracted by a simple melody repeated again and again by a feminine voice. A young woman with a child on her shoulders and engaged in cooking her food was singing. She had just lost her father. Her husband was a very bad character ; she had been obliged to leave him and to take refuge in her father's village, and, lo, he had died ! Feeling lonely and abandoned by all her natural helpers, she was expressing her grief in a low tone by the following words sung to a tune full of sadness (No. 41).

Tatana a ndji siya	My father has left me !
Na ndji nga li na mumben !	And I had no other except him !
Ndji se psanga libalen	I remain alone on the earth !
Sha ndji ta ya kwini mbuu !	Where shall I go then, Alas !

I am afraid Bantu lyrics have more than once found occasion to celebrate the selfishness and *rudeness of the White race* ! I remember travelling through the desert with three Zoutpansberg colonists, and some of their black servants. The White masters were not exactly gentle with their boys. A road had to be cut through the bush and it was hard work to remove the·stones, and to cut down the trees. The shambock was sometimes resorted to in order to stimulate the Natives. I once heard one of them, who had just been castigated, murmuring in a low tone his monotonous complaint, whilst chopping at a stem. I caught the following words : (Tune 9)

Ba hi shanisa !	They treat us badly !
Ba ku hi hlupa !	They are hard on us !
Ba nwa makhofi !	They drink their coffee !
Ba nga hi nyike !	And they give us none !

189

The Life of a South African Tribe

Of course the colonists, who only knew "Kitchen Kafir," could not understand the complaint of the Nkuna boy!

The *song of the crab* is more tragic! (Tune No. 10). In a deep minor key a man cries for help! He went to hunt the big crabs which dwell in the mud of the mangrove forest, or on the seashore. He followed one ; the animal hastily hid itself in its hole. The imprudent hunter tried to catch it there ; he put his arm into the hole and attempted to pull the crab out. But the crustacean seized his finger in its claws so firmly that the man could not get free. He remained tightly held down, fixed to the ground. The tide is rising ; soon it will cover him! And he cries :

> Yo-o ! Lomo tjukeni ku na mani ? — Hala yi khomi litiho !
> Alas ! - On the shore is there some one ? — The crab has caught me by the finger !

This is almost dramatic poetry and the scene is worthy of a true literary description.

The *erotic style* is cultivated by boys and girls on different occasions though it must be said that love, as we understand it, plays but little part in Thonga life. Boys in love generally express their feelings to the accompaniment of the unicord harp (see Chap. III) in the evening in the neighbourhood of the village of their beloved one ; I have never been able to catch the words of these songs, which are said to be sometimes very long, and are sung in a very loud voice ; they are not precisely chaste, according to one of our Native ministers, who considered that the use of the unicord harp ought to be forbidden to Christian boys! But here is a *love song* probably composed by a girl who was not allowed to marry the boy of her choice :

> To-morrow, to-morrow, my mother, I will start,
> To-morrow, father, I will start,
> I will start with an axe ;
> With this axe I will cut the stump,
> The stump on which my friend has hurt his leg,
> My friend whose belt of tails hangs from his waist,
> The one for whom I draw my legs out of the way. (1)

(1) Perhaps an allusion to the fact that it is taboo to pass over any one's outstretched legs. She draws in her legs to give him the means of passing and coming to sit beside her.

The stump is perhaps some ill-disposed person whose opposition the energetic maid is determined to overcome!

As a counterpart, here is the *complaint of a jilted lover*, who gives vent to his annoyance with the girl and her family :

> Refuse me if you will, girl !
> The grains of maize you eat in your village are human eyes !
> The tumblers from which you drink are human skulls !
> The manioc roots you eat are human tibia !
> The sweet potatoes are human fingers !
> Refuse me, if you will, girl !

The vexation of a jilted lover is of short duration. He has the money, he is sure to find a girl! But it would be erroneous to think Native lovers or husbands are not capable of deep and lasting affection. I know of a case, near Shiluvane, in which a Nkuna committed suicide because his wife had deceived him, and had relations with another man.

See, I. p. 286, the song in which the *despised wife* gives vent to her anger : her husband has plucked her little pumpkin and given it to the wife he preferred. No doubt the *bukwele*, the special feeling of jealousy existing between co-wives, has inspired more than one song which could find no equivalent in our own literature!

Mourning songs are numerous ; they are sung just after the burial. They are touching ; note the simple cry :

> Mamane ! You have left us ! whither have you gone ?

The tune (No. 14) is striking : a very high and prolonged note, followed by double crochets sounded very rapidly and ending in another long note with a short sharp conclusion, like a cry of anguish.

One of those present rises and sings, as if he were playing the part of the bereaved :

> A ba ndji ya'ange-ke lepsi ?
> Have they not hated me, treating me in this way ?

All the throng of the mourners answer :

> Ba ku yalile, wene, wa ka manyana !
> They have hated you, son of so and so !

He answers :

Ba tekile nkhao !
They have taken my intimate friend !

This is no doubt an allusion to the wizards, who are supposed to cause most of the deaths. They are cursed in another very curious song, half Zulu, noted down by Mrs Audéoud in Maputju. (Tune 16.)

Hamban, Muthakati ! Bulela bantu ! — U teka b'sikwin !
Go away, wizard ! Killer of men ! — You take them during the night !

Or the mourning song may be a complaint, in which the family bewails its bereavement, like the old Nkuna song. (Tune 15) :

Hi bana ba Nhumba ya ntima ! Hi bana ba Malala ni ngobe.
We are the sons of the black house (the house of misfortune and defilement)

The following is strangely stoic :

A li beni mombo ! A li beni mombo !
Ku tshubuka, ku baba ka psone !
Let it beat the face ! Let it beat the face !
To run away, what a bitter thing !

Death is like a foe. Look at it face to face ! Do not lose your courage in this last fight.

I quote in Part VI another mourning song, a very curious one, where an allusion is made to Heaven, the mysterious power which kills and gives life, which we have already heard mentioned in the song of the widows (I, p. 209), when they lament their bereavement.

This *stoic* song is also a *war* song ; it is customary to sing the war songs at the death of any important personage. The following belongs to the same category, and is used on both occasions :

Ketle-ketle, ntlubane ! Fumo dji wile ! A dlawa hi nomo, Tatana !
Hear this noise of weapons ! The assagai has fallen ! He has been killed on account of his words, father !

The chief has been killed in a fight which had been caused by his imprudent words : he wished to free himself from his

192

suzerain (the Ngoni chief?) ; war ensued, and he was put to death! So the sorrow caused by death has certainly furnished Thonga poets with touching themes.

The heart of the whole tribe was also stirred, at the close of the before-mentioned war of 1894-1896, when the young chief Ñwamantibyane, only 18 or 20 years of age, was caught and deported to West Africa. *The lament of the child* was then composed by an unknown author ; but he had so well understood the feelings of the Black nation that it at once became popular ; and it was heard everywhere on the wharf, hummed by hundreds of boys carrying loads or pushing trucks, and chanting the sad fate of the child ; in the villages, far and wide, they sang the recital of Ñwamantibyane's sufferings :

> Ndumakazulu ! The glorious ! Known as far as Zululand !
> He fought bravely ! He was obliged to fly !
> He was caught and deported... etc.

And ever and again came the chorus, in a sad, resigned tone : (Tune 11).

> Hi ñwanao! Hi ñwana ba dlele ! Ñwamantibyane !
> It is the child ! The child they have killed ! Ñwamantibyane !

Eleven years later, when travelling far away in the Manyisa district, I heard a tall, thin boy playing on his unicord harp in a Banyan store, and muttering some words, which he accompanied by beating his instrument. This was the same old lament of the child :

> It is the child, the child whom they have killed !
> He was not yet grown up !

The melody had greatly changed (tune 12) and the pain had passed out of it. But the national song had not yet entirely died away.

This is a kind of elegy, and forms a transition to the patriotic and epic songs.

III. *Epic poetry.*

The war songs have already been quoted when dealing with the Army (I. p. 460), those performed in the mukhumbi, at the coronation of the chief (I. p. 372) when preparing to go to fight, when returned from battle, as well as those sung during the march of the troop. I give the striking music of some of these in the next chapter. Tune 24 is the "Sabela nkosi" the great Mpfumo song, also adopted by other clans. Tune 25, with its splendid change from the minor to the major key, is the Tembe and Maputju classical war song. No. 29 is an old Nkuna war song, dating as far back as 1820, before the Zulu invasion ; No. 27 is the principal modern Nkuna song, and No. 28 the Nkuna equivalent to the Ronga *Giraffe song*. These old chants are sung to the accompaniment of the military dance, which consists in trampling on the ground, while rhythmically brandishing the assagais, lifting them first to the right, then to the left, bending them sideways, then downwards, as if to pierce (I. p. 463). They are certainly wonderfully fine compositions.

I include in the same category the laudatory song of the *mbongi* (I. p. 424), a branch of literature in which Court poets display considerable imagination and an extraordinary gift for unbounded hyperbole. All the important chiefs have their mbongi and it is required of the man holding this office that he should have a good chest (shifuba), the chest being to the Thongas the seat of eloquence (as it was to the ancient Romans : Pectus est quod oratorem facit!). The elucubrations of these poet laureates sometimes last a very long time and may have real poetic value.

As we saw (I. p. 361) each clan and even each family possesses its own laudatory phrase ; this is the *shibongo*, a word which generally means family name, but which etymologically signifies the formula by which the clan or family glorifies (bonga) itself. These formulae are usually short and often contain archaic expressions or allusions to unknown facts which make them very difficult to understand. I have given some of those from the Ronga territory. Here are two others, collected by the Rev. A. Jaques amongst the Transvaal Thongas, who seem to cultivate this custom more than the coast clans ; they are perhaps encouraged to do so by their Pedi neighbours, who are very fond of these formulae, called by them *mireto*.

Hlangwini wa ka Shitlhelane ; hi ba ka Nkandamuri ; hi ba ka Manyubele ni Mbowo ; hi ba ka Gidjigidji, ba tilo. —. Akane ka psitjunga ! Lomu nkobeni mi ta muka hi kona...

Hlangwini of (the house of) Shitlhelane ; we are of (the house of) Nkandamuri ; we are of (the house of) Manyubele and Mbowo ; we are of (the house of) Gidjigidji, the people of Heaven. —. Build (your huts) on the hills. In the valley you will have to leave (?)

It would seem that these Hlangwinis are a clan of rain-makers, people having the power of Heaven. They advise others to settle on the hills and not in the valleys, because otherwise their huts would be swept away by the floods, owing to the terrible rains which the Hlangwinis have the power of causing to fall.

The second is not very refined, but is characteristic. Erotic allusions are frequent in those formulae :

Nkuna wa Mabutane ; mabuta, ba yi bonile ku basa ka yona.
Nkuna of Mabutane ; when wooing a girl, he has seen that she was pure.

Mabutane is probably a surname of Nkuna. There is in this formula a play on the word buta which means to woo (I. p. 101). Before choosing a girl, the ancestor first made sure that she was untouched ; this denotes a species of wisdom which his descendants still boast of to-day!

In epic poetry may be included also the *pshiphato,* a Zulu expression which means the laudatory sentence with which warriors praise themselves according to the Zulu fashion. Private individuals, and even women sometimes have their shiphato ; for instance a girl bearing the name of Yandea will glorify herself in these words : Yendea, madjaha ! Yendea, the young men ! This formula does not throw a very favourable light on the habits of the girl, and scarcely belongs to literature!

A more elaborate product of Thonga poetry is found in the *hunting songs.* I have already mentioned these (p. 60) and here give as a typical example the Elephant's song. I have been told by my informant, Zebedea Mbenyana, a Native of Bilen, that the hunters performed it whilst dancing on the body of the enormous beast, after having transfixed it.

195

The Life of a South African Tribe

1st Strophe.

They march in single file, the Elephants, the mighty ones,
They go to slake their thirst.

Antistrophe.

Let us go too ! They're drinking amongst the thickets ! Hurrah !

2nd Strophe.

Hark ! the smothered roarings in the forest.

Antistrophe.

'Tis a grand sound, the roaring in the forest. Hurrah !

3rd Strophe.

The crying of the elephant, the mother ! 'Tis she who calls the hunters to the thickets.

Antistrophe.

Hurrah ! 'tis she who calls the hunters ! Ho ! Hurrah !

4th Strophe.

Yonder's the one with ears so large and drooping.

Antistrophe.

Hurrah ! the big-eared one has just passed us. Hurrah !

5th Strophe.

The boys are there ; the sound of knives being sharpened, there from the spot where the elephant lies slain.

Antistrophe.

Hurrah ! the sound of knives being sharpened. Hurrah !

This composition certainly exhibits wonderful poetic power and grandeur, describing marvellously the emotions of the courageous band, who have finally succeeded in obtaining the precious tusks of the elephant, and vast quantities of meat. This song of triumph is worthy of a place amongst the best productions of the Muse of primitive races.

To the imaginative mind of the Bantu everything that causes a deep impression, even material objects, affords an occasion for the utterance of lofty phrases and words of praise. Once when travelling south of Delagoa Bay through the desert, our party arrived in the neighbourhood of the Umbelozi railway. The train was heard in the distance. One of my servants was busy cleaning the pots ; I heard him muttering the following words :

The one who roars in the distance... The one who crushes in pieces the braves and smashes them ! The one who debauches our wives : they abandon us, they go (to the towns to lead a bad life) ! The seducer ! And we remain alone.

He was extolling the huge thing and lamenting his misfortune and the curse it has brought upon the country.

IV. *Satiric poetry.*

I have already mentioned the peculiar custom of Thonga literati of speaking in a round-about fashion, and using figurative language, especially when they want to say something disagreeable or to give vent to their humour. It is but one step from such forms to satire. They generally indulge in this satiric vein when dealing with relatives-in-law, women being especially prone to it. When the sisters and aunts of a married woman go to pay a visit to her, they convey all kinds of equivocal compliments. These must not be taken seriously! It is a round-about — exceedingly round-about — way of making graceful allusions and expressing their mutual esteem. I will quote the series of these songs of friendly chaff and invective as it was given to me by Shigiyane, with a running commentary to render them comprehensible. These lively and pointed choruses give a fitting finishing-touch to the marriage customs, and illustrate the curious relations existing between allied families, which I explained in Vol. I, p. 249-253.

On the wedding day the women who take the bride to her husband sing the *tjeka song* :

Let us go with her, but let us go back to our homes!

This is an ironical way of saying : "She is going to find trouble : we won't follow her as far as that!." The same idea runs through all the songs which these women sing during the next few days.

197

When they accompany the bride to her new home, they sing :

U ya kwi, Mamano ! — Whither goest thou, mother ?
U ya kwi shana ? — Whither goest thou ?
Ba ta tshaha shihundju ni lihlelo, mamano !
They will bring thee the basket full of maize and the fan, my mother !
Ba ta kuma u tlokoli, ba tlokolisa, mamano !
When thou hast finished crushing it, they will·make thee crush it again, my mother !
Ba ta kuma u kopoli, ba kopolisa, mamano !
When thou hast plastered the floor, they will make thee plaster it again, my mother !

But when they come on a visit, carrying jars of beer as presents to the newly married couple, they are much less guarded in their language, ridiculing the poor husband and his family, and making fun of every one in general. They begin singing on the way, with the jars on their heads :

He ntshonga, banhwanyana, he nga batjanana
He la libango ; fa hi nga labi, we manyana.
Ku laba manyana ka ñwan'a manyana.
We are a small band, young girls ; there are few of us.
We are looking for a piece of meat on the spit ; formerly we should not have known where to find any, our sister (so and so) !
Now our sister will get some for us from her husband !

Hi kokobisa lobe, hi ya kwihi shana ?
Hi bhanu ba ku yalwa !
He fambaka ni khombo, ni khombo dji le kaya !
Where are we going, thus dragging the hook behind us ? (1)
We are the people that are hated.
We walk in misfortune (2), the misfortune that has befallen our house !

Ka ku kandja ñwana a ku na kule.
Wo khunga he lihanyi, we koko !
Ya kokowela : kowe-kowe-kowe.
Where a daughter lives it cannot be very far off.
Go there, grannie, limping and leaning on thy staff !
Listen to the hen cackling. She says : kowe, kowe, kowe. (3)

(1) They compare themselves to women who have been in the fields, picking kwakwa fruits (p. 17), and are so heavily laden that they cannot carry the hook used for pulling the fruit off the trees ; they have had to tie it to their belt, and drag it behind them on their way home. The travellers give it to be understood that they are not out for pleasure !
(2) That of having to go and see a brother-in-law who ill-treats their sister.
(3) This line is an encouragement to the old woman who finds the walk long and tiring. The other women promise her a fowl at the end of their journey, which the son-in-law will kill for her. Note the first line of the third verse : it is a kind of proverb.

On arriving at the village they stop at the edge of the stream :

Fulamelani, banhwanyana, hi ya nwa mati nkobeni.
Stoop down, young women, let us drink water in the valley.

Finally they settle themselves in the home of their *bakoñwana*, their relatives-in-law, and begin to insult their hosts.

Ba yala na wo mbengana loko a boleka !
Ba li : " Famba, u ya teka kwenu u buya wa ta sila "
Ba yala ni shudana, ba yala ni musana
Ba li : " U ya teka kwenu u buya wa ta tlokola. "
They won't lend (our sister) a grindstone when she wants to borrow one.
They say to her : " Go home and fetch one and then come back and grind. "
They won't lend her the small pestle and mortar.
They say : " Go home and get your own, and then come back and crush your maize. "

Then they make fun of the mother-in-law, who is whispering with the other women of the village, making arrangements, doubtless, for the good entertainment of the visitors. They pretend to discover in these asides some terrible plot.

A li ñwono-ñwono !   Mabulela ya nsati lweyi ! Hi file ! Hi lobile !
That woman over there is whispering !   What can she be saying !
We are dead !   We are lost !

As for the head of the village, these shrewish visitors accost him thus :

Ñwenyi wa muti, hi wene ?   A ku hi hi mati, hi ñwene ?
A he hlayi wone, ya nhlobo !   Hi hla byala ne sope !
Are you the master of the village ?   Are you not going to give us any water to drink ?
We don't mean well-water ; we mean beer and brandy !

The villagers approach to salute the new-comers, who sulk and refuse to say a word.   Large pots are made ready for cooking food.

Mi kokela matambeko, mi kokela bamane ?
Kambe hi balala, hi nga ka manyana !
You prepare the large pots...   For whom are you making them ready ?
We are enemies, we are !

199

The young folks catch fowls in order to feast them properly
They raise objections.

> A hi djyule kwee !   A hi djyule kwee !
> Hi djyule nkoka-hi-pindja !
> We will have nothing to do with that which cries kwee.   (The cry of the
>   fowl when being killed.)
> We want the animal which is led with a string (a goat).

But it is the husband who has to put up with the worst insults.

> Ha ! matinga-tingela ya nhunu lwe ! Loko a hi bona a ku tlhanya psirubu.
> Ah ! see how he wants to avoid us !   As soon as he sees us he runs and hides
>   behind the houses !   (He is afraid of us !)
> Hi laba tima-mbilu ! hi djyula mafura ya ku nona phobo.
> We want something to satisfy the heart !   We must have our fat very rich !
> Nyoka ya nyoka !   Mbyana ya mbyana ! Yi whee !
> Serpent that thou art !   Dog that thou art !   Thou sayest bow-wow !

Then to show him that they really like and appreciate him,
they add, with the true untutored rudeness which they maintain
to the end of the visit :

> A ku hi lobolele ? Na wene, bana ba ku ba ku lobolela ki khume ni ntlhanu !
> Won't you buy another wife from us !   Later on your daughters will bring you
>   a dowry worth fifteen pounds sterling !

Finally, after having had plenty to eat and to drink and a
good dance, they will remark, on leaving :

> Hi tlhome nyonga ya mbuti, hi muka
> Twine the goat's bladder in our hair, that we may go home.

All this is not very high-flown poetry.   The general intercourse
between relatives-in-law is by no means refined and this rudeness
contrasts with the ordinary civility of Native life.   Let us
remember that this way of speaking is not intended to show a
want of politeness on the part of the visitors, but, on the contrary,
is the behaviour suited to the occasion!   I have the music of some
of these songs, which were noted down by Mrs Audéoud, in
Maputju.   In No. 13, the bridesmaids actually exhort the bride
not to follow her husband!   But they are the last to expect her to
follow their advice.

V. *Dramatic poetry.*

This is perhaps too lofty a term by which to designate the kind of songs, or other literary productions, which I am going to describe. Primitive folk have no theatre, no elaborate tragedies or comedies. But our tribe certainly possesses the rudiments of histrionic art in the dances accompanied by songs, which are called *tinsimu ta Ronge*, the songs of Ronge. The word *Ronge* does not seem to be related in any way to Ronga. It is applied to an old collection of songs in which dancing played the principal part and which were quite peculiar to the clans of the Coast. They were performed after harvest, when the storehouses were full and when the Ba-Ronga bid themselves : "Eat, drink and be merry!" Boys and girls used to remain in the bush for many weeks learning these dances, in a kind of school, which may have taken the place of the circumcision school ; the latter has been suppressed for more than a century in these districts. I say, these songs *were* performed, — because they are now fast disappearing, having been replaced by Zulu songs, called *mudjatu* and *muthimbo*. These are, in their turn, giving way to new dances called *gumpsa*, in which young boys and girls put on milala palm leaf dresses. These were the great novelty in 1908 and pupils of the Mission schools were deserting them to play gumpsa. Another new dance is called *shiloyi*, and consists in the imitation of boatmen : the performers sit down and execute movements similar to those of sailors pulling a boat, to the accompaniment of song. The *shindjekandjeka* was another dance executed by the wives of Mubvesha (I, p. 287). Most of these dances take place in the capital, and the Chief summons all the boys to take part in them. This is not absolutely obligatory, but should any one begin the training, and then leave before it is finished, he will be fined. No doubt these complicated dances mark the beginning of a theatre, as will be seen shortly : they at any rate give the impression of an organised ballet.

Many of the songs refer to *historical events* in the life of the clan, or to by-gone occurrences, almost forgotten, and it is for

201

this reason that some of them are so difficult to understand ; they also vary from one clan to another. The following, according to Spoon, is the most popular song in Nondwane. An individual performs on a drum to give the time to the dancers. Around the drummer, in a semicircle, are arranged the girls who sing the refrains (tekelela), and clap their hands to encourage the soloist (musimi). Farther away, in concentric semi-circles, stand the

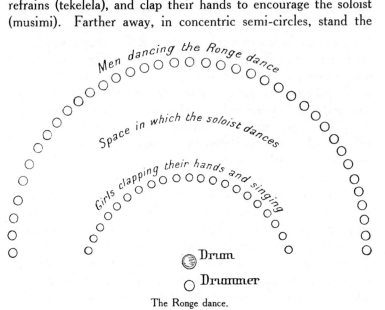

The Ronge dance.

men of the village, dancing but not singing. Between the two semicircular ranks the soloist has free play. He commences by saying :

> Ndji pfumala shigoba sha nakulori.
> Why ? I haven't got a partner for the dance !

The girls reply :

> Hi hlula hi mbilu yi babisaka.
> Our hearts are indeed very sad.

He continues :

> A psi na ntshumu ! Makweru Ñwakubyele a fanaka ni pataka dja balungu.
> Never mind ! My brother Ñwakubyele (will do very well), for he shines like
> one of the Whites' silver pieces !

N̄wakubyele was a Counsellor whose home was about three quarters of an hour's walk from Rikatla. He was probably a famous dancer. The words of this song would hardly seem very inspiring, but the noise of the drum, the clapping of hands, the dancing, — and the flow of beer, — all helps to account for the intense pleasure which these games afford to the Ba-Ronga.

Another Ronge song is in praise of another dancer :

> Nwahangwa ! Nwahangwa ! Loka ba shi bona, shi ne nkaukelo !
> Shi bombisa tinsimo ta ku tala ta Ronge !
> Nwahangwa ! N̄wahangwa ! When one sees him (one admires) his beautiful
> figure. . . .
> He is the perfect performer of the numberless Ronge songs.

Still another, on the same theme, celebrates Gilela, a choregraphic artist who must have rejoiced in a marvellously slim figure :

> U tlanga, Gilela ! Wa tlanga, likhalo li fana ni ngoti !
> N̄watshibeni ! tlanga ! tlanga ! Ku tjhongo ; hi nga tolobele !
> Thou dancest, Gilela ! Thou dancest and thy waist is no thicker than a string !
> Son of Tshimbeni ! Dance, dance. — That was too little. — We have not
> yet had enough !

I came across three other songs which seem to refer to actual historical events, but only one of these is sufficiently comprehensible to be worth transcribing. The music of the first phrase is very characteristic. (Tune 37.)

> Ndji wela, ndji wela, N̄watembe ! Ndji wela, ndji tjike ndji wela.
> Ndji koka mabyatsho ; ndji tjutjuma, ndji ya tlhasa ka Ntshangane.
> Sala muti wa Muhari ! — Ndji tjike, ndji wela !
> I cross the stream. I cross the stream. Oh Tembe ! I cross the stream, let
> me cross the river !
> I tow the boats. I fly away as far as Ntshangane.
> Good bye, village of Muhari ! — Let me cross the river.

The two men of Tembe who sang this song to me, telling me that it was a very popular one, were unable to explain its meaning. It is not difficult however to imagine the circumstances under which it was composed. It probably refers to fugitives, coming from the South, arriving at the Bay of Lourenço Marques, and asking the Coast dwellers, subjects of Muhari (a chief of Tembe in the XVIIIth century), for permission to cross the water and to continue their journey northward to Ntshangane (1), that is to say Bilene, where they wished to take refuge. The memory of their wanderings has thus been preserved in a popular song.

These examples will show that the Ronge repertoire is a varied one, but I have still to transcribe that which is, at least as far as my knowledge goes, the most curious of the whole collection. It was explained to me in detail by Shigiyane who, in the Shirindja country some fifty years ago, in the Mpatshiki district, (on the borders of Nondwane), had often taken part in the performance, always in the rôle of soloist. In her opinion it is an absolutely typical song. It is no exaggeration to say that it is almost a dramatic production, and we might rightly call it the *Shirindja comedy*. It comprises five parts — I was on the point of saying five acts, — which follow one another, but without, it must be admitted, any kind of logical sequence.

The *First Act* may be entitled "The old men's march." All the adults of the village go out into the bush, — let us say to the west, — whence they return to the square, halting and limping and dragging their limbs along, as if suffering from some complaint which prevents their walking. To a monotonous air they sing the following words :

Ndji laba batlhaben ! Angati leyi ya masengwe ya tshabisa !
Lomo kweru, mamana, we, angati leyi yi ndji tsimba ku famba ;
Ndji teka mumphinyi, ndji tshebukela ku djima,
Yi yengeta yi ndji tsimba ku famba !
Psi yengeta, psi ba roma loko ndji tjhama.
Psi ka ne mpuri, nsasi wa ku famba.
I am looking for some one to put leeches on me ! This complaint, this cursed lumbago is terrible !
In our village, oh ! my mother ! alas ! this trouble prevents my walking.
Take the handle (of my hoe). I start for the fields to till them. — And this thing stops me !
And it annoys (my relatives) to see me sitting down (doing no work). She may well be annoyed, the beauty, the good walker !

(1) Ntshangane is a surname of Manukosi who did not establish himself in Bilene much before 1820 or 1830. But for various reasons it is probable that this name already belonged to an ancient chief of the country, and that Manukosi simply adopted it as his surname. If this song really dated from the time of Muhari (a chief who reigned in the Tembe clan in the middle of the XVIIIth century), it would be the oldest of the Thonga literary productions yet collected. This fact would prove also that *Shangaan*, the name commonly given to Thongas in Johannesburg, is a very ancient one.

During this song, the old folks come to the village ; then the young ones go out, in the opposite direction, returning in due course to sing their verse, which forms the second act.

Second Act. Their story is that of a son-in-law who turned his mother-in-law out of his house, because she was suffering from smallpox. The poor old woman went out to die in the bush, in spite of the protestations of her daughter against her husband's cruelty. The husband and wife are heard giving expression to their feelings :

> *The son-in-law :* (Solo) Ndja famba, ndja famba, na ndji nyenyemuka...
> Ba mu hlongola, a famba a ya fela ahangale.
> I am going away ! I am going away ! I am going away in disgust
> Let her be turned out and let her go and die in the bush !
> *The daughter :* (her part is sung by all the actors in chorus)
> Ndji tjetja shitlambutana, shi fambaka shi hona abuhlambo.
> Lomo kweru, ka Mpatshiki, hi nga hanyi ! Hi yabana timpsalo ni mashaka.
> Psi yentsha he yo ngati ya kutane !
> Ngati ya kutane ya tshabisa, hosi ya nga !
> Psa ku hlongola ni mukoñwana, a famba : a buya a kulubisa ku hlaya, shi hundja hi la, ba mu hlongola, a famba, a ya fela hangale.
> I feel pity (when I see) smallpox making its ravages and ruining the face.
> Here, at home, in the village of Mpatshiki we no longer live ! We no longer are kind to each other, even amongst relatives.
> It is the fault of this terrible disease.
> This disease is truly terrible, my lord !
> It has driven the son-in-law from his home ; he goes, but returns with cruel words. The old woman comes this way, she is turned out ; she goes away and dies in the bush !

The Third Act begins when young and old are assembled on the village square. It is a dialogue (shibalekana) introducing a certain Gebuza, a man of Nondwane, who took refuge in Shirindja some time in the middle of the last century, when Zihlahla's warriors, led by Machaquene, went to fight in Nondwane on behalf of the Whites. This Gebuza was much beloved by Mpatshiki, a sub-chief living in the South of Shirindja, as we shall see in the fifth act. In any case he was a great dancer, and also possessed a marvellous faculty of saying a great deal and meaning very little! Listen to the following : a voluble dialogue is kept up between this individual and a young man named Mahlahlane.

205

Gebuza. Nanjduwe, Mahlahlane ?	My friend, Mahlahlane ?
Mahlahlane. Ha makweru !	Say on, my brother !
G. Tlanga, makweru !	Dance, my brother !
M. U tlanga, u ndji tlula,	You dance better than I do,
makweru ! A psi na ntshumu.	my brother ! That doesn't matter.
G. A ndji psi tibanga	I did not know that,
lepsako, nambe u le makweru,	although you are my brother.
inha ndja ku tlangisile	I could please you with my dancing,
Nhaviyana.	Nhaviyane.

Here the sense begins to be lacking... it concludes with a cross-fire of utterly meaningless remarks.

Mahlahlane. Eee !	That's it !
Gebuza. Nhaviyana bantsindja.	Nhaviyana, the people of the capital.
M. Eee !	That's it !
G. Nhaviyane basurumana.	Nhaviyana, the Mahometans.
Yi banga mahlolana !	That works wonders.
Khumbu-khumbu dja Mayingandlela	? ? ? ? ?
A siku dja tolo.	Yesterday.
Ku ta wa shikumbu sha ndladla	? ? ? ? ?
Ndji ndjuluka ndji nha,	I go back, that's what I do.
Kupa-kupa ha matikeriñwane.	Etc. etc...

On hearing this extraordinary production, quite as unintelligible as our Swiss children's "empros" — eena, meena, mina, mo, etc.,— the whole company dance in silence, going through various contortions which are doubtless as full of meaning as the dialogue which precedes them.

In the *Fourth Act* all the actors re-enter the stage and commence the *shiombelane*, the hand-clapping with which they so often accompany their songs. They sing the following chorus :

> Mamana, n'ta ku yini ?
> Ina, hi tlakula Mpatshiki, ñwa-matlanga-ni-tinsana-ta-batjongwana !
> He tlanga psigaba, Mpatshiki !
> Ntlhamulo, ndji nyike hi psikwembo, ankulweni !
> My mother, what shall I say ?
> Oh ! yes ! let us praise our Chief Mpatshiki, he who loves to play with little
>   children !
> We dance the Ronge dance, Mpatshiki !
> The echo (of our songs) comes back to us from the gods along the whole length
>   of our villages !

Evidently the singers are celebrating the joyous gaiety of this fête, where all are happy, the Chief good-natured, and wherein the gods themselves (the deceased ancestors, probably buried in the sacred wood near the village) join the living.

Fifth Act. A few songs in which Gebuza plays a prominent part, constitute the finale. He was an interminable braggart

206

when once he started on stories of the contests between the Nondwane and Zihlahla clans. Instead of tilling his fields, he idled away his time in his village, in the shade of a nkanye, the tree of bitter fruits (nunge)... Hence the following dialogue :

Gebuza. Tjikan, ndji hlayô !	Let me tell you...
Chorus of Shirindja : U hlaya tshini ?	What silly tales do you want to tell us ?
G. Tjikan, ndi hlayô.	Let me tell you...
Chorus : He baka Bidjiankomo...	We folks of Bidjiankomo (1) (this is what we say) :
Psigaba psi ne nsiku, i ka leyi ;	There is a day for singing, it is to-day ;
A ku djima, a ku psi koti.	As for work, you are incapable of it.
Gebuza ! Ankanyen lo'kulu lo'wa nunge ; psigaba psi ni nsiku i ka leyi.	Gebuza (you who are lazy), under your big nkanye of bitter fruit there is a day for singing ; this is the day !

The moral of this is sufficiently obvious : "To-day we sing, we dance : but this is not everything. To-morrow we must start with the tillage for the new year."

Doubtless in each small Ronga clan similar songs and dances are performed. They seem to us exceedingly childish, but also very innocent, and show us the taste possessed by these people for musical and literary productions (2).

VI. *Action songs, or songs sung while at work.*

I remember once ordering one of my boys to roll along an empty cask, in which we were collecting the rain water. There was a little water in it, and this made a gurgling sound inside.

---

(1) The forefathers of Mpatshiki, who was the chief then reigning.

(2) I should like to include in this category one of the songs of which Mungamane, the blind minstrel (p. 187) was particularly proud, and which he performed when the dancers paid him an extra fee of 200 reis. It is a dialogue between a husband who is not satisfied with the wife he has bought and the men of his village :

The husband. I have gone to lobola a woman ; I have paid twenty-eight pounds ; I expected she was worth something, and lo ! she is a woman of no account. How did you dare, you, her father, to claim such a big sum, saying that she would be a help to me, when she is so utterly bad ? I will take her ; I will give her back to her parents and claim my money in order to buy another.

The men of the village. No ! Have patience with her ! Do not send her home. Do you not see that you will bring misfortune upon yourself ? Did she not bear you children ? Who will cook your food ? Who will clean your clothing ? When strangers pass through your village, who will give them food ? To go and claim one's herd is troublesome ! Send your children to fetch water ! Send them to gather fuel !

Rolling it with vigour, the boy imitated the noise of the gurgling all the while, apparently with great pleasure. Natives are very fond of singing and shouting when at work ; they evidently find help in the conjunction of music and labour.

Many Thonga songs belong to this category. There are songs sung by women when pounding their mealies (I. p. 334), or when carrying their jars of beer or of bukanye to the capital. One of these *psirwalo* songs, extolling Mzila, the hawk that is in heaven, has been quoted I. p. 402. I heard it in February 1893, when an extraordinary inundation had filled all the little ponds in the hollows, and the lake of Rikatla had swollen to ten times its usual size. Beginning with the word : "Chwe! Chwe!" a descriptive adverb which renders the impression caused by a wide surface of water shining in the sun, the women sang :

Chwe ! Nambyana wu tele !
The lake has overflowed !
We seek the hawk who soars in the sky !
Who is the hawk ? It is Mzila !

For the music of the song see tune 17.

On the wharf at Lourenço Marques, one could collect a good number of the carrier songs, sung by the boys who carry loads from the ships to the Custom House. Some are highly impressive, full of guttural sounds such as : Ama-haussa-haussa! There is generally a soloist who intones (sima) and all the boys, covered with dust, clad in sacks, their eyes beaming, seize the heavy piece of iron, the bulky case, raise it rhythmically to their shoulders, and carry it with measured tread to the shed. To have a clever soloist who keeps good time is essential, and I was told that such artists are well paid.

I would remind the reader of the *travellers' songs*, an example of which has been given when speaking of the journeys of the traders in the interior (p. 144).

But the richest collection is that of *sailors' songs*. I heard one of these, (tune 18), on the Nkomati, repeated a hundred times in a monotonous fashion by a boy who was pushing the boat along the shore with his pole, from Morakwen to Lourenço Marques :

"I siloyi, I ndandale," he said — (these words have no more

208

meaning than tra-la-la) "They are starving at Ntimane, siloyi..."
He was journeying from the Ntimane country, near Khosen, and
having heard that the crops had failed, went muttering this great
news all down the river! Perhaps the song was not of his own
composition, but was an old refrain which had been preserved on
account of its catching tune.

Mrs Audéoud, during her long journeys on the Maputju river,
noted down many of the tunes, Nos. 19-22, some in two or even
three parts, curiously harmonised. The Native sailors seek in
this way to vary the monotony of rowing, punting or towing the
boat. No doubt a great many more such tunes could be collected.

VII. *Incantations.*

Children, as we saw, (I. p. 68), are fond of singing curious
little melodies to various animals : to the big *galagala* lizard,
to the *chameleon*, to the *crab* with one claw, to the *owl*. The
tune of the words addressed to the owl is No. 31. The boys of
Rikatla used to salute our ox-waggon, when it appeared on the
plain, with song No. 30 : "Gweymanâo! — here are the oxen",
they said running all round the span, the girls following them and
lifting up the babies in their arms, to show them the strange
machine and the long-horned oxen walking slowly, with impassive
looks, through the little black throng.

Incantations of a more serious type are the *songs of exorcism*,
performed to the accompaniment of rattles, big tins and drums,
close to the ears of the person supposed to be possessed, in order
to induce the spirit to reveal its name and to " come out". No. 32
is one of the most celebrated songs of this category, and has really
a great deal of character. I shall speak of it again when dealing
with possession.

VIII. *Songs accompanying tales and games.*

As we shall see, little songs are very frequently introduced
into the tales to embellish them, and are generally repeated
three or four times over, as if the narrator wished to exhaust

all their charm. Some are very primitive, like No. 33, the murmuring of a little boy who has been swallowed together with his oxen by an ogre called Nyandzumulandengela ; imprisoned in the stomach of the monster, he entreats him to let him out! Another, more elaborate, is the lament of the mother whose child has been stolen by the Baboon, and who follows the animal weeping and asking it to give the little one back to her. (Tune No. 35.) Tune No. 36 belongs to another ogre tale, concerning the suitors of pretty girls who are really only hyenas transformed into men. Some one knows their true nature, and forces them to appear as they really are, by chanting their song :

Manyange, the leg belongs to me !

the song in which they dispute with each other about the leg of the girl they are wooing! The most complicated of these songs is that in the tale of Zili (No. 34) ; it is a duet, and was sung to me by two Mpfumo girls so distinctly that I could easily take it down. It is very interesting as an illustration of the laws of harmony amongst the Thongas.

C. FOLK-TALES.

Folk-tales are by far the most interesting and valuable part of the Thonga Folklore, and before citing any new examples of those curious and charming stories, I shall try to show their importance in the Life of the Tribe, their literary, ethnographic and philosophic value.

I. *The place occupied by Folk-tales in the Life of the Tribe.*

In Vol. I. p. 350, we have seen the inhabitants of the village, after their evening meal, gathered round the fireplace, devoting themselves to innocent amusements ; first, guessing the piece of charcoal, pulling their fingers, asking each other riddles, — those who are beaten in the contest having to pay a forfeit which they redeem by telling a tale. So the tale is the conclusion of the game, the object of the whole entertainment. I have often seen exactly the same order followed in a European company playing parlour games.

This interesting scene may be witnessed from one end of the tribe to the other : "This is their evening prayer" said one of our converts to me, a woman who was also a clever story-teller, i. e. as we Christians have our worship every night before going to sleep, so the heathen gladden their hearts by their tales. Everywhere story-telling (ku tha psihitana) is considered the most refined and most pleasing of the games. The tales are called *shihetana* or *nsingo* (mu-mi) in Ronga, *ntyeketo* (mu-mi) or *nkaringana* (mu-mi) in the Northern clans.

Story-tellers are of all ages and of both sexes. I have heard little girls of ten amusing their play-mates with tales. Those I have collected were told by young girls of eighteen (Nkulunkulu and Ñwanawatilo), young men of twenty, (Khwezu, Maganyele, Simeon Makwakwa), and men of thirty and forty (Spoon, Jim Tandane) ; but the majority come from adult women, the most skillful being Shigiyane-Camilla, Sofia Midomingo, Martha and Lois. Some only know one tale, and repeat it on every occasion, like Jim Tandane, who used to narrate the story of an ogre, Ñwatlakulalambimbi, with such gusto that he was surnamed after his hero! But others can recite six, ten or twenty tales. Shigiyane, for instance, could entertain the company for many nights with her tales, some of which were very long. (See for instance "The little hated one," 24 pages, "Mubia, an ogre tale," 19 pages, in my *Chants et Contes des Ba-Ronga*). This woman's memory was wonderful, and the graceful manner in which she told her stories was no less astonishing. Nkulukulu had heard *her* tale ("The girl and the whale") only once in the Maputju country, and she had memorised it immediately with the little songs which enliven it.

Strange to say, there is a curious precaution to be observed in connection with story-telling : it is taboo to devote oneself to this occupation at noon ; it must remain an evening entertainment ;

if this rule is not followed, the transgressor will become bald! This is one of the most surprising of the lesser taboos of the tribe. What is its origin? Have the Natives noticed that famous story-tellers, those who practised their art day and night, were liable to this misfortune? I could get no information on this point. I rather think the prohibition comes from the fact that this game is so popular that they are afraid to devote too much time to it : people would lose all inclination for work, if they started it during the day. So they instinctively forbade story-telling in the day-time!

Another curious custom in connection with tales is this : when a story-teller comes to the end of his tale, he concludes with the following words : "Tju-tju... famba ka Gwambe ni Dzabana!" — "Run away, go to Gwambe and Dzabana." These two personages are believed, at least amongst the Northern clans, to have been the first man and the first woman (see Part VI), and I suppose that the object of this kind of incantation is to prevent the marvellous story haunting the hearers during the night, and troubling their sleep by disagreeable dreams. It is a means of returning from fairyland to the realms of every-day life! All these details tend to show the importance of folk-tales in the Native life, and their popularity amongst the tribe.

Phot.
A. Borel.

Martha, a Ronga story-teller.

II. *Classification of Thonga Folklore and its literary value.*

But of what does this folklore consist? How does it happen that men, girls, youngsters, will sit quietly for hours, listening to an old woman who keeps them under the spell of her tale? In reality, these products of primitive imagination are much more varied than would at first appear. Let us open the casket, whose key is kept by Gwambe and Dzabana, and make an inventory of the "treasures" of this lore, to use the words of the Rev. E. Jacottet in his publications regarding the Ba-Sutho.

It would certainly be pretentious to apply a strictly philosophical, or even literary, classification to our tales. It is, however, obvious that they present many different styles which are, it is true, often combined, but between which it is quite possible to differentiate.

1) The first and most noteworthy class is that of *animal folk-tales*, in which the "Romance (1) of the Hare" takes a prominent place; the Hare, the Tortoise and the Small Toad are seen playing clever tricks upon huge beasts such as the Elephant, the Lion, the Hippopotamus and even upon men, getting the better of them by their cunning.

2) In a second category, the same idea of the victory of the small over powerful enemies is illustrated by stories in which human beings, children, the miserable and despised, triumph over their elders and those who hate them. The type of such tales, amongst ourselves, is Cinderella. Thongas have a number of similar stories, which I would entitle *the wisdom of the little ones.*

3) The third category comprises the *Ogre tales*, where the triumph of the wisdom of feeble creatures over these horrible and cruel monsters is again celebrated.

4) Other tales, to which I may give the name of *moral tales,* are stories which are evidently intended to enforce some moral teaching. The moralising aim may be unconscious, but the

---

(1) I employ the term *Romance* in the same sense as the corresponding French term is used when speaking of the "Roman du Renard", the celebrated series of deeds performed by Reynard the Fox, the well-known example of mediaeval literature.

conclusion of the tales is unquestionably moral, showing, as it does, that bad deeds or bad characters meet with due punishment.

5) Another variety of stories of this kind, though they are called tales and told as such, seems based on *actual facts* which happened somewhere, and have been preserved in the memory of the tribe. But they are not regarded as actual historical traditions. As they are told for the entertainment of the hearers, no difference is made between them and ordinary tales. They cannot be called legends, a legend being an historical fact, transformed by the popular imagination, and held as such by those who narrate it. They are rather the contrary of legends, being regarded *as purely imaginative*, while the facts seem to be more or less historic.

6) The last category of Thonga folk-tales are the *foreign tales*, which have come from Moslem, Portuguese or English sources, but have been altered in a very curious way, thus affording interesting material for the study of the Native mind. Foreign infiltrations can be detected even in those tales which bear most distinctly the Bantu stamp, but in this last category, they seem to constitute the actual subject matter of the story.

These six classes, once more, are by no means sharply defined. One tale might be placed in two or three of them. An animal sometimes appears in a tale where the other actors are all human. Though animal folklore is generally absolutely devoid of moral purpose, a moral idea may be detected in some of the episodes, for instance, when we see the Elephant punished for having contemptuously crushed the spawn of the Small Toad, etc.

The literary value of these stories varies greatly according to the story itself, and to the narrator. Some tales are very short and insignificant, or they may be a hap-hazard collection of episodes without any plan. Others are *true compositions* in which there is order and design, a position is taken up and a conclusion reached. I recommend the perusal of the "Epic of the Small Toad" and the story of the "Little Hated One," in *Les Chants et les Contes des Ba-Ronga*. They are amongst the best and most elaborate examples of Bantu folklore, and show real literary talent. Very often, as already mentioned, *a little song* or several little songs form the framework of the story. They are repeated at least three times, the story-teller arranging his narrative in such a way that the refrain recurs again and again. Native speakers do not fear repetition ; they seem to think that to hear a catching tune once only is not sufficient, and that upon a second or third occurrence it will be more appreciated. So they make a real art of repetition. While it may make the recital somewhat monotonous, this literary procedure is by no means tedious. Some one once said to me, after having heard the tale of Nabandji, the toad-eating girl : "I should never have thought there could be so much charm in monotony!"

As regards the *narrators*, they also vary greatly. Some of them, the beginners, are dull, slow, and tedious. They mingle the episodes without any order, frequently assuming that things are known which have not before been mentioned. But others are full of life, and one feels a true literary pleasure in listening to them. It was a real treat, for instance, to hear Shigiyane, Spoon, his wife, and Simeon Makwakwa! Their gestures, their mimicry, their play of feature, the wealth of descriptive adverbs introduced into the narrative, added a great interest to the story. They imitated little children, or old people without teeth, with great effect. I even saw Spoon's wife have recourse to *imitative action* in order to increase the charm of one of the songs, No. 36, a kind of incantation by which deceitful suitors are transformed into hyenas. This song, according to the story, was sung by a woman whilst grinding her mealies. So Magugu brought with her an earthen-ware mortar, and vigorously worked with her pestle each time the song was repeated. The listeners seemed to take great delight in this performance.

III. *The Ethnographic Value of the Tales.*

When asked the origin of the tales they tell, Thongas invariably say : "These are old stories which we heard from our fathers. No one would dream of inventing a tale now-a-days." This assertion is certainly true. Bantu tales are very old. It is not without good

215

cause that story-tellers, when afraid of being haunted by the harrowing details, send them back to Gwambe and Dzabana, the first man and the first woman!

Another fact confirms the testimony of the Natives, and shows, at the same time, the ethnographic value of the tales. It has been noticed when comparing tales collected in various parts of South Africa, that there is a great similarity amongst them. Bantu folklore, whatever may be the differences met with amongst the tribes, possesses a true unity. More than that : this similarity is found in the folk-tales of all mankind. A number of stories seem to be found from one end of the planet to the other. Reviewing my book *Les Chants et les Contes des Ba-Ronga* in the *Revue des Traditions populaires* of June 1898, Mr. René Basset, who is perhaps the greatest authority in this domain, showed that certain episodes written in Lourenço Marques, at the dictation of a Ronga story-teller, were to be found in the folklore of the ancient Greeks and Romans, of the modern Germans, French, Greeks, Italians, Lithuanians, Siberians, Kirghizes, Indians ; in Brazil, Portugal, the Punjab, Scotland, Roumania, Guatemala, British Guiana, Morocco, etc! This is a truly wonderful phenomenon and it is very difficult to account for it. Three explanations may be given of the fact, which is one of the most interesting problems of Ethnography :

1) These stories belong to primitive humanity, and all the races carried them with them in their migrations.

2) There was, in a more or less remote past, direct contact between the various human races, by means of which the tales have been transmitted from one tribe to another, in such a way that, in the course of time, they have spread all over the world.

3) There is such a similarity in the mentality of the various races, when still in the primitive phase of their development, that they have all invented the same stories independently of each other. Hence the unity of folklore everywhere.

I do not think any one of these explanations excludes the others. There is probably a portion of truth in each of them. The difficulty is to define that portion exactly, and this cannot be done until we have more material at hand. For South Africa we have already a great deal of information owing to the work of Callaway, Theal, Torrend for the Zulu-Kafirs, Bleak and Mrs Lloyd for the Hottentots and Bushmen, Casalis, Arbousset, Jacottet for the Ba-Sutho, and my own for the Thongas. But there is still more to be collected. I am under the impression that, having now collected about fifty Thonga tales of different lengths, amounting to a total of 300 pages, in-8vo size, I possess only a fifth, or perhaps a tenth part of the whole folklore of our tribe!

However, Science cannot wait until all the tales have been reduced to writing and published. It will try to come to a conclusion as soon as possible, and perhaps the best plan would be to restrict the field of investigation, and to investigate thoroughly one, at least, of the regions of this vast land. That is the suggestion I would take the liberty of making to my fellow-inquirers in the field of Bantu folklore. Let us choose a characteristic portion of it, for instance, that which I have called the "Romance of the Hare", which is more clearly defined than any other section of this primitive and oral literature. Let all the episodes of this long story be first published in a form which may be regarded as typical, preferably in the form in which they are found in any one given tribe ; let a short résumé of each be made and assigned a distinguishing number by which it will henceforth be known. Then let a folklorist, if he has the necessary time and information at his disposal, make the following investigation : — In which tribes are these episodes met with? How do they differ from the typical version? Do they appear outside Africa (amongst American Negroes, for instance) ? This inquiry would throw light on many important points, viz., what is strictly Bantu in the "Romance of the Hare", and what is common to other races ? Are there episodes which belong to one tribe only, to a group of tribes only, or to tribes widely separated from each other ? To what extent do the wording and the content differ ? Are there not new episodes invented, possibly unconsciously, in recent times by Native story-tellers ? I think, that when this was done important conclusions might be drawn which would greatly assist Ethnography in the solution of this problem, and of many questions bearing on primitive humanity.

I hope later to publish the résumé and classification, of the 56 episodes of the " Romance of the Hare ", which I have collected. I may be able to make this collection more complete, as I know that a number of other stories are told about the "Wily Trickster", as the Thongas call him! This attempt may serve as a starting point for the inquiry which I propose, and should this inquiry ever be conducted on an extended scale, under the auspices of the S.A.A.A.S., for instance, and the result be published in its Journal, the Science of Folklore would certainly greatly profit by such an undertaking.

The antiquity of the tales is beyond any doubt: they are certainly, very old. This antiquity, however, is only relative: that is to say they are constantly transformed by the narrators, and these transformations go much further than is generally supposed, further even than the Natives themselves are aware of. After having heard the same stories told by different story-tellers, I must confess that I never met twice with exactly the same version. First of all *words* differ. Each narrator has his own style, speaks freely and does not feel in any way bound by the expressions used by the person who taught him the tale. It would be a great error to think that, writing a story at the dictation of a Native, we possess the recognized standard form of the tale. There is no standard at all! For this reason I cannot attribute any great importance to the *texts* of the tales. They are examples of the language as spoken by so and so in such and such a district, and therefore have a linguistic value, just as any report or address they may make or deliver. But they are by no means stereotyped texts, transmitted as such from old times. The words of the songs, which occasionally accompany the narration, are probably the most ancient and stable element of the tales. They are often half Zulu in those of the tales which have been borrowed from the neighbouring tribe, and contain archaic expressions. Some sentences also, especially when they are quotations, have the same character and are reproduced by different narrators in an identical form ; for instance, when the Small Toad, Shinana, deposits its eggs on the road and says, as a kind of challenge : "Let the passer-by pass. If he crushes them, let him crush them. If he spares them, let him spare them". I heard this sentence repeated in almost exactly the same terms by two Thongas, one from Khosen, the other from Rikatla. But these fixed elements are rare and, as a rule, Natives change the words with the greatest freedom.

The same may be said with regard to *the sequence of the episodes* ; although these often form definite cycles, it is rare to hear two narrators follow exactly the same order. They arrange their material as they like, sometimes in a very awkward fashion. The tricks of the Hare are sometimes attributed to the Small Toad. In Zulu folklore they are all given as the deeds of a dwarf, called Hlakanyana. I have heard Natives mixing up elements of totally different styles. For instance, in the ritornello of the "Hare's Hoe", which will be found later on and belongs to the animal or semi-animal folklore, the conclusion is borrowed from the well-known episode of the "Year of Famine", which belongs to the class of moral tales (or tales originating in an historic event). New combinations thus constantly take place, sometimes absurd when the literary sense is lacking.

I will go further : *New elements* are also introduced, owing to the tendency of Native story-tellers always to apply the circumstances of their environment to the narrative. This is one of the charms of Native tales. They are living, viz., they are not told as if they were past and remote events, in an abstract manner, but considered as happening amongst the hearers themselves, the names of listeners being often given to the heroes of the story, which is, so to speak, forced into the frame of everyday life. So all the new objects brought in by civilisation are, without the slightest difficulty, made use of by the narrator. He speaks of rifles and guns, of square houses and of clothing, which were not dreamt of by the ancient authors of the tales, and that not only in tales which are distinctly of foreign origin but also in those which are thoroughly Bantu. Thus Magugu, Spoon's wife, in her tale about the hyena-suitors, which otherwise has a strongly Bantu character, concluded by making the girl, the heroine of the story, come to the Missionary Station to be married in the Church! There is not the remotest shadow of historic or ethnographic criticism in the minds of Bantu story-tellers : hence the changes which are constantly deforming old traditions.

Lastly, my experience leads me to think that, in certain cases, the *contents of the stories* themselves are changed by oral transmission, thus giving birth to numerous versions of a tale, often very different from each other and sometimes hardly recognisable. See, for instance, the splendid tale of Zili which I now publish : a man kills his wife and cuts her flesh into strips which he gives to his relatives-in-law to eat. A bird reveals his crime by a little song ; he is found out, and put to death with his whole family. The theme is very popular, and forms one of the most typical moral tales. I possess a version of the story in which it is the wife who calls her parents and, with their help, kills her husband, because he ill-treated her. They cut off the flesh and hang it in strips on the fence of the village. The husband's mother comes to pay a visit to her grandson, and they give her the poor man's flesh to eat. She stays in the village many days, wondering why they feast her with meat of which they do not partake. When she expresses her astonishment, they say to her : "We kept it for you!" When returning home, having taken a supply of meat with her, the old woman hears a bird singing :

> Tsenengu! tsenengu! There is one who fell down!
> He fell down on the square of the village,
> His flesh hangs and swings;
> It is that which you carry on your head.

This song is totally different from that in Zili. The bird repeats it until she understands the words, and then she cries :

> My son! Alas! Alas!

The source of the two stories is evidently the same, but how great are the differences between them! Such alterations have evidently taken place, and are still taking place, every day in Bantu folklore.

How far can these alterations go? To answer this question I would ask my readers to study the charming tale which I have called the "Epic of the Small Toad" (*Chants et Contes des Ba-Ronga*, p. 109). What I call the Small Toad is not our little European green frog but a curious Batrachian, the Breviceps mossambicus, in Ronga the *shinana*. It can swell up to double its natural size and cover itself with an exudation which keeps its enemies away. It buries itself in the ground during the winter, and comes out in spring. This interesting little animal is, in the Ronga folklore, the equal of the Hare, and even surpasses it. Some of its great deeds are the same as those well known in the "Romance of the Hare." The Small Toad begins by killing an antelope by its tricks, and uses its horn as a trumpet to deceive the other beasts. This brings about a fight between the Small Toad and the Hippopotamus, followed by another between it and the Elephant, which has wilfully crushed its eggs. The Small Toad, accompanied by the Chameleon, forges assagais, kills the Elephant, and all the beasts make their submission. So it becomes a Great Chief. It would seem that the presence in the sandy country of Delagoa Bay of this kind of Batrachian with its curious habits, coupled with the example of the Ngoni chiefs who subjugated the clans of the coast by warlike expeditions, has given birth in our tribe to a new modern type of folklore, the type of the Breviceps : all the tricks previously and still told of the Hare are attributed to it, though it keeps its own definite character, viz., that of a warrior. If this be true, there has been a *real creation*, though most of the elements of the "Epic of the Small Toad" were previously in existence.

In conclusion I would say : — The Bantu tales are very old, at least the material of which they are formed is very ancient. But they are still plastic matter unconsciously undergoing constant and extensive modifications in the hands of the story-tellers. These facts are interesting, as they show the conditions of literary production amongst uncivilised tribes. This production is *essentially collective* : tales are not created on all sides by individual authors ; but they are modified, altered and enriched, as they are transmitted from one person to another, from one tribe to another, from one race to another, to such an extent that new types, new combinations, are adopted and a true development takes place (1). This is obvious if, in addition to these transform-

(1) To illustrate this theory, I published in *Folk-Lore*, Dec. 1924, an article under the title ; *La Genèse des Contes Africains ou comme quoi les Noirs inventent des Contes sans le savoir.* The reader will find in it three tales differing widely from each other. Yet they are inspired by the same fundamental idea which is frequently met with in Bantu Folklore : "Accept the advice of old, despised people, and do not have confidence in yourself ". The present conditions of the country round Delagoa Bay may very well explain the transformation of the old Bantu story and it is quite possible to take the view that these three tales have after all the same origin.

ations, that which I have called the fifth category really exists, viz., if it be true that facts which really happened are told in such a way that they come to be classed amongst the fabulous. So it is quite possible that the impression shared by all the story-tellers that all the tales are ancient, that the era of creation has passed, is after all erroneous or, at any rate, only relatively true. A development is still taking place and has perhaps never been more active than now. If this is correct, the hypothesis of Callaway, that our tribes have passed through a stage of greater literary production than is now apparent, cannot be maintained.

IV. *The Moral and Philosophical Value of the Tales.*

In some of the Thonga tales the moral lesson is so clear that I did not hesitate to place them in a special category, the moral tales. They are as wide-spread as the others. I do not pretend that those who tell them have a moral purpose. But the teaching naturally arises from the narratives, and it would be worth while studying them to extract therefrom a kind of code of Native elementary morals. In them we see just punishment following on faults, such as : the *curiosity* of Namashuke (Chants et Contes, p. 22) ; the *jealousy* of Mutipi's friends (p. 158) ; and of Longoloka (Les Ba-Ronga, p. 327) ; *the obstinacy* of .Sidiulu's wife ; the *unkindness* of an elder sister (p. 229) ; the *presumption* of a younger sister (p. 337) ; the *disobedience* of Halandi (p. 242) and of the elder brother in the "Disobedient child and the Snake ;" the *self-confidence* of a man who marries against his parents' will (p. 246) ; the *laziness* of the wives (p. 257) ; the *selfishness* of the husband (p. 260) the *homicide* of Zili. On the other hand we also see *kindness rewarded*, and also *pity*, in a tale not yet published, told in connection with that of The disobedient child (1).

(1) After having told how the little child saved his disobedient brother, (see later), the narrator goes on with a totally different story which, originally, had certainly no connection with the other episode. During the famine, the child who was now several years older, went away to another country. A headman received him, and ordered one of his wives to take care of him, but she refused, saying that her own children had nothing to eat. All the others did the same except one, who consented to feed him.

The animal folklore and Ogre tales seem to be absolutely devoid of such moral lessons. But, as we have already pointed out, they are all more or less illustrations of the triumph of wisdom over mere brute force. This seems to be the root idea of all this folklore, and is not this indeed a highly moral and philosophical idea?

To illustrate this very interesting argument, the story-tellers, in the first instance, narrate the doings of the animals, choosing for the heroes of their tales the smallest and most defenceless. Thus we have the Hare, the cunning trickster, up to all sorts of dodges ; the Small Toad, cold and calculating, the Chameleon, with its crafty prudence. The same idea runs through the group of stories which I have called "the wisdom of the little ones ;" those who were thought to be dullards, the disinherited, and the hated, end by succeeding in life better than their persecutors, of whom they often become the benefactors. On the other hand the Ogres, as representing brute force and all that is merely material, are defeated, are punished for their misdeeds and are generally cut open (to provide an exit for the victims they have swallowed!). So the exaltation of wisdom or goodness is clearly noticeable in almost all the tales, and even foreign tales seem to show, beneath a more or less exotic colouring, that they owe their origin to the same idea. The African story-teller undoubtedly endeavours, above all, to interest his hearers by picturesque, laughable or sensational narratives : but, consciously or unconsciously, he is certainly doing work the philosophical bearing of which is undeniable.

Why does this theme of the triumph of wisdom over strength reappear so frequently and under so many aspects in this popular literature? Doubtless because the thought is natural and eminently satisfying to the mind of man. It underlies our fairy tales of *Cinderella, Hop o'my thumb* and many other European

The child sowed seeds of all kinds and, his enchanted hoe having tilled large fields in a moment, a splendid harvest was the result, and the store houses of his adopted mother were well filled. The others said : "If we had only accepted him!" On his way home, he killed an army and took their assagais, killed a troop of merchants and seized their loads of goods, killed all his relatives and took their hoes,—an episode which resembles that of the conclusion of Mutipi's tale. (Chants et Contes p. 160.)

fables and stories. But may there not have been, in regard to the African tribes, some special circumstances which contributed to the development of this idea, and impelled them to give vent to it in a hundred different ways?

Among the Bantus, the Chief is all powerful. Surrounded by Counsellors, protected by warriors always ready to do his bidding, he is an autocrat with power of life and death over his subjects, especially where the primitive clan has evolved into a confederation of tribes united by military power. If the Bantu clan is in a sense democratic, the hierarchy is, nevertheless, all powerful in its midst. Before the Chief and before the invincible custom of which he is the representative, every one bows and trembles. In every village the headman possesses similar power over his subordinates, and elder brothers reign as despots over the younger. From the top to the bottom of the social ladder the strong dominate over the weak and combine, in a wonderful way, to assure the submission of the inferior. In the evening, round the fire, the women and the children take their revenge in the Black man's usual way, i. e., by saying what they think in a round-about manner. They do not try to upset the existing state of affairs. Far from it! But they take a malicious pleasure in telling of the clever tricks of the Hare and his associates! Why? Because Mr. Hare represents the little one, the subject, the ordinary private individual, who has received no special advantages, either by birth or from nature, and yet who, by his own personal wit or common sense, gets the better of the great ones of the community and even of the chiefs. Is it a mere coincidence that three of the tales I have collected conclude with the death of a chief brought about by the machiavellian astuteness of that rascal, the Hare? Or, sometimes, it is the youngest sister who figures in the story; the despised one, covered with a loathsome skin disease; the insignificant little goat-herd; the son of the neglected wife; all of whom accomplish great deeds, entirely unexpectedly.

I see in these stories, as it were, a discreet protest of weakness against strength, a protest of spiritual against material force; possibly they may contain a warning to those in power from those who suffer. And who knows if their ultimate object be not to assert the value of the individual amongst this down-trodden people where the individual counts for nothing? If this is so, then African folklore possesses a greater and more philosophical value than would appear at first sight. In the collective state of human society it represents an aspiration to a state of things where the individual will have his due place. In this way, it is prophetic. It can no longer be classed merely as an amusement for old women during the long evenings, or as a more or less intellectual parlour-game : it is a monument upon which the soul of the race has recorded, unconsciously perhaps, its ideas and its aspirations. It is thus doubly worthy of our study.

The scope of this book does not allow me to publish more than one or two tales of each category, and I must also abstain from any technical comment upon them, leaving the work of annotation and comparison to professional folklorists. My aim is to describe the South African tribe, and they constitute a sufficient illustration in themselves of its psychic life.

V. *Animal Folklore.*

I have published nearly thirty episodes of the Romance of the Hare in the works already referred to ; those which I collected in later years form three cycles : that of the *Wily Trickster*, a collection of episodes told by Martha and heard by her in the Maputju country ; the most noteworthy of these describe the victory of the Hare over the Lion ; *the Hare and the Lion*, told by Simeon Makwakwa of Bilen, containing episodes quite different from those of the first cycle ; *the Hare and the Baboon*, written for me by one of my pupils, Mbike Dzengen from Khosen, a very amusing story also known in Bilen with some variations. To these three cycles I have added the story of the *Hare's Hoe*, a curious specimen of a popular literary genus, the *ritornello*, or anadiplosis not frequently met with in Bantu folklore.

225

THE LIFE OF A SOUTH AFRICAN TRIBE

1) Ñwashisisana, the Hare. (1)

The Hare, that wily trickster (2), went to live with the Grey Antelope (3). One day he said to her : "Suppose we go and till our fields and plant some beans!" So off they went, and set to work. The Antelope stole the Hare's beans, and the Hare stole the Antelope's beans, but the Hare did the most of the stealing.

The Hare set a trap in his field, and the Antelope was caught by the leg. In the early morning the cunning rascal went out and found the Antelope caught in the trap : — "Don't you think you deserve to be killed" said he, "now that I have found you out?" — "No! No!" replied she. "Let me go, and we will go back to my house, where I will give you a hoe." So he let her go, and she gave him the hoe.

The Hare then packed his beans, harvested all his fields, and made ready to be off : — "Good-bye," said he to the Antelope, "I won't stay with you any longer, you are a thief!"

*

*   *

He soon came across the Great Lizard, the Varan (Ñwakhwahle) lying at the edge of a water hole. It was the Chief's water hole, where they drew their water, and he had been placed there on guard to find out who it was that was continually disturbing it, and making it muddy : — "What are you doing here?" said the Hare. — "I am watching this hole to see who it is that muddies the chief's water." — "I'll tell you what," said the Hare, "we had much better go and till a field together." — "How can I dig?" said the Varan, "I can't stand on my hind legs and hold the hoe in my fore-paws." — "That doesn't matter : just you come along ; I will tie the hoe to your tail, and you will be able to dig beautifully." So the hoe was tied on ; but when this was done, the Varan couldn't move. Then the Hare ran back to the hole, drank his fill of water, and finished by stirring it up well, making it as muddy as possible. After this he walked all over the Varan's fields, and regaled

---

(1) For the English translation of this and most of the following tales I am greatly indebted to Mr. G. D. Fearon and to Miss G. Quin, editor of the *Student World*, who has kindly translated the two new tales published below.

(2) Ñwashisisana is the surname for the Hare, which is generally called Ñwampfundla. The word is derived from the verb *shisa* to deceive.

(3) Ñwamhunti, the duiker of the Boers.

himself on his groundnuts. In the heat of the day he came back and
said : — "Ho! An army has passed through the country. I hear that the
warriors have dirtied the water in the hole... I hear too that they have
ravaged all your crop of ground-nuts!" — "Untie me" said the Varan,
"I can't budge." — "All right, but only on condition that you don't go
and accuse me, the Hare, of having stirred up the water." — "But
who told you this story about those soldiers who did all the mischief?"
— "Don't ask me so many questions ; if you do, I won't untie you!"
— "Very well! I'll be quiet ; but take away this hoe ; it hurts me!" —
"Listen! first of all I'll go and draw some water for you. You must
be thirsty." — "No, I'm not thirsty. Only let me go!" — "If you
are not thirsty, all right! I won't untie the hoe." — "Oh! very well I am
thirsty. Hurry up, and come back as fast as you can."

The Hare went to the Varan's village, took the wooden goblet he
always drank out of, drew some water, and once again stirred up the
hole. He took a drink to the Varan, and said to him : "If any one
asks you whether I have disturbed the water, you must say that you
did it. If you don't promise me this, I won't untie you." — "All
right! Very well." Then the Hare ran to call the chiefs : Lord Elephant
(Ñwandlopfu), Lord Lion (Ñwandjawandjawana) and the rest. They
all came and asked the Varan : "Who has been drawing our water and
making it all muddy?" — "It is I," said the Varan ; and the rascal of a
Hare added : "Yes, I found him committing this crime, and I tied him
up to a hoe, so that he couldn't run away."

The chiefs congratulated the Hare : "Ah! you have been very clever!
You have discovered the villain who has been muddying our pond!"
And they immediately killed the Varan.

The wily trickster took the hoe, and went to look for the Grey
Antelope (Ñwamhunti). She was on sentry duty, on the edge of a
pool, for guards were placed at all the pools to prevent any one approaching, as the water still continued to be muddied during the night.
The Hare, not being able to get anything to drink, said to the Antelope :
"What are you doing there, close to the water?" — "I am guarding the
Chief's pool." — "You will all get thin and die of hunger, if you stay
like that at the edge of the pools. Listen! You would do much better
to come with me, and till a field ; then, in time of famine, you would have
something to eat." — "Let us go!" said the Antelope.

The Hare set to work in grand style. He gave the Antelope a hoe
and told her to dig too. — "I can't get on my hind legs," said she,
"and hold the hoe with my forelegs." — "Let me have a look at your

227

forelegs : I'll tie the hoe to them, and you will be able to dig all right."
The Antelope tried, but she couldn't do it. — "Never mind," said
the Hare. "Wait a minute." He ran back to the pool, quenched
his thirst, and muddied the water. Then he filled a calabash, and hid
it in the bush. On returning to the Antelope, he said : "Hello!
Haven't you done any hoeing yet?" — "No, I can't manage it." —
"Would you believe it? An army has passed by, and they have stirred
up the pool." — "No! Truly? Untie me, Hare!" — "I won't untie you
unless you swear that what I said is true." — "Very well! Untie me."
Off he went to get the calabash to give her a drink, and made her
promise to confess that it was she who had disturbed the water ; then he
called the Chiefs, who killed the Antelope.

*

* *

But there was one creature that outdid the Hare in cunning, and
that was the Tortoise (Ñwamfutju). She mounted guard at the pond.
The Hare arrived on the scene. — "You will all die of hunger, if you
stay at the edge of the pools with nothing to do. We had much better
go and till a field together." — "How can I hoe with such short legs?"
— "Oh! that will be all right. I'll show you how to do it." — "Eh! No
thank you! I think not!" — "Well then! Let's go and help ourselves to
some of the Wild Boar's sweet potatoes." — "No," said the Tortoise
uncompromisingly, "no pilfering!"

However, before very long, she began to feel hungry, so much so
that, when the Hare again proposed a marauding expedition, she
overcame her scruples, and they went off together to root up the sweet
potatoes. Then they lit a fire of grass in the bush and roasted them.
— "Tortoise," said the Hare, "just go and see if the owners of these
fields are anywhere about, as we must not let them catch us." — "Yes,
but let us both go. You go one way and I'll go the other." Off
went the Hare, but the Tortoise, instead of following his example,
stayed behind and crawled into his wallet. The Hare soon came back,
filled up his wallet with sweet potatoes, threw it over his back and ran
away to escape the proprietors, shouting at the top of his voice : "Hi,
Tortoise! Look out! They will catch you! I'm off! Fly!" He
ran as hard as he could to escape capture ; the Tortoise, inside the sack,
ate the sweet potatoes ; she picked out all the best ones and finished
the lot! She said (descriptive adverb), "kutlu." After a while the

Hare was tired out, and lay down quite exhausted. He felt the pangs of hunger. — "Aha!" said he to himself, "I will have a good feed!" He sat down in a shady spot, opened his wallet, put his hand inside, and pulled out one very small sweet potato. — "This is much too small for me" said he, and, putting his hand in again, felt a nice big one. — "Oho! here's a beauty!" When he had pulled it out of his bag, what was his surprise to find that his prize turned out to be... Mistress Tortoise. — "Hello! (He shoyawe!) Why! It's you!" he cried in disgust, and threw her on the ground. She scuttled away as fast and as far as she could. The Hare began to weep : — "When I think that I have been carrying her all this time! ..." He felt very crestfallen.

*

*   *

Continuing his travels he next met King Lion surrounded by his courtiers. He, at once asked permission to *nkonza*, viz., to swear allegiance to the King, and to settle in his country. But every day he went out to steal other folk's ground-nuts. When the owners of the fields came to look at their crops, they exclaimed : "Who can it be that digs up our ground-nuts ?" The Hare went off to find the Lion, and said to him : "Sire, your subjects are not what they should be (a ba lulamanga), for they are in the habit of stealing." — "You don't say so?" said the Lion. "Go and keep watch, and if you discover any one stealing, catch him."

The Hare went off to take up his position in the fields, but the Lion followed him, and surprised him in the very act of feasting on ground-nuts. — "Ha! ha! You tell me that my subjects are not honest folks, while it is you who do the thieving!" — "Not at all! I was only keeping a look out! Come here, and I will show you the footprints of your subjects, for I know them well!"

So they went to a large shady banyan tree. The Hare made a strong string of one of the long tendrils (lisiha), and said to the Lion : "As you think I don't speak the truth, just sit down here and you will soon see the thieves passing by ; I will wile away the time by making you a crown of wax (khehla ngiyana. I. p. 129)." — "All right," said the Lion, "make me a crown." The Hare began by parting the Lion's mane down the middle and arranging the hairs carefully, one by one, on either side of his neck, as if he were preparing a spot on the top of his head for the crown. Then he made holes

229

through the bark of the tree, on both sides of the trunk, and passed the hairs of the mane right through them, some on one side, some on the other.   This done, he tied all the hairs securely together at the back of the tree with the string he had made, and said to the Lion : "I've finished the job.   Jump up quickly and you will see one of your subjects stealing in the fields!"   The Lion tried to jump up.   He couldn't!   He half killed himself struggling to get on his feet!   The Hare ran to the village. — "Come," he shouted, "and see who it is who ravages your fields!"   He had previously torn up a lot of ground-nut leaves and thrown them down close to the Lion.   The villagers hurried to the spot. — "There! don't you see him?   Haven't I found him out, eh?"   The Lion didn't dare to say a single word.   Then his subjects cut great staves and beat him to death : — "Ah! Hare, you are very clever, and we are very grateful!" said they.

*

*   *

The Hare cut the Lion up in pieces ; then he took the skin and wrapped himself in it ; thus disguised, he went to the Lion's village and entered the Queen's hut.   He said : "I am not well," and shut himself up refusing to see anyone.   He gave orders to the servants to kill an ox because he was ill ; then he had a second one slaughtered, then a third!   The women said to him : "Are you going to move to another place, as you are killing all your oxen?" — "No" said he, "I have no intention of moving any more.   I am killing them because I know very well that I shall never get over this illness."   So he had a general slaughtering of all the Lion's oxen, goats and sheep, to the very last head of cattle.   When all were killed, he said to the Queen : "Haven't you got my money in your keeping? — "Yes" she replied. — "Well, bring it all out, and put it, together with my royal mat, and all my valuables, on the village square."

The Lion's skin was becoming rather odoriferous, the flies were settling upon it in swarms, and the Hare was by no means comfortable inside it. — "What sort of complaint have you got?" said the Queen, "it is something that smells very nasty." — "Oh! I have only got some sores, I must go and find a doctor.   Good-bye : I shall start at once."   The Lion's wife replied : "Then I will go with you, my husband. — "No," said he, "no occasion for that, for I know exactly where I must go."   He went out on to the square, picked up the mat

230

in which all the money and valuables had been packed ; then throwing off the Lion's skin, he tore away as fast as his legs could carry him with all the village in pursuit!

*

*   *

He came to a burrow, and in he ran. The pursuers got a hooked stick to pull him out ; they tried to hook him and managed to get hold of his leg. —"Oh! pull away!" cried he, "pull away! you've only got hold of the root of a tree!"   So they left of pulling, and had another try. This time they really hooked on to a root — "Hi! hi!" he yelled, "Hi! hi! Take care! You're hurting me! You're killing me! Ow! Ow!"... They all pulled as hard as they could, and pulled and pulled until the hook broke and they all fell over backwards ; they said : "Qaa," (descriptive adv.). Finally they were tired out and said : "Oh! let us give it up and leave him where he is!" So they stopped up the burrow with a bunch of grass and went away.

The South wind sprang up, and blew the grass deeper into the burrow. — "I am done for," said the Hare to himself, as he fancied they were succeeding in getting nearer to him. He was suffering the pangs of hunger and was terribly thirsty, but did not dare to leave the burrow, supposing his enemies to be close at hand. At length he cried out : "Have pity on me and let me go, my good fathers (ba baba), I beseech you!" He crept cautiously towards the entrance to the burrow, and found only a bunch of grass. Then he made off at once, leaving all his treasures behind him, and not even giving them a single thought.

*

*   *

He ran on and on. He became thin and ill. He ate grass, but it did not remain in his inside : it passed through him immediately. He came to the home of the Grey Antelope. — "Say, Antelope, suppose we sew one another up! You stitch me up, but not completely, you know! It will keep the grass much longer in our insides when we browse, and we shall get much more nourishment out of it." She consented, and stitched him up partially. He sewed her up entirely. The Antelope swelled and died. But, fortunately for her, she fell in a

231

field belonging to a woman who picked her up, put her in her basket, on the top of her head, and carried her to the village to be eaten. She gave her to her husband to cut up ; he set to work, and began by cutting the stitches that the Hare had sewn. All that was in the Antelope's interior at once came out ; she jumped to her legs, and galloped away. She met the Hare and said to him : "All right! I've found you out now!.. Never again do I call you my friend!"

*

*   *

The Hare being thirsty was looking for a pool but couldn't find one. At last he came across one where no one was on guard. The Tortoise was really in charge, but she was in the water. The Hare walked in : "What luck! How nice and cool it is!" said he, quenching his thirst, and swimming about. The Tortoise snapped at one of his legs, then at another... — "Hello! let me go! I'll promise you a goat if you will let go!" They came out of the pool together, and the Hare said to her : "Come along to my house, and get your goat." They reached his home, but no goat! Nothing! The Hare did not give her anything. Then he remembered the money that he left in the burrow and said : "Let us go and see Mr. Chameleon. He has got my valuables, for he borrowed a lot of money from me. I'll just run round and fetch my brother ; he knows all about the business and will be my witness." Having said this, he decamped. The Tortoise arrived at the Chameleon's abode and said : "Give me the Hare's money which you have got!" — "What? I haven't got anything belonging to the Hare!" Whereupon the Chameleon blew into her eyes. She swelled, and swelled, and died.

That's the end.

2) The Hare and the Lion.

One day the Hare was looking into a pool and saw the sky reflected in the water. —"Hello!" said he to himself, "there is a fine large country down there, where I can always hide if any one tries to do me any harm. I can go and be rude to the Elephants now with impunity." Off he went to insult the Elephants, who promptly chased him. He rushed into the pool, but he was soon caught.

— "Hi! hi! my grandfathers! Let me go!" (The Hare calls all the other animals "grandfather"). — "What shall we do to you? Shall we kill you?" —"What! Kill me? You will no longer have a grandson then..." — "Very well ! Then we will beat you ! " — "Why? You can't find any spot on me big enough to hit, I am so small..." — "Well then! we will just roll you in the mud, and smother you all over with it, inside and out!" They did so, and left him lying on the ground, choked and smothered with mud.

*

*　　*

The Hyena came along. She is very fond of flesh, but it must be dead flesh. She lets the other animals kill it for her. She picked up the Hare and thought she had found a choice morsel. — "But," said she, "this is too dirty! it is all covered with mud! I must wash it." So she washed it. — "Now, the meat will be all wet and nasty ; I must dry it." So she laid it out, and sat down in the shade to wait. Suddenly the Hare jumped up and made off at full speed!

*

*　　*

He came to Lord Lion's village and this Chief took him into his service. The Lion went hunting every day, and it was the Hare's duty to look after the Lion's children, and teach them their lessons. When the Lion returned from hunting, he stopped some distance from the village and sent meat by the Hare for his three little children, saying to him : "Give the little ones the tender meat, for they are young, and you can eat the bones!" The Hare told the children : "Your father says you are to eat the bones, for they are hard and will make you strong, and I will eat the meat." Thus he regaled himself.

Then he taught them a nice little game. He collected a lot of wood, made a fire and said : "I will teach you how to jump. You know that your father catches animals by springing upon them, so you too had better learn how to spring properly." He began first : "I will show you the way I jump, and you must do just as I do." He easily cleared the fire in one bound, but, when the little Lion cub tried, he jumped right into the flames and was burnt. Then the Hare ate him up. When the Lion returned in the evening, he said to the

233

Hare : "Show me my little ones." He had stopped, as usual, a short way off, so the Hare lifted up one of the cubs saying : "Here is No. 1 ;" then another : "Here is No. 2 ;" and, lifting the same one twice : "Here is No. 3." — " 'T is well!" said the Lion. The next day the Hare repeated his game with the fire. Another cub perished, and was eaten. In the evening he lifted up the one cub that was left three times, and the Lion was quite satisfied. The day following the third cub was cooked and made away with. Then the Hare climbed into a thorny tree and scratched his skin so badly that he was bleeding in several places. The Lion came back towards nightfall : — "What is the matter with you?" said he. — "Alas! my grandfather, a whole band of enemies have been here! They have killed all your children! Just see the wounds their assagays have made all over my body!" He had also taken care to make a quantity of marks on the ground : "You can see their footprints all around. I will go and find out which way they have gone, and we will pursue them!"

*

*   *

The Hare ran off to the mountains, where he found an enormous boulder, so poised that it would only require the slightest push to send it crashing down the steep slope. — "This will do!" said he, "it is just exactly what I want!" He went back to the Lion and said to him : "Come along! and hide yourself just where I tell you to. If you hear a great noise, don't look up, don't even raise your head. It will be the enemy coming along, and, if you make any movement, they may see you, and run away. You can kill them when they pass close by you. Here is the spot! Hide yourself in here!" He placed him just below the rocking boulder. Then up he climbed. —"Look out! Here they come!" He pushed the rock ; down it fell, crushing the Lion. The "Slayer of flesh" (1) died! The Hare came hurriedly down the slope, cut off the Lion's claws and decamped.

*

*   *

He married the Grey Antelope, for he wanted her little horns to make a trumpet. The Hare is so full of cunning that he can induce

(1) Ñwangonyama, is the surname of the Lion.

any animal to marry him. After some time had elapsed, he said to her : "Let us play at cooking each other! (A hi psekane!) This is how we will do ; we'll get a big cauldron, I'll get into it. You light a fire underneath. When the water begins to get warm, I will call out to you to take me out, and you will pull me out at once." No sooner said than done. The Antelope pulled the Hare out before the water was too hot. Then the Antelope got in, in her turn. The wily plotter put the cover on the cauldron, and plastered it down with dung (p. 38), filling every aperture, and saying : "You will be warmer if I do this." Then he sat down, and smoked his hemp-pipe. When the Antelope called out : "Come and help me! I am boiling!", he said : "Wait a minute, my pipe doesn't draw properly! I must pull at it a bit." She twisted about and cried for mercy. He put more wood on the fire, and, when the Antelope was thoroughly cooked, he ate the meat and kept the horns!

*

* *

He went farther on, taking with him the jaw bone of the Lion he had killed, built an immense enclosure with stakes, and put the jawbone at the entrance. Then he sent this proclamation all through the land : "Come and see! A new and wonderful thing! Teeth growing out of the ground! Quantities of them!" He summoned everyone with his trumpet, and all the animals came into the enclosure, without noticing that there was no way out of it. He closed the entrance and all were prisoners. Then he said to them : "It is well, you are in the Chief's enclosure. I will go and tell him you have arrived. He will soon be here." He went and decked himself out in a dress entirely covered with small pieces of looking-glass : it was so resplendent that it quite dazzled the eyes of all who looked at him. "Here is the King," said they all, on seeing him approach. Then he addressed them and proclaimed this law : "Know ye all! Hawks, Lions, Tigers, that from henceforth no beast of the field is allowed to kill any other one, or to eat his flesh. Nothing is to be eaten but grass." He appointed a shepherd to see that the animals did not kill each other. The Lions and Tigers grew thin on this diet : it made them ill, and none but the herbivorous animals were in good health.

One day the Hare, having sent all the animals away, took off his glittering coat, and began to browse near the enclosure. Now it happened that a Lion, who was unwell, and could not go out with the others, had remained behind. He saw the Hare browsing close by, and, casting a glance around, to make sure no one was watching, with a single bound he was upon him and devoured him! In the evening all the animals returned, but as the King did not put in an appearance for eight or ten days, their spirits began to revive. They plucked up courage and flew at each other's throats : a terrible carnage was the result ; the stakes of the enclosure rotted and all the survivors dispersed. Amongst these was one of the Hare's brothers, who at once stepped into the shoes of the deceased deceiver and continued his evil ways.

*

*   *

One day the Hen invited the Hare to drink some beer at her house. There he saw the Hen cooking and the Cock roosting with his head under his wing. "Where is his head?" he asked the Hen. —"Oh! he cut it off and sent it round to invite our friends to come. It is only his body that you see there : his head will soon come back." — "No! really! You don't say so? Honour bright?" — "Why certainly!" — "What sort of drugs do you use for this wonderful operation?" — "Oh! none at all! You just take a knife, sharpen it well, and cut your head off!" — "Ah! is that all? I must try it!"

Later on the Hare asked the Hen to drink beer with him. He cut off his head and killed himself. Henceforth the Hen was the most cunning of all the animals!

That is the end!

3) THE HARE AND THE BABOON.

The Hare and the Baboon built a village together. One day, when they were tipsy, the Hare said to the Baboon : "Let us go and kill our wives!" The idea pleased the Baboon immensely : so they set off to kill them. The Hare went inside the hut and began to hit the big basket (ngula), telling his wife at the same time to shriek and cry out. The Baboon heard the cries, and was satisfied that the Hare was indeed killing his wife ; so he took a big stick and belaboured his wife so that she died, whilst the Hare had not done his wife any harm, having only belaboured the big basket!

One day the Baboon overheard the Hare talking to his wife. He was greatly astonished. "Ha! ha!" he said, "the rascal has played a trick on me ; I have killed my wife, and he never killed his!"

*

*　　*

Another day the Hare proposed to the Baboon that they should go and steal ground-nuts in other folks' fields. The Baboon was quite agreeable, as he was suffering from hunger, having no wife to till his land, or to give him any good food. When they got to the fields they began helping themselves to the ground-nuts, dug them up, and eat them. Whilst they were thus employed the Hare said : "Grand-father, don't tire yourself digging up these ground-nuts ; leave them alone ; just sit down in the shade and I will dig them up for you." The Baboon was very pleased, and took a seat under a shady tree which was close by : then the Hare dug up ground-nuts, and threw them down in front of the Baboon in such quantities that he was completely hidden behind the pile. He eat them greedily, and with great gusto. When the Hare saw that the pile was big enough, he went behind the Baboon and said : "Will you let me kill the fleas in your tail?" — "Certainly, little one!" said he. So the Hare set to work, pretending to be killing fleas, and all the while he was digging a deep hole, as deep as the tail was long, in which he intended to fix it, when he should get an opportunity! He tried to put the tail in the hole, but, in doing so, hurt the Baboon who said : "You are hurting me, grandson!" — "No," replied the Hare, "I'm not hurting you ; I am only playing with your tail!" When the Hare saw that the Baboon had nearly finished his ground-nuts, he hurried off to fetch a fresh supply in order to divert the Baboon's attention, while he continued his digging operations. Once more he tried to insert the tail in the hole ; but the Baboon called out : "What are you doing, grandson?"—"I'm not doing anything, grandfather!" said he, and continued digging until he had made the hole quite as deep as was necessary. Then he succeeded in putting the entire tail in the hole, right up to the stump ; he filled in the earth all round it, and hammered it down with a stick as hard as he could. He tried to pull it out, but couldn't ; it was so securely fixed in. Seeing the Baboon had again nearly finished his

237

ground-nuts, he got another lot, and went behind him to put the finishing touches to his handiwork.

When all was completed to his entire satisfaction, he ran off and clambered to the top of an ant-hill, and began to shout, at the top of his voice : "Hello! Here's the Baboon eating up other folks' ground nuts!" Hearing this the Baboon scolded the Hare, and told him not to make such a noise : "My grandson, you must not shout like that before I have finished my ground-nuts! You can shout as much as you like when I have done, and we will then run away together." But the Hare would not obey him, and went on shouting as loud as he could until, at last, the women of the fields heard him and people came running up with their bows and arrows and guns. Then the Hare came down from his ant-hill and took to his heels. As for the Baboon, he was in a great fright, dropped the ground-nuts, and tried to make off ; but he couldn't move, as his tail was hard and fast in the ground! When he saw the folks approaching nearer and nearer, he made the most frantic efforts to get loose, throwing himself first on one side and then on the other, until finally, groaning with pain and terror, with one tremendous bound, he wrenched his tail free ; but it was only the bone! With a skeleton-tail waving and dripping blood (lwa ku dzu-dzu-dzu, descript. adv.) he rushed away. He jumped, and dodged, fearing lest an arrow or a bullet should hit him, until he got safely into the wood.

When he reached home he found the Hare seated in his wife's hut, but he made no remark. During the night the Hare went back to the spot where they had been eating ground-nuts, and unearthed the remains of the tail, which he took home to his wife telling her to cook it ; this she did with great care, beginning by rubbing off all the hairs ; she then stewed it with some ground-nuts. She also cooked some flour. When everything was done to a turn, she dished up the food on separate plates, one containing the flour, and the other the savoury stewed tail. Then the Hare sent his son to call the Baboon, who came with much pleasure, as he knew he was being asked to a meal. On his arrival he went into the hut, sat down and was served with the flour and its seasoning, the stew. He enjoyed the food, took some of the meat and ate it. — "Why!" said he, "here is meat! Wherever did you get it, my grandson?" He had no idea it was his own tail! He ate it, emptied the plate and went home.

Some days later, the Hare told his wife to make some beer, which she did ; when it was properly brewed, he invited all the countryside to come to a beer-drinking. They all came and drank beer. Grand-father Baboon was among the guests. While they were all enjoying themselves, the Hare raised his hand for silence, and requested permission to make a few remarks. When all the noise had subsided, he raised his voice, and asked : "Have any of you ever seen any one who devoured his own tail?" They all said : "No, we have never seen such a person!" The Baboon also declared he had never even heard of such a thing. —"Well!" said the Hare, "shall I tell you who it is?" —"Yes, do! We should much like to know," said they. Then the Hare exclaimed : "It is he, the Baboon! he has eaten the tail that he lost over there in the ground-nut field!" The Baboon was very angry, and left the gathering with a scowling face ; he went home muttering to himself : "I wonder how I can manage to get the better of that rascal? I must try, for he is always making a fool of me, and annoys me horribly."

*
*   *

After some weeks, during which the Baboon had been cogitating how he could be revenged on the Hare, he hit upon a plan. "I'll go and get a wife" said he to himself, "and then I shall be able to trick him, and starve him to death!" So he began at once by making proposals to a girl in a distant village, and, when the time came to go and fetch her, he asked the Hare to accompany him on his journey. They each packed up their provisions and started. The Hare, when preparing for the trip, put his eatables in the bottom of his wallet, and three stones on top of them ; then he closed the package. The Baboon, who wanted to deceive the Hare, and get him to throw away his provisions, packed one stone with the eatables in his bag. When they were well on their way, they came to the bank of a river where they sat down to rest, and, beginning to feel hungry. thought they might as well have something to eat. Then said the Baboon : "Let us throw our provisions into the water, to see them float down the stream, for we are quite close to the village of my future parents-in-law." Now this was not true : the village was still a long way off. The Hare was quite willing to throw away the food, so the Baboon began and threw his stone into the water ; the Hare followed suit and also threw away a stone. Now, in the Baboon's bag only eatables were left, as he had only put one stone on the top, whilst the Hare,

239

having put into his bag three stones, and having only thrown one away, had still two remaining. — "Go on, my friend," said the Hare, "throw away another stone!" The Baboon had no more to throw, so he had to throw away his flour. The Hare then threw in his second stone. Continuing the game the Baboon flung his "seasonings" into the river, and had nothing left to eat. The Hare tossed his third stone into the water, but had all his provisions untouched. So the Baboon, failing to trick the Hare, was himself a martyr to the pangs of hunger ; for they were nowhere near the village of his relatives-in-law ; they had still four nights to sleep on the way! They jogged along on their journey and, whenever they stopped for a meal, the Baboon would seat himself at some distance from the Hare, and watch him eating ; he longed to share his provisions, but the Hare never offered him any, for the Baboon himself had stipulated that neither should ask the other for any of his eatables.

*

*　　*

When they had trudged on for four days, they arrived at the village, where they were well received. In the meanwhile the Baboon had arranged that if, when swallowing the good things provided, he should scald his throat, the Hare must run back and get the medicine for burns, to relieve the pain. Now this was only a dodge to get rid of the Hare, while he himself would eat up all the food, and the Hare find none on his return. However, the Hare suspected some trick and therefore stuck an arrow into the ground at the foot of the tree (muri) (1) which cures scalds and burns. Before reaching the village he said : "Oh! I have left one of my arrows over there ; I must run back and fetch it." — "Don't you go digging up the roots of that tree that I shewed you ; you must only do that if I happen to send you for some when we are having our meal." So the Hare ran back to the spot, where he had left his arrow. "He wants to trick me, does he?" said he to himself, and he dug up a root and put it carefully into his bag, so that the Baboon should not see it. On his return the Baboon questioned him as to what had kept him so long : — "You didn't dig up any roots of that tree, did you?" said he. — "Oh no!" replied the Hare. "I didn't take a single one!" And so they came to the village.

(1) Muri means both tree and remedy.

When food had been put before them, and they had commenced eating, the Baboon cried out : "I have burnt my throat! Oh! Oh!" Then the Hare hurried off, and got the remedy out of his bag : he had not very far to go. The Baboon was furious, and shouted : "I told you not to dig up the medicine, but only to do so if I should send you for it!" — "But, Grandfather," replied the Hare, "I did not like to keep you waiting in pain such a long time!" When the Baboon found he could not trick the Hare, he hurried up his wedding, and his return home, for he was very unhappy : he lost all his appetite owing to his fit of rage on seeing how short a time was needed for the Hare to fetch the medicine. On the other hand the Hare regaled himself heartily. The Baboon couldn't get over the disappointment ; he grew thinner and thinner and was nearly dying.

When they once more reached their home, they were each possessed of a wife, so they both started off to build their villages in different places.

*

*   *

The Hare used to go hunting to procure meat, but the Baboon was too lazy to hunt for himself, so lived by stealing meat from the Hare, and this is how he managed it : whenever the Hare had killed some game and cooked it in the open, the Baboon smeared himself all over with mud, and came rushing out of the marshes towards the Hare's village. Then the Hare and his wife and the little ones all fled away, for they were afraid of this great black beast. Now it was only the Baboon who frightened the Hare : he took the game and gave it to his wife. Thus it went on for several days, until, at last, the Hare concluded that he must look carefully into the matter. So, on a certain occasion, when the Baboon carried on his thieving in the same way, the Hare remained hidden in his village ; only his wife and children ran away. He hid in the hut so as to watch closely the animal who stole his meat and see how he could fight him. The Baboon crept up to the pot in which the meat was cooking, for the folks of the village had not yet begun their breakfast. He lifted the cover, pulled out a piece of meat, and ate it up. Then the Hare let fly an arrow and shot him right in the stomach. The Baboon ran off and went home to his wife. He was very ill. A day or two later, the Hare went to see his grandfather, and, on arriving, greeted him with : "How do you

241

do, Grandfather?" Now, before entering the hut, the Hare had heard groans, but, as soon as he stepped inside, all was quiet, for the Baboon was afraid his visitor might suspect that it was he who had been hit with the arrow. The Hare had, however, already recognised the Baboon as the culprit, and said to him : "Well, Grandfather, I hope you are feeling all right?" — "No," replied the Baboon, "I am not very well : I feel a pain in my side, which shoots right through me." — "I knew it was you who stole my meat," said the Hare, "so I shot you with an arrow." So the Baboon died and his wife lived in want and misery. — That's the end!

*
*   *

Simeon Makwakwa, a Native of Bilen, gave me a different version of the way in which the Baboon worked his vengeance, or tried to do so, on the Hare for having made him eat his own tail.

The Baboon set to work picking up all the Hare's excrement for several days, until he had collected quite a large quantity. The Hare, noticing this manœuvre, said to himself : "All right! We shall see!" He caught a fowl and pulled off one of its legs without killing it : the fowl survived. The Baboon invited the Hare to dinner, and the latter went quite happily with the fowl's leg in his pocket. "Here is the plat du jour," said the Baboon, pointing to the pot in which the Hare's excrement was cooking." — "Thanks! Thanks! said the Hare, who, as soon as his host's head was turned, dug a hole in the ground into which he emptied the contents of the pot, and began eating the hen's leg that he had brought with him. The Baboon returned. — "This chicken is very good" said the Hare, gnawing the bone. And so they parted.

A few days later, when the village was full of men playing *tshuba* (I. p. 345) the Baboon arrived on the scene, very cock-a-hoop, and called out : "Let me ask a question. Has any one here ever seen a person feasting on his own excrement?" —"Why certainly not" said every one present.—"Well! I know some one who has so feasted! It is the Hare." —"Are you quite sure of that?" said the accused, and holding up in sight of all assembled, the one-legged fowl, which he had taken care to bring with him, he told the whole story. So the laugh was turned against the Baboon ; everybody made fun of him, and the villagers caught him by his blackened and twisted-up stump of a tail, and chopped it off! — That's the end!

4) The Hare's Hoe.

One day the Hare said to the Grey Antelope : "Let us go and sow peas." — "I don't like peas, I prefer wild beans" said the Antelope. So the Hare went by himself to sow peas. When they began to sprout, he noticed that they were disappearing, so he hid himself in the field, and caught the Antelope digging up his peas : "Aha!" said he, "you are a thief. Pay the fine!" She gave him a hoe and he went off.

He met some women, who were digging clay with sticks. He said to them : "Haven't you got any hoes?" — "No," said they, "we haven't a single one." — "Then take this one," said he, "you can give it me back later on." When they had finished, the last one who used the hoe broke it. Then the Hare sang the following words :

> Clay-diggers, give back my hoe, my friends,
> My hoe which the Antelope gave me,
> The Antelope who paid the fine for my peas.

The women took one of their pots, and gave it to him.

*

*   *

He left, and met some men who were harvesting honey ; they were doing so in a piece of tree-bark. — "Haven't you got any pot to put your honey into?" said he. — "No" said the men, we haven't any." So he gave them his pot. The last one who handled it, broke it. When it was broken the Hare sang :

> Honey-harvesters, give me back my pot.
> My pot which the Clay-diggers gave me ;
> The Clay-diggers paid for my hoe,
> My hoe which the Antelope gave me,
> The Antelope who paid the fine for my peas.

They took some of their honey, and gave it to him.

*

*   *

He came to a village, and there he saw women pounding maize flour. He said to them : "Haven't you any honey to mix with your flour?" — "No," said they, "we have none." So he gave them his honey, saying : "Take it, but be careful to leave me some of it." But the last one finished it all. Then he sang :

> Pestle-pounders, give me back my honey.
> The honey which the Honey-harvesters gave me ;
> The Honey-harvesters paid for my pot,
> The pot which the Clay-diggers gave me ;
> The Clay-diggers paid for my hoe,
> The hoe which the Antelope gave me,
> The Antelope who paid the fine for my peas.

They took some of their dough, and gave it to him.

*

* *

He went on, and met some boys herding goats. —"Haven't you anything to eat?" said he, "your lips look very dry." — "No" they replied, "we have no food at all." So he gave them the dough, saying : "Eat away! but leave some for me." The last one eat the last bite. Then sang the Hare :

> Goat-herds, give me back my dough,
> The dough which the Pestle-pounders gave me ;
> The Pestle-pounders paid for my honey,
> The honey which the Honey-harvesters gave me ;
> The Honey-harvesters paid for my pot,
> The pot which the Clay-diggers gave me ;
> The Clay-diggers paid for my hoe,
> The hoe which the Antelope gave me,
> The Antelope who paid the fine for my peas.

They took a goat, and gave it to him.

*

* *

He met some young men tending the oxen while feeding. He said to them : "Your lips seem very dry ; haven't you anything to eat?" — "No," said they, "we have nothing." So he said : "Take this goat, but be sure to leave some for me." The last one devoured the last mite. Then the Hare sang :

> Cattle-men, give me back my goat
> The goat which the Goat-herds gave me ;
> The Goat-herds paid for my dough,
> My dough which the Pestle-pounders gave me ;

The Pestle-pounders paid for my honey,
My honey which the Honey-harvesters gave me ;
The Honey-harvesters paid for my pot,
My pot which the Clay-diggers gave me ;
The Clay-diggers paid for my hoe,
The hoe which the Antelope gave me,
The Antelope who paid the fine for my peas.

They gave him an ox.

*

*　　*

Still going on, he met some people who were tilling the fields. They were working for beer. — "Your lips look very dry," said he to them ; "haven't you anything to eat?" — "No!" said they. He gave them his ox saying : "You must leave a little of the meat for me." They went home with the ox, cooked it, and ate every mouthful ; nothing was left. Then the Hare came and sang :

Workers-for-beer, give back my ox,
My ox which the Cattle-men gave me ;
The Cattle-men paid for my goat.
My goat which the Goat-herds gave me ;
The Goat-herds paid for my dough,
My dough which the Pestle-pounders gave me ;
The Pestle-pounders paid for my honey,
My honey which the Honey-harvesters gave me ;
The Honey-harvesters paid for my pot,
My pot which the Clay-diggers gave me ;
The Clay-diggers paid for my hoe,
My hoe which the Antelope gave me,
The Antelope who paid the fine for my peas.

*

*　　*

They seized him and beat him. When he was quite unconscious, they took him out of the village, thinking he was dead. But he regained his senses and climbed up a tree, which was in the middle of the village, just on the spot where they were all drinking beer ; no one noticed him and, when he reached the top of the tree, he attracted in his direction all the light beer, and the water in the wells, in such a way that it all ran away into the ground, and folks soon found that there was nothing to drink. The little ones cried for water and there was none! The men and the women started out to fetch water, but they could not find any ; the rivers even were all dried up! The little ones died, and so did both women and men! Just a few survived. These went to the Hare, and said to him : "My Lord, we ask for water, as we are dying of thirst." — "Pull up this reed by the roots" said he. All the men, even the strongest, tried hard to pull up the reed, but could not succeed. — "Now," said the Hare, and with one finger he pulled it out of the ground, and forth flowed water and beer, light and strong. Then said he : "Give me five old women." He plunged them in the pond, and drowned them. After this they allotted to him a small province, where he reigned as chief.

*

*   *

The story of the Hare's Hoe is told from one end of the Thonga tribe to the other. I have another version, told me by a young man from Hutwene, near the confluence of the Lebvubye and the Limpopo, that is to say, at the North-Eastern boundary of the Transvaal (in the Maluleke clan). It is more or less identical with the Ronga version up to the moment where the Hare finds the women pounding maize ; they give him a basketful of maize as compensation. He comes to a village where the fowls have nothing to feed on but beetles, and offers his basket of maize to the owners, who throw the entire contents of the basket on the ground, and it is all eaten by the chickens. In compensation the Hare receives some feathers, which they pluck from the cocks and hens. He next comes across some young men dancing the "matangu" dance, and having no other ornaments than blades of grass twined in their hair. He gives them his feathers and, in return, they give him two assagais. The last meeting is with some men engaged in cutting up an elephant with large shells. The Hare gives them his assagais, and receives from them an elephant's tusk. The ending of the story is an adaptation — and to my mind a very inappropriate one — of an episode in the tale of the Year of the Famine, which is well known and often met with in the Ronga folklore. It concludes thus :

The Hare planted the elephant's tusk in his garden, and from it grew a beautiful fruit-bearing tree. There was a famine in the land. Then the Hare said to his wife and children : "I am going a long way off, to shoot eagles ;" but he only went as far as his fruit tree, climbed up it and sang :

> Tshoyo, tshoyo. mangayo !
> I will be the chief mourner for my father.
> I will be the chief mourner for my wife !

At the sound of this song, the fruit fell to the ground and he feasted on it. Returning home he would not eat the vegetables which his wife had prepared. "Give them to the children," said he, "they are hungry."

The next day he repeated the same performance ; pretended to go shooting eagles, but went to his tree and sang :

> Tshoyo, tshoyo mangayo !
> I will be the chief mourner for my father,
> I will be the chief mourner for my wife.

The fruit fell and he feasted on it.

One day his son followed him, without his being aware of it : he heard the singing and, when his father had gone, climbed up into the tree and sang the same words :

> Tshoyo, tshoyo, mangayo !
> I will be the chief mourner for my father,
> I will be the chief mourner for my wife!

The fruit fell and he feasted on it ; he also put a quantity of the fruit in his hair. When he got home he said to his mother: "Mother, fetch a basket, and take away in it all the lice which are biting me." She combed his hair, and fruit fell out of it. — "There" said he, "this is what father feasts upon, whilst we are dying of starvation. Come with me and I will show you where he finds it." She followed him and they sang the refrain :

> Tshoyo, tshoyo, mangayo!
> I will be the chief mourner for my father,
> I will be the chief mourner for my wife !

The fruit fell in quantities until there was no more left on the tree. They feasted on it, and she filled a basket full of it and buried it in her hut. The husband went again to his tree to find fruit, but all was gone. Then he returned home, and was glad to partake of the vegetables prepared for him by his wife. — "It is odd" said she, "you seem quite hungry to-day."

247

When the famine was over, the Hare's wife brewed a quantity of beer, and said to her husland : "Invite all your relatives to a beer-drinking, and I will ask all those on my side of the family." When all were assembled round the jars, in the hut, she said : "Allow me to pass," and went to the back of the hut ; there she unearthed the basket of fruit. Then she told all what the Hare had done during the famine. Her relatives, shocked and angry, took her away with them, together with her children, and she left her husband.

VI. *The Wisdom of the little ones.*

The following Thonga tales have already been published under this title :

The Man with the Big Sword (Ch. et C. (1), p. 144). *Piti* (Ch. et C., p. 151). *Mutipi* (Ch. et C., p. 158). *The Little Hated one* (Ch. et C., p. 170). *Sabulana, the friend of the gods* (Ch. et C., p. 266). *Sikulume* (Les Ba-Ronga, p. 286). *Mutikatika* (Les Ba-Ronga, p. 303).

I add to these the pretty story of *The Disobedient Child and the Big Snake* and a new tale, *The Magic Cattle*, which is very different from the others and, for this reason, is quite worthy of being published. It was written by one of the pupils of the Rikatla Training School.

THE DISOBEDIENT CHILD AND THE BIG SNAKE.

A man had three children. The eldest and the second one started out for a walk in the forest. Their mother said to them : "If you see any of that large fruit, the sala (2), you must not eat it, and if you come across any tracks of snakes you must not follow them." When they got into the forest, the elder of the two saw a fine sala hanging on a tree ; he plucked it, and broke it open (to eat the pulp.). His younger brother said : "Take care! Mother told us we were not to eat sala ;" but the elder beat him, and made him keep quiet. Soon they saw traces of a snake on the sand. The elder said : "I'm off!

(1) Ch. et C. abbreviation for "Les Chants et les Contes des Ba-Ronga," Lausanne, Bridel.

(2) The fruit with a hard shell, about the size of a large orange, which has often been mentioned. (See p. 16).

I'm going to follow the tracks!" — "No," said his brother, "mother told us not to!" but he only got another beating, and was forced to hold his tongue. The tracks led them to a spot where they found a boa, which the elder killed ; he then lit a fire by rubbing together two pieces of wood, cooked part of the boa and ate it. The younger one refused to eat his share, so the other cooked some more and ate that too ; in fact he went on cooking and eating, until he had swallowed the entire snake. When it was time to go home he found he couldn't move! Impossible to walk! The younger brother had almost to carry him, and at length, with great trouble, they managed to reach home. But the poor boy was very ill!

Then the parents sent a messenger to call the Big Snake, the great physician who was called "Chicken's Wing." The messenger went close to the hole, and sang as follows :

> Tse, tse, tse, tse, Zi-nkinto-nkinto !
> Do come and see the sick child, Tli-li-mamba,
> His father has sent me to you, Tli-li-mamba,
> He told me to seek for the doctor so clever,
> The doctor so wise. Chicken's Wing, Tli-li-mamba.

The Snake slowly poked his head out of the hole and looked around, when the messenger was so terror-stricken that he dropped his weapons and fled. Others tried and failed in the same manner. At last the mother said : "I can't let my son die thus ;" so she went herself to the Snake's hole and sang :

Tse, tse, tse, tse, etc.

The great head came slowly out of the hole, and the two big eyes glared at her! In her fright she threw away her basket, and ran away. Then the youngest child, who was not yet weaned, said : "I can't bear to see my poor brother die like this!" So he went off alone to the hole and sang in his baby tones :

> Tse, tse, tse, tse, Qi-to, ito !
> Do tum and see sz' sick tild, Ti-li-mamba.
> His fader has sent me to'oo, Ti-li-mamba.
> He told me to seek for sz' doctor so 'tever,
> Sz' doctor so wise, Ticken's Wing, Ti-li-mamba.

The Big Snake's head came slowly out of the hole, and looked straight at the child, who never moved, but sang once more :

Tse, tse, tse, tse, etc.

He stood where he was, perfectly fearless! Then the Big Snake said : "Very well! Just wait while I go and fetch my little calabash

249

of medicines, and my vapour bath apparatus." He came completely out of his hole. The child did not say a word. — "Carry me" said the Snake. — "How'tan I?" I not big'nuff!" — "Never mind, try and carry me all the same." The child still objecting, the Snake wound himself all round him, so that only his legs and eyes could be seen ; in this way the child carried the Doctor to the village. — "Is it very far?" asked the Snake. — "No, only a little way." In due course they arrived ; birds, fowls, and folks, all fled at the sight of them! The child entered the hut where his sick brother was lying, and the Snake unrolled himself. The patient was terribly swollen, for the sala which he had eaten had resumed its original shape, and the boa he had cooked had resuscitated inside him. Doctor Chicken's Wing administered his drugs, put up his mats round the boy, and gave him a vapour bath.

While the bath was in progress, the little child began to sing :

> Titilo ! Mother told us, you know, Titilo,
> Not to follow the tracks of the snake, Titilo.
> Yet you started by picking the sala, you know,
> And you swallowed it down just as fast as t'would go !

The Snake took up the words and sang in its turn :

> Tsungo, tsungo, ndlontiba !
> Mother told you, ndlontiba,
> After snakes not to go, ndlontiba,
> Yet the sala you plucked, ndlontiba,
> Broke the shell, the juice sucked, ndlontiba.

Then the boa which was inside the boy, began to crawl out of his mouth. The sala came out first, as the boa pushed it in front of him, and continued pushing it with his head until he reached the very spot in the forest where the disobedient boy had eaten it ; then the boa slid away to his own home.

*

*   *

The father then asked the Big Snake what reward he could give him for having cured his son. The doctor replied : "Give me an old iron ring which is of no more use to you." The father gave it. The Big Snake thanked him, and said to the youngest child : "Take me back again to my hole." But the father offered to send some grown up men to accompany him. — "No," said he, "I wish to be taken back by the little one." So he again rolled himself round the child, and together they left the village as they had entered it.

Later on the little one came safely home.

The Magic Cattle.

There was once a chief who ruled over a big country, as big as the district of Lourenço Marques. This chief possessed a very great many cattle, so many that they could not be counted. But an epidemic came to that country, and killed all the people ; only two little boys were left, who were twins, the children of the dead chief. These children lived on cows'milk ; they had never tasted food cooked in pots. The cattle too did not know anything of human beings, for they were very numerous, and the boys had only been seen by those quite near to them.

In a certain year a hunter set out from another country, the country of Mosapa ; he made a long journey, hunting wild beasts, and he came upon the cattle, which were so many that they had eaten up all the grass and only the earth was left to them. This hunter returned home, and told his chief that he had found a land which was full of cattle, and the chief organised a warlike expedition to go and carry them off. The soldiers came into the midst of the cattle which the hunter had shown to them ; they were very pleased, and looked forward greatly to eating the flesh of the oxen. But when the warriors tried to transfix one of them, the assegai was bent and all their other weapons broke, and the bullets from their rifles would not enter the bodies of the oxen. Then they were greatly astonished at seeing such oxen, and were very unhappy in their greed, for they saw the meat before their eyes, but could not eat it.

Then the general of the army sent troops from all sides to drive the cattle together ; some went to the right, some to the left, others remained in the centre, in the main body of the army. It took them fourteen days to get all the cattle together. Playing on their flutes, they tried to return back with them to their chief, but however much they beat them, the cattle would not move, and even though they bit them with their teeth, it was of no use. So the soldiers were in great distress because the cattle refused to move, and hunger came upon them and killed them.

On a certain day two young men climbed up a tree and looked at the herd from afar ; and they saw, in the midst of the cattle, two which were as big as the school building at Rikatla. The young men were greatly astonished to see such big oxen as that ; they went in that direction, passing through the herd until they came into the middle of it ; this took them seven days. It was here that the twin children were living, and now for the first time they saw human beings. They had no house ; they slept beneath the big ox, which always stood on its feet. And the vessels into which they milked the cows they put beneath the other big ox.

The young men asked the boys : "Whose cattle are these?" They answered : "They are ours ; our father left them to us." Then the young men said : "Come, let us go." So the boys fastened their wooden vessels on to one of the big oxen, and they themselves climbed on to the back of the other, and they began to sing the song with which they drive the cattle (1).

Then the ox on which they were mounted bellowed and began to run, and they came to the place where the army was. The soldiers were greatly astonished to see these boys on their ox ; they said : "It is a miracle." Then the young men who had found the boys said to the warriors : "Do not kill them!" So the soldiers asked them to give them an ox, so that they might kill it. The boys began to sing their song,

Let it die !

Then the soldiers killed a great number of oxen instead of only one.

After that the warriors asked that the cattle should be driven to the land of their chief, and the boys sang their song, saying :

Let them go !

and all the cattle began to run ; even the old ones found strength to run, the army following behind.

When they reached the land of the chief, he said : "Let the big ox be killed!" The boys sang their song and the ox died. When they had finished cutting it up, the sun was setting ; the chief commanded that it should be covered with grass, but that its limbs should not be pulled apart, saying that it could be prepared the next day.

In the middle of the night the boys sang :

Let it come to life again !

---

(1) This song is in Zulu, but I did not succeed in discovering its meaning.

and the ox came to life again ; they sang the song to drive the cattle, and all the cattle in the country and all the tame animals, from the biggest to the smallest, ran after the oxen of the boys. The people of the country slept that night a deep sleep, like death.

When they woke up in the middle of the day, there was nothing left in the country, not even a hen. The chief sent his army to pursue the boys and the cattle, but the boys crossed a big river in which the water was boiling, the army following close behind them. The boys sang the song to cross the river, and the water opened a way for them. When they had reached the other side, the water began to flow again. The army came up, and entered the water, and all the warriors who entered it were drowned. Only one man remained ; he waited, expecting to see all the warriors come out on the other side. When he saw no one, he tried to dip his stick into the water, but his stick caught fire. He ran away, horribly frightened, and told the story to his chief But the chief had now no one left to send in pursuit.

The two boys went to live in the place whence they had fled with their cattle.

This is the story : that is the end of it.

VII. *The Ogre Tales.*

See the following already published :

Nyandzumula-ndengela (Ch. et C., p. 198). *Ñwamubya* (Ch. C., p. 203). *Ngumba-ngumba* (Ch. et C., p. 200). *Namashuke* (Ch. et C., p. 221). *Ñwahungukuri* (Les Ba-Ronga, p. 311). *Mbukwana* (Les Ba-Ronga, p. 313). In the first edition I published the long story of *The Ogre Scaly-Heart*, in place of which I here give *The Ziniko Ogres.* This tale was also written for me by one of my pupils in Rikatla. I have chosen it because it affords a good example of the fact already mentioned that Thonga story-tellers are apt to mix tales of very different kinds in a way which is not always very intelligent. Here the ogre tale suddenly becomes an animal tale : the ogre Ziniko changes into the Hare. The narrator seems to have felt that this passing from one class to another was not desirable, and tried to justify it by stating that, as an ogre does not possess an altogether human character, he can transform himself into an animal !

253

The Ziniko Ogres.

There was once a man who was married to a woman.

This man set out for Johannesburg. As he was leaving, he commanded his wife never to drive away the hens. The woman obeyed his command for a long time, until her husband was on the point of returning home. But on a certain day the woman set to work to crush her mealies, and she placed her child on the ground a little way off. Whilst she was pounding the mealies, the baby woke up, and the mother went to it. Then the hens came to the mealies ; seeing this, the woman cried psaa (this is the expression used to drive away hens or birds) ; she had forgotten the command. Then all the hens flew away.

Seeing this, she set out in pursuit of them and went on till sunset ; but the hens flew across a river which was in that place, and she could not cross it. Close at hand she saw a little path, which she followed ; she came to a place where there was a hut standing alone ; there was nobody in it. She entered the hut ; on the ground there was a great quantity of animals' bones. She sat down there. Suddenly she heard a great noise ; it was the Zinikos coming back. She looked, and saw that they had all only one arm and one leg. Then she hid herself in the midst of the bones.

When they came to the entrance of the village, they placed themselves in line one behind another, the little ones in front and the big ones behind. They carried pieces of wood and the flesh of wild animals ; and they said :

"Ziniko - Ziniko ; Ziniko khogoloo ; Ziniko - Ziniko, Ziniko ppu khogoloo - Ziniko khogoloo - Ziniko khogolooo!"

They lit a fire, roasted their meat, and ate. When the time came to go to bed, they sent one of their number to go and light a fire in the hut ; he refused, and they disputed amongst themselves. Then another got up saying : "Ziniko - Ziniko ; Ziniko khogoloo - psee" and lit the fire. Suddenly he perceived an agreeable smell, and looked to see where it came from, but finding nothing, he called his companion : "Ziniko - Ziniko, come here." His comrade came, and he too perceived the agreeable smell ; they both looked carefully, and at last they discovered the woman. When they had found her, they called the others, who came up saying : "Ziniko - Ziniko - khogoloo - khogolooo."

Then they questioned the woman, asking her who she was ; but she trembled with fear. Then they said : "Give us your child's arm so

254

that we may eat it." She trembled and was terrified and said to them : "But he will die, my child!" They answered : "Are we dead? We have not got both our arms either ; we have only one arm and one leg! Give us the arm, so that we may eat it." They spoke angrily. Then she gave them her child's arm, and they ate it.

Then they asked for the leg, and she gave it to them ; they cut it off and ate it. Finally, they said : "Now give us what remains, to end up with." And they tore the child from her and cut it in two.

When they had finished, they said : "Now we want you, to eat." She began to cry, but they cut her in two and in a trice they had eaten her up. Then they took the two skulls and stuck them up on poles at the door of the hut.

Some days passed, and the husband came back from the Transvaal. Seeing that there was nobody in the house, he set out to follow the footprints of his wife along the way by which she had gone ; he too walked till sunset and saw the little path which his wife had taken and came to the hut where the Zinikos lived. Then all at once he saw the heads of his wife and child at the door of the hut, but he turned back and went home. He went to fetch his bow and many arrows ; then he returned to the Zinikos' dwelling, entered the hut and hid himself.

Then he heard the noise that they made as they came home ; when they came to the entrance of the village they stopped again as before, the little ones in front, saying :

"Ziniko - Ziniko ; Ziniko khogoloo ; Ziniko - Ziniko ; Ziniko khogo-looo." They lit a fire and roasted some meat. When they were ready to go to bed, they sent a little one to light the fire in the hut. He did not refuse, thinking perhaps that he would find meat there. He took a small lighted torch and said : "Ziniko - Ziniko ; Ziniko khogoloo - psee." But before he had time to blow up his fire, the man transfixed his face with an arrow and he fell dead, face downwards ; he did not even utter a cry.

Ten minutes passed, and he did not come out of the hut ; then they sent another, saying : "The first is enjoying himself, eating the bones, go and beat him." The second entered the hut, but the same thing happened to him as to the first ; and the same with a third, until they were all dead without knowing what was happening. Only the chief and his counsellor remained. Then the chief said to his counsellor : "They are all mad! Go and beat them." But the counsellor refused to go, saying : "Listen, chief, there is something in the hut." But the chief grew very angry and the counsellor made up his mind to go. As he was going into the hut, the man said to him : "Take that, then you will understand." The counsellor fell back, with his arms stretched out.

Seeing this, the chief grew afraid, and asked : "Ha, Ziniko, what are you doing, falling like that?" But the counsellor did not answer, for he was dead. The chief however had not noticed this, and continued to question him, walking angrily up and down, and saying : "Aha, Ziniko, why did you fall down?"

The man saw that the chief was running away, so he shot an arrow after him, but he missed him, he did not transfix him. The chief continued to run, shouting : "Ziniko - Ziniko - Ziniko," for he could not be silent. He ran in the direction of a certain little hut. When he reached it, he took down an arm and a leg, and fitted them on. At that moment the man came up, and not recognising him, said : "Have you not seen the chief of the Zinikos?" He answered : "No, I have not seen him." The man questioned him closely, but he continued to deny it, until at length the man stopped questioning him. He remained in that place and the two made friends, but the man did not know that it was Ziniko.

*

*   *

Then they went to buy some goats. Ziniko bought a billy- goat and the man a nanny-goat, but there was very little water in that place. So they tried to think of a trick to get water. Ziniko at once hit on a very clever plan. He said : "Let us prepare the skin of a hare, and I will put it on." (This is not surprising, for we know that he was not altogether a man.) So they prepared the skin and they sought also for some bees' honey. They put this honey into a calabash, and they took another calabash to put their water in ; they prepared everything with great care, for the well from which they could draw water was guarded by very clever and powerful beings, so they had to act with great cunning.

The next morning Ziniko took his calabashes and went to the well, (1) but now he is no longer Ziniko, he is the Hare. Having come to it,

---

(1) This is the well-known episode of the well in the Romance of the Hare. We have already met with another version of the story (p. 226). This seems to be the typical one. It has been published in a more complete and picturesque form in Ch. et C. p. 127.

he began to knock the calabashes together, so that they said : "Gelebete - gelebete - gelebete, gelebete - gelebete - gelebetee..." Then the guardian of the well answered : "Who are you?" He said : "It is I, the Hare!" "What do you want?" "I should like some water." The guardian said : "Come!" thinking that he would be able to seize him, and bind him. But just as he was approaching the well, the Hare said : "Taste that!" (1) The guardian, having tasted the honey, forgot all about seizing him, and said : "Give me some more." The Hare answered : "No, that honey is not good. It will only be good if I tie your legs together behind ; then it will be really excellent." The guardian of the well said at once : "Very well, tie me ;" and the Hare tied his legs together with a very strong rope. Then he began to beat him, saying : "There, that is the good taste of the honey!" Then he went to draw water, and bathed in the well. When he had had enough of this, he hung the two calabashes round his neck and returned home without having unbound the guardian. When the Lord Elephant and the Lord Lion arrived, they found the guardian of the well bound. They asked him : "What is the meaning of this?" He answered : "It is the Hare who has bound me!" They put another guardian in his place, but the same thing happened ; they put still another, but the same thing happened. In the end, they put the Toad there, so that he might catch the Hare without being seen.

In the morning the Hare arrived, swinging his calabashes : Gelebete - gelebete - gelebeteee, gelebete - gelebete - gelebeteee, gelebete - gelebete - gelebeteee... He knocked his calabashes together three times, because nobody answered ; then, seeing that all was quiet, he said to himself : "They have given up! They dare not try again!" Then he went in, drew water, and bathed ; but when he tried to go out, he felt that he was caught. He tried very hard to see what it was that had seized him by the leg, and discovered that it was the Toad. Then he took him, killed him, and hung him up on a tree.

When the others came back, they found the Toad hung up ; then they put in his place the Frog, who seized the Hare and did not let him go until the others had come up and found him. They made him prisoner. He said to them : "It would be a good thing if you were to learn from me how to kill somebody with a bow ; place me a little way off, and

(1) In Ronga : A ku mu nampsiso, a nice example of a derivative descriptive adverb. A = he ; ku = said ; mu = him ; nampsiso, from nampsa = ku taste ; derivative causative nampsisa = to make one taste ; o, final vowel employed to form descriptive adverbs.

then you can shoot at me." So they took him and placed him where he had told them, but he took to his heels and ran away. They ran after him, but could not catch him ; he left them far behind.

*

*   *

Now the Hare had bought a goat, and also his companion, the young man who had killed all the Zinikos. The young man's goat gave birth to a kid during the night. The Hare took the kid and put it beside his billy-goat. Then he called his companion and said to him : "See! my goat has given birth to a kid!" The man was greatly astonished, and said : "Is it really possible for a billy-goat to produce a kid?" The Hare answered : "Certainly ; it has produced it." They disputed together a long time. At length the young man ceased to argue, and said : "Very well, it is your kid." But another day, the young man set out, saying : "I am going home, I am going to see my father." On the way, he bought some mourning clothes, and came back without having been home at all. The Hare was startled when he saw him, because the young man had put on his mourning clothes. He asked : "What has happened at your home?" He answered : "My father has lost a child to which he had given birth." Then the Hare was astonished, and said : "Has it ever been known for a man to give birth to a child?" The young man answered : "But did you not say that your billy-goat had given birth to a kid?" The Hare said goo (was greatly embarrassed) and drove·his comrade away.

*

*   *

However, those whom he had left behind in his flight were still in pursuit of him. On a certain day Madam Antelope met him. On seeing her, he greeted her : "Good day, Madam Antelope." She said to him : "Oho! Now you are caught!" But he said : "Why, what harm have I done?" She said : "Was it not you who ran away from the well?" But he answered : "No, it was not I." Then they lived together and became friends. Whilst they were living together, the Hare said : "It would be a good thing if we were to kill our mothers." (1)

(1) See a similar episode p. 236, another proof of the plasticity of Thonga folklore.

258

So the Antelope went and killed her mother, but the Hare did not kill his, and he went and brought her food secretly, so that the Antelope should not know. But in the end the Antelope noticed it, and she killed the Hare's mother whilst he was away. When he went to give her food, he found her dead ; then he came back very sad, and went and sat down on the side where the smoke was blowing, and began to shed tears, as if it was the smoke that annoyed him, but this was a trick of his so that he could cry. His companion said to him : "Why are you shedding tears?" He answered : "It is the smoke which annoys me." She said : "Come on this side." But there too it was the same thing. Then she questioned him again, and he answered : "You have killed my mother, and now you ask why I am crying?" The Antelope said : "Was it not you who deceived me?" She drove him away, and so they parted company.

VIII. *Moral Tales.*

The following have been already published :

The Girl and the Whale (Ch. et C., p. 277) ; *The Road to Heaven* (Ch. et C., p. 237) ; *Nabandji, the Toad's Girl* (Ch. et C., p. 264) ; *Halandi and Mayiwane* (Ch. et C., p. 242) ; *Titishane's Cat* (Ch. et C., p. 253) ; *The Lazy Woman* (Ch. et C., p. 257) ; *Charity rewarded* (Ch. et C., p. 270) ; *Longoloka* (Les Ba-Ronga, p. 327) ; *The Bounder-of-the-plain* (Les Ba-Ronga, p. 353), a totemic tale, similar to Titishanes'cat.

I reproduce here the tale of *Zili*, which was first published in the Report of the S. A. A. A. S. for 1904, Vol. III, p. 250. It is one of the most striking of all and its graphic description of the torments of conscience is wonderful. The song illustrating it, in two parts, is also very curious and will be again mentioned. (See tune 34, later on.)

ZILI.

A man named Zili married a woman. One day he said to her : "It is a long time since we went to visit thy parents. Prepare a pot of beer and let us go." She put the pot on her head and set out. He led her by a path which was new to her, a road which no one used. — "Why dost thou lead me here?" she said. — "Never mind, it is another way," answered he. They came to a tree and rested beneath it. The woman objected : — "There is no room to sit down." — "Just sit down and set down thy pot of beer, that I may drink" said he. She gave it to him. He drank. Then he caught hold of her and killed her. He cut off her head, her arms, her legs, everything that had human shape. Those limbs he wrapped in a truss of grass, and went and hung them up at the top of the tree. As for the remainder of the body, he skinned it, cut the flesh into strips, which he also wrapped up in grass, and took them with him on his way.

Soon a bird began to sing :

> Zili! Amasesendini, amasendi baba! — Si loyile, sesendini!
> I nyama mune yakunhati! Sesendin!
> I kala nkila ka lihondjo! Sesendin!
> Zili! Amasesendini, amasendi, old man! — You are a witch, sesendini!
> What's that kind of meat ? Sesendin !
> It has got no tail ! It has no horn ! Sesendin !

— "What bird is this that sings and calls me by name?" said he. He threw his stick at the bird and killed it. Then he lifted his burden, and went on his way. But the bird rose again ; it followed him, passed close to him, flapping its wings, *pfu... pfu...*, perched on another tree, and sang its song once more. Zili astonished, exclaimed : "How is it the bird follows me thus? Is it possible that I did not kill it outright?" He gave chase to it, knocked it down, tore it limb from limb and threw the mangled remains to the winds. Once more he picked up his load, and continued his journey.

But behold, the bird gathered together its scattered limbs, and came back to life. Zili again pursued it a long way, and again killed it. He lighted a fire with the wooden flint. Then he laid the dead bird on the wood and watched it slowly burn to ashes. He then ground the ashes to powder, and scattered it far and wide. He remained sitting a long time at this place. As the bird did not return, he said to himself : "This time it is quite dead." He then resumed his journey and duly arrived with his load at the village of his parents-in-law.

They hastened to meet him : — "Here is Zili. Good-day, Zili!" They took from his hands the truss of grass filled with flesh ; they bade him enter the hut, and, before untying the bundle, they asked for news of his home. Then his mother-in-law took up the bundle ; — "To-day" said she, "thou dost treat us as princes!" And she began to open it. But, lo! swiftly and silently the bird arrived, and, perching on the top of the hut in which they were sitting, it began its song :

> Zili ! Amasesendini, amasendi, old man ! — You are a witch, sesendini !
> What's that kind of meat ? Sesendin !
> It has got no tail ! It has no horn ! Sesendin !

Zili kept quiet. —"What a curious bird's song that is!" said his parents-in-law. Others said, however : "Oh, it is only a bird." And the bird sang on.

"How did you leave our daughter at home?" inquired the parents. — "Quite well" answered he. "She will soon come herself." But the bird continued its song : "Zili, etc."

At last the bird flew into the hut. They drove it out, but it would not keep silent. The people began to understand what it said. Zili trembled, but said not a word. The bird then went to sing in the ears of the mother, as she began to roast the flesh Zili had brought. She understood and fell fainting.

Then the men of the village turned to Zili : — "What does this mean? What bird is this that follows thee and calls thee by name?" But Zili declared : "The bird came not with me. I heard it here for the first time in your hut." — "If that is so, come and let us see our child," said they.

They set off, the bird flying before them, and they following its guidance. It led them to the big tree in the bush, and began to sing loudly close to the truss of grass which Zili had hung up. Some one climbed up the tree, and untied the bundle. They opened it, and, at once, the men recognized the girl's face and the bracelets she wore on her wrists and ankles. They seized Zili and bound him. Some of them went on to summon Zili's relations all into one hut. When the others arrived they threw Zili, still bound, into the hut and then set fire to it.

So died Zili and his relations.

IX. *Tales founded on real facts.*

This is a new category which I have not mentioned in previous publications, but which is, I think, well defined. In it I would include the well-known and wide-spread theme of the *Year of famine* (Ch. et C. p. 260) and the following two curious stories : "*The Child that was carried off by the Baboon*" (a fact which may very well have happened), and "*Those who laugh but once.*" The latter is an example of ironic popular folklore, a branch of literature which is met with in many countries, and consists in making fun of people of a certain village or region. In Switzerland the village of which one makes fun and tells stories is never lacking!

Those who only laugh once are said to dwell near Inyaka Island, in the Maputju Country. But the story-teller, to whom I owe this amusing tale, Jeremia Lomben, asserted that they are an imaginary clan. However, the words *Makwetjhu, tjhwala,* quoted as pronounced by them, are a deformation of makweshju and shjwala, their ordinary form in the Maputju dialect, and it is said, that, in a certain spot of Inyaka Island, this altered pronunciation is really met with. So this tale has probably been applied to the Inyaka people, although it originally concerned another clan now forgotten. Natives take an immense delight in making fun of what they esteem an erroneous pronunciation, each clan laughing at the other for peculiarities of dialect.

The child that was carried off by a baboon.

A man started out with all his belongings and went to marry a wife in a foreign country. The woman lived with him for a long time, and had a daughter. One morning she went out to work in the fields, but could find no one to carry her baby. When she got to the field, she hoed a large plot of ground ; she laid her baby on the ground, and put it to sleep. A baboon arrived on the scene, and began to play with the child without anyone seeing it. Soon after the mother saw what was going on, but said nothing, for she knew that, if she made a noise, the baboon might kill the little one. But the baboon presently picked up the child and climbed up into a high tree. The woman said : "You can play with him, if you like, but be gentle and don't hurt him." The baboon replied : "If you make any noise, and if you call the folks to help you, I can easily crush him against the tree." So she kept quiet, and the baboon jumped from tree to tree. When she lost sight of it, she did not say anything, but went on hoeing, and soon the baboon managed to slip away unobserved. When she finally lifted her head, and looked around, she could not see the baboon anywhere, neither could she find her child. She looked intently at the tops of all the trees, without seeing anything. Then she threw down her hoe, and went to search for the baby. She walked a long way and shouted loudly, but with no result. She climbed to the top of a hill, for, she said : "As the baboon went by the tops of the trees perhaps he will hear me better if I get on a high place too." There she sang a song, which was both an appeal and a lament for her little one. (See tune 35, later on.)

> Baboon! Ravisher! What have you done with my child? Tell me! My
> heart is anxious,
> I must go, I must go home quickly to my master! Alas! (1)

Not knowing in which direction to continue the pursuit, she went to enquire at a village. She said : "Have you, by any chance, seen a baboon, which had a child with it?" — "Yes," they replied, "one has just passed by : there are its footprints still in the sand, and the hole it made to hold the little one's calabash." She started on again, in all haste, walked a long way, following the marks as much as possible, but she could not find the pair, for the baboons are curious animals, and when they are tired, they spring from one tree-top to another. The woman searched in many places and went everywhere singing her lament and weeping. She sang :

> Baboon! Ravisher! What have you done with my child? Tell me! My
> heart is anxious.
> I must go, I must go home quickly to my master! Alas!

Then she turned homeward. Night was coming on. Before reaching her home, she cut down the trunk of a tree, which was about the size round of a child. She cut it so that it was rather fatter in the middle, and thinner at the two ends : then she put this in the skin which she had used for carrying her baby, and, feeling very sad, went back to her village. She took care to cover the piece of wood with a cloth so that folks could not, at once, see what she was carrying. She went into the yard of her mother-in-law's house, who said to her : "What does this mean? How is it that you are coming back so late at night?" — "It isn't my fault," said she, "it is the child's : she is feverish." — "Well! if she is feverish, that is just why you ought to have come home earlier!" — "No, I wanted to hoe a small patch and sow my maize, but even now, I have not been able to hoe a piece worth mentioning, and have brought my seeds back with me." The mother-in-law was silent ; but shortly afterwards she said : "Put the child down, so that I can have a look at her ; you are not going to sleep with her on your back to-night, are you?" — "I will put her down when she wakes up," said she, and the mother-in-law said nothing more.

(1) The words of this song are half Zulu.

When the husband came home, he asked his wife similar questions. He said : "Put the child down on the ground so that I can see her ; it won't hurt her, even if she is not very well." The wife went about from spot to spot, doing her work, and hoping thus to distract her husband's attention, and prevent him asking her any awkward questions ; at last she went into her hut to go to bed. Her husband said to her : "Didn't I tell you to lay the child on the ground, so that I might have a look at her? If she is ill, never mind ; she will die in my arms, I who am her father!" In spite of his insisting, the woman would not obey him. Then the man became very angry ; he took his assagai and slit open the skin in which the baby was carried, when out fell the log of wood! — "Is this what you were hiding?" cried he. "Is this my child?" Irritated to a degree, he went out and called his relations to come and see what had taken place in the hut and to look at the block of wood. He wanted to kill his wife, but the relations said : "Don't kill her ; we will begin by examining her, and trying to find out how all this has happened, how it is that her child is changed into a log of wood." The poor woman, all faint and trembling said : "I fear it is all up with me to-day!" Then she told them just what had occurred saying : "It was while I was hoeing : and you know that I had no one to take care of the baby." Her relations replied : "It is quite clear to us that you have killed your baby ; she was not carried off by any baboon. If a baboon had done this, why didn't you rush home and tell us about it? We would have aroused all the men in the village, and they would have followed it until they caught it."

They turned the woman out of the village : perhaps they killed her, I am not quite sure.

THOSE WHO ONLY LAUGH ONCE (BA KA MAHLEKA-KANWE).

These folks lived in a country by the sea, a country that was quite cut off from all other countries by an immense marsh of papyrus. They were all able to go across this quagmire, for they knew just where to plant their feet. (No one ever went to see them, for those who were not accustomed to jump from one clod of earth to another were apt to fall into the slimy mud). They were called "Those who only laugh once," for when they burst out laughing, they only got as far as "Ha! ;" they could not go on : "Ha! ha! ha! ha!" That was their infirmity. — Now their chief never had any occasion to assemble the army for warlike expeditions, because his people were entirely separated from all the rest of the world. However, some of his folks, having gone to visit a neighbouring country, heard that the army had gone out to battle, and saw the warriors dancing and celebrating their doughty deeds before the chief. On their return home, they said to their own chief : "Call our army together too and let us go out to fight wild boars!" So they started out for the big forest, where the wild boars are to be found, and roused them up about noon ; one man ran his assagai through a boar and cried out : "Tjhokota makwetjhu, ndi tlhabile sha ku tjhwala nkumbu ndi nomu!" — "Ho! my brother, extol my prowess! I have slain a beast which carries his nose on top of his mouth!" The other replied : "Ho! it is a wild boar." They returned home, and their chief entertained them quite royally, because they had shown themselves so valiant in the fight.

On another occasion they heard far off in the distance a noise : "Huuum!" They cried : "Chief, call the army together! To arms, every one of you!" They all went to get their assagais. Again they heard a quail: "Huuum!" — "It is over there!" they said, and proceeded very slowly and cautiously in the direction of the sound. Once more they heard : "Huuum!" — "It is some huge wild beast," they cried ; "Let us be after it!" So they all began to stamp on the ground together : "Rji, rji, rji," and holding the assagai in one hand and the shield in the other they formed a circle round the enemy and gradually closed in on him. Suddenly : "Whirrr!!" (1) and up got a quail! The whole army were so startled that they fell over backwards! When they recovered from the shock, they all went home, feeling very much ashamed of themselves.

X. *Foreign Tales.*

Under this title I have already published in "Les Chants et les Contes des Ba-Ronga" : *Bonawasi* (p. 291) ; *The three Vessels* (p. 364) ; *Likanga* (p. 309) ; *The Boy and the Big Snake* (p. 314) ; *The King's Daughter* (p. 317) ; and in Les Ba-Ronga : *The Mice* (p. 352) ; *Big Head* (p. 339).

I have since collected others and now publish one of them, the *Unnatural Mother*. The beginning of the tale is very much the same as that of Longoloka, and may be Bantu. The hunting expedition of the

---

(1) Whirrrr ! is the usual way of expressing the *rising* of a quail or a partridge.

father to Mosapa has certainly been inspired by local circumstances. But the story soon takes on a very different character, and we hear of White people who are cannibals (a strange occurence indeed), and work sugar-mills, and of a man who would like to take a second wife, but is prevented from doing so by the monogamic scruples of his relatives ; the birth of twins is looked on as a misfortune in the true Bantu manner, etc., an extraordinary mixture of wholly incongruous elements. I leave to professional folklorists the task of determining the origin of all these episodes. This tale comes from a middle-aged woman named Martha, (p. 212) who heard it from her grandmother in the Southern part of the Maputju country, when she was a little girl (1875?), at a time "when there were few White people in the country." Those able to reach this remote part of Thongaland were Banyans, rather than Europeans.

These foreign tales, altered as they are by the Native mind, present a special interest, because they show how episodes conceived by the European or Asiatic brain, are changed when related by Africans. I listened to a girl who had stayed in Basutoland, and had brought back with her the story of Cinderella. It was easily recognisable but, instead of the fairy who consoles and advises the heroine of the tale, it was her deceased mother, who, as an ancestor-god (shikwembo), appeared to her on her grave.

The Unnatural Mother and the Girl with a Star on her Forehead.

This is how the tale begins : Once upon a time there was a woman who had a moon on her forehead. In her childhood she lived with her parents. Her parents died. She had a large mirror which had been given to her by her mother. When she was grown up she was married, and went away to her husband, taking her mirror with her. She was fond of bathing, and when she had bathed and arranged her curly hair, she placed her mirror on the table, and said to it : "My mother's mirror, is there any one in the country more beautiful than I am?" The mirror answered : "You are only surpassed in beauty by that which is in heaven" (ṅwa nya ka tilo). Then she felt very happy, took her mirror off the table, and sat down, her mind thoroughly at rest. She became pregnant. Before the child was born her husband left for Mosapa (1).

(1) A country to the North of Gazaland where elephants are still to be found. (I. p. 28.)

He left with his wife the following strict instructions. "I am going to Mosapa to kill elephants. When the child is born, should it die, you just keep for me one of its bones." — "Very well," said she, and the man went off elephant-hunting.

The woman remained at home with her servant, who stayed in the house until she was about to be delivered. When she began to feel the pangs of labour she said to her servant : "Heat some water for me, I would like to take a bath." He put the water on the fire to heat ; afterwards she had a bath, placed her mirror on the table, combed her hair and said to the mirror : "My mother's mirror, is there any one in this country more beautiful than I am?" — "You are only surpassed in beauty by that which is in heaven," was the reply. Then she put away the mirror, spread some blankets on the floor, and gave birth to a daughter. The baby was born after sunset, but she saw that there was a bright light in the house. The villagers were terrified and said : "It looks as if the house were on fire!" This light came from a brilliant star that was on the baby's forehead.

The mother took good care of her little one and laid her on a bed. She bathed and combed her hair as usual but forgot her mirror. The child grew and began to sit up ; she could even stand and walk a few steps . She toddled about in her mother's hut. The village folks were astonished, and said : "What can it be that is burning in the chief's hut?" They did not know that a child had been born. Then the servant told them : "My Mistress (1) has a daughter!"

*

*　　*

The child grew and walked out, holding her mother's hand. One day the mother took the mirror, and bathed the child, and combed her hair. The little one's hair was still more lovely than the mother's, because the star sent out rays of light, like beads upon her head. The mother gazed at her daughter, and began to feel afraid of her. She again asked her mirror : "My mother's mirror, is there any one in the country more beautiful than I am?" The mirror answered : "Think carefully. I told you that you were only surpassed in beauty by that which is in heaven, and by that I meant the infant that was in your

(1) Muhanu, a term by which White women are designated in Ronga. — " Was she really a White woman ?," I asked Martha.   "Yes," she replied.

womb. You are only surpassed in beauty by your child." The woman took the mirror, and broke it ; she was angry, because it had said : "You are only surpassed in beauty by your child." She picked up the pieces and threw them behind a box. She went to her hut, dressed the child and put on its hat. Then she dressed herself and put on her own hat. She put a pretty umbrella into the child's hands, took her own, and they set out together.

They went up a mountain where there was a high road along which many people passed ; the mother said to the folks : "Look at me, and tell me if you think there is any one more beautiful than I am?" They replied: "You are certainly very beautiful, Mother, but the child who is with you is more beautiful than you are." The woman began to feel unhappy, and went home with the child. Each day she went to the mountain road and asked the same question of the passers-by, and they answered : "Assuredly (nyambo) you are beautiful, but you are not so beautiful as your child who has a star on her forehead."

When the child had grown still more, and was about as tall as Nhwanene (1) her mother found a small calabash, which she gave her and sent her to draw water saying : "Don't go to the place where folks generally go to draw water, but go to the spot where there is a high preci- pice." She said to herself : "The child will tumble over and be killed." But the girl did not go to the high precipice; she went to the place where everybody went. When she got home her mother said : "Didn't you hear me when I told you to draw water at the spot where there is a high precipice?" The girl replied : "Mother, I went where you told me to go," for she knew quite well that her mother wanted to kill her.

The woman called her Kafirs (a name given by the Rongas to Native servants), and said to them : "If I told you to kill this girl, would you obey me? I would give you a bag full of money." They said : "Yes." Then she said : "Take the child and kill her. When you have killed her, cut off her little finger and cut out her heart and liver, bringing them back to me, that I may be sure you have really killed her."

The Kafirs said to the young girl : "Let us be off!" They started away together. When they came to a certain spot, they said to her : "Listen! Your mother told us to kill you. If we let you go, will you be able to run far away by yourself?" — "Certainly," said she, "I can easily run away alone. Although I don't know the country, I could easily find

(1) A girl of about ten years of age in the village of Rikatla, where this tale was told.

a home somewhere." — "Will you be brave," they said, "and let us cut off your little finger?" She held up her little finger and told them to cut it off. They did so. She stooped down, tore off a piece of her dress and bandaged the stump : then she ran away, and bathed in the river and in the sea ; wherever she went she bathed.

As for the Kafirs, an antelope suddenly sprang out of the bush, which they hunted until they caught it ; they cut it up, took out the heart and liver, and brought them together with the little finger (1) to their mistress. The woman then thanked them heartily, saying : "You have done well, for my daughter was more beautiful than I am, and that was what depressed me. That is why I wandered about on the mountains, because she was more beautiful than I. Now I ought to be happy!"

* ·
*　　*

The child continued on her way, and came to a large house belonging to White folks, the people of Yibane. She reached this house in the evening, after sunset, and went into it ; it was the chief's house, but it was quite empty : every one had gone out to steal ; those folks stole men, shut them up and ate them. Yibane was their chief. It was for him that they kidnapped people.

As these robbers were returning home they saw a bright light in Yibane's house and started running as fast as they could, crying out : "The house is on fire!" Yibane threw open the door and found the young girl seated on his bed. He said to her : "My daughter, whence do you come?" and embraced her adding : "Now I have indeed found something really beautiful!" Then he changed his mind, and said : "You are not my daughter, you will be my wife ; you will grow up, and you will be my spouse. I will give up all my evil ways, and will cast them away from me!" Accordingly he gave the order : "Go and find all the people you have imprisoned, and set them free. Never again hunt men to kill and eat them." His people thanked him and said : "We will never again eat men as we now have such a beautiful princess!" Yibane said : "Go and bathe and come back clean, all of you, for I have found a lovely wife!" When the girl had grown to be about the height of

---

(1) The story-teller has probably forgotten to state here that the husband returned from Mosapa and that the unnatural mother showed him the little finger, pretending that the child had died.

Shihahanhlanga (1), Yibane ordered the wedding feast to be prepared ; the people went into the marshes to steal sugar-cane and built a large mill (pikawusi) to crush the cane. He went out on this business with all his people, and the young girl remained alone, knowing that she was soon to be married. Just then the little servant who used to play with her when she was quite young, happened to pass by. The girl was at the window and the servant saw her ; he said to himself : "I have never seen any one like this woman, although I have travelled through many lands." He never suspected that it was his former playmate that he saw. He ran back to the girl's mother, and said : "I have seen a girl with a star on her forehead, but she did not see me." The mother said : "See! Take these beautiful slippers ; don't you think she would like to buy them?" The servant replied : "Give them to me ; I will take them to her." He went off in haste, and reached the house one day when Yibane was away, busy crushing sugar-cane. He found the girl at home and offered to sell her the slippers. — "How much do you want for them?" said she. — "Whatever you like to give me," he replied ; "they are very pretty ones." — "Wait a moment : I must just try them on."

She went into the house and put on the slippers. No sooner had she done so than she died. The boy ran home to the mother and told her that the girl was dead. "That is well," said she. "You certainly had the last word!" When Yibane returned from the sugar-mill, and regained his own home, his wife did not come out to meet him. He opened the door and found her lying on the bed ; he thought she was asleep and tried to awaken her, but could not ; then he saw that she was lifeless. His people heard him weeping, turning everything topsy-turvy and saying : "I shall never be able to find a wife as beautiful as she! The best thing I can do is to live alone, for I had centred all my hopes in her!"

He procured a coffin, and lined it with cloth, putting some money into it ; then they carried off the young girl to bury her. But Yibane said: "My wife shall never be put in the ground. Place her on a tree and build a canopy over her, a large canopy of planks, stretching a long way round!" They had to use force to restrain him, for he wanted to kill himself. The people took some silken stuff and made a canopy over the coffin, so that the heat should not hurt it.

(1) Surname of a young girl of Rikatla, named Madonge, who might be about 18 years old.

Thonga Folklore

*

*   *

The chief of that country, as it might be Matlotlomane, (1) had a son. This son went out hunting. He came to the spot, and looking up into the tree said to his servant : "What is it that glitters up there?" He had caught sight of the golden nails which had been used to close the coffin. The servants said : "Let us run and see who can touch the tree first!" The chief's son got there first, the servants later. He said to them : "Climb up the tree and bring down that box : be careful not to let it fall too heavily."

When the coffin was brought down, he unlocked it with the key that was attached to it, and tried to open it. He had hardly raised the lid, when he saw a light inside ; so he closed it again at once, and said to his servants : "Carry it home." They all helped one another, for the box was heavy, and arrived at their village when it was dark. The young man told the servants not to say a word to his father of what they had found : "Only tell him," said he, "that I am not feeling well." He gave them all the game he had killed and said : "Don't bring me any meat : you can eat all the game yourselves ; no one may enter my room!"

He shut himself up in his room, lifted the girl out of the coffin and laid her on the bed ; he sat on the ground weeping, and saying : "I have found my wife : how lovely she is, but, alas, she is dead!" He called his youngest brother, who lived in another room, and said to him : "Bring me some water ; I want to bathe myself." But he used the water to bathe the young girl, thinking she might possibly revive. The parents were astonished to see a bright light in his room. They questioned the servants who had been hunting with him, but they only said : "We don't know anything about it." Then the parents asked : "What is the matter with our son?" The servants replied : "We don't know ; he only told us that he had a headache."

Several days passed. He ate nothing, and drank nothing. He forbade anyone to enter his room. He placed the young girl on another bed, and mourned, and mourned, and mourned her.

One day he placed her on his own bed ; it was in the morning. His brother came in, and found him washing the girl's face. The young

---

(1) Surname given to the Portuguese Administrator, at the post of Morakwen, about one hour and a half's distance from Rikatla.

271

brother said : "Where did you manage to find this lovely thing? I congratulate you ;" and to congratulate him, he shook the girl's leg and took off her slipper ; then he took off the other one, upon which she suddenly awoke, and came to life again. The chief's son thanked his youngest brother and said : "You have acted with great wisdom! I thought you were but a little boy, and you have been wise enough to bring my wife to life again!"

He took two shillings out of his purse, and gave them to the boy. He would not leave his room ; he would not go and visit his mother ; he only wanted to stay and look at the young girl. The elder brother sent the younger to his mother to get some water to bathe the girl. There were many rooms in the house. Then he asked the young girl : "Do you think you could walk?" He took her by both hands, for her limbs were stiff, and led her into one of the rooms, where there was a large bath, and plunged her into it. When she had taken her bath, they were greatly rejoiced, for they saw the star shining brightly on her forehead. The youngest brother went out, but did not dare to tell all these things to his mother, for all the servants had told him : "If you are asked any questions you must conceal the truth." He only went to ask for food for his brother saying : "He is a little better now."

His parents were very glad to know he was recovering. They killed chickens for him, thinking it was he who eat all the meat. They didn't know he had a wife who was soon well enough to eat. She became fat and strong, and nobody knew anything about her.

When the elder brother saw that the girl was in good health once more, he sent the younger out of the room saying : "Now you had better go back to our mother." The younger was annoyed at being turned out like that, so he went and told everything to the parents. He said : "My brother has a wife, but she is not a woman of this country ; when you look at her you are so dazzled that you have to turn your eyes away, but when once you are accustomed to her face, you can't keep your eyes off her." His parents said : "We will go and see her." — "Yes," said he, "but don't let him know that I told you! Go quietly, and when she is seated at table, you will see her." So the parents started to go to their son's room. They saw it was all lit up, and asked the younger brother : "Is it the light of lamps that we see?" — "No," said he, "it is a star that she has on her forehead." They entered the room, while the husband and wife were at table. They greatly admired the beauty of the girl, and were very happy. The mother embraced her saying : "This is indeed a lovely girl!" The father was also much taken with her beauty and said : "This woman would suit me very well as a wife!" The mother rebuked him saying : "I will go away with all my children, if you take this woman as a wife! She is not for you! I am your wife! You have sinned!" (1)

He replied : "That is true! I have sinned. My head was turned by her beauty!" They said to him : "Don't do such a thing again!"

*

*   *

A splendid feast was prepared when the chief's son was married to the young girl. She became with child. Her husband said to her : "I am going to Mosapa to hunt elephants." His wife began to weep. "Oh," said he, "I will come back again, but I can't forget the elephants." Time went on, and the woman became the mother of twins — a boy and a girl. She wrote a letter to her husband, at Mosapa, to tell him the news and sent it to him by a servant. This man passed by the old home of the girl with the star, where the mother was living. Everyone was drinking, and they asked him to drink with them. When he had fallen asleep, the mother took the letter and read it. She saw that it was signed : "she who has a star on her forehead." — "It is from her," cried she, "then she is still alive!" She tore up the letter, burnt it, took another piece of paper and wrote : "Your wife has given birth to two monkeys," putting the paper into the servant's pocket. The servant found the husband, who read : "Your wife has given birth to two monkeys!" Then he wrote in reply : "Never mind! They are mine, don't kill them. I will play with them when I get back." The servant started back on the return journey, and again passed by the village of the girl's mother ; there they made him drink once more, and the woman took the letter and wrote another one, to replace it, which said : "Put out her eyes, cut off the nipples of her breasts ; place one child on her back, and the other on her bosom ; make her walk through the bush, torn by thorns, and pierced by spines, and so let her suffer!" They woke the servant and said to him : "Be off, the sun is already set." He arrived safely at his mistress' village, and handed the letter to her father-in-law, who, when he had read it, burst into tears. The father and mother

---

(1) Monogamic scruples which certainly betray some foreign influence. The "tip of the ear" of Martha, who is upon occasion an earnest preacher of the Gospel, here appears, and this again shows how these tales are altered.

273

were afraid to give the letter to their daughter-in-law ; they said : "Our son has gone mad : he says the children must be killed because they are twins! (1) "They could not make up their minds what to do. Finally they decided that they must give the letter to their daughter-in-law, as it came from her husband, but they said to her : "As for us, we will not touch you to do you any harm. If he wants to have this done, he can do it himself!" The wife said : "No, you must do it." She felt sure this letter did not come from her husband, so she said : "Go and do it." — Then they put out her eyes, cut off the nipples of her breasts, tied one child in front of her, the other behind, and she started out ; she did not walk upright, but crawled along on her hands and knees. She reached the forest, all covered with blood. She got there just at sunset. The sky began to thunder, and spoke to her saying : "My daughter, what do you seek here?" She replied : "I seek nothing. They have put out my eyes, they have cut off the nipples of my breasts, and have driven me from home with one child tied on in front and one behind, so that I should be torn by thorns." The sky continued : "Don't be afraid, my daughter ; go straight on, and if you come to a river, cross it without fear." When she reached the river, she found it was a very big one. "My little ones may be drowned," said she, but added : "Never mind!" She threw herself into the water, and swam across. Under the water she found a steam boat, and when she came out of the river she was in the steam boat, her eyes were back in their places again and also the nipples of her breasts. She sat down, and saw some food prepared, but did not know whence it came. Then she began to eat, and her children played around her.

Now the husband returned from Mosapa with elephant tusks. It was after sunset. He looked all round for his wife, but could not find her anywhere. He made enquiries, and they told him everything. He made no fuss, but only said : "Show me the way she went," and they showed him. He followed her and found little pieces of clothing torn off and strewed all along the way. He came to the forest and passed through it ; he also reached the river without seeing anything of his wife. At last he found her ; the steamboat had disappeared. Once more he saw the star which lit up her face. He also saw her children ; the girl had a star on her forehead like her mother, and the boy had a moon like his grandmother. He smiled on them and took them home without asking any questions. His parents were afraid he would be very angry with them, but nothing even ruffled him.

(1) This idea is evidently Bantu.

*

*   *

When they were all at home again, the wife said to her husband :
"Let us prepare a grand feast, and invite all the country-side, to celebrate
your return and my wonderful cure." — "That's right," said he, "let all
the inhabitants of the country be invited."   Now the wife wanted to get
hold of her mother.   The steamboat brought crowds of people : all
Yibane's folk came and so did the girl's mother.   Quantities of food had
been prepared and all feasted right royally.   The young woman saw her
mother and pointed her out to her husband, saying : "Look, there she
is, the woman who had my finger cut off, who killed me with the slippers,
who put out my eyes and cut off the nipples of my breasts!"
 ' Now there was a large tent in which every one was seated on chairs.
The husband and wife came in, and seated themselves, dressed in their
holiday clothes.   The people were very anxious to look at the wife,
but could not do so, as the brightness of the star on her forehead dazzled
them.   She put a veil over her face and then they were able to gaze upon
her.   As for the mother, she was filled with shame ; she said to herself :
"And I thought I had killed her!"   She trembled.
When they had finished eating, the young wife addressed them :
"Silence!" said she.   "I am going to tell you a story!"   They all
applauded.   She added : "It is not a very long one.   Listen, princes and
subjects.   When you give birth to a beautiful child, do you dare to kill
it?"   The chiefs were astounded at such a question!   "We never
thought such a thing possible." — "Well, I have known such a thing,"
she said.   "Look at my finger!"   Then she began, and told them all
the story ; how her mother had killed her with the slippers, had put her
eyes out and cut off the nipples of her breasts.   The mother was there,
in full view of everyone.   Finally the young woman said to her husband :
"I wish my mother to be killed to day!"   The husband said : "No, leave
her alone." — "No, said she, she must be put to death."
She had a small gun of her own, and with it she shot the mother right
before them all.   The people picked up the body, and went off to bury
it.   As for the young woman, she gave a piece of land to her father, who
said to her : "You have done quite right : I did not know who you were."
She gave him a certain sum of money with which to procure another
wife, and he settled in her village.
That's the end.

CHAPTER III

Music.

Music in a more or less rudimentary form, plays a great part in the Life of the Bantu tribe. Some tribes are more gifted than others in this respect. In the Province of Mozambique the Ba-Chopi are certainly the best musicians, as we shall see. But Thongas are also great singers and players, and their dances are invariably accompanied by music. What is its character? The melodies and rhythms are very difficult to catch, and I do not pretend to give here a full and definite description of Thonga music ; but the following specimens will convey a fair idea of it, and a study of their musical instruments will help us, in some measure, to understand their musical system.

A. MUSICAL INSTRUMENTS.

1) Wind Instruments.

The simplest is the *shiwaya*, an empty sala shell, or the shell of a Kafir orange (p. 19) : it has two holes, one through which children sing, another which they alternately shut and open, the withdrawal of the hand allowing the sound to be emitted ; the result is a monotonous wu-wu-wu, which is sufficient to amuse little boys.

Next in importance comes the *nanga*, (yi-tin) the goatherd's flute, made of the tibia of a goat, or of some other animal, on which the boys play two notes, generally in thirds. This is truly the infancy of art, but the tone of these little flutes is very sweet and wonderfully in keeping with the bush life, the bleating

276

of the goats and the nudity of the artist! There are many kinds of goatherds' flutes. One is called *ndjwebe* ; its sound resembles mbvrrr.... mbvrrr.... Natives are in the habit of putting a feather inside their bone flutes in order to keep them clean.

Another more elaborate flute is made of a reed, having a hole at one extremity for the mouth, and three others at the other extremity for the fingers. According to the number of holes stopped, the sound varies. It is called *shitiringo* (Dj.), or *shitloti* (Ro.), and Native artists are capable of producing pleasing tunes upon it. No. 39 in my collection of tunes is a shitiringo melody, heard on the banks of the Great Tabi.

But the true tinanga are the trumpets which compose the *bunanga*, the band already referred to (I. p. 431) as being one of the manifestations of Court Life. They are also called *timha-lamhala*, from the name of the mhalamhala (Hippotragus niger), the large, dark antelope whose horns are employed for the manufacture of these trumpets, together with the horns of the mhala (impala) antelope. These instruments are tuned according to rule. Ten of them, each having a different sound, form a *simo*, a kind of orchestra, completed by the big and the small drum already described. They are used to accompany the special dances which take place in the little capital of the Ronga clans, and in which the players are themselves the dancers, marching behind each other, with peculiar contortions, narrowing and widening their circle according to the time beaten by the drum.

The bunanga players receive a regular training before going to the capital, to play before the chief. When they have prepared the numbers of their programme, they all go to the capital, each sub-chief leading his band, for a musical contest. The tinduna act as judges. Each *simo* plays in turn. The judges discuss their respective merits, and when they have come to a decision, they call a young man to proclaim the result of the competition. This proclamation is called *ku tjema shibangu*, to cut the contest, and is performed in a very curious way. The herald has an axe in his hand. With a loud voice, he pronounces the verdict : "So and so played badly ; so and so better ; the one who played best is so and so." — "Nkino hi nkhensa wa ka man." Then he beats the trunk of a tree with his axe, as if he wished to confirm the decision, and runs away.   This is to avoid protests and insults from those who did not win!

No. 40 is a tune played by the bunanga.   It is very monotonous and the music is evidently not so important as the dance, the rhythm, and the contortions.   There are only four notes in this tune.   However it is probable that the ten instruments of the simo form a whole octave, with two notes below it, the same as the ten keys of the timbila which will presently be described. Unfortunately I have not been able to ascertain if this is actually so, having only once witnessed the performance of the bunanga. I am afraid the bunanga orchestra of antelope horns has now entirely disappeared from Ronga territory.

2) STRINGED INSTRUMENTS.

As regards stringed instruments, they possess the *unicord harp* called *gubu*.   There are two different forms of it ; the *shitjendje*, which consists of a bent rod, a bow, both extremities of which are united by a string made of milala palm fibres (nkuha), or a piece of wire. On the lower part of the bow a calabash is fixed as sounding box.   The shitjendje is held upright ; one hand grasps it at its lower extremity, whilst the other beats on the lower third of the string with a little stick.   The hand which grasps the instrument places its finger on this lower third of the string in different places, so as to vary the length and produce different sounds.

A gubu player.

In the *nkaku*, the sounding box is fixed in the middle of the bow. From it a wire starts and is tied to the middle of the string, thus dividing it into two equal parts. The instrument is grasped near the calabash, and the fingers are extended on either half of the string to differentiate the sounds. The other hand beats on either side with a stick.

The tune No. 12 was accompanied by a shitjendje.

3) The Timbila or Bantu Xylophone.

The most completely characteristic musical instrument of our tribe is the *timbila*, which may be seen on the accompanying plate showing both the upper and the under side of this very interesting Native piano. It is composed of ten keys, made of very hard wood, attached to each other by straps of leather on a wooden frame consisting of a curved branch. The keys rest on shells of sala, which act as sounding boxes, and in which two holes are pierced, one in the upper part to receive the sound, and one at the side, covered by a membrane, generally a piece of a bat's wing, in order to cause the sound to vibrate. This piano is easy to carry. The player places it in front of him and beats on the keys with one or two sticks, furnished at one extremity with an india-rubber or a leather ball. (See the cover of *Les Chants et les Contes des Ba-Ronga*).

Comparing it with a European piano I have ascertained that the third key is a G flat, and that, if we strike the following ones, up to the last, we obtain a regular major scale, that of G flat, with its proper half tones between the third and fourth and the seventh and eighth intervals. The two lower keys are, the first E flat, the second F natural. The interval from E flat to G flat is a minor third, so that, should we start with the lower key and strike the seven following, we should obtain a minor scale of E flat corresponding to the major scale of G flat : but it would not entirely resemble our harmonic minor scale as there is no "sensible," viz., the seventh note of the scale is not raised. Only when descending from the eighth to the first we should have a perfect melodic minor scale. This minor scale, without the raised seventh, is well known in the history of music : it is called the Eolian scale.

So we find this interesting fact as the result of our examination :

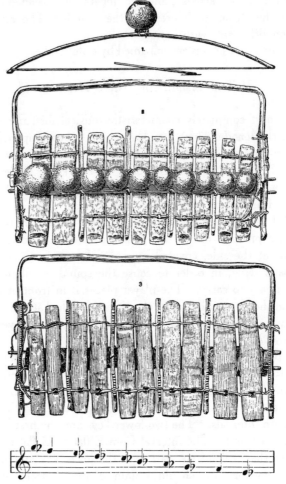

The timbila and its ten notes.

the timbila, in its ten notes, contains both the major and minor scales.

Is this accidental ?   Or are all the timbila tuned according to this method? The second hypothesis is highly probable. Of course there may be slight differences between the instruments, which is not astonishing, as they are made with primitive implements by unskilled workmen ; but the proof that they are all made according to a fixed rule is that many timbila are often played together by musicians who form an orchestra. This is rarely the case amongst Thongas but frequently amongst the

A timbila player.

Ba-Chopi, who are the true "masters" of this instrument. It is said that, in this very musical tribe, Native pianists sit in a line along the street of the village (for their villages are built in a straight line) and play together, all the throng of men dancing in front of them. I witnessed a similar performance when the Crown Prince of Portugal visited Lourenço Marques in 1907. Great feasts were given in his honour ; 25,000 armed warriors defiled before him, and thirty timbila played the National Portuguese Anthem. The Administrators who taught these Native artists to play that difficult tune on their xylophones deserve every congratulation! It was wonderful. The melody was quite recognisable and played in perfect tune. If the timbila had not been tuned to the same pitch, this concert would have become a dreadful cacophony! In the Johannesburg Compounds the East Coast boys manufacture timbila themselves, of smaller and larger sizes, some with enormous keys made of common pitch-pine boards, and emitting deep low tones, the sounding boxes being empty oil cans. They succeed in tuning them more or less perfectly. So every citizen of Johannesburg can hear their concerts, and witness their dances, in the Compounds of the Ferreira Mine and elsewhere on Sundays, and, though these ugly pitch pine timbila seem a parody on the beautiful instruments played at home, still the performance is worth a visit! (1)

The existence of the timbila is a proof that these tribes possess a real musical system. The Ba-Chopi are the "masters," and

(1) I have lately received some additional information on the timbila from my son, the Rev. H. Ph. Junod, who is living in Manjakaze, not far from the Chopi border. The keys are cut from a very hard tree, the mwendja. which is first put into a big fire in order to make all the sap run out. Large stems of that tree were used by the Ba-Chopi to built their strongholds when they fought against Gungunyana forty years ago. They have been exposed long enough to the rays of the sun to have dried perfectly, and the instrument makers employ them to furnish their keys. The artist begins with the lowest. His father was himself a timbila player and he tunes his keys in accordance with those of the paternal instrument, slightly diminishing the thickness of the little board till it gives exactly the same sound. This explains how all the instruments are tuned to the same pitch. It is not an easy job to find sala shells of all the required sizes. The vibrating membrane is made of the diaphragm of a small rodent called khweva. All the xylophones seen by my informant in Chopiland start from D (or E flat?). Some have 10, some 12, some 14 keys. Some have only four, but they are enormous and emit deep sounds like drums ; they are employed to accompany the others. It is' rare nowadays to hear orchestras of timbila, as most of the men are constantly away from their villages, working for the Whites ; but individual players are still frequently met with, some of them possessing great dexterity.

The xylophone is widely distributed all over the African Continent, Thongaland being the most southern point where this instrument is found. I saw a magnificent example in Vendaland, in the village of a counsellor named Chikhobokhobo. It had no less than 23 keys forming three complete octaves with two supplementary notes at the top. The owner of this piano was very proud of it and kept it in a special hut. I believe it to be the same which was greatly admired at Wembley where it was exhibited in 1925 by Mr C. T. Harries, the Native Commissioner. In Barotseland the xylophone is called sirimba, marimba amongst many other tribes of Central Africa, budimba or imbila amongst the Ba-Ila, and bala in the French Soudan. Mr Ch. Joyeux, who published an interesting paper on " Quelques manifestations musicales observées en Haute Guinée française" (Revue d'Ethnographie et des traditions populaires, Paris, 1924, p. 161-212) has analysed the xylophone of that country and found exactly the same succession of sounds as in the Thonga timbila. The prototype of this instrument is said to be found in the Dutch East Indies and in the Malay Peninsula.

this is generally admitted ; the Thongas, however, are not far behind them, some of them having learnt to manufacture the instrument, and a great many playing upon it quite artistically. In order to define this musical system more precisely, let me now give the 41 following tunes as examples, some of which I owe to Mrs Audéoud, whilst the majority have been noted down by myself.

B. A COLLECTION OF THONGA TUNES.

Tune 1.   The song of the Manyisa bard (p. 185).

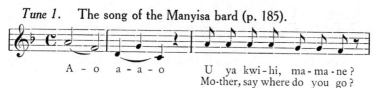

A - o   a - a - o   U   ya kwi - hi, ma - ma - ne ?
                       Mo - ther, say where do you go ?

Tunes 2. 3. 4. 5. 6., heard far away through the bush in the village of Muzila, sub-chief of Rikatla, in the years 1890-1893. In N⁰ 4 the singers were beating the ground with their feet to mark the time. In 5 and 6 boys answered to men and girls to women in the usual antiphonic fashion.

Tune 2.

Tune 3.

Tune 4.

Ha !
Foot   Foot   Foot   Foot   Foot   Foot

Tune 5.

(Voices of men)   (Voices of boys)

Tune 6.

(Women)   (Girls)   (Women)   (Girls)

Tune 7.   The Complaint of the childless woman (p. 188).

A ba bo‑le‑ki ñwa‑na? Ba bo‑le‑ka tshu‑ri ni nkamba!
They won't lend me a ba‑by! They lend me but a mortar...

. Ngi ndji ma‑nga tlu, Ngi ndji shi‑mu‑ngwe. Ngi n'ta ku u‑tla.
Were I an ea‑gle! Were I a bird of prey! Quick would I carry it away!

Tune 8.   Complaint of the boys going to Johannesburg (p. 189).

Stones are ve‑ry hard to break, Far from home in

fo‑reign land. Far from home, in fo‑reign

land, Stones are ve‑ry hard to break.

Tune 9.   Complaint of the Nkuna boy (p. 189).

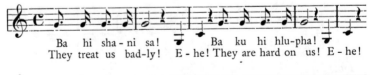

Ba hi sha‑ni sa!   Ba ku hi hlu‑pha!
They treat us bad‑ly! E‑he! They are hard on us! E‑he!

Ba nwa ma‑kho‑fi!   Ba nga hi nyi‑ki!
They drink their cof‑fee! E‑he! And they give us none! E‑he!

Tune 10. The song of the Crab (p. 190).

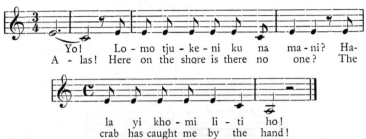

Yo! Lo - mo tju - ke - ni ku na ma - ni? Ha -ne -
A - las! Here on the shore is there no one? The

la yi kho - mi li - ti ho!
crab has caught me by the hand!

Tune 11. The lament over the deported chief Ñwamantibyane (See I. App. XI.).

Hi ñwa - na - o! Hi ñwa - na ba dle - le, Ñwa - ma - nti - byane!
It is the child! The child whom they have killed, Nwa - ma - nti - by - ane!

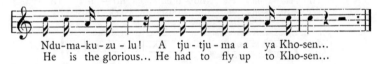

Ndu - ma - ku - zu - lu! A tju - tju - ma a ya Kho - sen...
He is the glorious... He had to fly up to Kho - sen...

Tune 12. The same lament as sung thirteen years later, with accompaniment of the shitjendje.

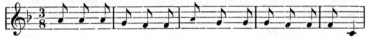

Hle Ndu - ma - ne, ñwa - na! Hlo - ngo - la Ñwa - ma - nti - bya - na
Have pi - ty on the child, They chased him, Nwa - ma - nti - bya - na

Hi ñwa - na ba dle - le, mbo - si!
'Tis the child they have killed, a - las!

Tune 13. The song of the bridesmaids : (p. 200) "Do not go with him". (Mrs. Audéoud, Makulane). (Comp. p. 197).

Au so ku so ma na ye!
Ye . . . . . ! Don't con-sent to go with him!

Tune 14. Mourning song heard after the death of Hamunde's wife who was drowned in the lake of Rikatla (1893) (p. 191).

Ma - ma - nee!   Ma - ma - nee!   U ndji si-
O my   mo - ther!   O my   mo - ther! You have left

yi - le   u   yi   kwi - ni!
me, where did you   go?

Tune 15. Old Nkuna mourning song (p. 192).

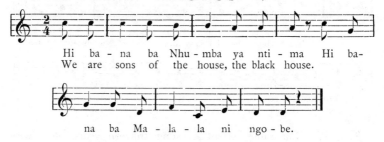

Hi ba - na   ba Nhu - mba ya nti - ma   Hi ba-
We are   sons   of   the house, the black house.

na   ba Ma - la - la   ni   ngo - be.

Tune 16. Mourning song at the death of Chief Tshutsha (Maputju. Mrs Audéoud) (p. 192).

Ha - mban mu - tha - ka - ti,   Ha - mban nu - tha - ka - ti,
Good   bye, you,   wi - zard, Good   bye, you,   wi - zard!

bu - le - la   ba - ntu,   Ha - mban mu - tha - ka - ti,
you kil - ler   of men! Good   bye, you,   wi - zard.

U ta ku bu - le - la   ba - ntu U te - ka b'si - kwin.
Why do you come and kill our folk, You come in the night.

Tune 17. Song of the women carrying "makanye" to Muzila (I. p. 402. II. p. 208).

Chwe! Chwe! Na-mbya-na u te - le! U te - le!
Hi la - ba shi-mun-gu Le - shi ka
Shi-mhu-ngu hi ma-ni? Hi Mzi - la!

U te - le!
Le ti - lwen!
Hi Mzi- la!

Tune 18. Sailors' song on the Nkomati River (1904) (p. 208).

A hi si - lo - yi, A hi nda - nda - le. Ku ni ndla-
A hi si - lo - yi, A hi nda - nda - le. They are starv-

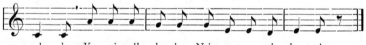

la ka Nti - ma - na, si - lo - yi. A hi si - lo - yi, A hi nda-
ing at Nti - ma - na, si - lo - yi. A hi si - lo - yi, A hi nda-

nda - le. Ku ni ndla - la ka Nti - ma - na, si - lo - yi.
nda - le. They are starv - ing at Nti - ma - na, si - lo - yi.

Tunes 19, 20, 21, 22. Sailors' songs on the Maputju River. (Mrs. Audéoud. 1906-1907).

Tune 20.

U fe - li ma - li, hm!... U fe - li ma - li, hm!... hm!

Tune 21.

A u na ti - nga - na   fa - mba b'si - kwin?
A - re you not a - shamed   to go at night?

yo yo yo   yo yo

A u na ti - nga - na   fa - mba bsi - kwin?
A - re you not a-shamed   to go at night?

yo   yo yo yo   yo yo yo

Tune 22.

Tune 23. Carriers song.

Tune 24. War song sung at the coronation of the Mpfumo chiefs (I. p. 373).

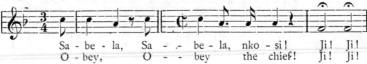

Sa - be - la, Sa - - be - la, nko - si!   Ji! Ji!
O - bey, O - - bey the chief!   Ji! Ji!

Si ya ku we - la mu - la - mbu mku - lu wa ka nko - si.
Let us go, let us cross the great ri - ver, that of the chief.

Tune 25. **The great war song of Maputju (p. 194).**

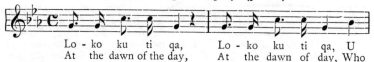

Lo - ko ku ti qa, Lo - ko ku ti qa, U
At the dawn of the day, At the dawn of day, Who

be-kwe ngu-ba - ne Mu-wa - yi? Mwai ka Ma - bu - du, Mwa-
is he that crowned thee, Muwayi? Mwai of Ma - pu - tju, Mwa-

yi, ka Ma - bu - du, U be - kwe ngu - ban !
yi of Ma - pu - tju, Who has crown - ed thee !

Tune 26. **Marching song of the army (I. p. 469).**

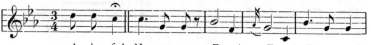

A - ba - fo! Na-ngu-ya, E - e! E - e! E - ne - na!
The en'my! Here they are, E - e! E - e! Here they are!

Ha - a! Ha - a!
Ha - a! Ha - a!

Tune 27. **The song of the spear (Nkuna) (I. p. 461).**

Hi yi-kwa ka ma-kho-si, Si phu-ma ka ma-
War comes from the chiefs. It is or-dered by the

kho - si, si ga - mbu - za! U-mkhonto se sa-ndhle-ni E-
chiefs. We go and kill! The spear is in our hands. E-

289

ji!　E - ji!　U - mkho-nto u　sao　go - bee...
ji!　E - ji!　The spear kills and bends　in the wound.

Tune 28. The Giraffe of the desert (Nkuna, Nondwane). I. p. 461.

O - ho ho - ho!　Nha si hu – hlu,　ya se ma - na - nga.
'T is the gi - raffe,　far in the de - sert.

E - ho ho - ho!　Nha si hu - hlu　ya se ma - na - nga.
'T is the gi - raffe,　far in the de - sert.

Tune 29. Oldest Nkuna war song (I. p. 461).

Hi ba yi - ma, hi ba yi - ma!　Hi ba yi - ma, hi ba yi-
Let us stand fast, let us stand fast!　Let us stand fast, let us stand

ma!　Mi te - ka bu - re - na mi nyi - ka　ti-nu-ba ta ba-mbe!
fast!　Do not let your strength go, it would help the en'my to con-quer!

Tune 30. Childrens'song welcoming the trek oxen (p. 209).

Gwey - ma - na - o, Gwey - ma - na - o, Gwey - ma-
See　the　o - xen!　See　the　o - xen!　See　the

na - o, Gwey - ma - na - o!
o - xen, See　the　o - xen!

Tune 31. Childrens' song to the owl (p. 209).

Shi - ko - ta-na gau - le - la fo - le, Ñwa-mbengen gau - le - la fo - le.

290

Tune 32. Incantation to the spirit during exorcism (p. 209) (Part VI).

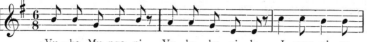

Vu - ka Mu-ngo - ni, Vu - ka, ku - si - le, I - nyo - ni ya
A - wake, o Zu - lu, The day has come, Now the bird is

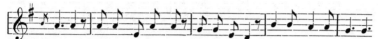

dhla - la. Dhla-la Mu-ngo-ni, Dhla-la va-len, I nyo-ni ya dhla-la.
sing-ing. Play al - so, Zu - lu, Play in the bush, Now the bird is singing.

Tune 33. Song of the tale of the ogre Nyandzumulandengela (Timbila song). (p. 210).

Nya-ndzu-mu - la - nde-nge - la, Ndzu-mu - la - nde-nge - la!

Ndji hwe ti - ho - mu ta nga ndji mu-ka! Nya ndzu-mu-la - nde - nge-
Give me my o-xen, please, that I may go!

la, Ndzu-mu - la - nde - nge - la! U - te - ki - le mi mhu-
You have ta - ken me and

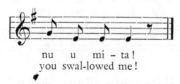

nu u mi - ta!
you swal-lowed me!

Tune 34. Song in two parts, in the tale of Zili (p. 259).

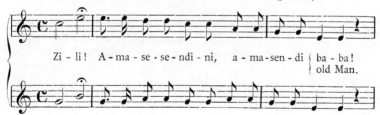

Zi - li! A - ma - se - se - ndi - ni, a - ma-sen - di ｛ ba - ba!
｛ old Man.

Si - lo - yi - le } se - se - ndi - ni,   I   nya - ma mu - ne, ya ku
You bad wi - zard }   —   What's that kind of meat, ve - ry

nha - ti { se - se - ndin,   I   ka - la nki - la ka li - ho - ndjo,
strange meat {   —   It   has got no tail, it has no horn.

se - se - ndin.   Zi - li!   A - ma - se - se - ndi - ni, A - ma -

se - ndi } ba - ba! Si - lo - yi - le } se - se - ndin!
      } old man, You bad wi - zard }

Tune 35. Song of the mother whose child has been carried off by the Baboon (p. 263).

Mfe - ne sa - ndhle - ni,   Mfe - ne sa - ndhle - ni,   A

u   ngi dhla - yi - se - le   mu - nta - na - me, si ya ndo - ndo

za! Si ngi-ya mu-ka, ngi ya mu-ka.

I - i In-ko-si ya mee I - i.

Tune 36. Incantation by which hyena-men are transformed into hyenas, in an ogre-tale (p. 210).

Ma-nya-nga, ma-nya-nga. { Wa nga hi ne-nge. { Ho!
 { The leg is for me. }

Tune 37. One of the Ronge songs (p. 203).

Ndji we - la, ndji we - la, Ñwa - Tem - bé, Ndji we-
I will cross, I will cross, Ñwa - Tem - bé, I will

la, ndji tchi - ké, ndji we - la!
cross, please let me, let me cross!

Tune 38. A tune played on the shitiringo flute on the banks of the Great Tabi (p. 277).

Tune 39. A shitiringo tune from Shiluvane.

Tune 40. A bunanga tune (I. p. 431, II. p. 277).

Tune 41 (p. 189).

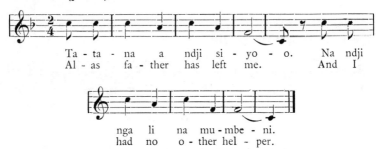

Ta - ta - na a ndji si - yo - o. Na ndji
Al - as fa - ther has left me. And I

nga li na mu - mbe - ni.
had no o - ther hel - per.

C. THE MUSICAL SYSTEM OF THE THONGAS.

Having now studied the instruments used by our tribe, and a certain number of tunes, we can try to come to some conclusions as regards its musical system. Let it be said, first of all, that such conclusions are only provisional, and I do not pretend that they are final. Noting down Native tunes is a very delicate task, as nothing is more plastic than sound, and however accurate we have tried to be, we may have introduced something of our own into this transcript. Nothing but phonograph records would be scientifically beyond suspicion! However between all these tunes there is enough similarity, enough family likeness, to convince students of primitive music that they are genuine, and that we are entitled to draw some deductions from this material.

As regards *rhythm*, it is generally very well marked, being emphasised by the accompanying instruments, and the movements of dancers : arms lowered in cadence, weapons brandished, feet stamping the ground at regular intervals, etc. However I did not always find it easy to catch, and there are certainly sudden changes in the time which put the hearer out of his reckoning. I have heard people assert that in primitive music rhythm is by far the most interesting element. Anybody having witnessed a war-dance, or the performance of the East Coast boys in the Johannesburg Compounds, will be able to certify that there is a wonderful sense of time in these productions. The binary combinations, 2/4 and 4/4 time, are met with more frequently than the ternary modes, 3/4 and 6/8.

The *melodic system* is evidently based on the scale of seven intervals, just the same as our own-music. The presence of the scale underlying all this music is proved by the preceding tunes, but more specially, as we noticed, by the timbila. Most of the tunes could be played on this primitive piano, which is evidently constructed according to the rules of the ordinary scale. I came to the same conclusion when teaching the sol-fa notation to raw Natives, and I remember having a class of boys, just from the bush, in Lourenço Marques, who, at the first lesson, after a quarter of an hour, were singing our scale without difficulty ; what seemed to be unknown was the name of the seven notes do, re, mi, etc., but the sounds themselves, in their regular succession, were quite familiar to their ears. One hears sometimes of a scale which has but three or four notes. Does it exist? Is not this succession of sounds "given" to the human ear, as also the succession of colours in the rainbow to the human eye? As we shall see, Natives do not distinguish all the colours. They use the same word, *libungu*, for yellow, and red ; black and dark blue are also both *ntima*. Their eye has not yet been fully trained. Their ear seems to me to be more developed, and to have attained a distinct perception of the elementary sounds.

Let it be remarked, however, that there are differences amongst them. Some sing more in tune than others. Often they are a third or a quarter of a tone flat or sharp. I would say that they do not precisely sing out of tune, but they are not yet true on the note. But this will come with due training. I very rarely met with Natives with no idea of tune. This occurrence is, I think, more frequent amongst the Whites than amongst the Blacks. As regards accidentals, I have seen some boys master the chromatic scale without much difficulty. But sharps and flats, viz., sounds which do not bear the ordinary, regular relation to those preceding or following them, are generally very difficult to catch, sometimes altogether beyond their reach. The use of European instruments will raise them to that higher level in the course of time.

But let us confine ourselves to their primitive state. They not only know our *major scale*, but frequently sing in the *minor one*. On the timbila, as we saw, they can play in the eolian method, viz., in a minor scale in which there is no raised seventh. In fact, even in the distinctly minor tunes, this raised seventh is never met with. We often notice the passage from the major to the minor, or vice versa, and our collection affords two striking examples of this musical procedure : in tune No. 33, the melody after 6 bars recommences a third lower : this is a characteristic timbila tune ; the melody, started on the third key, is played again starting on the first, passing from the major to the minor. In No. 25, at the end of the second bar, the reverse phenomenon takes place. The melody was first minor ; it is raised a third higher and becomes major for a while, returning later on to the minor.

The *character* of most of the Bantu melodies is rather sad, and this is generally explained by the assertion that they are in the minor key. I do not think this is true. Most of my tunes, 25, are undoubtedly major, 10 are minor, and 5 are mixed or doubtful. This impression comes rather from the fact that the melody almost invariably begins on a high note and descends to low notes, often ending on the lowest. The song starts brilliantly, triumphantly, and goes down, down, till it dies away on the lowest note. Hence the melancholy impression these tunes convey. The melody is very short, as a rule ; sometimes quite rudimentary ; its constant repetitions also produce a monotonous effect which enhances the sadness of the music. A professional musician, after having perused these tunes, once said to me : "Well, they are not 'jolly good fellows' your black people! Not a single dancing tune! Nothing merry about this music!"

The rules of *Native harmony* are very difficult to detect. They certainly exist. When you hear a chorus of beautiful voices singing in two or three parts, you at once perceive great differences between their system of harmony and ours. These choruses are by no means disagreeable, but are very strange to our European ear. It would be most interesting to seize them and note them down, but it would be a long job! I have succeeded at least in fixing the two parts of the song of Zili, which may be considered typical ; I owe it to two girls of Lourenço Marques, who had clear voices and lent themselves willingly and with great patience to the long investigation. A curious succession of fourths and sixths will be noticed, quite unusual in our music. The professional to whom I submitted this song told me it reminded him of similar chords found in the works of mediaeval composers like Bianchois, and Adam de la Halle. The fourth seems to be more acceptable to the Bantu ear than the third or the fifth. A collection of timbila music would be of great assistance in coming to a conclusion on the subject, as the artists invariably play with two hands, and a score of phonographic records taken in Johannesburg of a good player would be very valuable. Not having had the opportunity of making such an investigation, I must be satisfied to commend it to those who have time to devote themselves to it.

To sum up the result of this inquiry, I may say that Thonga music has certainly reached a certain stage of development, being based upon the seven intervals scale, recognizing the major and minor keys, and following a certain system of harmony ; but the melodies are still short and rudimentary and, although they may attain real grandeur when performed by hundreds of warriors, they are generally monotonous and sad. Notwithstanding this, the black race is essentially musical ; its gifts in this domain are real, and if properly developed they will certainly in time produce remarkable results.

We can guess to some extent what contribution the Blacks will make to the musical treasures of humanity when we hear the Negro artists who travel round Europe singing the striking plantation songs which they learned from their fathers. As far as I know, South African Bantus have not yet published many musical compositions comparable to those of their American brethren ; yet educated Natives, even school children, already invent songs for their own pleasure which are more elaborate than the old ones, but which retain the true Bantu character. I will quote three which I managed to seize in the neighbourhood of Lourenço Marques.

The first may be called *the song of the children who no longer wished to attend evening prayer*. I heard them singing it unnoticed on the Lourenço Marques hill. It must be said that on every Mission Station all the converts assemble every evening to attend a short service, bringing their children with them. It seems that, on one occasion, the missionary went away for a furlough and evening prayer was stopped for a while; it was however resumed when he came back home... much to the disappointment of the children, and they composed this song, whose words are perhaps not very edifying, though they ought not to be taken too seriously. The tune, at any rate, is charming :

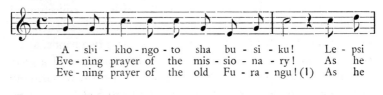

A - shi - kho - ngo - to sha bu - si - ku! Le - psi
Eve - ning prayer of the mis - sio - na - ry! As he
Eve - ning prayer of the old Fu - ra - ngu! (1) As he

ku tlha - si - ki ye - ne, A ta hi psa - u - la hi ku ba
has now come home a-gain, The bell will ring, ring, ring, and it will
has now come home a-gain, It will say nwe-nwe-nwe, and it will

a - nsi - mbi Ni bu - si - ku: Hi nga ye - tle - li!
vex our ears, Du - ring the night : No sleep a - ny more!
vex our ears Du - ring the night : No sleep a - ny more!

The second was composed *by a blind girl* of the Maputju country at the time of the Murimi Movement of which I shall speak later on (App. V). The prophet of this new god, Murimi, was travelling all over Thongaland to destroy witchcraft and to inaugurate a new

(1) "Old Furangu" is the church elder Frank whose name was transformed according to Thonga phonetics. In the following verses there are a number of descriptive adverbs imitating the ringing of the bell. It will say : go-go-go—rwa-rwa-rwa—nge-nge-nge...

era of prosperity and the chiefs called all their subjects, men and women, to take a snuff of a certain magical tobacco which would rid the country of all the killers by night. The young poetess imagines a woman, a witch, preparing to go to the meeting ordered by the chiefs in order to take the snuff. But she does not at all intend to renounce her criminal ways. She has in her power "psipoko" (see Part. VI, Witchcraft, and App. V), i. e. little folk no bigger than real babies, who are really dead people whom she has bewitched and whom she employs as slaves to till her gardens. During the day she hides them in the bush and during the night she makes them work. Now she takes leave of them before attending the meeting where she is determined to lie, pretending that she has nothing to do with witchcraft, whilst she is secretely determined to go on practising it. The song of the Christian girl reveals her duplicity and concludes by asserting that converts do not believe in this mass of absurdities.

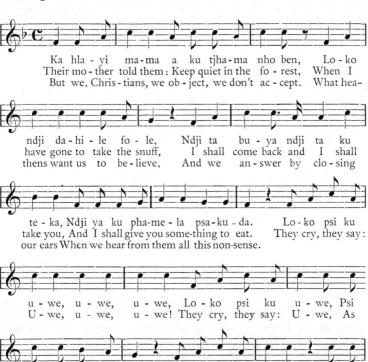

Ka hla-yi ma-ma a ku tjha-ma nho ben, Lo-ko
Their mo-ther told them: Keep quiet in the fo-rest, When I
But we, Chris-tians, we ob-ject, we don't ac-cept. What hea-

ndji da-hi-le fo-le, Ndji ta bu-ya ndji ta ku
have gone to take the snuff, I shall come back and I shall
thens want us to be-lieve, And we an-swer by clo-sing

te-ka, Ndji ya ku pha-me-la psa-ku-da. Lo-ko psi ku
take you, And I shall give you some-thing to eat. They cry, they say:
our ears When we hear from them all this non-sense.

u-we, u-we, u-we, Lo-ko psi ku u-we, Psi
U-we, u-we, u-we! They cry, they say: U-we, As

dji-le-la ku mam' Lo-ku psi ku: U-we! Bu-ya
they call for their mother. They cry, they say: U-we! Come back

ka - ya ! — Ndji ta ku pha - me - la psa - ku - da.
quick - ly ! — Yes ! I will give you some-thing to eat.

The third song is a sort of hymn whose author is a young evan-gelist belonging to the Chopi tribe, a tribe particularly gifted for music. This boy, named Onesime, was lame and lay for many years on his bed of suffering ; there he composed quite a number of melo-dies which he taught his pupils. Here is the *Song of the Star,* which he himself wrote for me in Sol-Fa Notation, and in which he expresses the feelings of his pious heart :

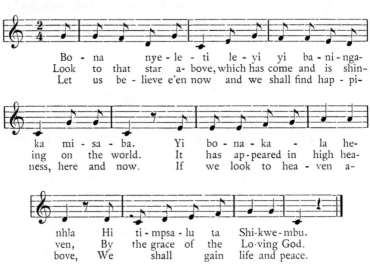

Bo - na nye - le - ti le - yi yi ba - ni - nga-
Look to that star a- bove, which has come and is shin-
Let us be - lieve e'en now and we shall find hap - pi-

ka mi - sa - ba. Yi bo - na - ka - la he-
ing on the world. It has ap - peared in high hea-
ness, here and now. If we look to hea - ven a-

nhla Hi ti - mpsa - lu ta Shi - kwe - mbu.
ven, By the grace of the Lo - ving God.
bove, We shall gain life and peace.

See at the end of this volume the Practical Conclusion of Part. V : *The Problem of Native Education.*

I have discovered that this melody is used in the congrega-tions of the French Basutoland Mission and is not originally Bantu. But it has been curiously transformed by Thonga children, a fact which is of common occurrence. The study of such alterations would greatly help in the understanding of the Bantu musical genius.

SIXTH PART

RELIGIOUS LIFE AND SUPERSTITIONS.

———

The mystery of the Psychic life! There is a mystery in any form of life, be it vegetable, animal, or intellectual. But how much deeper and more difficult it is to fathom, when we are dealing with those higher manifestations of the mental life, which seem peculiar to mankind : Religion, Morality and also, besides these, Magic of all kinds, Divination, Spirit-Possession, Witchcraft, all of which we include under the term Superstition. Amongst savage peoples Religion and Magic, Morality and Taboo, are not yet clearly differentiated. I believe them to proceed from different sources ; but they are more or less confounded in the rites, and this makes them all the more difficult to understand. I do not now claim to throw a perfect light on the dim, confused notions of the Bantu soul. The race is so little philosophical that it can accept conflicting ideas to an extent which would be impossible in more rational, more intellectually developed minds. My aim is, as ever, to be as impartial as possible. I have no preconceived idea as to what primitive man was, or ought to have been. I believe the evolutionist theory to be supported by a great number of probabilities and to be the best solution of many problems. Yet I think it to be merely a hypothesis, and that it would be unscientific to regard it as a dogma to the strengthening of which Science must devote all its labours. I may endeavour to reach some conclusions at the end of this VIth Part ; but my intention is to treat this subject by giving a faithful record of my own observations : professional anthropologists, or historians of Religion can do what they like with this material ; my only ambition is that it should be entirely reliable.

In the first chapter, I shall try to record the ideas of the Thongas on Nature and Man ; this is what might be called their *Natural Philosophy*, if the term were not somewhat pretentious.   In the second, their distinctively *religious notions and rites* will be explained.   In the third I shall describe the manifold manifestations of their *Magic*, in which I include the Practice of Medicine, Witchcraft, Possession and Divination.   In the fourth, the question of *Morality and Taboo* will be considered.

CHAPTER I

Conceptions of the Thongas regarding Nature and Man.

A. CONCEPTIONS REGARDING NATURE.

I. *Origin of the World:*

"What is it that created Heaven and Earth? — Nature!" This proverb or riddle, already quoted (p. 180), is perhaps the only answer given by the Thongas to the problem of creation. *Ntumbuluko*, the word I translate by Nature, comes from *ku tumbuluka*, to happen, to be formed.   It does not convey any clear idea of a Creation.   The sense of causality is very little developed amongst most of the Thongas.   So they are contented with this rather pantheistic notion, beyond which many very educated scientists of our age will not go, that Nature created the world, and they do not search further.   Some say that the originator of Heaven and Earth is Rivimbi, or Kudjwana, or Ñwari.   The first two of these names are the Venda or Pedi names of the first human beings ; Ñwali or Myali is a god of the Ba-Nyai whose legend has spread amongst the Northern clans of the Thongas, especially the Hlengwes and the Malulekes.   It is possible that the tribes from which these names have been borrowed, truly believe these personages to have created the world.   In

302

the story of Ñwali, for instance, it is said that, when he lived, stones were not yet hard, and so the implements of the first men left their impression on the rocks (Comp. I. p. 22). But they are in the first place the *creators of mankind*, as we shall notice.

I believe that the *origin of man* preoccupies the Bantu mind much more than the origin of the world as a whole. They can live their whole life without being troubled by this question, which has perplexed so many hearts in other lands. Only a few particularly serious spirits, the religious geniuses of the tribe, search eagerly for light on this subject. I have met with one of these. His name was Rangane, and he came from the Maluleke district. When quite a young boy he often asked his mother who it was who had made heaven and earth. She told him : "It is Khudjwana, but he died long ago. Even the place where he was buried is unknown." This did not satisfy the curiosity of the child : so she sent him to the old men to question them. They answered by the myth of the reed which we shall explain later on, saying : "All men came from a reed." This also failed to satisfy the thirst of this inquiring soul, desirous of knowing whence everything proceeds, and he told me how gladly surprised he was when, having come to Pretoria for work, he heard a convert say that God had created everything and teaching the Christian explanation of the world. I remember that his face beamed with joy when he told his story. But such earnest, philosophical natures are very rare amongst Natives, and Rangane was an exception. He died when still at the beginning of his course of study ; and he was vastly superior to most of his comrades as regards religious perception.

II. *The celestial world.*

(THONGA ASTRONOMY).

If Thongas do not bother much about the origin of heaven, and of its lights, what are their ideas concerning them?

Heaven (tilo, dji-ma) is for them an immense solid vault which rests on the earth. The point where heaven touches the earth is called *bugimamusi*, a curious word of the bu-ma class, the prefix *bu* meaning a place, viz., the place where the women can lean their pestles against the vault, (whilst everywhere else pestles must be leant against a wall or a tree). This expression is sometimes further explained by the following words : "Lomu ba kandjaka na ba khisamile" — "Where women pound their mealies on their knees ;" they cannot stand erect, or their pestles would strike against the vault! This vault rests on the earth, which is often called *libala*, viz., the great plain. On what does the earth itself rest? This question does not seem to trouble the Thonga mind and I never heard an answer to it. In this respect it may be said, in excuse for the African Natives, that the ancient Greeks, with all their intellectual ability, were not much in advance of them. Some people escape the difficulty by asserting that the earth is infinite, viz., that it is endlessly prolonged downwards and has no bottom. — In the next chapter we shall see that *Tilo*, heaven, is, for the Thongas, not only the material firmament which rests on the earth, but a spiritual principle which plays a considerable part in the religious conceptions of the tribe.

The *sun* (dambu, dji-ma) is never personified, nor worshipped. This word is perhaps related to Nyambe of the Ba-Rotse, Nzambi of the Vili, and a number of other similar words which are names of God. But if there was ever a time when the sun was regarded as a personal being, the notion has now entirely faded away. On the seashore, in the Makaneta district, according to Mboza, people believe that the sun emerges from the water. The reflection of light which remains on the sea, after the appearance of the sun, is considered as a kind of source of light from which the sun emerges and renews itself every morning : it is "cut out from the provision of fire," adheres to heaven, follows its course and *dies* in the West. To-morrow another sun will come out from the "provision," and so on. But others object to this explanation and assert that the sun passes under the earth and comes back the following day : so there is only one sun. To this theory the first retort that the earth having no bottom, the sun cannot pass under it !

The dawn is called *mpundju* ; then comes *tlhabela sana*, the

304

time when the rays of the sun (sana) are piercing ; *hisa ka sana,* when they are burning ; *nhlekanhi,* the middle of the sky, or *shitakataka,* the maximum point of the heat ; then *ndjenga* (Dj.), or *lihungu* (Ro.), the afternoon, the time when the sun goes down (renga) ; *ku pela* or *ku hlwa,* when it reaches the horizon, and *mpimabayeni* (Dj.) the twilight, literally "the time when you do not easily recognize strangers coming to your village because it grows dark." These are the divisions of the day (siku). Then comes the night (busiku).

Eclipses do not seem to have ever much impressed the imagination of the Thongas. At any rate, they never caused panics (Mboza). When, warned that an eclipse will take place, they see that, indeed, the sun or moon is "turning dark" (dji yentsha ntima), Natives are more struck with wonder at the supernatural knowledge of the White people, than with fear of the phenomenon itself.

I have already dealt with the notion of the *year,* (lembe, dji-ma), which is very vague ; it begins at two different periods : that of tilling and that of harvesting the first fruits (I, p. 396, II, p. 20). Thongas do not make any difference between a solar and a lunar year, their knowledge of months being very imperfect, as we shall shortly see.

Before leaving the source of light, I may add that the *light* itself is called *ku bonekisa* (Ro.), or *ku bonakala* (Dj.), litt. that which makes to appear. Of course Natives have no explanation to give of it. Moonlight is called by another name, viz. *n̄weti,* connected with hweti, moon. *Colours* are very imperfectly perceived, at least if we are to base our judgment on the vocabulary. *Ntima* means both black and dark blue. *Libungu* is carmine, red, purple, and also yellow. Yellow is not perceived as a distinct colour. *Psuka* is the tinge of dawn, and of the rising sun. *Nkushe,* which means sea-weed, is applied to the *blue* sky ; *nkwalala* is grey, *lihlaza* (Ro.) is green, the green of grass in the spring, and the corresponding term in Djonga is *rilambyana,* that which makes dogs howl. Very green grass has this effect on Native dogs.

The *moon* (n̄hweti (Dj.), hweti (Ro.) cl. yi-tin), was perhaps personified in former times, as it bears the feminine suffix *eti,* which is also met with in *nyeleti* (star) and in the names of certain rivers. (I. p. 36.) At the present time there is no trace of worship or of mythological conceptions in connection with it. Natives see in its spots a woman carrying a shirundju basket or a bundle of sticks, but they do not attach to that image more importance than we do when we talk of the man in the moon.

I have described (I. p. 52) how the new moon is received with exclamations of joy : in the villages the first person who sees it shouts : "Kengelekezeeee,"—"the Crescent! the Crescent!" and this word is passed on from one village to another, and dancers rejoice because they will have moonlight to illuminate their feasts! Such is, at least, the reason now given by the Rongas for this custom. There were perhaps other ideas connected with the new moon in former times. — According to a Nkuna informant the day of the new moon is a *shimusi*, a day of rest. It is taboo to till the fields and cut the roots of the trees with a hoe. The moon must be left to become firm (tiyela). It is still tender as a new born child. Destroying winds might blow and hail fall if this taboo were transgressed. — The appearance of the crescent was also carefully examined, says the same informant. If its horns were turned towards the earth, this showed that there was nothing to fear, all the dangers contained in this month had been poured out : "mafumo ma hangalakile" — "the assagais were dispersed." On the contrary, if the horns were turned towards heaven, this showed that the moon was full of weapons and misfortunes. — The new moon is of great importance in the customs connected with exorcism and possession, as every exorcist must undergo the *haza* purification at each new moon (Chapter III). Moreover Thongas, like many civilised people, also believe that some persons at this time have an attack of madness which is called *rihuhe ra ñhweti*, the lunar madness.

When the first quarter appears, the moon is said to *thwaza*, a Zulu word which corresponds to *tjhama* in Thonga, and is very much used in the terminology of possession. Eight days later, it is said to *basa*, to be white or brilliant ; full moon is said to *sima* or to *lata batjongwana*, to put the little children to bed, because when it rises, it finds them already sleeping on their mats.

306

The wane is called *ku shwela dambo* : the moon is then found by the rising sun to be still in the sky, not having yet dipped below the horizon. When, at last, it disappears, it is *munyama*, the obscurity; the moon is said *to fa*, to have died. Is this meant figuratively, as is often the case with the word ku fa, or do the Thongas really think that each moon dies and is replaced by a new moon? It is difficult to say ; most of them believe in an actual destruction and a new creation of the moon each month (Timotheo), and this would explain why they have the same word for moon and month ; they evidently identify the two ideas. Some, however, told me that they believed it to be the same celestial body which appeared anew each month.

Spoon, who is endowed with a very vivid imagination, believed that the sun and the moon have a race each month : the moon when it first appears is not yet firm (a yi si tiyela), like a new born child, so its light is feeble ; it is dominated by the sun ; but it grows and fights. When it is full, the sun sees "that now it is the moon!" : it is something to be reckoned with! During the second half of the month, as it decreases, it lingers in the sky and the sun soon overtakes it again and compels it to pass behind. Then the moon is entirely vanquished! How far these were Spoon's personal explanations or generally accepted ideas, I could not say. The term *shwela*, applied to the last quarter and meaning : "to be surprised in the morning" (See Ch. III), seems to convey a similar idea, and it is probable that Spoon rightly interpreted the ancient ideas of the tribe.

Each moon, being new, bears a special name. These names of the months, or moons, are now almost completely forgotten, at least in the Southern clans. This is indeed curious, when we think of the custom of presenting little children to the moon and telling them the name of their month (I. p. 53). This rite ought to have prevented the names from becoming obsolete. In the Northern clans they have been better preserved, and one of my colleagues, the Rev. H. Berthoud, succeeded in identifying them more or less. His attempt to revive the nomenclature for use among civilised Natives did not, however, succeed any better than the attempt of the scientists of the French Revolution.

Amongst the Ba-Ronga those which are still known are : *Nhlangula*, the month in which the flowers are swept (hlangula) from the trees, probably October, when all the minkuhlu, minkanye, etc., blossom ; *Ñwendjamhala*, the month in which the antelope mhala, brings forth its young (November?) ; *Mawuwana*, when the *tihuhlu* (p. 18) are plucked, because the people shout : "Wuwana! wuwana!" in their joy at having plenty of almonds to suck, corresponds to December. *Hukuri* is said to be the month when the fruits of the *nkwakwa* (p. 17) are ripe (December also?). *Ndjati*, or *ndjata*, viz., I am coming, is the time of *nwebo*, when everyone is in his fields eating the new cobs of mealies, and if you call a person he will answer : "I will come directly! Have patience! I am busy here!" "This may be January or February. *Sunguti* is also one of the summer months. *Sibamesoko*, the moon which closes the paths, also called *Dwebindlela* or *Sibandlela*, is easy to identify : it is February, the time when the grass grows so high that it hides the paths leading to the nkanye trees. This is the end of the bukanye time (I. p. 397). *Nyenyana, Nywenywankulu* are the ·months of the birds (nyanyana), when one spends all one's time in chasing the winged marauders from the fields of sorghum and millet (March. April). *Mudashini*, viz., what am I to eat? is the month when you have harvested so many different kinds of food that you do not know which to choose : this is the time directly after harvest, May or June. *Khotabushika*, viz., when winter comes, probably June or July.

The *stars* are called *tinyeleti* (yin-tin) and play a remarkably small part in the ideas of the tribe. The modern theory according to which all religions started from the worship of stars, finds no confirmation at all in the South African Bantu tribes.

It is taboo to try to count the stars. If any one attempts to do so people will say to him : "Keep quiet or you will wet the hut during the night!" Counting stars represents the torments of the soul! If a child has been deprived of food as a punishment for an offence, his parents will tell him, when he goes to sleep : "Go and count the stars," viz., "you will feel hungry and not be able to go to sleep ; you will be as unhappy as if you had to count the stars."

I never heard a distinction made between fixed stars and planets. They are all called tinyeleti. The best-known is Venus, which bears many names. Not knowing that the evening and morning star are one and the same, they have given it different names. The evening star is *Gumbashilalelo*, the one which steals the evening meal, because it appears when people are eating it, or *khwekhweti*, the brilliant star, or *Nkata wa hweti*, the moon's husband (as the two are often seen close together) ; the morning star is called *Ngongomela*, or *Khwezu*, and is greatly lauded as the herald of day. It gives the warriors the signal for starting on a war-like expedition : the warriors can easily kill their enemies under cover of the darkness, and the sun will soon appear and help them to complete their victory. Travellers also start on their journey when they see it : the dawn will soon be here ! Lit by its light, candidates for circumcision leave the village of the chief to go to the house of initiation. According to one of my informants (I. p. 75) there is a profound and mystic idea in this custom : Ngongomela announces the day ; so little boys must be conducted by the morning star when they abandon their childhood and all its ignorance to enter the adult life with all its knowledge. It leads them from darkness into the light! So Venus plays a great part in Thonga customs. It is the great star. Notice the feminine suffix *eti* in one of its names. It may have been personified in former times.

The *Pleiades* are the only constellation which bears a name in Thonga. They call it *shirimelo*, the one which announces the tilling season, because, in fact, in the lands situated in the Tropic of Cancer, it rises in July or August, when tilling is resumed. I have not heard of any other constellation known to the Natives. They have no notion whatever of constellations : their mind does not seem to have tried to group the stars, or to have seen figures of animals, or objects, in the sky ; their imagination in this domain is very poor, and they remain far behind the Oriental nations in this respect.

Falling stars are looked on as a bad omen. When they see one falling towards a certain point of the horizon, Natives think that a Chief must have died in the country towards which the

star is directing its course, and they have a formula of incantation
to get rid of the misfortune attending this phenomenon. They
say : "Thu! Thu! Nkulunkulu ndjuwee, famba psa ku u nga fa u
ku bi." — "You great thing, go away alone (without me, leaving
me behind) and die and disappear entirely." This is more an
imprecation (shiruketelo) than an incantation. The syllable *thu*
indicates, and accompanies, the emission of a little saliva. It is
different from the sacramental *tsu*, employed to invoke the spirits
of the ancestors : it is an insult. It is spitting *at* something, not an
act of respect and an offering, like *tsu* (1). This is the Ronga
formula ; the one used in Northern clans has the same meaning :
"*Rura, rura weshe*" (Move, move alone!).

Comets greatly impress the imagination of the Thongas ;
they are called *shimusana*, or *nyeleti ya musana*, the star of dust,
or *nyeleti ya nkila*, the star with a tail, and when they appear
they also mean the death of a chief. People say : "See ! A chief
has died, but they have not yet published the mourning" (I. p. 414).
The star which is said to have appeared the year of the death of
Manukosi was probably a comet. (See Report of the S.A.A.A.S.
1905, Vol. III, p. 232.)

These few superstitions and observations comprise all the
Astronomy of the Thongas. The sidereal world is almost entirely
outside the range of their preoccupations.

III. *Cosmographic and Meteorological Phenonomena.*

1) THE WIND.

The wind is called *moya*, an interesting word which means
also spirit (the human breath and the spiritual part of man),
and is applied to the acting, living agent, or to the smell, or taste,
of some objects. For instance it is said of an alcoholic beverage

---

(1) They spit at a child who is causing an unpleasant smell, saying to him : "Thu!
u ya tinyela matjimba." "Go away to ease yourself." Should you do this to a
person older than yourself, he will say to you : "What ! you make *thu* to me (wa ndji
tjhuka), you want me to ease myself !"

which has lost its strength that its "moya" has gone. It is also the moya which gives their potency to medical charms.

Another word for wind is *mheho*. Strong winds are called *shidzedze*. When they break trees and damage the mealies they are attributed to baloyi, wizards, who fight during the night, quarelling over the cobs.

One frequently hears about *timheho ta mune*, the four winds. They are called : Ñwalungu, the north wind, (a curious word perhaps connected with Balungu, the White men ; see later on) ; *Nyingitimu* (Ro.), or *Djonga* (Dj.), the South wind ; *Mupfanyaka*, the one coming from the plain of the black earth, the West Wind ; *Mfenya*, the sea breeze, coming from the East. Sailors who are great connoisseurs in this domain distinguish further the South Westerly wind, which they call *Mfenyakulu*, the great Mfenya. In Shiluvane, the West wind, which sometimes blows with great violence, coming down from the mountains of the Transvaal Plateau, is called *Burwa*, place of habitation of the Ba-Rwa (bu, locative prefix indicating a country). (Compare I. p. 18). Two other terms of the bu-ma class, also applied to East and West in all the clans, are : *Busha*, the spot where the sun rises (ku sha), the East, and *Bupeladambu*, the spot where the sun sets, the West. So there is no doubt that the Thongas possess the idea of the four cardinal points.

2) NATIVE GEOGRAPHY.

The geographical notions of the tribe are, on the other hand, very scanty. As a rule, they do not think it possible to know a country, or place, where they have not travelled. Every one must compile his own geography. Hunters, and men engaged in commercial journeys, had some knowledge of the Spelonken (Bvesha), of Pietermaritzburg (Umgungundhlovu), of Kimberley (Dayiman), and now practically every grown-up Thonga has been to Johannesburg (Nkamben). But those who have always remained at home, women especially, show gross ignorance regarding their own country. I met some who were totally ignorant of the fact that the Nkomati River, which leaves the

311

Transvaal at Komati Poort (a place known to all), was the same as the Nkomati which enters the sea near Morakwen, northwards of Lourenço Marques, at a distance of 60 miles from Komati Poort. It must be said, in excuse for them, that in Morakwen the river is called Morako (locative Morakwen) and thus many people have never been aware of the identity of the two!

If you wish to impress Natives greatly with your knowledge, tell them the names of all the countries of Thongaland in their geographical order, as you may have learnt them in conversation, or by studying the map. They will be amazed, and say : "What a wonderful traveller you are, knowing so many spots so far distant from each other !" The teaching of Geography in the schools tends, of course, to alter this state of things.

3) Earthquakes and Rainbows.

Earthquakes are not frequent in this part of the world ; so they are rarely spoken of. Thongas have, however, a name for them, *shimbeti*. They do not give any explanation of them and believe that they are perhaps caused by the gods. I remember having once heard a mysterious sound accompanied by a slight tremor of the soil. It was during the Boer war and was, I think, caused by the blowing up of a bridge somewhere on the other side of the range. All the Natives covered their heads with their hands and seemed greatly impressed.

The *rainbow* is called *shikwangulatilo*, viz., the one which removes the danger from the sky. Notice the stem *kwangula*, to inaugurate, which we have already met with, when dealing with pottery (p. 117). The sky after rain is compared to a new pot, from which the *nkangu* must be removed. But this is merely an expression. No one can say what the danger is that is thus removed ; it is probable that the tribe had more precise ideas on the subject in former times, and that these have become obsolete. In some of the northern clans (Nkhabelane, Mathiye, Shiburi, Mongwe) the rainbow is called the Bow of Nyandziyo. Nyandziyo is said to be a man of the olden times who made the rainbow ; he dwells in heaven and the rainbow is his bow. He it is who taught men the use of the bow.

The two great phenomena which mostly impress South Africans are lightning and rain, and of these you hear wonderful and endless stories!

4) LIGHTNING.

This is called *lihati* (li-tin), and is said to be caused by a bird called *ndlati* (yi-tin). These two words, etymologically speaking, seem to be related to each other. They possess the feminine suffix *ti* which is met with in the forms *eti, ati, oti*. This bird is also called *nkuku wa tilo* amongst the Ba-Ronga, the cock of heaven, or *psele dja tilo*, the hen of heaven, and magicians know how to determine its sex when the bird has fallen.

The thunder is attributed either to the bird itself or, more frequently, to Heaven. The proper expression for "It thunders" is : "Tilo dji djuma" — "Heaven roars."

In the Northern clans those who practise magical arts add many other particulars to the story, some of which may have been borrowed from the Pedi magicians, who seem to possess a more complete explanation of the phenomenon. According to them, the *ndlati* (Pedi, *dali*) is a bird of four colours, green, red, black and white, which lives in the mountains, by preference at the confluence of rivers. The medicine-men of former times knew its hiding place and had even found the eggs of the bird in a nest floating on the water. When a thunderstorm breaks, the bird flies to heaven into the clouds ; there may be scores of them, but one only will be dangerous (lebya) and cause death. It rushes down to the ground, striking a tree on its way, tearing its bark and its wood, and throwing it down ; or it falls on a hut and burns it, or on a man and kills him. Having reached the soil, the bird can be caught, and I heard people seriously assert that four of these birds, unable to fly away, had been found the previous year in Sikororo's country. Or the bird enters the ground, to a depth of two to three feet, and either remains there in its own form, or (this is the most common saying) deposits its urine (murundju), which had caused the flash of lightning, and flies away back to the mountains. The magician who understands the "treatment of Heaven" comes and digs at the spot ; there he finds a kind of gelatinous substance which solidifies after a little time. I possess a little of this curious drug given to me by a Pedi magician, by name Mudjumi ; it resembles a piece of chalk, and is considered very valuable on account of its rareness, and because it is used in the manufacture of the wonderful medicine of Heaven. Should a village have been struck by lightning, the magician of Heaven will come and dig out this foreign body ; if he finds it, the taboo is removed. If he does not, the whole village must move to another place. In the same way, it is taboo to warm oneself at a fire made of the wood of a tree that has been struck by lightning, or to use it as fuel.

The flute of Heaven.

Drawn by J. Wavre.

Happily this dreadful bird can be prevented from killing and burning by magical means. Both the Pedi Mudjumi and the Thonga Makasane possessed the enchanted flute, by which they could force Heaven — or the bird of Heaven — to spare them. Mudjumi having sold me his flute, I can describe it at length. It is made of a hollow bone five inches long, covered with Varan skin, filled at its larger extremity with a black substance like wax. Inside, to keep it clean, there is a vulture's feather. The bone is said to have been taken from the ndlati bird ; the wax substance was made from powder obtained by drying up and pulverising a little of the heart, the eye, the bones, the feathers, and the flesh of the bird. In the wax are embedded three seeds of Abrus precatorius, the "lucky bean" well-known in South Africa, a round seed of a splendid coral colour with a black spot, very much used in Thonga magic. This addition of Abrus precatorius intensifies the sound of the flute and enables it to reach heaven. The magician, seeing the thunderstorm approaching, climbs up the hill without any fear, blows in his flute : psee... psee... psee..., and shouts : "You! Heaven! Go further! I have nothing against you! I do not fight against you!" He may add in a threatening tone : "If you are sent by my enemies against me, I will cut you open with this knife of mine." The thunderstorm will then pass away!

This invocation to Heaven is curious, and we shall better understand it when studying the part played by Heaven in Thonga religion. Here I am merely considering the superstition as an attempt at explaining a natural phenomenon. And we may well ask : how is it possible for such absurdities to be believed, and firmly believed, by men who are not at all devoid of a sense of observation? The idea that lightning is a bird comes perhaps from the fact that its movements in falling from above resemble the evolutions of a bird in the air. After all the phenomenon is so sudden that this explanation could easily be accepted by the imagination of the savage. As regards the statements about the coagulated urine of the bird, I must admit that I was unable to understand on what they could be based, until I saw some samples of fulgurites found where lightning had struck the ground ; the heat of the electric current vitrifies the sand, forming a kind of pipe, which enters the soil, where it ramifies to a certain depth. These fulgurites, though not perfectly answering to the description given by Native magicians, may have been the natural substratum upon which Bantu imagination built up all the other superstitions.

5) THE PROBLEM OF RAIN AND THE WAY THONGAS DEAL

WITH IT.

All over the earth the question of rainfall is of primary importance, but this is especially the case in Subtropical Africa, even more than anywhere else. Rain may not fall during seven months, from April to October, and nobody worries about it. But if it fails in November and December, at the beginning of the rainy season, it is a dreadful misfortune, a calamity more serious than any other. The life of every individual, and consequently of the whole clan, is threatened. Famine will certainly follow, as cereals can only be sown during these two months and famine means not only suffering and anguish, but often death, in a primitive tribe which is totally ignorant of trade with out-lying countries, and does not possess any means of conveyance for food bought in other lands. No wonder therefore that the imagination of the South African Native has invented ways and means of regularising the rainfall, and that rites, and charms, and all the powers of magic have been resorted to with a view to ensuring the precious rain to the tribe at the right time.

These methods may be classified in two categories : the rites which aim at removing the causes which are believed to prevent rain and the charms by which the rain is made to fall, irrespective of any preventing cause.

a) *The causes which prevent rainfall and the rites by which they are removed.*

The general view is that rain comes *from the gods* : "Psikwembu psi nisa mpfula" — "the spirits of the ancestors cause rain to fall." So, should the spring showers not come in due time, the first idea will be to offer a sacrifice to the ancestor-gods, especially if the bones consulted have revealed that the anger of the gods is the real cause. Men will go to the sacred wood where the ancestors have been buried, sing there an ancient mourning song (I suppose No. 15, page 286, is used for the purpose), and some of them will beat the graves with sticks. As regards the sacrifice, it consists of a black victim, or it may even be the offering of a living human being to the gods ; these rites will be described later on.

Or it may be that a certain individual, *a wizard*, endowed with magical power, or rather possessing enchanted drugs, prevents the rain from falling (a siba mpfula) through wickedness, or hatred of his countrymen. This is a rarer occurrence.

But the terrible calamity of drought is brought into direct

relation with some physiological phenomena which no one would have thought of in this connection : the miscarriage of women when the foetus has not been dealt with according to rule, the birth of twins, the death of children not yet received into the tribe by the ceremony of *boha puri* (I. p. 56) and not buried in wet ground ; these are the great natural causes which prevent rain from falling ! I have met with this conception all over the Thonga tribe. I found it also amongst the Pedis of the Transvaal, who firmly believe it, and it would be most interesting to know if Suthos, Zulus, and Hottentots have the same superstitions. Let me quote the *ipsissima verba* of Mankhelu, the great medicine-man of the Nkuna Court. I shall never forget the earnest tone of his voice, his deep conviction, when he uttered to me the following words, as a kind of revelation : "When a woman has had a miscarriage, when she has let her blood flow secretly and has buried the abortive child in an unknown place, it is enough to make the burning winds blow, and to dry up all the land : the rain can no longer fall, because the country is no longer right (tiko a ra ha lulami). Rain fears that spot. It must stop at that very place and can go no further. This woman has been very guilty. She has spoilt the country of the chief, because she has hidden blood which had not yet properly united to make a human being. That blood is taboo ! What she has done is taboo. It causes starvation."

"What then must be done ?" — "The chief will collect his men and ask them : 'Are you in a normal state ?' (lit. are you right ?). They answer : 'Such and such a woman was pregnant but nobody knows what she has brought forth.' This woman will be arrested and told to go and show us where she has put it. The earth is dug up ; the hole is sprinkled with a decoction made of two drugs prepared in a special pot, the *mbendula* and *nyangale* ; the woman herself must wash her body every day with that medicine. Then a little of the earth taken from the hole will be scraped up and thrown into the river ; water drawn from the river will be poured into the hole : the country will be well again, and then the rain will come.

"Moreover, we, the medicine-men, after having sent old

women to the river to throw away the contaminated earth, order them to make a ball of that earth, and to bring it back to us in the early morning. We grind it, we put it into a pot where it must remain for five days, and then we prepare the great drug to sprinkle the land. The medicine is put into oxen horns and they go to all the drifts, to the boundaries of the country, on the borders of the Ṅwebeti and of the Thabina rivers, on the road to Sibila's country, to Diskop (Leydsdorp); they must not however cross rivers. Our neighbours do the same on their own side. One of the girls digs the earth, the others dip a stick into the horn and sprinkle the drug into the hole. We also sprinkle the road on which these women have trodden, when they had their blood; we remove the misfortune caused by these women on the roads. The country is pure again. Rain can fall."

This is the purifying rite in the Nkuna clan. Mankhelu asserts that the Pedis do the same. He did not know if the custom existed amongst other Thonga clans. But Viguet described the same custom to me as being in force on the borders of the Limpopo, under the name of *mbelele*. The bones having revealed that the country is impure, the chief orders the mbelele : it is a period of mourning (nkosi) for the land. First the *phoḳolo*, or sacrifice of the black victim is performed (See Part VI). Then the women assemble. They must remove all their clothing, only putting some grass round their loins and, with a peculiar skipping step, singing a special song : "Mpfula nana" — "rain fall," — they go to all the spots where children prematurely born have been buried in dry ground, on the hills, take away what they find in the broken pots and collect all that impure matter in a secret place, so that children may see nothing of what they are doing. Water is poured on these graves in order to "quench them (timula)." On the evening of the same day they go and bury these impurities; this is done in the mud, near the river. No man must approach during this operation : the women would have the right to strike the imprudent one and ask him questions on the obscene formulae of circumcision ; the man would answer in the most impure words he could find, as all language taboos are suspended on that day ; nakedness even is no longer taboo, "because," says Viguet, "it is the law of the country!" Every one consents to the suspension of the ordinary laws! (1)

Amongst the Rongas, I did not hear of any connection between prematurely born children and rain. When the mbelele rite is performed, a mother of twins must lead the procession of women who draw water and pour it on the graves of the twins in order to secure the rain. They also clean all the wells (kuha tinhlobo), digging them afresh and removing any filth in the water. It may be that the corpse of a twin, if it has been buried in dry ground, will be dug out of its grave and buried again near the river, or they will go in procession and pour water on the grave. This will influence Heaven, which is killing the earth by the terrible heat of the sun. The burning October winds will cease and the rain will fall.

There is something mysterious about all these customs. Considered merely as ideas regarding Nature and natural phenomena, I believe their essential meaning to be this : — there are some cases of human birth which are taboo. While any birth is taboo, owing to the lochia, that of children prematurely born is doubly dangerous. Abnormal children, such as twins, children who have died before the "boha puri" rite (I. p. 56), in some clans also children who cut their upper teeth first, share this noxious character. They are a calamity for the whole land as they are connected with the mysterious power of Heaven, and so prevent the rain from falling. The great remedy for the evil, the only means of counteracting this influence, is to bury these children in wet ground. Should this not been done, the chief must order these little corpses to be exhumed and buried near the river : this is the aim and object of the mbelele. If wet, these graves will cause no harm (2).

How did these extraordinary conceptions first originate ?

(1) This rite of *mbelele* shows striking analogies with the Passage rites which we have already often met with in Thonga customs. This is a special period, a mourning period for the land, says Viguet, a marginal period which, as such, is accompanied by obscene manifestations, both in speech and in absence of clothing.

(2) In the Maluleke clan, as previously mentioned, these three categories of children must be *cremated*, and foreigners dying in the midst of the clan are also burnt after their death, from fear that they might belong to one of these categories and so prevent the rain from falling, if they were buried in dry ground. The mbelele rite there is called *nkelenkele*. Rangane describes it as follows: — Women collect the bones of twins,

What is the connection between abnormal births of human beings and the rain-fall? I think it can be found in the conception of Heaven which has inspired so many curious rites, and which I shall explain in the next chapter. So it is possible that, after all, the mbelele rite has a religious idea at its base.

b) *Rain charms.*

The removal of the corpses of abnormal children from dry ground and their burial near the river probably sometimes proves ineffective to produce rain. So Bantu magicians have invented a great many charms to obtain the greatly desired showers, and the power of the rain-makers is enormous. Our tribe does not seem to have developed this art as much as others. The Sutho-Pedis are masters in this domain and Mankhelu, who had been taught by them and had become a great and renowned rain-maker, revealed all his secrets to me. He possessed the drug and used it frequently, he said, having often been called in by Sutho chiefs dwelling in far distant districts, as far off as Pretoria. He assured me that he had met with so much success that these chiefs had given him oxen, horses, a waggon, precious beads, etc.! Where had he found this marvellous drug? At Rivimbi (in Venda : Luvimbi), a country north of Spelonken, not far from the Limpopo and to which he went, as far as I could make out, in 1865 or 1866. The Luvimbi people are the descendants of Luvimbi, (1) a chief of the old times (as old as Nkuna, says Mankhelu) who, after his death, went to heaven and became king of heaven ; he still exists there as a spirit, hearing and knowing everything that is done on earth. This Luvimbi is probably the same whom the Vendas call the first man, and concerning whom they have a number of traditions

and those of still-born children or those who died at birth ; to these they add their old rags (perhaps the cloths used for their menses ?) ; they bring all these impurities to the cross-ways and *burn them* there, singing impure songs, saying : "To-day is a great day ! There is no taboo any more ! If you prohibit anything, it will be an insult to the rain ; it will not fall." The smoke of all that they have burnt constitutes a religious offering : now the country will be pure and the rain will fall. The conception prevailing among the Malulekes is somewhat different from that of the Rongas.

(1) I have published an account of the Venda traditions connected with Luvimbi or Raluvimbi in *The S. A Journal of Science*, April 1921, where more details will be found concerning this personage.

which I shall mention a little later. They all invoke him to obtain rain, asserts Mankhelu, even Modjadji, the great queen who has acquired such fame : she does not pretend to be superior to Luvimbi ; she owes her rain-making power to him! His successors have kept the famous recipe for rainmaking. Mankhelu visited them. He brought with him "bukosi," viz., riches, and they gave him horns full of the drug. One of them is in my possession ; it seems to be the horn of a he-goat. These people manufacture the rain-producing medicine on an extensive scale. Baskets are seen in their huts, full of the ingredients of which it is composed. Strange to say, these ingredients all come *from the sea* ; as far as I could identify them from Mankhelu's description, they are : sea-urchins, (shinana sha mitwa), sea-weeds (pindja ra lwandle, lit. rope of the sea), bones of whales, or sea-fish, bivalve sea-shells, pieces of wood from wrecked vessels run aground, etc. All these are roasted and, when the process is sufficiently advanced, sea-water is poured on them to cool them (timula). They are then pulverised and "salted" with another drug called "shinyuke," something black which I could not identify. The powder so obtained is put into the horns, half of which are dipped into sheep's fat and so become female drugs. Having been given the four horns, two male and two female, Mankhelu was told that these would retain their virtue for ever ; when he saw that their contents were nearly finished, he could always prepare a fresh supply by roasting marine products, but he would have to grind a little of the original drug with the new powder in order to *pfusha*, viz., to raise its strength, according to the universal practice of Bantu medicine-men. The original drug is the well-spring (shihlobo). Should any one try to manufacture the drug himself, using exactly the same ingredients, he would meet with total failure, as the virtue of the drug is derived from two sources : the produce of the sea, and the power of the first inventor, Luvimbi.

Having returned with the precious charm, when summoned by any chief to act as rain-maker, Mankhelu employed it in the following way.

He first asked the chief to kill a black goat or sheep (a he-goat, or a ram, if the bones said so) ; the head, at any rate, had

321

to be black. The heart was pierced with a puncheon and the blood flowed. He carefully washed the horns with the blood and smeared them later on (horola) with the "psanyi" found in the intestines of the animal. Then he took his *ntsiko*, viz., the two pieces of wood which served as his flint, poured a little of the powder into the notch of the female stick and made fire by the rapid friction described on p. 34. In the meantime Mankhelu prayed as follows : "Here are the drugs, Rivimbi of Tsome (Rivimbi's father)! Give us rain." Then he invoked his own gods, saying : "Go to Rivimbi for me and come along here all of you to make the rain fall." This performance is a "mhamba," a means of calling the gods, especially Rivimbi, "the master of this mhamba." After a while the wood began to burn ; leaves of the "nembe-nembe" bush (Cassia petersiana) were placed on it and a black smoke rose and ascended to heaven. Then the clouds appeared and soon the thunderstorm broke. A feather of the ndlati bird of lightning was placed amongst the leaves as a protection against thunderbolts.

Mankhelu was absolutely convinced of the efficacy of this means of rain-making, and there seems to be more sense in this rite than in many others. To use the sea to cause rain to fall, is not after all so absurd! I would not assert that Natives have a clear idea as to the formation of clouds, *mapapa* (Dj.), *matlabi* (Ro.), and know that the water from above comes from the water below, but at any rate they know that the sea is water and rain is also water. To obtain rain by smoke rising from burning sea products is a procedure which is in keeping with one of the most common beliefs of primitive man, that like produces like, a belief which has found its expression in the famous principle of the old physicians : "Similia similibus curantur."

When practising his rain-making art at home, Mankhelu proceeded with less ceremonial pomp. After having consulted his bones, he took four leaves of the tjeke plant (p. 14), smeared them with the magical powder and exposed them to the rays of the burning sun. As soon as these leaves were fully dry, "Heaven began to roar" and the rain came.

The great rain medicine is of Pedi or Venda origin. In addition to the sacrifice of the black victim and to the mbelele rite of purification of the land,which are characteristic Thonga customs, it seems that another old Thonga way of obtaining rain was the *tjeba fishing* which I described on p. 86. When the whole clan had gone to catch the barbels in the almost dried up ponds, a thunderstorm would come and rain would fall. This was especially the case with certain small lakes such as Malangotiba in Nondwane, and that in Nsime near Morakwen, because battles had taken place on their borders and the enemies' corpses had been thrown into the water. So these lakes had become "great sacred woods" (ntimu). I suppose the spirits of the deceased, which were certainly "gods of bitterness," (see next chapter), were supposed to prevent the rain, and the *tjeba* either appeased them or made them powerless.

To sum up this very complicated subject, I would say rain rites belong to three different categories: 1) The religious rites connected with ancestor worship (black offering, visit to the sacred woods, old songs and sometimes offering of a human victim). 2) Rites of purification of the land, those which are derived from the mysterious relations established between the power of Heaven and abnormal births (mbelele, cleaning of wells by women accompanied by the mother of twins) ; these present some features of the ordinary passage rites, either because the fall of rain inaugurates a new season, or because drought is a calamity comparable with death and attended with contamination. 3) The magic rites, in which sea charms play the most important part.

Hail, shihangu (Dj.), mabyana, lit. little stones (Ro.), is frequent in Thongaland ; according to Mboza, it is not the object of any peculiar superstitions. Amongst the Pedis the day on which it has fallen must be kept as a sabbath. It is taboo to till the fields on that day.

IV. *The Inorganic World.*

Water is called *mati*, a noun of the bu-ma class, the class of liquids, employed only in the plural form. Notice the suffix *ti*, which seems to show that, at a period when mythological conceptions were still current, it was considered as a feminine principle. This supposition is confirmed by the fact that *rivers* (nambu. pl. milambu) also have the feminine termination (I. p. 36, Note). I find the following names of rivers ending in *ti* : Nkomati, Nfoloti (Umbelosi), Nwebeti, Shalati, Timbati ; the termination *etsi*, *edzi*, may be another form of the same suffix (Nwanetsi, Ntsatsi, Shingwedzi, Madzi, etc.). A very curious fact, which shows the same conception, is that the river which crosses the territory of the Tembe clan is called Mi-Tembe. I first thought this to be a plural form of the mu-mi class ; but it is more natural to explain this *mi* as the feminine prefix (1) which means daughter of, as Migogwe, etc. (I. p. 352).

Crossing rivers is subject to a curious rule. It is taboo to bathe in the stream before crossing it ; taboo also for the traveller to cook his food on the hither side of the river ; he must first cross, and then take his meal. This rule is still universally observed by waggon trekkers in South Africa. In this case there may be a reason for the taboo : South African rivers are apt to be swollen in a moment by sudden rain, and the crossing made impossible for days : the traveller therefore makes haste ; he will have plenty of time to stop on the other side! When the river is dangerous, a Thonga will first chew (phora) a little of his *ndjao*, the root of a juncus, which is supposed to increase courage and to ensure victory over hostile influences. (See Part VI.)

Some *Lakes* and *Rivers* are believed to be inhabited by spirits, but not in the ordinary fetichistic way, in which a special spiritual being is incorporated with the natural object ; these spirits are *psikwembo*, spirits of the deceased ancestors of the owners of the land, and are propitiated by their descendants. Should another clan have invaded the territory where these lakes are, and crocodiles threaten the fishermen, (p. 88) they will call some one belonging to the clan of the old possessors of the country and ask him to make an offering to appease *his* gods. This is the ordinary course, and the more closely we search the more completely these lake and

---

(1) A number of river names have the prefix *li* or *ri*, especially those which are of Sutho origin : Lebvubye. Ritabi (Letaba) Ritshindjele (Letsitele), Rimbelule (Lepalula, Olifant). Others begin with ñwa, ma, and may be ancient names of men.

river spirits become identified with ancestor-gods. In my investigations I found one case, however, where a special spirit, a kind of Nature spirit seemed to be invoked. This was on the sea shore, in the northern part of Nondwane, at a place called Mahilane, where there are two great rocks on the beach. When the great waves dash against them, with a fearful roar, people go and sacrifice (hahla) ; they pray thus : "Tsu! Oh sea! Let vessels be wrecked, and steamers also, and let their riches come to us and help us." In former times, a young girl was sometimes exposed there as a prey, or an offering to the power of Mahilane. Now this is exactly what is done in the sacred woods for the ancestor gods and, in fact, Mboza asserts that : "When abandoning the girl, the officiant says : You, Psikwembo, ancestor-gods, drive on the sea that it may wreck vessels."

When urged to speak with more precision, my informant answered : "Mahilane and the sea are one and the same thing (ntshumu muñwe). When the sea is roaring people exclaim : 'Mahilane roars'! Near the island of Shefin, where two branches of the Nkomati river meet in the estuary, people say : 'Makaneta is roaring'. Here it is Makaneta and no longer Mahilane."

This information is extremely interesting. As regards Makaneta, we know him perfectly well ; he is the ancestor of Mboza and descendant of Mazwaya (I. p. 360). This ancestor-god begins to be confused with a natural phenomenon taking place in the country where he lived. The religious fear of the spirit of the deceased mingles with the awe inspired by the roaring of the sea to such an extent that both notions coincide in the imagination of the savage. We here note the exact point where *an ancestral spirit evolves into a Nature spirit*, and this instance proves, in the clearest possible manner, that the conception of the ancestor spirit preceded that of the Nature spirit. Here, at any rate, Ancestrolatry is anterior to both Fetichism and Naturism. These later forms of the belief can be easily accounted for by the development of Ancestrolatry : the reverse process would be much more difficult to explain.

The *sea*, with its immensity and its wonderful power, deeply impresses the Thongas dwelling near it. They do not however tell many stories about it, nor did I hear of any explanation regarding its confines and the shore on the other side. Some magicians claim to have gone and stayed for some time down in the depths : to have "crossed the sea" is for them a kind of diploma, which gives them the right of exercising their art. (See Chapter III.)

The *tide* (byaela) is considered to be caused by a whale (nkomu) which alternately swallows and vomits the sea-water : this is the common idea. Some Natives, however, connect it with the moon, having noticed that the tide is higher at full moon and at the wane ·

The sea must be feared : it is jealous. "When some one is taken away by the great wave, do not shout! Do not exclaim : 'He is lost!', else you will never see him again. On the contrary, if you say : 'All right, let him go , then the returning wave will bring him back." These are the assertions of Spoon. And old Makhani expressed his approval by nodding his head!

"It is the same with *fire*," Spoon also remarked. There was a terrible bush fire in Rikatla on the 18th of September 1908. As always happens at the end of winter, the bush was absolutely dry. A leper woman, tilling her fields, wished to cook a little manioc. The fire leapt to the weeds which she had gathered and from these to the bush. Two huts were burnt. "It is their own fault," said Spoon, "when the bush fire comes you must put it out quietly. If you make any noise, if you shout, it comes straight at you. That is what happened. In the first village people fought calmly and succeeded in saving their huts. At Jeck's village, they cried out. The fire leapt on to a hut, the small hut of the son. The mother cried : 'Yo! yo! Where shall I put my child?' She went on crying out until the hut was burnt to the ground. So the fire leapt on to the big hut and burnt it. She has only herself to blame!" (1)

The origin of *stones* is absolutely unknown. Pikinini, a Nkuna boy, who was endowed with an extraordinary imagination, once drew my attention to the stratification of a large dolomite boulder on which different concentric layers were visible, and said to me :

(1) Silence is always recommended to prevent misfortune : in the case of war (I, p. 470) women at home must keep silent ; likewise when the husband is hunting hippopotami (p. 69), when a child is seized with convulsions owing to the power of *tilo* (heaven). See also my remarks on the kunga rite. (I, p. 124).

"You see! Stones also grow!" Another Native geologist, who had heard the European story of creation, coming from the Coast, a country of sand and sand only, and visiting the Drakensberg Mountains near Shiluvane, was amazed by the enormous cliffs of the Mamotswiri and gave vent to the following reflection : "No wonder we have no stones in our sandy land. When God created the earth, he used them all to build these mountains!"

Fossils are rare in Thongaland, where sand covers almost the whole country. There is however in the southern part of the Maputju region an outcrop of cretaceous rock which belongs to the Gault and which contains ammonites, Nautillus etc. Natives call them *nsongo stones* and are very much afraid of them. They say that "these stones with ribs" can walk. They bring bad luck (singita). Should a child pick up one of these fossils and bring it into the village, he will fall ill ; he must therefore undergo a special treatment.

Crystal greatly pleases the Natives. It is rare in South Africa. When magicians can secure a white or a black crystal they generally wear it round their necks together with the claws, or teeth, of wild animals, or with their little skin bags which they use as amulets. For this reason I once had the good fortune to be able to exchange a crystal I had brought from Switzerland for one of these charms !

The *earth* (misaba) is also a great and important thing. First because it is identified with the people dwelling on it, with the clan. *Tiko*, the land, means both the soil and the people. Further than this, the earth is the chief (I. p. 382) ; hence many laws : e. g. the tusk of the elephant which fell on the earth when the beast was killed, belongs to the chief, etc. (p. 57). The most solemn oath is that which is taken with earth (ku funga u hahla hi misaba). Should a man be accused of stealing or of being a wizard, if he puts a little earth in his mouth, says *tsu*, and declares : "I do not know anything about it," those who care for his safety will look for a medicine-man to treat him : it is a *mondjo* (a magical method of divination. See Chapter III). The same thing is done when an oath has been taken by sucking a piece of iron.

A curious superstition regarding the earth is this : after moving from one country to another, you should for some days mix with your food a little of the earth of the country which you have left ; this will provide the transition between the old and the new domicile (See I. p. 49).

Metals known to the tribe before the coming of the Whites were few. (See page 137). *Nhumbu* or *nsimbi*, iron, *nsuku*, copper, and *ntchopfa*, a name applied to all white metals (tin, silver, etc.) are the only Native names for metals. There is no word for gold.

V. *The Vegetable World. Thonga Botany.*

While Bantus possess a very limited knowledge of Astronomy, Geography, Mineralogy, etc., while their ideas in these domains are in no way deserving of the name of Science, they are much more advanced as regards Plants. Here it is quite allowable to speak of a Science, a rudimentary Science, no doubt, but a true, precise knowledge which has been transmitted from past ages and which denotes a real power of observation.

The Delagoa flora is not very rich. I have succeeded in collecting between four and five hundred different kinds in a herbarium which I sent many years ago for classification to the Herbier Boissier in Geneva. In February 1893, before forwarding the second lot of exsiccata, I gathered together some Natives of Rikatla in the hut which I had pompously styled a Museum and, having promised them 1 s. each if they consented to remain till the end of the examination, I submitted the dried plants to them, asking them their names, their uses, etc. The result of the inquiry was marvellous. My areopagus did not seem to be a very choice one : an old woman, as dry as my exsiccata and smoking her pipe, another with ochre-smeared hair, a young one, with a baby on her shoulder, an elderly one-eyed man named Hamunde, my milkman. After them came the young chief Muzila, walking slowly, swinging the tails of his belt. This chief, notwithstanding his social rank, showed gross ignorance of botany ; but some of the others knew the name of almost every plant ; had I had a *ñanga*, a medicine-man, amongst them, I am sure I should have obtained the names of all the specimens of the collection, for they are the great connoisseurs in this domain, their drugs being almost entirely obtained from the vegetable world.

A study of these names undoubtedly proves that Natives have the notion of the *genus*. This had been denied ; it seems that, when naming animals, Bantus distinguish correctly between species, but do not classify species into genera. In Botany it is not so. Under the same name they bring together forms which are sometimes widely different, but which belong to the same genus. Here are some of these names.

Tsuna means fern and applies to the Acrostichum tenuifolium, which climbs up the palm trees in the marsh, as well as to the few other kinds of Filicea found in the district of Lourenço Marques ; *goñhwa* is the name for Liliaceae, many kinds of which blossom in the spring : the Crinum Forbesii, with its big white and pink flower, and other kinds forming a bowl at the extremity of the stem ; there are five kinds of Commelina in my collection, which were called *Nkompfana*, both those with blue flowers, and the yellow ; a certain Papillionaceae genus, the Eriosema, is called *Rongole*. All the Strigae, a genus of the Scrophulariaceae family, are known under the name of *Shitshinyambita*, those which prevent the pot from boiling, as they are believed to have this effect when put into the fire. The Lobeliae are called *Shilawana*, etc.

The notion of the *genus* is so truly present that Thongas distinguish between various species in the same genus. So the tree called *Nkahlu*, an Apocynea, the Tabaernaemontana ventricosa, a valuable tree whose sap is used as a styptic, and whose roots are used to make a decoction for lung complaints, has a congener, found in the palm-tree marsh, the Voacanga Dregei, which is called *Nkahlutjobo*, nkahlu of the marsh. The two genera are very closely akin to each other.

Cognate species found in various regions are thus distinguished by the mention of their habitat, either the hill (ntlhaba), or the black earth (nyaka), or the forest (mutju). There is the *Muhlu wa ntlhaba*, of the hill, and *Muhlu-tjhobo*, of the marsh (Secamone sp. tree of the Asclepiadaceae family). This is even more striking in the case of the Hibiscus genus. Its name is *Ntjhesi* ; there are the Ntjhesi of the hill (Hibiscus surratensis, etc.), the Ntjhensi of the nyaka, another species found in Morakwen in the black earth ; and there is the *shitjhesinyana sha ntlhaba*, double diminutive of ntjhesi, the Sida cordifolia, a pretty little Malvacea, a near relative of the Hibiscus, very much used in treating children's complaints, a panacea for babies, as it cures their vomiting, headache, wounds and internal troubles!

I find the same correct connection established between two Anonaceae shrubs, the Artabotrys brachypetala, called *Ntiti*, and the Art. Monteiroae, called *Shintitane*, little Ntiti, of the same genus, but a shrub of a very different appearance.

However there is, of course, no anatomical study at the base of this classification : so their ideas of genus are not always, scientifically speaking, correct. They call any parasite *Phakama*, whatever may be its form, and have a superstitious fear of them, especially of the larger ones, growing on other trees, such as the nkanye and nkuhlu : "Phakama dja singita!" (1)

Nkushe means sea-weed, either the true algae, as Lagarosiphon muscoides, or other plants growing in water and belonging to totally different families, such as Urticularia stellaris, found in the same locality. *Nkaka*, or *Nkakana*, is the little Cucumber already described (p. 14), whilst *Nkaka wa tjhobo* is a Convolvulvus (Ipomea cairica). The *Shirimbyati*, one of the names most employed, designates first the Helichrysum parviflorum, a yellow Composita which covers the sandy dunes, and blossoms during the winter ; but *Shirimbyati sha tjhune*, the male one, is Gnaphalium stenophyllum, and *Shirimbyati sha mutju*, the one of the forest, an Indigofera belonging to the Leguminosae family ; these three plants have in common small hard leaves : hence the same name is given to them, although they are by no means related botanically speaking. So shirimbyati corresponds to our word heath, which is applied to many forms of evergreen undergrowth.

---

(1) "The parasite stem *singita*," i. e. is of bad omen. They do not say *yila*, is taboo, though some rules apply to it similar to those concerning the tree struck by lightning. One does not warm oneself at its fire ; its wood is not employed to cook food, for fear lest men should suffer from hydrocele.

The want of an enlightened botanical sense is further seen in the following fact : three different kinds of Vernonia, though belonging to the same genus, are called by different names, as if the Thongas had altogether failed to perceive their relation. The Vernonia cinerea is called *Ntshontshongori* ; the V. Perotteti, *Nkukulashibuya* (the plant with which one sweeps the threshing floor) ; the V. Tigna, *Hlunguhlungu*.

Another case of one and the same name applied to plants of different families having merely an external resemblance is the following : the *Ndjiba* is a Leguminosa tree of large proportions, Apalatoa delagoensis (Schinz), and the *Shindjibana*, viz., the little Ndjiba, is a small shrub with leaves somewhat similar to those of the Ndjiba. Its scientific name is Synaptolepis Oliveriana and it belongs to the Thymeleaceae family.

It is no wonder that the notion of genus, though existant, has not always been correctly and universally applied. Thongas have no idea of the anatomy of plants ; they have never dissected a flower, and are totally ignorant of the presence of male and female elements in it. They know, however, that these sexual differences exist. They have noticed, for instance, amongst the nkanye stems, which are of a dioecious species, that some are male and some female, and they carefully preserve some of the male stems in order to fecundate the female ones ; but they believe that this fecundation takes place through the roots of the trees!

Thus, when the name of a plant can be explained, we see that, in naming it, *its external characters, or its uses,* have alone been considered. For instance the beautiful yellow Sterculiacea, Melhania Forbesii, is called *Muhlwadambu*, Setting Sun, because its deep colour is similar to that of the sun when dipping below the horizon. A certain plant whose seeds explode when crushed is the *Buputwana*, because, "it says bu-bu-bu." A climbing Composita with juicy stem is the *Kamele*, "the one which is pressed," (kama) to squeeze out its juice, which is said to have a medicinal value. A Euphorbiacea whose fruit is eaten by the partridges (Fluggea obovata) is the *Midyañhwari*, partridges' food. Those named after their uses are, for instance, *Nkukulashibuya*, the one which sweeps the threshing floor (Vernonia Perotteti) ; *Nhlangulaba-*

tjongwana, the one employed to wipe little children when dirty!
(This plant is tomentous and answers well for the purpose);
Psekamafura, a large tree (Casearia Junodi, Schinz), a tree whose
fuel is particularly good for melting mafureira fat (p. 18), etc.
The Asparagus bearst he name of *Nkwangulatilo*, the same as
that of the rainbow. When asked why this is so, Natives say
that it is because the colour of the asparagus leaves resembles
that of the rainbow, but another explanation which seems to
me more probable is this : it is because this plant is given as a
medicine to little children to prevent the roaring of thunder from
"tearing out their diaphragm (handjula lipfalo)."

The great use of the vegetable world is to provide men with
food and medicine. If plants bear names and have been carefully
studied by the Bantus this is, in the first place, because they are
useful in these two respects. We have already considered Thonga
vegetarian food (p. 9-19), and I shall devote some pages to the
medical art in Chapter III.

In Appendix II, I give a list of Thonga botanical names with
their scientific equivalents. These plants have been identified
by Dr. Schinz, who published a flora of Delagoa Bay in the
"Bulletin de l'Herbier Boissier," No. 10, 1900.

The conclusion reached from this study of Thonga names of
plants is that the vegetable world has been the subject of a true and,
in a certain sense, scientific observation on their part. Their
botanical knowledge can be compared with that of our forefathers
of two or three hundred years ago, before Botany became a true
science, when plants were still named from their external characteristics, and studied as medicinal herbs ; I would even say that
this knowledge, though of an inferior type, is more general amongst
Thongas than, for instance, amongst the European peasantry ;
a fact which shows that their powers of observation and scientific
study are not inferior to those of other more advanced races.

Do plants play a part in Thonga religion? (1)

When travelling through the country, you may come across

(1) The Vendas plant the bulbs of an Amaryllida which they call Lohome near
the stone which they use as an altar. See *S. A. Journal of Science*, Vol. XVII.
p. 215.

a tree round which a rag has been tied, evidently for some religious purpose. One's first idea would be that this tree is worshipped, but this is by no means the case. The tree is probably that which the divinatory bones have singled out as the one around which the village should be built, and the offering of this rag is made to the spirits of the ancestors, exactly as is done when the rag is placed near the grave, or at the door of the little hut built on it, in the case of those possessed. (See I. p. 141 and later on Chapter III). The tree is only sacred on account of this association. I have sometimes called the *Nkanye* a sacred tree, and the Thongas call it the king of trees, but it is not so in itself, or in virtue of any Nature spirit dwelling in it ; anybody can cut it without transgressing a taboo ; it is venerated because it provides the tribe with the national beer, and because its branches are used as pillows for the dead and its twigs as *mhamba* in the funeral service (I. p. 138). The religious and social *luma*, to which the bukanyi is subject (I. p. 397), is observed from fear of the ancestral spirits and not because the tree itself is in any way worshipped. In fact I never met with any worship offered to a plant as such.

VI. *The Animal World.*

Plants, *psimili or psa-ku-mila*, things which grow (ku mila), are distinguished from animals, called *psibandjana*, or *psihari*, which are said to *kula*, become great, and not *mila*.

The knowledge possessed by the Thongas with regard to animals is extensive. They give names to all the larger ones, especially, of course, to those which are eaten, but also to some which are smaller, insignificant and useless.

The *Annelida* are called by the generic name of *tinyokana*, diminutive of *nyoka* (yin-tin), snake ; leeches, *ntjundju* (mumi) ; lumbrics, *nshikwa* (yin-tin), both those living in the earth and parasites in the intestines of children.

Amongst *Myriapoda* the Julideae are called *Khongoloti* (dji-ma) ; the Millepedes, *Ndlandlalati* (yin-tin). When one of these has stung a Native, you will see him swallow a little earth, and a

333

mouthful of water after it, to prevent swelling. "The milleped will die at once and you will not suffer much, because you have been wiser than it (u yi rangelile butlharin)."

The same precaution is taken with regard to Scorpions, *shiphame* (Dj.), *mubalane* (Ro.). Other Arachnida are Spiders (*pume* (dji-ma) *ripe* (dji-ma), Ticks *(shikalana)*, and the Itch *(shinwayana)*, which Thongas know but too well without being aware that it is caused by a microscopic animal. To this group probably belongs the *maroda*, a parasite met with in the huts of Bilen and other remote parts of the country, whose bite causes actual disease.

The *insect world*, so richly represented in Tropical countries (1) is pretty well known, though many of its representatives are of no practical use to the Natives.

Orthoptera. Acridius peregrinus, the locust which ravages the fields, is called *humbi* (yin-tin) in Ronga and *ndjiya* (yin-tin) in Djonga. (See p. '81). The first "clouds" which appeared greatly impressed the Natives when they were seen at the beginning of the war of 1894. I heard some one say that this phenomenon had been foretold by a "mulungwana," a little man fallen from heaven to announce this calamity which threatened the land. (See next Chapter). Other Acridians are called *mhera* (yin-tin); the larvae of locusts, which abound at certain times in the gardens, are the *hondje* (yin-tin). The Pamphygus, a fat, heavy, grey locust, the female apterous, are called *phuphu* (dji-ma). The Grillus is *Shiyendlwa* (shi- psi), and is eaten by some. But the best known Orthoptera are those of the Mantidae family whose representatives are numerous in the country. They are called *Ñwambyevu* (Dj.) or *Ñwambyevulane* (Ro.), viz., the one which cuts the hair, probably on account of its claws, which move like scissors. This insect plays a great part in the superstitions of the Bushmen, who worship it. Amongst the Thongas there is a similar custom ; young shepherds, when they meet with a Mantis,

---

(1) See my publications on the Entomology of Delagoa Bay; I. *Coleoptera*, in collaboration with Dr. Bugnion ; II *Orthoptera*, by Dr. A. von Schulthess Rechberg ; III *Hemiptera* by Prof. Montandon in the "Bulletin de la Société vaudoise des Sciences Naturelles." XXV, p. 132-220; IV), *Lepidoptera*, "Bulletin de la Société Neuchâteloise des Sciences Naturelles" Tome XXVII, p. 177-250.

tear out a little hair from the skins of their belt and offer it to the insect saying : "Take, Grandfather!" They say that in old times they were looked on as gods (psikwembu), or rather emissaries of the ancestor-gods, just like the little green snakes (Chapter II) ; their name was Mahulwahulwane, and when one of them entered a hut, no one interfered with it, as it was thought that perhaps some god had come to pay a visit to his descendants. These ideas regarding Mantidae seem to be now disappearing and the offering made to them is merely a little children's game. Another Orthoptera is the *Shipfalapfapfa*, an onomatopoeia, describing a flying locust, and the *Shishirikoko*, a large species which emits saliva through its thorax. When it flies the Thongas say to it : "Go to the place where people eat meat!"

Hemiptera. Bugs are well, too well, known in Thongaland, having taken up their abode in most of the huts, where they are tolerated. They are called *Nsiketi* (yin-tin) and the wild bugs *Nsiketi ya nhoba*, bug of the bush. Lice, *Nhwala* (yin-tin), are regarded as vermin, and often as the result of bewitchment, especially when seen swarming on children. Many Aphidae (grubs) cause an exudation on certain shrubs, a kind of wax, the *Mubodi*, which is used for the manufacture of the black crowns (I, p. 130) ; others are called *Shibungubungu*, the red ones, probably a kind of cochineal.

Neuroptera. *Diptera*. The equivalent of these names of flies is *Nhongana* (yin-tin). Mosquitoes are called *Busuna* and fleas *Butseka*, with the prefix *bu* which here means a collection, a great number. *Busokoti*, a similar word, designates ants. The big gad-flies are the *Bawa* (dji-ma). The Libellulidae are called *Mungutane* (mu-ba) and the Termitideae *Muhlwa* (mu-mi).

Lepidoptera. Butterflies and moths are designated by a single word, *Phaphalati* (Dj. Notice the feminine suffix), or *Phaphatane* (Ro.) (dji-ma), and their caterpillars by the term *Hukwa* (yin-tin) or *Tomane* (dji-ma), this last word especially applying to the large Saturnidae caterpillars which are eaten by the Natives (p. 80). The relation between the caterpillar and the butterfly is not generally known ; only once did I find a boy who knew that a certain white cocoon, used as an ornament in dances (p. 102) gave

335

birth to the big green moth with long tails, the Queen Moth. The reason why butterflies, though plentiful in Thongaland, have so little attracted the attention of Natives is, no doubt, the fact that they do not in any way contribute to their food. I have told the story of a woman who tried to force a child to eat a butterfly. (I. p. 445.)

Coleoptera. The general term for Coleoptera is *Shifufununu*, and it especially applies to the big Tenebrionidae (Psammodes Bertoloni), called *shifufununu sha paripari* (p. 68) and to the large black Carabidae of the Anthia genus which abound on the roads in spring ; one of them, marked with small depressions on the elytra is, for that reason, called the small-pox shifufununu (sha nyedzane). Travelling once with a grown-up Thonga we saw a black Carabida which had four white spots on the back. It was the charming Eccoptoptera mutilloides. I saw him trace a circle round it in the sand saying : "To-day I shall eat to my heart's content !" — "Namunhla ndji ta shura !" — "What are you doing ?" I said. — "Oh ! This is the *Shurwa-shurwane*," he answered. "When you meet it it is a sign that you will have plenty to eat !" He was mistaken ! The real shurwa-shurwane is the Mutilla, a kind of apterous wasp, which has also four white spots on its back, and the beetle we met was so similar to it that he mistook it for a Mutilla ; is it not called mutilloides, pseudo-mutilla ? (1) — The Copridæ are called *Gadlen* (dji-ma) and these strange dung-eaters, which are extremely abundant in the country, are thought to be under the command of the wizards who can introduce them into your body to kill you. The pretty Cerambycidæ, with their long horns, are the *Ñwahomurikotjo*, the ox of Rikotcho, or, according to a truer etymology, the ox with horns bent backwards (kotjeka). Children sing an incantation before them, clapping their hands (I, p. 68). Their big white larvae, the *Shipungwana*, ˙dig channels in the stems of nkanye, nkuhlu, mphesa, etc., and are readily eaten as well as the *Shimhukuta*, the

(1) This custom reminds one of the action of Swiss children when they send the ladybird to heaven, to ask God to give them fine weather to-morrow, or of their saying that crushing a golden Carabus on the road will cause rain to fall. Certain Coleoptera are of good omen everywhere ! Only, if in Europe they foretell fine weather, in Africa they announce a good meal. The difference is significant !

larva of a large Calandra which swarms in the stems of the palm trees of the marsh (p. 4). The *Shitambela*, a big Buprestida (Sternocera Orissa) is roasted by the shepherds and eaten after they have torn off its elytra.

Hymenoptera. Wasps are called *Mupfi* or *Mupfu* (mu-mi), and are divided into four different classes : the *Mupfu* proper (Belonogaster), the *Tlatlanhongana*, the *Bamaandlopfu*, a grey species, and the *Mumpfundlopfu*, a large black species which burrows in the soil. When someone has been stung by a wasp, the others laugh at him. If he resents being made fun of, they say to him : "Be not angry ; we do this to help you." They are really trying to divert his attention from the pain in order to comfort him. *Bees* are called *Nyoshi* (yin-tin) and are greatly appreciated for their honey (p. 44). Natives know the males (*djongwe*, dji-ma) the larvae *(shipungwa)*, which they eat with as much pleasure as the honey itself. They call the honeycombs *hahla* (dji-ma) or *shihlenga*, the wax *mumpfu* (mu-mi) and the pollen brought by the bees, *nsindjo*. The curious *Mbonga* (yin-tin) *Bee* is worth special mention, owing to the superstitions which are current regarding it, and the part it plays in certain rites (I. p. 390). This species, which does not sting, digs a narrow passage of two or three feet deep in the soil and excavates a hole of one or two feet broad where it builds its round nest. Natives say that nobody knows what the mbonga does with the earth which it digs out of the cavity in which it makes its nest. No heap of earth is ever seen in the vicinity. The hole is continued under the nest and has no end. It probably extends to subterranean pools where the insects go to drink, — as it is said that no one has ever seen a mbonga drinking from the lake or the well, as the other bees do. Moreover the entrance to a mbonga nest is invisible to the majority of people. It is only certain families who can see it and consequently dig out the precious honey (1). For all these reasons the mbonga is

(1) The Libombo family was one of those "which the mbonga loves" (randja). Elias who belongs to it told me that he once paid a visit to one of his neighbours who had just cleaned his village ; he discovered a mbonga hole and said to his friend : "There is a mbonga nest in your village." But the man was unable to find it. Elias then dug as deep as his shoulders and found the nest all surrounded by "calabashes" full of honey. He says that when rain falls the little bees cover the entrance of

surrounded with a certain mystery, and this is no doubt why its honey is used in the manufacture of the *nyokwekulu*. Its scientific name is Trigona togoensis, var. Junodi (Friese).

Amongst the *Mollusca*, a great many are eaten : the *Mbatsana* (yin-tin) of the sea (bivalve shells), *Likatla* (li-tin) of the lakes, and the *Hwaru* (yi-tin), oysters of the Tembe shore. The land snails are called *Humba* (yi-tin) ; the big ones (Achatina Lamarkiana) are used as safes for the deposit of pounds sterling and are often buried in the huts ; hence the expression *Humba ya bupfundji*, shell of riches! The smaller ones, resembling our snails (Aerope caffra), are rarer and it is considered a bad omen to meet with them on the road. — "Where you go you will hear cries of mourning!" Their name is *Shikumbukwane*. The slugs are called *Holokompfa* (yin-tin) and the smaller snails, *Shihumbanyana*, diminutive of *humba*.

Fish all have names, but having never dwelt in the close vicinity of the sea, I have not learnt them. I know the *Mfungwe* (yi-tin), the fish whose mouth ends in a saw, the *Mangapfi* (dji-ma), the name of a kind of hawk given to the flying fish of Delagoa Bay, the *Nhempfane* (yi-tin) found in the fresh water ponds, the *Ntima* (yi-tin) the barbel, the black fish which must not be eaten by lovers before their marriage (l, p. 107).

Amphibia. *Ntlambya* (mu-mi) is the ordinary frog (Rana oxyrhynca) whose young are known and called *Shilungula* ; another black species is the *Rebya* (dji-ma) ; the tree-frogs are called *Shilungwalungwana* (Rappia marmorata and argus) ; the toad *Kele* (dji-ma), Bufo regularis ; the famous Breviceps mossambicus is *Shinana* (I. p. 87) the great warrior of the tales (p. 221).

Reptilia. There are many kinds of *Lizards*. The common kind found in the houses, under the verandas is the *Mponondjo* (mu-mi) (Mabuia striata), ; the Lygodactylus capensis, found on the hills, is the *Nkolombya* (mu-mi) ; the little Agama

the hole with their wings to prevent water from inundating the nest. When it lasts too long they quickly go down to close the entrance of the nest ; the water then leaks down the pipe which descends into the interior of the earth. He added : "If a man does not belong to a family which "knows" the mbonga and if he happens to find a nest he will meet with misfortune ; one of his relatives will die. The bees will bring him ill-luck (singita)."

aculeata, which runs on the sand, *Shipyindji* or *Shihonokamahlo*, the one which gazes at you ; the large gheko, Agama atricollis, with a head of which the grey colour can change into blue, *Galagala* or *Phululu* (dji-ma) (I. p. 173) the grey one, which hides itself in dark places, in hollow stems or under roofs is the *Hoko-kwana* (dji-ma) (Hemidactylus grenatus) ; it is said that when this lizard sucks at the breast of a human being, it is impossible to remove it, and the only means of getting rid of it is to go and suckle a dog!

But the most curious lizard of these countries, that which most strikes the Native imagination is the Chameleon (Chameleon Petersii), *Lumpfana* (dji-ma). Herd boys throw ground tobacco into its mouth to avenge themselves for the bad turn it did mankind when it lingered on the road and came too late to bring the message of eternal life (as we shall learn in a moment). It is used by certain magicians to discover thieves. They smear a chameleon with a drug which makes it turn white and then let it go : "Then the thief, wherever he may be, also turns white, and if he does not confess his theft, he dies!"

The flesh of none of these lizards is eaten, but that of the big Varan which lives near the rivers, *Kwahle* (dji-ma), is considered a delicacy. The kwahle is said to be very hard to kill. About *Crocodiles* (*ngwenya*, yin-tin) all sorts of stories are told. When one of them has been killed, the contents of its stomach are carefully preserved ; Thongas assert that each year, when the rains begin, crocodiles swallow a stone, so that their age can be known by counting them. These stones are taboo ; for a subject to swallow them is a cause of death, but one of them is chosen, treated with certain drugs and swallowed by the chief to warn him of his death, as we have already seen (I, p. 393). Crocodile stones play an important part in divination. (See Part VI. Ch. III. D).

Tortoises, whose generic name is *Mfutju* (yin-tin), are eaten and also used in the divinatory art, as we shall see. Some lake tortoises are called *Gamba* (dji-ma) and sea tortoises *Hasi* (dji-ma).

Snakes (nyoka, yin-tin) are generally dreaded and considered dangerous, although many kinds are quite harmless. The

Shipyahla (Ro.), *Mhiri* (yin-tin, Dj.) is the big, lazy, grey puff adder, which creeps along the ground, and is one of the most venomous kinds, together with the *Mhamba* (yin-tin), a slender species, very swift and often found on trees. "When you meet a mhiri," say the Nkunas, "throw a little earth on it and you will soon see its brother!" Of course magicians have plenty of drugs to cure snake bites. For this purpose they use the head of the adder roasted and pulverised. *Shibatlankombe*, (Naja nigricollis), "the one which carves a spoon" is the name of a species which curves its neck till it looks like a spoon. The *Hhlaru* (yin-tin) is the boa. It is eaten. Another member of the Clapidae family is the *Likure*, a pretty greyish violet species (Causus Lichtensteinii). Amongst the harmless snakes are those little blue ones, *Shihundje* (Dendrophis subcarinatus), which are considered as emissaries of the ancestor spirits. I shall mention them again later on. The *Nsoma* (yin-tin), very common and harmless, is probably Dispholidus typus. Some small ones, not larger than worms, but hard and shining like metal, are called *Tumbi-tumbi*, because they hide (tumba) in the sand. One of them seems to be Xenocalamus bicolor.

There are also the legendary snakes of the Thongas. On the Coast they speak of the *Buwumati*, which dwells in the lakes and is invisible. It is only heard crying "bu-wu-bu-wu" when rain is falling, and its voice is as loud as that of an antelope. If it shows itself to a traveller, it is a very bad sign. The story is told of a man who came back from consulting a bone-thrower. He saw the buwumati lying on the ground, its coils extending to a great distance, closing all the passages. He retraced his steps, but after three days he died. In the Transvaal, this dreadful snake is called *Shimhemhemhe*, the name being an imitation of its cry. This superstition is perhaps of Pedi origin, but it has been accepted by the Nkunas. The shimhemhemhe dwells in certain dark woody ravines on the slopes of the Drakensberg mountains. If anyone imprudently penetrates there, the snake pursues him, creeping along the branches above, and bites him on the top of the head. A man met with it once on the way to Thabina; he saw it on the road, its head raised, a shining head of two colours. There was no end to its body. He tried to avoid it by making a long circuit ; he reached home, but died because he had seen the snake which it is death to see!

Birds (Tinyanyana, yin-tin). As I have made no regular collection of birds, I cannot here give the scientific names corresponding to the vernacular ones. These are very numerous, and they are not always the same in the different clans. Here is the list which I made by questioning the pupils of my school who came from all parts of Thongaland : (1)

Palmipeda. *Sekwa* (dji-ma) duck. *Sekwanyari, Sekwamhala, Shikukubi,* (Mal. Kho.). *Ñwafamben* (Mal. Nku.). *Shihlaka-hlaka, Lingubi* (Mal.). *Shiyankaken, Tutwana,* (Mpf. Bil.). *Ngululwana* (yin-tin), (Mpf.).

Long-legged birds. (Tinyanyana ta psikokoko). *Kukolwe* (Mpf. Bil. Mal.). *Munyangana, Ñwantjangantjangana* (mu-ba) (Mpf.). *Makhondjwawa, Gumba* (dji-ma), *Mayiwabembe, Tshebane* (Mal.). *Mugalandlopfu* (Mpf. Mal.) ; *Tshembyana* (Mal.). *Tjololwane* (Mal. Mpf.). *Yindwa, Randjane,* (Kho. Mal.). *Ñwamahlanga* (Mpf.). *Mampfana,* or *Shisibaliyendjo* (I. p. 339).

Gallinacea. *Huku,* domestic hen. *Nkuku* (mu-mi cock. *Hwari* (yin-tin) partridge. *Mhangelane* (yin-tin), Guinea fowl. *Shitjatjatja* (Mpf. Nku.). *Nkungu* (Mpf.). *Matjyatjyana* (Nku.). *Teentana,* or *keenkana* (dji-ma), quail, (Mpf.). *Nkwahla,* (Mpf. Kho.). *Hukumati,* (Mpf. Nku.). *Mangoko* (Mal.). *Makokwe,* or *Makwekwe* (Mpf.). *Hlokoyo* (Mal.). *Shibotshe* (Mal.). *Djyedjyedjye,* (Mal.). *Ndjendjenle* (Mal.). *Ndura,* (Nku.). *Ngukulukwana* (Nku.), or *Shitiwitiwi* (Mpf.). *Nkulunkulu* (Mpf. Kho.) a splendid bird, red, green and blue, called the bird of the chiefs, because chiefs used to adorn themselves with its feathers ; it is the Gallirex porphyreolophus.

Pigeons. *Tuba* (dji-ma), pigeon. *Shibambalana,* or *bombokonyi* (Mpf.) ; same as *Mbabawunyi* (Nku. Mal.). *Gororotwana* (Mpf.) corresponds to *Gugurwana* (Mal. Kho.). *Nyakungufe* (Mpf.) corresponds to *Kopolo,* or *Mangobolo* (Nku. Mal.). *Ngalane* or *Shidjuvapepe* (Mal.).

(1) Abbrev. Mal. = Maluleke ; Kho. = Khosen, Antioka ; Nku. = Nkuna ; Mpf. = Mpfumo ; Bil. = Bilene ; Spel. = Spelonken.

Sparrows. *Mbawulwane* (yin-tin), (Mpf.) or *Mbeulwane* (Kho. Nku.) swallow. *Psikidyana* (Spel. Mal.). *Tinhwana* (Mpf. Bil.). *Tinkata* (Kho.). *Nkapa* (mu-mi) (Mpf.). *Nsongwana*, (Mpf.). *Nhlekwana*, *Tshamatisa*, *Shindjengeletana* (Mpf. Nku.). *Nadwa-ngafolen* (mu-ba) (Mpf.). *Ñwamutjalatana* (mu-ba) (Mpf.). *Lidja-djana*, (Spel. Mal.). *Timhatana* (Mpf.). *Tinhelwa* (Mpf.). *Ngodzi* (Spel. Mal.). *Khwezu, Kololwana*, etc., *Sowa* (dji-ma), sparrow.

Creepers. *Gongondjwane*, lit. the one who knocks. *Shitjemaha-ngala* (Mal.). *Munywane* (Mal.). *Ngobo* (Nku). *Hokwe, Ndhlazi, Nkoro.*

Rapaces. *Gama* (dji-ma) eagle. *Khoti* (dji-ma) vulture. *Shikotana, Mangapfi, Shimungu, Shihununu*, (Mpf.), or *Khukhunu* (Kho. Mal.). *Shikotlwane, Hwati, Fukwana* (dji-ma). *Manhe-ngana*, etc.

Runners. *Yintjya* (yin-tin), ostrich.

Some birds are the objects of superstitious ideas. First, the mythical lightning bird whose story has been told p. 313. Then the Mampfana, the one who stops travellers (I. p. 339), and the Nhlalala. The *Nhlalala* is the honey-bird. It is a little sparrow of a greyish colour. When a traveller crosses the uninhabited country, it calls his attention by emitting short and repeated cries ; it jumps from one branch to another and does not rest until it has induced the traveller to follow it. It then leads him to a hollow stem where bees have gathered honey. The fortunate wayfarer can eat to his heart's content and afterwards gives the bird the wax. If he desires to be shown a second tree, he has only to burn the wax : the nhlalala not having had its full share of the treat will lead him to another stem, hoping for another chance ; there is so much honey in the second spot that you will certainly leave some for your kind guide! Such are some of the stories told by a boy named Pikinini about the honey-bird.

Mammalia. My information, on this subject, is far from complete. One ought to join a Native hunting party, and hear the hunters tell their mighty deeds round the fire in the evening, if one wishes to acquire all their knowledge and learn all their queer ideas about the beasts of the bush, which they have carefully observed, and regarding which a great number of stories are in circulation (p. 63-76). I shall have to content myself with giving the names of some Mammalia and relating some superstitions concerning them.

Edentata : two kinds are known, the *Mpandjana* (yin-tin), the ant-bear, which is covered with hair, and the *Kwara* (dji-ma) which has scales. The only Cetacea known is the *Nkomu* (yin-tin), the whale.

Solipedes : *Mangwa* (yin-tin) means zebra, and this term is sometimes applied to horses ; this latter animal is called *Hanshi* (dji-ma), evidently a corruption of the English word. *Mbongolo* (yin-tin), donkey. *Mula* or *Mewula*, mule.

Pachyderma : *Ngulube* (yin-tin), wild boar and also, by extension, domesticated pig. *Mpfubu* (yin-tin), hippopotamus.

Ruminantia : *Homu* (yin-tin), ox. *Nyari* (yin-tin), buffalo. *Hamba* (yin-tin, Ro.), *Nyimpfu* (yin-tin, Dj.), sheep. *Mbuti* (yin-tin), goat. *Mhalamhala* (yin-tin), sable antelope, Hippotragus niger. *Mhala* (yin-tin) (Zulu impala). *Mhunti* (yin-tin), duiker *Hongonyi* (yin-tin), gnu. *Mangulwe* (mu-ba). *Mhetlwa* (yin-tin), water buck. *Nhlangu* (yin-tin), reed buck. *Mhofu* (yin-tin), eland, *Nhutlwa* (yin-tin), giraffe, etc.

Proboscidea : *Ndlopfu* (yin-tin), elephant.

Rodentia : *Mpfundla* (mu-mi), hare, *Nhlolo* (yin-tin), rabbit. *Khondlo* (dj -ma), mouse. *Vondo* (dj -ma), *Phephe* (dji-ma), *Ngole* (yin-tin), etc.

Insectivora : *Shitlulandlela*, mole, lit. the one which crosses the road ; it is a bad omen for a mole to cross your path. *Tjukunyana*, a brownish mole which digs its burrows just below the surface of the ground. Hence the fact that a bracelet made of its skin is employed as medicine against the Filaria, a parasite which makes its way under the skin!

Carnivora : *Nsimba* (yin-tin), civet cat. *Shipakana*, cat. *Mbyana* (yin-tin), dog. *Mhisi* (yin-tin), hyena. *Hlolwa*, *Nhlati* (mu-ba), fox. *Yingwe* (yin-tin), leopard. *Ndjau* (Ro.), *nghala* (Dj.), lion, etc.

Chiroptera : *Tangadana* (dji-ma, Ro.), *Mangadyana*, (mu-ba. Dj.), bat.

Primates : *Mfene* (yin-tin), baboon. *Habu* (yin-tin), monkey.

343

Monkeys are thought to be degenerate human beings, who have lost the habit of working and tilling fields, and thus fallen into their present miserable condition.

The collection of Native names of animals which I have compiled is interesting ; first from the linguistic point of view, for purposes of comparison. Bantu philology needs such lists of words on which to base its conclusions. Let me point out that there seems to be a great uniformity in the various South African dialects as regards the names of large animals, the root being the same although the names have been differentiated by the regular phonetic permutations (1) ; names of trees, on the contrary, vary very much, even from one Thonga clan to the other. But these names also interest us as throwing some light on the Bantu conceptions of Nature. The notion of *genus* is not so marked as amongst plants. It is not, however, absent. The different kinds of ducks are called *sekwa*, sekwa-nyari, sekwa-mhala, the word sekwa being a true genus name. The notion of *order* may even be discovered in the classification of mammalia made by Mankhelu when he said : "Women eat only the flesh of animals having *hoofs*, and not that of animals having *paws*" (p. 83).

It is curious to inquire to which of the grammatical classes these names belong. Most of them are of the *yin-tin* class, the animal class proper. Torrend makes a connection between the prefix *tin* and the stem *psala*, to beget, to bring forth, and this may be correct. But many are of the *dji-ma* class, which often contains objects forming groups ; animals roaming in companies, as well as the regiments of the army (mabotshu, mabandla, I. p. 456), frequently belong to this class. (Sekwa, duck ; sowa, sparrow ; khoti, vulture ; hanshi, the horse of White people, of the cavalry, etc.). Some mammalia have the personal prefix *ba* for the plural. The mu-ba prefixes are always employed in tales when the animal is personified ; in the few cases here referred to, however, *ba* is used without any idea of personifying the animal ; the bat, the fox and a kind of red antelope (mangulwe) are designated in this way, and I

(1) Compare the names in my list with the Zulu and Nyandja names collected by Miss Werner in the *Revue d'Ethnographie et de Sociologie*. Jan. April 1911.

am really unable to give any reason for the fact. A few other names of animals begin with *bu*, the singular prefix in the bu-ma class, which has evidently a collective meaning. *Busuna* is the immense number of mosquitoes which one hears buzzing in the night during the rainy season, whilst one mosquito is *nsuna*, pl. tinsuna ; *busukoti* is the crowd of ants swarming in the ants'nest, whilst *nsukoti*, (cl. yin-tin) is one ant, etc.

Phot. A. Borel.

Gebuza, whose nose was torn off by a hyena.

Thus, amongst the Bantus, scientific knowledge of animals is still in a very primitive stage and may be compared to that possessed, for instance, by the author of Leviticus. On the other hand, the animal world is not in their eyes so far removed from man as it is with us. Man lives in close connection with the animals, not only when he hunts them and tries to transform himself into "a thing of the bush" (p. 79), but even in ordinary life, and considers them as very similar to himself. For instance, some Thongas believe that animals have a *language*, and try to speak to them. I have already mentioned Pikinini ; he was a boy from the Bilen country who stayed with me for a time at Shiluvane, having left Bilene after the defeat of Guṅgunyana. As he

345

was working one day together with some little Pedi boys, I heard him talking volubly. Evidently he did not expect any answer from his helpers, who knew Thonga but imperfectly :

— "What are you saying?" I asked him. — "Oh! I am speaking to the cock." — "What do you mean?" — "I am asking it if it knows what is going on in our country, at Gungunyana. It answers that it does. This cock is a clever cock. It is a man. When cocks do not know what one asks them, they say *hwi* (descriptive adverb meaning to keep quiet)." — "Are there any other beasts to which one can talk?" — "Certainly, those which belong to the village." — "Dogs?" — "No! Pigeons! When someone dies in the village, the headman must go and gather together all the pigeons, giving them some water or some food, and tell them about the death. Then they begin to coo ; they are satisfied to have been informed, treated like people of the home. If this precaution is omitted, the pigeons will leave the village in the afternoon and never return (1). This happened to a Ngoni of Bilen."

Enchanted animals can also speak, for instance a hyena which has been sent by a wizard. In Rikatla there was a man named Gebuza whose face was entirely disfigured, his nose having been torn off by a hyena ; his story was told as follows. Once a hyena entered the village in the early morning when every one was still asleep. It saluted the people saying :

— "Good morning, you people." — "Good morning" answered the people in the hut. — "Give me fire" demanded the hyena. — "Open the door and take an ember" they said. — "No, open it yourselves!" Gebuza opened the door and the hyena seized his nose in its teeth, and bit it off. This is one of the countless wizard stories. With the exception of these instances I do not think the Natives, as a rule, believe that animals have a language, or that men can speak with them. They do not, however, feel

---

(1) A curious resemblance may be noted here. Amongst French Swiss peasants and in parts of England and of Germany, when the master of the farm dies the bees must be officially informed of the fact, and some one goes to the bee hives and tells them what has happened ; misfortune would otherwise befall them.

themselves so far removed from the animal world as is the case amongst more civilised races.

Another point on which Thongas see a resemblance between man and the animal is this : they believe that both possess the *nuru* (I. p. 478 ; II, p. 77-80). It is true that the nuru is only found in some animals : the eland, the ndakazi antelope, the elephant, the hippopotamus, etc. We shall have to consider this superstition again when dealing with Thonga Animism.

Is this idea of identity between man and the animal pushed so far as a belief that men can transform themselves into animals, and vice-versa? It is certain that in tales men are often changed into hyenas, lions, etc. (See Dukuli, *Les Ba-Ronga*, p. 283 and the story of the Ogre Ziniko (p. 256).) But these are purely fictitious. The theory is by no means generally accepted. In the ordinary course of life such transformations would not be considered possible. But they are certainly thoroughly believed in in the domain of magic. Magicians claim that they can fly through the air, with their axes, transform themselves into the lightning bird and so kill their enemy. But it is the wizards (baloyi) who are considered to possess this power par excellence, especially the faculty of changing human beings into beasts to make them work on their behalf. These ideas will be studied in Chapter III.

I have already mentioned the bird which "stops travellers" (I. p. 339) ; amongst Mammalia a certain Antelope is the object of the same superstitious fear. This is the little red *magulwe* (or *shipene*) whose astragalus bone is employed in divination under the name of malumbi (See Part VI. Letter D). — "When it crosses the road, in front of a travelling party," says Mankhelu, "the leader of the company stops his comrades, goes forward, sits down alone at the spot where the antelope passed, and pours his magical powder into the footprints of the animal. Then he shouts to his companions to come and follow him. Having walked for some time, he takes off all his clothing, and lies down quite naked, as if he were dead. The others continue their march forward. After a while, he jumps to his feet and, making a circuit through the bush, outruns them, without being noticed, and sits down on the road, further on.

They come up to him and wonder how he got there. By this rite he has prevented the misfortune which the antelope would have caused to the travellers."

B. CONCEPTIONS REGARDING MAN.

I. *The origin of man.*

While the Thonga mind is very little puzzled by the question of the creation of heaven and earth, the origin of man preoccupies it more deeply. I must now enter into some details as to the story of human origin which has been already mentioned (I. p. 21). It contains two parts : the creation of man and the cause of death.

1) THE CREATION OF MAN.

The first human beings came out of the *lihlanga*, the reed, as some say, or the *nhlanga*, the marsh of reeds, according to others. These two versions seem to answer to two different conceptions. The first is that one man and one woman suddenly came out of one reed, which exploded (baleka), and there they were! According to the second, men of different tribes emerged from a marsh of reeds, each tribe already having its peculiar costume, implements and customs. So when you ask about the origin of the iron hoe amongst the Vendas, who possessed it before the Thongas, you will be told : "The Vendas emerged from the marsh of reeds holding them" (1).

The first man and woman are called in the Northern clans

(1) I believe the first version to be the true Thonga one. It may be that the idea that all races came out of the marsh of reeds is an alteration of the primitive conception under Nyai influence. The Ba-Nyai say that all men emerged from a big hole, the hole of Myali or Ñwari, in the earth, at a time when stones and rocks were still so soft that foot-prints remained marked on them. It has been supposed that the myth of the reed is simply an allusion to a physiological phenomenon, but I do not believe this.

Gwambe and Dzabana. No special story is told of these ancestors of mankind, but their names are still used under certain circumstances. When expelling a disease, in the *hondlola* rite, the medicine man says : "Go away to Gwambe and Dzabana," an expression used concurrently with this : "Go away to Shiburi and Nkhabelane," viz., to the extremity of the land, a long way off ; again, when many tales have been told and folks are going to sleep, these tales are also sent away back to Gwambe and Dzabana (p. 212). Why? Perhaps because they are the old, old people, and the tales which are so ancient belong to them! At any rate, by this kind of incantation story-tellers aim at preventing the hearers' sleep from being disturbed by the remembrance of the marvellous things they have been told. In the legends relating to old migrations the "Road of Gwambe" (1) is mentioned. When the ancient peoples passed along it, the earth was not yet solid, so they left the print of their feet, of their mortars, etc., in the rocks, where they are still to be seen on the edge of a river called Hlantsabuhlalu. (Nyai idea? I. p. 22.)

In the Ronga clans, these two ancestors of mankind are called *Likalahumba* and *Nsilambowa.* The first name means : the one who brought a glowing cinder in a shell, viz., the originator of fire, (Compare the Hlengwe tradition, I. p. 24). Nsilambowa, the name of the woman, means the one who grinds vegetables. The first human beings, according to these names, were those who

---

(1) What is the connection between this *Gwambe* and the name of *Ma-Gwamba* commonly given to the Thongas of Spelonken (I. p. 19)? It is difficult to say. According to some, there is still a clan descended from Gwambe, the first man, whose chief calls himself Gwambe. The Ba-Venda, when they saw the Thonga merchants bringing their goods from Delagoa Bay or Inhambane, called them Makwapa, Balungwana ba Kwapen, the little White people from Kwapa or Gwamba country, viz., those who bring clothes, beads bought from the Whites. It seems certain that there exists a Gwamba clan somewhere in Gazaland, not far from the Chopi border. A story is told of this Gwamba chief, who sent messengers to Modjadji to obtain rain from her. On their return they refused to cooperate in gathering fuel for their fire and died on the road, where their graves are still to be seen. Other informants give a totally different version of the origin of the term Ma-Gwamba : Gwambe was a chief dwelling on the banks of the Oliphant, near the Dunduli villages; his men, while on a journey, said to the Vendas : "We people of Gwambe even accept old women," viz,, if they receive us well, we call them our wives to please them ! Hence the name they were given. Still other explanations might be found and I think there is no real connection between Gwambe, the first man, and the Ma-Gwamba.

introduced fire and the culinary art into the world! This idea is interesting and seems to show that, to the Native mind, the cooking of food is the pursuit which differentiates man from the animals.

In the clans of Maluleke and Spelonken there is a third tradition relating to the first man, but it has certainly been borrowed from the Venda or Pedi tribes. They say the first man was *Rivimbi* and his son *Khudjana* (name transformed into Hobyana according to Thonga phonetics). The Thongas only say that Hobyana is the creator of Heaven and Earth and the first ancestor of the race. But the Vendas and Pedis have a number of traditions about these two heroes (1).

2) THE CAUSE OF DEATH.

When the first human beings emerged from the marsh of reeds, the chief of this marsh sent the Chameleon (Lumpfana) to them, with this message: "Men will die, but they will rise again." The Chameleon started walking slowly, according to his habit. Then the big lizard with the blue head, the Galagala, was sent to tell men: "You shall die and rot." Galagala started with his swift gait and soon passed Lumpfana. He delivered his message, and when Lumpfana arrived with his errand, men said to him: "You are too late. We have already

(1) Here is one of the most curious of these traditions, a strange story indeed, when we reflect that these two personages are the great gods who created the universe! Once, in olden times, Khudjana planted a big pole in the earth, and passed spokes through it, right to the top. Rivimbi having climbed up, Khudjana took out the lower spokes and went home. His father being unable to get down, the son stole the food prepared for him and ate it at his ease. Then he again put the spokes in their places and the old man came home. But when he wished to have his meal, he found that nothing was left. His wife then gave him Khudjana's portion!

There is great confusion amongst these traditions. According to Mankhelu this Rivimbi, or Luvimbi, is the same as the great rain-maker to whose descendants he went to obtain the rain medicine (p. 320). He is not only the creator of the earth, but the protector of all men, who are his sons. So, if some one wishes to harm a man who is not guilty, the Vendas say to him: "Do not kill Luvimbi's man." If you steal a partridge caught in a trap which was not set by you, they say: "Luvimbi, who stands on that tree, sees you." He would seem to be a superior being, a god (shikwembu), even the chief of gods, endowed with omnipresence and omniscience. Moreover there is a relation between Rivimbi and Nwali, the Ba-Nyai god, who is represented either as father or son of Rivimbi, or identical with him. It may be that the Rivimbi tradition, which is both Pedi and Venda and seems to refer definitely to a first ancestor who has become the great god, has been mixed with the Ñwali tradition, which is Nyai, so that ideas of different origins have been intermingled.

accepted another message." That is why men are subject to death.

This myth is so strongly believed that shepherds, when they see a chameleon climbing slowly up a tree, begin to tease it, and, when it opens its mouth, throw a pinch of tobacco into it, and are greatly amused to see the poor thing change colour, passing from green to orange, and from orange to black, in agony, to the great delight of the little boys ; they thus avenge themselves on the chameleon ! (p. 339).

The same story is told amongst the Zulus, and other myths of a similar character are found all over Africa, especially amongst the Ba-Rotsi (1). It would be an interesting study to collect them all, and thus to compile the African Genesis. We should probably find that the origin of man and death are the two great subjects on which the imagination of the Bantus has tried to throw some light, and that, though the moral element is strangely lacking in these myths, yet there is a striking resemblance between them and the Biblical story, where an answer to the same questions is given.

II. *The various human races.*

Have Bantus a clear idea of the human race? What they call *banhu* in Thonga, *bantu* in Zulu, evidently means "black people," the first inhabitants of the country. The Zulus are regarded, owing to their military ability, as a superior race, not however to such an extent as they themselves believe to be the case! Whatever may be their hostility or repugnance to their fellow blacks, they know that they belong to the same species. I am not sure that they hold this idea regarding White people, who are not *banhu* but *balungu*.

What is the origin of this word? As it is also used in Zulu (abelungo), the etymology suggested is the verb *ku lunga*, to be right, good. White people would then be correct, nice people, to

(1) Compare *Foi et Vie*. Oct. 1910. Les Origines. A. Jalla.

the Native (1). However complimentary to us this explanation may be, I very much doubt its accuracy. Firstly, Black people have not generally such a good opinion of us. They admit our superiority in intelligence, but unfortunately have not always found that White people behaved correctly in their dealings with them. Secondly, when we compare the word balungu with Ñwalungu, North, balungwana, inhabitants of Heaven, (see Chapter II), and with Mulungu, the great name for God in Central Africa, we are led to suppose that there may have been ancient mythological traditions, now forgotten, relating to White people, when they were not yet well known.

To account for the superiority of the White race, Mankhelu assured me he had heard the following story many years ago, told by his grandfather in the village of Shiluvane, long before the arrival of the missionaries. When Ñwali created the first man, from whom both Whites and Blacks are descended, they were all naked. Gwambe slept with his sister, an act which had been forbidden, and she had a child. Since that time children are born ; but this was not the intention of Ñwali, who wished to create adult human beings only! The Gwambe (first ancestor) of the White people showed respect to his father, who was naked, whilst the Gwambe of the Blacks did not ; hence the deterioration (onhakala) of the Blacks. "We were fools and have been deprived of everything, and Ñwali said : You Blacks shall wear down your nails to the quick by digging the earth to find food!" As already pointed out, Mankhelu had not the slightest trace of the critical sense. This is evidently the Biblical story very curiously transformed. The idea of an original fault committed by the Black race in the beginning having resulted in the inferior position it now occupies, is, however, met with in many parts of Africa, and is probably autochthonous amongst the Thongas.

"Balungu ba hlulwa hi lifu ntsena" has become a kind of proverb, quoted by Natives when they see the marvels of

---

(1) Others say that their forefather named the White people balungu because they were clean (lunga having also that meaning). "They are always clean though they do not wash their bodies ! They have no dirt." But these explanations are not quite satisfactory.

civilisation and means : "White people are only overcome by death." I once heard a little boy muttering it when I was playing the harmonium.

Their notions regarding the several European races are very crude. Once when I asked one of them if he knew whence the Whites came, he told me : "The Portuguese came from the sea, the Boers from the mountains." — "And we, missionaries, who are neither Portuguese nor Boers?" — "You come from Heaven," he answered with a charming smile!

Pikinini, who knew how to converse with the cock, once told me what the Bilen people think of the Whites. It was just after the deportation of Gungunyana :

— "Gungunyana is dead. The Portuguese have eaten him!"

— "How is that?"

— "Certainly! The Portuguese eat human flesh. Every one knows it. They have no legs ; they are fishes (tinhlampfi). They have a tail instead of legs. They live in water."

— "Then how do they manage to fight with you and to beat you if they are fishes and have no legs?"

— "Ho! Those who come to fight against us are the young men ; they have legs. They take us and put us all in a steamer which goes far away, far away. This steamer reaches a large rock which is surrounded by water on all sides. This is their country. We are taken out and placed on an island, whilst the soldiers go and fire shots to announce to the great White men-fishes that we have arrived. They choose one of us and make a little cut in his little finger to see if he is fat enough ; if not, he is put into a big basket full of ground-nuts which he must eat in order to become fat. When he is fat enough, they place him in a big, elongated pot of the size of a man, and red-hot. We know these particulars because a man, Ngomongomo, gave us the full explanation. He had been caught, but on the road his gods helped him ; he was covered with an eruption of pimples which was so disgusting that he was left in the island, and brought back here. He saw everything. We first refused to believe that. Now we know that it is the truth!"

Evidently Pikinini was in earnest and these absurd ideas were

353

accepted as facts by the majority of his countrymen in Bilen. Is it not strange to notice that, whilst a great number of Europeans think of the Blacks as being all cannibals, these savages, on the other hand, believe exactly the same thing of us! Of course a closer contact with White people has already led them to a truer knowledge of what we really are, and they have discovered that, after all, there is not such a great difference between the various human races!

In former times the Thongas would seem to have believed that all White people, not only the Portuguese, dwelt in water. They were said to have eyes in front and behind and to see on all sides, so that it was impossible to escape from them. They used to kidnap Black people and take them away.

III. *The human body.*

1) Ideas of Anatomy.

The Thongas have never made an anatomic study of a human corpse. They have a riddle to this effect : "Ku pfura ndjilo mungema? — Ba lahla munhu wa ku fa." — "A fire of live coals? — They bury a dead man." As you never put your hand in the fire, so you would not touch a corpse. Nor have they ever made a post mortem examination! What they know of the human body is entirely derived from the inductions they have drawn from oxen, pigs and game which they cut open. Considering that the source of their knowledge is so indirect, one wonders that they have learnt so much of the human physical structure.

Having taught a little anatomy to the students of our Institute, I can bear testimony that they have names for most of the bones of the skeleton. *Pala* (dji-ma) means skull ; *lihlaya* (li-ti), maxillary bone ; *tinyo*, pl. menyo, teeth ; *tshuri* (dji-ma), molar tooth (same word as mortar) ; *litlatla*, clavicle ; *likhongotlo*, spine ; *khatla* (dji-ma), shoulder blade ; *shintjintji*, sternum ; *shikangana*, extremity of the sternum ; *libambo*, rib ; (they believe there are *ten* ribs on each side!) ; *shikukwana*, humerus ; *nkono* (mu-mi), cubitus ;

ñwalihlanga, (mu-ba) femur ; *lihandja*, tibia ; they seem to know nothing of the radius and the peroneus ; *guywa-guywana*, rotula ; *nhlolo*, astragalus ; other bones are called by the name of the region, or the organ, to which they belong : the bone of the pelvis, *nyongwa* (yin-tin), the hip ; the wrist bones, *hlakala* ; those of the palm, *shipapa* ; those of the fingers, *litiho* ; those of the toes, *shikuñwana* ; those of the ankle, *shirendje* ; of the sole, *nkondjo* (mu-mi) ; the thumb is called *khudju* (dji-ma), and the big toe, *the great shiku-ñwana*.

The different organs are also known : *byongwe* (bu-ma) (Dj.) *bongwe* (Ro.) is the brain ; *tihlo*, pl. *mahlo*, the eye ; *ndlebe* (yin-tin), the ear ; *nhompfu* (yin-tin), the nose ; *nomo*, pl. *milomo*, the lips and the mouth ; *lidjimi*, the tongue ; *nkolo* (mu-mi), the throat ; they know that there are two pipes, one for food, the other for air, but they are not sure which is in front and which behind ! *Hahu* (dji-ma), (Ro.), *phaphu* (Dj.), lungs ; *shidyelo*, the stomach ; *mbilu* (yin-tin), the heart ; *shibindji*, the liver ; *libengo*, the spleen ; *lipfalo*, the diaphragm ; *rumbu* (dji-ma), the bowels, including the male internal genitalia ; external genitalia of man and woman are taboo ; *yinso* (yin-tin) means kidneys ; *nhlonge* (yin-tin), skin ; *nwala* (mu-mi) nail ; *nsisi* (mu-mi), hair, etc.

But on pushing the inquiry somewhat further, we begin to notice a gross ignorance of important facts. The one word *nsiha* (mu-mi) means nerves, tendons, ligaments, veins and arteries ; *nyimba* is the uterus, but also means pregnancy. Natives seem to think that a new nyimba is created at each pregnancy. They know nothing of the glands and I never discovered a name for the pancreas.

2) Physiological notions.

For this reason it is obvious that they cannot know what really happens in the body, and the marvellous and complicated system of our physical life. The mystery of the nervous system is entirely unknown, as is also the way in which blood (*ngati*, yin-tin) is formed from food, the digestive process, the circulation of the blood and the action of the air upon it, etc. We must not be surprised at this ignorance ; our forefathers, three hundred years ago, were not much more advanced than the Natives are now.

On the other hand, Bantus, and especially Thongas, have a number of physiological ideas, which are pure superstitions, being devoid of any scientific foundation, but are, nevertheless, firmly believed and give rise to a number of practices, rites, and purifications. This is a most interesting subject and its study throws much light on the condition of primitive man. I have tried to explain these physiological conceptions in an article published in "La Revue d'Ethnographie et de Sociologie, Mai 1910." It is not possible to enter into all the details here, and I am obliged to refer the reader to that article for more particulars. However my description of the Life of the Tribe would not be complete if this subject were entirely omitted ; so I will rapidly give a general idea of this curious Native physiology.

In the Thonga mind, human life is composed of a certain number of periods which follow each other, each having its particular character.

As we have seen in the Evolution of man (Part I), *the first period* (busahana) extends from birth to the fall of the umbilical cord ; the baby is in a state of contamination owing to the lochia and must not be touched ; from the eighth or ninth day till the weaning takes place, is *the nursing period*, divided into two or three sub-periods by the presentation to the moon and the tying of the cotton string. The child has been progressively received into human society. Up to this day he has been considered as under treatment, because a child is not a complete healthy human being ; he is but *water* (mati), not yet firm ; he is always threatened with disease and so he must continually drink his *milombyana*. The *hondlola* ceremony closes this period and, by the act of weaning, he enters into the *childhood* period. (I. p. 59).

Infancy is a *bukhuna*, a state of incompleteness fraught with a certain defilement. Childhood is also a bukhuna, and this contemptible inferiority must be removed by the circumcision rites, the significance of which is both physiological and social. When they wish to marry, viz., *to pass from the class of unmarried to that of married people*, young men and women must again undergo a number of ceremonies of a social rather than of a physiological character.

But, in addition to these conceptions of human life, which determine so many acts and customs, there are at least *five phy-siological phenomena* which are believed to be attended with defilement, and which call for special precautions and rites : the menstrual flow, the lochia, disease, death and the birth of twins. To protect individuals, the family, or the clan, against these dangerous defilements, is one of the main preoccupations of any adult Thonga ; and to gain this end they submit to endless ceremonies of purification,and observe innumerable taboos ; thus it is plain that these physiological conceptions, absolutely unscien-tific and wrong as they are, play an immense part in their lives and cause them any amount of unnecessary trouble.

I need not deal at length with these five greatly dreaded physiological events. As regards menses, the subject has been treated in Vol. I, p. 187. (Compare Vol. II, p. 47) ; as regards lochia, see Vol. I, p. 43 ; concerning disease, we shall hear further in our third chapter. The tremendous contaminating power of death has been shown in the explanation of funeral rites, and the birth of twins will be studied more closely in the next chapter. The importance of these facts in the system of taboos will also be explained in Chap. IV.

The sexual act, though not considered as attended with con-tamination in the same manner as the five other physiological facts just referred to, is, however, subject to very characteristic restrictions. I have already explained them when dealing with conjugal life (I. p. 188). It will, however, perhaps not be superfluous to treat of this question again, considering it in its physiological aspect and in relation to the Bantu conception of Nature, and giving at the same time precise references to all the cases hitherto met with.

Let us first remark that, as some of my informants said, the sexual act when indulged in before marriage, by boys and girls in their gangisa (I. p. 150) has quite another bearing than when accomplished by married people. It would seem that it is not the physical act in itself which is attended with all these taboos,

357

but the act in as far as it is a regular manifestation of the collective life of the family ; in this case only does it have its terrible repercussion on the life of the community. Married people who have regular sexual relations, "who are hot," constitute a danger in the three following connections.

1) They are dangerous to those *individual members of the community* who are in a weak state of health and in whom disease would gain new strength if they entered into contact with married people. This is true of the master of the village when he is seriously ill (I. p. 133), of the mother who has given birth to a baby (I. p. 43), of the baby itself which is considered as "being not yet firm," (and sexual relations are forbidden to its parents until they have tied the cotton string round its loins) (I. p. 45, 58) ; of circumcised boys (I. p. 80, 93) ; of convalescents, who must not tread on the same paths as married folk or, if they do so, must tie round their ankles a root of the *sungi* juncus as a protection against the emanation, or perspiration (nyuku) which married people have left in their footprints or on the grass. During their whole convalescence sexual relations have been strictly forbidden to them (Ch. III. B. III. 4).

2) Sexual relations constitute a danger *to the community itself* as a whole, when its existence is threatened. They are prohibited in time of epidemic. Mboza, having heard that a proclamation had been issued in Lourenço Marques on account of an epidemic, was convinced that the object of the decree was to suspend sexual relations amongst the White community! The same law applies to all marginal periods, because these are critical times in which the life of the community is threatened. This is the case during the Great Mourning (I. p. 150). Mourners must *keep quiet ;* if not, there might be quarrels, the mourning might "overcome them." Again when moving the village to another place (I. p. 320), the same rule must be observed.

3) Married people again are taboo in certain operations or pursuits, the success of which would be endangered if they took part in them or if they indulged in their ordinary relations. It must not be a married person who sets fire to the furnace in which

the potteress fires her pots (1) (p. 115). Why is this so? No doubt because if married people, who are hot, did it, the fire would become uncontrollable and all the pots would crack. The same reason explains why sexual relations are so strongly prohibited in hunting and fishing. The game or fish would be so wild that it would be impossible to catch it ; big game would probably kill the hunters (p. 61).

This conception of the sexual act explains why certain functions in the ritual must be performed by young children, still without knowledge of sexual matters, or by old women past the time of childbearing and consequently belonging to the asexual class (I. p. 466).

How is it possible to explain, on the other hand, that this act, so severely prohibited on so many occasions, should be the great purifying act by which the community gets rid of the defilement of death and returns to normal life? We have seen that this is the case after the death of an important person in the village as well as when the village itself moves to another place, probably in conse-quence of defilement by the loss of some of its members. Notice that the sexual act, in order to obtain the desired result, must be accomplished in the ritual fashion, i. e. s. n. i. (I. Annotatio 2 and 13). It would seem that, in the Thonga mind, death defiles not only the belongings of the deceased, his implements, his assegais, even his fire, but also his parents, even the parents of his wife, and above all, those secretions of the genital organs which are the very fountain of their life, and through which the community is maintained and multiplied. They must be cleansed in order that the social group may re-enter upon a normal state. The ceremonies which we have described (I. p. 152-156 and 320-328) are highly significant. Each couple must perform the rite in turn and all must participate in a collective lustration which takes

(1) According to the Rev. Ed. W. Smith the same rule is observed in the smel-ting operations of the Ba-Ila. A little boy and a little girl are put into the kiln when it is about a foot high and they must crack a bean in their mouths and swallow it. We have here a very good example of Bantu primitive philosophy. The innocence or, as we may say, the *cool'ness*, of the little ones will prevent the flame from being too fierce and spoiling the whole operation, whilst the slow cracking of the bean will ensure the success of the smelting process (Smith and Dale, *The Ila-Speaking People*, I. p. 205).

place at a given spot and according to a given order of precedence. This will bring about the definite restoration of the village and a new and pure life will henceforth be possible.

I ought perhaps to offer some excuse for having dwelt at some length on a subject which is generally left alone as indelicate. I hope however that my readers will agree with me that all these physiological conceptions and all these strange customs, far from being of a lascivious or licentious character, denote, on the contrary, a deep and earnest conception of life and an aspiration towards purity which it is most interesting to observe. They are at the same time amongst the most striking manifestations of Bantu Dynamism.

Beside these great principles of Thonga physiology, I may mention a few other ideas relating to the various secretions of the human body.

Spitting (ku thuka) is a sign of want of respect, as we have seen (p. 310). It is especially prohibited in the presence of people who are eating, and if any one should spit, they will insult the culprit, saying to him : "Eat your own shikohlolo!" — When some one expectorates, others present will cover the phlegm with sand, not on account of taboo, but from disgust.

Blood (ngati, yin-tin) is also instinctively covered with sand, as soon as it has been shed. This is a taboo, because wizards might use it to bewitch you! The charms of the wizards are commonly called *tingati*, bloods.

As regards *sweat* (nyuku, mu-mi), although I cannot assert that the idea is universal, I think it is conceived as coming from outside and falling on men like the dew (mbere) on the grass. When they enter a place which is close, Natives say : "There is sweat here." The etymology of this word is *ku nyuka*, to melt.

Excrement (matjimba) is looked upon as disgusting, but there is no taboo in connection with it.

Yawning (yahlamula) is attended with no superstition.

Hiccough (shitikwane) is not feared in children, but very much so in the case of sick people.

Belching (bisa) is sometimes considered as the result of having been bewitched, especially if the patient becomes thin. Magicians also belch, to show the mysterious power hidden within them.

When any one *sneezes* it is the signal for bestowing upon him good wishes : "Butomi ni burongo!" — "Life and sleep!" The sneezer himself may begin to pray as follows : "Bupsayi! Bukwari! (two liturgical words of invocation to the gods) I pray to you! I have no anger against you! Be with me, and let me sneeze! Let me know sleep and let me know life, that I may go by the road, that I may find an antelope (dead in the bush), that I may take it on my shoulders ; or that I may go and kill 'ndlopfu bukene,' an elephant, (viz., meet with a girl and obtain her favour), etc. Now I say it is enough, you my nose!"

Cutting the *hair* has been referred to already (I, p. 146, II. p. 99). In Tembe and Nondwane there is a curious superstition regarding hair : it is taboo to throw it away without precaution, otherwise a bird called *makhondjwana*, or *n̄wantshekuto*, might find it and line its nest with it, and your hair would not grow any more!

IV. *The human soul.*

Thongas have a quantity of names to designate the *psychic faculties* and generally locate them in various organs of the body. *Patience* resides in the liver, and the identification is so complete that there is but one word to express both the organ and the virtue : *shibindji!* *Hatred* is located in the spleen, and both are called *libengo* (from ku benga, to hate). *Mbilu*, the heart, is the seat of *genius* and intellectual gifts. A man expert in certain arts and crafts has been taught by his heart. From the heart come the decisions of the will : a heathen cannot be converted to Christianity because his heart has not yet told him to be so (mbilu a yi si hlaya). To have a good heart implies kindness, compassion. The chest, *shifuba*, not the lungs, is the seat of intelligence and eloquence (as pectus in Latin). A dumb man is a man "whose chest is dead." The diaphragm either *lipfalo*, sing., or *timpfalo*, plur., or *mapfalo*, is the conscience ; its contractions are identical with qualms of conscience (p. 75). The head and the bowels do not seem to be the seat of any special faculty.•

But although Natives locate the psychic faculties in the different organs, they certainly believe in an independent psychic principle, in a *soul*. On this point, however, their ideas are most confused. They call it *moya*, spirit, and in the Ronga clans, *hika*, breath (the plural mahika, in the expression "ku ba ni mahika," means to be out of breath). This is the vital principle of man, and when a person is dying, his relatives sit near him "waiting for the departure of breath" (langusela ku suka ka hika). "The spirit has gone," — "moya wu sukile," they say, when death has come. They have no theory as regards the way the breath goes out of the body, nor do they stop the nostrils or the mouth to prevent its escape (1).

A third name for soul is *ntjhuti* (mu-mi), or *shitjhuti* (Ro.), *ndjuti* (Dj.) *shadow*. It seems to apply more especially to the departed soul rather than to the psychic principle of the living. I have been assured that one cannot dream of the shintjuti of any one still alive, but only if he is dead. The shadow, as such, is not subject to many taboos or superstitious fears. They do not fear to tread on the shadow of a chief, for instance. It may even be questioned if they identify the material shadow with the shitjhuti, the spiritual part of man which separates from his body at death (2). At any rate many think that it is the shitjhuti which becomes shikwembu, the ancestor god.

In former times Thongas feared to look at their own reflection in a pool. They seem to have passed that stage now. The reason was perhaps that they thought their spiritual principle to be

---

(1) A Native of Botshabelo, near Middleburg, Transvaal, asserted in my hearing that in this part of the Sutho nation it was believed that the human soul escaped from the body at death in the form of a Copris beetle. The grave is not filled up with earth until a Copris has been seen in the neighbourhood ; and if a hawk appears at the same time the satisfaction is still greater ; the beetle has transformed itself into a hawk and the soul has in truth found its way out. Strange to say, when these Ba-Sutho give a patient medicine and see that it has had the desired effect, they say : "It has agreed with the Copris;" whilst if the patient dies they say : "The Copris has refused the medicine."

(2) In the following story a direct relation is established between the real shadow and the vital principle. A Ronga magician, Shidzabalane, used to show his super-natural power in the following way : he slept on the ground and ordered a mortar to be placed on his chest and three women to pound mealies in it. This seemed to make no impression on him (a fact which can easily be explained if he was in a state of cata-lepsy). But it suddenly occurred to one of these women that he had perhaps passed into his shadow, so she hit the shadow with her pestle. The magician at once rose, crying out ; he had really left his body and entered into his shadow !

identical with their image. This notion seems to be at the root of the fear they show of being photographed, as we shall see directly.

We see therefore that Thongas are not at all dogmatic on this subject. The soul is at the same time the breath, viz., something of the nature of the wind, the shadow, the image, the external likeness, or fashion of man as opposed to his flesh.

Whatever may be the original notion, they consider the human being as double and capable of unsheathing itself on certain occasions ; their conception on this point may throw more light on their ideas concerning the nature of the soul.

Some believe that the *unsheathing* always takes place during the night and that the soul comes back when its owner awakes ; this is, par excellence, the case in regard to witches, who unsheath by their magical power and bewitch people during the night, as we shall see. But, though the belief is not universal, some think that all souls go away (or die) during sleep. I heard a boy earnestly praying one evening that his soul might come back to him next morning! This is a kind of physiological normal unsheathing which is attended with no bad results. But a pathological unsheathing also exists, and is very dangerous. It may be caused by the photograph of a man being taken. Ignorant Natives instinctively object to being photographed. They say : "These White people want to steal us (pepula) and take us with them, far away into lands which we do not know, and we shall remain only incomplete beings." When shown the magic lantern, you hear them pitying the men shown on the pictures, and saying : "That is how they ill-treat us when they take our photographs! (1)"

But the great and dangerous parting of soul and body, which causes certain death, is that which wizards operate by their magic charms. We shall study these strange conceptions in Chapter III. They firmly believe that such is the result of witchcraft ; so, when some one is dying, and the divinatory bones have revealed that the disease was caused by a certain *noyi* (witch or wizard), the

(1) The following reflection well illustrates the superstitious fear which Natives have of likenesses of the dead. Before the 1894 war broke out, I had gone to show the magic lantern in remote heathen villages, and people accused me of having caused the disturbance by bringing to life again (pfusha) men who had died long ago.

magician shuts him in with the dying man in the hut and gives him the following command : "Bring back the spirit which you have taken and hidden somewhere." Some magicians, who are more powerful than the wizards, pretend to be able to find the stolen spirit and so to restore the patient to health. In cases of epilepsy, or of any psychic trouble attended with unconsciousness, when the sick person returns to his senses, they triumph : have they not brought back the soul? But they say that this must be done in haste. No time must be lost!

Lastly, the final unsheathing of personality takes place at death. The body becomes rotten, but the shadow goes away and continues its life as a god, shikwembu. The belief in the continuation of life after death is universal, being at the base of Ancestrolatry, which is the religion of the tribe. We shall study the ideas relating to the future life when dealing with the gods.

What Thongas can absolutely not understand is the resurrection of the body. "Mbuti yi fa, yi bola ; homu yi fa, yi bola ; munhu a fa, a bola!" — "The goat dies and rots, the ox dies and rots, man dies and rots!" answers the sceptical Thonga when he hears the story of the resurrection.

On the whole their ideas of future life are not so very different from those of the ancient Greeks, who believed that the human soul went after death to the realm of shadows.

Dreams are not generally liked by the Thongas. If something they happened to dream really takes place, it "disgusts" them (nyenyetsa). When a man has seen a woman several times in his dreams, especially if she was pregnant, he will consult the bones. If he dreams that he has relations with her, he may go next day and hit her with a stick. He leaves the stick on the ground and goes away without a word. According to Mboza, this is done to get rid of the obsession, and to prevent the dream from becoming reality. That is the reason, I suppose, why a Christian boy once said to his missionary : "I dream of many people, but I keep quiet!" Amongst Thongas dreams do not seem to play the great part which the animistic theory attributes to them in the formation of primitive beliefs.

Conceptions Regarding Nature and Man

Conclusion of Chapter i. Classification of Thonga Conceptions of Nature and Man.

During the World Missionary Conference at Edinburgh, the question of the various religions was discussed one day in connection with the preaching of the missionary message. Speakers frequently mentioned Animism in their discourses. In the gallery which was reserved for missionaries' wives, a lady wrote a few words on a slip of paper and passed it to a gentleman who happened to be sitting not far from her : — "Can you tell me what animistic religions are?" was the question it contained. Unfortunately the answer given by the gentleman is unknown. He probably felt somewhat embarrassed... The lady was quite right in putting the question, as few people really understand what is meant by this term! It is not so easy to give at a moment's notice, a thorough and adequate definition of its meaning on a slip of paper.

The South African tribes are regarded as animistic in their beliefs. They belong to that section of mankind which is said to profess the animistic religion. But in what does their Animism consist? Since Tylor first invented the word Animism and defined it as "the belief in spiritual beings," it has acquired a wonderful popularity, but it has been used so indiscriminately that it has lost very much of its definiteness and it has been necessary for modern Anthropology to restrict its meaning in order to maintain scientific precision.

Animism according to Prof. Marett (*The Threshold of Religion*, p. 15.) implies not merely the attribution of personality and will, but of "soul or spirit." He terms *Animatism* conceptions according to which natural objects are endowed with personality and will only, but not with a distinct existence as spirits. In as far as the power attributed to natural objects is not clearly personified, but conceived of as a more or less independent energy, or virtue, we are dealing with *Dynamism* and not Animism. To these distinctions I would add another, which is essential. When speaking with savages or semi-primitive men, you sometimes hear them expressing ideas, giving explanations which are purely *personal*, whilst others of their notions are *collective*. When we wish to ascertain the conceptions of a tribe as a whole, we must lay much more stress on this latter kind ; they are generally incorporated in rites and customs which every one accepts ; they are really *beliefs*, whilst those of the first category are merely *ideas* springing from the imagination of the savage.

The Life of a South African Tribe

Having traced the broad lines of our classification let us now see how far the Thonga conceptions are animistic, animatic or dynamistic.

1) Individual ideas.

In a certain year, the *mintjhopfa* trees (p. 19) did not bear fruit. A Rikatla boy, named Zinyao, took a stick and walked through the bush, belabouring all the ntjhopfa shrubs, scolding them because they had not done their duty. An ethnographer, anxious to penetrate into the mysteries of primitive souls, might infer from this fact that Thongas believe in the personality of trees, and that each tree possesses a spirit ; this would however be absolutely false. Zinyao was doing the same thing as a little boy who hits the table against which he has knocked his head, or as a little girl who breaks her doll because she is angry with it. The same boy, who was evidently endowed with a strongly animistic tendency, once saw a big moth fall to the ground ; a hen at once ran towards it and devoured it. Zinyao watched very attentively, and I heard him muttering to himself : "The Son-of-Moth goes to the Son-of-Hen, yonder, and asks him to pay a fine, because, says he, I have been eaten by you there on the earth." If this reflection were taken seriously, it would mean that, to the Thonga mind, each animal has a soul which continues to exist after death, and even that wrongs done to an animal during its earthly life must be repaired in the after world. This conclusion would be absolutely erroneous. No one seriously believes in a continued existence of animals after death ; and, as to a final judgment, there is no idea of it, even as regards human beings, who are believed to be immortal! These were the *personal views* of Zinyao.

I would place in the same category the description of the fight between the moon and the sun, as given by Spoon (p. 307). The same informant on another occasion gave me an eloquent and graphic account of the battle of the water near the lake of Rikatla, when the rain has been falling for many days : "In the hollow there is a papyrus marsh which becomes filled with water ; at a quarter of an hour's distance the lake itself is swollen by the rain ; there is a canal which joins marsh and lake ; so the waters flow into that canal from both sides ; they meet in the middle and fight : but the water from the papyrus marsh comes with greater force, and after a while it overcomes the other current and makes its way triumphantly to the lake!" These individual ideas are either animatic (idea of trees, of sun and moon, of water,

366

lightning), or animistic (Son-of-the-Moth). But they are not of much importance. They belong to the same category as the description given by the Psalmist of the sun as a bridegroom coming out of his chamber, or to that of Homer comparing the break of the day to a young damsel with rosy fingers. This is poetry, mere personification of natural objects, or forces, and not beliefs. The poetical tendency is very marked amongst primitive races. It may be that ideas of this kind were more firmly held in former times, if the tribe has really passed through a more mythological phase, a hypothesis for which there are some grounds.

2) COLLECTIVE BELIEFS.

The beliefs of the Thongas which deserve to be called by that name because they are universal and express themselves in important rites and customs, are the following :

1. The human soul continues its existence after death, when it is endowed with new powers which make it an object of awe and fear. *The spirits of the ancestors* are the main objects of religious worship. They form the principal category of spirits (psikwembu).

2. Although the spirits of the departed generally have nothing to do with people other than their descendants, some of them, especially *those belonging to foreign tribes*, can take possession of living men and cause troubles which must be cured by a process of exorcism. This is the second category of spirits.

3. Some individuals have the power of magically unsheathing themselves during the night, and their spirit goes out to torment, or to kill and eat other people. These are *the wizards* (baloyi) ; this third category of spirits accomplish their wicked deeds when separated from the body, but their body is still living and they re-enter it. These three beliefs are distinctly animistic.

4. There is in man, and in a few large animals, a semi-spiritual principle, the *nuru*, which escapes from the body when the individual is killed in war, or in hunting, and through which the dead man, or animal, avenges himself or itself on the murderer. What is the relation between the nuru and the shadow (sitjhuti)? This is not stated. The nuru seems to be of a more material nature, as it can enter a root, and it remains attached to the corpse and the bones of the person or animal killed. This category of spiritual enemies, probably invented under the influence of fear and remorse, has no connection with ordinary people,

and only troubles those who have killed, rendering them, as is generally believed, insane. — The nuru belief seems to be a compromise between Animism and Dynamism. (See p. 77-80.)

5. There are in plants, animals, stones, hidden virtues which can be either useful or harmful to man. Medicine-men (tinanga) possess a more or less esoteric knowledge of such, and magicians (bangoma), endowed with special powers, can acquire a control over these virtues and use them in medical art, or in magic. — This is true Dynamism.

6. Certain natural objects, such as the sea, the bush fire, are sometimes vaguely personified. — This is Animatism.

7. But above them all is Heaven, Tilo, which is sometimes looked on as a real being, sometimes as an impersonal power, a number of mysterious superstitions finding their explanation in this strange and perhaps obsolete notion of Heaven. — This is more than Animatism and seems to be a vague theistic, even monotheistic, idea.

The essential difference between Animism and Dynamism seems to me clear. But it is by no means absolute. We shall often meet with rites which belong to both domains, or bear an intermediate character. In the following chapters the exact nature and influence of these various kinds of spirits and impersonal forces will be studied, and I hope that an explanation of all the facts concerning them will throw more light on the subject and show that, at any rate, Thonga Animism is very different from the Animism of the Dutch East Indies, for instance, where men speak of thousands of spirits of the earth, air, water, mountains and trees ; very different also from the fetichism met with in other Bantu tribes of Central and Western Africa.

*

* *

Before leaving this chapter, in which I have tried to sketch what I have called by the rather pretentious term of The Natural Philosophy of the Bantus, and as a preparation for the explanation of the religious and dynamistic rites described in the following chapters, I think it advisable to set forth the principles which seem to underlie most of these rites, and which may be called the *axioms of primitive mentality*.

As regards what are commonly called *magic rites* I contend that they are in no sense purely arbitrary but that they rest on certain definite principles. These axioms of primitive mentality are what anthropologists fittingly call collective representations, viz., everybody believes them. Whatever may be their origin, they form a part of the mental make up of every Native. A careful study of the rites reveals at least three such axioms : Like acts on like and produces like ; the part represents the whole and acts on the whole ; the spoken wish produces the desired result.

1) *Like acts on like and produces like.* All the elements of Nature are dependent on each other, and if there is a similarity between two of them, they are at once brought into a special relation with each other and begin to influence each other. The application of this principle is universal, in the religious as well as in the dynamistic domain. The Native mind is extremely quick at perceiving a similarity between the most heterogeneous objects or phenomena, and immediately establishes a causal relation between them. We have already met with scores of instances of this law. *Colour* acts on colour ; black sheep and black smoke produce a black cloud full of rain (p. 318). *Form* produces a similar form ; a necklace of maize grains round the neck of a small-pox patient produces an eruption of small, transparent, pustules which are not dangerous, in place of the large, thick, deadly ones. (See Chapter III. A.) *Disintegration* produces disintegration ; the chewing of a bean ensures the melting of the iron ore in the kiln (p. 359). *A certain state of mind* produces a similar condition in living beings, and even in material phenomena ; the continence of little children ensures control over the flame of the furnace (p. 115) whilst the passion of married people accelerates disease, and increases the fury of wild beasts, (p. 61) etc. (1)

This kind of magic has been called *imitative magic.* A corollary of this principle is that the image or object representing a thing is in close relation with the thing itself, and any action performed on the image will have its repercussion on the thing represented.

---

(1) To show how far this action of like on like can go, let me quote this final example which I gave in my paper on *The Magic Conception of Nature amongst Bantus (South African Journal of Scien e,* Nov. 1920). A magician has had the good luck to discover a crow's nest full of young. He climbs up the tree, and ties all the little birds together by their feet. The mother crow, however, is not at a loss to deliver her progeny. She brings each day a leaf taken from different trees, and places it in the nest. The magician keeps watch. He climbs the tree, looks at the leaf, and recognizes the tree from which it has been taken. He then goes and digs up a piece of root from that tree. After a few days he will have collected quite a bundle of different roots. By that time the little crows will be free, the string which bound them having given way, or having rotted, and the magician will possess a medicine of first rate quality. By means of it he will be able to free any patient from any disease or worry by which he is held fast.

2) *The portion of a complexus acts on the whole.* The elements of
Nature are considered as forming complexuses in which the component
parts are united in such a manner that they react on each other. The
body forms such a complexus ; an isolated organ can therefore act on the
whole body or replace it. (See the case of the trumpet of heaven (p. 314)
which is the femur of the bird of lightning and which is used to expel the
thunderstorm). But there are much more complicated complexuses, for
instance the village, muti. When death strikes its chief or any of its
members, everything is contaminated (I. p. 143). Material contact is
of paramount importance here ; but more spiritual considerations are
also taken into account in establishing these complexuses. Why is it
the first wife of the hunter who must shut herself up in the hut in order
to save her husband from the fury of the hippopotamus (p. 69)?
Because she is united to him by a mysterious tie, being the lawful, true
wife (I. p. 284). The community of life is more complete between her
and her husband than between the hunter and his minor wives. For
this reason, I prefer to call this form of magic *communionist magic* rather
than sympathetic magic, the term generally employed. In many
magic rites imitative magic and communionist magic are combined.

3) *The words in which a wish is emphatically expressed produce the
desired result.* Primitive man in the hierarchic form of his social
group, is accustomed to command and to be obeyed. He attaches great
importance to his word, and intends natural forces to accomplish his
will as well as his subordinates. This may be one of the reasons for the
prevalence of this kind of magic, which has inspired incantations,
imprecations, etc. There are no doubt other reasons, and the forms of
verbal magic are numerous.

It is evident that we cannot assign any scientific value to any of these
axioms of primitive mentality. They are absolutely false. It is not
true in actual life that like produces like, that the part acts on the whole,
and that the expressed wish produces the desired result. The magic
rite may be attended with some objective result in as much as its performance gives the performer greater confidence in himself, thus producing
an auto-suggestion favourable to the success of the operation. Moreover
the magician develops certain subliminal powers which are not yet well
understood but which are real and may be effective (especially in the
domain of divination). But magic rites are utterly irrational ; they are
doomed to disappear before the advance of Civilization and Science.

CHAPTER II

RELIGION.

About the end of the XVIIIth century, a Portuguese military commander visited the Bay, and, after having spent a year and eight months in the country, sent to the Prelate of Mozambique a very curious report on the cultivation, trade and civilisation of the land (p. 141). The following sentence is found in his report : — "All the inhabitants are Hottentots, and have no religion." That he should have had erroneous ideas concerning the distinction between Bantu and Hottentot tribes is but natural ; the ethnology of South Africa was not yet known. But that, after such a long sojourn amongst the Natives, he should have declared that these people had no religion seems indeed strange ! I can, however, understand the error, and excuse it. Amongst the Thongas there are no temples, no special day set apart for worship, no priest class, in fact, nothing external to attract attention to their religion. Even if he had been present at any of the religious ceremonies, the visitor might very well have mistaken them for ordinary family gatherings, as he would not have noticed anything like religious awe in the offering of the sacrifice, stolen by the *batukulu* (I. p. 162), in the prayer cut short amidst laughter, or in the songs, which would be of the usual type, perhaps even of a somewhat obscene character. Yet, notwithstanding all this, how real is the *Ancestrolatry*, the Religion of the Thongas, of, in fact, all the South African Bantus ! How frequent and manifold are its manifestations ! This is *the first, and most perceptible of their religious intuitions*, and any European who has stayed in their villages, learnt their language, and tried to understand their customs, will have had an opportunity of familiarizing himself with this religion. But there is a *second set of religious intuitions*, less

371

easy to perceive. In the quartz of the South African veldt, miners, in their investigations, sometimes strike a reef : they crush the hard stone, wash it, apply to it certain chemical tests and find there is gold in the reef. This is similar to an experience which I once had when conversing with Thonga natives. Quite unexpectedly I heard them speaking of *Heaven*, not as a kind of impersonal being, but as a king, endowed with great power and omniscience, who must be feared by thieves, because he knows them. Persevering in my inquiries, I discovered this second set of religious intuitions, quite distinct from the first, viz., the *Deistic Conception of Heaven*. I intend now to describe these two parts of the Thonga religious system. Later on we may discuss their relation to each other. "System" is perhaps too big a word, for no Native philosopher or theologian has ever classified this somewhat confused mass of religious ideas, and we must not look for anything logical and organic. We may even meet with contradictions, conflicting statements... While trying to bring some order into the subject, I will endeavour at the same time to give a faithful and reverent explanation of Native ideas.

A. ANCESTROLATRY.

I. *The Ancestor-Gods (Psikwembu).*

1) The name of the ancestor-gods.

Any man who has departed this earthly life, becomes a *shikwembu*, a god. We shall show, later on, that to translate "shikwembu" by god (with a small "g") is by no means incorrect. The word is indeed interesting, but unhappily no light is thrown on it by etymology. It belongs to the shi-psi class, the class of instruments. Take the verb "famba" to walk ; put the prefix "shi" in front of it, and change the final "a" into "o" and you obtain "shifambo" — "the thing with which one walks!" So shikwembu would mean "the thing with which one *kwemba*." Only this stem *kwemba* is never used, and its meaning is unknown. There is another form, *nkwembu*, of the class mu-mi, very rarely used, and having the same meaning, and the word *bukwembu*, the abstract noun derived from the same root. Bukwembu is the "power which creates life and death, which gives riches, or which makes poor," says Viguet. In Pedi the ancestor-gods are called *badimo*, a word which seems to be related to *Khedimo* (above, in heaven). But I have heard this connection doubted (1). In Zulu the etymology of *indhlozi* and *itongo*, employed to designate the ancestor-gods, is also unknown, which is a pity, as it would have been interesting to see if the stem from which they come also means above. Is it not strange that in these three closely-connected languages the terms used for the spirits, about which they have exactly the same ideas, are absolutely without any linguistic relation? In Sutho, these spirits belong to the class "mu-ba," the class of persons, which seems natural. In Zulu their two names are of the class yin-tin and dji-ma, respectively ; in Thonga they belong to the shi-psi class. This dissimilarity is indeed curious.

2) Categories of Ancestor-Gods.

Since every human being becomes a shikwembu after death, there are consequently many categories of these. What is the fate of little children? If they die in infancy no religious ceremony is performed over their grave, nor are any prayers offered to them. The twig rite (I. p. 142) only begins for children who have died at the age of puberty. Infants are, however, seen in the sacred woods amongst the adult gods. This is one of the points about

(1) The Vendas call the ancestor-gods *badzimo*, which is evidently the same word as the Sutho badimo. The Rev. Th. Schwellnus told me he thought that the etymology of this word was the verb dzima (in Thonga tima) which means to extinguish (Timula tora means to quench the thirst). The badzimo would thus be those who bring relief, who remove anguish. As this stem dzimo under various forms is widespread amongst the Bantu tribes to designate the ancestor-gods, it would be interesting to know if the corresponding verb dzima also exists and if this etymology is clearly established. The word *ntimu*, sacred wood, in Thonga, may perhaps come from the same root.

which there is no very clear explanation ; doubtless the matter did not seem worthy of inquiry!

The two great categories of gods are *those of the family*, and *those of the country*, the latter being those of the reigning family. They do not differ as regards their nature. In national calamities those of the country are invoked, whilst, for purely family matters, those of the family are called upon.

Moreover, each family has two sets of gods, those *on the father's side* and *those on the mother's*, those of "kweru" and those of "bakokwana" (I. p. 268). They are equal in dignity. Both can be invoked, and the divinatory bones are always called on to decide to which the offering must be made. It would seem, however, as if the gods of the mother's side were more tender-hearted and more popular than those of the father's. The reason for this is, perhaps, that relations are easier with the family of the mother than with that of the father. It is also just possible that it is a relic of the matriarchal period, when the ancestors of the mother alone were known, and consequently invoked. At any rate, the part played by batukulu nephews in the offerings shows that they are the true representatives of the gods, not of those of their father, but of their mother.

Two other categories of gods, which I have sometimes heard mentioned, are the *Gods of assagais* (psikwembu psa matlhari) and *the Gods of bitterness* (psa shibiti). The former are those who have been killed in battle ; the latter are those who have been drowned, killed by a wild beast, or who have committed suicide, or the pregnant woman who has been buried without being cut open (I. p. 166). In most of these cases, as is evident, the corpse has not been buried with the due rites and ceremonies ; the deceased has not been properly cared for : hence his bitterness ; or, as in the case of the pregnant woman, something has been buried without having first breathed its last breath (I. p. 140). In the case of the suicide, the poor man who hanged himself was full of sadness : "The great bitterness is the rope", said Mboza. In most of these cases no one was present at the death! These gods are therefore angry, and are the most to be feared.

The *Gods of the Bush, Psikwembu psa Nhoba*, are also especially dreaded. There is a little song which is sung as a welcome to travellers who reach their home safely :

> Shikwembu sha nhoba shi etlele !
> Shi etlele, banhwanyana !
> Amadikeo-dikeo-dikeo !
> The god of the bush has remained asleep!
> He has remained asleep, young girls !
> Hurrah ! hurrah ! hurrah !

The spirits of the departed who wander about in the bush, not having been properly buried, try to attack innocent travellers. You are fortunate to escape their anger! For this reason they often say to a relative who is starting out on a journey : "Go with your god," viz., the special ancestor-god who can protect you against the dangers of the bush.

I have also heard mention of *Shikwembu sha tihanye*, the god of quarrels. When an offering prescribed by the bones and presented to a certain ancestor-god has not had the desired result, people say : "This god is a god of quarrels. Let us make an offering to the others so that they may scold him."

3) The Abode of the Ancestor-Gods and their Mode of Life.

Ideas on these two points are very confused, even contradictory. Some say that the departed go to a great village *under the earth*, a village where everything is white (or pure, "ku basa") ; there they till the fields, reap great harvests, and live in abundance, and they take of this abundance to give to their descendants on earth. They have also a great many cattle. The place where they live seems to be a kind of Hades or Paradise (1). But it would seem, when we consider the funeral rites, that the deceased, on the contrary,

(1) The Ba-Ila (see Smith and Dale, *The Ila-speaking people*, II p. 119) believe that the ghosts go *Kwiwe*, to the East, to Chilenga, the Creator. But they have the same contradictory ideas as the Thongas concerning the abode of their deceased ancestors.

Amongst the Natives of Barotseland, on the Zambezi, it is said that the dead go to Nyambe, the God of Heaven. They pierce the lobe of their ears and make other incisions in their bodies as a sign that they belong to Nyambe. When they die and reach the end of the earth at the great river Walamba (the Styx of the Zambezian tribes) the ferryman who conveys the dead to the other bank looks at them to see if

remains *in his grave.* Is not his grave his house (I. p. 137)? Does
he not sit on his square, where his mats have been unrolled? Thus
the life of the shikwembu seems to be the exact continuation of his
earthly existence. That such is the idea is proved by the two
bones which represent the gods in the set of divinatory bones :
1) the astragalus or nail of an ant-bear, because ant-bears live in
the earth, and come out only during the night ; 2) the astragalus
of an antelope, found in the excrement of a hyena ; the hyena ate
the antelope, and swallowed the bone, which came to light again ;
in the same way the gods have been buried in the ground, and
reveal themselves later on. (Compare Ch. III. D.) A third idea,
more or less intermediate between the other two, is that the gods
reside *in the sacred woods,* and there lead their family life in
human form, parents and children, even little children, who are
carried on their mothers'shoulders. Mboza went so far as to say
that they are married and bring forth children, as children are seen
on their mothers'backs. Here again, we find the life of the other
world regarded as the exact reproduction of this terrestrial
existence.

4) THE SACRED WOODS.

These are vast, almost impenetrable thickets, in which the
ancient chiefs have been buried ; they are called *ntimu,* (mu-mi)
cemeteries. Every clan owns one or more of these burying places.
The ntimu is reserved for the men of the royal family, those who
have been the owners of the land. They are buried in different
sections of the forest, "according to their villages," in such a way
that the wood represents separate cemeteries, corresponding to the

they bear the marks, and only in that case does he take them to Nyambe (See *Ames
primitives*, Th. Burnier, Paris Mission, 102, Boulevard Arago).

The Ba-Chopi believe that their ancestor-gods dwell in rivers. They have no fear
of the graves where the deceased have been buried, and even till the ground over
them, asserting that the bones alone remain in the earth, the ghosts themselves having
departed into the river where they are heard singing, dancing, and playing on antelope
horns. When the chiefs make a national offering, they mix the meat with water when
they present it to their gods, and the one officiating turns his eyes towards the river
when he prays. He places the part of the victim which has been cut out for the gods
on the bank of the river, and everybody goes home. The gods come when all have
gone and take the offering. It is taboo to remain on the spot and to be seen by them!

villages of the living. No woman, and no uterine nephew is buried in the official cemeteries.

These woods are taboo. It is forbidden to gather fuel there, to cut down any tree, or to allow the bush fire to enter them. Should anyone have imprudently set fire to the grass in the neighbourhood, and be unable to extinguish the blaze, and should the fire thus pass over a grave, he must provide a goat for sacrifice, in order to "extinguish" (timula) the sacred wood. All entry is strictly prohibited except to the guardian of the wood (mutameli wa ntimu), the priest, who is the descendant of the gods of the forest. He goes there from time to time, to offer the sacrifices. He penetrates into the dense foliage by a narrow path, hardly perceptible. I have often visited one of the most celebrated woods, that of Libombo, two miles east of the Rikatla station. The old Libombo chiefs were buried there, and Nkolele, the proprietor of the forest, was very proud of it. He asserted that Mahazule, the chief of Nondwane, belonging to the reigning family of Mazwaya, whose forefathers had conquered the land of Nondwane, feared the spot and, in order to avoid it, took a circuitous route to Lourenço-Marques, or, if forced to take that road, stopped near the wood to pay his respects to the old chiefs buried there. I did not see anything remarkable in that wood. Forcing my way through the bushes, brambles, and creepers I at length came to a sort of tumulus, but very slightly raised, on which were to be seen some dried leaves of maize, the remains of offerings placed there some time previously. The young man who acted as my guide — considerably against his inclination, I fancy, — turned away his face, with a terrified expression, when we came upon this grave. In another spot I found some other tombs. Snakes thrive, naturally, in these thickets, where they are undisturbed, but I did not see any on that occasion. No mausoleum has been built over any of these venerated sepulchres ; a few pieces of old blackened pottery were all we saw — the remnants of the jugs and plates belonging to the deceased, which were broken on the spot after his death.

The dread in which these sacred woods are held by the Natives is certainly not due to any unusual objects they may have seen there. It is inculcated, and kept alive, by the truly terrifying tales which are told concerning them. These are related in the evening, in low tones, and with frightened looks, and the feeling of awe is fed and maintained by these legends. I intend to narrate here those I heard from various informants ; these stories will illustrate better than any philosophical explanation the ideas of the Natives concerning their gods. Those connected with the Libombo wood are the most typical. I owe them to Spoon and the aged Nkolele. I will begin with those which are of most ancient origin, and whose legendary character is most unmistakable.

One day a woman was passing close by the forest of Libombo : she plucked a sala (p. 16) from a tree and ate it, after which she went to till her garden. On another occasion, just as she was cracking another sala against the trunk of a tree before eating it, she saw that the fruit, instead of having a stone inside, was filled with small vipers. She threw it away, but the vipers said to her : "Go on! Eat away! Haven't we seen you every day picking sala ? And these sala are ours, and not yours. What shall we gods have to eat ? Have we not made this tree to grow ?" And she went home and died, because she had been cursed by the gods.

Another woman was passing by the forest on a rainy day, and saw a child, who had climbed a tree, and was eating berries. She approached the child and said : "Give me some of those berries!" The boy made no reply, so she began to pick some for herself. When she had picked enough, she said : "Are you going on picking berries in such a rain as this! Where is your mother?" He still remained silent. She felt sorry for the child, thinking he was indeed to be pitied : — "Come," said she, "and let me carry you on my back." So she went up to the tree, and lifted down the child, and tied him on her back with her shawl ; then, putting her conical basket on her head, she started for home. On arriving at her hut, she saw that a fire had been lighted on account of the rain. — "Put on some more wood," said she, "for the sake of this little one, whom I found on the road eating berries." She untied the shawl, and tried to place the child on her hips, but he refused to be moved, and clung to her back, where he kept quite still. The folks said to the woman : "Put him down on the ground, so that he can go and warm himself near the embers." He refused. Then they said to him : "Get down!" But he still refused to move. Then the villagers said to the woman : "Didn't you pass by the Libombo forest?" — "Yes! I did," she replied, "and there I found this child gathering berries, and

brought him along with me." — "This is no child! It is a god!" they
cried ; "a child never has a hard head like this one has. And look at his
legs! What strength! How ever did you come to think it was a child?"
—"But," said she, "I certainly thought it was a child — and can it
be a god?" — They sent for magicians, who threw the bones. At
once the magicians knew what was wrong : — "Ha! Hé! You found
him at Libombo, did you not?" They tried to remove him by force,
but he clung still more closely to the woman's back, stiffening his legs
round her waist, and his arms around her neck. They tried to unclench
his hands, but it was impossible! Then they begged her to go back
to Libombo, and implore the owners of the forest to set her free from
this child. She took her basket, and returned to the tree where
she had found him. The guardian of the forest soon appeared. It
was Makundju, the ancestor of Nkolele. He inveighed against the
woman and those who accompanied her, saying : — "When you find
fruit in the forest, do not pick it! If it be maize, leave it alone, or,
if you pick it, spare at least one ear. If your chicken flies into the
wood, do not go after it. If your goat runs away into it, you must
not follow it. We are worn out, we folks of Libombo, with offering
sacrifices for you passers-by... Your troubles are the consequences
of the sins (psihono) you commit in this place." A white hen was
caught, and sacrificed on behalf of the woman. Emitting the "tsu"
the priest said : "Behold our ox, by which we present our petition.
Let this god leave her back. She did not do it on purpose. She
thought it was a child ; she did not know it was a god. Which way
can people go henceforth if you, gods, put obstacles in the way?" While
this sacrifice was being offered, the being suddenly left her back,
disappeared, and no one knew how, or whither he went. As for the
woman, she trembled violently and died...

A man once defied the prohibition of cutting dry wood in the forest.
Suddenly he was pelted from behind with kwakwa and sala fruits.
It was the gods. He tried to fly, but was unable to find the path out
of the thicket. He was lost, and tired of wandering about he let his
bundle of faggots fall. Then the gods allowed him to find his way
out again, but, when he found himself in the open, he perceived that
he was carrying nothing, even his axe had been taken from him.

Sometimes the gods made themselves heard ; when they were
especially happy they played on trumpets, sang and danced.
Passers-by often tried to get a glimpse of them, but the noise

ceased at once, and would commence again suddenly right behind the listeners. The people of the country know quite well whence this music comes, and, at Libombo, they can even report the song which is heard in this forest. It is a great pity that I was not able to obtain the music of this ode of the gods! I can, however, give the words, which will probably be found to smack considerably of the earth, earthy! —

> With ground- nuts and onions, nté, nté, nté!
> Make a good sauce in the pan!

However, here are one or two facts of quite recent occurrence, showing that the age of sacred wood miracles is not yet over, or that, at least, the religious awe still survives in some faithful hearts!

Spoon assured me that he saw on one occasion a whole herd of goats in the forest, while he was picking tihuhlu nuts. He ran to tell his grandfather, Nkolele, and to ask if he might appropriate them. Nkolele reproved him with bitter words : "Unhappy man! Don't dare to touch them! They belong to the gods! Don't even speak of them! It is taboo! (psa yila)."

The young folks of Libombo used to blaspheme in their hearts, saying: "There are no gods." "But," added Spoon, "we very soon saw that there were some, when they killed one of us, named Mapfindlen. He was walking along the path, singing and jumping, when he trod on a snake, which he had not seen, and hurt it. During the night the gods came to him. He began to scratch himself all over his body. He saw them against the wall : they were like snakes, and they said : 'Thou hast hurt us!' No one else saw them. His mother tried to quiet him, but he shrieked, and said to her : 'Leave me alone! The gods are killing me because I trod on them! Help!' They threw the bones. The diviner said : 'This comes from your household gods! Has he not trodden on a snake?' His parents procured an offering, and sacrificed to the gods, trying to propitiate them ; but the gods were angry and Mapfindlen died."

The following is the most recent of the stories. It was related to me by the hero himself, Nkolele, the aged priest of Libombo.

RELIGION

After the war of 1894-1895, the Portuguese Authorities established a camp at Morakwen, and decided to build a town there. To do this it became necessary to widen the primitive pathway which led to Lourenço Marques, and Natives had to cede trees and grass lands, to the extent of several metres on each side of the path ; then a fine road was built of some 20 kilometres in length. This road passed close by the sacred wood, as it had been decided to follow the line of the pathway, which skirted this wood for a distance of about half a mile. Amongst many other trees was one huge mahogany, under whose shade I have frequently passed, which sent out a low branch, right over the path ; it was necessary to cut off this branch, and the people living in the neighbourhood were intrusted with the job. "When they began the work," said Nkolele to me, on the 28th November, 1895, "I went to see what they were doing with the mahogany tree. As I was seated the gods came to me, saying : 'What are you doing here ? You ought to have stayed at home.' I fell backwards unconscious, and remained in that state for four days. I couldn't eat : they had closed my mouth. I could not speak! My people picked me up and carried me home. My relatives and my children were all summoned : the villagers said : 'Our medicine-man has left us! He is dead!' Then my eldest son went to offer a sacrifice in the sacred wood. He let loose a fowl, which flew away and never returned ; he prayed : 'Oh! my ancestors! Here is my ox. Do not slay my father!' Then I got up. Ah! It was he, who saved me, Ngeleñwana, my eldest son! I looked around and said : 'What have all these people come here for ?' They were terror stricken. Then they told me that the gods of Libombo were angry with me. The gods said to me (doubtless by means of the bones) : 'Take an ox-cock' (meaning an ox, an animal for sacrifice, which may be a cock), 'and go to your brother Shihubane. Let him give you a fowl, and go and sacrifice. Why did you go there ? You ought to have stayed at home, and have sent your children.' I did not go any more by the big road. I go by the path through the marshes, and never by the avenue made by the Whites. Now I can go that way, for I have sacrificed, and the gods have said : 'He has asked our pardon by means of his gifts.'"

Is there not something significant and touching about this tale ? Civilisation penetrates irresistibly, crushing everything in its way, and cutting remorselessly, perhaps unwittingly, through the edge of the sacred wood! And there, under the mahogany tree, the aged priest, the guardian of its traditions, swoons away and asks forgiveness for having been an involuntary witness of the sacrilege!

These stories are by no means restricted to the Libombo sacred wood. Similar tales are told of all the forests. Mboza says :

A woman was imprudent enough to cut some dry branches in the sacred wood of Masinge, near Morakwen. She at once heard an unusual voice : bi... bi... and received blows. She ran away home leaving her garment in the bush. Having arrived home, she asked her husband to go and fetch it, but he refused, from fear. Nkomuza, the guardian of the forest, went to fetch it, but they had to reward him with a bottle of wine.

An older story about the same forest runs as follows : — In olden times the gods were frequently seen marching in file, going to draw water from the well. They had their own road. They were of short stature, the women carrying babies in the *ntehe*, but, strange to say, with the feet up and the head downwards! A man, called Mishimhongo, built his village near to the forest. The gods, angry with him, entered his huts while he was busy with all his people working in the fields. Only a little child remained in the village, and the gods wrapped him up in a mat, and hid him somewhere behind the huts. Then they went to the garden and shouted : "Mishimhongo! There are visitors in your village." The man looked to see who was calling him, but saw no one. He went home, and found that the child had disappeared. In the evening the gods came and said to him : "Look behind the huts. But move at once ; do not remain near our road! If you do so, we shall kill you and your child." The poor man needed no second warning!

Not far from this place, in the Nkanyen district, is the sacred wood of Tlhatlha. An enormous pot is said to have been placed there long ago, a marvellous pot which possesses the faculty of locomotion. It can move as far as that village yonder (half a mile). But though it may have arrived only yesterday at the spot where you see it, it is quite hidden in the grass and shrubs, as if it had been there for years! It takes its walk from one end of the graves to the other. It is taboo to touch it! When the Portuguese tried to establish a camp there, they heard strange noises during the night, drums, trumpets, etc. The Landis (Natives) said to them : "Take care! There are gods here." So they removed their camp to Morakwen. (Mboza.)

The wood of Tembe, called Mudlomadlomana, is very celebrated.

It is said that, in olden days, there was an anchor there, and before sacrificing, the priest always used to lift it up, and let it fall to the ground, saying : "Shawan! (I salute thee) Tembe!" If the sacrifice was acceptable the sound of a trumpet : "bvé... bvé...," was heard, far away in the depths of the woods, but no form was ever seen. This anchor also possessed extraordinary powers. When the country was at war with its neighbours, and matters did not go well with Tembe, the anchor would move off by itself into the Matjolo district. This was the portent of some terrible catastrophe!

No one ever penetrated very far into the sacred wood of Tiyini, of the Matjolo clan, for it was said that any one doing so would be lost, and unable to find his way out. When the people of Matjolo were in need of rain, they took a young man of the country into the wood, and there abandoned him. The gods accepted their offering, and the young man, struck with paralysis, was unable to follow in their retreat those who had led him to martyrdom! He saw them going away, but remained behind to be devoured by the gods. The others hastened to sacrifice and returned home ; they were forbidden to look behind them. Once home, they told how they had seen on the ground, in the wood, foot-prints of adults, and even of little ones who must have been old enough to crawl on their hands and knees! Often, they say, they brought back the rain with them!

According to all these stories, it is evident that, in the Thonga mind, the ancestor-gods dwell in the sacred woods, and lead a life there in the earth, and occasionally outside, very similar to the terrestrial one. Mankhelu had, however, another idea, which is difficult to reconcile with this representation. On his forked magic pole he had a long shining grey branch of a climbing shrub called ñwabola. This has enormous thorns, which are supposed to have the power of calling the precious things which are far away, and of gathering them in the hut : money, oxen, girls to marry, etc., and also the ancestor-gods : "When they pass through the country, coming from our old domicile, near the Limpopo, they are caught by the thorns, and settle here to bless us." This idea that the gods fly through the air, is very rarely met with. I never heard it said that the gods were in heaven, not-withstanding the Sutho term badimo, which is believed by some to mean those who are above.

5. RELATIONS BETWEEN ANCESTOR-GODS AND THEIR LIVING DESCENDANTS.

The apparitions of ancestor-gods in a human form in the sacred woods are not of frequent occurrence. The gods reveal themselves to their descendants by other and more common means ; first, by their appearance *in the form of animals*, such as the Mantis (p. 335) or more often as little bluish green snakes called *shihundje* (p. 340). These charming and harmless reptiles are frequently seen in the huts, crawling in the thatch of the roof, or along the reeds of the walls (1). Natives never touch them, thinking that they are some of their gods who have come to pay them a visit. It is taboo to kill them. If a disease breaks out in the village the bones may reveal that some one in the hut has hurt the gods, and a sacrifice will be required in order to appease them. They also appear in the form of the large grey puff-adder (shiphyahla) (2).

Secondly, the ancestor-gods communicate with the living *in their dreams*. If some one dreams of one of his dead relatives, he is very much frightened, and consults the bones, in order

(1) This is the story which I heard from one of my informants of the Khosen country : All his family was once assembled together for a marriage feast. The people were playing on the village square and enjoying themselves. The old women had remained in the hut, and suddenly they saw two little green snakes crawling along the reeds of the wall. They were much afraid, and at once called the headman. He came in, saw the snakes, and said : "Do not fear ! These are our ancestor-gods ! They have come to share in our feast."

(2) Describing to me a sacrifice at which he officiated either in September or October 1895, the old priest Nkolele told me as a fact the following story, which I will now quote word for word :

"I myself went into the wood with the offering I had prepared for the gods, and then *it came out*. It was a snake ; it was the father of Makundju, the Master of the Forest, Mombo-wa-ndlopfu, Elephant's-Face. He came out and circled round all those present. The women rushed away terrified. But he had only come to thank us. He didn't come to bite us. He thanked us saying : 'Thank you ! Thank you ! So you are still there, my children ! You came to load me with presents, and to

to know exactly what the god desires of him (Viguet). If the apparition was painful, if the god came as an enemy, fighting, the dreamer, when he awakes, will take some tobacco, or a small piece of cloth, and hang it somewhere in the reeds of the wall, near the door, as an offering. Or possibly the god has ordered him to give him something to drink. He will then buy a bottle of ginor wine, and pour a little outside the door ; whatever remains he will drink with his companions. If the dream takes place during a journey and the ancestor-god seems to be happy, the traveller will throw some tobacco on the ground when he awakes and say : "I had prayed thee to help me on my road ; thou hast come indeed! Help me to go further." But if the ancestor-god has an angry look and tells him : "Why do you not give me a piece of calico print? You have forgotten me"—the traveller will fetch a piece and tie it round a tree and say : "When I return home after making money, I will give thee some."

But the great means by which the will of the gods is revealed is the *set of divinatory bones*, which are cast on every occasion, and are called the "Bula," the Word. Does this mean the Word of the gods? Not precisely, but in most cases the diviner thinks he owes his divinatory power to a dead relative, who used to cast lots himself, and who transmitted his spirit of interpretation to him. Whatever may be the real explanation, the fact remains that it is by means of the bones that Thongas believe they know what their gods think and wish, and this is the reason, as we shall

bring me fruit ! T'is well !' — He came to thank us for our chicken. Even if one only kills a chicken, he is quite content. For him, it has just the same value as an ox. It was an enormous viper, as thick as my leg, down there (he pointed to his ankle). It came close up to me, and kept quite still, never biting me. I looked at it. It said : 'Thank you ! So you are still there, my grandson !' "

— "But," said I to Nkolele, "what you are telling me, is it really fact, or just fancy?"

— "Undoubted fact ! These are great truths ! After that I prayed, and said : 'Thou, Mombo-wa-Ndlopfu, the Master of this land, thou who hast given it to thy son Makundju ; Makundju gave it to his son Hati ; Hati gave it to Makhumbi ; Makhumbi gave it to Kinini ; Kinini gave it to Mikabyana ; Mikabyana gave it to Mawatle... ('Mawatle gave it to me, his son' is here understood)... Look upon my offering. Is it not a beautiful one ? And here am I, left all alone. If I had not brought this with me, who would have given you anything? Is it not just so ? I ask of thee, my ancestor, I ask of thee all the trees ; the palm trees for building, the trunks which can be hollowed out for canoes ; and let it be that these trunks shall not fall on the people and crush them, when they go to cut them down, over there in the marsh.' "

see, why divination plays such an important part in their life. It is of the utmost importance to know what their gods think and do, as the very existence of the village, and of the clan, and the welfare of every member of the clan depends on them. Is not Bukwembo, Divinity "the power of killing or of making alive, of enriching or of making poor?" Natives believe firmly in these two opposite actions of their gods. They are the masters of everything : earth, fields, trees, rain, men, children, even of baloyi, wizards! They have full control over all these objects or persons.

The gods can *bless* : if the trees bear plenty of fruit, it is because they have made it grow (I. p. 414) ; if the crops are plentiful, it is because they forced wizards to increase them, or hindered them from spoiling them (I. p. 396) ; if you come across a pot of palm wine, it is your god who has sent you that windfall (p. 44). When Mboza escaped from the Morakwen battle, one of his relatives exclaimed on his return home : "The gods of Makaneta have still been with you!" (Psikwembu psa ka Makaneta psa ha ku yimelele.) Often when a man has narrowly escaped drowning, or spraining his ankle on a stump which has caught his foot, he will say : "The gods have saved me."

But they can also *curse*, and bring untold misfortune on their descendants. If the rain fails, it is owing to their anger ; if a tree falls on you, they have directed its fall ; if a crocodile bites you, the gods have sent it ; if your child has fever and is delirious, they are in him, tormenting his soul ; if your wife is sterile, they have prevented her from childbearing ; perhaps the gods of your mother have done this, because you had not given your maternal uncle the *tjhumba* part of the lobolo, which he has the right to claim (I. p. 267) ; in fact any disease, any calamity may come from them. There are, of course, other sources of misfortune : the baloyi, for instance, or Heaven, and the bones will show who has caused the mischief ; but the ancestor-gods are certainly the most powerful spiritual agency acting on man's life. Hence the necessity of propitiating them by prayers and sacrifices.

II. *The Means of Propitiation. Offerings and Sacrifices.*

It is no wonder, since these spirits are so terrible, that their descendants have sought means of propitiating them. The study of these rites is very interesting, and will throw more light on the ideas of the Bantus concerning their ancestor-gods. Some of these means of propitiation bear a magical character. For instance, when Mankhelu wished to induce the gods to sleep and leave him in peace, he took roots which had been brought to light naturally by a swollen river that had washed away the ground. The reason is clear ; the gods are in the earth, therefore things found in the earth can influence them. So he cut these roots in small pieces, cooked them with the flesh of a goat, and drank the broth ; the assagai which killed the goat had been first smeared with a powder made of these roots. He fastened the astragalus of the goat on his ankle, on the right side if the god to be propitiated belonged to his father's family, and on the left if it was one of his mother's ancestors. If the propitiatory ceremony was performed for a woman, the astragalus was tied with a strap "en bandouillère" round her body.

We shall often see such *magic acts* performed in the ancestor worship of the Thongas. This is in keeping with their general conception of Nature, as already explained (p. 369), and with the magic principles or axioms of primitive mentality. But to the magic element is added the religious ; the officiant is aware that he intends to influence living, conscious and superior beings, therefore he has recourse above all to specifically *religious means*, viz., to offerings and prayers. He presents to his gods what he calls a *mhamba*, and not *miri*, charms or medicines similar to those employed in magic proper. We shall understand more fully what the word mhamba means when we have described the various kinds of offerings.

1) CLASSIFICATION OF OFFERINGS.

These offerings are much more complicated and varied than they at first seem. The following principles of classification may be applied to them :

1) *Individual and family offerings* — those which concern a man or his family alone, — and *national offerings* — those which concern the whole clan.

2) The *simple offerings* called *gandjela*, and the *sacramental ones*, accompanied by the famous *tsu* which constitutes them a *hahla* (Ro.) or a *phahla* (Dj.).

3) Offerings attended with *bloodshed*, and those where no victim is killed.

4) The *regular offerings*, made at certain dates, or in connection with definite events in the life of the family or of the clan, and those made in *special* circumstances.

a) *Individual and Family Offerings.*

Simple Offerings (Gandjela).

Here the ritual is reduced to its minimum. The offering is made by the father of the family at the gandjelo, the altar, or place of worship. This is, as has already been pointed out, a little pot, placed at the right side of the entrance to the village, or under the tree designated by the bones (I. p. 320) (1). In some cases, especially if the headman is a medicine-man or magician, the gandjelo consists of a forked branch planted in the ground, either inside his hut, or in the very middle of the square. Such was the case in the village of Mankhelu (See illustration I. p. 5). His gandjelo was a branch of *nkonola* (or *nkonono*) ; this tree, the *mpfilu* and *shisalala* are the only trees which are used for the purpose. He had removed the bark in some places, and smeared the stems with his black powders, so that there were two dark rings of about 3 inches wide on the branch. A lot of curious things were to be seen hanging from the lateral branches : bags

---

(1) If there are people of different clans inhabiting the same village owing to the fact that foreigners have "kondza" i. e, have put themselves under the authority of the headman (I. p. 433), there will be a central gandjelo, the altar of the master of the village, at the foot of the sacred tree where offerings will be made for himself and his relatives ; but people of the other clans will have their own altars which will be placed near the main entrance, on the spot where the representatives of each of these clans assemble when discussing their own affairs.

full of roots, calabashes of different sizes, containing the precious drugs, pieces of the ñwabola shrub (p. 383), etc. When he had earned some money or acquired something by accident, Mankhelu used to put these objects near the stem, and leave them there for the night in order to inform his gods of his good fortune. At the foot of the branch the earth was smeared with black clay, forming a circle with a little furrow traced round the outside of it. Men who are not so important as this great ñanga, are contented with the

Sokis mug. The altar of primitive mankind.

small pot I described before. This can be placed on the grave, if it happens to be near the village.

In the case of Sokis (I. p. 139) it was the *deceased's own mug* which was used, pierced at the bottom in order to allow the beer to sink easily into the ground, when an offering was made to the recently deceased by his relatives (1).

Regular offerings are brought to the altar by the headman. When he has finished preparing his *tobacco* for use, he carefully puts aside some leaves of it, and places them near the pot. When he has ground the tobacco for snuff he puts two little spoonsful

(1) I had the good fortune to obtain this mug, which may well be called the altar of primitive humanity! I offered Sokis' wife a small pig in exchange for it. She was quite willing to accept the bargain, but her sister-in-law made objections, doubtless fearing that the deceased might be angry... The widow answered her thus: "When he was living you refused him beer often enough! You may do the same now, and accept the little pig." Thanks to the common-sense view taken by Sokis'wife I am now in possession of this precious pierced mug, and in a position to give its facsimile in the accompanying plate.

into the pot, one for the paternal, the other for the maternal gods, saying as he does so :

Fole hi ledji! Tlanganan mi djaha, mi nga ndji hobilise loko ndji djaha fole, mi ku ndji mi tjona.

Here is some tobacco! Come all of you and take a pinch, and do not be angry with me when I snuff, nor say that I deprive you of your share.

Having made his offering, the headman must return to his seat, on the hubo, without looking behind him : this is a taboo.

Another way of gandjela is the offering of a piece of cloth (nturu), which may be tied at the entrance, or to the tree of the village (p. 333). Liquids also are poured into the gandjelo (I. p. 341) : beer, when a beer feast is to take place ; wine, when it has been bought at the neighbouring store ; palm-wine, when the big pot called gandjelo (see p. 43 for the explanation of this word in this particular connection) has been filled, and the precious drink has been brought to the village.

Occasional offerings are made, for instance, in a case of *shirwalo* (I. p. 406) when relatives-in-law have brought jars of beer. A little of the beer is first offered to the gods, in order that the pots may not get broken during the return journey. Another case is after a dream, in which the gods have asked for such and such an offering to be made (p. 385).

Sacramental Offerings or Ku Hahla (Ro.), Phahla (Dj.).

These are of much greater importance than the simple ones and also differ from them in two ways, viz., they are always ordered by the divinatory bones, and accompanied by the sacramental *tsu*. The bones are first consulted, and give many indications, e. g., what must be the nature of the offering ; to which god it must be consecrated ; in what place the act of worship must be performed, (in the hut, behind it, at the door, in the square, in the sacred wood, or in the bush). When the ceremony takes place over the grave the bones reveal whether the officiant must stand at the head or at the foot. (See Chap. III, D. for the consultation of the bones).

The Offering of Bitterness. There is a progressive character in the offerings, according to the value of the gift accompanying the *tsu*. In some cases, all that is given to the gods is the small amount of saliva emitted in pronouncing the sacramental sound. These offerings are called "Offerings of Bitterness" (ku hahla hi shibiti), and form a most curious category. They are generally presented by a headman who is overwhelmed with sorrow, and deprived of everything. "He shows his misery by offering nothing but his saliva. He leans his head upon his shoulder with a look of profound sadness. His heart is bitter! He has nothing! He therefore does not try to win over his gods by presenting rich gifts to them. He wishes rather to gain their blessing by this appearance of abject misery. And they will indeed have pity on him!" (Mboza). This is certainly touching! But this kind of offering, though showing more individual piety than others, must only be made ritually, i. e., by order of the bones. The sacrifice of bitterness may be resorted to when no evil has as yet fallen on the village, as a preventive against misfortune.

The Offering of Charcoal. When a headman is in great difficulties, (quarrels in his village, disease amongst his people), the bones may order him to *hahla* with a piece of charcoal. He takes an extinct charcoal, puts it to his lips, utters the *tsu* and adds :

Akhwari! i. e. Smoothly! You, so and so. What you want is this. Abupsayi! i. e. Gently! This is fire! This is the mouth of the lion! Let what troubles me come to an end, etc.

The Offering of Earth. Earth is the offering of the chiefs, because they are the masters of the soil (I. p. 405). It can, however, also be used by subjects on various occasions. When the bones have not revealed that the disease was sent by the ancestor-gods, when they have not said that it was the work of wizards, then it is caused by "the earth, misaba" i. e. by some unknown people of the land (bhanu ba misaba). The bones say : "Go and seek the navel of the earth." The navel of the earth is the ant-heap. The officiant then takes a piece of termite nest and *hahla* with it. He addresses his prayer to his ancestor-gods in order to be delivered from his enemies.

The Offering of a Thorn (Mhamba ya Mutwa). This is also called *ku hahla ka shihlahla*, the sacrifice of the forest. The headman has seen that misfortune has fallen on his village ; all his people die, the village is about to disappear, to become merely a part of the bush. He goes to the forest, picks up a thorn there and accomplishes the religious act by sucking the thorn, and emitting his saliva. Then he returns to the forest and places the thorn where the bones have ordered him.

The Offering of Contempt (Mhamba ya Litsañwa). We have already seen a case in which this offering is made. It is a component part of the burial ritual (I. p. 142) and we have called it the rite of the twig. But it can be performed on other occasions also. In certain clans (Nkuna-Khosa, Hlengwe) it does not take place at the burial, but is of common use when someone wishes *to avoid contempt*, to be well received by those to whom he goes ; for instance when he goes to his debtors and fears that they may despise him and perhaps refuse to accept his claim, or when a young man goes to woo a girl and is afraid that she may not look favourably on his suit. The religious act is performed as follows. The officiant cuts a twig of the nkanye tree. We have often mentioned this tree, whose fruits are used to prepare the famous bukanye beer ; it is everywhere regarded as the best of trees, and highly valued. It is dioecious, as we have seen (I. p. 397). The twig must come from a female stem, if a man *hahla* for himself, from a male stem if a woman does so. The officiant bites the extremity of the twig till he has drawn a little of the sap into his mouth; then he emits that sap together with his saliva, and proceeds to his prayer.

The Offering of the Fig Tree (Mhamba ya Hlulawumbe). This tree is called shihlampfana or hlulawumbe. It frequently grows as a parasite on another tree ; or surrounds it, growing close to its stem, and in this way kills it. If a man has enemies, if there are people who hate him, he digs up a bit of the root of this fig tree and uses it in making his prayer. These troublesome persons will be choked, destroyed, just like the stem close to which the hlulawumbe grows, (Hlulawumbe means to overcome others) (1).

Offerings of the Medicine-men. The Native physicians are, as has already been pointed out, very pious. Their art having been handed down to them by their forefathers, as a family secret, they always implore the blessing of their ancestors on their various treatments. This is done by true offerings, performed with the *tsu* and a liturgical prayer. In Vol. I. p. 55, the religious ceremony which accompanies the monthly vapour bath administered to infants was described ; a religious rite takes place also in the hondola of the weaning (I. p. 59). These are typical cases. Another offering of the same nature is made on behalf of the man who is about to *start out on a journey,* for instance to Johannesburg. The doctor, having prepared the protective drugs in a pot, brings them to the entrance of the traveller's hut, and calls his "patient,"; then, taking a little of the decoction in his mouth, he spits it at him with the sacramental *tsu,* and prays in the following words :

Akhwari! Abusayi! Ndji hlaya psolepso! Khongelwa a nga dlawi. Ku dlawa phalaburena! Khombo a dji suke, dji ya ka Shiburi, dji ya ka Nkhabelane! A a fambe psinene, a kandjetela balala, mitwa mi yetlele, ku yetlela ni tindjau. A a ye nwa mati ya kone, ma mu tjhabisa hi djo tluka ledji.

Gently! Smoothly! I say so. Death does not come to him for whom prayer is made ; death only comes to him who trusts in his own strength! Let misfortune depart, let it go to Shiburi, and Nkhabelane (2). Let him travel safely ; let him trample on his enemies ; let thorns sleep, let lions sleep ; let him drink water wherever he goes, and let that water make him happy, by the strength of this leaf (viz., of my medicinal herbs).

---

(1) I may mention here another religious ceremony which is also called a mhamba, though I am not sure that a regular prayer is offered. It is the *Offering of a Stone.* Stones are almost totally lacking in Thongaland. But on the Swazi border, in the Lebombo hills, there are porphyreous rocks, and when a Native passes a certain spot, on the Estatuen road, he picks up a stone, spits on it, touches both his knees with it and throws it on a heap made of the stones thrown by those who passed before him. This heap of stones is called *shititane.* This rite is said to be performed in order to call a blessing on the journey ; thus the traveller will find a favourable reception in the villages and be given plenty of food. This custom is wide-spread in many other tribes.

(2) The extremity of the land (Comp. I, p. 55).

To these words is generally added an invocation to the medicine-man's gods, who are entreated to bless the drugs they have given to their descendant, and to join with the traveller's gods in order to insure his success in this undertaking. The decoction is then used to wash the body of the young man. He will pay the fee on his return home.

Offerings of Hunters. This is called *byalwa bya ngenge*, the beer of ngenge. This beer is made of maize grains which have been crushed but not softened by long steeping in water, as is generally done in brewing ; they are then reduced to flour ; some water is poured on this and it is offered in that form by the head hunter, all his companions standing near him. They must start at once ; there is therefore no time to brew proper beer.

Offerings of Travellers. These also have their particular mhamba, which is called *Lehika.* It consists of water alone which the officiant takes in his mouth and spits out, saying : "*Pff!*" (amongst the Hlengwes : "*Phaaa*"). "My ancestor-gods! May I find no difficulty on my road, etc." This *water offering* is also made by a headman whose village is troubled by endless disputes. The way of bringing them to an end is not clear. So he entreats his gods to "open the road, pfula ndlela," so that all hearts may be relieved. This will help him to "herd his village, ku byisa muti." The idea of finding a road clearly accounts for the fact that this offering is made under two sets of circumstances so different from one another. Why water is used to attain this end I do not know.

The offerings hitherto described bear a more or less individual character. Let us now consider those which are in direct relation to the life of the family.

Regular Family Sacrifices. We have seen these performed in connection with the most important events in life. At the *weaning* (I. p. 58, this might however be termed a medical sacrifice), *on the marriage day,* either publicly, as amongst the Ronga clans (I. p. 110), or privately, by the bride's father alone, as is the custom amongst the Nkunas (I. p. 118). The gods are entreated to give the newly married woman "timbeleko," births, i. e., children, as it seems that the power of begetting depends directly on the gods. Regular acts of worship are performed also at the *burial* (I. p. 142), at the *crushing of the hut* (I. p. 158-163), on the days of *mahloko* (I. p. 215), and at the *adjudication of the inheritance* (I. p. 208).

I have already mentioned the stringent taboo in regard to the victims killed in these sacrifices. The portions distributed amongst the different relations must not be eaten either in the village of the deceased, or in those of the various visitors. This meat must be roasted on the road, and eaten on the spot, and it is likewise taboo to season it in any way. The inhabitants of the deceased's village can eat the meat boiled, but it is prohibited to add ground-nuts to the broth.

These are the great family sacrifices, in which the uterine nephews play their curious part, and on the occasion of which family matters are brought up and settled. They play a most important part in the life of the family, and I have therefore described them at length, when treating of the social life of the tribe, as religion and social life are here intimately united. There is therefore no need for me to add much more regarding them here. With their clearly established and typical ritual they form the most definite and settled element of the religious life of the tribe.

Rangane asserts that another offering is regularly performed in the Maluleke district. On the first occasion of the *cooking of the new mealies*, each headman prepares a little of the flour, takes a spoonful of it, and throws it away, praying at the same time to the Ba-Nyai spirits, i. e., the gods of the Ba-Nyai, who have been conquered by the Malulekes. He calls this "magandjelo ya ku ñwantseka," i. e., "sacrifice tasted and thrown away." This is evidently to propitiate the gods, who were the first owners of the country and who might harm or destroy the invaders. Compare p. 377 the respect shown by Mahazule to the Libombo sacred wood, and also the curious request of the Samaritans, II Kings. XVII.

Special Family Sacrifices. By these, I mean particularly those offered *in cases of disease.* The bones having revealed that the disease is caused by the gods (and not by wizards, nor by Heaven, nor by contamination, which are three other possibilities), and also that it comes from such and such a god, a god of bitterness, or a god of the paternal or the maternal line, now indicate the nature of the offering which must be made, the place, and sometimes even the person who must make it. Here is the detailed description, given by Viguet, of a sacrifice made for a ntukulu, a uterine nephew, who is ill : — "Suppose," says Viguet, "that I am the sick child. The bones have said that an offering must be made to the gods of our *bakokwana* (mother's family) ; so we go to our maternal relatives, to my *malume*, and ask him to perform the sacrifice. The offering may consist of a hen or an ornament like a bracelet. If it is a hen, my malume will kill it in accordance with the ceremonial rite, take a few of the feathers of the neck, which have been soiled by the blood, put them to his mouth, and spit on them, making *tsu* (the blood of the victim thus mingles with the saliva of the priest), and say (bulabulela) :

You, our gods, and you so and so, here is our mhamba (offering)! Bless this child, and make him live and grow ; make him rich, so that when we visit him, he may be able to kill an ox for us... You are useless, you gods ; you only give us trouble! For, although we give you offerings, you do not listen to us! We are deprived of everything! You, so and so (naming the god, to whom the offering must be addressed in accordance with the decree pronounced by the bones, i. e., the god who was angry, and who induced the other gods to come and do harm to the village, by making the child ill), you are full of hatred! You do not enrich us! All those who succeed, do so by the help of their gods! — Now we have made you this gift! Call your ancestors so and so ; call also the gods of this sick boy's father, because his father's people did not steal his mother : these people, of such and such a clan, came in the daylight (to lobola the mother). So come here to the altar! Eat and distribute amongst yourselves our ox (the hen!) according to your wisdom.

Then the priest takes a feather from one of the wings, a claw of the left foot and the beak, and after tying them together, attaches them to the left wrist or left ankle of the child, or to his neck, passing the string over the shoulder and under the left arm ; (all is on the left side, because it is an offering to the gods of the mother's family ; it would be on the right side if it were to the gods of the father). These parts of the victim are called *psirungulo*, the religious amulet.

When the offering consists of a bracelet, the bones having so ordered, the priest will pour consecrated beer over it, and say his prayer. The bracelet will then be fastened to the child's foot. He may not remove it, nor exchange it for anything else : it belongs to the gods.

This description, given by Viguet, is typical of sacrifices offered in the case of disease. In the Maluleke clan the sacrifice made for a sick person is as follows. The headman takes beer, which has been specially prepared for the gods and is very much diluted, the beer called *byala bosila*, and a twig of male nkanye. He orders the patient to sit near the altar, and after dipping the twig into the beer, sucks it and says the following words :

Phaa! (this word corresponds to tsu) : this is byala bosila, you Makhima! Take it and convey it to your father Mashakadzi ; call each other and come here together to drink! Let all disease depart! Heal this man!

I must also mention the sacrifice performed in the curious ceremony of *dlaya shilongo*, in the case of marriage between near relatives (I. p. 258), and will now proceed to describe two others, viz., the sacrifice on behalf of the son who has just returned from Johannesburg, and the sacrifice of reconciliation.

When a young man, who has been absent from home for a long time, *returns to his village,* he cannot be received again into the community without special precautions being taken. If there has been a death in the kraal he must be purified from the collective contamination before eating the food of the village. This is the luma milomo (I. p. 146), and is connected with the defilement from death. Some of the provisions of the deceased, kept in a pot and diluted with hot water, must be poured between his two great toes, and he must afterwards rub them together. But, before this, a religious act is performed. Before the boy, who is on the return journey, is allowed to enter his native village, he has to stay for a short time just outside, while his father, seated at the main entrance, cuts open the neck of a hen, which he has previously selected, and throws it on the boy's luggage. The victim leaps about (phuphumela) in its agony. The officiant then plucks out some of the bloodstained feathers, pronounces the tsu, and says :

Here is your son. He has returned home safely, because you have accompanied him! Perhaps he has brought back pounds sterling with him to lobola. Perhaps he will now take a wife! I do not know. The great thing is that he is healthy, and you have brought him back safely.

The Offering of Reconciliation. One of the most curious of the religious acts performed in connection with the family is called *ku hahlela madjieta*, viz., to perform a sacramental act in connection with the madjieta. *Djieta* (dji-ma) means a *rash oath*, or an oath *with imprecation*. If two brothers quarrel, and the younger believing himself to be the injured one, breaks off all connection with his brother, he may say to the latter in his anger : "Never" will I speak to you again, or come any more to your village!" This is a djieta. To give greater weight to the imprecation, the angry brother will put his nail beneath one of his incisor teeth, push it from within outwards and say : "U ta kota u ñwoo psi nga yentshekanga!" This probably means : "May you die if this does not happen," viz. if I do not keep my oath. Or he will pinch up the skin below his eye, and pull it out, saying : "U ta kota wao *hum!*" (Same meaning). The two men may remain for years without the slightest intercourse with each other. But if a serious disease should break out in the village of the younger, and the bones order him to make an offering, he is at once in a difficulty. He has no right to present it himself, for, according to the great law of priesthood in ancestrolatry, it is his elder brother who must do it for him. The bones, on being again consulted, give the response : — "There is something in the way. You two have tied a knot. Untie it first, then offer the sacrifice." The younger brother will then go to the elder, and say : "I have sinned in swearing that I would never come again to your village. Let us hahlela djieta, i. e., accomplish the sacrificial act, which will cancel the rash oath (1). The elder will scold him severely, but will eventually accept his excuses. This meeting for confession and reconciliation is called ku hahlela madjieta, even if no other act, no *tsu*, or prayer, is performed. — The reconciliation may, however, be celebrated in a more solemn manner by a ceremony, which is attended by the elder members of the family. The brother who pronounced the imprecation prepares a decoction of a special herb, called mudahomu, and pours it into a sala shell. Everyone assembles on the square, and the two former enemies sit in the midst, on the bare ground. The offender raises the shell to his lips, sips the decoction, spits it out with the customary tsu, and says : "This is our djieta. We pronounced it, because our hearts were bitter. To-day it must come to an end. It is right that we make peace." The other brother, the offended one, then takes the shell, and after going through the same rite of the tsu, says : "I was justly angry, because it was he who first offended me ! But let it be ended to-day ; let us eat out of the same spoon, drink out of the same cup, and be friends again." Then he breaks the shell, and they drink and enjoy themselves together.

In the Northern clans this offering is called *byalwa bya huwa, the beer of noise* (on account of the noise made by those who quarrelled). It is considered as necessary, not only to reconcile the estranged brothers, but as a protection against wizards. Wizards might be encouraged to bewitch these men, thinking that, if one of them met with misfortune, people would say that his brother had cast a spell over him ; the wizards would then have an opportunity of killing him without fear of being discovered ! The offering consists of *many sorts of cereals*, mealies, millet, sorgho taken from the granaries of all those who have fought ; two handfuls of the

---

(1) See also my article on "The Sacrifice of Reconciliation" amongst the Ba-Ronga (*South African Journal of Science*, February 1911). The djieta is any rash oath, and not only one pronounced against a brother. If a man swears that he will never enter a pool again (because he has been stung), or a river (because he has been followed by a crocodile), it is likewise a *djieta*. Should he find it necessary to enter this lake or this river again, he must first hahlela djieta, i. e. cancel his oath by a sacramental act. This is not necessarily a prayer to his gods, but only an invocation addressed to the imprecation itself : "You djieta, I said I would enter this lake no more, but I want to *tjeba* (p. 86) and to eat fish ! Don't cause me to suffer for it." Then he takes some water in his hands, and throws it into the pool.

grains are brought to the altar and thrown on to it and the brothers who wish to be reconciled recount their grievances. The offering, though called beer of noise, is not really beer at all, (the cereals offered are not ground nor cooked). However, as my informant said, it is truly beer, as these raw cereals *represent* beer. Natives do not think that they have said anything contradictory in expressing themselves in this way! Notice the fact that these cereals are collected from all the granaries (Tembe). In the same manner the members of the whole family must be reconciled.

The same offering is resorted to in *cases of protracted births* (I. p. 40) when it is known that the woman in labour lived on bad terms with another woman. The latter will be called ; she will take a little water in her mouth and spit it out against the hypogastrium of the other, saying *phaa* with the following words : "The angry words which we have spoken must come to an end. May you find help. (Lepsi hi nga bulabula psi fanele ku hela, u pfuneka)". This prayer will not be accompanied by an invocation of the ancestor-gods of either of these women. A similar ceremony is performed when the bones have revealed that delay in parturition or in the child's taking the maternal breast is due to the *bitterness* of its parents in their previous relations. The diviner will tell the father "Hahlela shibiti, make an offering on account of bitterness." This will be performed in the hut. The father will come, and without putting anything into his mouth he will say *tsu* and add the following words : "Let her give birth to the child! What I had (in my heart) I have left ! Let us be united again. (A a beleke! Lepsi ndji nga na psu ndji psi tjikile! Hi tlhangana kambe)." In this case the offering is also called an offering of bitterness, though it is very different from the one previously described under that name.

Offering of "the Big millet" (mabele makuku). The millet (mabele or ñwahuba) is the smallest of the cereals cultivated by the Thongas ; this offering, however, is called "big" on account of its importance and its character. It is a true *thanksgiving offering*. When the family has special cause for rejoicing, for instance if there has been serious illness and the patient has recovered, all its members are called together for the offering of the "big millet."

Let us remember that this cereal is probably the most ancient known to the Thongas. If a daughter is living far away at her husband's home, she must come and bring him with her, because an ox will be killed, if possible, or at any rate a goat. A preliminary ceremony is performed to announce (hlehleleta) to the ancestor-gods that an ox is prepared for them. If the cause of the rejoicing is the safe return of a son who has been absent for a long time, working at Kimberley, for instance, his gun is brought to the altar and also the living ox, and the officiant thanks his gods by offering "byala bosila, ground beer". (See later). When the true beer is brewed, i. e. some days later, the second ceremony takes place, all being present ; the ox is killed, and the offering of the animal and of the millet beer is made, the *psanyi* of the victim being poured on to the altar, and also a little of the beer. During the prayer of thanksgiving the women shout their mikulungwana after each sentence of which they particularly approve. This is one of the rare offerings not dictated by fear or misfortune.

Before passing to the next topic, the National Offerings, I wish to quote a graphic description of a religious ceremony performed near the Shiluvane Mission Station by the Makaringe family, and attended by 200 members of this sub-clan. These Makaringes live amongst the Nkunas, but belong to the clan of Ba-ka- Baloyi, settled near the confluence of the Olifant and the Limpopo. I owe this description to the Rev.A. Jaques, together with the photograph which accompanies it. I do not know to what category this offering belongs. No particularly sad event had happened to account for it, so that it is quite possible that it was also a thanksgiving offering. I will let the Rev. A. Jaques describe the event :

"In January 1924 I had the opportunity of attending a sacrifice of the Makaringes. The ceremony took place on the graves of their ancestors, on the hill which is at the foot of the Marobunye mountain. Those present numbered about 200.

A first libation of beer was made on the spot where the old men knew the graves to be. The chief of the clan, the old induna Mugwaleni, officiated. Squatting on his heels, he held in his hands the twig of a female nkanye ; this he put into his mouth and spat twice, producing the sacramental sound tsu. Then he poured out some beer, invoking the

ancestor-gods. All the members of the clan squatting in a circle round
him clapped their hands in cadence, the palms slightly curved, in such
a way that the clapping produces a hollow noise. This is the respectful
manner of saluting the bakoñwana, the wife's parents and the mpse-
lekulobye, (a term which designates the father and mother of a son-in-
law or of a daughter-in-law). This way of saluting intimates the
respect shown to the ancestors.

Then the victim (in this case a cow) was killed. A young man tried to

Photo A. Jaques.

The sacrifice offered by the Makaringe family to its
ancestor-gods in Shiluvane (January 1924).

pierce its heart with an assegai. (Curiously enough I have observed
that the Thongas always stab the animal on the right side.) But on
this occasion the ill-directed weapon struck the breast plate, and the
badly-tempered iron was bent aside. It was a painful sight, but
happily somebody knocked the animal down with an axe.

When it had been cut open, the second sacrifice took place. Someone
brought on a plate the portion reserved for the spirits, consisting of a
piece of the ear, of the tongue, of the forelegs, of one of the hindlegs, of
the heart, of the liver, of the bowels and all the grass contained in the
first stomach.

The circle is again formed and those present take up the same
positions. Mugwaleni seizes each of the portions one after the other
and places them on the ground, addressing himself to the dead; he calls
them by their names, speaking to them in a familiar manner and begs for

their protection : "May the harvest be plentiful ; may the cattle multiply ; may all our wives become pregnant." He uses by preference negative expressions : "Be not angry against us ; may the cows not slip their calves ; may our wives have no miscarriages, etc." In the meantime the people continue the same clapping of hands (called ku diya or ku losa gupsi, gupsi expressing exactly the hollow sound produced by the curved hands).

Notwithstanding this ritual clapping of hands, not much respect is shown by those present. They chat and joke whilst the chief of the clan is praying. A little tobacco has been spread as a libation on the graves and all help themselves to it. The influence of European ideas can be noticed ; a man cries : "Take off your hats !" and most of the men obey, showing that they are conscious that this is a religious ceremony worthy of respect.

As soon as the ceremony is over, they begin to dance. Immediately the clapping changes. It is now done with the hands held flat. It is chiefly the women, especially the old ones, who dance. Gabaze, the principal wife of the Nkuna chief Muhlaba, who is a Makaringe, the sister of Mugwaleni, makes herself conspicuous by her contortions. These are the ordinary dances.

They eat the roasted meat ; they drink the beer brought by the women. The portions offered to the manes are eaten as well as the rest, and I did not observe that they were reserved to special persons. The skin of the victim is cut into small strips which the men tie round the right wrist, the women round the left."

b) *National Offerings.*

These are those offered at the capital, to the ancestors of the chief, but on behalf of the whole clan, because the gods of the reigning family have control over the clan, just as the chief has over the families of his subjects.

The regular national offering is the *luma* of the first fruits, their consecration, which I have described at length as one of the principal manifestations of the National life (I. p. 396-406). The Bantu conception of hierarchy is clearly illustrated by this custom : the gods must be the first to enjoy the produce of the new year, then the chief, the sub-chiefs, the counsellors, the headmen, then the younger brothers in order of age. There is a stringent taboo directed against the person who precedes his superiors in the enjoyment of the first fruits, this law being applicable to Kafir corn or bukanye in certain clans, and also to sorghum, pumpkin leaves and beer, etc., in others (1).

The sexual taboo is also enforced. Those who contravene this law are said to "destroy the efficacity of the offering, nyumbisa mhamba." At the Ngoni Court, where sexual excesses were prevalent (see I. Annotatio 14) it is said that the chiefs used to remain continent for a fortnight at the time of luma. The reason of this taboo is probably the fact that the luma signifies the entering upon a new year, a new season, and is thus a rite of passage.

The religious meaning of the rite is clear : the gods, if deprived of the right they possess by virtue of their hierarchical position, would avenge themselves by threatening the harvest ; so they must be given their share first.

In the Maluleke clan, in which the customs seem to have been influenced by the Ba-Nyai, there is also a regular offering at the capital, when *the crops are still growing*. Rangane describes it as follows : "When the chief sees that the Kafir corn is threatened by the vermin in the fields, he says : "Perhaps the masters of the country (i. e. my ancestors who are dead) are angry ; perhaps I have not worshipped them fittingly." He summons the sons of the royal family.(mangalakana) from all parts of the country, prepares beer, and selects a goat for the sacrifice ; they assemble around the graves with the sons and the uterine nephews, where they worship, and then, after eating all that is to be eaten, they return."

The special national offerings are those in connection with rain. If the rain falls at the right season, the sacrifice will not be made ; but should it fail to do so, the whole ritual will be gone through. This sacrifice for rain, is, as has already been mentioned (p. 318) called *phokolo* amongst the Bilen clans, and is performed in the

(1) Amongst the Malulekes a *second luma* is necessary after harvest, when brewing the first beer. It seems that the sub-chiefs or even headmen, settled in districts far away from the capital, can obtain a special license to perform the luma ceremony on their own account, but they must first apply for this permission, and after having finished, they must forward the chief's share to him.

following way. The bones are consulted, and a special pot, called phokolo, is buried just below the surface of the ground, in the middle of a clean spot well hidden in a dense thicket of thorny shrubs. The victim, a black ram without any white spot, is brought there, and killed in accordance with the ceremonial rites. The grass of the paunch is squeezed over the pot, so that the green liquid drips into it, and the blood is spread all over the ground. Four furrows have been dug in the form of a cross with the pot as a centre, and pointing towards the four cardinal points. Little girls ("who are not yet wise," i. e. they are not yet informed regarding sexual matters) are sent to fetch water and fill the pot until it overflows into the furrows. This being done, they go back to their mothers. The *mbelele* rite will immediately follow (p. 318). This phokolo sacrifice is the religious act in connection with ancestrolatry, the mbelele being actuated by entirely different ideas. The phokolo rite is replaced in the Nkuna clan by the official visit to the graves, accompanied by an old mourning song, and the custom of beating the mounds with sticks ; (whether to awaken the gods or to show them the dissatisfaction of the worshippers, I do not know). In many sacred woods, a living *human victim* is offered to the gods, as already mentioned (p. 383). The phokolo rite is a regular sacrifice attended with bloodshed.

In the case of war threatening the country, another offering is made which is called *Mhamba ya Burena, the Offering of Valour*. The general of the army chooses a thorn, a large thorn taken from a munga tree (the Accacia horrida), not a crooked one ; he sucks it without biting it, and emits his saliva saying : "Tsu! You, the ancestor-gods, so and so and so, enemies wish to take your country! Give us valour! May we stab them with this thorn, with the assegai! (N̄wi, psikwembu, man, man, man. Yimpi yi ta, yi ta teka tiko djenu! Hi nyikan burena, hi ba tlhaba hi mutwa lo, hi tlhari!)" This offering resembles the offering of the thorn made by the headman, but it has an entirely different meaning, and it is probable that the kind of thorn employed is different.

Another national act of worship, which recalls the rite of the nkanye twig in funeral ceremonies, is performed with the aid of the *great mhamha*, to which I have already referred

(I. p. 386). This is a most curious object, the mhamba par excellence, in the Tembe and Zihlahla clans. It is so highly venerated that people fear to call it by its own name, and refer to it as hlengwe, riches. According to the description of Hlekisa, (a Tembe Native), it consists of the nails and hair of the deceased chiefs. When a chief dies, the more or less imperishable portions of his body, such as the nails and the hair of his head and beard, are carefully cut, kneaded together with the dung of the oxen which have been killed at his death, and a kind of pellet is thus made. This is bound round with thongs of hide. When another chief dies, a second pellet is made and added to the first, and so on down through centuries. The mhamba of the Tembe clan is at the present time about one foot in length, says my informant, who is a cousin of the man to whose custody this sacred relic has been committed, and who has seen it often. The guardian must be of a particularly calm temperament, and must not be given to the use of strong language, nor to intoxication. The chief gives him money or perhaps a wife, for his trouble, because of the responsibility which he has undertaken towards the country. He keeps the mhamba in a hut specially built for the purpose, at the back of his own village. Whenever he is called upon to use it for a religious purpose, he must abstain from sexual relations for a whole month. The sacrifice then performed will consist of a goat, slaughtered in the usual way, but consecrated without the ordinary tsu. The tsu is replaced by the mhamba, which the officiant will brandish in the same way as the nkanye twig (I. p. 142) in the funeral ceremony, tracing circles in the air, and invoking the gods. — This object is wrapped in great mystery. Mboza thinks that the *ntjobo* of the Nondwane, kept in the sacred hut of nyokwekulu (I. p. 386), the national medicine, was the same thing, but most people were ignorant of what it consisted. At any rate the same law applied to both : it was looked on as the greatest calamity for it to fall into the hands of enemies in time of war. When the clan is forced to seek refuge in flight, the keeper of the mhamba is the first to flee. The whole army stands between the guardian of the precious amulet of the clan and the enemy. It is more than its flag, and will not be taken until all the warriors have been killed or dispersed. — It is said that once during the war between Tembe and Maputju, the latter succeeded in gaining possession of the mhamba ; a terrible drought ensued, for the gods of Maputju were irritated, as they were of the same family as those of Tembe (I. p. 329). Not knowing what to do with it, the Maputjus at length cut open a goat between the hind legs, and introduced the mhamba into its body. They then led the goat to the river which marks the boundary of the Tembe country, and threw it into the water. Hlekisa's grandfather, a Tembe man, who had settled in Maputju, was asked to lead the goat. — Thus the rightful owners recovered their mhamba. (Is there not a striking resemblance between this story and that of the capture of the ark of the covenant by the Philistines ?)

The mhamba of the Zihlahla country used to be kept by a man named Petshela, who carried it with him from place to place, when fleeing, refusing to trust it to the care of any save his own children. Is it still in existence, since the clan was deprived of its independence? In Nondwane the national amulet was in the care of the Godhlela family, as already mentioned in I. p. 388, and this function was hereditary.

The story *of the great mhamba of the Shirindja clan* (between Nondwane and Manyisa) is even more impressive than those told about the palladium of Tembe and Zihlahla. The man who revealed these mysteries to me did so somewhat reluctantly, saying that those who give information about them may die! In this clan the mhamba consists of *the skin of the faces of the deceased chiefs.* As soon as a chief is dead, the great ñanga Manketwana removes the skin from his forehead down to his chin and spreads it on the ground, the edges being fixed down by sticks all round in order that it shall dry without shrivelling. He also cuts off the fingers. The whole is then handed over to an old woman who no longer has sexual relations, the wife of one of the sub-chiefs. She adds this skin to those of the ancient chiefs and keeps the bundle in a special hut, the hut of the mhamba, built behind the principal hut of the new chief, in which she sleeps. No one is allowed to enter it ; married men in particular must not do so ; and a woman only if the child she carries on her shoulders has not yet passed through

407

the ceremony of tying the cotton string (I. p. 56. Sexual relations have been prohibited to her from the birth of her child up to the performance of this rite. She is consequently pure). The chief may penetrate into it, but only if he has abstained from intercourse with his wives for a whole week. Mankentwane himself must observe this law, otherwise the "medicine, muri" would be spoiled and lose all its virtue. (The sexual taboo, in this case, is evidently dictated by the fact that the mhamba is directly connected with military matters, as we shall see. Compare I. p. 470.) In this sacred hut the old woman constantly keeps up a fire which is maintained with the logs of a certain tree, called shibondjwane, cut by the subjects at the command of the chief. Now and again she exposes the skins to the rays of the sun in order to kill the worms which attack them. Should enemies invade the country, she escapes, carrying the bundle in a mat. If they come up with her, she at once disappears (nyumba) leaving the mat on the spot. As soon as an enemy has taken hold of it, he becomes insane ; he begins to wander about in the bush, unable to return home. When the war is over, the old woman goes to the place where she left the mhamba ; if she does not immediately find it there, her heart is not in the least troubled. The bones are thrown, and reveal where the mhamba has been put by the enemy. Two days do not elapse before it is found! The great mhamba is used first of all for the preparation of military expeditions. A small portion of the fingers and of the faces is cut off and these pieces are mixed with the other war charms ; a pill is made and placed on a piece of broken pottery over a fire in the sacred wood. All the warriors pass by one after the other and expose their assegais, their legs, and their faces to the smoke ; finally the great ñanga puts the fire out and the army is ready to start. But the Shirindja mhamba also plays a great part in the National religious ceremonies, as in the other clans (1).

(1) It is interesting to compare the Thonga *great mhamba* with two objects found amongst other Bantu tribes. The first of these is the *byiri* of the Pahuins of the French Congo. This is a most powerful fetish consisting of a skull kept in a box in the huts of these people, in a dark corner; it is used as a means of obtaining wealth and of discovering wizards. In former times it is said to have been the skull of the father of the owner of the hut which had been dug up by him and smeared with drugs. In

RELIGION

2) THE MAIN ELEMENTS OF ANCESTOR WORSHIP.

The sequence of the religious ceremonies in a typical sacrifice, like that performed at the crushing of the hut, is as follows :

1) The bones are first consulted, and reveal to what god, when, how, and by whom the sacrifice must be made.

2) The officiant, who is as a rule the eldest male member of the family, comes and presides over the sacrifice.

3) The victims are brought by those who have either been designated, or who have volunteered to provide them.

4) They are killed by the uterine nephews, the goats or sheep by piercing the heart, the hens by cutting the throat. Sometimes the face of the goat is directed to a certain point of the horizon.

5) The victim bleats, or if it is a hen, jumps about on the ground in its agony. At each thrust of the assagay, or of the

order to secure this much desired object as soon as possible, the son would go so far as to poison his father. Now, according to the testimony of Mr. F. Grébert (*Au Gabon*, p. 154), the byeri is not necessarily the skull of an ancestor. Any skull can be used, either that of a traveller found dead on the caravan route or even the skull of a man belonging to a foreign clan who has been assassinated. The byeri, whatever may be its origin, acts by its own power and no longer on account of its connection with the spirit of an ancestor. It is a true fetish, a material, magical object which is able to kill or to enrich in virtue of its own power. The Thonga mhamba is not a fetish. Its power is never dissociated from the spirits of the old chiefs whose nails, hair or faces have been used to produce it. Whatever action it may have is due to the fact that these nails, hair or faces influence the dead chiefs to whom they belonged, according to the magic principle that the part acts on the whole. The origin of the byeri is certainly ancestor-worship, but here ancestrolatry has evolved into fetichism, and I conclude from these facts that Thonga ancestrolatry is simpler, more spiritualistic and must therefore be more ancient than the present Pahuin system.

Amongst the Ba-Ganda (see Rev. J. Roscoe, *the Baganda*) there are powerful gods who have their priests and mediums, and are worshipped according to a complicated ritual, one of them being the war-god Kibuka. They have their temples, in which there is a sacred shrine placed on a stool. The shrine of Kibuka was secured and sent to the Museum of Ethnology at Cambridge, and it was found to contain, together with other objects, a bag with a human jawbone, the male organ and a decorated umbilical cord. This is a proof that the god Kibuka is an ancestor-god, whatever may be the splendour to which his worship has attained in the course of time. And here again we are in presence of what seems to be a later form of ancestrolatry, most probably evolved in consequence of the development of the social system of the Baganda. They form a nation with a powerful royal family, more than one thousand years old. With them the spirits of the dead kings hover round their jawbones, just as they are influenced by their nails, hair or faces amongst the Thongas, who would seem to be in a less advanced stage of evolution.

409

knife, the uterine nephews utter their cries of joy (1). This is their way of consenting (pfumela) or answering, for they accept the offering on behalf of the gods (2). The whole crowd joins in these manifestations of joy.

6) The victim is cut open, and one limb, or small pieces of each limb, are put aside for the gods ; the half digested grass, *psanyi*, found in the intestines, especially in the *shihlakahla* stomach, is carefully put aside.

7) The priest takes a little of the psanyi mixed with the blood of the victim, puts it to his lips, emits a little saliva, and spits out the whole, pronouncing the *tsu*, this being the means of consecrating the offering, or, as we may say, despatching it to the gods.

8) He pronounces the prayer — occasionally interrupted by some member of the family, who has a complaint to make.

9) In certain cases of special misfortune, whilst praying he squeezes the green liquid contained in the psanyi over his hearers, who rub their bodies with it.

10) One of the nephews "cuts his prayer" (i. e. brings it to an end) by taking in his mouth a little of the consecrated beer or wine, or part of the hen's gizzard.

11) The uterine nephews steal the offering and run away, followed by the throng, who throw pellets of psanyi at them. They eat the portion of the gods.

12) Should the offering have been made on behalf of a particular individual, the astragalus of the goat, or some portions of the hen are tied to him and worn for a time on the left or right side of the body : the left if the offering was made to the maternal ancestors, the right if it was made to the paternal gods.

Let us examine more closely some of these acts, so that we may better understand the elements of this ceremony.

(1) Amongst the Ba Nyai they clap their hands and shout : "Ndiyo !" — " all right."

(2) It is not necessary to add more about the part played by the uterine nephews in the sacrifice, for it has been explained in detail in Vol. I, p. 269 when treating of the family system. The two great reasons for their taking such a prominent part in the religious ritual seem to be the following : 1) during the life of their maternal uncle, and also of all their mother's family, they were on very intimate terms with them, "even eating from the same piece of food, not fearing their saliva." Therefore they now eat the flesh of the victim instead of the ancestor-gods of their mother. 2) Maternal relatives have a special religious duty towards their nephews. They act as their priests

RELIGION

a) The Priesthood.

The Thongas have no sacerdotal caste, but, as has already been pointed out, the right of officiating in religious ceremonies is strictly confined to *the eldest brother*. All offerings must be made through him. To supplant him is a great taboo, and would entail the malediction of the gods, and even the death of the offender. There are, however, some minor offerings which anyone is allowed to make to his gods ; for instance, a lover who has been jilted, may, after having consulted the bones, give something to his god in order to obtain his aid in regaining the favour of the girl he loves. But, as a rule, no one must *hahla*, or even *gandjela*, before the death of his parents. If, after their death, their son should happen to dream of them, he must offer worship to the deceased by pouring some ground tobacco on to his wooden pillow, this being the commencement of his religious functions : "he begins to learn to gandjela" (Rangane), and, if he is the eldest, he may in course of time become the priest of the whole family. I heard, however, a man from Tembe assert that he had *hahla* when his father was still living, but in this case he had been designated by the bones. A little child may even perform the office if the bones order it ; his father will then hold him in his arms and pray in his stead. The bones often call on *women* to pronounce the prayer, especially the elder sister ; there is no anti-feminism in Thonga religion. In the *luma* ceremony, however, it must always be a man, the chief himself, who is the principal officiant. The wives of the clansmen naturally cannot take a prominent part in the offerings made for the clan, being themselves members of another clan and having their own ancestor-gods, to

(I. p. 268), offerings being frequently made to the gods of the mother's family through the agency of the maternal uncle. Hence the fact that uterine nephews take such a peculiar part in the ritual of the worship.

I must add that according to information just received from the Rev. A. Jaques, in the Northern clans uterine nephews do not steal the portion of the offerings put apart for the ancestor-gods. It seems that this custom, which I believe to be ancient, is met with essentially amongst the Ronga clans, where the special term *mupsyana* (an old Bantu word corresponding to *um-tshana* in Xosa and *mochana* in Sutho) has also been preserved to designate the uterine nephew, whilst it has fallen into disuse in the Northern clans. (Compare I. p, 162, 232, 498.)

411

whom they sometimes pray in the hut (See App. IV). Amongst Thongas the wife does not adopt the gods of her husband's family (1).

The beginnings of the *constitution of a sacerdotal caste* may be seen in the fact that in each clan, the mhamba, the sacred object used by the royal family to invoke its gods, or the drug on which national invulnerability depends, is entrusted to the care of a certain man, whose office is hereditary. As soon as the political tie becomes stronger, and the power of the paramount chief greater, the religious acts which are performed at the capital gain in importance, and the person who officiates becomes a kind of high priest. Should this evolution continue, it is easy to see how a sacerdotal class may be formed at the expense of the primitive family worship, which thus increasingly loses its importance. Amongst the Thongas this has not yet taken place, and their religious system seems to correspond to a very ancient state of things ; it is in all probability the pure form of primitive Ancestrolatry.

b) The Thonga Conception of the Offerings.

With the help of new information obtained since writing the first edition of this book, I think it now possible to attain to a fuller understanding of the meaning of this great Thonga word *mhamba* which I have translated either by offering or by sacrifice, in connection with the killing of a victim. Under this designation come objects of two distinct categories : articles of food, clothing, etc. which are of immediate service to human existence and which are *given* to the ancestor-gods, and magic or magico-religious objects which are not given but only employed in the act of worship. The aim is the same, whatever may be the nature of the object, viz. to obtain the favour and help of the ancestor-gods, but in the first case the officiant adresses himself to living, conscious

---

(1) There seems to be a profound difference between Thongas and Suthos on this point. The Rev. P. Ramseyer assured me on very good evidence that in Basutoland "a wife takes the family name (seboko) of her husband and abandons her *midimo*." The midimo, says my informant, are not only the *badimo* proper, i. e. the ancestor-gods, but all the supernatural powers in which a given clan trusts, the totem, the spirit (moea) of hail, of rain, of lightning, of disease. A Sutho woman can become a Tebele by marriage, though this seldom actually happens.

spirits, endowed with intelligence, feelings and will, and tries to induce them to respond to his needs, whilst, in the second case he trusts that his offering will act on them magically, i. e. automatically, according to the principles of magic explained above. Let us consider these two kinds of mhamba more closely.

1) *The gifts.* As regards their nature these are indeed most varied, consisting in the first place of *domestic animals*, the ox, goat, fowl, which are only used by subjects, the sheep being the offering proper to the chief (p. 50). Pigs are not accepted for the altar, neither are antelopes, or other kinds of game. I have never heard of any offering consisting of the flesh of wild beasts. The victim is generally killed, but there are cases of its being consecrated *living*. If a living hen or goat is given to the gods, (a ring sometimes being attached to the leg of the fowl), it is taboo henceforth to kill or sell it ; if it dies, it must not be eaten, and it must also be replaced by another (1). Another kind of living offering is the *human sacrifice* made in certain sacred woods in order to obtain rain, but this is rarely resorted to. "The victim wanders about in the forest till he dies," says Mboza ; "the gods take him."

The most common kind of offering is *the produce of the fields*, chiefly the Kafir Corn in the official luma, but also other cereals, sorghum maize, likoro (p. 11), various kinds of pumpkins. Ground nuts are never offered. But the ancestor-gods appreciate drinks, not only the national beer, but also the wine of the Whites. They like narcotics as well as intoxicants, and tobacco is one of the gifts most frequently made to them.

Clothing, especially handkerchiefs of various designs (these designs being often prescribed by the bones) is often offered, even ornaments, e. g. the bracelet in the sacrifice for the uterine nephew (p. 396) ; but it is the sick boy who wears it, probably instead of the gods.

Lastly one sometimes finds on the graves "wealth, hlengwe,"

---

(1) I have heard of two cases of a *living human offering* in the Bilen and Manyisa regions. A girl had been consecrated to the ancestor-gods ; she was therefore a mhamba. In the first case a goat had been given to them also, as a living mhamba. The girl died, and the goat ought to have been burnt together with all her belongings, but her parents presented it to Christian Natives, who were free from the fear of the ancestor-gods.

elephants' tusks or hippopotamus'teeth. (Nkolele). I never heard of any money being consecrated to the ancestor-gods, but generally speaking it may be said that most of the things which rejoice the heart of a human being may be placed on the altar and employed to win the favour of the ancestral spirits.

But what is *the actual value of these gifts?* All things considered, it must be confessed that it is very small. The sacrificing Jew made a burnt offering : he burnt the victim in order that Jehovah might be gratified with the smoke of the roasting flesh, which ascended to heaven! Nothing of this sort is met with amongst the Thongas. When the offering is a living one, there is actually a certain element of self-denial, in that the sacrificer renounces the possibility of eating it or selling it ; but the bones rarely order such offerings. Generally the offerings cost nothing. Thongas present their gods with a goat, but they eat it themselves. From each limb a small piece is cut ; this is enough for the gods, and the uterine nephews will steal even that. If the bones have ordered the sacrifice of an ox, it may happen that the officiating headman, having none to offer, will go to one of his neighbours who possesses an old, dry oxhide, and cut a small piece from it; this will serve as his ox. As for fowls, a feather or the bones are placed on the altar, but the meat is eaten by the people ; only, whether it be a fowl or a goat which is sacrificed, the animal must be in perfect condition ; it is not stated if this is in honour of the gods or for the satisfaction of the eaters. The same thing happens with regard to cereals. The bones frequently prescribe a mhamba called *byala bosila*. What is this? It is prepared as follows. The officiant takes a handful of maize grains and softens them by steeping them for a time in water. Then he stirs the mixture, takes a little in his mouth and emits his tsu. He may even content himself with the scum produced by this stirring. Nobody would eat byala bosila nor dare to offer it to a visitor. The particles of bran which remain in the sieve when beer is brewed are also quite good enough for the gods. But observe, said my informant, that thus no one, not even the poorest, will ever want for a mhamba to offer to his gods.

How is this to be explained? Mboza assured me that it was done to *deceive* (kanganyisa) the spirits of the ancestors, as if they were still the wretched old people from whom the grandchildren used to steal their food (I. p. 132). But I doubt the truth of this explanation. The valueless nature of the offerings is rather due to the fact that Natives know perfectly well that the gods neither eat nor take what is offered to them, and that it is devoured by the fowls running about the place. When telling the story of the theophany described on p. 384, the old priest Nkolele made the following remark : "Even if one only kills a chicken, the god is quite content, for, to him, it has the same value as an ox." This seems to be the true explanation. The gods do not ask for real food, or wealth ; they only regard the "mhamba" as a token of love from their descendants, and a sign that these have not forgotten them, but will do their duty towards them (1). If this be the case, the offerings, which have little material worth, acquire a real religious or spiritual value. But it must be confessed that, although this may really have been the original idea, the chief anxiety of the worshippers now-a-days is to observe exactly the details of the *prescribed ritual*. This is what makes an offering acceptable, and not the disposition of the heart towards the gods... It is possible that an offering may be refused by the gods. A worshipper may be "overcome" by his mhamba, and will then return home shivering, having only increased the anger of the spirits. Therefore, let the rules of the ritual be well observed, and especially the indications of the divinatory bones.

Some features of this ritual are most interesting, especially the *tsu* so often mentioned, by which the offering is consecrated. What does it mean? The Natives themselves are unable to explain it, so we are reduced to mere supposition. It consists in an emission of saliva, generally mixed with something from the victim : some of the short feathers of the neck soiled with blood, in the case of a fowl, or a little psanyi also kneaded with blood, in that of a goat. But in the offering of bitterness (p. 391) there is

(1) In Chinese Ancestrolatry the same thing occurs. Worshippers do not offer their ancestors real money, etc., but paper representations, which they burn for the ancestors, thinking that the spirits of the various articles will enter the other world, and be accepted by the spirits of the deceased. Probably Bantu worshippers are unconsciously influenced by a similar idea.

merely saliva ; this, however, is a true "hahla," and this fact shows that the saliva is a gift, the *personal gift of the worshipper*. He first gives his gods something emanating from himself, mingling it with the blood or psanyi of the victim, and only then does he approach them. So there seems to be a deep meaning underlying this sacramental act, though most of the worshippers are not aware of it (a circumstance which unhappily occurs in all religions) ; though unconscious, it exists and has given rise to the rite ; the gift of oneself is necessary to obtain the favour of the Divinity. — What is the intention in adding the blood and psanyi ? Is there any meaning in the *choice of the blood* which is mixed with saliva in order to despatch the offering to the gods (sungulisa mhamba) ? Is the blood (ngati) regarded as containing the life of the animal, as was the case amongst the Jews, who used it in sacrifices "to cover the soul" or the sins of the worshipper (hence the idea of atonement) ? There is no sign of a similar conception among the Thongas. It is true that they prefer to resort to sacrifices with blood in cases of misfortune, disease and death, when some idea of guilt may be entertained. The moral element, however, if it ever really existed, has entirely disappeared from the actual horizon of ancestrolatry.

On the other hand, the use of the *psanyi*, the half digested grass found in the shihlakahla stomach, is easier to explain. It is evidently a means of purification for the family, if not exactly from sin, at least from misfortune (khombo) ; hence their custom of washing their bodies with the green liquid extracted from it, a religious ceremony which to us seems very disgusting, but to the Natives quite clean, their ideas about dung being very different from ours (p. 38). A large ball of psanyi is put on the head of the bride after the dlaya shilongo ceremony (I. p. 257) in order to remove the dangers of consanguineous marriage, and so make it easier for her to have children. Pellets of this substance are thrown too at the uterine nephews, when they run away after stealing the offering (I. p. 162) ; or on to the roof of the deceased's hut, when this is officially closed, with the aim of removing the danger of death ; the slaughtered goat has thus to contribute to the restoration of peace and happiness to the family.

No special use is made of the *bones* of the victim, except, as we shall see later, in offerings on behalf of those possessed. The only part kept is the *astragalus*, or the *psirungulo* just described, which are tied to the person on whose behalf the sacrifice has been made, probably to insure for him a permanent blessing from the gods.

It must be observed that the sacrificial ritual, as well as the medical art, lays great stress on the *sex* of the offerings. As a rule, there must be opposition between the sex of the victim and that of the person for whom, or to whom, the sacrifice is made. A woman is prayed for by means of a he-goat or a cock, and a man by a she-goat or a hen.

What is the reason of this rule? — "Psi yaka muti," says my informant. "It builds up the village." As a village can only grow and multiply by the union of the male and the female element, so in order to succeed in any pursuit it is necessary to unite both sexes. This principle is universally applied : when a girl is ill, a boy will bring her medicine, and vice-versa. The rule is also followed in another case. It may be that a mhamba has been wrongly performed and threatens to bring misfortune instead of appeasing the gods. This mhamba must consequently be "quenched, timula" "so that it may keep quiet and cool down, because it might cause annoyance and overcome them" (Mboza). This will be done by offering a mhamba of the opposite sex, which will correct the first. So if a female nkanye twig has been employed in the funeral ceremony, when the ritual ought to have been performed with a twig taken from a male stem, the ceremony will be repeated with a male twig in order to quench the first mhamba.

The last observation to be made about the gifts presented to the ancestor-gods is that the *psirungulo*, viz. the part of the victim which is tied to the person for whose sake it has been sacrificed, must be attached to the left part of the body if this person belongs to the female, to the right if to the male sex ; moreover in the sacrifices offered to maternal gods, the attachment is always done on the left side, whatever may be the sex of the person. Why is this? Because the left side belongs to the woman, the right to the man. We have seen that this is the case in the hut (I. p. 187).

Shimantji is the term used for left ; its etymology is unknown.
Shinene means right ; it also indicates nice, good, true.   In this as
in many other instances the male sex has arrogated to itself the
better part!

2) *The magical objects used in worship.* First of all comes *the
great mhamba*, the nails, hair or faces of deceased chiefs. We are
evidently dealing here with a case of *communionist magic*. I
explain in the same way the use of roots brought to light by a river
which has washed away the ground (p. 387), but it may be that this
is also an instance of *imitative magic* : the roots were hidden in the
soil and have come to light ; in the same way the ancestor-gods
have been buried in the ground and have again come forth to bless
or curse their descendants. The curious astragalus bone of an
antelope which had been swallowed by a hyena and found later in
its stools and which Mankhelu employed to represent the gods in
his divinatory set of bones, would favour this second explanation.
In fact most of these objects are supposed to act in virtue of the
principle of similarity : the nkanye twig, because this venerated
tree will ensure respect to the person, living or dead, for whom it is
used ; the piece of charcoal, because the enemy will be reduced to
impotence just as the piece of wood has been consumed by fire ;
the thorn employed by the general of the army, because the
warriors will be able to pierce their opponents and kill them, etc.
Is the number of magic objects used in this connection limited to
those I have mentioned ? I do not think so. It is probable that
some others may be found in the various parts of the tribe. I even
have proof that new objets of a magic character are still invented by
worshippers who are gifted with special imaginative powers. My
old friend Mankhelu was telling me the particulars of the battle of
Nov. 1901, during the Sikororo war (I. p. 513), when suddenly
jumping to his feet and taking a small bundle of grass, he said :
"Listen! I will show you the mhamba I made when the enemy
rushed on us. I took a bundle of grass like those which women
use for binding their sticks, and feverishly separated the blades,
saying : 'Let them fail to surround us, or decoy us!' Then I
scattered them in all directions and said : 'Let them be so dispersed,
carried off and destroyed!' And this is exactly what happened.

On my return from the battle I showed all the army how I had prayed." The old general's spontaneous appeal to the gods on behalf of his country in its hour of supreme danger is indeed worthy of notice, and also furnishes a proof that ancestor-worship is still a living force and has not become a mere matter of ritual amongst those who practise it. This prayer of the Nkuna general, this exclamation of an anguished soul in the presence of a great danger, may be regarded as *verbal magic*, as it is not expressedly addressed to the gods, and the same may be said of the formula employed to cancel an oath in the offering of reconciliation, the mention of the gods being absent in this case also. All these acts, however, are mhamba. They are in reality accomplished with the idea that the gods hear and see what is said and done and will be induced to deliver their worshippers.

The magic character of these rites is most marked in the cases of communionist magic ; those which are classed under imitative magic may perhaps be more properly called *symbols*, or at least some of them (1).

Elias Libombo once came to me and said : "My brother, Klass, died. He was *the mhamba of the Libombos*. Now his younger

(1) But what is a *symbol* in religion, and what is the difference between the symbol and the magic rite ? I cannot treat this important subject here in all the necessary detail and length. Let us take only one instance. The offering of incense which took place every evening in the Temple of Jerusalem and which is also widespread in certain branches of the Christian Church is regarded as a symbol. The perfumed smoke which ascends towards heaven corresponds to the prayers of the worshippers, which are thought of as ascending to God and pleasing Him, just as the agreeable smell of incense gratifies the nostrils of the man who perceives it. But in the Hebrew religion it is not thought that incense conveys prayers to God in some actual and magical fashion. It is a symbol. Psychologically speaking this use of incense is probably to be explained in the following manner : The material representation of a religious act (or a religious truth) tends to induce in the worshipper a stronger faith in the efficacy of the act or the reality of the tru'h. His soul thus finds satisfaction in the performance of the symbolic act through which he feels himself brought into closer communion with his God. It is easy to understand that in the course of the religious evolution, a higher conception of God should have caused the magic act to evolve into the symbol, and that the symbol itself should be abandoned or reduced to a minimum when the idea of God has become perfectly spiritualised and communion with the Father who is in Heaven is realized without any external and intermediary means. A comparison of the great mhamba with the relics of saints or other relics used in certain religions would probably show a similar type of evolution.

Some scientists believe that religious evolution contained a *preanimistic phase*, in which the worship of spirits had not yet come into existence, and in which primitive man employed only magic means to influence the supernatural powers. This

brother will be so called." Nkolele, the father of these two men, was the Libombo mhamba before them. This is another meaning of this great word mhamba. Klass was neither a gift made to the ancestor-gods of the Libombos, nor a magic object employed to win their favour, but he was the elder member of the family, the one who was the official and indispensable intermediary between all the Libombos and their gods. For this reason he was a mhamba. This leads me to propose the following definition of the word : *A mhamba is any object or act or even person which is used to establish a bond between the gods and their worshippers.*

Having thus analysed all the elements contained in the Thonga mhamba, we may safely conclude that its spiritual and religious value cannot be denied. Whatever place ritual may hold in the ceremonies of ancestrolatry, whatever mixture of devotional and magic elements may be found in them, the offering is not a mere external gift which appeases the gods by its material value, nor a simple means of coercion which forces them to submit to the will of the worshipper. By means of the mhamba the Thonga really aims at entering into relationship with those powerful spirits who control his life (1).

may be true, but as regards Bantus, they have long outgrown this stage. Even when they have recourse to magic processes in order to influence their ancestor-gods, these have a distinctive character, different from that of the ordinary magic which they practise when they wish to affect the impersonal forces of Nature. Everything done in order to obtain the favour of the ancestor-gods is a *mhamba*, not a *muri*, as I have already pointed out.

(1) Religious and magic practices are more or less mingled in Thonga ritual and it is evident that the smaller the degree of·magic contained in a rite, the more genuine religious feeling there will be in it. I owe to my Venda informant the description of a sacrifice performed in his tribe for a sick child, where the two elements are combined to an extraordinary extent. It is called *the offering of the goat with clothes* (mbudzi ya u dzwindisa).

A goat is provided. It is placed before a basin of water mixed with certain drugs and forced to drink, to drink till it is fully distended, and dies. It is then skinned and cut open. The large intestine is extracted from the body, and a part of it is cut off and stitched up at one end so as to form a kind of pouch. From each limb a bit of meat is taken, and a provision of the seeds of various cereals, brought to the spot together with drugs. All these different kinds of food are introduced into the pouch, the process of filling it being accompanied by prayers to the ancestor-god. The officiant, whilst proceeding with his task, puts seeds into the goat's intestine with one hand, and, with the other, takes other seeds and places them apart. These he will keep carefully in order to sow them later on. And continually he prays : "Eat your fill and be satisfied, and leave us some for our use." Thus the ancestor-god has been fed, well and duly stuffed. The pouch is then stitched at its other end. But now the ancestor-god must be clothed

RELIGION

c) Prayers.

The act of prayer is called *khongota* (Ro.), *khongela* (Dj.) (the same word being also employed to mean "supplicate") ; or *bulabulela*, to speak to, or scold the gods ; *bukutjela* means a long, meandering prayer in which the officiant says the same thing over and over again. I have given twenty-two different forms of prayer when describing the manifold religious acts of the Thongas : two prayers of medicine men (I. 55, II. 393) ; those pronounced on the day of marriage (I. p. 111) ; of death, with the nkanye twig (I. p. 142) ; in the ceremony of crushing down the hut (I. 161) ; at the distribution of the widows (I. 208) ; at the death of a sister (I. 216) ; in the ceremony of killing the tie of consanguinity (I. 258) ; on journeys (I. p. 340. II. p. 394, 398) ; on offering the first fruits (I. 396) ; before the tjeba fishing (II. p. 87) ; when sneezing (II. 361) ; on offering tobacco at the altar (II. p. 390) ; for a sick nephew (II. p. 396) ; at the sacrifice of reconciliation (II. p. 399) ; at the worship of the Makaringe family (II. p. 403) ;

also ! A strap is cut from the goat's skin and the sacrificer winds it all round the pouch. Carrying the offering with him he now goes to the grave of the grandfather, digs, and lays the pouch in the earth parallel to the body beneath; he then prays again : "We worship you, grandfather ! And we have clothed you. This is your food. Eat and be full and be contented. And leave us food, plenty of food that we also may be contented, and bless the sick child."

Let us try to analyse this rite according to the ideas of magic which we have explained, p. 369. We are dealing here with the ancestor-god complexus. A goat is provided, a gift made. This is religion. This goat has now become one of the possessions of the ancestor-god, a part of him. Henceforth the goat represents the god and an action performed upon it will be at the same time performed on the god. The goat is filled with water to quench the thirst of the god. A pouch is made of the intestine, a part of the animal which will now represent the whole, and food is introduced into it to feed the god. All these acts are instances of *communionist magic*, and the prayer which accompanies them is the religious element of the sacrifice. Some seeds are put apart to be sown later on. As they belonged to the provision made for the offering, these seeds partake of the nature of the whole of that provision ; they have entered into the ancestor-god complexus ; they are therefore particularly suitable for sowing, since the blessing of the powerful god will rest upon them. This is communionist magic again, whilst the filling up of the goat with water and food and the clothing its intestine with a strap may be regarded as *imitative magic*. The placing of the pouch in the grave facing the same way as the body of the ancestor once more signifies the identity of both, and the sacrificer is definitely persuaded that by all these rites he has really exercised a strong and compelling influence on his god (See my paper on "Some Features of the Religion of the Ba-Venda" *S. A. Journal of Science*, April 1921).

in the offering of charcoal (II. p. 391) ; of valour (II. p. 405) ;
see also Mankhelu's prayers before the battle (II. p. 418), and
Nkolele's invocation in the Libombo wood (II. p. 384).

Most of these prayers have an *extremely liturgical* character ;
all know what must be said on each occasion of regular sacrifice ;
the personal element is almost totally wanting. Here are the
principal parts of a typical prayer.

After the consecration of the offering with the sacramental
tsu, a kind of *dedication*, the officiant sometimes begins with the
words : "Abusayi! Akhwari!", or "Ibusayi! Ikhwari!" These
words mean : Gently! Smoothly! They are pronounced with a
gentle intonation as if to express deep feeling. According to
Mboza the worshipper wishes to say : "I am not angry with you!"
"It is the *tisola* of the heathen," said the same informant. Tisola,
in the Christian language of the Thongas, means to humble or
condemn oneself in asking for forgiveness.

Then comes the *invocation*. If the sacrifice is on behalf of
a sick person, the god to whom the offering is made, he having
been designated by the bones as the cause of the misfortune, is
called, and asked to bring thither all the other gods whom he
had induced to aid him in punishing the patient ; or the priest
may call first his own father, and entreat him to go and bring
his grandfather, the latter to bring his progenitor, and so on till
the last named. The ancestors in the main line are then sent
to call all the great-uncles, and all the deceased of collateral lines.
Or, if praying for the welfare of the country, the officiant will
address his remotest ancestor first, because it was he who gave the
land to his descendants, and then proceed to call the son and
grandson of this ancient founder of the dynasty, continuing
the succession of generations until he reaches his own father.
It seems as if it were desired to have as many gods as possible
present at the ceremony. The gods of the father's family may
also be summoned, if the sacrifice is made to the gods of the
mother's (p. 396).

The *petition* follows the invocation, and this naturally differs
with circumstances. At the luma sacrifice (January) the priest
asks the gods to increase the produce of the fields. At the family

422

gatherings, after a death, the elder brother entreats the gods to bless the family, to prevent bad feeling,' or strife, to give wisdom and strength to the new headman, that he may be successful in his rule over the village (1).

When some great misfortune is the occasion for this religious act being performed, the petition is preceded, or followed, by a regular *insulting* of the gods. There are two words used to designate this curious part of the prayer : *holobela*, or *holobisa*, to scold the gods, or *rukatela*, the actual word for "to insult." There is an instance of this strangely impertinent manner of addressing the gods in the sacrifice for the sick nephew (p. 396). These insults are generally uttered while the priest is squeezing the psanyi over the shoulders of his subordinates.

The last part of the prayer is *its sudden termination*, when one of the uterine nephews puts a portion of the victim into the officiant's mouth, thus "cutting his oration" (tjema). This is a true part of the ritual. When the victim is a hen, it is the gizzard, which has been half roasted during the long prayer, that is used for this purpose. The priest eats it, and so is the first to partake of the flesh of the offering.

Prayers to the ancestors do not show very much religious feeling, and are, at any rate, absolutely devoid of awe. Whilst

---

(1) *Music* plays no part in Thonga religious ritual. During the preparation of the offering those present often sing, but these songs are those which accompany the ordinary dances and bear no religious character. I only once heard of a true sacred chant. Mungomane, the distinguished dancer and musician who made his living by the exercise of his art in the neighbourhood of Lourenço Marques (p. 187) told me that when he presided over the worship in his village, he used to *sing his prayer.* He gave me the words, but unfortunately not the notes. They are worth quoting :

"Let the meat not stick in your throats ! Eat, you chiefs, you ancestor-gods... They are coming (the oxen) ; they see me, whilst I mourn you, my father and my mother, whilst I remain outside, where I receive life from you, who are below ; I remain, I am a miserable wretch.

"The oxen are slain ! Slay the oxen ! Here they are. I mourn you. Let us eat them together, you father and mother. Give me life and give it also to my children. Let us eat these oxen which I possess, but I possess them for you. Let us not suffer from complaints of the chest here in our home.

"This is the song by which we accompany you, as you return below. Let us remain in good health."

At a given moment the uterine nephew answered by saying:

"I magnify you, my father ! You shall see me, father and mother !"

And all those present, seeing that they would have plenty of meat to eat, joined in a chorus of praise, clapping their hands.

sacrificing, the Natives laugh, talk in loud tones, dance, sing obscene songs, even interrupt the prayer with their remarks, and insult each other about family matters. The officiant himself sits on the seat designated by the bones, and speaks in a monotonous manner, looking straight in front of him with utter indifference. There is nothing in his demeanour which denotes fear. An exception must perhaps be made in the case of those members of the Makaringe family who clapped their hands during the prayer in the same manner as when saluting "bakonwana" (p. 402). They have as much respect for the ancestor-gods as for their relatives-in-law, and that is, indeed, saying much. I have heard that in the Maputju country people kneel down during the prayer. In Nondwane women alone kneel, whilst the men sit on their heels, the customary attitude in worship (1). If the gods were actually old people, still living, they could not be addressed with more familiarity. This leads us finally to consider in what the divinity of the ancestor-gods consists.

d) The Divine Nature of the Ancestor-Gods.

I have brought together in a preceding paragraph (p. 372-386) all that the Natives say about their gods. Now let us return to them, after having studied the religious ritual, and ask : What

(1) The Ma-Lemba, that curious tribe settled amongst the Thongas and Vendas of Spelonken which has certain Semitic customs (I p. 73) are much more respectful towards their ancestor-gods. They have prayer meetings at which the old men of many families assemble together ; one of them, he who knows the ancestors best, leads the others in prayer, "quoting all their mountains" viz. all the sacred hills where the ancestors have been buried, and at the end of each sentence they all answer : "hundjiii..." When the prayer is finished, they each raise an arm and say : "Amen !" This is one of the customs borrowed by them from the Semitic populations with which they came into contact in former times. When they heard Christians pronouncing the same word to conclude their prayers, they were very much astonished. One of them told me ; "This shows that we were Christians formerly and have become back-sliders." One of their formulae when praying is as follows. "You, so and so and so, help us and enable us to reach Mudzimu." Mudzimu is the name by which they designate the Supreme Being in whom they believe and of whom they say : "All that you eat, it is Mudzimu who gives it to you!" If a child refuses to obey, they say to him : "Mudzimu will see you !" For them the ancestor-gods are but intermediaries between themselves and Mudzimu. They often call themselves Basilamusi, Moslems, and claim that there were Moslems belonging to their tribes (A ba ri ba ka hina).

do all these ceremonies reveal as to the conceptions of the Thongas concerning the ancestral spirits which they worship? A striking contrast exists in their ideas. On the one hand, the ancestor-gods are *true gods*, endowed with the attributes of divinity, whilst, on the other, they seem to be merely *human beings*, exactly on the same level as their worshippers.

1) *They are divine*! When an old decrepit man or woman dies, he at once becomes a god : he has entered the domain of infinity. The Thongas have no very clear idea of infinity. They have, however, a technical term for it : "lepsi nga yiki helo (Dj.), or mbangu (Ro.)" — "that which does not reach the point where it ends." This idea has certainly been extented to the shades which have attained the rank of psikwembu. The psikwembu are *omnipresent*. As Mankelu says : "For them there is no such thing as distance (a psi na kule) ; they are everywhere present (psi kone hikwaku). They are like heaven, the sun and the moon. There is no place where it can be said that the moon is not." The notion of *omnipresence* is perhaps that which has been understood most clearly. *Omniscience* is also believed in : the gods know what their descendants do, though they may be separated from them, perhaps dwelling in distant lands. *Omnipotence* results from the fact that they control everything in the life of their descendants. They are superior to wizards in this respect. As regards their connection with Heaven, I have never heard the point discussed. Natives do not philosophise. Thus the ancestral spirits are true gods endowed with divine attributes.

2) *They are still, however, only men*! They are not transcendent beings before whom miserable sinners tremble and offer prayers. The attitude of the worshippers, which I have just described, the freedom they show in insulting their gods, indicates that they consider them as exactly on the same level as themselves. This human nature of the gods is clearly shown by two facts : the limits of their power and their want of moral character. The domain in which they exercise their power is limited, being only *that of their own family* ; they watch over their descendants, bless or punish them, but they are absolutely indifferent to other men, and do not trouble about their affairs more than they did when still alive

on earth. I have nothing to fear or to hope from my neighbour's gods, if I do not belong to the same "shibongo" (I. p. 360). The gods of the royal family are invoked on behalf of the whole country, and have power to give rain to the land ; but it is the chief and his uncles who must approach and sacrifice to them. I have no right to do so. It is true that an exception seems to be made in the case of the gods of bitterness, or of the bush, who attack the traveller, although he belongs to another family. But this is indeed only an exceptional case, it being their kinsfolk, who neglected to bury them, who are most exposed to their wrath.

Another proof that they are men is this : although as gods they have acquired these divine ontological powers, they have made no real moral progress. They are not better than they were as men. Their *character* is that of suspicious old people, who resent any want of respect, or attention, on the part of their descendants. They wish to be thought of, and presented with offerings. It would seem that they are not actually in need of anything, for they live in abundance, but they exact a punctual observance of the duties of their descendants in regard to them. They must *luma*, eat the first fruits, and have their share of the tobacco leaves and also of the ground tobacco. They are jealous, and avenge themselves when forgotten (1). The only sin which seems to be deserving of punishment is to neglect them. There are, however, two other faults which they strongly condemn, and for which they may even kill their descendants : the first is any serious *transgression against the law of hierarchy* (as we saw, when dealing with the sacrifice of reconciliation) ; they punish especially the young man, even though he be the chief, who dares thus to

(1) In a very interesting tale, which is unique, and which I owe to Camilla and have published in *Les Chants et Contes des Ba-Ronga*, p, 264, we hear of the people of Mashaken, near Lourenço Marques forgetting for many years to make offerings to their gods. Famine ensues. The men go to the marsh to cut sugar canes. They are unable to break them, and the gods chase them away. The women, who come to a place where honey is flowing from a tree, try to take the combs, but their hands break off and remain fixed to the spot ! The bones order Sabulana, a young girl, to go to the sacred wood to sacrifice. She enters the forest and sees the gods assembled. They say to her : "Tell your people that they have sinned, because they have tilled the ground and harvested without presenting us with any offerings. Now we are glad, because they have come to invoke us." This story was told me as a tale, not as a legend of the sacred woods.

426

encroach upon the right of the *regular priest*, which is a great taboo ; secondly, they kill a man who loses all restraint in sexual relations ; when any one yields to that sin, people say : "The gods will lead him into the thick bush and kill him there." To other sins they are quite indifferent. Mboza even asserted, with a sadness which reminded me of the complaints of Asaph in Ps. LXXII, that men of bad habits do not fall ill or meet with misfortune ; the cough only attacks the good ; wizards bewitch them and do not go to the bad fellows, "for the gods see that they are not worth anything!"

In conclusion, I should say that what is wanting in the conception of the ancestor-gods, as compared with the God of higher religions, is both transcendence and the moral attributes.

III. *General Characteristics of Ancestrolatry.*

If I had to characterise Thonga ancestrolatry, I would say :

It is a *spiritualistic* religion, in the sense that no idols are adored ; there is neither idolatry nor fetichism in it. Spirits and spirits alone are worshipped.

It is an *animistic* religion, as defined in the preceding chapter, the categories of spirit gods being numerous, and these spirits being worshipped in order to win their favour, and propitiated when they are angry.

Though consisting essentially of offerings and prayers, which are distinctly religious acts, *it is mingled with magic* to a considerable extent.

It is a *particularistic family* religion, each family having its own particular gods. We may also see in it the beginings of a *particularistic national* religion (the great mhamba).

It is a *social* religion, its prescriptions being aimed at keeping alive and strengthening the hierarchy, which is the main feature of the social order.

It is an *unsacerdotal* religion, there being no sacerdotal order, but at the same time the priesthood of the elder brother is strictly enforced.

It is a *non-moral* religion, by which I do not mean that it is *immoral*, i. e. opposed to the laws of morality, but that it has no, or at least very

427

little, connection with the moral conduct of the individual. It has no moral prescriptions except those which insure the observance of the hierarchical order in the family. It neither promises reward nor threatens punishment after death.

Consequently it is purely *eudemonistic*, the religious ceremonies having as their sole aim material benefits connected with the terrestrial life, e. g. abundance, health, peace, and good sleep!

It is *unphilosophical*, that is to say, it does not attempt to answer the great problems about the origin and purpose of the world and human existence. These questions of causality and finality are absolutely beyond its horizon.

It is essentially *ritualistic*, and leaves very little place for true religious feeling. Adoration is practically non-existent. However, elements of *personal religion* are not altogether wanting. Some expressions in the liturgical prayers reveal humility and trust, e. g. "Death doth not come to the man who is prayed for, but only to the one who trusts in his own strength" (p. 393) ; thankfulness for escape from danger is sometimes expressed in a spontaneous and genuine way ; and may not also the sacrifice of bitterness (p. 391) be actuated by a real and touching feeling of dependency ; the old formula of invocation and the sacramental word *tsu*, now inexplicable, seem to show that there was, even in former times, such a thing as *self dedication*, and some aspiration towards a real communion between the worshipper and his gods. (See Appendix III on Personal Religion amongst Thongas.)

Animism is generally spoken of as a *religion of fear*. Applied to Thonga ancestrolatry, this statement would be an exaggeration. There is indeed no deep love for the ancestor-gods in the hearts of the Thongas; how could it be so when these "psikwembu" are so jealous, and show so little love themselves? But there is no perpetual fear. The attitude is rather that of *indifference*. Natives ask for one thing only : that they may live in peace, and that their gods may interfere with them as little as possible.

B. THE CONCEPTION OF HEAVEN.

When studying the classic tragedies of Greece, and more especially those of Aeschylus and Sophocles, one is led to the conclusion that the gods of Olympus, in whom may be recognised, more or less distinctly, the personification of the forces of Nature, or heroes glorified by apotheosis, were not the only beings in whom that intellectually gifted people believed, nor the sole objects of their veneration. Higher than Olympus, and dwelling in the more remote heavens, a mysterious divinity looks down upon mankind, a divinity wiser and nobler than the capricious Zeus, or the voluptuous Artemis ; sometimes this being is called Nemesis, the avenger, inexorable fate, and sometimes it is a god more human and more moral in character. But this Supreme Being is vaguely conceived, and its form is, as it were, closely veiled, In the religion of the Thongas we meet with a similar phenomenon. Above the gods whom the common people know, worship, and call by name, there exists a power which to the majority remains ill-defined and which they express by the word *Heaven* (Tilo). This word *Tilo*, which, in the ordinary language, is used to designate the blue sky (p. 304), contains a far deeper and more comprehensive meaning. I shall not attempt to throw complete light on these ideas, which are so dim in the Native mind. But the reader who studies carefully the facts and customs which I am just about to describe, will certainly be convinced that there really exist two parallel series of religious ideas in the Thonga Religion. We have already dealt with those which first manifest themselves to the observer. Let us now consider the others ; they are not less interesting, nor less picturesque ; they are indeed perhaps deeper than those of the ordinary Ancestrolatry. This belief is in such an embryonic state that it very easily escapes observation. As already pointed out, it is a vein, a reef of gold, which has been discovered through some fortuitous circumstance, and must be worked with great care.

I. *The definition of Heaven.*

Tilo is a grand word ; it comes from the same root as *Zulu*, the honoured name of a great and powerful tribe.

"Before you came to teach us that there is an All-Good Being, a Father in Heaven, we already knew there was a Heaven, but did not know there was anyone in it." Such was the declaration of one of the most intelligent women of our congregation at Lourenço Marques, who was also the best acquainted with all the ancient Ba-Ronga customs. Timotheo Mandlati said to me, on the other hand : "Our fathers all believed that life existed in Heaven" (butomi byi kone tilwen). It is quite certain that, according to the ideas of the Thongas, as well as to those of many other tribes, Heaven was a *place* ; a place much to be desired, where was to be found that which is so seldom met with on earth, namely rest. Hence a song, which is to be found in a very similar form amongst the Zulus (1), and even amongst the Ba-Sutho, and runs thus :

(Solo)   Bukali bya ngoti !
(Tutti)   Nha ndji yahliya ngoti, ndji ya Tilwen !
         Ndji ya kuma ku wisa !
(Solo)   What a rare thing is string !
(Tutti)   Oh ! how I should love to plait a string, and go up to Heaven, I would go there to find rest !

An old refrain which has come down through the ages, and has in no wise been inspired by the Christian religion : it is pure, authentic Bantu! Thus the warriors, when threatening their adversaries, and hurling defiance from one troop to another, say : "Make ready your string, and climb up to Heaven, there is no place for you here below. Here you will find nothing but misfortune" (I. p. 472) (2).

Thongas, however, never declare as a belief that men go to Heaven after death. They become "psikwembu," and we have already seen where their abode is. Nevertheless Viguet told me the story of a Hlengwe, whom he knew in times long gone by, in the Bilen country, who used to address the people in mysterious tones as follows :

(1) "Who could make a cord, whereby to go to Heaven ?" Such is the Zulu version given by Callaway.

(2) When a bone-thrower has decided that his consultant must make an offering, he often tells him, looking towards heaven : "Go, make the offering and say : It is good if I overcome the people who are below by the country which is afar." The people who are below are the wizards. The country which is afar is heaven. Another version is as follows : "It is good if I overcome the people who are below and reach the country which is far away." In the first case Heaven is considered as possessing a power greater than that of wizards ; in the second it means evidently the place of rest.

RELIGION

Though you eat plenty of fat and of honey, and drink plenty of beer, the day will come when you will say "Huku-huku" (fall on your back, i. e. die) ; people will say "Woo" (i. e. mourn you), and ask you : "Where are you going?" Then answer : "I am going to Ngundju-ya-mapsele, the Source-of-Grace, to the place where the oxen are herded by vultures (because there is no hatred and no death there), where the mosquito is killed with a stick (because everything is so flourishing and big there), where the fowl dies from fat (because there is no disease nor dearth in that blessed land) — to Heaven!"

This Hlengwe 'had either heard these words in his home or had invented them himself.

But Tilo is something more than a place. It is a *power* which acts and manifests itself in various ways. It is sometimes called *Hosi*, Lord. But this power is generally regarded as something entirely impersonal. Thongas appear to think that Heaven regulates and presides over certain great cosmic phenomena to which men must, willingly or unwillingly, submit, more especially those of a sudden and unexpected nature, by which I mean above all rain, storms, and, in human affairs, death, convulsions and the birth of twins. From this idea spring certain very characteristic customs, which I shall proceed to describe briefly.

It is Heaven that afflicts children with those terrible and mysterious *convulsions*, which carry them off without their having been really ill, in a manner of speaking... "He is ill from Heaven" — "A ni Tilò," said an old Native doctor to me in a low tone, referring to a case of this description. So Heaven is the great nombo (infantile disease), (I. p. 48), whilst diarrhea is the small nombo.

But more than this, *it is Heaven which kills and makes live.* Hence the frequent expression : "Heaven loved him," when someone has escaped some deadly danger, or is particularly prosperous, and "Heaven hated him," when he has been very unfortunate, or has died.

The same idea is expressed in the following dirge.

Wa hi kanganyisa, Tshabane !
Hi yingeli Tilo, dji ku dja buya nininini !
Hi kumi babanuna babiri, ba famba ba hlahluba Tilo.
Wa nga yingela psa bambe, u ta yingela ni psa ku !

You deceive us, Tshabane !
We have heard Heaven thunder... The roaring will soon come.
We have seen two men who were going to throw the bones with reference to
    Heaven...
Doubtless you have heard tell of the misfortunes of others :
You will hear them talking of your own !

Enigmatic words, but, with the help of the Natives, I have unravelled their meaning : — You are deceiving us, Tshabane, you who are trying to reassure us. We have heard Heaven. A storm has burst, there was a sudden downpour, a flash of lightning ; Heaven has struck! It has killed some one. Two men passed by, terrified ; they went to consult the bones, to try and find means to ward off these strokes of Heaven. Useless! If you have seen the sorrow of those who mourn, do not imagine that you will escape. It will soon be your turn!

Another song which contains a similar allusion to Heaven as the power which kills, has already been quoted when describing the customs of widowhood (I. p. 207). "What shall we say to thee! King!"

The tale of "the Road to Heaven" (See *Les Chants et les Contes des Ba-Ronga*, p. 237) is also very significant in this respect. It tells the story of a young girl, who, having broken her jar, and fearing a scolding from her mother, *climbs up her string* and goes to Heaven. (Always the same idea of shelter from all evils.) (1) There she finds a village ; a child is given to her, because she is so gentle and obedient. Her sister tries to do the same thing. But she is ill-tempered and wicked. Heaven explodes (baleka), kills her (by lightning), and her bones are blown right to her parents' house. In the tale of the Adventures of Bonawasi (Ch. & C. p. 295) Heaven intervenes to endow a young Native with peculiar wisdom, by means of which he gets the better of the Governor of the town. Possibly some idea of the God of the Europeans may have found its way into the composition of this tale, in which may be recognized certain traces of foreign influence. But this is assuredly not the

(1) The mention of this string is perhaps due to a tradition common in other African tribes. According to the Ba-Rotse, Leza, God, who dwelt on earth, ascended to Heaven one day by a spider's web. Several human beings tried to climb up the same way, but fell and failed in the attempt. (Comp. A. Jalla, *Foi et Vie*, Oct. 1910.)

case in respect to the story of Ñwahungukuri, which I have published in *Les Ba-Ronga*, p. 312, and in which Heaven is credited with the full knowledge of a hidden crime committed by a murderer. This idea is so far from being an innovation due to European influence that thoughtful Natives all agree that, in former times, it was more usual to attribute death to the power of Heaven. It was a common saying that "Heaven has fallen (ku we Tilo) on such and such a village." Nowadays it is rather the gods, or the wizards, who are believed to cause death.

But this belief in Heaven has not only inspired these sayings, songs, and tales ; it has also given rise to curious customs, a description of which will throw more light on this conception of the Thongas. Their existence proves that we are not here dealing with the "animatic" invention of some person gifted with a vivid imagination (p. 366), but with a true tribal belief.

II. *Customs Connected with the Conception of Heaven.*

1) HEAVEN, TWINS AND RAIN.

This power, which causes lightning and death, also presides, in a very special way, at the *birth of twins*, so much so that the mother is called by the name of "Tilo," — "Heaven," — and the children "Bana ba Tilo," — "Children of Heaven" (1). Now the arrival of two or three babies at the same time is looked upon by the Thongas as a great misfortune, a defilement in respect of which very special rites must be performed. I give the details of these rites as practised in the Zihlahla, Nondwane, and Nkuna clans, as they were described to me by Tobane, Mboza, Mankhelu, etc.

Twins (hahla, or bandjwa, dji-ma) are now both allowed to live. But in former times, one of them, the one which appeared to be the feebler, was always put to death, being left to die of

---

(1) In our school at Lourenço Marques there was a charming young girl, who was named Nwana-wa-Tilo, Daughter of Heaven, because she had a twin brother.

starvation, or strangled by a rope. It was buried in a broken pot, like other infants (I. p. 165), just below the surface of the ground, a hole being left for the air to enter, so that the "spirit (moya) may go out," in order that, for the mother also, the "spirit may get out," may be able to fly out and not close (the passages), this being a primary condition of her having other children (1).

But even the death of one of the twins is not considered sufficient to remove the curse. Directly after birth a particular doctor is sent for, who keeps the drugs needed in such a case. Shimhuntana and Manganyele were the medicine-men who were capable of dealing with the twin defilement in the district of Lebombo, and Ñwashïhuhuri of the Matimela family in the Zihlahla clan. They were held only to be surpassed by the medicine-man who treated cases of leprosy. The mother has to leave the village immediately, and they build for her a miserable little hut behind the others, where she goes to live with her twins. Her former hut is burnt with all her possessions.

In *Zihlahla*, all the women assemble that same day and start out in all directions, North, South, East and West to draw water in old calabashes from all the lakes and wells of the neighbourhood. They go skipping along, and singing

"Mbelele ! Mbelele ! Let rain fall"

This is the mbelele song (p. 318).

Then they return. The mother is seated with her two babes in her arms. They throw the water over her, intoning all the while the same monotonous refrain. This ceremony is to begin the removal of the "misfortune of twin birth, which is a death," (khombo dja lihahla, dji nga lifu). To complete the purification the magician gives to the father and mother a certain drug, which is kept in the Matimela family. The mother will put some of this into the little milombyana calabash, containing the diet-drink of newly born infants.

In *Khosen* the purification is performed by the medicine-man

(1) Even if a child dies at the age of ten days or more, if it is buried in the ground, its grave must be quite shallow ; for if it were buried too deep the mother would have no other children.

alone (See *Les Ba-Ronga*, p. 414). He pours his drugs into one of the pots brought by the women, adds to them the psanyi of the goat sacrificed for the occasion, and pours all the contents on to the shoulders of the mother, who holds the babes in her lap. After this he pours from some other pot, which contains pure water, and the woman conscientiously washes herself and her children all the while. Until her purification no inhabitant of the village is allowed to eat anything, and the following day it is taboo to work in the fields, for this would prevent the rain from falling.

Amongst the *Nkunas*, the mother of twins sits at the entrance of the hut, and the drug is poured over the roof above the doorway ; it leaks through the thatch on to her, and thus both the mother and the hut are purified at the same time.

This preliminary purification being thus accomplished, the woman goes to live in "her shelter," outside the village. She is absolutely shut off from all the other inhabitants. She has her own pots, axe, mortar, pestle, and does all her own cooking. Nobody even pays her a visit, and people only speak to her from a distance. Her children see no one but her. To each is allotted one breast, always the same. To help her in the nursing of twins the mother must "buy" a girl, to whom the care of one of the children is committed. This is a law. It is taboo for a girl, even should she be the elder sister, to "play" with a twin. The payment of £ 1 or ten shillings removes this taboo and the defilement (shisila) connected with it.

Women fear that, if they touch anything belonging to the mother of twins, if they smear themselves with her provision of fat, or if the defiled one smears herself with their fat, they will also incur the dreadful misfortune of giving birth to twins. For this reason it is taboo for a mother of twins to draw water except at a certain spot. She must select one place and always go there. When she returns from drawing water, she must pay attention to the little wreath of grass which she wears on her head to help her balance her pot ; it must not be thrown away with those used by other women, for fear that they also should become contaminated (tekela).

All these regulations clearly show that, for the time being, the mother of twins, like the widow, (I. p. 200) is regarded as outside the pale of society. But her defilement is worse than that of the widow; so, in order to be purified from it, the rite of *lahla khombo* (casting away the malediction) through which she must pass is much more severe. According to Mboza she must "deceive" four men one after the other, in the bush, all of whom will die. She hears that so and so says *djoo-djoo*, viz., becomes livid, that his body swells, that he is dead! She knows the reason. He has taken her defilement! Perhaps the fourth does not die but only becomes consumptive. These men have been pointed out to her by the divinatory bones. Each time she succeeds in performing the purification ceremony described in I. p. 205, she informs her medicine-man, who "prepares for her a vapour bath." Afterwards, she goes to reside at her parents' house, has relations with a lover, and gives birth to another child. Then her purification is complete, and her husband goes with 10/- to fetch her, and bring her home. The lover completed the removal of the "buhahla" i. e. the condition in which a mother of twins is. He has washed her (hlampsa). A new hut will be built for her, furnished with new utensils, and the ordinary family life will begin afresh.

As regards the twins themselves, they do not pass through the ceremony of presentation to the moon (I. p. 52) as other children do. They are weaned earlier; immediately after the reappearance of the menses the mother begins her *lahla khombo*, which at the same time is a *lumula*, a weaning of the children. They are then fed with goat's milk.

Twins are not liked by other people. They are looked upon as bad characters. When the little ones begin to crawl, and chance to go towards the other huts, people throw cinders at them and drive them away, saying: "These are children of Heaven. Be off! You annoy us!" If any ordinary child has a particularly bad disposition, they often say: "You are naughty! You are just like a twin!" — "Hahla dja karata" — "Twins are troublesome" is another common saying; and if a child is really exceptionally difficult to deal with, people say: "It is a twin! You cannot do anything with it! (A dji koteki!)"

Special precautions are taken in respect to twins when they pay a mourning visit. One of the grave-diggers meets them at the entrance of the village and says : "Do not fear, Children of Heaven." He then puts some ashes on their heads and on their fontanelles. This is done because twins are feeble (ma ni bushapu) and the defilement might affect them more than other children. They must therefore be protected by smearing the middle of the head, and the "extremity of the tree of life," viz., the fontanelle, with a preventive. The mother also undergoes a similar treatment. She must prostrate herself near the hut of the deceased, at the place where the wall has been pierced to make an exit for the corpse. Then the grave-digger brings some live embers in a broken pot, pours a little water on to them, and dips his fingers into the water ; he then presses both his hands against the woman's belly and brings them round her waist, pressing them all the while against the skin, until they meet on the spine ; thus she is "cured inside" (dahiwa ndjen). This will prevent her from suffering from internal troubles, to which she, having given birth to Tilo, Heaven, is particularly liable. (Comp. I. p. 151) (1).

From this brief description of the customs connected with twins in most of the Thonga clans, it may be seen that their explanation is twofold : 1) The birth of twins is a death, consequently a defilement, indeed the worst of all defilements. Hence the *purificatory rites* which bear the character of *passage rites* : the mother is secluded and passes through a period of isolation, after which she is again admitted to society after a painful "casting away of her misfortune." 2) But the cause of the defilement is not an ordinary death, but Heaven. *She is Heaven* ; she is said to have

---

(1) Another category of persons bearing a special relation to Heaven are the *albinos*. Cases of albinism are not frequent amongst South African Natives, yet they are sometimes met with. They are called in Thonga *Khalandlati*, a word which means literally *charcoal-lightning*. It is believed that they have been burnt (hisa) by lightning in their mother's womb before their birth. "Ba tlalile, a ba wupfanga, ba bengiwi hi tilo," viz. "they are uncomplete beings, they are not ripe, they have been hated by Heaven" ; these are the terms in which they are described. They are not however regarded as taboo (yila), they merely inspire disgust (nyenya) (p. 83). As regards women suffering from this kind of disgrace, other women do not smear themselves with the same ochre as they, lest they should give birth to albinos ; they do not drink from the same cup. Men do not marry them, and in this respect they are classed with leper women and witches, who are also looked on as repugnant.

made Heaven (a hambi Tilo), to have *carried Heaven* (a rwi Tilo), to
have *ascended to Heaven* (a khandjiyi Tilo). This connection
established between her and Heaven is clearly seen in the *rain
customs* previously described. Notice that the day following the
birth of twins is a *shimusi*, i. e. a day of rest. Nobody tills the
ground, fearing that it would prevent rain from falling. When the
mbelele takes place in Nondwane and Zihlahla (p. 318), the half
naked women who are sent to clean the wells take with them a
mother of twins. This is no doubt in order to show them where
the graves of twins are. But there is also another reason. In the
sacred wood of Libombo there is a hole into which the woman is
put ; her sisters then pour on to her the water which they have
drawn from all the wells, till the hole is half full, and the water
comes up to her breasts. This will cause the rain to fall. Why is
this? No doubt because, the woman of Heaven being wet,
Heaven itself will be wet. Spoon did not give this explanation
himself, but, when I suggested it to him, he accepted it readily.
For the same reason the graves of twins are watered. In certain
cases water is poured on the graves of the ancestors also, because
rain is attributed both to them and to Heaven, and this watering
the graves is meant to induce either Heaven or the ancestor-gods to
cause rain to fall. Hence again the precaution taken of burying
twins in damp places, and of exhuming them in times of drought if
they have been buried in dry ground (1).

The connection between twins and Heaven, so clearly to
be seen in these customs, appears again in respect to thunder-
storms, which, as we shall see, are another manifestation of Heaven.
When lightning threatens a village, people say to a twin : "Help us!
You are a Child of Heaven! You can therefore cope with Heaven
(mi kota Tilo), it will hear you when you speak." So the child

(1) In other clans this law is extended to children prematurely born, even though they
are not twins, and even to children who have not had the cotton string tied round their
waist or who have cut their upper teeth first. On the other hand, among the Nkunas
no special connection seems to be established between twins and Heaven. These differences may be explained by the fact that all these abnormal cases were ascribed to
Heaven in former times, and the connection has been preserved in the various clans in
respect to one or the other of these categories. Note that, in the song of the widows
(I. p. 207), the king Heaven appears to have caused the death of the husband ; this is
another proof that Heaven was formerly considered the most frequent cause of death.

goes out of the hut and prays to Heaven in the following words :
"Go away! Do not annoy us! We are afraid. Go and roar far
away." When the thunderstorm has ended, the child is
thanked (1). His mother can also help in the same way, for has
she not ascended to Heaven? "She can speak with it, she is at it
(or in it) — a li ku djone." (Spoon.)

We find in these rites a striking instance of the combination of the
three forms of magic which have been explained above (p. 368).
Heaven, rain, lightning, the mother of twins and the twins themselves
form a connected whole. Action brought to bear on the mother of
twins will therefore have its effect on Heaven ; this is *communionist
magic*. This action consists in pouring water over her, (not only in
plunging her into a lake). According to the principle of *imitative
magic*, Heaven will thus be watered and will pour rain upon the earth.
The act of the twin in commanding the lightning to spare the country is a
case of *verbal magic*. All this would be logical enough and the conclusions perfectly legitimate if only the premises were true!

Customs regarding twins vary from one clan to another. While
in one tribe they are put to death, in others their advent is
considered an event of great happiness. This is the case in
Tembe and Maputju, where women are said to wish for twins,
and, if certain mothers have enjoyed this piece of good fortune,
others ask them for some of the fat with which they have smeared
their bodies, hoping by the use of the same ointment to obtain a
like happy result. The hut is never burnt. The mother gives
birth to the twins behind the hut (fukwen, I. p. 37). When it is
time for her to re-enter her domicile, a hole is made in the wall at
the back. The husband is excluded from the hut till the day of
presentation to the moon (a ceremony which, in these clans, is not
omitted in the case of twins). When he is again admitted, his
wife strikes his legs with a stick, in order "to cure him" (ku mu

(1) Mrs. Junod, who was for years a missionary amongst the Fañ or Pahouin of
the French Congo, told me that, one day, after a tornado, the rainbow suddenly
appeared in the sky. One of her female pupils at once ran to her, and hid her face
in her schoolmistress'lap. On asking the reason of this fear the teacher was told that
this girl was a twin, and twins dare not look at the rainbow. So the connection between Heaven and twins exists also in this tribe of Western Africa.

daha). Striking is frequently one of the rites of aggregation. (See Van Gennep, *Rites de Passage*, p. 55). Let us remember that the Tembe clan is of Northern origin (I. p. 23) and has retained some customs which are different from those of the other Thongas (1).

2) HEAVEN AND THE "NUNU."

The following is a very extraordinary custom, and one which, in many respects, greatly resembles those I have already described. There is to be found, on the shores of Delagoa Bay, a small Coleoptera belonging to the Alcides genus of the Cucurlionidæ family. It has a proboscis-shaped mouth, a very hard carapace of half a centimetre in length, brown, and marked on each elytron with two longitudinal white bands. The Blacks call it the *nunu*. It is a scourge to the fields of beans and maize (much as cockchafers are with us). In December or January, when these insects begin to swarm, the chief men of the country order the diviners to throw the bones, and send the women to pick the "nunu" off the bean stalks. They gather them in "sala" shells. Then they choose (probably by casting lots) *a woman who has given birth to twins.*

(1) Amongst *the Hereros* a multiple birth is the happiest event which could possibly occur ! The Rev. E. Dannert published in the *Capetown Folklore Journal* an account of the customs practised on such occasions by the Natives of this tribe, which occupies the Western side of Southern Africa, at about the same latitude as the Thongas. The father and mother are condemned to complete silence, under penalty of bringing a curse on those who speak to them. All the members of the tribe are convened and bring their cattle with them. The twins' family has to appear before the whole assembly, and is received with lamentations. Each individual must present himself to the parents, and make them a gift of beads, or other ornaments, in return for which the father and mother purify them by means of a certain powder. After this the father has the right of going from village to village, and claiming an ox from each one, as a kind of ransom. He becomes quite a rich man. This is the *kunga rite*, which we have also met with on many occasions amongst the Thongas (I. p. 124.). How can this diversity between the customs of the Hereros and those of most of the Thongas be explained? No doubt by this vague mysterious idea of Heaven, which is behind the religious conceptions of these tribes and in which all these rites originated. This celestial power, when it manifests itself, stupefies the Natives, for it causes "a death," entails a curse. With the Thongas it is the mother and children who are the objects of this malediction, hence the purifying ceremonies imposed upon them. With the Hereros, it is the whole tribe which is affected. The family into which the twins are born has been distinguished and honoured by this heavenly visitation, and collects for itself the fines which all must pay to regain the celestial favour !

One of her daughters, who is one of the twins, is told to throw the whole "catch" of insects into the neighbouring lake. She is accompanied by a woman of mature age, and, without speaking a word, must go straight to the lake in question. Behind her marches the whole crowd of women, arms, waists and heads covered with grass, carrying branches of the big-leaved manioc, which they wave from side to side, and singing the following song, which has been composed for this occasion :

Nunu, muka! Hi da mabele !
Nunu, go away ! That we may eat mealies !

The twin throws her little calabash into the water without turning round (for she is not allowed to look behind). Then the savage yells are raised louder than ever, and the women sing their impure songs (ta ku ruketela), which they would never dare to utter on ordinary occasions, and which are reserved for these ceremonies, rain seeking and "nunu" hunting.

On that day, as during the mbelele, woe to the man who walks along the paths! He is pitilessly attacked by these viragos, who push him to one side, or even maltreat him, and none of his fellows will go to his assistance. They all keep out of the way, for they well know what would be in store for them, should they meet the savage crowd! So they mostly stay quietly at home in their huts!

The "nunu", is not always thrown into the water. Sometimes, to get rid of the plague, or rather to conjure it away, they start out in a band, armed with sticks, to throw these destructive insects on to neighbouring lands. It would seem that the men are mixed up in these underhand tricks, for it is said that this way of handing over the "nunu" to neighbours, often leads to pitched battles, in which sticks are wielded to some purpose, and blows rain thick and heavy! The people of Rikatla, citizens of Nondwane, used to make a present of their pseudo-cockchafers to the inhabitants of the district of Makunyule, belonging to the Mabota clan. But the true way of conjuring away the "nunu" is to drown them in the lake, and this custom, in common with the preceding ones, certainly has some connection with the notion of Heaven, the appearance of these pests being caused by that mysterious power, which

presides over all unaccountable and unavoidable phenomena of the
atmosphere and of the life of the fields, or of human existence.

We have seen how the two sets of religious customs play their
part side by side in the rites of rain-making. A similar coincidence
may be noticed here. The removal of the "nunu," a rite which
originated in the conception of Heaven, corresponds to the
sacrifice of the chief in the Maluleke country, who gathers his sons
together to pray to his ancestor-gods for the destruction of the
vermin (psidi) which eat the mealies and endanger the harvest
(p. 404).

3) Heaven, Storms and Robbers.

The most characteristic manifestation of Heaven is in the
storm. According to the statement of the credulous Natives, after
the women have finished cleaning the wells, and have watered
the graves of twins, clouds appear, a whirlwind arises, and "Heaven
begins to thunder" — "Tilo dji djuma." — I have already described
Thonga ideas about thunder and the lightning bird (p. 313), and
the powerful charm made from the flesh, feathers and urine of this
marvellous creature! There is still another use made of this
extraordinary drug. It is a powerful aid in *tracing thieves*! The
magician who possesses this powder of Heaven, (Ñwagwalen of
Shikhabele in the Mabota clan), when called upon to point out the
thief, acts in the following way. Suppose some one finds that some
valuable article has disappeared from his hut, he will say to his near
relatives, to those whom he suspects of having committed the
larceny : "Take care! If you don't confess, we will go to Ñwagwalen, who lives at Shikhabele!" This threat may possibly be
sufficient to elicit an avowal. If not, the individual who has been
wronged goes to the diviner, and asks his assistance ; the latter
takes his "bag of tricks," his drugs, and his big black stick, i. e., the
stick which he was carrying when he dug in the earth and found the
urine of the bird, or the bird itself. A notch has been made in the
stick, to show the depth of the hole in which he has discovered
Heaven. Carrying these charms, he goes to find the chief. An
audience being granted, he cries aloud : "O Chief! a theft has been

committed! Now, no one ought ever to rob me. What shall I do!" Then the Chief assembles his subjects and invites the guilty one to confess. If all deny it, Ñwagwalen starts off, with all his apparatus, for the place where the theft was committed, and "treats it medicinally" (a dahela mbangu). He spreads out his drugs, raises his stick in the air, and addresses Heaven as follows :

> We, Tilo, hi wene u ka ni mahlu, u bonaka busiku ni nhlekanhi !
> Ba tekile psa nga ba kaneta ! Tana u ba komba ba psha !
> Oh Heaven, thou it is who hast eyes which see as well by night as by day...
> They have stolen my goods, and they deny it ! Come and discover them ;
> may they be consumed !

Then the clouds begin to gather, and, towards evening, the storm breaks. Lightning strikes the thief in his hut, and causes the stolen articles to reappear. — "I saw this happen at Hoñwana," declared Spoon, "but of late years such occurrences have been less frequent."

According to Camilla, the guilty person is sometimes punished by a terrible attack of vermin, of which he is unable to rid himself ; or he is confronted with several palm leaves, which, by a kind of supernatural judgment, turn into snakes, if he be truly guilty of having stolen the missing property.

The intervention of Heaven in the matter of detecting thieves is also an accepted fact in Khosen. My colleague, the Rev. A. Grandjean, told me of the following significant custom. When there is a storm, those who have missed any belongings go and stand at the door of the hut of the suspected thief, and it is quite possible that the inmate, terrified by the thunder, may throw out the stolen articles.

It may be concluded, from these perfectly authenticated customs, that the Natives attribute to Heaven the power of *omniscience*, more especially in respect to the detection of theft. The basket of bones is never consulted for this purpose. Moreover as Heaven guarantees property and makes people afraid to steal, it acts as a kind of *moralising influence*.

I have also been told by witnesses from the Nkuna region that into the composition of the charm used to protect gardens against thieves, (p. 30) there enters a little powder obtained by burning a stem which has been struck by lightning, i. e. by Heaven ; or the magician will burn branches of the same tree in the garden itself and bring them near to the stalks in order that these may be surrounded by the smoke emanating from them. If a thief enters the garden with evil intentions, "Tilo dji ta mu dlaya, i. e. Heaven will kill him."

4) HEAVEN AND THE BALUNGWANA.

In 1894, as previously stated, locusts, which had not been seen for some fifty years, made their appearance on the shores of Delagoa Bay, and also in Natal and the Transvaal. The popular imagination was, naturally, greatly stirred by this unusual phenomenon, which was at first greeted with smiles and astonishment, but which, later on, was the cause of endless lamentation. I was one day walking up the hill of Lourenço Marques with an old man, the counsellor of one of the sub-chiefs of Tembe, a thoughtful and intelligent person, when he said to me, with great earnestness, in a low voice, as if referring to some important event : "Have you not heard that in Maputju two dwarfs (psimhu-ñwanyana) fell from Heaven ; a little man and a little woman. They came to say to the people : "Do not kill the grasshoppers! They belong to us!" This counsellor only repeated what all thought and were saying in all the native villages ; these grasshoppers, arriving unexpectedly from on high, were a manifestation of Heaven, just like the lightning, rain, twins, or the nunu, and these celestial beings had come to announce it to men.

But belief in the existence of *special personages* in Heaven did not originate in connection with these terribly destructive insects. The idea had been familiar, for a long time past, to the Rongas, and probably to all the Thongas. These personages were not only described as dwarfs, but also as balungwana (p. 352). They were said to fall from Heaven at the time of the great rains. Thus, Timoteo Mandlati told me people had seen some of them appear, a long time ago, in the Nkuna country, and that they had gone back to heaven in a cloud ; they live in celestial space, and when it thunders without any rain falling, the Nkunas say :

"Balungwana ba tlanga henhla" — "The balungwana are at play up there." Or it is they who are singing in heaven when there is a prolonged roar of thunder, saying : "wuwu-wuwu!"

When some one passes along the road, they dispute up above as to who he may be. One says : "It is so and so," and the others contradict him. Then they spit on the traveller, who is quite astonished to see some saliva on his hand. He mistakes it for rain, and looks up to the sky to see where the rain is coming from. The balungwana then have a chance to see his face, and the one who has guessed rightly says to the others : "You see! I was right."

In Bilen I heard of a man who prevented children from picking the beautiful red flowers of Tecoma capensis, telling them that the balungwana wanted them for dresses. The same individual believed that these little men would bring oxen to him.

The Rongas say that a little man fell on the hill of Lourenço Marques, near the house of Sithini, the son of Mashaken, just before the famous war between Mozila and Mawewe (I. p. 28), the rival claimants to the kingdom of Gaza, and that this dwarf came as a presage of the troubles which were to follow. "Lots of folk saw him" said Charlie in 1895 ; (he was then a man of some forty years of age). "We were too young to be allowed to look at him ; the Whites took him and carried him off to Mozambique." — Heaven is therefore inhabited. This is generally admitted, but the idea, from all that one can gather, remains very vague.

C. CONCLUDING REMARKS ON THONGA RELIGION.

I. *The Origin of the Conception of Heaven.*

Ancestrolatry forms a clear, well-defined religion, with its theology (i. e., the ideas as regards the psikwembu), its sacrifices, and its prayers. The dim, mysterious ideas about Heaven, incorporated in or rather lying behind some of the most extraordinary rites of the tribe, bear a very different character. There is something incoherent, vague and unexpected in them, and it would seem that, bearing as they do an essentially deistic character, and accompanied by no true worship, they might as well be absent from the horizon of the Thonga mind.

However, when we study other Bantu tribes, we come to exactly the opposite conclusion, i. e., that it would be indeed strange if no religious ideas of this kind were found amongst our tribe. In fact, this occurrence of a double set of religious ideas is universal amongst Bantus. They all believe in a kind of Supreme Being, an All-Father, who bears many different names, *Nzame* amongst the Fan and a great number of West African tribes, *Nyambe* amongst the Ba-Rotsi, *Leza* in some Zambezi and Rhodesian districts, *Mulungu* amongst fifteen East African tribes (1), *Unkulunkulu* in Zululand, *Nungungulu* round Inhambane, and *Mudimo* amongst the Ba-Sutho, etc., etc. The Thonga *Tilo* is, most likely, one of these names. The word probably comes from the root *ulu*, high, elevated, and *ilu*, heaven, which the Rev. P. Sacleux has found with that meaning amongst Central or West African tribes. (*Mulu*, amongst the Bembas ; *Liulu*, in Kimbundu ; *Diulu*, in Luba ; *Wilu*, in Luyi ; *Egulu* in Ganda ; *Idjulu*, amongst the Tongas of Zambezi, etc.). This root, with the personal prefix, has given birth to the term *Mugulu*, designating God in Tabwa and *Mukuru* in Herero. It may be that Mukuru is rather related to the *Unkulunkulu* of the Zulus, the Great One. (See Mgr. Le Roy, "La Religion des Primitifs," 1909, p. 498.)

In the South African tribes, however, the conception of the Supreme Being is not nearly so precise as in most parts of Central Africa. The Thonga Tilo, although sometimes invoked, is hardly a being, but seems rather to be a personification of Nature. Is this the original conception of the Supreme Being, or is it rather a transformation of this? I abstained, in *Les Ba-Ronga*, from expressing any definite opinion on this point. Further study has now led me to believe that the latter conclusion is the more probable, and that ideas concerning Heaven were more definite in former times. This, at any rate, is also the conviction of intelligent elderly Natives, who are able to remember the former ideas held by the tribe. They say : "As regards death, people now commonly affirm that it is caused by witchcraft, whilst formerly they attributed it to the agency of Heaven." Let us also notice the name of the dwarfs who are believed to inhabit Heaven, the *balungwana*. This word is a

---

(1) Comp. J. Torrend's *Comparative Grammar of the S. A. Bantu Languages,* p. 68.

diminutive of *Mulungu, balungu*, by which are designated, amongst the Zulus and Thongas, White people of every description, whether Europeans or Asiatics. Could the inhabitants of Heaven have been called "balungwana," on account of their resemblance to the Whites? It would hardly seem probable, for the name of the balungwana, and the ideas connected with them, were in existence long before White people were generally known, or had settled in the country. It is much more reasonable to suppose that the name of these mythical beings, as also that by which the Whites are designated, is a derivative of some other pre-existent term ; and what should this be if not the famous vocable "Mulungu," which stands for God, the One Supreme God, in so many of the Bantu dialects of East Africa, from Lake Victoria Nyanza to the Zambesi, to Senna and Quilimane? I should be inclined to think that the tribes in the neighbourhood of Delagoa were also acquainted with this name, which is so widely known, and that it has, in the course of centuries, disappeared from their theology, only leaving, as a last trace, the term balungwana, applied to the heavenly beings who occasionally descend to earth, and balungu, designating that superior race whose wisdom has always impressed the Blacks as supernatural. If this hypothesis were confirmed, we should have the right to conclude that the idea of Heaven, such as it is described in this chapter, is the dis-figured remnant of a higher and monotheistic conception, held by the primitive Bantus before their dispersion, which has evolved in various ways amongst the different tribes.

II. *The Antiquity of Ancestrolatry.*

Ancestor Worship seems, on the other hand, to be an extremely ancient religion amongst mankind. There have been discovered of late years sepulchres of prehistoric date, which seem to show that the funeral rites of the first races were very similar to those practised by the Bantus of the present day. In comparing the burial of Sokis (I. p. 139) with that of a human being of the Mousterian age, whose remains were recently discovered by Hauser in the celebrated "Abri du Moustier" (Dordogne) (1) I noticed the following resemblances :

(1) See my paper "Deux enterrements à 20,000 ans de distance." *Anthropos*, 1900, I. v. Comp. also *L'homme préhistorique.* January, 1909.

1) In both cases, the corpse was treated with great, even affectionate care, protected against the earth, and provided with a pillow.

2) The legs and arms had been bent towards the body, a custom widespread amongst primitive races, and directly due to the belief in an after-life.

3) The deceased is regarded as sleeping : hence the pillow provided for him.

4) His after-life is believed to be an exact continuation of his existence on earth. Hence the fact that the articles which he was accustomed to use are put on to, or inside, his grave, the mats, rugs, mug in one case, and silex or "coups de poing" in the other.

5) If the rites performed for Sokis may be explained by the hypothesis that he has become a *shikwembu*, a god endowed with divine powers, if they are in truth acts of worship, it is but reasonable to suppose that the same religious conceptions gave birth to the similar rites of the Mousterian Primitives. The Mousterian Age is one of the first periods of the Quaternary. Some palaeontologists believe it to be anterior to the last glacial period, and think that the dwellers in la Dordogne lived 20,000, even 50,000 years ago! They possessed, then, a religion, and this religion was probably Ancestrolatry.

III. *The Relation between Ancestrolatry and the Conception of Heaven.*

The conclusion which may be drawn from the two preceding paragraphs is that both Ancestor Worship and the Conception of a Supreme Being are of very ancient date, and the question naturally arises as to which is the older. I do not pretend here to be able to supply a solution to this great problem, but merely to draw the attention of my readers to the following facts.

1) When questioned as to the relative antiquity of their two sets of religious ideas, Thongas reply that they are unable to give an answer. Their conception of Heaven is so impersonal that they cannot draw any comparison between the two. Their neighbours, the Swazis and the Zulus, however, are very decided upon this point. The Rev. W. Challis, in *The East and the West* of July, 1908, summarises their statements as follows :

448

"Long ago a great and noble Bantu king was in the habit of climbing a twin-peaked mountain at daybreak, there to intercede with the Great Great One (Unkulunkulu) on behalf of his people. His son, who succeeded him, was afraid to draw near to the Great God whom his father worshipped, so he called upon the spirit of his father to intercede for him and his people before the Creator of all. Gradually each head of a house adopted this method of approaching God, until each family had its own ancestral spirits as mediators first, then merely as beings who brought good or bad luck, and who needed to be propitiated by sacrifice and constant flattery and attention. But God is not in their thoughts now ; only a vague tradition among the old men survives as to the existence of the Great Great One."

The Zulus affirm, so Callaway says, that the same proceeding took place amongst their ancestors. This seems to be a phenomenon similar to the adoration of saints in medieval times, after a period when religion had had a much purer and more transcendental character.

2) A second fact, which points in the same direction, is the contrast which exists in the conception of the ancestral spirits. On the one hand they are but men, who may be insulted (as was often the case with the saints to whom reference has just been made ; take, for instance, the incident of the striking of the image of St Antony of Padua by a worshipper, because the saint had not helped him to recover some lost property) ; on the other hand they are endowed with the qualities of omnipresence, omniscience and omnipotence in their relations with their descendants. It would seem as if the idea of divinity, which was not originally connected with the spirits of the departed, had been applied to them in an awkward and merely external fashion.

3) It is wonderful to notice how easily the idea of the Christian God is accepted by the Bantus. They have scarcely any difficulty in believing that this is the real God to whom worship is due. Livingstone long ago remarked this, and the truth of it has been confirmed by Miss Kingsley, for one, in regard to the Northern Bantus, and also by most of those who have endeavoured to win over these tribes to Christianity. It seems as if one were telling them an old story, with which they had been quite familiar but had now half forgotten. In regard to the Thongas I believe the psychological process to be as follows. When they hear of the *Shikwembu*, who is *in Heaven*, there at once takes place in their minds a coalescence, or reunion of the two main characteristics of their two religions ; — their *shikwembu* is personal but not transcendental ; their *Heaven* is transcendental but not personal.

God, the real God who is preached to them, is both personal and transcendental ; it is as if two different kinds of electricity suddenly came in contact with each other in their minds and produced a flash of light... The result is decisive. The two ideas can no longer be kept apart. When the Native has adopted the living God of Christianity, he either understands Him more and more fully, and is able to find great joy and satisfaction of soul in his new religion, or he abandons Him, and becomes godless, if he is unwilling to accept the morality of a true Christian life ; he very seldom returns to Ancestrolatry, nor to his former deistic and naturalistic conceptions. This is another proof that the knowledge of the one and only God, who reigns over all, was indeed sleeping in his heart and conscience, no doubt as a result of the ancient monotheistic conceptions of the Bantus.

The evolution of mankind has been a long one! Even if the Bantus formerly had the idea of God, this would not go to prove anything as regards the primitive religion of humanity. This question is entirely beyond the range of the present work, and even Science may perhaps never be able to answer it. I can therefore leave it out of consideration.

My last observation has shown the caducity of the Thonga religion. It is not able to stand before the advance of the higher revealed religions, Mohammedanism and Christianity. Hence the facility with which Thongas are converted to one or other of these beliefs. This fact is of considerable importance in respect to the future of the tribe, and it will be necessary for us to consider it in our Conclusion.

(See also *Some additional remarks on the idea of the Supreme Being and on Ancestor-worship in relation to Religious History.* App. IV.)

CHAPTER III

Magic

Without pretending here to give definitions applicable to all the primitive races, well knowing how difficult the subject is, yet, I think I ought at the beginning of this Chapter to explain as clearly as possible the distinction which I draw between Religion, Magic and Science, as they are represented amongst the South African tribes.

I include under the term *Religious* all the rites, practices, conceptions, or feelings which presuppose the belief in personal or semi-personal spirits endowed with the attributes of Deity, and with which man tries to enter into relation, either to win their assistance or to avert their anger, essentially by means of offerings and prayers.

Under *Magic* I include all the rites, practices, and conceptions which aim at dealing with hostile, neutral, or favourable influences, either impersonal forces of Nature, or living men acting as wizards, or personal spirits, whether ancestor-gods or the hostile ghosts which are supposed to take possession of their victims, these rites and practices being inspired by the magic principles explained above (p. 368). I recognise two kinds of magic : *White magic*, by which man tries to protect himself against these influences, or turn them to his advantage, and *Black magic*, by which man attempts to make use of these forces against his fellows.

I call *Scientific* all the rites, practices, and conceptions which are inspired by a true observation of facts. I include in this category certain medical treatments, ideas as to botany and zoology, etc.

These different elements are intermingled in practice to such an extent that, as explained in the preceeding Chapter, Religion is largely adulterated with Magic. On the other hand, Magic often admits religious elements (see Possession), and the true domain of Science is invaded on all sides by conceptions of a magical character. This will be shown by the study of the four subjects which I include in the Chapter on Magic, viz. : Medical Art, Possession, Witchcraft and Divination.

The confusion between these three domains also accounts for the composite character of those individuals who practise the medical, or magical art. The medicine-man (ñanga) is far from being purely a man of science, he partakes more or less of the nature of the magician, and prays to the ancestors who transmitted their charms to him. The magician (mungoma) is sometimes a kind of priest when he undertakes to exorcise the spirits of possession. The diviner (wa bula), whose art is entirely based on magical conceptions, occasionally prays to his ancestor-gods to help him in throwing the bones which he has received from them. I am convinced that the three domains are essentially distinct, and that the Thongas have a dim perception of this distinction. But they grade into each other with the greatest ease, and I shall try to follow these gradations, faithfully endeavouring not to alter the original ideas, whilst trying to explain them intelligibly.

A. MEDICAL ART.

The medicinal practices of the South African Bantus are very interesting from the ethnographic point of view, but their study has also a practical importance. In all civilised lands the medical profession is subject to restrictions; the candidate must pass examinations showing that he is capable of treating his future patients. Nothing of this kind is to be found amongst the Thongas. The only qualification of the doctor is that of having inherited some recipes from one of his ancestors, and of using them with more or less success on voluntary patients. Should steps be taken by Colonial Governments to stop, or at any rate to regularise, the action of the medicine-men?

A precise knowledge of their practices is necessary in order to come to a conclusion on this point. Missionaries have also a great interest in this study. They have all noticed how often their converts, when sickness overcomes them, abandon the Mission Station and run to their quacks, sometimes brusquely interrupting a treatment which had been prescribed to them by a fully trained medical missionary. The result is almost sure to be the eventual loss of their health and of their faith. Let us, therefore, try to understand the Native medical art and see how far we can trust its representatives.

I *The Medicine-men*.

I came across a good many *ñanga* (yin-tin), the technical name given to Native physicians. They are all very proud of their

452

knowledge, and it must be remarked that this knowledge is mostly *hereditary*. Certain drugs have been tried, and used for years, by a certain individual, who probably owed them to his father, or to another of his ancestors. Before his death he transmitted his art to his son, or to his uterine nephew, the one of his descendants who seemed to be "induced by his heart" (mbilu) to enter the profession. This being the case, medicine-men differ very greatly as regards competence. Some only treat one complaint, or one category of patients, because they only know the medicine which applies to them. For instance *Eliashib*, one of our first converts, a native of Khosen, had only one drug, the bark of a certain tree which possessed terrible purgative powers, and he prescribed it in every case, half killing those who came to him for treatment, and who had all the more confidence in the drug because it came from a distant land. Eliashib was hardly a ñanga. *Sam Ngwetsa*, my Rikatla neighbour, was a physician for infantile diseases only. He knew the milombyana prescription and how to biyeketa (I. p. 48, 54), and people used to ask for his assistance as a specialist in this domain alone. We have seen that there is also a special doctor who boasts of being able to treat the dangerous condition of the mother of twins, and another who treats leprosy, this latter being regarded as the most skilful of all. *Spoon-Elias* had a more extensive knowledge of the popular "materia medica" than Sam, but he was still only a beginner. His Nondwane colleague, *Kokolo*, was vastly superior, — an individual in the prime of life, wearing the black crown which distinguishes the notables of the land. He belonged to an ancient family of doctors ; his father Mankena and his grandfather Mahlahlana practised before him, and bequeathed to him the valuable legacy of their experience. Tobane, to whom I applied to put me in touch with some really clever practitioners, said of this man : "Awa daha!" — "He is one who succeeds in his cures!", adding with a look of profound respect : "It seems that even the Whites of Lourenço Marques consult him!" And Kokolo, without too much persuasion, showed me his drugs, and went to "dig" for some for my special benefit. I had to pay him fairly generously, as the gentleman does not work for nothing, and it was with an evident consciousness of his talent and powers that he explained to me the uses of his medicines.

But the most distinguished medicine-man I ever met was old *Mankhelu*, who may be looked upon as one of the masters of the profession in the Thonga tribe. "It is no play, what I am doing! I have beaten an ox (i. e. made a present of an ox) to my maternal uncle Hlomendhlen! I even gave him two oxen, and he taught me his medical art! He led me everywhere, showing me all his drugs." So Mankhelu became a regular nanga, in addition to being a diviner, a master of the art of throwing bones, a rain-maker, a counsellor, and general of the army. His whole family shared his professional character, and helped him in his work. Every year, at the time of bukanye, the drugs had to be renewed. His wives went all over the bush to dig out the medicinal roots and to collect them in their *lihlelo* baskets (p. 123). On their return home the bones were consulted to find out who was to cut the roots in pieces (gemela). This having been done, they pounded them in their mortars; a portion of this material was dried outside, and reduced to powder without having been cooked; these were the *male medicines*. The other portion was roasted in pieces of broken pots, burnt until it was like charcoal, ground and made into a black powder; these were the *female medicines*. The whole village assembled and inhaled the smoke through reeds during the operation. A goat was killed and a sacrifice performed; the liquid contained in the *psanyi* (p. 410) was squeezed on the burning drugs to put them out; a little bukanye beer was also used for the same purpose. In the meantime Mankhelu said "*tsu*," and addressed this prayer to his gods, and especially to the ancestor who had taught him his science :

"You! so and so! Let these drugs of yours rise (pfuka, i. e. find new strength). Let people come from the Zulus, from Mosilekatse, from Mpfumu! Let them think of our leaves (matluka, the common name for drugs). Let them bring elephant tusks, marriageable girls, etc. Let them dream of us!"

This operation of renewing the drugs aims at giving them new strength. Mankhelu said : "We let our drugs *luma* for the new year ; we raise our calabashes, so that the new season may not be too difficult for us... This will consolidate our home ; bad coughs will not attack us too severely. It will shut out the wind ; we shall no longer be very ill, because these are new drugs. As regards the old ones, they have been contaminated (khuma) by the misfortunes of last year. They are mad (hungukile). A new rain falls ; let there be also new drugs, and we can undertake our journeys to sell our goods." So the ñanga removed a little of the old powder from each calabash ; he threw this on the path at a crossway ; then he washed the calabashes at the same spot : "Misfortune is thus thrown away. Passers-by will take it with them as it has been thrown out there by us." Then the new powder was added to the remainder of the old, which was "raised" by it.

In order to throw more light on the nature of Mankhelu's art, let me briefly mention *the roots* (rimetju), or *the leaves* (tluka, ri-ma), or, to use the great, the generic name, *the drugs* (muri, mu-mi) which composed the marvellous powder of the calabashes. He was not a man of one drug. He claimed to be a universal physician, so he mixed together all kinds of drugs, being sure that, in this way, they would certainly be effective in any case brought to him. Here is the description given by him.

Ntjebe : that by which we find strength to trample on our enemies ; we trample also on the winds which spoil the mealies ; we drive out the bad cold (or wind) which has come to us and made us cough. (Notice the triple use of this drug).

Shikuku : that which tramples on misfortune.

Mpoñwana wa burisi matuba-tubana : vanquisher of the enemy and of misfortune.

Shinano : that which induces the enemies to sleep ; you hang some leaves of it on your shield and they are overcome by drowsiness, they do not see you coming towards them.

Nembe-nembe. By it you reach your enemy while he still sleeps and kill him before he can defend himself.

Mpetshu wa milomo : that of the lips ! It overcomes the curses and the assagais of the others !

455

Rihinga ra ndlela : a root found on the path ; it helps you to go on, though others may seek to hinder you in your progress.

Shivunge : that which attracts patients to the doctor.

Nandjiyane : that which makes his words agreeable, so that patients will like them ; (from ku nandjiya, to be agreeable).

Mvakazi, phuphuma ra matlhari : that which is used to make the slayers vomit the main drug of the *tintebe* (I. p. 479).

Mbendjula : that which strengthens all the other drugs.

These are the principal trees, or plants, used for the preparation of the powder. They must be *salted* by the addition of the *sea*, viz., of the medicines taken from the sea, which Mankhelu uses to cause rain to fall (p. 321).

The sexual character of the drugs is essential. The female are used principally for sprinkling the army and the assagais, the male for treating diseases. We find here again the law of opposition of sexes ; the military domain is the male domain par excellence : it must be treated by means of female drugs. On the contrary, when slaughtering a she-goat for the sacrifice, a little of the male drugs must be placed in its mouth and the weapon used to kill it must be smeared with the same, and vice-versa for the he-goat. "To act otherwise is taboo. All the ñanga do this" (p. 417).

There may be some true scientific elements in Thonga medical practice. Experiments have been made in using certain roots to cure certain diseases, and tradition has handed down some prescriptions from father to son. Why should there not be effective curative properties in plants of their country just as in the Cinchona bark, or in Castor oil seeds? And why should they not have discovered them? However the Native ñanga is by no means a scientific man, and the best, the most renowned, are perhaps the least scientific. Those who treat only one complaint, and only know one drug, are perhaps those most resembling real physicians ; they act on the results of experiment. But the line between science and superstition is very soon crossed, and the medical art passes with the greatest ease into the domain of magic, all the more so as the difference between Science and Magic is not perceived. *Muri*, which means originally tree, plant, medicinal herb, is at the same time any means of producing any effect, natural or supernatural, on any influence, hostile or favourable, personal or impersonal (1). That is why the *ntjebe* shrub helps Mankhelu to attain three objects at the same time : cure a bad cough, protect the mealies, and rout the enemy.

The question has often been put : Are these medicine-men sincere? or are they mere quacks living on the stupidity of the patients whom they deceive? I am convinced, after having listened to their talk, that most of them thoroughly believe in the value of their drugs ; this does not prevent them from occasionally using tricks in order to impress their patients with their miraculous power. One of my pupils, who had accompanied a ñanga for a long time, wishing to enter the profession himself, and had thus had an opportunity to watch his master in his medical work, assured me that, as a rule, the man administered his drugs honestly and in good faith ; but if somebody came suffering from toothache and asked for relief, the doctor first procured a little worm found in the berry of a solaneous shrub called rulane. This he placed in a pot filled with boiling water. The patient had then to inhale the vapour from the pot, his head being covered with a cloth. When the inhalation was over the ñanga took a piece of charcoal and rubbed his forehead with it ; he did the same all round his eyes and told him : "Now your eyes are open and you will be able to see what it was that caused your suffering." He emptied the pot and the little white worm appeared at the bottom, resembling the caries of a decaying tooth : "This is what they had brought on you" the ñanga would add." ("They" evidently means the wizards.) This is clearly a trick pure and simple. But, according to my informant, it was also a medical treatment, because the aim of the trick was to convince the patient that he had been cured. It was thus what we should call a means of suggestion. If, after that, the suffering did not cease, the ñanga would tell his patient that he had not paid enough to effect the cure, that his ancestor-gods (those of the ñanga, who had given him his drugs) were angry at receiving such a small fee, etc. The trick of making patients believe that a harmful object has been extracted from their body is frequently used. We have

(1) The following story, which I owe to one of my colleagues, fittingly illustrates the ideas held by most of the Thongas concerning *muri*, remedy. A man of the Libombo clan found a bottle filled with a white salt which he at once recognized as being most probably a *muri*. He picked up the bottle and kept it carefully in his hut. One day, feeling unwell, he thought the occasion had come to use his precious drug. His wife bade him be careful, but he secretly swallowed a good dose. Was it not a *muri* ? He was poisoned, and would have died if my colleague had not succeeded in saving him by means of an antidote.

seen another instance of this (p. 188). It is in keeping with two ideas which are very familiar to Natives and which we shall meet with again later, viz. that disease is a material thing and that it is generally caused by this thing being introduced into the body by wizards.

The mixed character of the medical art of the primitives, which is so evident in their medicine-men, will appear clearly as we continue our study.

II. *Medical Practices.*

Surgical cases are treated in the worst possible way, any intervention with a knife being looked on as absurd, if not culpable (1). When dealing with *sores*, the aim of the ñanga seems to be to conceal them under a black powder, so as to give the patient a false impression; he thinks himself healed, as he can no longer see his sore. Mankhelu used to grind the bark of the *Ndjupfura* tree (a tree with a white sap), and put the powder on the sore to make it dry up, renewing the application on the fourth day, then five days later, then six days later. — For *wounds* Kokolo used the sap of the *Shilangamahlo*, letting it fall in drops on the bleeding wound. The *Nkahlu* (p. 329), with its milky sap, is commonly used for this purpose. — "But," says Kokolo, "the chief is *Shilangamahlo*." *Bruises* are treated by the *rimba* method. When a person has fallen and some complication is feared, a fire is made; when there are enough glowing embers, and the soil is very hot, the ashes are pushed aside and a little sand taken from the river is poured on the spot, and some nkuhlu leaves on top of it. The patient leans over the place "which has been so treated;" this is an unexpected application of the principle "similia similibus curantur;" — as the soil has been burnt, but afterwards "quenched" (timula) by the cool sand, so the bruise will be prevented from burning him dangerously! — *Decayed teeth* are not extracted, properly speaking; they are broken down with a piece of iron, on which the Native dentist beats with a hammer

(1) Gungunyana, who killed thousands of poor Ba-Chopi without the slightest remorse, could not conceal his horror of Dr. Liengme, who dared to amputate limbs, or to cut open the body in order to cure patients!

until he has removed as much as he can of the tooth! Sometimes
he breaks the jaw also ; the jaw may even pass through the cheek,
causing a frightful wound! Once one of my colleagues had to
perform the operation of the removal of the inferior maxillary bone,
which was protruding as the result of the so-called extraction of a
tooth by a ñanga! — *Snake bites* are treated with a powder made
of a snake burnt to ashes, and some ingredients mixed with it,
the whole being *salted* with common salt. Incisions are made in
all the joints, wrist, ankle, elbow, and also in front of the neck, and
the powder introduced into them. Children are inoculated as a
means of prevention, so that, when bitten, the venom will not
affect them ; the doctor has "preceded the snake" (yi yi rangerile).

Medical cases are generally treated more rationally than surgical
cases. Here are some of Kokolo's and Spoon's prescriptions.

To begin with the drug used when one "feels his head," in other
words has a *headache* ; this is the root of a shrub called *Nhlangula*,
which seems to be a regular anaesthetic, and is used as follows.
The fresh bark is scraped with a knife, and a certain quantity is
folded up in a cloth and applied to the forehead for half a day.
In case of *toothache* the same drug is used together with another
called *Ndjenga* : they are boiled ; a little of the decoction thus
obtained is held in the mouth, and the pain should disappear.

When it "bites inside," that is to say when one suffers from
colic or looseness of the bowels, the remedy is *Munwangati*,
Shimbyati and *Shidlanyoka* made up into a bunch. The doctor
prepares this medicine with great care, cutting the roots into equal
lengths and tying them together with a band of palm leaf. (See
illustration, No. 2.) He concocts his remedy with a larger
quantity of the roots of the milder type, and only a few pieces
of those which act more violently. The bunch called *shitsimbo*
is then boiled to bring out the active principles of the drugs, and
the decoction is taken by the patient, just as it is. Sometimes
it is mixed with maize, when preparing the meal, and taken in
that way. As the bunch, or packet, of these roots retains its
medicinal properties for a long time, a single packet may be
used over and over again during a whole week.

The prescription for *dysentery* is as follows : *Shimbyati, Shi-*

459

dlambangi, Likalahumba, Nkonono (Terminalia sericea) and *Nsala* (Strychnos spinosa). That for *bronchitis*, or for a cold in the head, is *Menyomamba, Mphesu* (a kind of mimosa, Albizzia versicolor) *Shongwe, Ntshatshe* (a papilionaceous shrub), *Gowane* (Zygia fastigiata, a large mimosa) and *Muhlandlopfu*. The last is a very powerful drug ; the last but one less so. For *hydrocele* the following are used : *Lihlehlwa, Ntshatshe, Nkonono, Mamuntana*.

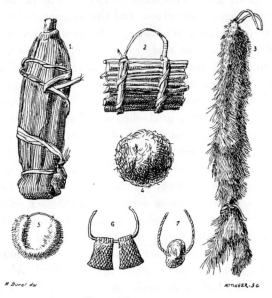

Thonga Pharmacopoeia.

1. Box made of maize bracts, containing medicine. 2. Shitsimbo. 3. Skin of a mole, containing powdered drugs. 4. Pill (Mhula). 5. Bracelet of *tjukunyana*. 6. *Timfisa*, amulets. 7. *Sungi* root tied round the ankle.

The Natives regard this complaint as contagious, and as being transmitted by matrimonial relations.

I obtained two *purgatives* from my Native doctors. The first is *an aloe*, or cactus, a species of which grows plentifully on the sand dunes. The sap is squeezed on to grains of millet or sorghum, which are kept in neatly constructed boxes of maize leaves ; these are made by plucking an ear of maize, breaking off the cob and leaving the large bracts which enclose it and which adhere to the stalk at its base. This is a very primitive receptacle, and easily procurable (No. 1). The medicine is thus kept until required for use, when it is ground to a powder and taken in water. The second of these purgatives is the bark of a tree growing in the Nkomati valley in the Khosen country. This is the one, already alluded to, which was appropriated by one of our Christians, named Eliashib, who administered it to the Rikatla folk in such generous doses that it generally did more harm than good.

Three or four other roots form part of the packet for children ; these are called, as previously explained (I. p. 48), by the general term milombyana, medicines to promote the growth of newly-born infants. If an intestinal parasite be expelled by *dlanyoka*, it is burnt to cinders and reduced to a powder ; an incision is made in the belly and loins of the child, into which the powder is rubbed. This is a kind of inoculation, a further application of the principle "like cures like."

The packet used for treating *haematuria* contains six drugs : *Humbutlo, Ntshopfa, Shintitana* (an Apocynea shrub related to the Artabotrys, p. 330), *Likalahumba, Ndjindjila* and *Shimbyati*. According to doctor's directions these are boiled in a pot with beans ; after a while the packet is taken out. The patient must then transfix one bean with a thorn and throw it over his left shoulder ; he pierces a second in the same way and throws it over his right shoulder, then a third, which he swallows. The first two beans are used to "try the earth," that is to say, to propitiate the several evil influences existing in the soil, which have probably been the cause of the illness. Such is the first part of the treatment. The second part consists in pounding large white tubers (something like elongated potatoes) in a mortar. The paste thus obtained is squeezed into a jar, and the patient must take this juice as well as the beans, seasoned as aforesaid! Every evening he must drink a cup of the bitter mixture (the packet broth), and also a cup of the sweet medicine made from the tubers. If, after this, the haematuria does not stop, the patient will be given a *phungulo*, a turkish bath, which I shall describe later on. The foregoing is Spoon's method of treatment. — Dr. Kokolo had another cure for the same complaint ; he used *Shirole, Nembe-nembe, Likumba-kumba* and *Nhlanhlana*, which he recommended to be taken in the usual way as a tisane, cutting them up in small pieces in a pot. They are roasted on a brazier and the smoke inhaled through a hollow reed ; the carbonised pieces are ground to a powder which is mixed with ordinary food. A curious fact to be noted with regard to this complaint is that the patient's wife, if he be married, has to undergo the same treatment. — *Gonorrhea* is treated with *Shilangamahlo, Hlahlana, Nembe-nembe* (Cassia petersiana) and *Ntinti* (Artabotrys Monteiroi). If necessary *Shimbyati* is added as an adjuvant. It is with the leaves of this latter plant that Kokolo made the huge pill which he presented to me (No. 4).

For the last named illness, as for haematuria, if internal treatment does not suffice, a more efficacious method "for outward application only," is resorted to. A certain number of roots will be burned and pulverised, the black powder thus obtained being mixed with fat taken from the paunch of an ox. This is rolled up into a ball and placed on red-hot embers, and the patient must expose the part affected to the heat thrown out, and to the smoke thus engendered.

Fever is not considered very dangerous by the Thongas, and strange to say, has no special name. It is called "to feel one's head", or "to have a hot body". Natives are so accustomed to it, and its attacks are generally so mild, that they do not take much heed of it. They lie on the ground, exposed to the burning sun, wrapped in a blanket, and perspire to their heart's content. "Take the root of *Mbalatangati*, cook it in a little pot and drink it with a spoon ; you will have a good sleep," says Mankhelu.

Consumption (lifuba) is treated as follows by Mankhelu. Part of the lungs of a crocodile, and of a sheep, is mixed with fat taken from a gnu and a root of the *Khawa* tree. All the ingredients are burnt in a broken pot and the patient must inhale the smoke through a reed ; this will dry up his chest, because the fat of the gnu is always dry and cannot melt!

Leprosy, "the vanquisher of physicians," is treated by some specialists. There was one near Rikatla, but he absolutely refused to communicate his secret. He belonged to the Chopi tribe. The Ba-Pedi forbid sexual relations to lepers.

A nursing woman who has no milk must take a certain Euphorbiacea shrub called *nete*, containing a milky juice, crush it in the mortar, cook it in water and drink it. When a cow refuses to feed her calf Natives smear the calf with the *ribvumbara* herb, which has a pleasant odour. The cow smells this, and allows the calf to suck.

The treatment of *sterility* has already been described (I. p. 190) Mankhelu tried to cure it by digging a root of *Nembe-nembe* and one of *Nhlangowume* ; he cooked both together, and ordered the woman to eat them during a period of six days, mixing them with her food. This drug was considered as "closing her" (pfala), so that she would no longer have her "tihweti, "and thus be enabled to conceive. In the meantime, she had to undergo the horola or hondlola rite, which I shall describe presently.

Small-pox, nyedzane, was on several occasions introduced by the Whites, or by the Zulu armies on their return from their Northern raids. There have been at least five or six epidemics in the neighbourhood of Lourenço Marques during the last fifty years. I had the opportunity of witnessing the last in 1918 in Rikatla and thus obtained first-hand information on the way Natives treat this disease and on their strange ideas concerning it. I published a detailed account of these in the S. A. *Journal of Science*, July 1919, and will give here a description of the most important of these *customs connected with small-pox amongst the Ba-Ronga*. When small-pox has invaded the country and reached the borders of the territory of a clan, the headmen assemble at the chief's residence and decide to proceed to the general inoculation of the population. This is a remedy which they have long been accustomed to use. They have noticed that the disease is milder when produced by inoculation with the virus than when it *hahela*, i. e. flies to the person. (There is some truth in this assertion ; the protection afforded however is not very effective, and severe and even fatal cases often follow the inoculation. It does not always secure immunity from a second attack.) The virus is provided by the people of a neighbouring clan who have already been attacked by the disease, and it is the *batukulu* of the chief, his nephews, the sons of his sisters, who are sent to procure it. Are they not the favourites of their maternal uncle? (I. p. 222). Nobody could suspect them of bringing misfortune into the village of their *bakokwana*! The particular ntukulu who must render this service to the country is designated by the bones. The bones also indicate the village of the neighbouring clan to which he must go to fetch the virus. The serous fluid is taken from old people or from children, who have no sexual intercourse ; we already know the reason for this. The ntukulu inoculates himself and his comrades and returns home ; when their pustules are ripe, they inoculate all the members of the clan who have not yet suffered from the disease. From this day begins for the whole clan a distinct marginal period, with all the taboos accompanying the critical phases of the life of the community. No one is allowed to wash his body. Absolute continence is imposed on all. Salt is prohibited, as it is said to make the blood flow more quickly in the body and it may cause the wounds to become sore.

But in addition to the ordinary taboos, some other measures are taken which are dictated by the special nature of small-pox. This disease, amongst Black people, manifests itself in two forms, which may be called the white and the black. The former is much milder than the latter. In it the pustules are large, superficial, scattered all over the body and well separated from each other ; the skin is discoloured over them and becomes whitish ; they soon dry up and do not leave deep marks. In the second form, which is the confluent and haemorrhagic type of the disease, the pustules are small, black, continuous with each other, and full of blood ; they soon discharge a nasty fluid ; fever is high and death may intervene. The whole aim of the treatment is to promote the mild, white form of small-pox and to prevent the black form. It is therefore taboo to eat any meat containing blood, which is black and must therefore be avoided. On the contrary, fish meat is allowed because it is white and contains no dark blood. Another device of Native doctors to obtain this result is to place before the eyes of their patients grains of mealies, which are white like the desired pustules and are also similar to them in form, and to prevent their

seeing grains of Kafir corn, which are of a dark colour. Grains of
mealies are softened in water, pierced through and made into
necklaces which patients wear round their necks, whilst the spikes
of Kafir corn, which are to be found in every hut fixed to the reeds
of the roof as seeds for the next season, are carefully taken away and
hidden somewhere in the bush during the whole time of the
epidemic. Should the malignant form of small-pox develop
notwithstanding all these precautions, the headman will shake his
head and tell the parents of the patient : "Hahlani! — Make an
offering." But in this particular hahla no real offering will be
made, and the prayer will not be addressed to the ancestor-gods.
The principal words of this prayer are : "Mavuzane, dhlula!"
These are Zulu expressions which correspond in Ronga to :
"Mabutise, tlula!" i. e. "Questioner, pass on your way!" Who is
this Questioner? It is small-pox itself, Nyedzana, which is more or
less personified and looked on as a real and terrible visitor coming
at given intervals to examine the country and search for sinners.
The great sin which Questioner especially wishes to discover is
buloyi, murder by witchcraft. Let the patient then confess the
acts of bewitchment which he has committed, and he will be
spared. If he conceals them, small-pox will kill him. Suppose
that the patient so seriously ill is a grown-up woman, the wife of one
of the men of the village. Her parents will first be called. The
headman and all the inmates of the village will attend the meeting
in the hut. "Confess your guilt!" they will all say to the woman.
She may answer : "No! I am not a witch" *(A ndi noyi!)* They
insist : "Do not hide anything." And under the strain of their
questions she may say : "Yes! I am a walker in the night! I have
eaten so-and-so! I have eaten my own child!" If the patient is a
little child, his father will have to make the confession in his stead.
He will take the infant in his arms and say : "Mavuzane dhlula!
Questioner, pass on your way! Yes! We are baloyi. I have
taught my child to eat human bodies! But we will not persist in
our bad doings! Go away and leave us in peace!" (1).

(1) We have here one of the cases in which an impersonal force of Nature is treated as
if it were a personal being endowed with superhuman power, and invoked. The prayer

When the disease has run its course, and the pustules have dried up, a day is appointed on which the marginal period will come to an end, and the clan return to its regular life. This return is marked by the special *Reintegration and Purification rites*, which aim at removing the defilement acquired by the disease. The main purificatory rite, that which regularly closes a marginal period, is *the smearing of all the huts* with a new layer of clay, either mixed with cow's dung or not. The old ground is for ever covered. It is a way of saying : "Behold, the former things are passed away, everything has become new." On the morning of that day, every patient must go and wash his body *on the road*, as if to pour all the filth of the disease on to it. Moreover, the ashes found in the fire-places inside the huts, the necklaces of mealie grains, the implements used by the people who have been seriously ill, sometimes their garments, the ochre with which they anointed themselves, all the things which were employed in connection with the scourge, are collected and thrown indiscriminately on to the large paths, preferably on the places where two roads cross each other, a rite which is by no means altruistic, and still less antiseptic! We shall see shortly how it is to be explained.

Nervous diseases are peculiarly feared by Natives. *Melancholia* is believed to be caused by those spirits of possession which will form the subject of the next paragraph. *Idiocy* has no remedy ; nothing can be done with an idiot : "It is death! It has found him!" (Mankhelu). *Delirium* (mihahamo) is cured by *Mbulula khutla*. The patient must enter the hole from which clay is taken for smearing the huts, and is washed with a decoction of the drug when in this hole. Moreover a stick of the same tree is cut and kept in the roof of the hut, and the person who sleeps with the patient will take it every night and place it near his head. "Thus we kill delirium." (Mankhelu). — Another form of insanity is called *rihuhe*, "the disease which comes from far away with the winds" — "ri pfa timhehwen" (Mankhelu). A drug is prepared with the *shiromo* root, mixed with the lung of a sheep and the blood

to Small-Pox (with capital letters) may be compared with that pronounced when an imprecation has been uttered or when someone wishes to cancel his oath (p. 399).

found inside its heart.   All these things are burnt in a broken pot, and made into a medicinal powder.   The patient is brought to the broken pot ; a cut is made in his head, so that it bleeds abundantly until the pot is filled with blood ; the blood boils in the pot, it solidifies and is burnt.   The ñanga takes it and buries it in an ant's nest, according to the timula rite described below.   The wound of the patient is filled with the medicine ; he eats the meat, he sleeps : — "If you have been equal to the occasion, he will be cured ; you have given him lots of sleep. — You have killed the *rihuhe*" (Mankhelu).   The *wutleka* disease means both the *convulsions* of little children generally explained by the agency of Heaven, called Tilo (p. 431), and epilepsy.   The great remedy for the latter disease, which greatly terrifies the Natives, is provided by monkeys and baboons.   Pieces of their skin and their excrement are roasted in a broken pot.   Some pieces of lion's skin are added ; when the powder is prepared, the limbs of the patient are smeared with it ; his body is also sprinkled with a decoction made of these drugs, or an ointment is prepared from them and applied to the head, the fingers, and all the limbs, which are then pulled with some force (olola).   The patient is laid down and leaves of the hlampfura tree (Kigelia pinnata) are put on his head : — "He sleeps, he passes water, he evacuates stools, he is cured!"   But to confirm the healing, a very curious ceremony is performed which reminds one of the rite of the scapegoat, so often met with amongst primitives. The doctor makes the image of a monkey (habu) with a kind of grass called *muhulane* ; this image is smeared with the drugs just described, and fastened to a long rope ; a little boy must then drag the dummy out of the village, and all his comrades hit him with sticks, saying : "Go away!   Go away!"   He runs until he reaches a tree far away in the bush.   All the boys hang the figure to it, and it remains there swinging in the wind.   The disease has thus been expelled.

When folly is accompanied by great excitement, and there is danger of the people of the village being mishandled by the sufferer, he is prevented from doing harm by means of fetters.   These consist of a log of wood pierced through by a lozenge-shaped hole into which the foot of the madman is introduced ; a wooden bolt is then fixed across the hole in such a way that he will be unable to withdraw it. When he wishes to walk he is obliged to drag along the heavy log. He very soon loses his strength, being ill-fed, and covered with vermin, and dies in a terrible condition.

*

* *

In our study of these various treatments, we have met with about twenty different prescriptions of Native physicians, containing, in all, some 40 to 50 different drugs, to be made use of in various ways : outward application, inhalation, fumigation, infusion, decoction, inoculation, manducation of carbonised or pulverised drugs, etc. We are then entitled to assert that, up to a certain point, the Blacks do possess an *ars medica*. To complete our review of medical matters, I must further mention a few curious practices of the Thonga doctors, which forcibly remind us of those to which our own practitioners sometimes have recourse.

Let us begin with *cupping*. A full account of this will be found in the story of the ",Gambadeur de la Plaine" (*Chants et Contes des Ba-Ronga*, page 357) where a young girl resuscitates a buffalo by performing this operation. She proceeds as follows. Water is boiled and in it is placed the packet of roots required ; a spot in the temporal region is carefully washed, and a few incisions are made with a razor (likari). A particular horn (nhluku ya ku lumeka), which is open at both ends, is placed over the incisions and the operator, putting his mouth to the horn, draws in his breath, causing the blood to flow freely. The wound is then exposed to the vapour emanating from the boiling *shitsimbo* packet, and smeared with a particular ointment, kept in a calabash.

The next in order of the practices which we are noticing, is the *phungulo* (Dj.), or *hungulo* (Ro.), a kind of *Turkish or vapour bath*, which is administered in certain complaints and also after the funeral rites, in order to remove the contamination of death (I. p. 145). A circular enclosure is made, with a screen of matting, in the middle of which the patient is placed, and, close by him, on live embers, a pot containing leaves which are supposed to possess medicinal properties. A second mat is then spread over the top of the enclosure, thus shutting the patient up in a sort of small hut. The smoke from the live embers makes him cough terribly. The hot vapour from the pot induces profuse perspiration from every pore, and the victim of this treatment is left for a very considerable time in this intensely uncomfortable condition! When, at length, the remedy is supposed to have had sufficient time to act efficaciously, the mats are removed. The patient suddenly finds himself in the open air, absolutely dripping with perspiration. I saw a man remain in this condition, in the chill of the evening, apparently risking inflamation of the lungs. The doctor rubs his cheeks, or some other parts of his body, with either a white or a black powder. Such is the Thonga Turkish bath, which is frequently referred to in their folklore. — The phungulo is administered in most cases where ritual defilement is feared, or is believed to have caused the disease. The kind of poisoning caused by the impurities connected with death, menses, lochia, etc., manifests itself by swelling of the joints, of the hands and feet, pains in the bones, etc. This vapour bath is also resorted to in order to cure married people who do not succeed in having children. The physician makes for them a shitsimbo packet of the following roots : *Nhlangawume, Mpoñwana, Ritiyi* ; he cooks this in the pot inside the mat enclosure ; and into the fire, under the pot, he puts part of the flesh of the goat which has been sacrificed for the occasion, in particular the uterus. This flesh has been previously smeared with drugs. So, by means either of the vapour, or of the smoke, the medicine enters the patients. "Ba wupfa," — "they ripen" or "are cooked." When the mat is removed, a pot full of cold water is poured over them and extinguishes the phungulo which has "cooked them." They will have to take home the meat, and cook it in their hut together with the packet of roots. Another packet is put into the pot in which they keep their beer.

A third practice, quite as old as the foregoing, is the *tlhema* or *cautery*. This may be done with a packet of roots, which are heated and applied to the part affected. But, as a general rule, cautery is done *with the foot*. This is undoubtedly a curious proceeding! Kokolo gave me a detailed description of it. A hoe is made red-hot; an obliging individual lends his foot, a foot which has rarely been encased in a shoe and possesses a sole with a skin like leather! This natural sole is rubbed with the leaves of a plant called *Shungwe*, which has been chewed and mixed in the palm of the hand with saliva and grease. For the same purpose Mankhelu employed a fat containing among other ingredients, the following drugs: *Hlampfura* and *Ñwambula-wamitwa*. Then the obliging operator places his foot on the red-hot hoe and, with a quick movement, plants it on the spot to be cauterised, the patient being hardly able to bear the contact. As for the owner of the foot, the horny sole is apparently so thick that he feels no pain at all. This is the remedy for the *shitjebe blood*, probably pleurisy.

The last practice to be noticed, the one by which the doctor gives his patient a clean bill of health, is the *hondlola* or *hondla* (Ro.) or *horola* (Dj.); it is a ceremony of purification, performed *after the cure is effected*, to remove the defilement (nsila) of disease. "In this way," says Mankhelu, "we disperse (hulurisa) the blood which has made the patient ill, so that it cannot return to him violently." The hondla is obligatory after all serious diseases and after weaning. I have described how it is performed in this latter case (I. p. 59). According to Mankhelu, a sacrifice is always made in connection with the hondlola. In the case of adults, a goat is slaughtered. The doctor having carefully taken a piece of each limb of the goat, prays "by means of them" to his gods, saying:

You so and so! This is my ox which I have slaughtered... Give me strength (ndji thwasane matimba) that I may cure this man. I have no other drugs! I do not add any others to those which you gave me. So give me strength; accept me with both hands, that I may be able to cure.

The psanyi of the goat is then mixed with various drugs, especially the *Shireti* and the powder of the calabashes. The patient, sitting on a mat, rubs his whole body (tihorola) vigorously with this psanyi; all the particles (timhore, or timhorola, or timbhorola) which fall on the mat are carefully gathered together, and the bones are consulted to know where they must be thrown (See Letter D). This is the *tumba* rite, following the hondḻola. The bones may perhaps have indicated a hole in the trunk of a tree, or the river, or the mud of the marsh, or an ants' nest, or the entrance to a molehill. The physician takes the timbhorola in a piece of broken pot, or sala shell, and introduces them into the hole, which he closes with a little clay ; he has with him water in a little calabash, of which he takes a sip and says : "Tsuu! or

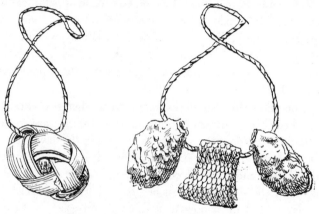

Fowa and timfisa, medico-magical amulets.

pheuuu! Let the misfortune remain here." On the way home no looking back is allowed : this is taboo. Should the tumba be made in an ants' nest, and should the ants themselves close the hole, this is a very good sign! The bones may perhaps order the particles contained in the sala shell to be placed in another kind of ants' nest, made of grass ; the ñanga will go during the day and prepare a place for the shell. In the evening, when it is dark, he will put the shell into the hole without looking back towards it. The ants will take all the timbhorola down into their nest, and so "the misfortune will remain with them." (Mboza.) — The hondḻola rite is generally accompanied by the preparation of *protective amulets (timfisa)*. The nails and hair of the patient are cut, put into small bags of lizard skin and tied round his neck.

471

One frequently meets people wearing this ornament, which also aims at making the cure permanent. Sometimes the nails are those from one hand and foot only. The *psirungulo* i. e. the astragalus of the slaughtered goat, or the beak, claws and some feathers of the hen (p. 410) are also tied round the neck of the patient. This is the *religious amulet*, whilst the lizard bag is the *medico-magical* one. Convalescents are moreover provided with the *fowa*, a kind of rattle, consisting of a root called *sungi* (there is no connection between this word and the sungi of the circumcision school, I. p. 77) contained in a kind of round box made of palm leaf which is tied round the ankle. This is intended to protect them against the perspiration of those who have sexual relations (p. 358). They sometimes wear a little piece of reed filled with a protective powder, as do also nursing mothers during the whole nursing period (1) (I. p. 48).

The hondlola rite also marks the moment when sexual relations, which had been suspended during the disease, are resumed Celebrating as it does the victory over disease, the day of hondlola is regarded as a fête-day. Beer is prepared as a mark of gratitude to the doctor and "to rejoice his heart." It is also the day of reckoning ; the physician must be paid. This individual has not, however, waited until now to ask for a "refresher." From the commencement of the case it has been necessary to *pfula hwama*, that is to say, to lift the cover of the medicine wallet by means of sixpence or a shilling. At times he has been very anxious to change the medicine, in order to produce a greater effect ; on such

---

(1) I may here mention two other articles which are frequently worn by Thonga Natives : one is the dried seed-pod of the flower of the large Protea bush (sugar bush) which is so common on the slopes of the Drakensberg. It looks like a hard brownish cone, all covered with concentric layers of little square ledges. This cures *verti o*. Why ? No doubt because when it is turned round rapidly, it makes the spectator giddy. It is hung round the neck with a string. This curious remedy is brought back from the Barberton mountains by those who go to work in the Transvaal. The second is a bracelet often seen round little children's wrists, and is made from the skin of a kind of tawny mole, called *tjukunyana*, which digs its burrows almost on the level of the ground. You can see the earth a little raised all along its track. The *Filaria* parasite, which is often met with in our tribe, also creeps under the skin in a similar way (p. 343). See illustration No. 5. These are two new instances of the principle "similia similibus curantur." Bags filled with snake powder are also often worn as a preventive.

occasions he has been presented with a chicken as an encouragment; but on the day of the hondlola, when his skill is joyfully affirmed, and the cure an accomplished fact, accounts must be definitely settled with the ñanga, who will henceforth discontinue his visits.

III. Conception of Disease.

The preceding details make it possible for us to understand the conceptions which underlie these rites and ceremonies. Possessing as they do so few and such inaccurate notions regarding Anatomy or Physiology, it is not surprising that correct pathological knowledge is absolutely non-existent amongst South African Bantus. In fact this knowledge is both superficial and superstitious. I shall try to prove this by a study of the *names* given to the diseases, the *causes* to which they are attributed, the *notion* of contagion, and the ideas underlying the *rites which mark the end of a disease*.

1) As regards the method of *naming diseases*, it is most childish. Thongas call the complaint from which they suffer by the name of the organ affected ; for instance "I have a foot, I have a hand, I have a neck" (ndji ni nenge, boko, nkolo) means "I have a pain in my foot, my hand or my neck." These curious expressions doubtless arise from the fact that no notice is taken of the existence of any particular organ until something goes wrong with it. "He has a head" means "He is mad." For "I have a headache," the expression "ndji yingela nhloko," meaning "I feel my head," would generally be used. Very often one hears complaints of "a blood" (ngati) which moves from spot to spot, finally taking up its abode in the side or in the stomach, or elsewhere. This is an idea similar to that of the morbid humours of olden days. There are then as many diseases as there are organs, and we are often asked for remedies for the "nape of the neck complaint," or for the "inside trouble." This latter might be gastritis, congestion of the liver, or dysentery, and we should often be wholly at a loss how to prescribe were it not for the highly picturesque, and often particularly appropriate, imagery used by the patients, or by their friends, in describing the various symptoms ; for instance when

473

a sufferer from "inside trouble" says that "it bites" (luma), we know that it is a case of intestinal colic. But it becomes somewhat puzzling when a patient declares that he suffers from an intestinal worm which passes from his stomach into his neck and returns through his lungs, when it does not happen to take a fancy to remain in his head! "It makes a sound like *pfie...pfie...*," said an old man to me when describing this animal, which plays an important part in the medical science of the Natives (1). (I. p. 48.)

There are, however, certain technical terms which are used to designate some diseases ; thus *mukuhlwana* means cough and the mucous catarrh of the throat and nose. The ordinary *mbukulu* seems to be tonsilitis, while the special *mbukulu* is an affliction accompanied by fever, vertigo, delirium and madness, which is generally attributed to the malign influences of the spirits of the departed. — Hydrocele *(masangu,* or *masenge)* is wide-spread and well-known, as is also bilharzia, a form of haematuria called *shinyalu* or *ndjundjwane,* which appears in severe forms and is due to a special parasite. Rheumatism is called *shifambo,* the runner, as it moves from spot to spot. Syphilis, imported long ago by Europeans, is universally known, and is, alas, so general in the neighbourhood of the town of Lourenço Marques that almost all Natives suffer from it. The Natives call it *buba* (probably from bubo). Gonorrhea is of more recent importation, and dates — according to my informant Tobane — from the time of the construction of the Pretoria Railway ; it is called *shikandjameti,* the disease which crushes the villages.

The eruptive diseases are perhaps those best recognized by the Natives. *Shintshinana* is the name for measles, but seems also applicable to scarlet fever. Small-pox is called *nyedzana,* and, as regards psychic or nervous troubles, the treatment of which

---

(1) I may here mention that the tape worm and the lumbric, both called *tinyokana,* small snakes, are very common amongst Natives, and are well known to them. They even think that these worms are necessary for digestion. An old woman had asked one of my colleagues to give her a vermifuge, and the drug had been successful. But she came back to ask him to give her another medicine to prevent all the inhabitants from escaping. Some of them must remain in her body "because," as the old woman said, "who would eat my food afterwards" ?

we have just studied, they are attributed either to Heaven or to evil spirits or to the winds. The name of the *wutleka* disease is worthy of notice. This word comes from *wutla*, which means to rob, to seize ; wutleka, the qualificative derivative (Thonga Grammar § 196) means the condition of something taken away. This would seem to be a passive meaning, as if the patient had been robbed by some agent. However, Mankhelu explains the term by saying : "The patient has stolen the *rirabi*" — "a wutle rirabi". *Rirabi* is very closely allied to a word meaning stick ; the old doctor says it is the name of the disease. If this etymology be correct the patient would be considered as having taken the disease by a kind of robbery. But Native etymology must always be accepted with caution.

All these names show how unprecise is the pathological knowledge of the Thongas.

2) As regards the *causes of diseases*, Thongas are groping in the grossest superstition. When a medical man wishes to treat a disease, he first tries to diagnose its cause. The Bantu nanga does the same, only the difference is that he takes very little notice of the physical symptoms. There is no auscultation, no palpation, no examination of the secretions, blood, saliva, or urine, as these are disgusting and must be covered with sand as soon as possible! The great means of diagnosing a disease is the throwing of bones. There are three great causes of disease : the spirits of the gods, the wizards and the makhumo, defilement from death or from impure persons. A fourth less common cause is Heaven. The bones will reveal by the way in which they fall which is the one to be combated.

3) Their ideas of *contagion* are not much in advance of their other pathological conceptions. The two most dreaded diseases in this respect are consumption (lifuba) and leprosy (nhlokonho). *Consumption* is by no means a new ailment due to civilisation, though it has increased enormously since Thonga boys have gone to the towns. A proof that it has been known for a long time is to be found in its great importance in the ritual. To the Thonga mind it is caused by the *makhumo*, i. e., the contamination of death, or the defilement resulting from contact with a woman in

a state of physiological impurity. Hence the law ordering
people affected with any of these kinds of makhumo to eat with
spoons ; they thus protect themselves against the poison which
might cause them to become consumptive. A curious feature in
the conception of *contagion* is the following. When Sokis died
(I. p. 139) I heard some of those present saying to his sister, who
was carrying a child on her shoulders : "Do not cry! If you cry
the disease will jump to your baby!" There were two reasons
for this warning ; to cry in the presence of misfortune increases
the danger tenfold (compare p. 326) ; moreover the contagion of
disease is especially to be feared in connection with the relatives
of the sick or dead person. Hence the strange custom illustrated
on plate p. 26 : when a man dies of consumption his relatives are
absolutely forbidden to eat any of the food he may have left. The
"luma milomo" ceremony (I. p. 146) is of no use in this case. In
former times all his mealies were burnt. Nowadays, however, it is
allowable for people outside his family to buy and consume his
provision. The large storehouse, illustrated on p. 26, contained
the mealies harvested in Sokis' fields. These were sold to
strangers, whilst relatives bought other mealies which were stored
in the small hut for the use of his widow and children (p. 111).
The same reason no doubt explains why the widow of a consumptive must *lahla khombo* with strangers, and not with men
of the village (I. p. 206).

This peculiar idea of contagion also gives rise to the rules
for *burying lepers*. Their relatives must not have anything to
do with the burial (I. p. 508). Relatives-in-law can perform
this painful duty, or possibly the family of the deceased leper
will ask a friend to help them in their distress. "Have you
prepared something as a reward for me?" he asks, and if this is the
case he digs a grave just outside the wall of the hut where the
patient died, removes the reeds of the wall, and pulls the corpse
down into the hole without any funeral ceremony. The relatives
are assembled far away on the square, and do not even dare to look
on at the burial. All the implements are broken in the depths of
the forest, at a great distance, for fear that a relative might touch
one of them and die. Or they are left in the hut, and the whole

village is at once removed. Leprosy is called *nhlulabadahi*, the disease which is stronger than the doctors. It is very much dreaded ; lepers are not, however, segregated ; they live in the village with other people and even attend beer-parties, but they bring their own mugs, whilst every other guest receives a drinking utensil from the master of the village.

Another disease which is believed to be contagious is "possession" by the *Bandjao spirits*. Should you pick up on the road some object which belonged to one of the possessed, his madness will jump to you (tlulela). — Epilepsy is also dreaded on that account. A nursing woman must not see any one suffering from an attack of this disease, or the child which is on her shoulders will become epileptic.

Speaking of the conception of disease, I must remind the reader of the fact that *sexual relations* between the inhabitants of the village are believed to aggravate the condition of the patient dwelling in it (I. p. 133, II. p. 358), and are consequently forbidden during epidemics and in any case of serious illness. Hence the precautions which convalescents must take of wearing the *sungi*, as we have just seen.

4) The special rites which mark the end of an illness throw much light on the Thonga conception of disease. A serious illness constitutes a marginal period either for the individual concerned, or, in the case of an epidemic, for the community, and the hondlola rite is the method by which the patient is reintegrated into society ; it clearly has the character of a passage rite. The rubbing with psanyi, the removal of the defilement of disease, the throwing away of the "timbhorola," the cutting of nails and hair, all these are rites of separation from the period of disease, whilst the feast of the hondlola day, and the resuming of sexual relations (1) are rites of reintegration. In the disease of possession, as we shall see, it is the reintegration into the society of spirit-possessed persons, and amounts to an initiation.

(1) We often hear of a Christian woman, who has gone to a heathen medicine-man for treatment, having sexual intercourse with him. We generally attribute this fact to immorality alone, but it was probably a part of the treatment, at the precise moment when sexual taboos were removed.

In the case of an epidemic, it is the whole clan which passe through the marginal period, and all its members have to perform the reintegration rites, by means of which they re-inter upon normal life.

But these rites have another meaning as well. They aim at "dispersing the disease." In the hondlola proper, the particles which have fallen on the mat during the rubbing operation are cast away into an ants' nest; this is the *tumba,* which corresponds to the throwing away of all the "nsila", i. e. the "filth" of the small-pox patients at a cross-roads. In this case the body of the patient is also washed at that spot ; this is likewise done at the conclusion of measles. The same idea underlies all these customs, that by their means the patient or clan will *definitely get rid of the disease.* Disease forms an organic whole, an important element of which consists of the dried perspiration of the patient, the dirt covering his skin, the implements he has used during his confinement, the dust of his hut, etc. All these are thrown either into an ants' nest to be disposed of there by the insects, or on to the road to be trampled under foot by travellers. The latter, by coming into contact with this filth, will at the same time take upon themselves the disease which it represents and carry it away into far distant countries. Thus the request of the medicine man will be granted, (I. p. 55, II. p. 393) : "Let the bad blood go to Nkhabelene, to Shiburi... to the ends of the earth." I do not think that in this apparently hostile act of throwing the dust of a contaminated hut on to the road Thongas are actuated by the wish that travellers should be infected with the disease. Their principal aim is to disperse the contagion according to the principles of communionist and imitative magic. It is however dangerous to tread upon it. It is one of those "makhumo" which can cause disease.

The medical system of the Bantus is mingled to such an extent with superstition and error that very little reliance can be placed upon it. The question which I put at the beginning of this section is therefore very difficult to answer. What is the duty of the White Government in regard to the Native quacks? The ideal would be to replace them by fully qualified, civilised doctors. As this is impossible, let medical missionaries at least be encouraged, and their number increased, and a medical course be open to educated Natives, if not a complete University course, at least such instruction as would allow them to treat their fellow men in a scientific manner, the medicine-men being gradually prevented from practising their very questionable art.

B. POSSESSION.

The curious psychic phenomenon which I am now about to describe belongs to the domain of medecine ; it is "the disease," or rather the "madness of the gods" (bubabyi bya psikwembu). But at the same time it bears a distinctly religious character, the spirits which are believed to cause the disease being *psi-kwembu*, spirits of deceased people, to whom worship will be addressed. On the other hand, the rites connected with the treatment of this kind of madness are definitely magical, and those who have suffered from it often become recognised magicians, claiming to possess supernatural powers.

This is a very interesting subject from the point of view of psychology and psychiatry. Phenomena of possession exist amongst most uncivilised races, even amongst more advanced peoples, and it would be useful to compare the manifestations of this disease amongst Bantus with those met with in other parts of the world. I shall however leave this task to professionals, and only try faithfully and clearly to describe and, if possible, to understand, the facts which I witnessed myself. This disease has spread enormously amongst the Thongas in the last fifty years. It is said to have been previously very rare, or even unknown ; since that time it has become quite an epidemic, although it is at the present moment rather on the decrease. Possession is more frequent amongst the Ba-Ronga than in the Northern clans.

I. *The Spirits which Cause the Disease.*

Strange to say, the gods or spirits which are credited with the power of possessing people, are not the ancestors of the Thongas themselves, the ancestor-gods, but Zulu spirits and those of the Ba-Ndjao tribe, who inhabit the country beyond the Sabie, as far as the neighbourhood of Beira. It appears that the possessions which first occurred were due to the Zulu and Ngoni spirits ; possibly they coincided with the invasion of the warriors of Manukosi, and with the ever-increasing exodus of young men who go to work in the diamond mines at Kimberley, or the gold mines at Johannesburg, or Natal, and travel through territory occupied by Zulus. As regards the Ba-Ndjao spirits they are sometimes called *amandiki*, and are said to have followed the Thonga and Ngoni soldiers of Gungunyana, who established themselves for some years at Mosapa, right in the middle of the Ndjao country, to the North of the Sabie, and who, later on, came down again from that mountainous region into the fertile plain of Bilene. (Lower Limpopo.) On the other hand, when the war of 1894 to 1895 compelled the Northern Ba-Ronga, those from Mabota, Zihlahla and Nondwane to flee, they took with them, so the story goes, the gods who had possessed them, and "scattered" them so thoroughly in the countries of the North that, when they returned to their own homes, they were no longer molested by these *psikwembu*. That is what I was told by a Native. We must carefully note, at the outset, these two ideas : the tormenting spirits are the *manes of strangers* and not of the people of the country, and they frequently attack Thongas who happen to be travelling in such countries, and follow them in their further migrations (1).

The Ndjao possessions appear to be worse than the Zulu. "Bundjao bya karata" — "the Ndjao possession is painful." If the incantations used are in Zulu for Zulu possessions, they are in the Ndjao language when such are caused by Ndjao spirits, and those who suffer from this affliction are known by the large white beads which they wear in their hair. Sometimes they have merely a short string of small beads, hanging down somewhere from the head. I well remember on the banks of a stream, in a

---

(1) However, in the case of Mholombo, the spirit was an old Tembe chief, a true ancestor, and in that of Nwashinhwana there was a throng of occupants, amongst them her own son, Manuel, who had died some time before. In the case of Mboza it was also a Ronga, but he had died in a foreign country (See later).

wooded valley called Nhlalalene, where we had made a halt during one of our journeyings, seeing a good-looking young woman wearing one of these curious ornaments. I was struck with the sight, and asked my companion why she was thus decorated. — "She invokes the spirits of the Ba-Ndjao," was the reply.

II. *Beginning and Diagnosis of the Disease.*

I have carefully studied the story of many cases of possession amongst the Ba-Ronga (See *Bulletin de la Société Neuchâteloise de Géographie*. Tome X, p. 388). Most of them began by a distinct crisis, in which the patient was unconscious, but this does not seem to have been brought about by any previous nervous trouble. A woman of the neighbourhood of Lourenço Marques, *Ñwashinhwana*, fled from her home and threw herself into the Bay. The contact with the cold water restored her to her senses, after which the bones declared that she had *psikwembu*. Another, *Mholombo*, heard a voice calling her during a dream ; it was the possessing spirit, which revealed itself later on as a chief long since dead. I will now give full details of the case of *Mboza*, who was himself possessed at one time, and later on became a regular exorcist. After having worked in Kimberley for some time, he returned home in good health. Soon afterwards, however, he became lame for six months. He attributed his difficulty in walking to rheumatism (shifambo). There was some improvement in his condition, but he began to feel other symptoms ; he lost his appetite and almost entirely ceased to eat. Here is his testimony : "One day, having gone with another young man to gather juncus, in order to manufacture a mat, the psikwembu suddenly started in me" (ndji sunguleka hi psikwembu psikañwe). I came back home, trembling in all my limbs. I entered the hut, but suddenly I rose to my feet and began to attack the people of the village ; then I ran away, followed by my friends, who seized me, and at once the spirits were scattered (hangalaka). When I became conscious again, I was told I had hurt a *khehla* (a man with the wax crown (I. p. 129), and had struck other people on their backs :

"Ha!" they said, "he has the gods (or he is sick from the gods, a ni psikwembu)." Thus the first signs of possession seem to be a nervous crisis, but also the occurence of certain suspicious symptoms : a persistant pain in the chest, irrepressible hiccough, unusual yawning, emaciation without apparent cause, etc. These symptoms, however, are not sufficient grounds for a diagnosis, and the bones are always consulted in order to arrive at a conclusion. The amulets of the patient (called "his shade") are placed on the mat, and the bones thrown near them. We shall see, under letter D, how they must fall to confirm the diagnosis. Should they do so, a second consultation takes place in order to ascertain to what doctor the treatment must be entrusted. There are medicine-men who are specialists for this disease. They are not true ñanga, but are called gobela (dji-ma), at least amongst the Ba-Ronga, who suffer from possession more than the other clans. These gobela have formed many rival schools in which the drugs used, and the rites followed, differ slightly ; the schools of Kkongosa, Sindondondo, Ñwatshulu, who are men, and those of Ñwamutheto (in the Shifimbatello district) and of Thambula-nyoka, viz., Snake-bone, both of whom are women, etc. Ñwashinhwana was treated by a disciple of Khongosa ; Mboza by Ñwatshulu.

III. *The Treatment of Possession, or Exorcism.*

In former times, the only remedy was waving a large palm-leaf (milala) in front of the patient. This was deemed sufficient to "scatter the spirits." Now the treatment is much more complicated. Though it varies slightly in the various schools above mentioned, it comprises four principal rites : the drum performance, the ablution in the gobo calabash, the drinking of the blood and the hondlola ceremony. In the Khongosa treatment the gobo rite comes first, and is called *baselo*. A certain root, the *phuphumane*, is prepared, and dipped into water in a big calabash cut in two so as to form a large basin. The mixture is stirred ; an abundant foam is thus produced and the patient must wash himself with it ; or he must take the basin on his knees, suck in a little of this foam between his lips and spit it out in the direction of the four winds, saying *tsu*, evidently as a preliminary means of propitiating the possessing spirits, which will be invoked and entreated to reveal themselves in the following rite.

In the case of Mboza, the calabash came as the second phase of the treatment, the first being the drum performance.

1) THE DRUM PERFORMANCE (GONGONDJELA). .

This extraordinary rite reminds one of the witches' sabbaths of medieval times by the infernal din and uproar through which the possessed will have to pass. However, notwithstanding the external resemblance, it is totally different, having nothing to do with witchcraft proper, and being only a "medical practice" in the eyes of the Thongas. — A strange medical practice, indeed, devised rather to kill than to heal the patient!

In the first place the bones must be consulted to find out in what spot the sabbath should be held. If the bone which represents the patient falls in the middle of all the rest, this shows that the tambourines, or "tom-toms," must be beaten in the interior of the hut itself. If the bone falls on the outer edge, the sabbath must be in the doorway ; if it falls further to one side, beyond all the others, the treatment must take place on the village square (hubyen) ; if it rolls still further off, and if the astragalus of the roaming gazelle is also separated from the rest, this shows that the meeting must take place in the bush, quite away from the village. If the bones remain silent, revealing nothing, then the throwing will be continued behind the hut, or on the square, until they speak. It is also necessary that the four shells Oliva, and Cypraea, which form part of the set of bones, should fall on their backs, exposing their crack or mouth. This signifies that the possessing gods, the spirits, will come out ; there will be an egress for them, whilst if, on the contrary, the shells fall differently, shewing their convex sides, the diviner will say : "Ma tikarata ntsena" — "all your trouble is in vain :" the sabbath

483

will have no effect ; no means of egress for the gods will be found!
(Compare Letter D. Divination). But a way will soon be found
to get over this difficulty, and it will not be long before the sabbath
is in full swing.

In the hut, right in the middle, the patient is seated. Dejected,
with downcast eyes, and fixed expression, he waits... Everyone throughout the country knows that to-day, to-night, on the
appearance of the new moon, the strange and terrible exorcism
will begin. All those who have once been possessed will officiate.
The director of the ceremony, the *gobela*, who has been appointed
by the bones, holds his tambourine, made of the skin of the big
varan lizard stretched over a circular wooden frame. (See
Illustration p. 124, No. 9.) In the calm quiet of the evening air
the first blow is struck. It reverberates, and is heard afar off on
all sides ; it penetrates the thickets and reaches the neighbouring
villages, where it inspires a strange emotion, a transcendent delight
born of curiosity, malice, and I know not what feeling of unconscious satisfaction. All rush in the direction of the well-known
sound ; each one hurries to the hut of the possessed ; all desire to
take part in this struggle, this conflict with the invisible world.

They all assemble, some with tambourines, others with large
tin cases picked up on the outskirts of the town (tins in which
kerosine oil is sold in Lourenço Marques), still others with
calabashes, filled with small objects, which do duty as rattles
(ndjele, yin-tin) ; and now, crowding round the patient, they
begin their hideous din, striking, brandishing, shaking their
various instruments of torture with all their might and main.
Some lightly touch the head or ears of the unfortunate sufferer.
It is a frightful hubbub, which continues, with but short inter-
ruptions, during the whole night, or until the performers in this
fantastic concert are compelled to stop from sheer fatigue.

But this is merely the orchestra, the accompaniment. That
which is most essential is the *singing*, the human voice, the *chorus
of exorcists*, a short refrain, following on a still shorter solo, repeated
a hundred or a thousand times, always with the same object in
view, toward which all strive seriously and persistently, namely to
compel the spiritual being, the mysterious possessing spirit which

is there present, to reveal itself, and declare its name, after which it will be duly overcome. These songs are at the same time both simple and poetic. They address the spirit in laudatory terms, trying to cajole it by flattery, to get on the right side of it, and thus induce it to grant the signal favour of a final surrender. Here follows the first of these songs which I heard. — One day, when I was travelling, hearing the uproar of a sabbath behind some bushes, I jumped off my waggon, and found myself right in the midst of an exorcism ceremony.

> Shibendjana ! u vukele bantu !
> Rhinoceros ! thou attackest men !

These were the words shouted by the singers round a poor woman who appeared to be in some sort of a dream, and was seemingly unconscious ; my arrival had scarcely any effect on the unearthly hubbub, in spite of the fact that the appearance of a White man in the villages of that district was generally regarded as quite an event.

When the hours pass without any visible effect being produced on the patient, the chorus is changed. The night may be far spent, and day-light at hand :

> Come out, spirit, you make us weep till sun-rise !
> Why are we thus ill-treated ?

Or, perhaps by way of bringing greater pressure to bear, they will threaten to leave the spirit, for good and all, if it will not heed the chidings of the frenzied tambourine players :

> Come, let us be off ! bird of the chiefs ! Let us go away (as thou treatest us so harshly).

The melodies of the exorcists' incantations have a singularly persistent, incisive, penetrating character. I had the opportunity of noting down one which was sung with a strange alto accompaniment in fourths. This tune is No. 32 in the collection (p. 291). The disturbing effect of this music was intensified by a very pronounced sforzando when the chorus took up the dominant phrase. This is the song, as universally known and sung in the neighbourhood of Lourenço Marques.

> Awake ! Awake! The daylight breaks ! Now the bird is singing !
> Play also, Zulu, play in the bush. Now the bird is singing.

The meaning is not difficult to gather. "Day is dawning. Awake then, sleeping spirit! (This spirit is called Mu-Ngoni, Zulu, for the case is supposed to be one of Zulu possession). The birds are already sporting in the thickets. Soon we shall be obliged to go to our work and leave you! It is your last chance ; come out and salute the morning and reveal yourself to us!"

This insistence is renewed. The patient begins to show signs of assent. The shikwembu is preparing to come out. Those present encourage it :

Shawane! Mu-Ngoni. Huma ha hombe hi tindlela ta hu lulama...
We salute thee, spirit! Come out gently by the straight way.

Meaning : Do not hurt the afflicted one! Spare him!

Overcome at length by this noisy concert the patient enters into a condition of nervous exaltation. The crisis occurs, evidently as a result of hypnotic suggestion. He rises and dances wildly in the hut. The hubbub is redoubled. They implore the spirit to *declare its name*. A name is shouted, a Zulu name, that of some ancient departed chief, such as Manukosi, or Mozila ; sometimes, strange to say, the name of Gungunyana himself, although he was still living. An old woman, formerly possessed, told me that she cried out the name of Pitlikeza, and it appeared that this Pitlikesa was an itinerant Zulu bard, who wandered about the district of Delagoa when she was a young girl. She was quite convinced that the spirit of that individual had taken up its abode in her, years after Pitlikeza's passage through the country.

In the case of Mboza the patient was covered with a large piece of calico during the whole drum performance. A first medicinal pellet was burnt under the calico, in a broken pot full of embers, a male pellet (made of the fat of an ox or a he-goat) ; no result having been obtained, a second pellet, a female one, made from the fat of a she-goat, was introduced. The exorcist, N̆watshulu prayed to the gods as follows :

Help us, you Ngoni spirits (or gods, psikwembu). I received this medicine from your hands, so "they" must come out at once from my patient. Should he have swallowed a snake, or a toad, should these prevent the spirits from coming out, let these animals run away, far away, and provide an egress for the spirits.

486

MAGIC

When the second pellet was nearly all burnt, Mboza began to tremble ; the women sang louder. The *gobela* shouted amidst the uproar : "Come out, Ngoni!" Then he ordered the singers to keep quiet, crept beneath the veil and said : "You who dance there, who are you? A Zulu? A Ndjao? Are you a hyena?" The patient nodded his head and answered : "No!" — "Then you are a Zulu?" — "Yes, I am..." And, during a pause, he said : "I am Mboza." Mboza was a Ronga who died in Kimberley many years ago. The uproar was resumed and the third pellet was introduced. This is the "pellet par excellence," neither male nor female, the one which is expected to have the strongest effect. Mboza suddenly rose, threw himself upon those present, beat them on the head, scattered them all right and left, and ran out of the hut under the impression that the spirits were beating him! "Every one saw that day that I had terrible spirits in me." In the crisis of madness the patient sometimes throws himself into the fire and feels no pain, or falls in catalepsy (a womile, lit. becomes dry), and strikes his head against wood, or the ground, without feeling anything.

Sometimes the concert of tambourines continues for three or four days, a week, or a fortnight. I know a woman (since converted to Christianity under the name of Monica) who underwent a seven days treatment of this description. All depends upon the patient's nervous condition, and upon the degree of depression to which fasting and suffering have reduced him.

The spirit, having disclosed its name and title, is henceforward known and can be interrogated. Spoon, the diviner, whose wife had been twice possessed, once by the Zulus and once by the Ba-Ndjao, told me the story of one of these conversations. He happened to be in one of the neighbouring villages when he was suddenly sent for in great haste and told that his wife, who had attended a sabbath at such and such a spot, was taken with the madness of the gods. He went as fast as he could to the place indicated, and found that his wife was really beside herself, and dancing like a person possessed. He had never before noticed in her the slightest sign of possession. The spirit began to speak, as soon as she was somewhat calmed down, and gave answers to the

487

questions put to it : "I entered into this *ligodo*, i. e. into this body, this vessel, in such and such a manner. Her husband had gone to work in the gold mines. I entered into him while he was seated on a stone, and when he returned home I left him and entered into his wife." — "Are you alone, spirit?" is the usual question, to which it may reply : "No, I have my son and my grandson with me ;" and, if the witnesses suspect that there really are several spirits in the patient, the tambourine symphony is again resorted to, in order to dislodge the entire company. Sometimes the possessed pronounces as many as ten different names.

Or it may be that the gobela only asks the name of the father and grandfather of the possessing spirit, in order the better to know the latter with all his genealogy. Such was the case with Mboza. "My father is Ndlebende," said the spirit. — "Ho!" answered the gobela, "then you are Mboza, son of Ndlebende." And he identified the spirit in that way.

It may be that, at the first sitting, the spirit will claim some satisfaction : a "nturu," a piece of calico of such and such a colour. It is also generally at this time that the patient will *sing his song*. Every possessed person invents a song which will be henceforth *his*, and by means of which crises, or trances will be provoked or cured. Nwashinhwana sang :

> Alas ! my father ! Medicine-men can do nothing for me !
> Who will deliver me ?

Mboza :
I am the one who wanders about, I come out from the body of magicians.

These songs are generally in Zulu, and it is asserted that, even if the patient does not know this language, he will be able to use it in his conversation, by a kind of miracle of tongues!

The first rite is now completed. It has succeeded in forcing the spirit to reveal its name (1).

(1) Exorcism by drum beating is the classical method of expelling spirits. Of late years, since 1910, another method has been invented called *ku femba* which, strange to say, is connected with a new word borrowed from European Animism, the word *shipoko*, now current in Thonga terminology. Shipoko comes from the Boer spook, which means ghost. According to the Native idea, wizards have power to enslave ghosts and make them work in their own fields during the night. They can also send them to take possession of their victims and torment them. If a patient is supposed to

Magic

2) The rite of the gobo basin.

When Mboza had finished revealing the name of the spirit possessing him, he had to undergo the rite of the *gobo*. His head was dipped into this, not entirely, but so that his eyes, at least, were plunged in the water. Then the gobela said : "Open your eyes." He felt a sensation of burning, and saw nothing but a red space with black dots running to and fro through the field of vision. He was kept in that position for a good long time. Then he raised his head, and the water ran all over his face and on to his body : he was purified (a basile). But this rite does not seem to be strictly a purification rite. By this kind of baptism the patient is said to have "crossed the sea." He enters upon a new life, and it is clearly a rite of passage. Now he will be able to speak, because "he has seen everything." It is the drug which "makes one see" (muri wa ku bonisa). Some are said to have learnt divination by this gobo ablution.

Having undergone these two first parts of the treatment, Mboza says he slept soundly. Next day, came the third.

3) The appeasement by blood (ku thwaza).

During the confabulation following the concert of tambourines, the spirits speaking through the mouth of the patient, although

be possessed by one of these shipoko, the exorcist will proceed with the femba in the following manner. He prepares a little crown made of medicinal roots woven together, similar to the *hari* which women place on their heads when carrying their water jugs. The patient lies down in his hut, surrounded by the mathwaza beating their drums. The magician touches one of his limbs with the hari, blows upon it, brings it close to his lips and draws in his breath. If nothing happens, he touches another limb, the arm, the side, the leg, the head, drawing in his breath each time, searching for the ghost. Suddenly he is seized by a fit, and falls down unconscious ! The ghost has entered him, he has swallowed it. His attendants raise him up and take him outside the hut. They begin to ask him : "Who are you ?" He tells them his name ; he also informs them that he has been sent by so and so, a wizard. This wizard may be "an inhabitant of your village, someone with whom you eat porridge every day !" The shipoko continues his confession :" Yes ! this man has sent me to kill the patient."

We shall hear more of these shipoko when dealing with witchcraft. We find here a curious mixture of witchcraft and the ideas of possession, with the addition of a European element. My informant assures me that this femba rite is quite modern, and I can readily believe it.

perfectly distinct from him, had already demanded some presents ;
but there is one in particular that must be given in order to

The great exorcist Hokoza with his companions (Tembe).

propitiate them and to get rid of them (hangalasa). The refrain
of the second verse of the exorcists' song, which I have already
quoted, mentions this offering, and half promises it, as an

490

inducement to the spirit to disclose its name. This is what is called the *thwaza*.

Aba ka Khongosa ba thwaza hi huku!

meaning : the patients of Khongosa's school treat with fowl's blood. Blood, an abundance of blood, is necessary to effect the cure of the patient, and to obtain an assurance from the objectionable tenant in possession that it will do no further harm. As a general rule it is given something better than fowl's blood. In most schools a she-goat is taken, if the patient be a man, or a he-goat in the case of a woman. The exorcist who has been in charge of the cure orders the by-standers to repeat the song which had induced the first crisis. The possessed again shows excitement, and exhibits the same symptoms of raving madness that I have previously described. Then the animal is pierced beneath the foreleg (in the case of Mboza this took place at the entrance of his own hut), and the patient throws himself on the wound, greedily sucking the flowing blood, and, in frenzy, filling his stomach with it. When he has drunk his fill, he has to be dragged away from the animal by main force ; certain medicines (one of which is called *ntshatshu*, apparently an emetic) are administered, his throat is tickled with a feather and he retires behind the hut to vomit all the blood he has absorbed. By this means the spirit, or spirits, have been duly appeased and expelled.

The sufferer, who is now recovering, is next washed again, and smeared with ochre. The spirits will have ochre on the day of thwaza, and torment him if he does not satisfy their desire ; Sometimes the *kunga* rite is also practised for the exorcised, viz., no one is allowed to speak to him before having given him a present. (Compare I. p. 124) (1).

(1) The accompanying illustration represents a well known exorcist named Hokoza, who had won great fame in the Tembe and Maputju regions, a kindly man who had even some sympathy for Christianity, to which most of these magicians are strongly opposed, as may easily be understood. According to the Rev. A. Aubert, Hokoza used to begin teaching the magic art to his patients on the day of thwaza. Whilst the exorcised was seated in his hut, after having vomited the blood, some of the disciples of the magician took that part of the skull of the goat to which the horns are attached, its astragalus and gall-bladder, and went to a certain spot to hide these objects. When they returned to the patient's village, the latter began to dance, to sing his song, to put

It is interesting to note what is done with the different parts of the sacrificed goat : the *bile-bladder* is stuck in the patient's hair according to custom (p. 50), to symbolise the happiness and good fortune that the sacrifice has ensured ; afterwards he is clothed with *strips of the skin* of the animal. All the tambourine players, who are themselves *mathwaza*, i. e. who have already gone through the torture of possession, decorate themselves also with these strips of skin, crossing them over the breast. The strips must be tied together with *munganazi*, i. e. strings made from the roots of the munga tree, which have a pleasant odour ; this has the property of "rejoicing the nose" of the spirits, and is always used in the ritual of possession. In former times people wearing strips were often met with, as these ornaments had to be worn, at that time, during *a whole year*, until the hondlola. — The *flesh* of the sacrificed goat also supplies the means of finally exorcising these mysterious spirit powers. From each limb a small piece is cut, and these pieces are cooked in a separate saucepan, with a powdered drug prepared for this special purpose. The head exorcist breaks off the branch of an acacia bearing enormous shiny white thorns, on each of which is spitted a piece of meat. The patient runs at full speed towards the branch, and seizes a piece of meat between his teeth in passing. While eating it, he rushes towards the East. He comes back, seizes another piece in the same manner, and runs towards the West, and so on towards all the four cardinal points. In this way he propitiates the gods, the spirits of every country, in whatever direction they may lie. The young *mathwaza*, viz., those who have lately passed through this initiation, must also seize the pieces of meat with their teeth, but not the gobela, nor the old mathwaza. This is one of the rites of the Khongosa school. Ñwatshulu used not to observe it. The remainder of the goat is then cooked and eaten. A feast is celebrated, in which the chief exorcist dances and sings his song,

himself into a state of trance, and ran outside in search of the hidden objects. It was a species of trial ; Hokoza wished to know if the exorcised possessed the gift of divination. If he succeeded in finding the astragalus, he tied it to his left foot ; the gallbladder he fixed in his hair. Hokoza was then satisfied and predicted a bright future for his pupil.

all the people clapping their hands (wombela), to encourage him, as an accompaniment. — The *horns and hoofs* will be carefully kept, and placed on the roof of the hut, just over the door (shiranwin) by which the afflicted one enters, evidently to protect the abode from malign influences. — The *astragalus* will be tied, together with the strips, on the sternum of the patient. — The *bones* of the goat are the objects of special care. They must not be broken to eat the marrow, but burnt in the shade of a large tree, where it is "cool." So the possessing spirit will also be cool (titimela) and not too wild. Sometimes they are preserved in a special pot, and burnt on the day of the hondlola.

The period of convalescence then begins. It lasts one year, and is a distinct marginal period, as clearly appears from the fact that sexual relations are absolutely forbidden during that phase, and until the hondlola. It is also, more or less, a period of apprenticeship, as the possessed will become an exorcist himself, if his magical powers become sufficiently developed. He accompanies the gobela everywhere, assists him in his cures, and so learns the art of exorcism. The apprentice will also have to practise the rites of protection, which I shall shortly describe, and which are obligatory during the whole period of convalescence, and even later.

4) The final purification of the hondlola and investing with amulets (timfisa).

As we saw, the hondlola, the removal of defilement of disease, is necessary at the close of any illness. So, when a possessed person is regarded as healed, he will have to pass through this rite. It can however only be carried out on the one condition that the possessed husband, or wife, has remained in a state of continence during the period of convalescence. In order to know if they have obeyed this law, a fowl will be placed on the head of the patient. If he, or she, has been continent according to order, the bird will remain quiet ; it will not fly away, even should someone approach and pass close by. If it flies off making a great noise, the angry exorcist will also take his leave, saying :

493

"You have sinned and, in so doing, have marred the efficacy of all my medicines (mi honile miri)." On the other hand, if the rule has been properly observed, the bird will remain quite still, when it will be stabbed with a knife and its blood will be used in connection with the hondlola friction. Afterwards the fowl will be plucked and eaten by the village folk, but neither the patient, nor his spouse, nor the exorcist-in-chief will be allowed to partake of it. Thenceforth the husband and wife are permitted to live together as in the past.

The hondlola rites seem particularly complicated in cases of possession. Their sequence was as follows in that of Mboza. 1) He had to pay £ 1 to Ñwatshulu, as a reward for his medical attendance. He gave him the money, together with a pot of beer. 2) Then the doctor took his *gobo* calabash, stirred the medicine in order to make it froth abundantly, invoking his gods all the time, and saying : "Awake, you who spit on the road, you, Zulus, who have ears capable of hearing, etc... 3) Then he shouted : "Mboza! Eat!" The exorcised had to kneel down and swallow the froth. 4) The exorcist took mafureira fat, mixed it in his hand with medicinal powder, smeared and rubbed the body of the convalescent, from the knees to the feet, the arms, the chest, the belly, and the head. 5) He cut the nails of the hands and feet with a knife, and also a little of the hair on the forehead, and put the whole into the timfisa bags (p. 471) together with medicinal powder. 6) Then followed the ordinary hondlola friction. A pellet (shibuwu) had been prepared by crushing roots of the *bamhuntane* and *shilewana* trees in a mortar, and a hen had been killed. Mboza sat on a mat and the doctor rubbed his whole body with the pellet. He gathered the *timhora*, the particles fallen on the mat, mixed them with the blood of the hen, and again rubbed the patient. 7) Fresh timhora fell on the mat. They were gathered up a second time. Some were put into the amulet bags, the remainder were made into a ball, which was not thrown away as in ordinary diseases, but carefully placed at the back of the hut, where the forked branch was to be planted.

Let us remember that, in the case of the exorcised, the hondlola does not only mean the re-introduction of the patient into the society of the healthy, but his reception into the society of the magicians. It is the last act of *initiation* : he himself becomes a magician, a doctor able to treat those who are possessed. This new dignity is symbolised by the *shiphandje* (forked branch) which will be given to him to-day, as it is to medicine-men (p. 388), or diviners (See later on). It was Nwatshulu who chose and cut the branch for Mboza from the tree called *shiralala*. He dug a hole in the back part of Mboza's hut, chewed his sungi or ndjao root, and blew against the foot of the branch before planting it in the hole. Then he made the branch firm in the ground, and hung to it the baskets full of drugs and calabashes full of medicinal powders which he gave to his disciple. This branch will be the drug store of the new magician, the place where he keeps all his magic drugs ; it will also be his *altar* (gandjelo), not the altar of the ancestor-gods, who have no part here, but that of the possessing spirits, to whom he will also henceforth address his worship. (Compare with Mankhelu's forked branch, letter D). This leads us on to the next division of the subject.

IV. *The new Condition of the Exorcised.*

It is interesting to note the stages in the process of initiation through which the possessed passes in the different acts of his treatment. The tambourine performance has provoked, or accentuated, the manifestation of his dual personality, viz., the person possessed and the spirit possessing. The baptism in the calabash has helped him to cross the sea and to reach the land beyond, the land of miracles and of magic powers! By the drinking of blood, he has become a superior being, a man who does not fear that which makes others tremble ; he has *thwaza*. This word is the same as that employed for the renewal of the moon (p. 306) ; like the moon, he has been born again ; a new light has appeared after a period of darkness. He has entered a new life. The period of convalescence, with its taboos, is his last trial ; by the hondlola he finally enters the society of the initiated.

Henceforth he will lead a special life, characterised by protective and propitiatory rites, which tend to the development of his subliminal faculties.

1) Protective rites.

As soon as he was "born again" in the thwaza ceremony, but to a still higher degree later on, after being elevated to the dignity of the magician, the exorcised, having entered the mysterious world of those endowed with powers, becomes the butt of all his colleagues in the magical arts ; first the baloyi, the witches, who *try* him, to see if he is able to discover their evil deeds, and secondly the other magicians, who are annoyed at seeing a rival ready to dispute their practice with them. So he must be continually on his guard ; in the evening, especially, he must protect himself against their nightly charms. The great protective medicine is a pellet made of the powder of many roots, which have been burned and bound together with fat taken from the bowels of a goat. The first of these roots comes from a tree called *mabophe*, found in the Bilen country. This has the power of tying (bopha, in Zulu, means to tie) the knees of the wizards who come during the night, so that they will be found in the morning, stark naked, in the hut of the exorcised. The *nulu* root seems to be used for the same purpose ; the *nsala*, which also enters into the composition of the protective pellets, rather aims at ensuring the success of the treatment undertaken by the new gobela ; as its fruits are plentiful (p. 16), so will the possessed come in great numbers to the doctor. The pellet is used for medical treatment, but the same drugs are also kept in the form of powder, in a piece of reed, or in the calabashes hanging from the forked pole. Every night the exorcised swallows a pinch, and throws another pinch on the fire in his hut. This will prevent enemies from entering, or make them prisoners. Before eating, he must also protect himself by chewing (phora) a little of the *manono*, a kind of antiseptic or anti-witchcraft root as big as a stick, which he always carries with him ; this is the special *luma* (I. p. 146) of the exorcised. Who knows if his food has not been poisoned by the malpractices of his rivals ?

When undertaking a journey, he must always chew his *ndjao*, the juncus root which has often been mentioned and which "cleans roads ;" this is "his shield," because the ndjao knows and tries (djinga) everything, and overcomes the hostility of man and things. It is the universal remedy against any hostile influence. So, after having chewed, he spits on his stick, rubs it and starts on

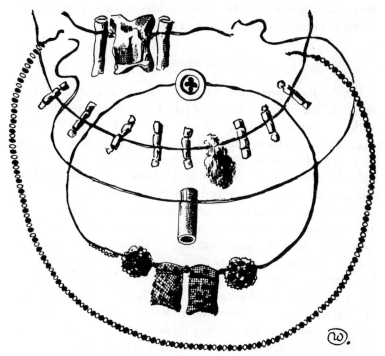

Protective amulets worn by exorcised.

his journey, saying : "The road is ripe (wupfile), let us go !" — The astragalus will be the principal charm that the possessed will have to wear, and will be tied round his neck between two little amulet bags or reeds.

The exorcised leads a life of constant fighting against evil spiritual influences. These protective rites are observed all through the year of convalescence.

Another rite, which is observed after the hondlola only, is

497

the *haza*, viz., the monthly purification of the exorcist. He fills his gobo calabash with a decoction made of the roots of the mphesu and ntjebe trees, drinks the whole, tickles his throat with a feather and vomits the medicine. "A tibasisa ndjen" — "he purifies his inside." This is done at every new moon. The connection between the possessed and the moon, which was first established by the fact that he had *thwaza* as well as the moon, is maintained and intensified by this rite.

2) PROPITIATORY RITES.

Besides these protective drugs, the exorcised wears a necklace made of little pieces of a creeper called *mayambatju*, tied together with a munganazi string. See the second necklace in the illustration. This is intended *to calm his gods*, and to scatter them when they desire to come upon him with violence. This is indeed a great danger ; the exorcised is liable to nervous attacks of ·a dangerous nature, especially during the first few weeks following the exorcism. Perhaps his song is heard in the distance. Then suddenly he is seized with madness, and furiously assaults his neighbours with the small hatchet, or the assagay used in the dances. People run away ; or, on the contrary, they collect and begin to clap their hands, and make their infuriated companion dance and sing his own song. This may help to dispel the spirits, and calm him down. Sometimes, feeling uneasy, foreseeing a crisis, the poor man himself asks them to sing. But he may also be led, in his frenzy, to the bush, far away, unconscious, quite mad, tearing his clothes and his skin with the thorns. This often happened to Ñwashinhwana. Her husband then followed her, and, when the crisis was over, saw her fall down exhausted and brought her home ; there, having returned to her senses, she became very sad and wept bitterly. So, in order to avoid being tormented, the exorcised propitiate their spirits ; they worship them, in truth, and this gives birth to *a new religion* totally different from ancestrolatry, which has its rites and its duties.

As already pointed out, the exorcised has *his own altar* in his hut. It is the forked branch, round which a circle of raised clay is carefully maintained, and regularly smeared. He puts his offerings there, principally tobacco. The snuff box is deposited there. Does he want snuff? He enters the hut clapping his hands, saluting his spirits, and, taking the box, throws a pinch of it at the foot of the branch, and says : "You! Ngoni, you see that I have not stolen! I first gave you your share." His wife will do the same. This is a "mhamba." — When ready to undertake a journey, he will come to the altar, sit on his ankles (a woman will kneel down) and take leave of the spirits. Holding his assagay, and his manono root, he says : "Good-bye, Ba-Ngoni! This hut is yours ; keep it well! I go to such and such a place," and asks them to bless his journeying. On his return he will inform the spirits that he has succeeded in his trip. If he is sick, and the bones have revealed that the disease has been caused by the spirits, he again comes to the altar, and says : "You! Ba-Ngoni, why are you angry with me?" These acts of worship are not only performed at the altar. Wherever he may be, before drinking beer, the exorcised will pour out a little for his spirits. He will also throw a little food for them before eating. This will be *a daily worship*, much more constant and individual than the rites of ancestrolatry, a real communion with the spirits who, after having tormented the exorcist, have become his benefactors, giving him the power of healing others and thus of making money! There is much more religiosity in the exorcised than in ordinary people.

3) DEVELOPMENT OF SUBLIMINAL FACULTIES.

All these nervous crises, natural or provoked, the double psychological existence which is fostered by them, the regular participation in the exorcism of others, generally greatly injure the mind of the exorcised ; they have an extraordinary look, something wild about them, as if they were not in their right senses. They may be heard sometimes groaning, or emitting a sudden cry without any reason. This nervous instability may pass away and they may return to their normal state, but it may be that if they possess those strange mental powers, which modern psychology calls subliminal, and which are more or less dormant in every individual, these faculties will suddenly develop and the exorcised will become a real magician. A faculty of *second sight* may reveal itself. Or he will become a *diviner*, either by ecstasy or by bone throwing (See Letter D). Or he will be a *wonder-worker*, a *prophet*, etc. Mholombo, who was an extraordinarily acute woman, had possessed all these gifts. She could discover wizards ; one night, crossing the Mabota country, she met one of the indunas of the chief accompanied by two other men, leading his own wife to the marsh, in order to eat her. They were acting in their capacity of wizards (See Letter C). Mholombo knew them at once and said to them : "No use eating her. Her meat is bitter sour." Terrified, the wizards fled, and confessed their guilt next morning! I have related in the *Bulletin de la Société Neuchâteloise de Géographie*, of 1910, how she received divinatory bones from her possessing spirit, prophesied the arrival of missionaries, showed up the man who had stolen £ 8 to the Mpfumo chief, was given the power to cross the Nkomati river by walking on the water, etc. By this same power Shidzabalane was able to leave his body, and to go and dwell in his own shadow (p. 362). Reference will again be made to the profession of magician when dealing with witchcraft.

4) The society of the exorcised.

If the power of an exorcised person becomes very great, if he succeeds in his cures, all his *mathwaza* join him, and he becomes the founder of a school. He starts new rites, discovers more powerful drugs, and so attracts patients to himself from all parts. We have seen that five or six schools existed northward of Lourenço Marques, in the Mabota and Nondwane countries. Mboza might have started a new one, as he had already cured two patients.

Each school of exorcists celebrates *an annual feast*, in winter, at the close of the harvest season, a feast to which all the disciples of the master are summoned. This is the rite of the *renewal of the drugs*, which we have already noticed as a medical practice in the case of ordinary medicine-men. Mboza, who was the favourite of Ñwatshulu, was entrusted with the organisation of the feast. He stood at the main entrance of the village and welcomed the exorcised coming with their empty calabashes ; on their arrival, each of them gave two shillings, or half a crown, or a mat, or a fowl for the master ; this was their annual fee. Next day they all gathered fuel and burnt the drugs in broken pots, two or three mathwazana around each fire. Then they all inhaled the smoke through reeds, and absorbed the froth of the phuphumana and psekamafura decoction from the gobo basin. In the evening the old inhabitants began to grind the carbonised roots, and Mboza filled the calabashes of the disciples with the new protective medicines, after which dancing began, each of the exorcised singing his own song as well as the universally known refrains, such as : "Vuka Mungoni," etc. This was a great day of rejoicing!

As already pointed out, great rivalry exists between these schools. Professional hatred is carried to its extreme limits amongst magicians ; they not only *test* their colleagues, entering their huts during the night, but they steal each other's drugs. I have been told how Sindondondo overcame Khongosa. Sindondondo was a wonderful man, dwelling on the Western border of the Nkomati, at Shifukundju. He had disappeared for two or three years, and was regarded as dead, but he unexpectedly reappeared, saying that he had lived at the bottom of the sea during the whole time. There he had not eaten anything ; he was like a fish. The chiefs of that country, under the water, had given him his great drug called *ndzundzu*, and he returned home bringing with him a bunch of the precious roots. His people welcomed him and made a feast on his return. He then became a great magician, and exorcised a number of people. He and his one wife were the sole inhabitants of his village ; he was very particular as regards his food, eating only mealies of the preceding year, and drinking no beer. (The exorcised often observe special, individual alimentary taboos.) His forked pole was outside, on his hubo, not in the hut, and when he went on a journey, he ordered a neighbour to keep watch over his drugs and his fowls. Should some other man try to enter his village, he would find it full of enormous snakes, surrounding the magic branch. Khongosa, who inhabited the district called Nkanyen, on the Eastern border of the Nkomati, wished to possess the marvellous *ndzundzu* drug ; so one night he crossed the river and tried to steal it. But Sindondondo was on his guard, his protective charms were working. They caught his rival, who was *shwela*, viz., imprisoned till after sunrise. Sindondondo behaved magnanimously : "Why, my friend (gobelakulori), did you not come in daylight to ask for my medicine? I would have given it to you! I could cover you with shame now, and show all the people what kind of an exorcist you are! But I have pity on you! Go home." And he released him. Mboza was fully persuaded of the truth of this story.

It may happen that a disciple emancipates himself and founds a new society of the exorcised ; this is, of course, very unpleasant for his master, as the new doctor will start a dangerous competition and refuse to pay any more fees to his initiator ; he will proclaim himself as his superior. So the old gobela goes to his altar and prays his Ngoni gods to make the drugs of his rival powerless. This prayer is heard, and the young gobela is obliged to ask for forgiveness, and to pay a fine of £ 1 in order to obtain success in his future cures. He may perhaps *succeed* his master, but only when the latter is dead.

5) Funeral rites of the exorcised.

The burial of the exorcised is attended by other mathwazana, and by his disciples, if he was an exorcist and special rites are observed for his funeral. The corpse is taboo. It must be covered with ochre. The grave is smeared with clay, and the body is not laid down on its side, but is placed in a sitting position, its hand holding the assagay, or hatchet, which the deceased used when dancing and singing the songs of exorcism. A bunch of *shibowa*, a Urticaria which grows in water, is placed on his head : "*This is to cool him*, because his poor head has been so tired, it has suffered so much from anguish, pain, excitement!" The grass, being taken from the water, also appears *to cool the spirits*, who will thus remain in the grave, and not trouble other people. Moreover a little hut is built on the grave itself, as was the case for Sokis (I. p. 141), with the same intention, to protect the exorcised against heat and fatigue. If the deceased was not only a disciple but a master, his drugs will be stored in the hut till the adjudication of the inheritance. The most skilful of his followers, the one who best knows the use of these charms, will dance on the grave, all his companions clapping their hands to encourage him, and, when the mourning is ended, he will "raise the drugs," burning them as is done at the annual feast, and will eventually succeed his master.

6) CONCLUSION ON POSSESSION.

Cases of possession, such as those which occur amongst the Thongas, are met with in a great many other countries. A Swiss missionary, the Rev. H. Rusillon, working in the Paris Mission in Madagascar, has drawn attention to practices very similar to these, called the Tromba, amongst Hovas. It is impossible not to note the striking resemblance between the Thonga disease and that of the demoniacs of the New Testament. On hearing the story of the madman in Gadara, whose spirit called itself Legion, the Natives at once identify the phenomenon, and say : "These demoniacs had psikwembu."

These psychological phenomena are certainly of a morbid character. The fact that they generally appear in an epidemic form is significant. It has been noticed that similar epidemics have broken out in populations which have been weakened by the sufferings of a long war, when the nervous resistance had been reduced by privations. May not the progress of Alcoholism, together with the disintegration of the old social order caused by the influence of European civilisation, account for the spread of the disease amongst the Ba-Ronga in the last fifty years?

Whilst not pretending to analyse these phenomena scientifically and fully, I will here add two observations :

1) In the Jewish conception, phenomena of possession were due to *evil spirits*, devilish agencies, which tormented poor humanity, and were cured by the power of the real and true God. Dualism prevailed in their religious conceptions. This idea of dualism is altogether absent from the Thonga belief. South African Bantus have not yet reached that stage of religion where the antagonistic ideas of right and wrong are

transported into the realm of divinity, thus giving rise to the true gods and the devils. Possessing spirits are not worse than ancestor-gods. They all are non-moral. They can bless and curse, and their moral character is not taken into account at all.

2) The progress of modern psychology gives an explanation of many of these phenomena. The disease of the personality which manifests itself in the presence of a double psychological consciousness is well-known ; the hypnotic suggestion which the tambourine players unconsciously exert on their victims, sufficiently explains the origin of the disease, and the kind of life led by the exorcised is well calculated to develop their mediumistic faculties. So many of the so-called miracles of possession are easily accounted for. It would however be going too far to exclude, a priori, any possibility of external spiritual influences in those phenomena. There is one very striking fact which is a source of great wonder to the Natives. These patients, as soon as they put themselves under Christian influence, are healed at once and for ever. We have, amongst our converts, exorcists who had acquired great fame, and who recount, with glowing eyes, how they have been delivered from their terrible anguish by their new faith. For, whatever success they may have obtained in their career of exorcists, their condition was a disease, a painful disease, and they are extremely glad to have been delivered from it. This fact must certainly be remembered when trying to arrive at an explanation of possession.

C. WITCHCRAFT.

I have pointed out, in an article published in the Report of the S. A. A. A. S., of 1906, how little comprehension most White people have of this important but difficult subject. A confusion is almost always made between the *witches* and the *witch-doctors*. The French word *sorcier* and the English term *sorcerer*, indiscriminately used for those who cast spells and for magicians, lead to the same misconception. In order to avoid errors it is, I think, imperative first of all clearly to distinguish between *Black Magic* and *White Magic*. The adjectives black and white are not employed in this connection amongst South African Natives, but Thongas certainly do make the distinction and possess different terms for each. Black magic is called *Buloyi* ; it consists of the criminal magical practices by which wizards and witches bewitch innocent folk. Buloyi is a crime. White Magic is called *Bungoma*, and means the magical operations of those who combat evil influences and use their powers for the benefit, and not for the ruin, of their countrymen. The *mungoma* (magician) is consequently the great enemy of the *noyi* (caster of spells). It may be that the power of both is at bottom of the same nature. But the use they make of it is entirely opposed, the one exerting it in the interests of Society, the other against it. We shall therefore have to deal with these two categories of persons in two separate paragraphs.

I. Black Magic (Buloyi).

Buloyi, an abstract noun of the bu-ma class, as well as *noyi* (pl. *baloyi*), is derived from the verb *ku loya* (Ro.), *lowa* (Dj.), to bewitch. This word is very interesting. It seems to have been known already in the Ur-Bantu (Comp. Meinhof, *Grundriss*, p. 173) and exists in Swaheli, Herero, Xosa, Sutho, Thonga, etc. Strange to say, the stem is absent in Zulu, where it is replaced by *thakata*. In Thonga its most common meaning is to bewitch. But the word is also applied to the act of a man who marries his near cousin (I. p. 258). Moreover Nkolele, describing to me the sacrifice in the sacred wood, and speaking of the *ntukulu* who prepares to steal the offering, said : "Here is the *noyi*, ready to come and steal the beer..." I also heard the crocodile stone, used by the chief as a charm to protect his life, called *buloyi bya hosi*, the magical power of the chief (I. p. 393) ; these instances show that the word loya is sometimes, though rarely, used in a more general sense. Its technical meaning, however, is and remains : to injure or kill by enchantment. Who are these baloyi, and what crime do they perpetrate?

1) THE BALOYI.

The *baloyi*, or people possessing the evil eye, are numerous in each tribe. Their power is hereditary, but, strange to say, it is transmitted by the mother and not by the father. Therefore should a polygamist have three wives, one of whom is a noyi, all the children he will have by that "noyi" wife will be baloyi, and his other children will not be so. This dreadful power is sucked in at their mother's breast when they are still infants, but it must be strengthened by special medicines in order to be really efficient. The "noyi" mother chooses one of her sons to whom she does not give these drugs, and he will be free from buloyi. She does this in order that, if one of her offspring should later on be accused of having killed by witchcraft and be called to pass through the ordeal (of which we shall speak hereafter), the immune child may be sent in his place to undergo the trial. The chief will consent to this substitution, as it is well known that all the sons of a "noyi" woman are equally baloyi. But the intoxicating medicine of the ordeal will have no effect on the substitute, and therefore the true noyi will escape!

These baloyi know each other. They form a kind of *secret society* within the tribe, and they assemble during the night — in their spiritual bodies — to eat human flesh in the desert. There they form a true "hubo," that is, a meeting for discussion. They discuss what they will do to injure property or destroy life. They sometimes fight. If one of them is defeated in the discussion, suggesting, for instance, that there should be no mealies this year, a proposal which is not accepted by the others, they condemn him to pay a fine, and this fine will consist of a human body, which he will have to provide, after having killed it by witchcraft. It may be that he will choose his own child to bring to the horrible banquet! This shows that there are more and less powerful baloyi, and they are constantly trying to overcome each other in finding out more efficient charms.

As regards the other members of the tribe who are not witches, or wizards, they are regarded by them as stupid beings who deserve no better fate than to be eaten wholesale by the clever baloyi! These man-eaters are the truly intelligent, the superior, the wise ones! (Ba tlharihile). They are also called for that reason "bahanyi" — "those who live," no doubt because they possess a kind of superior life. They are, however, greatly feared by the others, and when a boy wishes to marry, the main thing to consider in the choice of his wife is that she should not belong to a family of witches. The accusation : "You are a noyi" is the gravest insult which one man can utter to another (1).

The activity of the baloyi is almost entirely nocturnal. For this reason they are sometimes called by the euphemism : "ba busiku" — "the men of night." In fact, they possess the faculty of getting out of themselves at night time ; they have large wings, and, after having left their huts by the crown of grass which covers the top, or by the closed door, they fly through the air and betake themselves to their horrible work.

As they are active in the darkness of night a connection is established between them and nocturnal birds, especially *owls* (kuhunu). When the sinister cry of this bird is heard, men take a torch upon which they have spit out of their mouths a little ndjao powder, and chase away the creature. Baloyi are also identified with the little moving lights sometimes seen in the marshes, the will-o'-the-wisps, the fires of the night (mindjilo ya busiku), the belief being that these fires are either the baloyi themselves, or that they are sent by the baloyi as a threat (2). We have seen (p. 720) that the wizards who ride on hippopotami during the night are credited with the power of producing flames similar to lamps.

Two questions here arise. Does the Native mind imagine that

---

(1) Thongas are extremely sensitive in regard to a possible suspicion that they are baloyi. When I proposed to my pupils in the Shiluvane Institution that they should move up for the bad season to the sanatorium which we had set up in the mountains, in order to avoid the dangers of fever in the Low Country, not wishing to abandon their comfortable accomodation at the station, they made great difficulties. I therefore said to them : "But if your devoted teacher, Miss So and So, catches the fever, on account of the heat and moisture of the malarial climate, will you not be responsible for whatever may happen?" This remark caused quite a commotion amongst the pupils. "What ?" they said. "We are then baloyi ! We have the power of killing people by witchcraft !"

(2) One of my informants says : "We are walking peacefully along the path at night-time, chatting pleasantly with our companions. Suddenly a will-o'-the-wisp appears. We at once stop on seeing this terrible object, for one of us must be the culprit. It cannot arise from any other cause. We organise a meeting for confession (rerela nyiwa, see below), and thus rebuke the noyi who is amongst us. Sometimes people who see the fires of the night trample on the ground, take a pinch of earth between their fingers and put it to their mouths (khabuta)." (This may be a kind of "mhamba" similar to that described on page 391, aimed at obtaining protection against the "enemies of the earth.")

a true unsheathing of the personality takes place when the baloyi go on their nocturnal expedition, or that they leave the hut themselves, in their entirety, in their ordinary persons? As far as I could make out, the Sutho theory is different from the Thonga. The Ba-Sutho say that the wizard goes altogether, soul and body. Nothing remains on the mat when he has departed for his nocturnal ride! He casts spells over the other inhabitants of the hut, and they sleep so heavily that they notice nothing. The Thongas tell a different story. According to them, the noyi is but a part of the personality. When he flies away, his "ntjhuti," his shadow, remains behind, lying on the mat. But it is not the true body that remains. It appears as such only to the foolish non-initiated. In reality what remains is a *wild beast*, with which the noyi has chosen to identify himself. This fact was disclosed to me by the following striking confession of S. Gana, a very intelligent Nkuna. "Suppose," he said, "my father is a noyi and I am not. I wish to marry a certain girl whom I love. My father knows that she is a noyi, because they all know each other, and he tells me : 'Don't do that! She is *clever* ; you will repent!' However, I persist in my idea. He urges me to abandon the plan, and threatens me with great misfortune. I marry her. One night, my father enters my hut and awakens me. He says to me : 'What did I tell you! Look! Your wife has gone!' I look at her place and find her sleeping calmly — 'No. Here she is.' — 'That is not she! She is away! Take this assagai and stab her. — 'No, father, I dare not.' — 'Do as I say!' And he puts the assagai into my hand and makes me strike her violently in her leg. A cry, the cry of a wild beast, is heard, and a hyena appears in the place of my wife, a hyena which deposits its faeces in its fear, and escapes from the hut, howling. My father gives me some powder to swallow so that I shall be able to recognise the baloyi and their ways and habits. He leaves me — trembling greatly from fear — and goes home. When the sun is about to rise, I hear a noise like that of the wind in the branches, and suddenly something falls down from the top of the hut beside me. It is my wife. She lies sleeping, but her leg shows a wound, the wound that had been made in the hyena!"

From this dramatic story it must be inferred that, according to the idea of the Ba-Thonga, there is a true unsheathing of the personality when the noyi goes about its nightly work.

A second question arises, which is this. As the baloyi lead a double existence, a day-light existence in which they are merely men, and a nightly existence, in which they perform their work as witches, are they aware, during the day, of what they have done during the night? In other words, are they conscious of their doings as witches? The question is difficult to answer, as there seems to be no clear idea on this point in the Native mind. The old, genuine view is that a noyi *does not know what he is doing* ; he is not even aware that he is a noyi until he has been revealed as such by the methods which will be explained later. Therefore he is unconscious. His nightly activity is unknown to him when he returns to his ordinary daily life. For instance, my informants assure me that a man may have sent a crocodile to kill another, during his noyi existence, but that he will be the first to show sympathy to the poor sufferer, and to deplore this sad accident. And he will be amazed when the diviner points him out as having caused the death by his buloyi, of which he was in entire ignorance. But those baloyi who have long practised their horrible tricks would seem to be aware and even proud of their doings, and therefore more or less conscious of their double life. Some of them go even further ; they renounce their evil deeds and become magicians, using the knowledge they have acquired to baffle the enchantments of other baloyi, as we shall see.

But let us hear what the dreadful acts are which they commit in their baloyi form.

2) THE CRIMES OF THE BALOYI.

(a) The baloyi are in the first place *thieves*. This is the least criminal aspect of their activity. They steal mostly mealies or the products of the fields. They empty the ground-nuts of their contents (p. 12). The magicians have a kind of medicine with which they plaster their mealie cobs in the gardens, and the noyi, when he wants to tear them from the stalk, remains a prisoner

on the spot, unable to withdraw his hand from the cob! But, what is even more curious, the baloyi of one country assemble and form an army and go to fight with the baloyi of another, in order to deprive them of their mealies and carry them away to their own fields. For instance, in 1900, there was a great war between the baloyi of Mpfumu, near Lourenço Marques, and those of the peninsula of Inyack, at the entrance of Delagoa Bay. That year the Kafir beans were plentiful at Mpfumu, and this was explained by the fact that the Mpfumu baloyi had won the victory over their Inyack enemies. They owed their success to the following trick. They gathered a large number of seeds of the little cucumber, called nkakana, and made with them a kind of enormous ladder, which was suspended midway between sky and sea ; upon it they crossed the 20 or 30 miles of the bay of Delagoa and stole all the Kafir beans of Inyack (1). If a tempest has uprooted trees and broken branches, people are sure to say that the "army (yimpi) of the baloyi" has passed in the shape of a terrific storm during the night.

b) But the great crime of the baloyi is that of *killing*. They are murderers, and all the more to be feared as they act unconsciously, without being seen or known. Two motives inspire their crimes — hatred and jealousy. If one of them has been offended, he is sure to revenge himself by putting his enemy to death. During the night he escapes from his hut (as we have seen above), opens his wings and flies directly to the dwelling of the man he hates. But the habitation of this man is well protected ; all round it there is a spiritual fence made up of charms, various

---

(1) On one of these expeditions to the Inyak Islands the baloyi of the Movumbi district wished to buy food from their colleagues beyond the Bay. A certain woman, who was a great noyi, took her daughter-in-law with her, but the latter was not a noyi. However she was led through the air, along the nkakana ladder, to the village of Magilankinsin, a headman of Inyak. This man refused to accept her, as she was ignorant of the buloyi art, and sent her back home. In the meantime the husband, Midlalen, noticed that his wife was not sleeping in the hut. When she reappeared in the morning he asked her : "Where have you been ?" — "To Inyaka." — "Indeed !" — "Yes ! I saw everything there." — "How did you go ?" — "I do not know." — "How did you return ?" — "I do not know." — "Have you seen Magilankinsin ?" — "Yes !" The husband suggested that his mother had played this trick by means of her buloyi and chased her away from his village. Mboza told the story as absolutely authentic, and added "these events occurred some ten years ago."

510

medicines which close the kraal against any invasion of witches. What must he do in order to perpetrate his crime? He has first made an agreement with another noyi residing in that village, who has made an opening in this spiritual fence, similar to one of the small holes in the material one! He then gets into the kraal, tries to penetrate into the hut by the door, finds it closed, beats on it and, being unable to enter that way, flies to the crown of the hut and descends through it into the abode of the enemy, calmly sleeping on his mat. Then he proceeds to the bewitching operation, and the poor bewitched man is condemned to die! "O loyiwile," — "he has been bewitched ;" "ku sa ntjhuti ntsena," — "only his shadow remains." They also say that only the "ntjhumbu," the corpse, has been left, his true self having been stolen and eaten. He is sometimes called *ntungulu*, a word used to designate a wasp whose nest has been destroyed, and which flies about disconcerted, not knowing where to go, unable to sting, because it has no home... The heart of the bewitched has been stolen and put somewhere in a hole or a cavern (mhakwen). "Ba mu pepulile," they have ravished him, (like a feather taken away by the wind). He will get up in the morning, and die some days later, but what will die will be only his shadow. He himself was killed during that frightful night. He is already eaten! Or he will become mad (lihlanyi) and people will say : "The living have had the better of him" — "Ba mu kotile bahanyi." Here we find again, in an even more mysterious form, the idea of the duality of the human personality. How it is possible for a man who has still some days or months to live to be regarded as already entirely eaten up, I do not pretend to explain. Such is however the Native idea. One of my informants tried to overcome the difficulty by saying that what the noyi takes with him to eat is the inside, the bowels ; the outward frame alone remains, and the man will soon die! Most of the Natives, when the absurdity of the idea is pointed out to them, laugh and say nothing.

In order to attain his criminal ends, the noyi may resort to various means ; he may point at his enemy *with the index finger*, which is a common method of bewitching in many nations. If, later on, you are overtaken by misfortune, you will remember that so and so has "shown you with the finger" (komba hi litiho), and will suspect him of having cast a spell over you. (Comp. I. p. 250.) Or he may obtain a hold on you by *taking your own blood*, if this has by chance been shed on the ground, and using it as a means of bewitching you, (a ku loyela ha yone). Hence the precaution universally taken of covering one's blood with earth, should any have dripped from a wound (p. 360). But the five chief methods which a noyi has at his disposal are the following : ruma, mitisa, matshelwa, ntshutshu and mpfulo.

The *ruma* (to send) consists in sending either a crocodile, or a lion, or more often a snake, to the place where the enemy is about to pass. He will be killed or wounded. We may recall the story of Gebuza, whose nose was torn off by a hyena ; this is a typical case of ruma. In Maputju, the heathen accused the converts of bewitching them by means of the owls which took shelter under the roof of the chapel ! In Khosen also the Christians were charged with having sent a crocodile from Nkomati River into the Sokotiba lake to kill those who refused to be converted to Christianity ! If the noyi does not wish to kill, he may only send antelopes to destroy the fields and eat the sweet potatoes. Even in the Christian village of Shiluvane, during the days when the "duykers" are plentiful, and become a nuisance, you may hear some one say : "*They* are sending us their duikers !" Who are *they*? A mystery ! *They* are the baloyi ! But do not call them by their name !

The *mitisa* (ku *mita*, to swallow, ku *mitisa*, to make somebody swallow) is the only one of these five methods of bewitching used during the day. It consists in giving to a visitor something to eat or drink into which certain drugs have been introduced. The mealie pap or the beer look just as usual, but, owing to the enchantments of buloyi, as soon as you have swallowed them, they are transformed, in your throat, into any kind of noxious creature, which threatens to suffocate you, and gives rise to a disease and perhaps produces death ! You may thus have swallowed a snake, a beetle of the Copris genus, one of those strange dung-eaters, a big fly, or certain kinds of flesh of animals. The great effort of the magician to whom you will apply for treatment will be to remove these foreign bodies, and, when you vomit, he will show you with triumph a bit of bone, a tooth, the famous beetle, or other objects which he himself had cleverly placed there beforehand (p. 457). There is a medicine which Natives are fond of having inoculated into their tongues, and which has the wonderful property of forcing the bewitched food to reveal its true character when you eat it. If you have been treated with this, you will hear the cracking of the elytra of the beetle, and at once be able to spit out of your mouth the death-containing food!

The *matshelwa* (ku tshela, to throw) are not only these foreign bodies which the noyi introduces into you by means of poisoned food, but may be *tingati* (blood) poured on you during the night in such quantity that the floor of the hut will be found quite wet in the morning (1).

The *ntchutchu* (ku tchutcha, to inspire) is another way of getting rid of an enemy. It is a *bewitching of the will* by which the noyi inspires his enemy with the idea of leaving the country. Without any motive, the poor bewitched person prepares to go to Johannesburg, or anywhere else. There he will become the prey of other baloyi, who will kill him. When a boy dies in the mines, as hundreds of them do, his parents think : — "He has been killed by such and such a disease." But the author of his death is not in Johannesburg, he is here at home ; it is the noyi who hated him and made him go by "ntchutchu."

The *mpfulo* is still worse. This word, which comes from the verb ku pfula, to open, designates the mysterious power which the baloyi possess of *opening* all kinds of things. One of them, a Nkuna, named Ñwayekeyeke, had charms to open *the oxen kraals* ;

(1) The following story fittingly illustrates this kind of "buloyi." An evangelist of the Manyisa region, named Abel M. had taken into his house his wife's daughter. He was himself without children. The girl fell on the threshold of the hut and injured her leg. Her parents took her home again, but found the leg very much emaciated, and consulted the bones. The diviner told them that Abel had "loya" his niece through sheer jealousy because he had no children ; he had "eaten the girl's leg," but, being a hunter, he had killed an antelope and introduced the femur of the animal into the leg in place of the bone ; the true bone was however still somewhere in Abel's hut and the magician offered to go to the evangelist's village, and boasted that he would be able to find it. Fearing a scandal, Abel entreated his wife's parents not to allow this. They said : "Then take the girl back into your home and treat her." He did so, and the girl eventually recovered.

during the night, he would come into a village holding a hyena tail daubed over with peculiar medicines, and would throw all the inhabitants into a deep sleep. Then, waving the tail, he would open the kraal and call the cattle out. Flying with the rapidity of the wind, he would then be followed by the whole herd which he had bewitched. When tired, he would jump on to a tree and rest for a while, fearing lest the oxen should run over him and tread him down, they being irresistibly attracted by the tail. Should anyone see him on his way, he would say : "Take an ox, I give it to you," until he reached his village and housed the stolen oxen in his own kraal. But there are other kinds of *mpfulo* : the power of *opening the hut*, removing the husband sleeping there without waking him, and committing adultery with his wife. However the great *mpfulo* consists in *opening a man*. The following story will show how this criminal act is accomplished. Some fifty years ago, a young man called Nkokana, the uncle of my informant, astonished the whole tribe by his marvellous skill in dancing like a chameleon. The circumcision school was just over, and on the last day of it all the boys had to enter solemnly the kraal of the chief, performing the ceremony which has been described I. p. 93, and which is called ku nenga. One of the men of the tribe, who was a noyi, was struck by the perfect performance of Nkokana, and, filled with jealousy, resolved to bewitch him. As the boys were going home that same day, happy to have reached the end of all their trials, they had to cross a thick wood ; suddenly a voice was heard calling : "Nkokana!" The boy said : "Yes, I am coming," and went to the place from which the voice came. But he found nobody. Instead of going back to his companions, who were waiting for him, he ran all through the bush, as if possessed by a kind of madness, always following the voice, but with no success. The night passed. He came back home entirely worn out, a mere shadow of himself, and died some days later. He had been "opened up" by the witch. When this sort of bewitching takes place it is probable that the noyi wishes to enslave his victim, and make him work for him.

c) This leads us to the last of the crimes of the baloyi. Their object may not be to kill their victims, but *to use them as their servants*, for ploughing their fields, cutting their wood, and so on. One day the footprints of a leopard were seen in a mealie garden near the Shiluvane station. People were convinced that this was nothing but a bewitched person, sent there during the night in the form of an animal (1) to serve the owner of the field; it is said that the baloyi, when assembled in their hubo, choose those whom they like amongst the victims they have overcome by the ntshutshu, by their magical inspiration, and change them into leopards, hyenas and snakes, compelling them either to till the fields, or to uproot mealies in the gardens of others, and to "lead" (byisa) the stems and plant them in the gardens of baloyi. A Nkuna of Thabina once claimed to have witnessed such a case of nocturnal theft, — and he was expelled from the country because, as people said, he could not know of such deeds if he were not himself a noyi. Of late years, since the word *shipoko* has been adopted by the Rongas (see p. 488, note 1) it is believed that these nocturnal servants of the baloyi are the ghosts of dead people and that they resemble little children. The baloyi hide them in the forests during the day and take them during the night to till their fields. As we shall see, these baby workers bewitched by the wizards were much spoken of during the strange Murimi revival which I shall describe later on. (See also the song of the Christian girl who ridicules the deceitful witch (p. 299) and compare with App. V.)

To be fair towards the wizards I must add that there are also some *good baloyi*, viz., baloyi who use their power to bless. They can do this when sent by the ancestor-spirits to increase the produce of the fields, if the prayer of the luma day has been heard by the gods (I. p. 396). In this case the wizards are said to have *loyela masimu*, bewitched the fields to make them produce more (loyela, applicative derivative of loya). This would seem to show

(1) The connection established between animals and baloyi is pushed even further in Maputju. My colleague, the late Rev. W. Audéoud, heard of baloyi who really look on themselves as the possessors of certain beasts. One of them owned a wild boar. A hunter killed the son of this wild boar and the noyi bewitched him, as he considered that he had a vested right of property in the son as well as in the father! We have seen, when dealing with hunting rites, that baloyi domesticate the hippopotami of the Komati river and use them as mounts (p. 72-74).

that baloyi are more or less subject to the ancestral gods. It may happen also that if somebody shows kindness to a noyi, this noyi will take him under his protection, and prevent his comrades from doing harm to his friend. But these are rare occurrences, and the baloyi are, and remain, criminals in the view of the Thongas.

Stealing, killing, enslaving are the principal crimes of these maleficent beings. But they can also cause any other species of harm to their infortunate victims. I have told the story of a young man who complained to me of having been deprived by the tricks of a noyi aunt of the power of having sexual intercourse with his wife ; she was pregnant and the witch wished to act on the offspring in such a way as to change it into a snake, a hare, a quail, or a duiker, so that the mother should die on the day of the birth. (I. p. 187.)

II. *White Magic and Magicians.*

1) DISTINCTION BETWEEN MAGICIANS AND WIZARDS.

As previously stated, the power which the magicians claim to possess is perhaps not essentially different from that of the baloyi. They even sometimes boast that they are themselves baloyi, baloyi more powerful than the ordinary witches, and that they are thus able to discover them and baffle all their tricks. So Mathuza, one of the most celebrated Ronga witch-doctors, used to say : "I am the great Noyi! I am the one who kills. I can fly. So I know them all and I disclose them." But magicians differ absolutely from wizards in four ways, at least :

1) Their activity is not secret, nocturnal and more or less unconscious. They act openly, in the light, during the day, and do not hide their magical powers ; on the contrary, they make a show of them, covering themselves with any number of charms ; most of them wear "tingoya" and smear themselves with ochre (p. 100).

2) They all undergo a preparation, or pass through an initiation, differing according to the different kinds of magic they practise.

So they possess, so to speak, letters patent, either because they have been received into the society of their fellow-magicians (as is the case with medicine-men, exorcists, and throwers of bones), or because they have found new and powerful drugs during a sojourn, real or pretended, in the sea, the desert, or elsewhere.

3) Whilst baloyi are said to use *tingati* (blood) poisons, the magicians employ *miri*, i. e., medicinal herbs or objects, drugs which, however, are all thought to possess special powers. I do not say "supernatural" powers, as the notion conveyed by this word cannot exist in any definite form amongst people who have hardly a true conception of Nature. The stronger the miri, the stronger the magician. — In addition to their drugs, they certainly believe themselves endowed with personal power due to the development of their faculties of second sight, etc., which they also attribute to the spirits (ancestor-gods) from whom they have inherited their drugs.

4) The last point of difference but by no means the least important, is this : magicians are the supporters and upholders of the social order, and not criminals attempting to destroy it. They foretell the future, cure diseases, prevent misfortune of all kinds, fight against baloyi, and are regularly consulted by the Native Court for the detection of wizards.

Between the unconscious baloyi whose crimes are purely imaginary and the bangoma who use their magical powers for the benefit of those who have recourse to them, there certainly exists another category, i. e. wicked individuals who kill their fellow-men by means of real poisons or by criminal practices and do this quite consciously, either to avenge themselves on their enemies or to help others to get rid of those whom they hate. Such acts may be called ku loya, by an extended use of the term ; but there is another word to designate these crimes, the word *ku dambika*, which we already met with when speaking of the jilted lover who wishes to play an evil trick on the girl who despised him (I. p. 101). In the neighbourhood of Rikatla, there was a man who claimed to be a noyi of this type, and to have at the same time the power of "treating" (daha) buloyi. He was a Mu-Sutho, a stranger. Wishing to kill an enemy, a Ronga of the country asked his help ;

the magician bade him first bring a sheep ; this he slew, took part of its fat, and smeared with it and with some very black drugs a root of the ntjhopfa tree (I. p. 58). This fat and these drugs were to give to the root the power of "taking away" the heart of the enemy ; the magician buried it in the road and assured his client that when the root was rotten his enemy would be dead. This root was discovered later on, owing to a revelation given by the bones, and the man who had consulted the magician had to pay a fine of £. 1. No doubt such conscious acts of witchcraft exist, but this is not the typical loya.

2) VARIOUS CATEGORIES OF MAGICIANS.

Some magicians specialise in one division of the immense domain of magic, but others claim to practise the magic arts in all their diversity.

1) Those whose activity bears a less magical character. These are the *ñanga* (yin-tin), or *ba-muri*, whom we met with when dealing with the medical art (Compare Chapter I. the Medicine-men).

2) Those who have passed through the ceremony of exorcism and have become exorcists. They are called *gobela*, and the character of their initiation has been sufficiently explained in Chapter II.

3) Those called *mungoma*, magicians proper, who have divinatory powers and can perform wonders, fight the baloyi, cause rain to fall, influence Heaven, etc., even if there has been no exorcism episode in their previous career.

4) Those whose principal qualification is the power to detect baloyi, and who are called for that reason *shinusa*, "smellers-out."

5) The bone-throwers *(ba-bula)*, whom we shall describe in Chapter IV.

The priests, *ba ku hahla*, do not enter into any of these cate-gories, their specific activity being of a totally different character ; they have recourse to Religion and not to Magic.

518

MAGIC

3) SOME THONGA MAGICIANS.

On calling to mind the various magicians with whom I came in contact, I observe that very few limited themselves to the medical art alone ; *Sam Ngwetsa* and *Kokolo* alone did this. The aim of the magician is to combine as many branches of the business as possible. — *Mankhelu*, with his forked branch, was a medicine-man of the highest rank, owing to his calabashes containing a mixture of all the most powerful drugs, salted with Rivimbi's sea charms. He was a magician, being a rain-maker, a detector of baloyi, and, in particular, a successful bone-thrower, but he seemed to be entirely ignorant of the art of exorcism. — *Makasana*, on the contrary, a Thonga from the Leydenburg district, had acquired his power after passing through the ordeal of exorcism and had obtained the drugs of his exorcist. This had made him into a regular *mungoma*. Round his neck he wore three necklaces of half transparent yellow beads, between which were small square lizard-skin bags, timfisa, containing : 1) drugs against snake bites ; 2) charms against the baloyi ; 3) the *maringo ya tilo*, the charms of Heaven. Birds' claws and a crocodile's tooth also hung round his neck ; his hair was pulled out, the *tingoya* radiating in all directions, and in the very middle, on the top of his head, he wore a little chain, in the form of a narrow turban, to which a brass cartridge was fixed ; this was his snuff box, resting comfortably on his thick thatch ! Possessing all these drugs Makasana was at the same time exorcist, witch-doctor, medicine-man, and magician of Heaven. The last qualification was perhaps his principal one ; he told me that he had to fight against his colleagues, who wished to test him by means of their own charms. — "At noon," he said, "when the sky is quite clear, I see a little cloud appearing over my head, quite black. The lightning bird is in it, and wants to kill me, having been sent by one of my enemies. Then I pour a little of the medicine of Heaven into the palm of my hand ; when I see the bird moving its wings and ready to rush down upon me, I blow a little of my drug towards the cloud and the bird will come and fall down powerless quite close to me. Then I take it, and cut it in half. I take a little of the heart, and of the eyes, I crush the bones, I make a powder with all these ingredients, and this is my great medicine. With one of the bones I make a flute ; I put a little powder into it, and, when a thunderstorm breaks, I go outside without danger and conjure the lightning by playing on my flute, etc." (p. 314).

Mathuza, the magician of Nondwane to whom I have just alluded, was essentially a detector of baloyi. — So was also *Ñwashihandjime*, the great Nkuna magician, a splendid creature, tall, his eyes beaming with a kind of supernatural light. I once saw him, after having performed the "smelling out" rite, point out a woman with the tail he always carried with him, an enormous tail fixed on a handle richly decorated with beads and copper wire. This tail, which is one of the most common attributes of the mungoma, is generally *a gnu tail*. It is said that when a mother gnu has dropped her offspring, she beats it (phyita) with her tail and thus gives the new-born gnu the necessary strength to walk and follow its mother. Hence the peculiar magic use of the gnu tail. In its very middle are hidden certain drugs which possess a revelatory virtue ; the magician puts his nose right amongst the hair before pronouncing his sentence and beating (phyita) the noyi. Ñwashihandjime is said to have disappeared from his village for months, and to have come back from the desert emaciated but full of new magical powers. I once tried to draw his attention to things more spiritual than his art and his drugs. He gazed at me with wild eyes, as if unable to follow my demonstration ; suddenly he emitted a cry very similar to a hiccough and turned his back. (Hiccoughing is a well-known symptom, showing either that one has been bewitched by "mitisa," or that one possesses magical power).

At the station of Shiluvane I once made an inventory of the charms of another Nkuna magician. In his hair the man wore a brass bracelet and some rings, and a necklace with a sixpence attached, all these objects having been inherited from his father, who was himself a mungoma ; moreover he hung round his neck a little piece of the skin of a goat, which had been sacrificed after the death of his father ; in this way he tried to acquire and keep the power of his initiator and of his god. Two panther's claws were fixed on his head, pointing towards each other, as if they wished to catch something ; this helped him to go and seize (to ba) the wizard in the *vumisa* rite, which I shall now describe. Two empty goats' bladders swung amidst his crop of tingoya as he walked, an unmistakable sign that he had cured patients and received goats as a reward. The noise they made in hitting against each other "called other goats to come to him." From his neck hung two crocodile's teeth, a piece of buffalo's horn, "psiboho psa nga" — "that which ties me, viz., makes me firm ;" another horn which had been broken by a bullet and in which he kept the *nulu* medicine (p. 496), the root of a white sea-weed, used to produce the foam of the *gobo* rite in the exorcism, and a goat's horn full of a powder which cures the "burwa" disease. The burwa is the strong Westerly wind in Shiluvane (I. p. 18) which the baloyi are said to use for bewitching through the ears. He rubbed the patient with the horn and placed it near one ear, then near the other, and could cure the bewitched in that way. Another drug, called "rishwala," helped him to acquire many wives, and to have many children ; a cock's spur was also worn in order to give him "courage and weight." This mungoma, who called at Shiluvane on the 28th of June 1899, sold me a "kaross" (a rug) made of skins of rock rabbits, the work of the Ba-Pedi, worth £ 6. He had earned it by the practice of his art.

I here give the picture of a true Ronga *gobela*, from Tembe, who once passed through Rikatla with two assistants ; he was on a tour to exorcise the possessed of the land. He had a terrifying appearance with all his military and magical attire, his big snake skins, and his gnu tail ; he hardly condescended to pronounce a word, maintaining all the time a most dignified demeanour. He was, before all else, an exorcist.

These few descriptions are sufficient to illustrate the composite character of the magicians. There is no end to their charms and their tricks, but they are certainly in earnest as regards the practice of their art, and are convinced that they are very useful and powerful personages.

III. *The Method of dealing with Wizards.*

All the power of the magicians is resorted to in order to check the enchantments of the baloyi. Their drugs are used with two objects, — protection and cure, the cure consisting mainly in the disclosure of the wizard.

1) Protective methods.

The village, as we have seen, (I. p. 311) is well protected with *anti-baloyi drugs*. The fence itself, the main entrance and the threshold of the headman's hut, have been magically treated when first built. But the magician, when he thinks it necessary, "revives" the drugs by burning his powder in a little fire on the road which enters the village. This protects the main entrance, and he does the same at the threshold of the headman's hut. The smoke will keep the wizards away. Stones, daubed with the powder, are placed in all directions to close the openings.

"These medicines act wonderfully," says Mankhelu. "Should a *noyi* succeed in entering the hut, the power of the smoke will be such that he will at once be revealed. The *noyi* will suddenly be seen there without any clothing, apparently dreaming, seeing nothing, knowing nothing. If it is a woman, I shall call her husband and show him his wife... 'What are you doing here?' he will say to her. She will not utter, a word. Then I shall say to him : 'Look here, my friend... I might be hard on you. But I have pity. Do not allow your wife to do anything of the kind again. Pay me one or two oxen, and I will keep silent.' He will consent. Then I beat the woman with my stick. She awakes, and, quite ashamed of being in another hut without any clothing, she will fly away home!" Such is the testimony of Mankhelu, and he is certain of having succeeded more than once!!

Mboza asserted to me that he had witnessed a similar case

A Ronga "gobela."

in Muthiyane (near Rikatla). A woman had been thus "surprised by the rising sun" (shwela, p. 307). She was stark naked and had something red, like fire, on both shoulders ; these were the remnants of her wings. Having been overcome by the magical drugs she had been unable to reabsorb these wings into her flesh, and part of them remained outside. Every one ran away at this sight, and the chief ordered the woman to be shut up in her hut.

Some magicians used to fight the baloyi by *running through the bush during the night* and catching them as they flew by with their wings of fire. Note how Mholombo prevented two wizards from killing a woman (p. 500), and how the exorcised protect themselves by means of the mabophe drug, and by swallowing their nulu powder (p. 496).

2) METHOD OF DISCLOSING THE BALOYI.

But should all the protective medicines which surround the village, together with those which have been swallowed by the inhabitants, or by which they have been inoculated, remain without effect, and should a serious case of illness occur, one of those evils which are generally attributed to the baloyi, the first thing to do is to *detect* the culprit.

Who may he be? The patient's relatives have most probably already some idea on this point, because, at the beginning of most buloyi cases, something happens which arouses *suspicion*, and this is a very important point to be noted if we wish to find the psychological explanation of these customs. Perhaps there has been a quarrel between two persons, and one of them, in his anger, has said to the other : "N'ta ku bona" i. e. "I shall see you." On hearing this the people immediately say : "This man is a noyi. He has revealed by daylight his crimes of the night." The man himself had perhaps not the slightest idea of such a thing. The same conclusion will be drawn if he points to another person with his index finger (I. p. 250). An imprudent word which at first sight would appear quite innocent may have the same result if hostile feelings already existed between two persons (1).

Jealousy alone is sufficient to give rise to the suspicion even without a word having been uttered (2).

The fact of a woman having lost many children is also a reason for suspecting her of being a witch, as the death of a baby is constantly considered as having been caused by its own mother, who wished "to eat it." The fact of belonging to a family of baloyi is also an indication to the same effect, buloyi being hereditary, as we have seen.

But a mere suspicion is not sufficient to warrant action being taken against the suspected noyi. An objective proof, a piece of convincing evidence is required, and this the magicians are asked to supply. The patient's relatives go *to the diviner* who will cast the bones and discover whether the disease is due to witchcraft or not. This consultation is secret, and is merely preliminary. There are, in the sets of bones employed in Thonga divination, some which,

(1) The evangelist Silas G. was one day speaking to Saul N., an elder of his Church, about Church contributions and said: "So and so does not pay his dues. It would be good to show him his duty." Saul answered: "I do not wonder; that man has a bad wife and you are sure to fail in your duty when you have a bad wife." — "No", said Silas. "Everyone ought to pay his contribution. You, for example, would certainly do your duty even if you had a bad wife !" — "Nevertheless I maintain that a wife who behaves badly takes away her husband's courage. Look at your own case, Silas. Your wife does harm to your work as an evangelist. Did she not say the other day when she saw my baby : 'How fat it is ! It is like a pumpkin !' " On hearing these words Silas starts ! They are an accusation of buloyi. To say that the baby was as fat as a pumpkin showed that the woman who used these words was ready to eat its body during the night; the evangelist's wife was a noyi ! An enquiry was at once started to ascertain if she had really pronounced these words, and the whole little Church was upset. Finally the elder was blamed for having brought an accusation of buloyi, which is forbidden in the Native Congregations, and he resigned his office. The evangelist and his wife "became thin" owing to the mental suffering caused by the insinuation of the elder.

(2) I had amongst my evangelists a very active and intelligent man who cultivated large gardens and was well provided with everything. His neighbours began to suspect him for this reason. He said to them : "We ought not to work on Sundays," and this increased their suspicions. "It is evident", they said, "that *he is not alone !* How does he manage to have such splendid harvests when he does not work on Sundays ? Surely he has others to till for him. He takes our backs and uses them to cultivate his big fields. And the reason why he has such wonderful crops is that he has taken our own mealies from our gardens by his witchcraft" — "But," said others, "you cannot complain ! Mealies are plentiful in your gardens too !" — "No," answered the enemies of the evangelist. "Though you see mealies in our gardens, they are no longer mealies ; they have been taken away by him." They meant that, just as a bewitched person is no longer normal but has been emptied of his viscera, so the cereals had been robbed of their virtue by buloyi.

represent the *baloyi*, in particular the astragalus of the reedbuck, or of the duiker, the small antelope which rambles about during the night, just at the time when witches are at work. Should this bone fall in a certain way near the bone representing the patient, or near his amulets, which have been placed on the mat, this shows that his disease is the result of buloyi. The name of the noyi will be sought, and perhaps ascertained, on that first day, but the parents of the victim will never venture to accuse him merely on the testimony of the bones. The next step will be to go to the *mungoma*, the magician who "smells out" the *baloyi*.

The magician employs various means to find out a noyi.

a) *The Enchanted Horn.*

In the Murchison Range there is a magician who possesses an enchanted horn, into which he introduces a short twig smeared with an anti-baloyi medicine. Persons suspected of having killed by witchcraft must try to pull the twig out of the horn. The noyi will be unable to do this, though he may declare, like the others : "I have not killed." Amongst the Nkunas, the magician who has succeeded in finding out a wizard, takes his coat and hangs it on a tree as a trophy.

b) *The Enchanted Flute.*

When some one dies and his relatives think he has been bewitched, they can call a certain mungoma who "treats the grave" with his drugs. If he thinks that he has discovered the noyi, he gives to the bereaved a small flute, telling him to go and play on it in the neighbourhood. This helps not only to detect the wizard but to punish him ; he will die. This rite is called "to play on the little flute (ku yimbelela shinangana) for somebody."

526

MAGIC

c) *The rera nyiwa, or ba hungwe.*

Rera nyiwa or *ba hungwe* means to summon an assembly for discovering wizards. This is done when the chief is ill, or when an epidemic has broken out and threatens the villages. The headman, or sub-chief, assembles all his people and says: "Hungwe!" (this word has the meaning of: "Take care!"). "The bones have declared it: It is so and so: a woman having two, three or four children... or married twice... or a widow... or a girl... or a man... or a medicine-man..... Cease your enchantments and make the patient live! We know you! Do not bring upon him bad influences during the night! If you do not restore him to health, we shall kill you!" All the people look at each other and try to discover who is meant by the bones and by the speaker. The rera nyiwa acts as a solemn warning to all the baloyi of the country, and may thus prolong the life of the chief.

This method of combating baloyi is also resorted to in connection with the products of the soil when some fields are in good condition and others not, or when caterpillars or locusts have spoiled some whilst others have been spared. This unequality is due to the baloyi! In the region of Matalane, near Rikatla, this kind of nyiwa was performed as follows at the end of 1918. The clansmen assembled in the little capital, whilst the women were ordered to stay at home. The men visited all the gardens, those in the marshes as well as those on the sandy hill, and took from each of them food of all the different kinds, sweet potatoes, manioc, mealies, pumpkins, even pine-apples. Then the whole throng assembled somewhere in the bush, a big pot was brought, and they all ate from it, the man who had been designated by the bones taking the first mouthful (luma) and offering a "mhamba." Then he said to the people: "We have seen where food is plentiful and where it is wanting!" The aim of the whole performance was evidently to show the supposed wizards that they must cease their bewitching of the fields. It was at the same time a symbolical meal in which all the members of the little community ate some food from each of the fields, thus asserting that all must remain equal (ba fanana) and that this equality must not be destroyed by the wizards' robbing the others by their enchantments, and becoming rich at their expense.

d) *The smelling-out procedure.*

But should it be desirable to ascertain the name of the noyi, in order to punish him (for instance, in a case of death, where nothing remains but to avenge oneself on the murderer), the mungoma will proceed to the *shinusa divination*, the regular smelling-out. This can be done in two ways, either by questioning or by ecstasy.

1) *Smelling-out by questioning.* The relatives of the bewitched come to the shinusa, pay him £ 1, and ask him to find out the murderer. He makes them sit down in a half-circle, and, facing them, begins to put questions to them. They always answer by the word *mamoo*, which means yes, in the language of *bungoma*. Hence the Zulu term *vumisa* viz., "to make somebody say yes," applied to this ceremony. The *mamoo* is cool or warm, doubtful or convinced, and the clever diviner easily perceives every shade of meaning in this perpetual *mamoo*. He is well aware of all the disputes and hatred between the people and, in his investigation, he draws nearer and nearer to the man of whom the consulting party is thinking. Their *mamoo* becomes bolder. The questions are more precise. At last, when he feels himself in agreement with the consultants, the *mungoma* pronounces the name and lets his tail fall. He is bathed in perspiration after the great strain, and remains silent, as if he were indeed infallible ; he has triumphantly "smelt out" the culprit. Next day, relatives of the patient go to the kraal of the noyi, waving branches, dance before him, and say : "So you are killing us !" The accused keeps silent. Then he says : "All right. We shall come to-morrow and also consult our *mungoma*." Both parties then go to another diviner. The performance of "smelling out" is again gone through, and very likely the verdict of the second *mungoma* will confirm that of the first ; the augurs know that they must not contradict each other if they wish to maintain their authority, and the terrible tail falls on the head of the accused. As soon as proof and counterproof have been obtained, the case becomes a judicial one. The plaintiff brings the matter before the chief, who will not condemn until the

guilt of the pretended noyi is confirmed by ordeal, the trial by the famous philter called *mondjo*.

2) *Smelling-out by ecstasy* partakes more or less of the character of the rera nyiwa. All the people have been assembled in the Capital. The chief wishes to collect together all the baloyi of the land. The diviner arrives, decked out with amulets and all the insignia of his power. In his hands he carries his magical

Photo D. Lenoir.

Smelling-out a wizard.

tail, by way of a whip, and an assagay. He begins to dance, the crowd seated all round him, clapping their hands (wombela), and singing a chorus peculiar to the occasion :

Ṅwashongana khalo ! Famba u ya teka, u ya teka, mungoma !
Beautiful dancer of slender figure ! Seek for it, seek for it, diviner !

He goes on dancing ; like Pythia of old he falls into a condition of extreme nervous excitement, ecstasy, inspiration. He bran-dishes his tail, dilates his nostrils, inhales the air on all sides, as if to smell out the spot from whence the evil influence has emanated, then takes to his heels in a certain direction, the assembly

529

still clapping their hands and singing. He approaches a hut, enters, and triumphantly plants his assagay in one corner. A hole is dug in that spot and — just where so and so places his wooden pillow when retiring to rest for the night — there are discovered a small gourd full of blood, packets of suspicious objects connected with enchantment, and perhaps a snake. It is quite possible that the diviner may have previously hidden these articles ; nevertheless he carries them exultingly away ; they are the wizards'weapons, the "bloods" (tingati) which they throw over their victims at night.

The shinusa returns to the village of the chief, who is veryangry, and orders him to go and show these objects to their owner. Then the magician, making a sign to the crowd to stop singing, will go and throw the articles in front of the occupant of the hut to put him to shame before the whole assembly. The mysterious charms, and the noyi's gourd, must in every case be consumed by fire, and then the sickness and deaths in the village should cease.

e) *The Mondjo ordeal.*

As already pointed out, the final and supreme method of unmasking baloyi is the *mondjo ordeal*. This is a legal procedure ordered by the chief, a true method of obtaining information in a criminal case. This custom calls to mind the judgment of God in the Middle Ages (ordeal is derived from "urtheil," judgment) ; it is practised by the majority of the Bantu tribes, varying from one tribe to another, but everywhere it has the same end in view, namely the discovery of the casters of spells by the imposition of an ordeal which is supposed to be fatal to such as are guilty.

This ordeal is called amongst the Ba-Ronga (as also from one end of the Thonga tribe to the other) *drinking the mondjo* (ku nwa mondjo). The mondjo is a plant of the Solaneae family, probably a Datura, which possesses intoxicating properties. With it a special magician prepares a beverage which is to act as a means of revelation. It can be resorted to by any individual accused of witchcraft, or of any other crime. A woman accused of adultery, for instance, may say : "Let us go and drink the mondjo." The mondjo magician will give both the accused and the plaintiff a little of his drug, and the one who becomes intoxicated, or unconscious, after having drunk the magic beverage will be convicted of guilt. But the mondjo ordeal can also be ordered by the chiefs, just the same as the rera nyiwa, not only as a warning, but with the object of revealing the wizards and in order to get rid of them.

This is how the ceremony is performed in Nondwane. When it has been decided at the capital that all subjects shall undergo this ordeal, the chief sends word to the Shihahu folk to prepare the mondjo. These particular folk are a small clan inhabiting the left bank of the Nkomati, not far from the sea, northward of the district of Manyisa. The mondjo is cultivated by the medicine-men of Shihahu, but they have by no means the monopoly of it, for my neighbour, Hamunde, who lived at Rikatla, a few steps from the station, had one of these plants growing in his village, where I myself saw it. But it is at Shihahu that the recipe is known for the preparation of this magic philter. This is very complicated and intricate. It contains several strange ingredients, amongst others, it may be noted, *the fat of a leper long since deceased*, or a little of his powdered bones! To make sure of the efficacy of the drink, the Shihahu folk experiment upon a certain individual named Mudlayi. This man is considered the very chief, the "bull" of all the wizards of the country (nkunzi ya baloyi). He is more powerful than all the others in casting spells. If, therefore, the decoction produces in him the characteristic intoxicating effect by which the spell-casters are discovered, it is certain that the brewing has been a success. If, by any chance, Mudlayi should not have been intoxicated, word will be sent to the chief that the decoction has failed (yi hi hlulile), and another brew will be made, until the mondjo has attained the strength required. Then the people of Shihahu do not go directly to the chief, but, according to the rules of etiquette, to the counsellor who looks after the interests of their country. The other counsellors come to greet them, but the whole business is kept a great secret. Messengers are then sent to all the sub-chiefs, telling them to assemble at a certain time, in a given place, bringing all their people with them. This general assembly takes place on the borders of a lake. Every man and every woman must defile before the proprietors of the decoction and take a small mouthful of it, tepid, from a particular receptacle. Already at this stage of the proceedings some few, terror-stricken, make a confession : "Ndja loya!" — "I am a caster of spells," they cry. These persons are then collected together and placed on one side under a tree. The rest sit down in a line, in the fiery glare of the noon-day sun. There they are, then, all seated and exposed to the torrid heat of the sun's rays. They have received the following order : "Do not move! You must not scratch yourselves! Remain motionless!"

Mudlayi begins to dance in front of them. With widely opened eyes he glares in a peculiar manner at those who have sipped the mondjo. In his hair is fixed a large feather, which he waves up and down by moving his head. Everyone gazes at him intently.

Suddenly some one scratches his arm. Sounding his trumpet, *nte-nte-nte*, Mudlayi approaches the individual and places the feather in his hair over the forehead. The man tries to pull it out, but only clutches the air on one side or the other, in front of the feather. He is quite incapable of catching hold of it. A second individual begins to show the same symptoms of intoxication (popya) a little way down the line. Mudlayi continues his comings and goings to the sound of his trumpet. A third and a fourth are overcome in turn. They try to get up, clutching the grass to assist them to do so, but fall to the ground, or crawl feebly about. The others keep away from them. It seems that the mondjo dries up the saliva of all who drink it, but, in the case of the truly guilty, this effect is greatly accentuated ; the jaws become locked. They try to speak, but can only say *be-be-be-be* (they stammer). They are carried off, and all placed together under the tree, where they are guarded by the chief's counsellors, who will not allow their friends or relations to come near them.

"*Selekan!*" — "Get up!" is the order given to all the others, the seated crowd who have not become intoxicated. Jumping to their feet, they must run at full tilt to the lake and bathe.

Some get into difficulties on the way, they jostle each other, fall to the ground, and remain there, unable to regain their legs. Some even fall down in the water ; all such are baloyi. The rest, who have successfully undergone the trial of the mondjo, come back and are restored to freedom, after having received three pinches of a special powder ; one of these is thrown over the right shoulder, another over the left, and the third is swallowed, in order to counteract the defilement consequent on having imbibed this drink of the wizards, which contained in solution... the fat of a human being! As to the poor, unfortunate hypnotised folk, their affair is settled. The magic potion has revealed their criminal character. They must be made to admit their evil deeds. The counsellors interrogate them. To restore the power of speech, a particular tisane, prepared from the herb called *tjeke*, is poured into the mouth ; they are shampooed *(tlhema)* on the cheeks and all over the body with its leaves. The saliva returns. They gradually revive and then begin to speak : "Yes! I devour men! I ate so and so and I still have some of his flesh in store!.. I hate so and so, and I would like to kill him, but I haven't done so yet... I bewitched the maize to hinder its growth." They are well reprimanded and told : "Cease your witchcraft and enchantments. Remove your spells from the cereals, let them grow properly, or we will kill you!"

How can the effect of the mondjo be explained? According to an old Native, the intoxication of the baloyi comes from the presence of these elements of human flesh contained in the solution. The noyi, who swallows them in drinking the philter, thus does during the day what he is accustomed to do during the night : hence the loss of his senses. As a matter of fact the man who administers the drug is clever enough to give a larger dose to those who are more or less supposed to be baloyi. Moreover there is a regular process of hypnotisation in Mudlayi's performance, and that is why some people fall into what seems to be a true cataleptic state.

3) THE PUNISHMENT OF WITCHCRAFT.

What is the punishment inflicted on those convicted of the crime of witchcraft? Let us remember that this is a crime, an act of homicide, doubly punishable by the Court. Chief Shiluvane had definitely prohibited it by a decree in the following words : "I do not allow anyone to die in my country except on account of old age. So let the baloyi at once cease their enchantments, or I shall kill them all." In former times the crime of witchcraft was punished by death and the culprit was immediately hanged. The last to be punished in this way, in the Nkuna clan, was Mudebane (I. p. 443), and Mankhelu himself executed him. The wizards are impaled or drowned, as the case may be. Flogging and banishment were also resorted to when the crime was not so heinous. In Khosen wizards were expelled from the villages and roamed about the country, sleeping in the ruins, mocked at and insulted by the children, and oxen sinews were tied round their biceps so tightly that they entered their flesh and caused great suffering.

One of my informants (Fenis), who drank the mondjo at the death of Zihlahla, chief of the Mpfumo district, about 1870, told me that the heaviest penalty imposed on the wizards on that occasion was a fine of one or two goats, or of one pound sterling. He attributed this leniency to the proximity of the Whites. The civilised Governments in Africa have certainly done their best to put down this method of smelling-out wizards, and their efforts have been by no means without result. Native chiefs are now content with fining the wizards £ 10 or £ 15, half of which remains in their own pockets. I heard of one of them who claimed to be a Christian, but did not object to the substantial increase to his civil list brought about by witchcraft suits.

IV. *Concluding Remarks on Witchcraft.*

Witchcraft is one of the greatest curses of Native Life. I attribute the enormous hold which this superstition has taken on the mind of the Bantu to three causes : 1) The *Animistic beliefs* explained on p. 367

which are at the root of the idea of the double existence of the baloyi.
2) *Cannibalism*, which has perhaps never existed as a general custom
in South Africa, but has been practised sporadically in times of famine,
and has left a feeling of disgust and horror in the minds of later
generations ; this feeling is also manifested in the numerous Ogre tales.
3) The *terrible hatred* of which the Native mind is capable. If some
people venture to accuse members of these tribes of such awful acts as
those of killing and eating human beings, it is because they know that
a Native who hates would not shrink from anything to satisfy his desire
of vengeance.

We must however remember that the witchcraft superstition was
universally found amongst our own forefathers, and that there were
epidemics of it in the XIVth, XVth and even the XVIth centuries,
hundreds of wizards having been tortured and burnt in most European
countries, after having been tried before regular Courts. I have tried
to establish a parallel between the ideas and practices of witchcraft in
French Switzerland and those of the Thongas. The results of the
comparison are very curious. I cannot give them all here, and must
refer the reader to the Paris Revue *Foi et Vie*, No. of October, 1910, in
which they were published. The most striking difference is this.
Amongst Thongas, we are still in the *predualistic age*, viz., the opposition
between a good, moral Spirit (God) and bad, wicked spirits (demons,
Satan) does not yet exist in Religion. So the power of God is not
invoked to reveal the wizards, or to protect the innocent against their
spells. But the same animistic conceptions evidently formed the basis
of European as of African witchcraft.

This superstition has a deadly effect on Native life. It is a continual
source of trouble, fear, quarrels, sorrow. Strange to say, it has been
on the increase in recent years. It ruins the villages. — "Formerly,"
say my informants, "you could see villages of ten or twenty huts. Now
the accusations of witchcraft have broken them up. Each man builds
his own hut apart, from fear of being bewitched, or because he is
suspected of being a noyi (1)."

(1) The evil affects the Native Christian communities also, fostering hatred amongst
them, and this animistic doctrine is much more difficult to overcome than ancestrolatry,
which is very quickly and completely abandoned by converts.
Some Christian Natives are so convinced that witchcraft is a reality that they interpret Matt. X. 28 by saying that "those who kill the body and who must not be
feared" are the baloyi. Unhappily a Zulu translation of the Greek word φαρμακοί
by the word corresponding to baloyi, in Revelation XXII, v. 15, confirmed them in

The Thonga tribe really suffers from the results of the witchcraft superstition and this explains a curious magico-religious movement which took place in the years 1914-1917, in which the tribe made a serious and touching attempt to free itself from this scourge. The story of "The Murimi Movement" will be found in Appendix V.

I have already explained how I think Government can and must interfere in order to check this terrible superstition. (I. p. 445.) But its eradication will only be possible under a twofold influence, the increase of the scientific spirit, which will conquer and destroy the absurdities of the animistic magical conceptions involved in these practices, and the Christian Religion, the Religion of Love and of Light, which banishes fear and hatred.

D. DIVINATION.

Divinatory practices are extremely common amongst Thongas. Surrounded by so many evil influences, having very little or no scientific knowledge, possessing no notion of a God capable of illumining the path of their life, they try to obtain directions by the various methods of divination which they have invented, and it must be confessed that they have reached a high degree of proficiency in this domain. The anxiety to know the future lies at the foundation both of omens and divinatory practices. Let us first briefly consider the former.

I. *Omens.*

These are of two kinds ; some objects are ill-omened, they *singita* or *hlolela*, foretell bad luck ; others are favourable and announce happiness and, more especially, plenty of meat !

their idea that wizards certainly exist, since they are even mentioned in the Bible ! Of course those who are further advanced see the absurdity of the witchcraft theory, but a great many do not. As a proof of this I may quote this letter addressed by a young convert to his father from Johannesburg: "If the Lord agrees with it, I shall return home in the month of February; expect me that month. I entreat you not to tell anyone, less they bewitch me by preparing (lit. placing) snakes for me (ba ndji bekela tinyoka)."

Amongst the first we have already noticed *falling stars* (p. 309) ; *the snail* (p. 338) : should you meet with it on the road, you will soon hear that one of your relatives has died ; *the stem of cuscuta* (yendje-yendje) ; (1) there are families, however, for which this is not of bad omen, but for other people it foretells misfortune ; *the mbonga bee* belongs to the same class (p. 337) ; the various kinds of *mistletoe* are also of bad omen. So also is the *puff-adder* (p. 340), the *likure* (p. 340), a greyish slender snake : if it blows upon you, or bites you, you will grow thin and turn grey, like the animal itself ; the long-legged bird *shitshinyariendjo* foretells misfortune on the road (I. p. 339) as do also the *buwumati* snake and the *nkangu bird*.

Other objects are of good omen ; the beetle *Eccopteptera* and the *Mutilla* (p. 336), and especially the beetle *Bombolosi*, belonging to the Curculionidae family, a curious insect which drops to the ground and counterfeits death when touched or frightened ; it is the symbol of riches. Natives hang it on a string at their door ; I have heard of others hanging it in their hair ; but in this case it is said to be placed there to eat lice !

All these superstitions are believed in more or less seriously. But, in order to know their fate and what they must do to avoid misfortune, Thongas have recourse to true methods of divination. Amongst these mantic practices some are simple and some more elaborate.

II. *Less important Means of Divination.*

1) Amongst these I may mention first the *pshapsha*, which corresponds to our "drawing lots" and is performed exactly in the same way by placing pieces of grass or sticks of different length between the fingers, and pulling out one of them, having

(1) The cuscuta sometimes covers large patches of ground on the sandy hills of Thongaland ; as is well-known, it has a regular root, but afterwards becomes a parasite on the vegetables to which it attaches itself, whilst its stem and root die. This fact has been noticed by the Natives, and has given the cuscuta a special value in their eyes. When they happen to find a plant which still retains its stem and root, magicians make use of these, especially in their exorcism rites. But this stem, which is so rare, is a bad omen for ordinary people.

first decided to act in such and such a way if the longer or the shorter grass be drawn. This is more or less a game and is employed mostly by children.

2) Another more serious method of divination is the *mondjo*, the enchanted philter, used as a regular means of procedure to obtain evidence in Court (I. p. 443), especially to discover wizards and adulterous women. It has been described at full length in the preceding paragraph.

3) A third is the *divination by ecstasy* which is employed by the magician when "smelling out" wizards. The old men assert that, in former times, there were diviners who could guess anything when in that peculiar psychological state in which the subliminal faculties may develop to a marvellous extent. Hendrick, a very old Native of Khosen, said to me, speaking of one of these *shinusa* (the term by which these diviners are known) : "He used to travel all through the land, practising his art in the villages. He was able to describe minutely a goat which he had never seen ; or if somebody had buried something in a certain place to test him, he would go straight to the spot and say : 'Dig in the earth here, and you will find it.' Viguet also asserted that there were formerly true and trustworthy diviners in the Hlabi clans, and I myself heard trustworthy witnesses assert that a certain diviner who had been called into a village near Rikatla actually discovered some pounds sterling which had been hidden by their owner, who was no longer in the country.

4 & 5) A young man of the Mabota clan described to me two other methods of divination employed by his father, old Tumben (I. p. 531). One was called the *Small Mug* (shintjekwana). The diviner took a wooden mug in his left hand and held it by the handle. He placed in it an antelope's or goat's horn, and with his right hand he struck his right leg, putting the question to which he wanted an answer. He would say : "Is the matter really as I say?" If he had guessed rightly, the horn began to move to and fro ; if not, it remained quiet. Tumben also consulted the oracles by means of the *Small Calabash* (nhungubane). This calabash had some rags hanging from its neck, and a string was passed round it by which he held it dandling from the thumb of his left hand. He

lifted that hand and with his right hand struck his right hip, meanwhile putting questions to the magical calabash, and calling it by the name he had given to it, viz., Nkoshi-wa-tihomu. To signify agreement, the calabash answered by means of the rags, which moved in all directions. Thereupon he said : "Keep quiet!" and the calabash remained quiet. — "He astonished us greatly, our father," added my informant! "His divinatory power came from the fact that certain incisions had been made in his hand and a special medicine inoculated into them. He had been taught by a man called Shitakule. Those who have not been initiated cannot consult the calabash ; the rags do not move for them, neither does the horn in the small mug."

All these are primitive means of divination. We now come to the more elaborate, the famous divinatory bones. But before entering upon this most curious and interesting subject, I will describe the *Hakati*, which is based on the same ideas, but, being very much more simple, affords a useful introduction to the study of the bones.

III. *The Hakati.*

Hakati (yin-tin) is the name given to the stone of a fruit growing in the desert. This stone is oval-shaped, and is cut in two so as to form two pointed cupules with a small notch at each extremity. These extremities are both called *nomu*, mouth, though there is undoubtedly an anterior part, that which is pointed, and a posterior part, that which is blunt. Six of these cupules constitute a whole set. Three are male (♂), three female (♀), the former being distinguished merely by their larger size. In the set which I possess, some cupules have been marked with brands of different kinds. These marks do not appear to have any significance, except that they help the diviner to recognise such and such a shell at once. The six shells are pierced through in the middle so that they can be passed through a string and hung round the neck. (See the left side of the accompanying plate.)

The hakati is mostly employed in Hlengweland (Gaza), and seems to have been invented by the Ndjao tribe ; the Ba-Ronga and

539

Thongas of other clans found it there during the hunting expeditions, and brought it back with them. It is used mostly by hunters to obtain directions and predictions in regard to their undertakings. Some also employ them for their domestic affairs (psa muti), but they are hardly sufficient for this purpose.

I have given an illustration of four cases which Spoon explained to me. The shells are thrown on a mat and two main things must be considered in the interpretation : the *direction* towards which they look and the *side* on which they fall, whether on their back, in the negative position, showing the concave side of the shell, or on their "legs," in the positive position, showing the convex side of the shell.

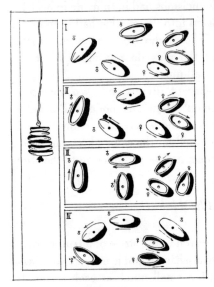

The Hakati.

No. 1. Two female shells on their backs looking to the right : the women have remained asleep in the village. One of them (♂ shell on her legs) is working. The male shell on the top is the hunter who starts in the early morning, and pursues the elephant (the ♂ shell to the right) with his gun (the ♂ shell at the bottom)... The hunter is on his back : he has missed the elephant, which runs away, being on its legs! The signs are unfavourable!

No. 2. Same scene : Women asleep at home ; early morning. But here the hunter is on his legs and the elephant on its back : the beast will be killed! The signs are favourable!

No. 3. A case of disease. Everybody on their backs, males and females! A very bad case, with no hope! They hardly breathe!

No. 4. Another case of disease. On the left, three shells ; the shell in the middle is the patient ; that at the bottom, in the negative position, is his grief, his mouth wide open, moaning ; that on the top is a female one, a woman who caused his disease, either by bewitching him, or because he had an unlawful connection with her. On the right three other shells : that at the top, the male one, is a friend going out of the village to fetch a remedy ; the two others, female, are two women opening their mouths, not to lament, but to laugh! They laugh at the man who was silly enough to expose himself to such a disgrace!

Those who practise the hakati art must also be initiated. They must bury their shells in the earth on the road, and when some one passes by on the path they unearth one shell, a male one if the passer-by be a man, a female one if it be a woman, (See later).

IV. *The Divinatory bones (Bula).*

The hakati shells are regarded as more or less childish. The divinatory bones, on the contrary, constitute an admirable system of divination and play a considerable part in the life of the tribe. They are called *nhlolo* (yin-tin), which is their little name ; the great one is *bula*, evidently the same word as *ku bula*, to speak, i. e. the *Word* with a capital letter, the Revelation! I remember old Maselesele, a Nkuna diviner, telling me : "You Christians believe in your Bible. Our Bible is much better than yours! It is the divinatory bones!"

I was initiated into the knowledge of this wonderful art by many masters. The first was *Spoon* (I. p. 4) ; he was only a beginner, and his set of bones was not complete ; but he understood the rules perfectly well and all that he told me was confirmed by subsequent study. The second was *Maselesele*, the old Nkuna just referred to, a blind man who knew his bones by the mere touch, and had a true veneration for them. Unhappily for this poor Nkuna, his hut was burnt during the Sikororo war (I. p. 512) and the precious basket containing his bones was destroyed. — "Why did they not warn you of the fate they were about to undergo?," I asked Maselesele one day. "They might have ordered you to save them if they knew everything!" He could find no answer to this remark, but his faith was absolutely unshakable. Such was also the case with *Mankhelu*, who had

541

practised the art all his life, and was attached to his divinatory
bones by every fibre of his being. His set was the most complete
I ever saw, containing as many as 64 objects. He even had two
sets, one contained in a leathern basket, the other in a kind of net
with small meshes ; the first he called the Father and the second the
Son. The Father always remained at home, whilst he took the
Son with him on his travels (1). I spent many hours with him,
trying fully to understand his teaching, and he took great trouble to
initiate me, concealing nothing from me, wondering sometimes at
his own readiness to do so, and saying : "This thing I would not
have told my own son." I had thus an opportunity of penetrating
into the depths of the Bantu mind, which has perhaps invented
nothing more elaborate or more typical than this divinatory system.
Of course no sensible person would for a moment believe in the
objective value of these practices. *Astragalomancy* has no more
real value than Cheiromancy, Necromancy and all the other
"mancies." But I am obliged to admit that the Thonga system is
far more ingenious than any other that I have met with, and that it
answers admirably to the wants of the Natives, comprehending all
the elements of their life, and photographing them, so to speak, in
such a manner that indications and directions can be obtained for
all possible . cases.

I have explained Spoon's art in detail in "Les Ba-Ronga."
I will here confine myself to Mankhelu's revelations, which were
more complete, as the old man was one of the masters of the
diviner's profession as well as of that of the medicine-man.

1) The objects composing the set of divinatory bones.

These may be divided into two kinds : the *bones* properly
speaking, most of which are *astragalus bones*, and the various
objects which are *not bones*. I shall now enumerate them, always

(1) I heard of another bone-thrower from Tembe who had also two baskets of
bones ; the first was called the basket of the chiefs, the second the basket of the subjects ;
the first was used in criminal cases to discover wizards : they were bones which "killed,"
and when they had accomplished their purpose, the diviner left them to rest for a
whole week, using in the meantime the second basket. He then washed them, and
they were ready to be used again.

giving the Native name of the object, as these names are technical and form quite a special vocabulary which seems to have an archaic character.

a) Amongst the bones some belong to *domestic animals*, goats and sheep, and consequently represent the *people dwelling in the village* :

Five astragalus of *he-goats* : 1) *Mbulwa*, the astragalus of an old castrated he-goat, the old man. 2) *Mbulwana* (diminutive of mbulwa), a he-goat not so old : men of ripe age. 3) *Shivimbiri*, a non-castrated he-goat : men in their prime. 4) *Shivimbidjana* (diminutive of the preceding), a non-castrated younger he-goat : young men of sixteen to twenty. 5) *Morisana wa timbuti shi-añwa-mafi*, the astragalus of a kid which is still a suckling : little boys, goatherds.

Six astragalus of she-goats : 1) *Gosha nkata wa mbulwa*, the old woman no longer capable of childbearing (1). 2) *Mihlangwana ya bukati, shinyuki sha timbuti*, a ripe woman still at the childbearing age, one who still smears her body with ochre. 3) *Ntibulana* (from tibula, to bring forth a child for the first time, I. p. 192) young married women, having had only one child. 4) *Nhombela*, a she-goat before parturition : girls practising the *gangisa* (I. p. 97), running about during the night but not yet married. 5) *Nhombe-djana* and *nhombedjana yo-anwa-mafi*, little goat and suckling goat : girls still without sexual knowledge, or babies at the breast.

The goats, here as everywhere else, stand for the subjects. The *sheep* indicate the chiefs. There are five astragalus of sheep : 1) *Hamba, nuna wa noni*, a castrated ram, the chief and the old men of the royal family. 2) *Shikwela sha timpfu* or *Khuna ra*

---

(1) This, like most of the bones, has a long story. When Mankhelu was empris- oned by the old Boer Government for having strangled a pretended wizard (I. p. 444), and condemned to death, a diviner consulted the bones for him, and advised him to draw the image of a Native village on the earth and to pray every day to his ancestor-gods on his mother's side, asserting that they would deliver him, and that, when he returned home, he should sacrifice a goat to them. He added : "If people offer you a cow on the road, refuse." Mankhelu was indeed released, owing to petitions made in his favour, and, on his way home, everybody came to welcome him. In one village, the people wanted to give him a cow, but he refused it. When he reached his kraal, one of the wives of his maternal uncle appeared with twenty jars of beer, five baskets of mealies and three goats. He sacrificed one of these, and the astragalus became the gos'ia of his set... He cannot look at it without a thrill of the heart !

timpfu, a non-castrated ram : the sons of the royal family, the εὐγενεῖς! (bana ba-ku-psalwa). 3) Another *Shikwela*, astragalus of the ram sacrified during the Sikororo war, the one whose psanyi was used for the sprinkling of the Nkuna army ; it designates the enemy, and is watched with special attention when casting the bones in connection with military affairs. 4) *Noni wa timpfu*, an old sheep, the widow of the chief. 5) *Nhombela ya timpfu*, a young sheep, the girls of the royal family. As regards the wife of the chief, she is represented by the astragalus of the female mhala antelope.

In one of his sets of bones Mankhelu also had two objects taken *from an ox*. One was an oval-shaped smooth bone, two inches long, the other, one of its hoofs decorated on one of its three sides with triangular marks (See plate). Both represent the *Nkuna* tribe, whose totem is the buffalo. (Comp. I. p. 364.) But this is a custom borrowed from the Sutho-Pedis. I never saw bones corresponding to totems used in Thonga divination ; the idea of totem is altogether absent from the minds of the Thongas when not influenced by their Pedi neighbours.

In addition to those of the domestic animals, there are a number of astragalus, or other bones, taken from *wild animals*.

First from *antelopes* : the male *mhala*, *tsombe ra mhala*, means the chief, and the female mhala, his wife ; the male mhunti, *tsombe ra mhunti*, *mhunti ya matlhari*, the duiker of the weapons, means fighting men, and the female mhunti, called *mbiri*, means women of loose character : *mbiri ya ku tola, nwashifamba ni mafura eku rimen*, the woman who smears herself with grease and ochre, even when she goes to her field (thus trying to attract the attention of men). The *nhlangu* (reed buck), wandering about during the night, means wizards, as these cast their spells by night. Mankhelu had only the astragalus of the female in his set. The *mbalala* antelope dwells in the forest ; it does not like to come out in the plains ; its astragalus therefore designates the chief who rests in his hut and does not expose himself to the toil and the heat of the day.

The astragalus of the *ngolube ya ku dya marambo, yi tjela mitshi yi ralarala, yi languta hi matlhelo*, the wild boar which eats bones, which digs holes, which looks about on all sides, is the medicine-man who searches for roots to prepare his drugs. The female wild pig is the medicine man's wife.

Three astragalus of a very different form come from *baboons, nuna wa mfene*, the male baboon, *nsati wa mfene*, the female

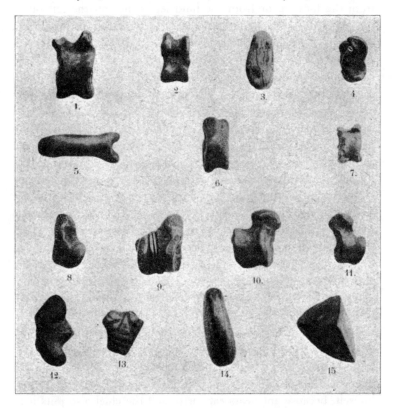

Objects specially worthy of note in Mankhelu's set of divinatory bones.

1. Mbalala antelope ☌. +. 2. Ram —. 3. Mhala antelope ☌ ×. 4. Reed buck ♀ :. 5. Phalanx of a Lion +. 6. Astragalus found in the dejecta of a hyena : Ancestor-god. 7. Malumbi +. 8. Ant-bear +. 9. Hyena +. 10. Leopard +. 11. Baboon +. 12. Kanye stone +. 13. Kanye : part of twig +. 14. Ox. 15. Ox hoof.

baboon, *nhombela ya mfene*, the young baboon. They symbolise the *village*, because baboons never move from their chosen spot. "You never see the ruins of their habitations ; though men may build in their neighbourhood, these apes do not leave permanently, you will see them coming back again next spring."

The following bones are asexual. There is only one of each kind in the set and it is not indicated whether it is male or female : the phalanx of a *lion* (ndjao), either male or female, taken either from the fore leg or from the hind leg, either on the left or on the right side. The lion is the chief of wild animals, so its phalanx represents the chief of the tribe, par excellence. It also designates White people, who are regarded as being as rich as kings! The astragalus of the *leopard, yingwe, shidya mafura,* the beast which eats fat and eats no grass, is also alone of its kind, the male only being taken ; it represents those who can choose their food, the rich, not the poor and wretched, "the chiefs and you White people," says Mankhelu! The *hyena, mhisi,* stands for the counsellors, the sycophants, the parasites ; they resemble the hyena, which follows the lion and the panther to eat the remains of their feasts, crunching the bones of a prey which it was not strong enough to kill! But the astragalus of the hyena also represents the wizards, because they eat the flesh of people whom they steal ; the ancestor-gods, because the hyena remains hidden in its hole during the day, like the psikwembu in their graves ; the chief himself, in as much as the chief also "eats" his subjects, and you cannot follow him and recover your property any more than you can a hyena!

The astragalus of the *ant-bear* (mhandjela), which digs the holes in which porcupines live, has also many meanings : the ancestor-gods, because they dwell in the earth and never come out in the day-time ; the power of death, because it digs the grave ; the chief himself, because ant-bears eat earth, and the chief also puts it to his mouth when sacrificing. He has the right to do so, when saying *tsu,* because the earth is his ; it belonged to his ancestors before him and he calls to them by its means (I. p. 405). Spoon used one of the claws of the ant-bear, instead of its astragalus.

A very curious bone is the one called *Shikwembu,* ancestor-god. It is a mhala astragalus found in the excrement of a hyena ; a most uncommon discovery, made by Mankhelu when on his way to Swaziland. The bone is worn down : it has evidently been bitten by sharp teeth. I have explained (p. 376) how fittingly this bone was chosen to represent the spirits of the departed. They also have been swallowed by the earth, as the astragalus by the hyena, but return again to light and life in a new and divine existence!

The last astragalus of the set is the *malumbi*, the astragalus of the *shipene* or *mangulwe* antelope ; it is also asexual : *shirombe sha matiko, malumbyana wa tintibo, ntsinyarendjo*! the miserable of the land, the little antelope with white spots, the one which stops travellers (p. 347)! It plays a special part in the divinatory system, representing everything which is violent (leba) : the chief, the enemy, and especially the mysterious power of Heaven. For that reason it is watched with great attention by those who cast bones in connection with rain. When it falls in the "mild" position, it means that "the eye of Heaven is open, the knot is untied, the mouth of Heaven is open, rain will fall!" Then Mankhelu will make the offering (mhamba) for rain ; first the four leaves, then, if this is not sufficient, and if the chief requires it, the sacrifice of the black ram (p. 322, 316).

I include in the category of bones the pieces of *Tortoise shell*, *mfutju*, four of which are found in Mankhelu's basket : *mbulwa wa mfutju*, the adult male tortoise, *nsati, ntibula ya mfutju*, the young tortoise. According to the way in which they fall, these objects designate peace or misfortune for the village, prosperity or starvation (1).

b) The second category comprises the objects which are not bones or parts of the body of an animal. The most conspicuous are the *sea-shells* (djuma, dji-ma) belonging to two different genera : the *Oliva* shells, representing the attributes of the male, assagais, virile courage, etc., the *Cypraea* shells, corresponding to the attributes of the female, baskets, pots, pregnancy, births, oxen for lobola, etc.

There are besides two *kanye stones* of an abnormal form, one

---

(1) One day, when travelling through heavy rain, Mankhelu found a tortoise and obtained one of his divinatory bones from it. Soon afterwards he came upon an animal (I did not catch its name) which had just died, and ate it. Some time later he was offered a big he-goat in a village. So when the tortoise falls together with the astragalus of that animal, it is a s gn that plenty of meat will be forthcoming !

found by a woman, the *female nkanye*, the other by a man, the *male nkanye*. These abnormal stones are very rare. They represent the vegetable world, especially *medicines, drugs*. They are supplemented by a little piece of nkanye twig, *nhombela ya nkanye*, the girl of nkanye, which was cut by a girl of Mankhelu's village on a certain day when he went to his "bakokwana" (to the relatives of his mother) to make a sacrifice. Being their uterine nephew, he had special rights and took the opportunity of enriching his divinatory set with their assistance.

Two *stones* are also to be found in the basket : the first is *ribye ra ngwenya* or *shimidjya sha ngwenya*, a stone found in the stomach of a crocodile ; these stones are generally of a dark colour, and frequently represent mourning, defilement (khumo, nsila) ; the second is *ribye ra dayiman*, the diamond stone, not a real diamond unhappily, but a stone with a striking design, found on the road, or in distant lands, by a traveller. It means luck, money, riches brought from foreign countries, gold which is extracted from the soil, in the same way as was this stone. I have shown in the accompanying plate (p. 545) the most curious and rare of the contents of Mankhelu's basket. In that of Maselesele there were also two pieces of white china, which represented the Whites ; another Nkuna diviner had chosen the shuttle of a sewing-machine for the same purpose. But these are new-comers in the basket, and are not met with in the old sets.

Comparing the explanations of the old Nkuna Mankhelu, who had been initiated long before and was an experienced diviner, with those of Spoon who belonged to the Coast clans, and was still a beginner in the art, I found a remarkable agreement between them. There are, however, some differences which can be explained by the wonderful imagination of the diviners. For instance, the wild pig indicated for Spoon the ancestor-gods, because they dwell in the sacred woods and dig the earth, and also old relatives who are on the eve of becoming gods ; the duiker meant the wizard because it also walks during the night, and the traveller because it rarely rests.

Though the bones have a fixed and definite meaning, they can also designate other objects if it is possible to establish a connection between the animal and these objects, and we know how quick the Bantu mind is at discovering such relations between men and animals.

2) THE CONSULTATION OF THE DIVINATORY BONES AND THE RULES FOR THEIR INTERPRETATION.

I owe to a Tembe informant the following full description of the sequence of acts performed in a consultation of the divinatory bones. Suppose one of the inmates of the village to have been suddenly taken ill. The people who dwell in the same hut will at once go to the headman, even if it is night-time ; he will come, inspect the patient, and, having convinced himself of the serious-ness of the case, he will start immediately for the diviner's village, not forgetting to take with him the necklace of the patient with his protective amulets (timfisa p. 471) ; if the man did not wear timfisa, the headman will replace these by some roots of a common plant, the tjeke, p. 14, or even of a common grass, the ntlangi ; these roots will be rubbed against his forehead and against his chest and will then be called his *ntjuleko*. Having reached the diviner's village, the consultant briefly states the object of his visit. A mat is unrolled and the ntjuleko placed on it, somewhere at the side ; the diviner takes all his bones in his hand, holds them firmly, and having chewed a little piece of a magic root, (1) spits on them and throws them on to the mat, saying with emphasis : "Mhamoo!" Those attending the consultation answer in the same tone : "Hizwaa! Si ya vuma!" — "Yes! We are agreed." This throwing is only preliminary. By spitting over his bones the diviner wishes to awaken them (pfusha) to make them see (hanyanyisa). He then passes them to the consultant, who will himself throw them throughout the whole consultation, the diviner only holding his little stick and pointing to them in order to explain their significance.

In the first place the consultant takes the necklace of the patient

(1) Mankhelu used for this purpose the bulb of a Liliacea called shirungulu, which has an agreeable scent.

or the above-mentioned roots, and rubs three or four bones against them. These objects having been in close contact with the patient and containing his "nsila," the exudation of his body, establish a connection between him and the bones. The bones will then "know him" and throughout the operation these astragalus, which have been, so to speak, anointed with the "nsila" of the patient, will be watched with special interest ; if they are "doubtful," hesitating (gome), the diviner will also have doubts about the revelations made by the others (1).

The consultant throws the bones for the first time, the diviner having asked : "What about the patient?" If the bones fall in a manner which corresponds to the state of the patient, all is well. The diviner will show with his stick that this correspondence exists. It is a proof that the bones have really awakened and are disposed to speak. The question is then put a second time in order that the first reply may be confirmed.

The way is now open for further inquiries ; in the first place, what is the cause of the disease? Does it come from the ancestor-gods? From a male ancestor-god? From one on the paternal side? From great-grandfather so and so? From great-grandmother so and so? When the bones answer in the negative, another name is tried, and so the consultation proceeds by a process of elimination ; the names of deceased great-uncles, parents, uncles, even of a son who may have died quite young are pronounced successively. If the ancestor-god who caused the disease is not found in the paternal line, then the same questions are put regarding the maternal ancestors, the bakokwana, the diviner himself suggesting to the consultant the names which are to be mentioned. It may be that the bones, which are often thrown two or three times for each name, will designate one of the ancestors. Then begins another series of questions. Why is the god angry? Is it because the patient has neglected his duties towards him? What does he ask for in order that he may be appeased? Goat's flesh? Clothing? Beer? Mealies? Who shall bring (tamela)

(1) If the diviner or his client consults for himself, he rubs these bones against his own forehead and his chest before throwing them on to the mat, and the connection is thus established.

the offering? The headman? An adult? A child? A certain relation who is on bad terms with the patient and has sworn never to enter his village again? If the latter is designated he will have to come, after having first made the offering of reconciliation (described p. 398). The bones must likewise designate the person who will have to stab the victim, as also the person who will say tsu and pronounce the prayer. This may be a baby, and, in

Consulting the bones.   *Phot. A. Borel.*

that case, his father will take him in his arms and pray instead of him. Women are often designated, as we saw on p. 411.

But it may happen that the bones do not agree that the disease has been caused by an ancestor-god at all. The consultation then takes another turn. Was it caused by a wizard? By a witch? Is it so and so? Or so and so? If no affirmative answer is given there then remains still another alternative. Has the patient been contaminated by the defilement of the bush (the dust of contaminated huts thrown down at crossroads) or of the footprints (mitila, p. 478)?

Such is the procedure followed in a consultation regarding disease. It will be modified according to circumstances, when the advice of the bones is asked for in other difficulties.

If from the beginning there is no correspondance whatever between the manner in which the bones have fallen and the case for which they are consulted, if they "refuse to speak," the diviner will perhaps roll up his mat and leave the hut ; he will then try to throw the bones on the square, or in the bush, or behind the hut, and the consultation will be continued there till a clear answer is given.

In order to see if the bones have really consented to speak, three or four things are specially examined : the *side* on which the bones have fallen, the *direction* towards which they look, their *disposition* or the position they have taken in regard to each other, and the *relation* of the male and the female bones towards each other, viz., are all the male or all the female bones on the same side ? Each object can fall on two sides, all of them having a *convex* and a *concave* side. If they fall so as to show the convex side (bukhatsha position), they are said *to be full* (ku tala), or *to stand on their legs* and to *march forward* (ku famba) ; this is the *positive side*, which I indicate by $+$; if they fall showing their concave side (lwandla position) they are *empty* (ku pshya, image of a lake which has dried up), or lie *on their back* : this is the *negative position* which I indicate by $-$. In the first case, the person or principal represented by the bones is happy (tjaka), at peace (rula), active, marching, powerful ; in the second he is tired (karala), ashamed (tingana), powerless, dying (fa). Astragalus of goats, and sheep on their convex side, show that the inhabitants of the village, or the chief, are in good health and good spirits, working, succeeding ; if on their concave side, they show that those persons are lying ill or dying. On the other hand, the astragalus of the ant-bear in the positive position indicates that the digger is digging a grave, that the ancestor-gods are awake and probably ready to punish, etc. So it would not be correct to call the convex the favourable, and the concave the unfavourable side. The first is the *active*

552

position, the second the *passive* one. Most of the astragalus may fall not only on these two principal sides, but also on the right or on the left side. The right side is called *ntjumba*, and is somewhat convex. Mankhelu explained to me its meaning by himself imitating the position (See the accompanying plate). He sits with his shield protecting him, with *his chest full*, ready to

Phot. H. A. Junod.

Mankhelu imitating the "ntjumba" position.

spit (like a cat), and his assagay lifted ready to be thrown ; this is the position of hostility, of anger. The left side is called *dzwari*, or *minkono*, viz., the elbows ; it is somewhat concave. It is the position of a man half leaning on his elbows, *his chest empty*, enjoying life and not threatening others, the assagay being turned towards the soil (See the next plate). These two positions, which I represent by ×, the sign of multiplication, for *ntjumba*, and :, the sign of division, for *minkono*, are rarely met with. Spoon knew nothing of them. They belong to a more elaborate art. In fact the two first positions are by far the most common. Let us see what is the meaning of some of the divinatory objects in these different positions :

Baboon +, the village is firm ; no ruins! Baboon —, the village is destroyed ; disease or death ; that which you eat does not remain inside : dysentery.

Ancestor-god +, the gods are happy and thankful. Ancestor-

Phot. H. A. Junod.

Mankhelu imitating the "minkono" position.

god —, they sleep ; there is nothing to fear ; ×, they are angry, they speak in a low voice ; : , they speak mildly.

Kanye +, the drugs have their eyes open (the two kernels inside the nkanye stone have been removed, and it appears to have two eyes, which are visible in the positive position and hidden in the negative) ; the drugs help, cure. Kanye —, the eyes of the drugs are closed ; the medicine-man will not succeed.

Crocodile stone +, the country is at peace, the village is happy,

554

no misfortune.   Crocodile stone —, the crocodile is hidden in the water, it waits for you and will kill you : starvation, death, defilement.

Tortoise-shells +, the village is smeared with ochre ; every one perspires agreeably, walking slowly as tortoises do when they come out to enjoy the rain, and eat grass.   People drink beer, and have plenty to eat.   Tortoise-shell —, misfortune in the village ; everything looks black (the concave side of the tortoise-shell is rough and more or less black).   Nothing is cared for on the square ; the grass grows there ; disorder, death, starvation.   The tortoises are hidden in their holes.

Female sea-shells +, the rivers are full ; pregnancy takes its normal course ; the wealth which comes by the sea in the steamers is well protected.   Female sea-shells —, the rivers are empty ; birth is imminent, either favourable or otherwise ; there has been a wreck at sea, and you will find riches on the shore!

Male sea-shells +, the assagais are in good condition ; men succeed in their undertakings.   Male sea-shells —, the assagais are broken ; the army will be defeated.

Sea-shells in the negative position, showing their opening, also mean a mouth open to laugh or to cry : if all are in this position, it means lamentation, because when all the people open their mouths together, it is always to lament ; when two or three only show their teeth, it means laughter, as people never laugh all together, but only a few at a time!

While the side on which the bones fall must be considered before all else in the interpretation, the *direction* in which they look is also very important, as it reveals the intentions and movements of all the personages represented ; their *arrangement* shows the relation between these persons ; moreover if all, or most, of the astragalus of the same sex fall in the same position, this is a sign to be particularly noted for the following reason. If a woman is ill and you wish to receive directions as to what to do for her, you cast the bones ; if the she-goat falls on the negative side, this proves that the Word is speaking; but if all the other feminine astragalus show their concave side also then no doubt remains ; the Word is really speaking ; a valuable confirmation has been given!

3) SOME CASES OF ASTRAGALOMANCY.

My informants explained to me a certain number of cases which will illustrate the system of astragalomancy better than anything else. I have published illustrations of seven of these in an article in the *Bulletin IX of the Society of Geography of Neuchâtel*. They were given to me by Spoon. I shall here re-publish one of them, the case of the sick mother, and two new ones, much more complex, which I owe to Mankhelu.

These three cases will be sufficient to illustrate the divinatory system. Let me give, as a preliminary, the two following instances :

Prediction of rain : Ram × and Mhala ×, the chief is full of confidence ; the He-goats, the headmen are glad and thankful ; Mbalala +, the chief is happy ; it will be wet in the forest! Tortoises —, there is black everywhere ; the soil is dark on account of the rain. Olivae +, all the huts are closed because nobody dares to go out lest he be soaked! Baboons +, the village will have plenty to eat. If Baboon were —, the rain would be accompanied by bad winds, which would break down the mealies and bring starvation.

The place where the timbhorola (the dirt which falls from the body of a convalescent during the hondlola rite, p. 471) *must be thrown*. Here the diviner proceeds by questions, in order to obtain the directions required. He asks : "In the river?" and throws the bones ; if the astragalus of the patient falls in the + position, Male Tortoise also, while the female astragalus are on their elbows, playing, smiling ; if the Lion is — (the bad bloods have been overcome) ; if Hyena is — (the disease which kills is vanquished), if the Ant-bear is — (the gods sleep), and the female Tortoises are +, meaning that women will soon be able to smear their bodies with ochre, then the answer is : yes. If this is not the case, he asks : "Into an ants'nest?" and again throws the bones, until the answer is positive.

The chiefs always consult the bones in order to know if the time has come *to sow the seeds* of pumpkins and millet. If all the Sea-Shells fall showing their mouths (yahlama), and the astragalus of the ram and ewe are in the + position, then you may sow.

See, p. 483, how the bones are consulted in order to obtain directions *in the rites of exorcism*, and, p. 525, how they help to *discover the wizards*.

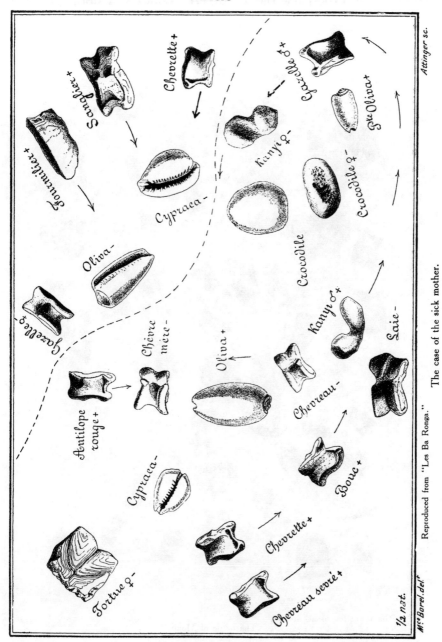

½ nat. McᵉBorel. delᵗ Reproduced from "Les Ba Ronga." The case of the sick mother.

Attinger sc.

557

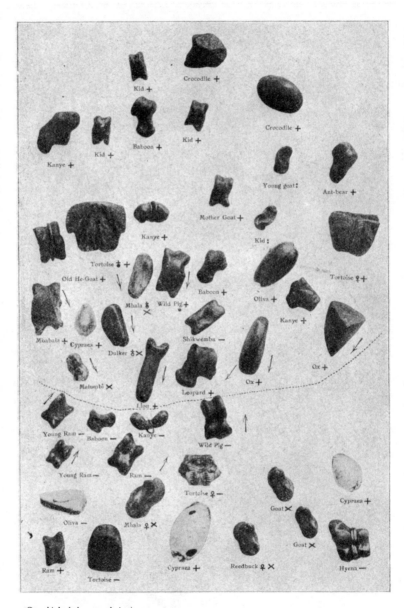

(One third of the natural size.)

The battle of Moudi.

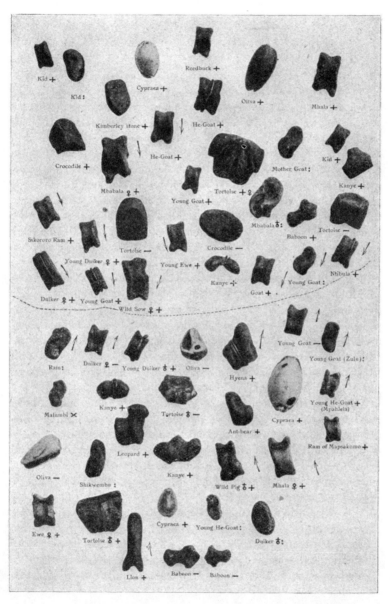

(One third of natural size).

Prophecy of a Migration.

a) *The case of the sick mother* (p. 557).

In the centre we see *She-Goat* —; the mother is sick, on her back! Above, the red Antelope, Malumbi + and below, Oliva +, are looking towards her ; these are the malignant influences which have thrown her into this state. *Cypraea* — wide-open, on her left, shows that she is suffering from dysentery! On the extreme left we see *Weaned Kid* + and *Young Goat* + on their legs, walking ; they are going towards *He-goat*, the father, who is also +, not quite discouraged, and pointing toward the *kanye*, the medicine by which he hopes to cure his wife. By so doing he keeps in check *Wild Sow* — the ancestor-god, who is thus prevented from adding his hostile influence to those already active. Near him is *Kid* — a young boy on his back, quite in despair, who keeps close to his mother. The father, having spoken with his children, starts for the bush, following the three arrows shown at the bottom of the plate. On the right, we see *Gazelle, Duiker* + ; this is he again returning from his walk as a traveller (the duiker, being always on his legs, often represents travellers). He holds the drug he has dug up *(Kanye* —). But this kanye stone is on the bad side ; it was difficult to find the roots, which penetrated into the soil, as do the two protuberances of the stone! Moreover two *Crocodiles' stones* speak of death, and the little *Oliva* + looks at the father in a hostile manner. The bones of the upper part, on the right, contain no encouragement whatever. *Wild Pig* + is an old relative coming to pay a visit to the sick woman ; he is accompanied by a girl, *Young She-Goat*, below him, who also goes towards the village with lamentations, shown by the open *Cypraea* in front of her ; on the top, *Ant-bear* + comes to dig the grave! Near him *Duiker* — is on its back, without strength, whilst *Tortoise* —, in the left hand corner, is also lying on her back ; no agreeable perspiration, no peace, no happiness.

The bones here give a triple revelation ; they depict the actual position, show its cause, and indicate its course and the remedy ; the disease is serious, but there is ground for hope if the father finds the right drug. If the astragalus of the He-Goat had been on its back, and that of the Wild Sow on its legs, directed against the patient, the case would have been hopeless.

MAGIC

b) *The battle of Moudi* (p. 558).

On the 6th of November, 1901, when the hostile army of Sikororo was signalled (I. p. 513), Mankhelu, seized with a terrible dread, consulted his bones. The Word spoke with such precision that one would be tempted to believe that the message was touched up post eventum. But Mankhelu asserts that many witnesses were present and testify to the prophecy of the victory which occurred the following day.

The bones fell in two lots, first, those on the upper two thirds of the plate, on the side of the diviner, and consequently representing his own army : complete victory! Second, those in the lower third of the plate, representing the enemy : absolute rout! I have separated these two parts with dots. Let us look at the lower part first. Three Rams on their backs : the chiefs killed ; the Ram is Rios, the acting chief of the Sikororo clan, the great enemy. Yesterday a ram was sacrificed to ask the gods to give victory. Its astragalus was taken and added to the other bones, to represent Rios ; here he is, dead on the battle-field! Close by, Wild Pig and Kanye are also on their backs : their medicine-man has been unable to protect them. Baboon is —, the village of Sikororo is destroyed! Tortoises —, no peace in that village, they are black! No resplendent ochre, but darkness and misfortune for them! Female Mhala ×, the women have their chests full of grief ; they cry. See all the female astragalus on their backs, or on their sides, in dreadful misfortune. Oliva —, the weapons broken, powerless. Two Cyprea +, no laughter, faces dark! Hyena —, Titus, a Pedi Christian who acted as counsellor to the chief, the sycophant of Rios, has been killed. See, in the left corner, at the bottom, Ram +. This is old Sikororo, the chief who dwelt in the mountains and had not given his consent to the treacherous attack. He is alone, unaware of what has been done by Rios, the chief regent. The Nkunas will not interfere with the good old man.

On the Nkuna side, Lion and Malumbi are in the foreground ; the one + the other ×, viz. full of courage : they represent the superior powers : you, Ba-Moneri (the missionaries), who helped us in that terrible hour! Leopard +, the sons of the chief are also running furiously towards the enemy. Ox +, the totem of the Nkuna clan is in good order ; he is safe. Shikwembu sleeps ; the ancestor-gods are not anxious about us ; they rest peacefully. Wild Pig +, the medicine-man who sprinkled the army is happy ; all his drugs (Kanye +) are

561

acting, they have their eyes open. Look behind Malumbi ; all the troops of warriors, Mhunti, Mhala, are in the ntjumba position, in high spirits, and their arms (Oliva +) are all strong and victorious ; the guns will not miss fire. Behind them, the kids and young goats, little boys and girls, are playing, quietly leaning on their elbows (minkono position). The chief (Mbabala +) who remained at home, is happy, as is also the old He-goat, his uncle, who did not take part in the battle. Ant-bear +, the ancestor-god of the village, is also quiet ; the two Tortoises + warm themselves in the rays of the sun ; the women still smear their bodies with fat and ochre!

The battle of the 6th of November, 1901, was a great event for the Nkuna tribe. For me it proved a wonderful opportunity of witnessing some of the most curious customs of the tribe. I owe to it this consultation, the narrative of Mankhelu's mhamba (p. 418) and the knowledge of many military rites (I. p. 476).

c) *Prophecy of a Migration* (p. 559).

On the day of the renewal of his drugs, which was a feast for his whole village (p. 454), Mankhelu threw his bones, which promised marvellous things : a throng of distinguished visitors were about to come and make their submission to him and increase his power ; princes, rich people laden with wealth! As Mankhelu was residing on the Mission farm, he said to me one day : "Be happy, my missionary, you will have new tenants who will increase the value of your farm! They are preparing their loads now... My god, Shiluvane, has revealed this to me. They will come before the tilling season begins. If they do not come I will give you an ox!" Some months later, no one having appeared on the horizon, I inquired from my old friend as to my ox. With a good-natured laugh he said : "Look! I will show you how the bones lied to me," and he placed his sixty-two bones on the mat as they had fallen on that day.

Once more we have the two halves, which I have separated by the dotted line ; in the lower part the migrating clan arriving, in the upper, Mankhelu's village welcoming it. Two Baboons —, the village is ruined, they leave it ; their chiefs are Lion, who is +, in good health, and Ram : laughing, smiling, playing. Malumbi is ×; his chest is full, because he is running away ; he is a powerful man, but he is out of breath. Near Ram we have his daughter Duiker ♀ on her back ; he offers her in marriage. She will even give us a child (young male Duiker near her!) The child will be a boy, as he is surrounded by Tortoise ♂ and the male shell Oliva. These chiefs may have been dispossessed of their own country ; this is shown by the Ram of Mapsakomo ; this astragalus was taken after a sacrifice made at the death of Mapsakomo, the rival of Muhlaba, who died of anger when his right to the chieftain-ship of the Nkuna clan was forfeited (I. p. 412). Young He-Goat, in front of him, also proves the foreign origin of the visitors ; it is an astragalus which Mankhelu obtained in the Mpahlela district, South of the Oliphant. Young goat, playing, indicates the same thing, its astragalus having come from Swaziland. In front of her is another Young goat — ; this is a girl who is offered to us in marriage, perhaps a second, perhaps the same as Duiker ♀; at any rate the prediction is confirmed. This Young goat is called that of *ringela bovumba*, because its astragalus has been taken from the animal sacrificed in the rite of removing the malediction of bovumba (I. p. 194). It may perhaps indicate that the misfortune of these noble strangers will also be removed when they come and dwell with us! Hyena is in the + position : they are cunning people ; nobody will dare to run after them! They keep firm hold of what they possess or have stolen! Leopard + : they are rich people, living on fat and flesh. The two Cypraea +, indicate the sea and the wealth brought into the country by the steamers, which they carry with them! One might think that they were White people! Wild Pig +, they have their medicine-man and their drugs (Kanye +) ; their children (young He-goat : and Duiker ♂) play and dance! Their women (Mhala + Ewe +) are covered with ochre as shown by Tortoise +. Their gods, Shikwembu and Ant-bear +, are with them and have "given them the road"; they are pointing in the same direction. "Look at Ewe, the old woman, the widow of the chiefs! What has she hanging round her neck? — Oliva, a crocodile-tooth, an amulet well smeared with protective drugs?" Such is the procession of the new-comers.

In the upper half, we see the village of Mankhelu welcoming the new-comers ; the young children and the women run in front (Duiker ♀+, Young Duiker +, Young Goats + and Young Ewe +, Ntibula +); they are curious, they are anxious to see who the visitors are. Behind them come the old people : Mbabala ♀+, the wife of the chief ; the chief himself, Muhlaba, Mbabala ♂:, is on his elbows, quiet and smiling, in no way fearing this peaceful invasion, whilst his mother, Mother-Goat, comes also, dancing. Baboon + ; does not this show that the village is secure? Mankhelu himself is represented by three bones : Ram +

and two He-Goats +. He comes with dignity to meet the arrivals. Behind, in the village itself (at the top of the plate), boys (kids) play beneath the shade of the trees (kanye) ; two women are killing each other's lice! i. e. Reedbuck and Cypraea, the female sea-shell! etc. One of the Tortoises is —, showing its black side. But this is not a sign of disease or defilement ; the village has been cleaned, the black soil is visible everywhere because it has been well swept and the huts also have been smeared afresh. The black colour also indicates that the bush has been burnt ; it prophesies the time when these strangers will come, when the bush-fire has reduced all the grass to ashes, in September or October, at the end of the winter The Tortoise in front of He-Goat is + ; this is the face of Mankhelu, radiant with joy. "Mahlwen ka mbulwa ku nyuka!" — "on the face of the old man there is sweet perspiration." His drugs are all right (kanye +, means both drugs and shade). Crocodile is —, the rivers are low ; this confirms the forecast of the time of the arrival. The Kimberley stone is + ; the earth is solid, firm. Oliva +, the sky is clear, we are happy! When we rise in the morning we look towards the East! etc.

—"Wonderful!" said I to Mankhelu. "Only they did not come!" — "Never mind," he answered. — "Then the bones have deceived you!" — "Not at all! If it is not this year, it will be next year! Moreover, we diviners are not afraid of being told that our bones lie. When, later on, our prophecies are fulfilled, then people wonder! They are convinced. And after all, if the Word lies, it is not my fault!" — "How is that?" — "We do not put our ideas into them (a hi ti rumeteli) ; we merely interpret them ; it is they who speak!" — "Then they have a power in themselves?" — "No! the power is in the chest of the diviner." Such was the conversation with which the demonstration closed. I shall return to it presently.

4) THE INITIATION OF THE DIVINERS.

Astragalomancy is not an esoteric art ; every one in the tribe knows the bones, and their significance, and all the men attend the consultations and help in the interpretation. However, every one is not a diviner and an initiation is necessary to become a fully qualified practitioner. If a young man feels that he has the qualities of perspicuity and shrewdness necessary for the practice of the art, he begins by collecting the astragalus one after another. This is a long job. Spoon told me that, having once been annoyed by a forecast made by a diviner, he thought : "I might as well consult the bones myself!" So he picked up the astragalus of a goat in a hut. He obtained others when hunting ; on the road to Johannesburg he saw a curious stone, which became the lucky stone in his set. When he had ten astragalus, he began to throw them for his comrades, giving them advice in their love affairs! Then he consulted his bones before going to hunt and noticed that, when the astragalus of the duiker fell in the negative position, he killed game. But he was still an apprentice ; he had not the right to receive money, but only bracelets which hung on the string of his basket (1). When the apprentice has earned enough of these bracelets, he goes to an old practitioner, gives them to him as a fee, and asks to be initiated, so that he may become a master himself. Shishakane, in the Movumbi district, and Ñwahoñwana, in the Mabota clan, were those to whom such applications were made. The following are the ceremonies of initiation amongst the Ba-Ronga.

The master takes all the bones collected by the apprentice, kills a fowl, introduces them into the body (2), and cooks the whole. Then the candidate eats the fowl, returns home with his bones and buries the astragalus on the road, at the entrance of the village. He hides himself at that spot, to watch. When a woman passes, he exhumes a female astragalus ; when a man, a male one ; the he-goat, in the case of a man of ripe age, the kid, in that of a boy, etc. In this way all his bones are said to "have returned to him." Then he again calls on the master. The old man orders him to close his eyes and places before him all his bones in a line ; the candidate must recognise them all by touch and take them all up one after the other, pronouncing the name of each. The examination evidently aims at ascertaining if he knows them thoroughly. Having successfully passed through the trial, the

---

(1) The divinatory basket of Spoon is shown on the plate p. 124 No. 2.
(2) I suppose that he adds his own bones to those of the applicant, in order that their divinatory virtue may enter the bones of the candidate. This is the rule followed in the Nkuna initiation. See later.

new diviner must undergo a hondlola, a long ablution with nkuhlu leaves, after which he is initiated ; he has the right of asking payment in cash, up to the sum of three pence. For a shilling, he will consent to throw the bones all day until they have revealed everything.

Amongst the Nkunas the initiation is somewhat different ; the apprentice does not practise his art until he has earned a goat. He practises in foreign villages, where he is not known and where people believe that he has already been initiated. Having succeeded, he brings the animal to his master and will then "have his bones cooked for him" (a ta psekeriwa bula). One of the forelegs and the diaphragm are put in a pot together with a root called banga. The set of bones of the master and that of the apprentice are added to them, and the whole is cooked. When the meat is done, the contents of the pot are poured into a lihlelo basket, and both suck in the broth with their lips. They then eat the meat, which has been cut into pieces, without touching it with their hands, seizing it with their teeth alone, "the same as vultures do, which scent meat from far away." The heart of one of these birds has been cooked with the other drugs "so that the new diviner will be able to dream of things which are far away and go straight to them." He will be able to go and guess anything at once without fear or hesitation.

The bones have remained in the lihlelo basket, and another drug is used to wash them ; this is the bark of a tree called *mbandjwa*. The new diviner must then show his powers of divination : all his astragalus being mixed with those of the master, he must pick them out without a mistake, calling them by the name he has given them. If he fails, the trial must be gone through again later ; he returns home and the bones are given a rest ; he then comes another day and the two sets are again dipped, this time into beer ; the beer is drunk by both the master and the apprentice, the bones are washed and thrown, and the latter must now pick them out again. He will probably succeed, and so becomes a master. But the old diviner gives him one of the bones of his own set, which will "reign over the set of the initiated." This bone will always be considered first ; it is the *father* and *mother* of the set.

If the other bones indicate a bad omen, the new diviner will not be troubled so long as the king of the set shows a good one. If, on the other hand, the king is in the — position, or in the × position, the young man will fear to give a favourable prophecy.

The diviner (wa bula) is in most cases at the same time a ñanga. a medicine-man, and he will probably initiate the candidate into the knowledge of his drugs also. "Because," said Mankhelu, "to possess the Word alone is of little use : you need also the *mbhulo*, the magic medicines." The price paid to the initiator was formerly 80 hoes, or a wife, and the initiated, when calling at the village of his master, used to sleep in the hut of this woman. Being in possession of these new qualifications the newly-qualified diviner has the right of *planting his magic forked branch* (shiphandje. See Illustration I. p. 5 and II. p. 495). This rite is subject to many rules, which the initiator teaches his pupil ; the latter must dig a certain quantity of white sand in a deep pool, and bury it in his hut where he intends placing the branch. This will then be "planted in the abyss" (shidziba). Should the hut burn, or should enemies set fire to it, water will spring from the depths and prevent the shipandje from being consumed. Moreover a sacrifice is made to the ancestors who transmitted their drugs to the initiator, and the psanyi of the slaughtered sheep is used to smear the branch. An intimate relation remains between the old doctor and his pupil. When the former dies, the latter must "raise," or "awaken his drugs" by a number of ceremonies which aim at removing the defilement brought upon them by this death. These are rules which apply to medicine-men as well as to diviners.

The forked pole is both the laboratory and the altar (it is also called gandjelo, p. 388) and also the museum of the magician. He hangs to it his calabashes of drugs, his basket of bones, the psirungulo (part of the victims preserved as religious amulets, p. 472) and any valuable objects that he may possess. When Mankhelu had made some money by his bone-throwing or his medical practice, he used to leave the coins during the night at the foot of the branch, in order to inform his gods of his success !

I am unable to say whether, in former times, the diviners *formed a class* apart within the tribe, better defined, more close and secret than is at present the case. It may be so, as the hondlola by which they pass from apprenticeship to mastership is a true rite of integration, by which they enter upon a new condition and acquire a special position. At every new moon henceforth they will have to wash their bones ritually in order to remove the defilement of the preceding month, after which they will smear them with psanyi.

When a diviner finds that he is not successful in his forecasts, he consults another member of the fraternity, who tells him to offer such and such a victim to an ancestor-god who was himself a bone-thrower, and who is supposed to have given the bones to his unsuccessful descendant. The spirit of interpretation of the deceased will then enter into the supplicant.

In order to attract customers, Mankhelu kept a little pellet of black .grease amongst his bones. When he arrived at a place to practise his art, he took a little of this grease and placed it on a glowing cinder, arranging the bones all round, and the smoke which rose from the fat acted as a summons to the people. "So I saw one coming from this direction with an ox, another from another direction with a goat, and made good profit!"

Women may also become bone-throwers, but this is a rare occurrence.

5) The importance of the divinatory bones.

From all the foregoing information it may easily be gathered that the art of bone-throwing is by no means child's play, nor mere quackery by which astute sooth-sayers deceive their credulous fellows. It is a true art which the diviners practise *in all sincerity*, themselves believing that they receive objective revelations through its means. This sincerity is attested by many proofs.

1) The fact, already mentioned, that it is not a secret, esoteric art, but that all know its rules and take part in the interpretation.

2) The confidence which diviners have in the power of their bones, and the strong attachment which they profess for their divinatory basket (1). Each of their astragalus bears a name which reminds them

(1) The conversation, just referred to, which I had with Mankhelu after his explanation of the unfulfilled prophecy, is very striking in this respect. It concluded as follows : — "Mankhelu," I said to him, "you see that your bones deceive you ! They

of the person who gave it to them, the circumstances in which it was found, and some of the triumphs of their career. Their whole life is connected with these bones, which they truly love and to which they are bound by all the fibres of their hearts!

Of course diviners are *shrewd*! Their interpretation does not proceed from mathematic evidence, but from their extraordinary powers of imagination. Tortoise in the negative position may at the same time mean black earth, death, defilement, a well-swept village, the burnt bush, according to the requirements of the case ; but this is fair play and everyone approves of their ingenuity ; it is not a conscious attempt to deceive. It is evident that the predictions often remain unfulfilled, as in the case of Mankhelu's prophecy. Or the exact reverse of the forecast happens. One of my evangelists, Filipi Mabemane, when still a heathen, went to consult a Matjolo diviner regarding the birth of a child which was shortly to take place. "It will be a boy, and he will live" was the answer. Actually, it was a girl and she died! So many people are more or less sceptical and say : "Tinhlolo i ntlhangana na pso!" — "The bones tell the truth when by chance it so happens!" However their faith is not impaired for long! The anxiety to know the future is so great that they consult anew, but not the same diviner. People say : "Psa mu hlula," — "He has been overcome," and go to another! Qualified doctors sometimes experience similar treatment even amongst the Whites! Viguet once quarelled with a bone-thrower. The man of art contended that he always told the truth. "What did you tell me?" said Viguet. "You told me that I should get plenty of oxen and goats. Where are they? And why did you not tell me : 'Hanya, hanya, hanya... Live, live, live... there will come a day when something will happen and we shall quarrel!'" But the sceptics are rare. Faith in the bones is blind, but it is great!

How is this confidence, which both diviners and their customers have in the divinatory bones, to be explained?

are old, dry, dead things which cannot help you ! Come to the light of the true Revelation of Jesus Christ." — "You are right, Moneri," answered my friend. "I am old! I cannot use my bones any more, as I no longer travel for trade or feasting ! I shall have to come to the Church by and by." — "If that is so, let me have your basket ; it interests me very much. I will pay for it." — "He ! Moneri ! Impossible !" — "Why ? At any rate sell me the Son, if you wish to keep the Father !" — "No ! I want to keep the Son." — "Then give me the Father !" — "Never !" said he quite scandalised. — "You see that your heart is still in it, old chap !" — "Yes. When a child has dysentery, can I leave it so ? Must I not consult the bones to know what drug to give ?..." I did not succeed that day in buying either Son or Father. However, the diviner died some years later and his heirs consented to sell me one of his sets, which is now in my possession.

Does it come from a *religious belief*? It is not easy to say definitely to what extent the divinatory art rests on religion. On the one hand, the power of interpretation of the bones comes from the ancestor-gods who were bone-throwers themselves, and they are invoked to give or to revive this power. Mankhelu even told me that the prophecy of the arrival of the strangers had been inspired in him by his deceased father Shiluvane. But the Bula, the Word, is not generally looked on as being the utterance of the ancestor-gods. The bones are, in a certain sense, *superior to the gods* whose intentions they disclose. The Bula is the revelation of a more or less impersonal power, independent of the gods.

It is undeniable that the divinatory art is *essentially magical* ; it rests on those universal axioms of primitive mentality which are deeply engrained in the Bantu mind (p. 368) and this is sufficient to account for the indisputable value which it possesses in the eyes of the Thongas. Like replaces like. By virtue of mere external similarity one object can signify another. Thus human beings are represented by animals which resemble them in a certain point. The reedbuck which wanders during the night stands for the wizards who do the same ; the hyena, which eats the remains of the lion's feast, is the parasite who follows the chief, etc. Thus there are representative and represented objects. But like also acts on like : in some mysterious way the fate of the representative object will be the fate of the object represented. There is no doubt that diviners sometimes claim not only the power to form a diagnosis, to discover causes and give advice, but to influence the course of events themselves and determinate certain results. Mankhelu believed that he had contributed to the defeat of the Sikororo tribe when the bones so vividly depicted the rout of their army. If imitative magic controls the divinatory art, the part played by communionist magic is equally great. The part represents the whole. The astragalus, which is but a small bone, represents the whole body, and its fate prophecies the fate of the entire animal or person represented by it. The Native mind has a much profounder conception of the unity of the animal and human worlds than we have. Spoon once said to me mysteriously : "The astragalus of the goat truly represents the people of the village, because these animals live in the village ; they know us, they know what is in us." Observe also how the consultant takes the amulets of the patient and rubs them against the bones in order that they may be able to speak the truth about him. These amulets contain the nails and hair of the patient if they have been tied round his neck in the hondlola ceremony. Moreover they are covered with his "nsila," the exudation of his body, the material representation of his personality. By this contact the patient has in a way become a part of the "complexus Bula" and what happens to the bones will also happen to him ; what is said by the bones will henceforth apply directly to him. This magic conception of Nature is probably the profound and secret reason why the diviners believe so firmly in their art.

On the other hand, this art is so perfect that bone-throwers can derive very great satisfaction from the practice of it. It must be born in mind that, in fact, all the elements of Native life are represented by the objects contained in the basket of divinatory bones. It is a resumé of their whole social order, of all their institutions, and the bones, when they fall, provide them with an instantaneous picture of all that may befall them. This system is so elaborate that I do not hesitate to say that, together with their language, their folklore, their lobola customs and their burial rites, it is the product of their psychic life which shows most intelligence. If the premises of divination are accepted, astragalomancy seems to me vastly superior to cheiromancy and all the other systems which have been invented by us. It is also superior to the divination by four tablets of ivory or wood practised by a certain number of South African tribes, a description of which will be found in Appendix VI (1).

But if this system of divination is a proof of great intelligence, it must be confessed that *its results*, as shown in the psychic life of the tribe,

---

(1) There are some grounds for thinking that divination by astragalus bones is very old in the history of mankind. The Greeks practised *astragalomancy*. In a paper to which I shall refer in App. VI, the Rev. N. Roberts mentions the temple of Dodone, in which, according to Cicero, there was a large brass basin with the statue of a man upon it, and this man held in his hands a whip with three straps from which hung small astragalus bones. When these bones were set in motion by the wind, they struck against the basin and the sounds thus produced had a prophetic character. This was astragalomancy, but of a very different kind from that just described. Aristotle makes frequent allusions to the astragalus bone and says, inter alia, that one of its sides, named *coon*, represents the figure 6 ; another, named *chion*, the figure I, etc. This shows that in his time the astragalus bone was already identified with the dice. The dice, also called $\alpha\sigma\tau\varrho\alpha\gamma\alpha\lambda o\varsigma$ in Greek is simply an astragalus bone whose sides have been cut so as to form a perfect cube. We find traces of the use of the astragalus even further back in the past. Angelo Mosso, quoted by the same author, asserts that he found many astragalus in Italy, where they were used in connection with primitive religion as far back as the neolithic period. The discovery in the lake of Neuchâtel of a collection of more than thirty astragalus in the lake dwellers' station of Auvernier may be a proof that these bones did in truth play a part in the customs of primitive humanity. If this is so, then the Bantus have preserved the astragalus as they did the wooden pillow of the old Egyptians, the ancestrolatry of the Mousterians and the "mbaya" (p. 93) of the Libyans. The astragalus is still employed in play to represent cattle by Swiss children in the Canton of Valais, and I am told that the South African Boers have the same custom, and call these bones dol-osse.

are most *deplorable*. These practices kill in ovo any serious attempt at the use of reason or experience in practical life. Native doctors might have arrived at a useful and beneficent knowledge of the medicinal virtues of vegetables, if they had studied them carefully. But why should they trouble themselves with study, when a single cast of the bones at once tells them what root must be taken to cure the disease? (Compare my account of diagnosis, p. 475). Further, the bones annihilate the moral conscience, or, at any rate, they prevent any healthy development of this precious faculty. When overtaken by misfortune the Bantu might be moved to introspection to review his conduct, and see what wrong actions he had committed. From this self-examination, moral progress might result. But such trouble is useless! The bones are thrown. They reveal that misfortune was caused by such and such spiritual influences, wizards, gods, defilement, Heaven, that it must be combated by such and such means, — a drug, or a packet of drugs, a victim, male or female, offered by so and so, in such and such a manner. This is all-sufficient and the conscience remains dormant (1) as does the reason. I am convinced that, however high the degree of astuteness engendered by the divinatory bones may be, they have been extremely detrimental to the intellectual and moral welfare of the Natives.

This leads us to our last chapter, in which the questions of Taboo and Morality will be considered.

(1) Wishing to know if the bones were sometimes used to obtain moral guidance, I once asked Mankhelu: "As you throw your bones on every occasion, would you consult them when going to a beer party? There might be trouble, perhaps quarrels, blows... If you wish to avoid these would the bones tell you to abstain from the party?" He laughed heartily. "No!" said he. "If I saw that the men were drinking too much I should leave before they were quite drunk." I have some doubts if he would really have done so, but it remains clear that the bones have nothing to do with morality!

CHAPTER IV

Taboo and Morality.

If we take the trouble to make a careful study of the life of so-called savages, we very soon notice that, instead of being free from all law and restraint, as superficial observers believe, their life is, on the contrary, subject to a great number of rules and prohibitions, by which primitive man is held captive in the bonds of custom and tradition. These prohibitions are of two principal kinds. Those which are most obvious are *the taboos*, which we have met with on each page of these two volumes. They play an immense part in the behaviour of the raw Native. But, in addition to these, there are other restraints which seem to spring from a totally different set of ideas, *the moral principles*. The relation between the taboo and moral notions is very difficult to determine. It is at the present time one of the most debated questions of Anthropology ; I shall try to show what the state of things is in that phase of human development to which the Thongas of South Africa have attained.

A. THE TABOO.

I ventured to give a provisional definition of the *yila*, or *taboo*, of the Thongas, when we met with the first interdiction of this type, Vol. I. page 37 : "Any object, act, or person that implies a danger for the individual or for the community, and that must consequently be avoided, this object, act or person being under a kind of ban." After explaining hundreds of taboos, I do not feel that this definition needs any alteration. Its main element is this :

the object, act or person tabooed constitutes a danger (1) ; it must therefore be avoided.

I. *Classification of Taboos.*

Let us now sum up our study of taboos by attempting to classify them.

The most primitive of all are those which are called by Modern Ethnographers *the sympathetic taboos,* those which man instinctively observes in order to preserve his life and avoid suffering. To touch a burning ember or a fire, is taboo. Thongas sometimes use the word yila for such prohibitions : they say for instance "psa yila" for a little child to play with a knife. But this category of taboos, which impose themselves on man with a certain self-evidence, play no special part in Thonga customs.

1) The first category on which I would dwell is that of the *physiological taboos.*

a) First, those connected with *defilement.* When dealing with physiological ideas (p. 357), we noticed that there were five or six physiological phenomena which are considered to be attended with special danger, because they are the great *agents of defilement* : the menstrual flow, the lochia, disease, death and the birth of twins. Those who have been defiled by one or other of these agencies are taboo ; they are subject to a number of interdictions, in order that fatal contagion may be avoided ; in most cases, they have to pass through a marginal period, at the end of which they are again received into society. Hence a great many taboos, which I would call the *physiological taboos proper.* The *sexual taboos,* and the *special feminine taboos* (I. p. 184) naturally belong to this category, in which I would also include the *military taboos* in connection with the slayers (I. p. 478), and those underlying the strange *hunting rites* (p. 77), as all these seem to proceed from the

---

(1) The word *yila* very closely corresponds to the term taboo so widely used in Anthropology. In current speech it is sometimes employed in a wider sense, in cases where the notion of danger is not clearly present, but this is certainly an extension of the meaning. In fact the *yila proper* exactly answers to the definition just given.

idea of defilement through death. *Adultery* is taboo because the husband fears "the bad bloods" by which his wife may have been contaminated through her misconduct. In as far as respect for the *totem* is considered necessary for the maintenance of the health of the clansman, I would also include the taboos of this order in the physiological category ; these are, however, very few in number amongst the Thongas (I. p. 366).

b) Another variety of the same category are *the taboos connected with growth* or *change of condition*, or *with the various initiations* through which a Native may be called on to pass. The whole life of primitive man consists, as has already been stated, in a succession of stages ; he must proceed from one to the other through ceremonies in connection with which a number of taboos are to be noticed. The individual who ascends from an inferior stage to a superior one, always passes through a marginal period by which he ·is separated from the former and received into the latter. In this .case the seclusion is not due to defilement properly speaking ; it is connected with the idea of *growth*. Hence the taboos of *tying the cotton string*, (I. p. 56), *weaning* (I. p. 58), when passing from infancy to childhood, *puberty*, when entering upon adult life through circumcision, *marriage* (p. 124), when being received into the group of married people ; initiation into the society of the possessed, and into the profession of magician, or diviner, is attended with similar taboos.

All the taboos of this category seem to have been actuated by the idea of danger accompanying ritual impurity, or passage from one condition to another.

2) A second category of taboos, much less numerous, are the *cosmic taboos*. Nature prohibits certain acts ; if they are committed, rain will not fall, and the community will suffer. The prohibition of cutting the roots at the new moon (p. 306), of tilling the fields when a shower falls in the morning (p. 28), of warming oneself at a fire of parasitic plants and at the ntjhopfa (p. 18), and some agricultural taboos belong to this category. Some of the most severe physiological taboos, those connected with twins and with unlawfully buried children, become cosmic, inasmuch as they prevent rain from falling (p. 317).

3) A third kind of taboos are those I call *taboos of prevision*. Foresight is dangerous on certain occasions : Do not build your hut before you are married! (I. p. 251). Do not prepare the ntehe before the birth of your child (I. p. 46), nor your ngula basket before harvest! The travellers' taboos (I. p. 339) might also be included in this class.

4) A fourth category comprises the manifold *social taboos*, *viz.*, those actions which are prohibited because they would be dangerous to the social order. Exogamous laws (I. p. 256), hlonipha customs, viz., the tabooing of certain words by the chief (I. p. 384), and especially the curious taboos to be observed in the intercourse of allied families (I. p. 250), are social. The taboos connected with the moving of a village (I. p. 320) are physiological in so far as they are actuated by the fear of defilement, and social in so far as they aim at maintaining the life of the social organism, which is the *muti*. But those which chiefly bear the character of social taboos are those connected with the idea of *hierarchy*. We have met with them in the ceremonies of the first fruits (1) (I. p. 394) and in the rules of sowing. It is taboo to "precede" a chief or an elder brother in agricultural operations, sowing or harvesting!

5) This leads us to a fifth category : the *religious taboos*. The ancestor-gods, being the elders of the actual members of the family, must be treated as hierarchically superior ; hence the religious taboo of luma : the interdiction of eating the new crop before having presented the gods with the first fruits ; the prohibition of infringing the sacerdotal rights of an elder brother (p. 398) is a taboo of the same kind. We here observe the intimate connection between social and religious life in Ancestrolatry. Forgetfulness in fulfilling duties towards the gods (p. 426), and killing green snakes (p. 384) are also religious taboos.

6) I include in a sixth category the *language taboos*, ku ruketela, viz., the use of obscene expressions not allowed in ordinary life.

---

(1) The *luma* taboos are social and religious; but they also belong to the first variety of physiological taboos in so far as they are actuated by the fear of defilement (food of a deceased person, Vol. I. p. 146) ; to the second variety in so far as they are connected with a change of condition : first use of a new crop (I. p. 394), of a new meat (p. 71), of a new implement (p. 117), or fishing trap (p. 85). (Notice the relation between khangula , to inaugurate, and luma).

The words designating the sexual act and the various parts of the genital organs are *yila* ; but there are substitutes for them, euphemisms which may be used in their stead. When a child employs such words, people scold him, and say to him : "Psa yila! Do you think we are cleaning the wells?" This remark is due to the fact that the language taboos are suspended during the marginal periods and especially during the "mourning of the land," when the rains are delayed and people try to cause them to fall by the rite of cleaning the wells (p. 318). The language taboos are related to the social taboos ; to use obscene words leads to the destruction of social order, and this is allowed only when that order is actually destroyed, for instance during the mbelele rite (p. 318), during the time of moving the village (I. p. 321), and during mourning ceremonies (I. p. 160).

These six categories, although they are not absolutely distinct, form a convenient method of classifying the taboos.

II. *Some remarks on the taboos.*

1) What is the *origin of taboos*? It is not impossible to trace it in a number of cases. The *hlonipha taboos*, for instance, are proclaimed by the chiefs under certain special circumstances (I. p. 384). The taboo concerning *the planting of new fruit trees* is explained by the coincidence of the desolation of a ruined village with the presence of such trees (p. 29). Such coincidences, amounting to bad omens, have no doubt given birth to numerous taboos. If misfortune has followed a certain act two or three times, a hasty generalisation is made by the primitive mind : post hoc ergo propter hoc! So the act is tabooed.

This is due to the fact that with primitive people, as with children, *the emotional element predominates over the rational*, and when unfortunate events have happened or are feared, disease, drought, death, when the mind is in a state of terror, anxiety, or merely of nervous expectation, the reasoning faculties are disturbed, and a distinctive mental phenomenon shows itself, called by the French philosopher Renouvier the *intellectual vertigo* (le vertige intellectuel). Prof. Raoul Allier, in his valuable book on *La Psychologie de la Conversion chez les peuples non civilisés* (Vol. I. p. 250-260), ably describes the psychological process which takes place in the soul of the savage. Suppose some event to have happened which has caused a deep emotion in the tribe, the arrival for instance of the first Europeans with a number of unknown objects which arouse fear in the Native population. This emotion may perhaps subside and eventually be forgotten, and the tribe will accustom itself to the presence of the new comers ; but if some great misfortune supervenes, for instance if a serious epidemic breaks out, a new emotion will be produced throughout the country. This will remind the people of the emotion previously experienced on the arrival of the Europeans, and, in the disturbed state of mind thus created, the association established between the two emotions will be extended to the two facts which gave birth to these emotions, and the tribe will declare that the first fact is the cause of the second. Europeans and everything they brought with them will henceforth be considered as taboo. This is utterly illogical and the conclusion absurd. Yet this is what actually happens amongst people whose reasoning faculties are but little developed. These observations help us greatly in our understanding of primitive mentality, and many taboos may be psychologically explained in this way. Most of them, however, are inexplicable. They originate in the animistic or dynamistic collective representations of the tribe (p. 368) and these representations are instinctive, unconscious and consequently unaccountable.

2) How are they *enforced*? In as far as taboos have been proclaimed by conscious agents, their transgression will meet with punishment by those agents. A chief will sue a subject using a hlonipha word. The gods will punish those who transgress the law of hierarchy, who pass all bounds in incontinence, who forget their duties towards them (p. 426). But, in most cases, the decree is not enforced by a conscious agent. The *taboo avenges itself directly*. Consumption, swelling of the legs, the impossibility of passing water, disease of one kind or another will follow the transgression, or the children will be covered with an eruption of pimples.

3) How are taboos *dealt with?*

Happily the danger of taboos can be removed, otherwise life would be almost impossible! The medicine-men have the necessary drugs to protect their poor fellow-men against the misfortune (khombo) which is always threatening them! Is not the whole arsenal of magic at their disposal? Rites in great numbers provide the necessary protection, especially the *luma rite*, which is the proper method of avoiding the special dangers connected with the *first use* of anything. The wish to obtain protection against all these dangers explains the immense influence of the medicine-men, of those who know the preventive drugs to be used against defilement and misfortune.

It is impossible to attain to a true knowledge of the taboos without studying the laws of *their suspension.* Taboos are sometimes suspended. The chief, for instance, is above them, at any rate above some of them, being himself a magical being, a tabooed personage (I. p. 382). The collectivity has a still greater power over them and can cancel them. There are times when all these prohibitions, or at least some of them, are withdrawn; these are the marginal periods, when we behold the strange spectacle that ordinary taboos are suspended (language taboos, relatives-in-law taboos), whilst others are enforced (sexual taboos). I have often drawn attention to this curious phenomenon.

B. MORAL RESTRAINTS.

But taboos are not the only kind of restraint to which primitive Bantus submit themselves. The following statements have been collected from old or young informants who were urged to express their inner feelings on this question :

1) The maternal uncle must provide the ntehe for the first child of his sister. However this is not *yila*, it is a *nau*, a law, and if it is transgressed no direct harm will follow. (I. p. 46.)

2) Men and women do not bathe in the same spot in the lake of Rikatla. Why? Not on account of a yila, but on account of

shitshabo, viz., fear, or respect (1). There is no danger in transgressing this law of decency, but to do so is condemned.

3) When a young man has transgressed the taboo of *matlulana* (I. p. 197), having had sexual relations with the same woman as another man, he is not allowed to attend the burial of his rival. It is a taboo. However, if the deceased is his own father, the culprit can be treated with drugs, and so fulfil his duty of grave-digger, being protected against the dangers of his condition : "The *yila* has been removed, but the *biha* remains." *Biha* means that which is bad.

So there are three domains, besides the yila, in which the Native is conscious of the restraints imposed upon him : law or custom, respect or decency, and duty or *fanelo*. To these might be added a fourth, the disgust for a certain food (p. 83). The great difference between the taboo and the other prohibitions is that the transgression of the latter is not necessarily attended with danger (2).

Let us consider more closely the idea of *fanelo*, or duty.

Fanelo comes from *ku fana*, to be alike ; fanela is what is seemly, becoming. This is not as yet a very high notion of morality. The moral sense, however, certainly exists and this is proved by three facts :

1) The richness of the vocabulary expressive of moral ideas. There are more words applicable to the negative side of the idea and signifying *bad*, than to the positive, signifying *good* ; a phenomenon which may be observed in most primitive languages, even in our French patois. *Ku biha* means to be bad, morally speaking, and to be ugly, esthetically speaking. The distinctiveness of the two domains exists, however, in the mind of the Native. He says : "behile mbilu" — "is bad in his heart," or "behile liso" — "is ugly as regards his face." *Shibi*, the derivative noun of the verb ku

---

(1) I have heard the mixed bathing of men and women also called a yila, but it is a special kind of yila, *the yila of tshabisa*, the taboo of respect or decency.

(2) I would not, however, insist too strongly on the distinctiveness of these five domains. Theft and murder are prohibited on account of *duty*, but they become taboo if the culprit is discovered, because they will bring punishment upon him. The moral wrong of these acts was perceived *before* their dangerous character, and we have here an instance of a taboo grafted on a moral, or social, prohibition.

biha, is regularly used in Djonga to mean *sin*. It also designates the offensive substance which a child or careless person may have left on the path, instead of observing the sanitary regulations of Native villages. (I. p. 311.) But in addition to biha we have *dyoha* (Dj.), *doha* (Ro.), to commit a wrong, *hona* (Ro.), *onha* (Dj.), which means to spoil, but also to sin, and from which comes *shihono*, the true word for sin in Ronga. *Somboloka* means to be irremediably bad, crooked, like a stem which cannot be straightened.

On the contrary the adjective *nene*, corresponding to biha, contains three meanings : good, nice, and true, the derivate *bunene* designating rather goodness and beauty, and another derivative, *psinene*, truth ; the verb used for to be good is *shonga* (Ro), or *saseka* (Dj.), and has both the moral and esthetic significance. *Ku lulama* is to be straight, like a stem, and the use of this word indicates a deep and clear sense of right doing. Many other expressions might be quoted, showing that the notion of moral good and evil is certainly present in the Native mind, quite independently of that of taboo. They also recognise the *conscience* (timpfalu), seated in the diaphragm (p. 361).

2) *Intercourse with Natives* proves the same thing. Though their ideas may differ from ours as regards what is good (1), they are undoubtedly moral beings, with a more or lees developed conscience.

3) Their *folklore* is the best and most objective proof that this is so. Vice is punished and virtue rewarded in all the tales which I have called *moral,* and they certainly contain a whole code of natural and elementary morality (p. 222). The pangs of conscience in a criminal are depicted in a wonderful fashion in Zili, for instance.

However, it must be confessed that this morality is low, that it does not possess a very strong hold on the Native soul, and that the imperative of conscience is by no means the categorical

---

(1) The idea of charity is particularly low : charity is due only to relatives, or to clansmen, and not to foreigners. I remember a man of the Manyisa clan who nearly died near the lake of Rikatla, having been hurt when working on the railway ; nobody took pity on him, because he belonged to another clan. He was saved by a converted woman, Lois, who had a wonderful understanding of the new principles of universal brotherhood.

imperative of Kant. If you can steal without being caught, you may steal! Such is the advice generally given. To tell lies is mere play, which few people take seriously, especially if the lies are not intended to do harm to your fellow-men. There is a great laxity in Native morals (1). Why is this? I am convinced that this weakness of the moral sense is due to the fact that the moral law is not regarded as having been proclaimed by a personal, transcendental God. No relation is established between duty and the divinity. Religion is non-moral ; the ancestor-gods themselves are non-moral. The absolute character of the moral law can only spring from the absolute character of a God who has established it. For the Bantu the law, *nau*, is the *interest of the clan*. Theft is bad because it ruins individual property, and it is necessary to respect property, otherwise collective life becomes impossible. So theft, blows, insults, murder, and witchcraft are condemned and punished, because these actions endanger society and its recognised modes of life. But if society is not aware of it, you may steal ; you are not guilty ; no one has been offended! This principle gives to the morality of Natives a very curious *legal character*, which White people are sometimes slow to understand. A man is not guilty if he has not been convicted of his fault by a regular judicial pronouncement. He does not even feel himself guilty. But if his sin is proved, he at once gives up all subterfuge (Compare Zidji, p. 206) (2). We thus come to this conclusion : if the great

(1) Let me observe, however, that the domain of morality is also the domain of liberty ; and where there is liberty there are also individual differences. This is certainly the case amongst South African Bantus as regards their moral conduct. Any European having Native servants under his direction will have noticed that some of them show real moral qualities, faithfulness, disinterestedness, straightforwardness, respect, even a capacity for self-sacrifice, whilst others are unmitigated liars and thieves and addicted to vices which endanger the welfare and the purity of the home. Even in the Native village such differences are met with. I knew, for instance, a young man who never adopted the gangisa custom, which almost every boy looks on as the legitimate amusement of his age (I. p. 97) ; something told him that it was not right, and he kept away from the girls.

(2) This tendency of the Bantu mind to consider as right and good any decision which has been taken by the group, irrespective of its real moral value, also accounts for a fact which those who have to deal with pupils of African Native Institutions have frequently observed. It may happen that the Principal of the Institution will voice an opinion, give an order or propose a measure which does not please the Native students, and opposition will manifest itself amongst the group. Some of the more obstinate

fault of Bantu religion is that it is non-moral, that of Bantu morality is that it is non-religious. No supreme legislator has ordained it. Hence the want of the idea of the absolute in the dictates of the Bantu conscience.

Nevertheless, the rudiments of morality are present in the Thonga conscience, the feeling of duty, the sense of right and wrong, and these are independent of the essentially self-interested idea of taboo.

C. RELATION BETWEEN TABOO, SACREDNESS AND MORALITY.

Some modern Ethnographers see in the taboo idea the origin of that of the sacred, and of morality. Amongst South African Bantus, the idea of sacredness is not a prominent one. It may be said that the person of the chief is sacred to them, being set apart ; the law of hierarchy, the right of precedence belonging to the elder brother is also sacred, and this conception is very closely allied to that of taboo, though it does not necessarily contain the idea of danger. But if sacredness has been in certain cases a natural development of taboo, I do not think this is the case with moral ideas.

In some·cases, morality distinctly preceded taboo ; speaking of theft, we have just seen the taboo conception grafted on to a

---

succeed in persuading their comrades to a unanimous refusal of obedience, and as soon as they feel themselves thus agreed they will oppose their Principal apparently with a good conscience, despite his most persuasive arguments and all the patience that he may display. Morally speaking, they are clearly wrong ; religiously also ; the principles which they have themselves adopted indubitably condemn them. Yet they will maintain their resistance as long as they can face their master with a united front. But if the Principal is clever enough to take one or two of them — the most sensible — apart, and convince them, then the charm is broken. Feeling themselves divided, the pupils at once come to the conclusion that they are wrong, and they readily submit to the will of their superior. Such events may take place in other colleges, and amongst other races, I am afraid, but the difference is that amongst Bantus, just emerging from the state of collectivism, where morality depended not on the laws of a clearly conceived, holy God, but on the will of the community, the feeling of being right or wrong is above all determined by the attitude of the group. (See my paper on The Magic Conception of Nature amongst Bantus. *South African Journal of Science.* Nov. 1920).

primitive moral idea ; we have also met with a taboo evolving from a notion of disgust (nyenya) (p. 83) ; or of decency (p. 580). I do not assert that it could be proved that the moral restriction in all cases preceded the taboo prohibition. There is on the other hand no ground for asserting that the moral ideas are a natural development of original taboos ; these two sets of ideas seem to be parallel in the domain of conduct, just as Ancestrolatry and the idea of an All-Father are in religion.

_____

APPENDIX I (See p. 169).

The Chronology of Shinangana, a Thonga of Spelonken.

Speaking in 1905, he says :

Sixty-seven years ago, Shiluvane and the other Thonga chiefs fled before Manukosi (1838, or 1839?).

Three years later, battle with Matshekwane, Manukosi's general, who pursued the Nkunas (1842).

In the sixteenth year of the era, battle of Gologodjwen, when the Nkuna chief, Shiluvane, fought against the Ba-Pedi of Sekukuni (1855). In the nineteenth year, Manukosi dies (1858 or 1859? His death may have taken place as early as 1856).

Henceforth each year is known by its principal event :

Expedition of Shihahen (1859).

Beginning of the great war of succession between Manukosi's sons, Muzila and Mawewe. Muzila fled to Spelonken (1860).

Circumcision school at Mudjadji (1861).

We are plundered by Djiwawa (or Joao Albasini, the Portuguese Commander who for many years was the chief of the Thonga refugees of Spelonken) (1862).

Djiwawa goes to fight against Mawewe (1863) (1).

We are plundered by the Swazi army (1864).

Shiluvane, the Nkuna chief, settles in the Nyarin country (1865).

Djiwawa kills Ribole and Magoro (1866).

The Modjadji army fights with the Nyari clan (1867).

The Swazis plunder Modjadji's country (Buluberi) (1868).

Djiwawa plunders the people of Mashao (Spelonken) (1869).

Muzila's army returns from Mosapa (Gaza), and plunders Spelonken (Bvesha) (1870).

The Swazis plunder Makandju (1871).

Circumcision school of Madori in Spelonken (1872).

Daiman! (Opening of the Kimberley mines where Natives begin to go to work) (1873).

(1) According to Portuguese documents, this intervention of Muzila and Albasini took place in 1862, Mawewe having been definitely beaten on the 20th August 1862.

Birth of my child Rihlangana. Death of Shiluvane (1874).

Famine of Magadingele (1875).

Death of Nkambi, son of Mhalamhala, a Khosa (1876).

War of Makhanana of the Loyi country. Refugees come to Spelonken (1877).

The Makandju people kill Ñwashitine of Rikotjo (1878).

Birth of my child Ntitiri (1879).

Circumcision school of Mayingwe (1880).

Djiwawa goes to seize Sekukuni (1881).

War between the Boers and the English (1882).

Year of the comet (1883). Djiwawa's son, Sambana, becomes chief. Sambana plunders the village of a Venda called Mbekwa (1884).

Phundjululu : the vermin destroy the mealies (1885).

Circumcision school of Ñwamutjungu, a Hlanganu who had come from Spelonken (1886).

A Gwamba chief quarrels with Girifi. (Mr. Grieve, an old colonist of Spelonken) (1887).

Sambana beats a policeman (1888).

Death of Djiwawa (1889).

Sambana calls statute labourers (1890).

Death of Sambana (1891).

Circumcision school at Modjadji (1892).

My son Magondjwen starts on a journey (1893).

He returns home (1894).

We are struck by hail. Four people die (1895).

My son-in-law goes away (1896).

Epidemic among cattle. War of Makhube. We accompany the Boers (1897).

Matshona : Plague among oxen (1898).

Bahehemuki! The people of Gungunyana take refuge in Spelonken (after the war of Magigwana with the Portuguese) (1899).

The Boers attack Phefu, the Venda chief (1900).

The Whites fight. (Anglo-Boer war) (1901).

The English column chases the Boers away from Pietersburg ; Ñwashimbutane! The Son-of-the-Kid! (General Beyers, compared with a kid on account of his swift movements through the country during the guerilla war.) (1902).

Mugayo! Ndlala! The mealie flour bought from the Whites on account of the famine! (1903).

Of course many of these dates are doubtful... Many are of very small importance ; it seems childish indeed to mention as the only noteworthy event of the year 1888 the fact that Sambana, Albasini's son, had beaten a policeman. This shows, however, the historical sense of Shinangana ; he wished to record that uneventful year in his chronicle, and he chose the most remarkable fact that had occurred in it, though it was, indeed, of no great importance. Thus he attained his object, which was to preserve a full record of all the years from 1858 to 1903. The chronology of Shinangana is a true feat of memory, and, as he remained free from any civilised influence, it is a feat that must be considered when dealing with phenomena of oral tradition amongst savages.

APPENDIX II (See p. 332).

List of Thonga botanic names with their scientific equivalents.

According to the publication of Hans Schinz and Henri-A. Junod :

"*Zur Kenntnis der Pflanzenwelt der Delago-Bay,*"

"Bulletin de l'Herbier Boissier," Tome VII, N° II, 1899.

Pteridophyta.	Tsuna.	Acrostichum tenuifolium (and other ferns).
Typhaceae.	Papala.	Typha australis (Used to make mats).
Pandanaceae.	Shihlowa.	Pandanus.
Aponogetonaceae.	Fenyana.	Aponogeton spathaceus (1).
Hydrocharitaceae.	Nkushe.	Lagarosiphon muscoides (2).
Gramina.	Luhlwa.	Imperata cylindrica (Used as thatch).
»	Byanyi.	Andropogon (and all the other grasses).
	Litlange. Ntlangi.	Cynodon dactylon.
Cyperaceae.	Nhlale.	Cyperus flabelliformis.
»	Bungu.	Cyperus prolifer (?) (Papyrus).
Commelinaceae.	Nkompfana.	Commelina africana, Forskalei, etc.
Liliaceae.	Goñhwa.	Crinum Forbesii, etc.
Orchidaceae.	Shishengane.	Eulophia papillosa.
Olacaceae.	Psautemu.	Opilia tomentella (3).
Amarantaceae.	Shinghalafumane.	Hermbstaedtia elegans.
	Tlabatlabane.	Cyphocarpa Zeyheri (4).
Nympheaceae.	Tibu.	Nymphaea coerulea (Bulb edible).
Menispermaceae.	Shimbyati.	Cissampelos Pareira (5).
»	Shihumbula.	Synclisia Junodi.
Anonaceae.	Ntiti.	Artabotrys brachypetala.
»	Shintitana.	Artabotrys Monteiroae.
Leguminosae.	Gowana.	Albizzia fastigiata.
»	Khawa.	Accacia kraussiana.
»	Ndjiba.	Apalatoa delagoensis.
»	Ntjenge.	Dichrostachys nutans.
»	Nembe-nembe.	Cassia petersiana.
»	Hlapfuta (Ro).	Afzelia Cuanzensis. (6)
»	Shene (Dj).	» »
»	Shirimbyati sha mutju.	Indigofera podophylla.
»	Shiringeti sha tchune.	Indigofera sp ?
»	Lisekaseka.	Sesbania aculeata.
»	Shekane.	Desmodium incanum.
»	Nwamahlanga.	Canavalia obtusifolia,
	Rongolo ra nhlohe.	Eriosema cajanoides (The white Rongolo).
Meliaceae.	Nyamari.	Ekebergia Meyeri.
Euphorbiaceae.	Midyanhwari.	Fluggea obovata.
»	Shinyandjana.	Phyllantus pentandrus.
Anacardiaceae.	Nkanye.	Sclerocarya caffra (King of trees!) (p. 17).
Hippocrateaceae.	Shikokombela.	Hippocratea sp.
»	Mphyinsha.	Salacia Kraussii (Fruit edible).
Sapindaceae.	Buputwane.	Cardiospermum halicacabum.
Malvaceae.	Ntjinsi.	Hibiscus surattensis, Trionum, etc.
»	Shintjinosana.	Sida cordifolia.
»	Bushale.	Gossypium herbaceum (Cotton).

Appendix

Sterculiaceae.	Muhlwadambu.	Melhania Forbesii.
»	Nkondlwahari.	Waltheria americana.
Ochnaceae.	Kelekele.	Ochna arborea.
Flacourtiaceae.	Psekamafura.	Casearia Junodii (Schinz).
»	Nhlungunu.	Flacourtia Ramontoli.
Passifloraceae.	Menyamamba.	Modecca Kirkii.
Thymeleaeaceae.	Shindjibane.	Synaptolepis Oliveriana.
Combretaceae.	Balekanhloko.	Combretum Gueinzii.
»	Nkonono.	Terminalia sericea (Used for handles, etc.).
Ebenaceae.	Nhlangulane.	Euclea natalensis.
»	Shirole.	Royena pentandra.
Sapotaceae.	Ndjole.	Mimusops caffra (Fruit edible).
Loganiaceae.	Nsala.	Strychnos spinosa (p. 16).
»	Nkwakwa.	Strychnos Ungasha (p. 17).
Apocynaceae.	Nulu.	Carissa Arduina.
»	Ntamunga,	Carissa sp. (Fruit edible).
»	Mbungu.	Landolphia Kirkii (7)
»	Nkahlu.	Tabaernaemontana ventricosa (Styptic).
»	Nkahlu-tjhobo.	Vocanga Dregei.
»	Ntjulu.	Strophanthus Petersianus (p. 58).
Asclepiadaceae.	Muhlu-tjhobo.	Secamone sp.
»	Ndjutlwane.	Sarcostoma viminale.
Convolvulaceae.	Nkaka-wa-tjhobo.	Ipomoea cairica.
»	Masinga.	Stictocardia Woodii.
Scrophulariaceae.	Shitsinyambita.	Striga orobanchoïdes.
»	Murilwane (Dj).	Striga lutea.
Solanaceae.	Rulane.	Solanum panduraeforme.
»	Mondjo.	Datura fastuosa (?) (8).
Bignoniaceae.	Mpfungura.	Kigelia aethiopica.
Pedaliaceae.	Hlehlwa.	Pretrea Forbesii.
Lentibulariaceae.	Nkushe.	Utricularia stellaris.
Rubiaceae.	Ngalangala.	Tricalysia Kraussiana.
Cucurbitaceae.	Nkaka.	Momordica Balsamina (Edible).
»	Shirakarana.	Citrullus Naudinianus.
»	Nkaka wa Batshopi.	Coccinia jatrophaefolia (Eaten by Chopis).
Campanulaceae.	Shihlangwana.	Wahlenbergia arenaria.
»	Shilawana.	Lobelia chilawana (Schinz).
Compositae.	Ntshontshongori.	Vernonia Cinerea.
»	Nkukula-shibuya.	» Perotteti.
»	Hlunguhlungu.	» tigna.
»	Shifodyana.	Ageratum conyzoides.
»	Kamele.	Mikania scandens (Medicinal).
»	Shirimbyati sha tchune.	Gnaphalium stenophyllum.
»	Shirimbyati.	Helichrysum parviflorum.
»	Mushidji.	Bidens africana.
»	Nhlangula-batjongwana.	Helichrysum damarense.

This list might be greatly extended by any one devoting more time to the study of Thonga botany. Though it is not complete, I publish it, knowing by experience how difficult accurate botanic classification is in South African flora. It may be used as a starting point.

(1) Dancers make crowns of it. (2) All the algae and generally plants growing in water are called Nkushe. (3) Banyans are said to use it to clean their teeth. (4) Used for rheumatism (5) Medicine for bowel complaints. (6) Used to manufacture canoes. (7) Indiarubber, Kafir orange, p. 19. (8) This plant, used as a means of divination, is a Datura, subspontaneous or cultivated in various spots. I cannot guarantee the name of the species (p. 530).

APPENDIX III (See p. 428).

On Personal Religion amongst the Thongas.

The following facts prove that though ancestor-worship is above all a collective and ritual affair, religious acts of a personal and individual character are not wanting.

A young man of the Hobyana family told me that when he was still a boy, he was employed by his father to convey travellers over the river in a boat. He was accused by his brothers of stealing the money paid to him for this service. His brothers did not like him; they took from him the money which he received from the travellers and accused him of keeping it for himself and of deceiving the owner of the boat. One evening, as he was returning home after his day's work, he heard a great noise in the village ; people were speaking of him in angry tones. A Portuguese official had passed through the country some time before and had shown him kindness. He decided to run away and seek refuge amongst the Whites. The night was pitch dark when he arrived on the borders of a great plain. He felt very lonely and was seized by a terrible fear of this great, empty space which he had to cross. Then "another heart" told him to pray to the ancestor-gods to help him in his anguish. He remembered how his father used to *hahla*, and thought of saying "tsu." But he did not dare to pronounce the sacramental syllable. A feeling of shame (tingana) prevented him from doing so. However, he knelt down, put the parcel containing his clothes under his left arm, crossed his hands before his breast and joined them (fumbarela). He decided not to address his prayer to his paternal ancestors, those of the Hobyana family, as it was his father and his brothers who were ill-treating him, but rather to those of his mother. One of these maternal ancestors bore a special relation to him, as his parents had named him after this ancestor, who had died without posterity and whose name they wished to "revive" (pfusha) in this way. The boy prayed as follows : "You, my ancestor-god, after whom I have been named, save me and lead me where I am going." While pronouncing these words, he kept his eyes towards the East, where the moon was just rising, and, adds the boy, "I felt a great peace and joy in my heart and continued my journey."

Another boy of the Mashaba family, going for the first time to work in Johannesburg, was suddenly seized by fear in the railway carriage, remembering that he had been told that the mines were full of water and that boys working underground contracted fatal diseases. Overcome by the idea that he was going to his death, he jumped out of the train at the third station after Komati Poort and began to walk in the direction of Barberton through the desert. Feeling tired, he lay down and tried to sleep. But he heard antelopes running about quite near him, saying "mpfi! mpfi!" — "If these animals were hyenas," thought he, "I should be lost." Then the idea came to him that he ought to call upon the psikwembu to help him, which he did without pronouncing the official tsu, saying : "My gods! Help me! Save me from dangers and from wild beasts! Keep me alive!"

One of my pupils of the Khosa clan had a great affection for his mother. He said that she frequently prayed in her hut when he was sick, asking the psikwembu to heal him (p. 412). She used to offer them a little of a special mealie pap, prepared with particular care, and to throw a pinch of ground tobacco on the threshold of the hut in the morning. When she was tilling her garden and felt very tired and unwell, she used to pray "according to what her heart instructed her to say."

An Inhambane boy told me that, when travellers cross the Inharrime drift, many take a little water in their mouths, say tsu, and pray to their ancestor-gods to take care of them in this dangerous passage. Though his father and mother were still living and it is the custom not to hahla before their death, he said tsu, as the others did.

At the Morakwen drift the river Nkomati is very broad, and when the South wind begins to blow in fury the ferryman who rows travellers across to the opposite side runs great danger. One of his relatives told me that when this happens, he spits out a little saliva (as an offering of bitterness) and says : "Tsu! Do not hate me! These heads are not mine," meaning : "The children I convey do not belong to me, and I should have a great responsibility towards their parents if they perished in the river." Another witness assured me that this ferryman also begged all those in the canoe to join in his prayer and to entreat their own ancestor-gods to save them.

A Native of the Manyisa country added : "Individual prayer undoubtedly exists! During the heat of battle, a warrior, feeling himself in great danger, will kneel down, plant his shield in front of him and invoke his ancestor-gods. Some have remained in this position so long that the enemy have been able to stab them while they were still kneeling."

Such spontaneous appeals to the ancestor-gods do certainly occur, and this shows that ancestrolatry, notwithstanding its strongly ritualistic character, sometimes affords religious souls real help and relief.

When asked what they wish to obtain by their ancestor-worship, Thongas often answer : *Butomi*. This word comes from the adjective *ntomi*, to which is prefixed *bu*, the prefix of abstraction. *Ntomi* designates a man who is in good health, and butomi means above all *good health* ; but it has also a wider connotation and may well be translated by *life*. Life for the greater number is merely good health, plenty to eat, the possession of many children, material blessings ; but for the finer types it means something more ; it is the full happiness, to which they vaguely aspire and from which the moral element is not altogether absent. At least such is the impression I sometimes had when I heard them speak about butomi.

APPENDIX IV (See p. 450).

Additional Remarks on the idea of the Supreme Being and on Ancestor-worship amongst Bantus in relation to the History of Religion.

Much new light has been thrown of late years on the subject of the relation between ancestrolatry and the belief in a Supreme Being, a subject which remains one of the greatest problems of the History of Religion. In the paragraph which I devoted to this question in my first edition and which is reproduced in the second (p. 448), I refrained from attempting a definite solution of the problem of the order of priority of these two beliefs. I still believe that it is safer to maintain an attitude of reserve on the subject, as such a solution ought to take into account not only Bantus, of whom I know something, but the whole of primitive humanity. I should like only to add a few remarks which have been suggested to me by a comparison with some other Bantu tribes, and to put forward tentatively an explanation which may be applicable to the Bantu domain.

As already pointed out, the belief in a Supreme Being is found in various forms amongst all the Bantus, but it is perhaps nowhere more clearly defined than amongst the Ba-Ila, so minutely described by the Rev. Ed. W. Smith in his book, already quoted, on the Ba-Ila speaking people. *Leza* is designated by a number of typical praise-names : the Creator, the Moulder, the Constructor, the One who has no end, the Guardian the Giver, the One who gives and who causes to rot, the

Master, Owner of things. He is also the Persecutor. He is sometimes
more or less confounded with rain, with lightning, and with the sky and
what comes from it. It is generally believed that the Supreme Being
amongst the Bantus is a divinity who has abandoned the world and
takes no more heed of mankind. Leza is sometimes described in this
light ; he is however invoked in prayers which are sometimes touching.
The chapter which Mr. Smith has devoted to Leza must be read by all
who wish to acquaint themselves with Bantu theology.

The Supreme Being amongst the Ba-Rotsi, *Nyambe,* whose name is
sometimes equivalent to Leza, seems to be more remote than Leza ; yet,
according to the Rev. Th. Burnier (*Ames Primitives,* p. 10) every
morning the Zambezian Native presents Nyambe with an offering of
water in a wooden plate placed on a little altar built in his kraal ; he
kneels down ; he turns his face towards the rising sun, and twice makes
the royal salute *Yo-Sho.* Then he bows his head and claps his hands
against each other, muttering certain words.

The Rev. E. Allegret (*Revue de l'Histoire des Religions,* 1904) heard
amongst the Fañ of the French Congo a list of epithets applied to *Nzam*
very similar to those by which Leza is praised. The old Native who
revealed these names to him did not understand their meaning, but it
was not difficult to discover it from their etymology . These mysterious
words, Mebeghe, Menkwa, Sokuma, Mbongwe, mean: The Upholder of
all men, the Judge who cuts, i. e. decides, everything, the King of Kings,
the Organiser, the Creator of generations. Nzam is looked upon as the
father of all men, and every one when quoting his own genealogy
comes finally to him as the first in the series ; when he pronounces his
name, however, the Fañ adds the praise-names just referred to. The
Supreme Being is often confounded with the originator of mankind, or
with heroes of past times, but the more thoroughly the question
is studied, the more clearly the transcendental nature of the divinity
amongst Bantu tribes appears.

As regards ancestor-worship, a comparison between the Thongas
and three other Bantu tribes which are particularly well described, the
Akamba, the Ba-Ila and the Ba-Ganda, shows that the nature and importance of the ancestor-gods is closely connected with the social system
of the tribes. Amongst *the Akamba,* living near Kilimandjaro (see
G. Lindblom, *The Akamba, Vol 17 Archives d'Etudes Orientales Ch.* X
and XIII), with the exception of totemic clans which play no part in
religion, the only social unit is *the family.* There are no chiefs except the
heads of families. There the power of the ancestor-gods is reduced

to its minimum ; though they are very much feared, they are thought to be mortal. Amongst the Thongas, we find *the composite clan* described in Part III. Here the social unit is larger, a family reigns over a country which comprises a number of people belonging to other families ; there are consequently *national* ancestor- gods, those of the royal family, who are of greater importance and power, as they control the whole country. We go a step further when we reach the Ba-Ila. Here, besides the family *bazhimu* worshipped by their descendants much in the same way as amongst Thongas, there are *communal gods*, i. e. the spirits of dead men who control a wide tract of country and are worshipped by all the inhabitants of the region, even by those who are not descended from them. There are more than 14 of these larger communities, and the ancestor-gods who preside over them have more importance and power than the simple family ghosts. Higher up in the scale than these communal divinities there is still another divinity called Bulongo, also a mudzimu, whose origin, however, is not known, but who is superior to the communal gods, being worshipped through the whole country, almost on an equality with Leza. The situation amongst the Baganda is again different. Here worship is addressed to the family ancestor-gods, but it is of small importance. In this country there are a number of *high gods*, more or less specialised as regards their attributes : Katonda, the Creator, Mukasa the benevolent, Kibuka, the war-god, Kitaka, the earth-god, — about twenty gods and godesses, most of whom have their temple, their mediums, their complicated ritual, their mythology. Uganda, on the other hand, is *an old kingdom* governed by a royal family which has been in existence many centuries, and thus the social system of the Ba-Ganda is very much in advance of the primitive forms of Bantu society. The ancestor-gods would seem to have undergone the same evolution. These great gods are human beings who lived centuries ago, a fact which is proved by the jawbone which was found in the shrine of the god Kibuku (p. 409). But they are greatly superior to the aimu, the psikwembu or the bazhimu of the Akamba, of the Thongas or of the Ba-Ila. A comparison between the ancestrolatry of these four tribes tends to show that the wider the original social unit has become, the greater the development of the power and importance of the ancestor-gods. We might therefore be inclined to conclude that the appearance of the idea of the Supreme Being is merely the last stage of this evolution, that ancestor-worship came first and that the notion of the Supreme Being was derived from it. There are however many objections to this theory ; it might as fairly

594

be argued that the idea of a Supreme Being came first and that the idea of divinity was later incorporated in the ancestral spirits in a degree corresponding to their importance, — itself connected with the social system of the tribe, — until these ancestor-gods absorbed, so to speak, all the attributes of the Supreme Being, as is the case amongst the Ba-Ganda. Moreover we meet with many peoples belonging to primitive humanity, who possess a remarkably clear idea of the Supreme Being, although their social system has undergone no such development, e. g. the tribes of South Eastern Australia. It must also be noticed that this belief contains elements of Naturism which do not belong to the definition of ancestor-worship and could hardly be derived from it.

When everything is taken into consideration, and all due respect paid to the evolutionist hypothesis which has proved so useful in many instances, is it absolutely necessary that the two beliefs should be derived one from the other? Is it not rather probable that both arose in the human heart simultaneously from different, parallel sources? What is religion? It is essentially the feeling of man's dependence on higher, supranormal powers to which he has recourse to help him in his distress. From the beginning, as soon as he became conscious of himself, man was sensible of his dependence on Nature, especially on the celestial phenomena. Heaven smiled on him in the rays of the sun and terrified him by lightning and the roar of thunder. Later, when he passed from the nomadic to the agricultural stage, he was more dependant than ever upon rain for his means of life. No wonder primitive humanity worshipped Nature and especially the sun and heaven. But from the beginning also, man was faced with family relationships, and in that domain also his experiences were similar. The tenderness of the mother, the authority of the male members of the family created around him an atmosphere in which he felt himself strongly dependant. When, with the development of animistic conceptions, he became convinced that his ancestors were still living in his vicinity, it was natural that he should think of calling on them for help in his difficulties (1). Later

(1) In a very suggestive little book, *Le sentiment religieux et la Psychologie de l'Enfant* (Delachaux et Niestlé, Neuchâtel), Mr. Pierre Bovet of the Institute J. J. Rousseau, has shown by some typical examples, that children, when left to themselves as far as their religious development is concerned, and driven by the religious instinct which is in them to create their own gods, worship either the sun or their parents. This correspondence between the religion of the child and that of primitive humanity, is, if it is confirmed, a most interesting fact. Physically speaking, during the pre-natal period, the child reproduces the main evolutionary forms of life of the animal world ; later, in the same way, when his mental and spiritual development begins, he passes through the stages which primitive humanity has traversed.

still, reflexion sets in. Man begins to think of causes and of the first cause. In many tribes we meet with men of a superior spiritual type who are preoccupied by the question of origin which leaves the mass cold (p. 303). This is causalism. It is a third source of religious beliefs and has given birth to the very wide-spread idea of the Moulder. Memories of the great deeds of ancient heroes, more or less legendary in character, may have also intervened to give individuality to the divinities created by popular imagination. This is the theory of the Greek philosopher Euhemerus and is called euhemerism. To all these sources, in a thousand different forms, primitive religion owes its origin, and it is unnecessary to establish a relation of cause and effect between its various elements. This explanation, which is in harmony with the polygenist theory of the origin of Religion advanced by Archbishop Söderblom in his book *Das Werden des Gottesglaubens*, seems to me the most satisfactory both from the scientific and from the religious point of view. Scientifically speaking it is in accordance with facts and does not distort them in order to force them into a preconceived system. The positivist thinker, even the philosopher who recognizes no objective value in religion, can accept this theory as to its origin. But what about the Christian thinker, who believes in the existence of God and in the objective reality of the spiritual world? In putting this question I abandon the purely scientific standpoint which this book claims to adopt. I am conscious of the fact, but I do so purposely. If the positivist sees in the origin and development of primitive religion a purely natural process, this is not the case with the thinker who believes in God. He takes the view that all through, God was striving to draw the human race to himself. Naturism, family relations, causalism, euhemerism have been His avenues of approach to the spirit of man, and in these rudimentary forms of religion I see a kind of revelation, very uncomplete indeed, but corresponding to the low stage of intellectual and moral development of primitive humanity, a progressive revelation on which further revelations, contributed by all the prophets of mankind, have since been grafted, until God has become fully known to us as Light, Holiness and Love. And for this reason I do not despise the childish rites of Animism nor the absurd representations of Naturism. In them I see not only an attempt on the part of man to know God, but an attempt on the part of God to make Himself known to man.

---

*The Murimi Movement, an attempt on the part of the Thonga Tribe
to get rid of witchcraft.*

In the year 1913 (or 1914) the members of one of the Hlengwe clans
living near the Sabie River, in the extreme north of the Thonga territory, seeing that the crops were bad, game wanting, and that even honey
was scarce, contributed each of them a small sum of money, collected
£ 10 and sent messengers to Myali, the Kalanga god who dwells in a
cave in Machonaland, in order to regain prosperity. They were well
received by the priests of Myali, who introduced them to the god they
serve. They had to pass through a tunnel, with a big rock hanging
over their heads. On the other side of this tunnel there was a kind of
amphitheatre of rocks, enclosing a very clean and well-swept space. A
voice from the rocks above greeted them in Zulu : "Good morning, my
children", and they were given a pouch full of tobacco with the following instructions : "When you reach your home, take a snuff of this
tobacco ; then go to your gardens, blow your noses and spread the nasal
mucus in the soil ; henceforth you will have abundant harvests." The
Hlengwe messengers returned home and began to use the precious drug,
but this tobacco of Murimi, as it was called, had a marvellous fate. It
found purchasers throughout the Thonga tribe, and during four years
all the Thonga clans performed the new rite, the rite of Murimi, in the
conviction that a new era had set in in which there would be no more
famine and in which witchcraft, that great enemy of humanity, which
causes disease, robs, and kills, would be expelled for ever.

Who is this Myali? He is the same personage who is called Ñwali
in other parts of the country, the same also as Ra-Luvimbi, the god of
the Ba-Venda, to whom they pray to obtain rain (See p. 321). His
sacred cave is in the Matoppo hills, in the midst of that extraordinary
desert of rocks in which Cecil Rhodes chose the spot for his grave, some
fifteen miles further south. Mr Eliott, who was Native Commissioner
in this region, told me that the description of the cave given above was
exact. I will not discuss here the origin of the cult of Myali, called
also Mlimo, a term probably corresponding to the Sutho Modimo,
which would seem to have been transformed into Murimi when it was
adopted by the Thongas. This is a most interesting subject to which I
would draw the attention of our Rhodesian colleagues. Myali has med-

iums, consecrated girls (bampouka) set apart from their youth to become the wives of his priests ; the rite of the magical tobacco, which is a fecundation rite, is unknown in South African ancestrolatry. Everything would appear to suggest that this cult is of foreign origin. A fact which is worthy of special notice is this : *Myali is the enemy of wizards.* If anyone guilty of witchcraft approaches his cave, he will be struck dead, and his priests will have nothing to do with witchcraft cases.

I cannot explain in detail how the new cult spread from the Hlengwe country down to the Maputju region, thus creating in the Thonga tribe a unity which has but seldom been attained. Certain individuals appear to have availed themselves of the new belief to do a profitable piece of business. They bought a part of the original tobacco of Murimi, mixed it with ordinary tobacco and went to the chiefs offering to let their subjects snuff the miraculous drug. I happened to meet one of these prophets of Murimi, who also called himself Murimi and who had been arrested by the Portuguese Administrator of Morakwen, as the Authorities seem to have feared at a certain moment that the agitation caused by this movement might have a political character. This particular Murimi appeared to be a very simple type of man. He was half lame, his arms were crooked, and he told me that his reason for fighting the wizards was that it was they who had reduced him to that miserable condition ; he was convinced that his efforts to combat them were very beneficial to the country. But notwithstanding these altruistic inclinations, he did not neglect his own interests ; anyone admitted to snuff the tobacco had to give the chief a fowl or a "nkinyenta", i. e. 500 reis, then of the value of I s. 6d, and Murimi received a considerable share of the fee.

Wonderful rumours preceded the distributor of tobacco. It was said that he had been emprisoned by one of the Administrators, further north, but had suffered nothing through this infringement of his liberty ; the following night he had been miraculously transported to the bed of the Commandant, whilst the latter had taken his place in the gaol! He was now approaching the town of Lourenço Marques in the form of a gigantic dragon before whom everyone fled!

The following is the description of the manner in which the Murimi rite was performed in the Matalane region, some 15 miles north of Lourenço Marques. The chief Magebeza summons all his subjects to assemble early in the morning in a forest (Sept. 1916). His counsellors are present and bring with them the lame prophet holding in his hands a sala shell containing the tobacco. A woman comes and, kneels down in front of him; she holds out her open hand, palm upwards. Murimi takes hold of one of the fingers in order that the hand may remain well open, pours a little tobacco into it and asks : "Are you a witch?" She answers: "No!" — "Then," says the prophet, "snuff!" The woman draws up all the precious tobacco into her nose, taking care not to let the least particle fall on the ground. If she carries a baby on her back, she puts a little of the powder into his nostrils, and if she is pregnant, she rubs her hypogastrium on both sides with the drug in order to "let the child who is inside snuff." Another woman comes; she answers in a hesitating manner, which does not escape the prophet ; she may go so far as to say : "I do not know ; perhaps I am a witch". Murimi looks at her with terrible eyes : "Take care," he says, "cast away your witchcraft immediately. If you do not do so, this goat's skin in which you are carrying your child will come to life again and belabour your breasts with its hoofs! And the day you begin to cast your spells again, you will be split in two (handjuka hi le makari)!" The worst case is when a woman who is a witch accepts the tobacco without confessing her evil deeds. Then, such was the rumour, the tobacco poured into her hand would suddenly increase in quantity, and upon that sign, Murimi would give her hand a blow from beneath, throwing all the tobacco over her shoulder, and the woman would fall to the ground unable to get up again and on the point of splitting in two.

When all the subjects had passed through the trial, Ndonga, one of the counsellors, addressed the throng in these words : "Now witchcraft is destroyed! You have all cast it far away. But let it not come back again. If any of you has *psipoko* (pl. of shipoko, p. 488) kill them, cut them in pieces with your axes or with your big knives, and let them not come back, because, if they do so, it would be a great calamity for you. They would beg you: 'Mother! give me something to eat' and if you should do so, you would die" He added: "A new era has begun. You have no longer anything to fear from wizards. If one of them approaches you to bewitch you, he will immediately split in two. Murimi has cut off the wings of the baloyi. They will not be able to come to do harm to you during the night. Henceforth we are free from the calamities which caused us to suffer so greatly."

This is the first part of the rite, which aims at destroying witchcraft for ever. But it has also a second aim, the bringing in of a new prosperity, a golden age in which everyone will have plenty to eat, in which even, according to some, death will no longer exist. The second part of the rite is connected with this great hope.

Whilst Murimi proceeded with the examination of the people, another counsellor, Phayindi, was preparing "the leaves"; these are the large bracts protecting mealie-cobs which he has torn from the stem and in the centre of which he has placed a little of the tobacco. These are now lying on the ground, and each woman must go to fetch one and return home with her husband. Keeping silent all the while, she takes a little pot full of water, pours a little of the drug into it and carries it to the threshold of the hut, where both husband and wife wash their hands and feet. She must not enter the hut herself; the husband enters, and carefully places the pot in the back part of the hut. The woman then sets out for her gardens, carrying the leaf. She follows the boundaries of each field, digging in the ground here and there, throws into the hole a little mucus from her nose, which is still full of the tobacco, and covers it with earth. She keeps to the end the largest field, in which there may be a nkuhlu tree (p. 18), the mafureira tree which is apparently preferred by Murimi. She digs a little hole at the foot of this tree and buries the leaf in it, in such a way that only the middle of the leaf which contains the tobacco will be covered with earth; both ends will remain visible. Thus the fields are "fattened (nonisa)" for ever. But if the mistress of the field should again begin to practise witchcraft, the leaf will come out of the soil and fly up to the chief's village, where the guilty woman will have to redeem it by paying a fine of £ 1.. Having finished performing the fecundation rite, the woman claps her hands and says: "Murimi! I ask thee to help me here in my gardens in order that I may have a plentiful harvest and become fat!". She then returns home, and leans her hoe against the sacred tree of the village. Her husband, who has waited for her, again washes her feet with the lustral water and the injunction of silence is removed.

These are the rites of the first day. But now begins a sacred period which lasts from ten to fifteen days, and is marked by three strong taboos. The labour taboo; no work is allowed in the fields until agricultural occupations are resumed by the collective tilling of the chief's field. The sexual taboo; at the end of the period the great wife will smear her hut with clay and have relations with her husband the following night; next day the other women will do the same, but woe to the one who should precede the great wife (I p. 324). The travelling taboo; travelling is forbidden during these days and everyone must stay at home till the chief has cancelled the prohibition by himself undertaking a journey.

This is still not the end. Those who have snuffed the tobacco of

Murimi constitute in some sort a new humanity; they have been *init-iated* into a new life; they must abstain from relations with those who do not belong to their society, and observe peculiar rules which will distinguish them from the uninitiated. If a man has not snuffed whilst his wife has done so, she must not allow him to have conjugal relations with her; if he was away from the country when Murimi passed, the husband must go to the capital and snuff there, a little of the tobacco having been preserved for those who were absent. He will be subject to the law of silence until he has ritually washed his hands and feet. (This is a form of the kunga rite as observed in the initiation ceremonies. (See I, p. 124.) If strangers pass through the village, no food will be offered to them unless they have snuffed, at any rate no food coming from the fields which have been "treated (daha)" with the drug. The following are some of the taboos regulating the life of the initiated. Language taboos: the word *fole*, which means tobacco, must only be used to designate the tobacco of Murimi; ordinary tobacco must be called by a new word, *shilandi*. The word *mpfula*, rain, is prohibited and must be replaced by *magayisa*, (which means a party of boys going to work). Alimentary taboos: no special food is prohibited, but certain articles of diet must be eaten according to new rules. This is particularly the case for the fruit of the nsala tree (p. 16). The shell must be broken in such a way that it forms two halves; the eater must lie on his belly, place the upper half of the shell on the soil, suck out the pulp round the stones to his heart's content and put all the stones back into the first half of the shell; when he has finished, he must place the second half over the first and deposit the fruit thus reconstituted at the foot of the tree, saying: "Murimi!" in order to show his gratefulness to his new god. If there are many ripe sala fruits on the stem, one must be left for Murimi. When digging sweet potatoes, sticks must be used rather than the hoe for the first ten days, during which tilling the ground with hoes is taboo; later on the hoe may be used, but one potato must be left in the earth as the share of Murimi. There are a number of other less important taboos to be observed; the stem of the cuscuta must not be employed to tie the bundle of dead wood gathered in the bush for fuel, because the cuscuta is the mat of Murimi. Certain kinds of snakes, the big Varan lizard, the tortoise and the small turtledove called shivamba-lane must not be killed. Should a hunter kill a shivambalane by mistake, he must place it on the branch of a tree, saying: "Murimi!". Above all, the initiated, the members of the new humanity, delivered from the fears of witchcraft by the all-powerful Murimi, must invoke him upon every occasion. At the conclusion of their speeches they pronounce his name. Though no special offering is made except the sweet potato and the sala fruit just referred to, and no special ceremony of worship is performed, Murimi has clearly become the object of adoration of his devotees and is much nearer their hearts and consciences than the ancestor-gods.

A year or two went by and the Thongas were obliged to confess that the produce of the fields in the meagre sand of their hills was not richer than in former years. People died just as before ; the great salvation which the worshippers of Murimi had expected did not come, and the tribe understood vaguely that it had been the victim of a gigantic hoax. At least when the question was put to the devotees of the new cult : "What about Murimi?" they smiled and did not answer a word, and very soon Murimi was forgotten.

It might be thought that this strange movement was the result of European influence ; it bears a strongly monotheistic character, and Murimi is certainly very different from the ancestor-gods and from Tilo, Heaven, and much more akin to the Christian God. It must however be observed that very little information was given about this god, who was to a certain extent identified with his prophets, the latter being named Murimi as well as himself. But setting aside the small part played by Murimi, we are forced to recognise that the new rite is essentially and authentically Bantu. It is directly connected with witchcraft, the old Thonga animistic belief ; we have already met, in connection with the treatment of smallpox, with the idea of destroying witchcraft by means of a collective confession and repudiation (p. 465). The taboos accompanying the new rite are those we have everywhere found in the marginal periods or when an initiation was taking place. The Murimi Movement is thus a genuine creation of primitive Thonga mentality. Changes are taking place so rapidly that it is probably the last. I am glad therefore to have had an opportunity of witnessing it and of publishing the record of such an interesting event. Further details will be found in a paper which appeared in *Le Journal de Psychologie normale et pathologique*. 15 Décembre 1924. Paris.

APPENDIX VI (See p. 571).

Divination by means of Ivory Tablets amongst the Ba-Pedi.

Astragalus bones are employed for purposes of divination in many South African tribes : Suthos of Basutoland, Pedis of the Transvaal, Ba-Rotse of the Zambezi plain, Nyandjas of Lake Nyassa etc. Wishing to ascertain if the interpretation of the bones was the same amongst the Ba-Khaha of Shiluvane as amongst their Nkuna neighbours, I asked

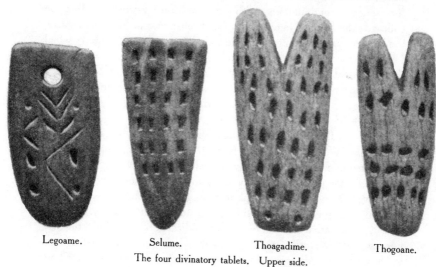

Legoame.   Selume.   Thoagadime.   Thogoane.

The four divinatory tablets. Upper side.

a diviner of this tribe to explain his art to me, which he very willingly did. It was in the year 1907; this man, Mutshezi, possessed most of the astragalus of the Thongas and used them in the same manner, but I noticed amongst them four ivory tablets of a triangular shape which were totally absent from all the sets belonging to Thonga diviners which I had ever seen. Setting aside his astragalus bones and confining himself to the four tablets, my informant showed me that, as their upper face was marked with dots whilst their lower face was quite plain and white, these four objects could fall in sixteen different ways, each of which had its own significance. This is mathematically speaking perfectly true, and I was greatly astonished to find an uneducated Bantu, belonging to a race so little developed from the point of view of

603

the arithmetical sense, possessed of such a surprising knowledge of the law of permutations! Pushing my questions further, I learned that two out of the four ivory tablets were male, one of them, named *Legoame*, being the adult male and the second, *Selume* the boy, whilst the two others, which have a notch on their smaller side, were female, the larger one called *Thoagadime* and the smaller *Thogoane*. It was evident that these four objects, representing the four principal divisions of the family, formed by themselves a complete system of divination independently of the astragalus which accompanied them. The information which I collected in 1907 was not sufficient to enable me to publish the sixteen combinations with the necessary accuracy. But my colleague the Rev A. Jaques, who has been living in Shiluvane during the last few years, has at my request kindly completed the study which I began and thanks to his valuable help I was able to write a full description of this species of mantic in the *Bulletin de la Société Neuchâteloise de Géographie*, 1925. I cannot reproduce it here in full, but I will give the main results of the researches of the Rev. A. Jaques and myself (1)

Let us call Legoame, the man, M, Selume, the boy, B, Thoagadime, the woman, W, and Thogoane, the girl, G. The tablets may fall showing their upper side, the side covered with dots ; they are then in the positive, active position, corresponding to the position of the astragalus showing its convex side. I shall indicate this position by +. Or they may fall showing their lower side, the plain side without any markings. This is the negative or inactive position, indicated by —. When the diviner has cast his ivories and sees how they have fallen, he first utters a word or a few words expressing the *formula* of the combination. Then

(1) The Rev. S. S. Dornan, in a paper published in Vol. XX of the *South African Journal of Science,* on Divination and Divining Bones, declares that the system of the four tablets is very much employed amongst the Bushmen, each individual possessing his set and using it for his own wants. He believes that the Bantus have borrowed it from the Bushmen. In a paper by Mr. H. W. Garbutt published in 1900 in the *Journal of the Royal Anthropological Society,* there are plates representing the divinatory tablets used amongst the Ma-Shona, the Ma-Tebele and the Ma-Kalanga of Rhodesia and amongst the Ba-Toka, Ba-Totela and the Ba-Leya of the Zambezi region. It seems evident that these, though generally rectangular in form and made of wood, are employed for the same purposes as amongst the Pedis. Amongst the Ma-Kalanga they are called Kwami, Tshilume, Lumwe and Dagwala and these names are very similar to those of the tablets in Pedi. I would further mention the paper of the Rev. N. Roberts in the *South African Journal of Science,* 1915, p. 367-370, in which he describes the four ivory tablets found by him in the Malaboch tribe, in the Northern Transvaal, not very far from Shiluvane. He discovered the same sixteen combinations and gives their names which, as a whole, correspond to those of the Khaha-Pedis, but he does not enter into a detailed explanation of their meaning.

he begins a kind of incantation, which is more or less uncomprehensible, consisting, as it does, of obsolete expressions of the meaning of which the diviner is almost entirely ignorant, but which evidently aim at stimulating his divinatory po rs. It is even possible that, according to the principle of verbal magic, the magician expects by this more or less lyric utterance of mysterious words to exert a real influence on the course of the events which he is about to predict. When the incantation is finished, the diviner proceeds to the *application* of the revelation made by the combination to the case for which he has been consulted. Leaving aside these incantations, which are so difficult to translate, I will now give : *a)* the formula of each combination, *b)* the general idea, sometimes very vague, which each contains, and *c)* some of the applications.

1. M+B+W+G+ . *a) Mphirifiri.* The coming and going of a throng of people. — *b)* Febrile activity (everyone is on his legs). — *c)* Dances, quarrels in the village. Thunderstorm or strong wind. Locusts. An object lost will not be found ; it is lost amongst the throng, etc.

2. M+B+W+G— . *a) Makhulela ea masadja.* (Dead things in the chief's village). — *b)* The chest is full (of violent feelings, bitterness, sadness. — *c)* There is much disease, the patient is panting. No rain. The enemies will capture the chief, etc.

3. M+B+W—G— . *a) Mashupia a sebimmpi* (The animal which has no horns, the secret thing which one keeps to oneself). — *b)* The heart is enchained. There is something hidden which people will not reveal. — *c)* No peace in the village. The disease is constipation, and the patient dies without having expressed his last wishes. The mother will give birth to a dead child

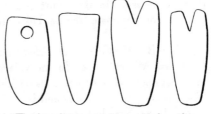

The four divinatory tablets. Under side.

and will not reveal the name of its father. No rain ; it is tied up, etc.

4. M+B—W—G—. *a) Legoame la makhuluho.* (The man, the father, flows out). — *b)* Something leaks away, gets lost. — *c)* The village is scattered. The disease is dysentery. If anyone dies it will be the father. Rain will fall abundantly. We shall kill the enemies' chief. This combination designates the father.

5. M—B—W—G— . *a) Muthakulana oa matzepe* (meaning un-

known). — *b)* Everything is lying on the ground ; everything is dead, everything black. — *c)* In the village, mats are unrolled ; people are sitting down talking. The disease comes from the mats on which the patient has had unlawful relations. Rain will fall and darken the soil. The lost object will not be found ; it is hidden in the dark ground, etc.

6. M—B+W+G+ . *a) Moraroana oa sili* (The little circle of vomiting?). — *b)* Things which produce nausea, disgust or which happen suddenly. — *c)* In the village, people are disgusted with each other on account of theft. The disease is accompanied by vomiting. On the war-path a warrior has had bleeding of the nose and the whole army has returned. In the Court, the judges will not accept the claim, finding it disgusting, etc.

7. M—B—W+G+ . *a) Bukhacha* (Kept back at home). — *b)* Rest. People remain at home. — *c)* In the village the women either quarrel or are satisfied, but they do not think of going away. The disease consists of great fatigue and will not soon be cured. Protracted birth. War is not brought to a conclusion. No travel is undertaken, etc.

8. M—B+W—G+ . *a) Thabadiva* (Bath in the river?). — *b)* Crossing rivers, and telling lies. — *c)* In the village, quarrels. The disease is not clear, the patient lies ; you think he will recover ; it is a lie ; he is near his death. No war : false rumours. The traveller will cross many rivers and reach a far distant country. Thunderstorm, but no rain, a deceptive noise. No harvest ; the fields do not make good their promises . In the Court you will be accused of lying. This combination designates the Ba-Tokwa tribe, which has the crocodile as totem.

9. M—B+W—G— . *a) Selume thudu* (The little boy alone?). — *b)* Tears! Misery! — *c)* In the village, poverty, bad feeling. The maternal uncle refuses to give his daughter to her motsoala (L. p. 293). The disease causes weeping and is fatal. War, travel accompanied by tears. If you have lost something, cry as much as you like, you will not find it again. The harvest fails : nothing but tears. This combination especially designates the maternal uncle.

10. M—B+W+G— . *a) Sefara* (Something which is attached to something else). — *b)* That which is attached to the body : the breasts, the suckling child ; two things at an angle with each other. — *c)* In the village you have taken in a stranger who is spoiling your life. The disease affects the breast, the ears, the arms. Difficult parturition : the child remains attached to his mother. In the battle, warriors fight

interlocked. The chief's wife must go with her baby in her arms to make an offering at the village gate, etc.

11. M+B—W+G—. *a)* *Mugolori oa rebatsalala* (The man and the woman are standing, satisfied?). — *b)* Double meaning : Happy family life and relations with the mogolo, elder brother (I p. 497). — *c)* Peace in the village. Pregnancy normal. No war. No travelling. Rain does not come, but remains where it is. On the other hand, anger of the elder brother ; his younger brother has had relations with his wife. If rain is wanting, ask your elder brother to make an offering.

12. M+B—W—G+. *a)* *Sethaku sa musepedi* (The sandal of the traveller). — *b)* The traveller. Quarrels. Disorder. — *c)* In the village they fight with knives. Dispute about the expected birth. In the war, desperate fighting. The traveller has put on his sandals : he will go far, etc. Ma-Kalanga clans, and those which have the lion as totem.

13. M—B—W+G—. *a)* *Murupi oa setshuga* (The hawk which frightens). — *b)* Fright! Terror! — *c)* The village is destroyed by a fire. Inside, the disease burns ; death will come in a way which will terrify you. The mother will give birth to something awful, perhaps to twins. In the war, enemies will set fire to your village, etc. This combination designates the principal wife and the grandmother.

14. M—B—W—G+. *a)* *Lenwe la thupuli la mavone.* (Alone ; thing which one picks up, which is seen?). — *b)* Loneliness (of a girl) and abduction. Things seen. — *c)* In the village you have shown kindness to somebody who abandons you with ingratitude. Women make denial, one of them says : "I am not pregnant" ; but it is no use lying : it has been clearly seen! No war near : you will only see it from afar, etc. This combination also designates the younger co-wife of your mother or your younger brother's wife.

15. M+B—W+G+ . *a)* *Moraro omogolo* (The great circle). — *b)* To turn round in a circle. — *c)* In the village people are sitting, apparently in peace, whilst they slander each other and thus burn the village. The disease affects the loins and the hips. (Moraro also means behind). The woman suffers from the intestinal worm which moves all round her body. The army of enemies will camp round your village, but will not enter it. No rain ; it falls all round the country, but not in it, etc. This combination designates the grandfather.

16. M+B+W—G+ . *a)* *Maviana ea lishada* (Small stones which make a noise). — *b)* Noise caused by small stones hitting each other or by locusts'wings. — *c)* In the village, quarrels and cries. Rival wives

fight. A sister insults her brother who refuses to give his daughter to her cousin, the woman's son (I. p. 293). The disease is itch or folly ; or it is caused by the anger of the ancestor-gods with the maternal uncle who refuses his daughter to her motswala. The traveller will go to a mourning ceremony, etc. This combination also designates the paternal aunt and the girls, because the wife has gone (thoagadime is on her back) and the husband has nobody to play with except his sister and the girls of the village.

This system of divination is much more difficult to understand than astragalomancy. Though it is easy to recognize in some of its features the magic principles which underly most of the Bantu practices of divination, yet there are also in the interpretation of the ivory tablets other elements and a large amount of conventionality , as I have tried to show in the paper quoted above, to which I must refer the reader for more details. It would be interesting to know whether the interpretation given by the Bushmen is similar to that of the Pedis ; are the words of the incantations used by the latter of Bushmen origin ? This is one of the subjects which South African ethnologists ought to study without delay.

PRACTICAL CONCLUSIONS

I. On Alcoholism and the South African tribe. (See p. 46)

The craving of the Bantu of South Africa for alcohol is by no means a result of civilisation. The race, being of a weak character, has always given way to drunkenness. Deprived of true religious and moral principles, it was exposed, as all primitive races are, to the excesses of that dangerous passion. The beer-drinking parties are as old as the tribe itself, or at any rate, as ancient as the introduction of cereals !

But it must be confessed that civilisation has developed this natural instinct to a terrible degree. In former times, Natives were able to get intoxicated from time to time, the chiefs more frequently than their subjects, owing to the shirwalo taxation (I. p. 405). But the brewing took nine days, and in the meantime the inmates of the village were obliged to keep sober. Now all that is changed. Where the law does not prohibit the sale of liquor to Natives, they can buy as much as they like at all times ; some of them are therefore constantly under the influence of drink as long as they have money to purchase it, and the progressive alcoholisation of the entire population is already to be observed. I lived for many years in a Colony where there is no liquor law. Formerly German rum was sold all over the country by thousands of flagons, and I even saw children drinking it with avidity, although they shivered whilst swallowing the deadly drug ! Later on it was prohibited and replaced by what is called "Vinho colonial", which, however, was no great improvement. According to the late E. Torre do Valle, a great friend of the Ba-Ronga, who strongly deprecated this liquor trade, it is an adulterated mixture in which tobacco, India-pepper, etc. are used to give pungency to the taste, and containing but little natural wine. When a White man enters an upcountry store and wants something to drink, the Banyan who retails this mixture from three barrels standing on the end of the counter, refuses to serve him with it, saying : "This is for Natives and not for White men". Round Lourenço Marques there are hundreds of such bars, and although the Authorities have tried to diminish their number, the drunkenness in the Native Location is terrible and almost incredible in extent. Let the visitor go on Saturday night or Sunday along the avenues of Majlanganen (I. p. 206), where the galvanised iron stores extend without interruption in all directions, and observe the women, men, youngsters dancing on the road in front of the

bars, falling on the ground, spending their last penny to get drink beneath the eyes of the amused storekeeper, and he will realise what the
unrestricted sale of drink to the Blacks means. It is simply horrible to
contemplate ; morally it is a most reprehensible, economically a most
deplorable, physically a most dangerous state of things. I shall not deal
here with the moral side of the question ; let us merely consider what is
the effect of this liquor trade on the health and on the economic future
of the Black race.

1) There can be no doubt that it *kills* hundreds of Natives. Whatever
stamina the race may possess, it cannot long resist the deadly effects of
an inferior, unwholesome type of liquor absorbed in such enormous
quantities. Coffee must be *kweba*, drunk in sips, but wine according
to Natives, must be *nwa*, viz., drunk "à plein gosier" like water ! We
saw the young chief Shongele, heir of the Klosen clan, son of Magudju,
die a miserable death from delirium tremens, and many other chiefs and
sub-chiefs followed his example. For years they led a disgusting life,
half drunk all the time, no longer able to preside over the tribal court, or
to govern their people, having entirely lost the dignity of manner and
the sense of position which was so remarkable amongst Bantu rulers,
clapping their hands and abjectly entreating the White visitor to give
them *sope* (the Native name for brandy).

Hand in hand with drunkenness goes immorality, and immorality as
practised in that hell means the unchecked propagation of syphilis.
According to medical authority, ninety per cent of the Natives round
the town of Lourenço Marques are now contaminated. The girls who
come on Saturday to sell their produce in the market and sleep two
nights in the Native town, give themselves, for a few pence, to one of the
hundreds of boys working on the wharf, and thus propagate the disease
in the interior, and all this means the rapid destruction of a race which
was made for life, and has great possibilities before it.

During the war of 1894, a merchant in the town of Lourenço Marques
said to me cynically : "The Natives are a nuisance ! Let them be given
as much alcohol as they want and we shall soon get rid of them."

2) Alcohol will kill the Black race in the long run. It is already
ruining the kafir trade. Those who uphold the liquor traffic, in order
to increase the Revenue of the Colony, ought to obtain the opinion of
the traders who do not deal in liquor. These merchants, who try to
create new wants, to develop a healthy and useful trade amongst Natives,
in a word to civilise them, would testify that selling strong drink
to the Natives prevents their buying anything else. The craving for

alcohol is such that they spend all their money on it and no longer care for clothing, better food, ploughs, live stock, etc. The *consuming power* of the Black race as regards European goods, which might become enormous, is thus curtailed ; and at the same time its capacity for work is destroyed. When drink was allowed to be sold in the Compounds of Johannesburg, the Mine Managers soon found that a third of their Black workers were constantly in a state of intoxication and unfit to go down into the mine. So the sale was happily stopped, not so much on moral as on purely practical grounds.

So, if we study the question seriously, we are forced to the conclusion that total prohibition of European liquor, and any similar product, is the one chance of salvation for the Natives. I know of only two classes of people who would oppose this conclusion : the liquor traders — whose judgment is not disinterested — and some educated Natives, and negrophiles, who resent any colour legislation and think such prohibition an insult to the Black race. There is no need to reply to the former. Let them consider the heavy responsibility which they incur when they enrich themselves by slowly killing a primitive, childish race which has not enough moral force to resist the danger ! To the second I would say : "Even if some of you have in reality attained that moral status in which you can use and not abuse your liberty, you must confess that your race, as a whole, has not yet reached this level. A great number of the best Native Christians have fallen irretrievably and been lost owing to the passion for drink ; how much more defenceless are the rank and file, raw heathen or weak Christians ! Accept the testimony of facts and recognize that the Black race, just emerging from savagery, is still in a state of moral infancy and must be treated with great consideration. Later on, let us hope, the time will come when it will have grown in strength and moral vigour, and no legal restrictions will be required."

As regards *Native drinks*, the use of *byala*, strong beer, is generally prohibited in Christian Congregations. Some Missions also exclude light beer, *buputju*, whilst some (amongst them the Swiss Romande Mission) allow it. *Buputju* proper, the Suto *leting*, is not very objectionable, containing but little alcohol ; but I have already pointed out the great difficulty of establishing a clear line of demarcation between buputju and byala. Our experience is that Native Christians readily approve the prohibition of byala... but, after a while, they begin to brew a buputju which is almost the equivalent of it, and the morality of their congregations sinks in proportion to the increase of alcohol in their drink. So, in a Synod held in Shiluvane in 1908, the question was earnestly discussed during a whole day. The following were the confessions made by the delegates "We have deceived our leaders! What we drink is byala, and not buputju! We ourselves, the elders, are drinking and leading the others into temptation ; thus we give strength to the beer. The beer is the hyena. It kills the soul ! It kills the work of salvation! Let it die once for all, the wild beast. Let a knife be provided to cut the throat of the wild beast", viz., let strict regulations be adopted to prevent drunkenness in the Church.

When Natives arrive at such a conviction of the danger of alcohol for their race, and take up such a position in regard to their own beer, should not we Whites be greatly to blame if we increased their difficulties by providing them with European drinks which are ten times more dangerous for them!

At the International Conference on Alcoholism which took place in Geneva, 1st to 3d September 1925, regulations for the Colonies were discussed and I had the honour of putting forward the following suggestions, especially as regards Mozambique ; they were supported by Gen. A Freire d'Andrade, the Portuguese delegate to this Conference.

"The ideal would be total prohibition of any foreign alcoholic liquor, as Natives already possess sufficient national drinks. If, however, it is felt to be impossible to adopt such a radical measure at the present time, the following restrictions are suggested, bearing on two categories of drinks, imported drinks and those manufactured in the Colony.

First Category. Imported drinks.

a) Prohibition of importation and sale of all *distilled* liquors.

b) Prohibition of adulterated wines, prepared for Native consumption (trade spirits, vinho colonial).

c) Compulsory analysis of all *fermented* drinks offered for sale and prohibition of all those which contain more than 12 % of alcohol and of those which are of a harmful character.

Second Category. Drinks manufactured in the Colony.

a) Prohibition of distillation of any liquors destined for consumption, whether manufactured by European or Native processes.

b) Periodical examination by the Sanitary Service of the Colony of all fermented drinks manufactured by Europeans or Natives, and prohibition of those which are prejudicial to public health, whether on account of a too high percentage of alcohol, on account of their mode of manufacture, or on account of the physical and moral disorders which they produce."

These proposals were favourably received by the Committee for the Colonies, but no vote was taken on details, only a general resolution being passed. It is clear that these recommendations are intended for the whole Native population. In the domain of the Church we should go much further, as pointed out above.

II. On the Problem of Native Education.

The study which we have made of the Bantu Intellect in Part V has paved the way for a consideration of this great question, which is one of the most important features of the Native problem in South Africa.

The wild buffalo has been made prisoner! A yoke has been placed on its neck. — The savage mind of the Bantu is now being trained to civilised methods, and the Elementary School gathers in the goatherds of the bush, all over South Africa. More than 220,000 children are attending a course of instruction. The wild buffalo has bowed its neck to the yoke with wonderful readiness! It is one of the promising features of the present situation of the Black race that it has so quickly accepted the school. This acceptance proves its vitality ; it understands that the acquisition of knowledge is, for it, the only way of adapting itself to altered circumstances. So, though primary education has nowhere yet been made compulsory, children are leaving their flocks and learning reading, writing, and arithmetic. This phenomenon is universal, and is to be observed not only in the towns, where big boys of twenty or thirty years of age crowd to the evening schools, patiently writing letters on slates with clumsy fingers, but in the most remote parts of the country, wherever a missionary or a Native teacher opens a school.

This spread of instruction is bound to have great results for the future of the race, and its intellectual development ; it is therefore of the utmost importance that rational and wise methods should be adopted in the conduct of this work, in order to help rather than injure the Bantu mind. Unfortunately it cannot be said that such has always been the case in past times. To avoid mistakes and errors I beg to put forward the following suggestion as to the first principle of Native Education.

THE LIFE OF A SOUTH AFRICAN TRIBE

1) THE NECESSITY OF A SPECIAL NATIVE CURRICULUM.

I should like in the first place to give a personal recollection.

When I was a young missionary on the Rikatla Station, I had the great misfortune to lose my Native teacher. He was not satisfied with the pay he received from the Mission, so he took leave without ceremony and went to town to earn more money. I remained alone to attend to all the spiritual and educational duties of the Station. Until then, I had left the entire charge of the school to him. Now I was obliged to go myself each day to teach the twenty or thirty boys and girls of the class. But what I at first regarded as a very sad occurrence proved a real blessing. Having to teach in a Native school for some months, I gained very valuable experience, and I at once saw that, with a language totally different from our own, and subject to other influences, and a different training in their homes, Native children could not be taught on exactly the same lines as Europeans ; in other circumstances, other methods had to be employed. In what way, and how far, the training must be different was a very interesting question, and its solution seemed to me to deserve every effort on the part of the friends of the Native.

What was my surprise, on visiting Cape Colony some years later, to find that, in this the most advanced of the South African States, the same course of instruction was followed in the schools for the Natives as in those for White children! The former had to pass through the six classical Standards just in the same way as the sons of the English or Dutch colonists. What was the reason for this strange regulation? Was it in the name of a liberal and generous negrophilism that Blacks were treated exactly the same as Whites? I was told that this was not altogether the true explanation, and that it was due rather to the indifference with which Native Education was regarded ; the Authorities had not taken the trouble to inquire into the matter, and ascertain if this was the proper method of dealing with it. The Natives, as a rule, were satisfied, believing that the more they were treated like Europeans, the more did they really resemble them. But there were signs of uneasiness. School Inspectors, intelligent Natives, were observing that such a system resulted in a superficial and useless education, in a denationalisation of Native children without any true progress towards a more civilised state. In fact, agitation on this question led to an official inquiry conducted by a Select Committee of the House of Parliament, and a number of complaints were brought forward condemning this system as actually harmful to the Native pupils.

Three times the South African General Missionary Conference discussed this important subject. It had a full right to do this ; it was in fact its undoubted duty to do so, since Native Education in South Africa is in the hands of the missionary bodies, who provide the teachers, and found the schools, the State only exercising a general supervision and paying part of the salaries. So on two occasions I had the privilege of impressing upon this Assembly the necessity of a special Native course of instruction, once in Johannesburg in 1904 and once in Bloemfontain in 1909 (1).

Before explaining the grounds for this necessity, let me remark that, *a priori*, it is entirely reasonable to make a difference between the instruction given to a young savage just emerging from the bush, and that afforded to a civilised child. The six Standards of the British Curriculum constitute indeed an excellent programme, and many educationists are so convinced of its perfection that they would apply it to all the children on the face of the earth. We may observe, however, that in foreign countries like France and Germany, where the schools have reached the same degree of excellence, the curriculum is slightly different. In a programme of primary education, there would seem to be two series of elements : the universal elements, which every human being must be taught if he wishes to be looked upon as educated, and the particular or national elements which answer to the special wants or gifts of the various nations. So we might say that the English course has a more practical, the German a more scientific, and the French a more literary character. If such differences exist amongst the civilised nations, is it not reasonable to expect to find them when we are educating on the one hand White children, and on the other children born in the bush, far away from European influences, in a totally different environment, amidst totally different traditions?

But the necessity for a special course of instruction for Natives does not only arise from the differences between the Bantu and European mind. It is forced upon us by the fact that these tribes possess and use their own languages ; the centre of the problem is the presence of these languages, and this being the most important point in the discussion, I must dwell at length upon it.

(1) See Reports of the South African General Missionary Conference of 1904 : "The place of the Native Language in Native Education," and in the Report of 1909 : "Native Education and Native Literature." Compare Journal of the African Society. October 1905.

615

2) THE PLACE OF THE VERNACULAR IN NATIVE EDUCATION.

If we wish to express a sound judgment on this subject, another question of a more general character must first be considered. What will be the fate of the Native languages in the course of evolution of the Black race in South Africa?

Some superficial observers have expressed their conviction that these dialects are bound to disappear in the near future before all-powerful civilisation and its vehicle, the European languages. This opinion is based on no substantial foundations. In the last 20 or 30 years, the use of Native languages has not decreased in the slightest, nor is there any sign of the Black populations abandoning them. In some places in the Orange Province a kind of Low Dutch has superseded Sesutho, or the old Hottentot dialect, but this is owing to the disintegration of the tribes and the prevalence of European influences. Where the Bantus still adhere to their tribal system, or where they dwell in locations, they retain their native tongue, and they are fully justified in doing so; these languages are altogether worthy of preservation, as has been shown in the first chapter of Part V. They are not degenerate, they are not inexpressive, they are rich in their own way, and, at any rate, they are admirably in keeping with those who invented them. Thus they are by far the best medium for the expression of their thoughts. I may quote here the Thonga proverb : "The strength of the crocodile is water." When speaking his own tongue, the Native is a crocodile in water. He is strong, he is eloquent, he is a personality! When speaking a foreign language, most of them are caricatures. Of course some of them master English perfectly, or Portuguese, or Dutch, if they have been in long and intimate contact with Whites. But this is a chance which falls to the share of very few, and it will probably not be the lot of the majority until social and political conditions have undergone an entire change. If our European patois have been preserved for centuries in so many countries where they have had to fight against a literary language, against books, School and Church, how much more probable is it that Sesutho, Zulu and Thonga will remain the languages of the South African tribes! The vernacular then will live, and it is worthy of being used both as a medium for instruction and as an object of study in Native schools.

On the other hand, European languages are making great progress amongst the Natives, and it is but natural and desirable that it should be so. The South African Native instinctively understands that he must be able to converse with his White master in his tongue, as the White master is much too busy (and perhaps too lazy) to learn the language of his boy. The greatest concession the White man will make is to speak a smattering of "Kitchen Kafir," that most deplorable mixture of Zulu, Dutch, English and Portuguese, lacking all grammatical construction, which flourishes on the docks and in the stores of half civilised South Africa. To kill this execrable product more promptly, let the Natives arrive at a true knowledge of the European language as quickly as possible. The Governments desire this, the storekeepers long for it, the mistress of the house demands it, and the missionaries have nothing to say against it!

In fact the *South African tribe must be bi-lingual*, the vernacular remaining the language of the home, of the soul, of religion, of intercourse between the Blacks ; while the European language, English, Portuguese, or Dutch, as the case may be, is used in the ever-increasing intercourse with the Whites. That the race can attain to such a level is beyond doubt ; its literary ability is quite equal to the effort.

If these premises are true, what conclusions are to be drawn from them as regards Native Education? The Native child enters school knowing only his vernacular. He must leave school having acquired a true training of the mind, and having become at the same time a useful member of the community, two aims, the educational and the practical, which must not be sacrificed one to the other. How are we to attain them both? I shall consider the question more especially from the point of view of language.

Without entering into technical details, let me say that Native primary education ought to comprise three stages :

1) *The Vernacular Stage*, a period of two years during which pupils who are just commencing their studies learn to read and write their own language. This will form a solid foundation which will be useful to them all their lives. At this stage, the European language is taught by ear only, colloquially, according to the method of the Berlitz School, as far as possible by establishing a direct connection between objects seen and the foreign words learned. This period corresponds to Sub-Standards A and B.

2) *The Mixed Stage*, corresponding to Standards I, II, III of the English course, forms the transition period. The pupils are still taught through the medium of their own tongue ; they receive lessons in its admirable and regular grammar, until they are able to parse sentences, a very good exercise which will accustom their minds to analyse and

classify (1). But Readers in a European language are now put into their hands, and they read these, the teachers always taking care to avoid a mere memorising of words without an understanding of their meaning. For this purpose we recommend for use during this stage, bilingual books containing a literal translation of the text in the Native language on the opposite page.

3) *The European Stage*, corresponding to Standards IV, V, VI. Some contact is still kept with the vernacular at this stage by reading the best of Native literature, when available ; but here the Native curriculum comes nearer to the European, some subjects, however, such as history, being taught in a somewhat different way, to answer to the needs of Natives. The European language, English, or Dutch, or Portuguese, is employed as a medium as much as possible.

This division into three stages will provide a sound evolution from the untrained bush life to adult and civilised life, and will do as little as possible to destroy the character of the Native.

I cannot here go into full details of the course of instruction which I proposed to the Bloemfontein Conference, in 1909, and which was included in the Report. I will only add that after an interesting discussion, the assembly passed a resolution, approving the system of the proposed three stages, which in the English Colonies would be termed the Vernacular, Anglo-Vernacular and English stages. In the Mozambique Province, Governor General Freire d'Andrade adopted a similar plan, combining it with the Portuguese Code of Education (1908). Natal has also changed its Code of Native Education exactly on the lines indicated in the Bloemfontein Conference.

As regards the Transvaal authorities, they only began to take an interest in Native Education after the Anglo-Boer war. Provisional Standards were adopted with two Sub-Standards, in which the requirements, as regards English, were very modest. The study of the Native language was nowhere mentioned ; the vernacular was entirely lost sight of. "Teach it as much as you like and have time to do so," said the Department, "but we cannot take it into account." Such a recommendation, however, cannot easily be carried out. A subject not mentioned in the curriculum, and not included in the examinations, will never receive study. This system, moreover, gave rise to the following

(1) This teaching of the Native grammar to Native pupils has been given in the Swiss Mission schools for years, and has proved very interesting. I am glad to observe that Bishop Cameron, of Cape Town, recommended it in the following words : "In order to train the mind to understand the process of thought, the Kafir grammar, which is elaborate, logical and on the whole regular, is a much more satisfactory instrument than the English grammar."

serious difficulty. Native children, on their first arrival at the school, had to be provided with two books, the vernacular Reader and the English Primer. They had therefore to begin by learning the same letters with two different values, *a* being pronounced like the Italian *a*, in the Bantu orthography, and like *é*, the French *é*, in the English book ; *e* being respectively the English *a* and the French *i* ; *i* the English *e* and the French *ae* ; *u* the French *ou* and the English *you*! The case is almost as bad with the consonants! This course is surely not desirable from a pedagogic point of view. Is it not cruel to force pupils, who are just beginners, to learn two alphabets at the outset? And are we not right in claiming that one of the axioms of Native Education should be the exclusion of any European book, as long as the child is still learning to read his Native Reader? If this plan is not adopted, the results will be deplorable. A teacher in Cape Colony who had occasion to examine pupils taught in out-stations according to such methods, said to me : "They are supposed to have passed Standard III. They easily read a St. III Reader, but they do not understand a word of it, and when I examine them in Kafir, they are unable to read the first Kafir Reader." So the result of this method has not been more favourable to the English language than it has to the vernacular. Four years of study on these lines have only resulted in a useless memorising of English words, and an almost complete inability to read Kafir. Out-station teachers may be blamed for this deplorable result ; but anti-pedagogic methods, or rather the want of reasonable methods, have had a great part in bringing it about.

The system I now advocate, insisting, as it does, on a real understanding of all subjects taught, is designed to correct the great fault in Native Education all over South Africa. The Bantu mind is endowed with a wonderful memory, as we have seen. Moreover, being the mind of a primitive race, it has a strong tendency to imitation. Hence the fact that Native children (and often teachers) are perfectly satisfied with a parrot-like learning of words and sounds which they do not understand. They commit to memory entire books in a purely mechanical manner, without bothering at all about the meaning of the words ; this knowledge is but a superficial veneer which will disappear as soon as they have left school, and most of them leave after Standard III. This parrot-like way of learning must be combated with the utmost determination and, realising that this is a weak point of the Bantus of this and perhaps of the next generation, the Native curriculum must provide a means of checking the spread of this evil, which I have ventured to call the blight of Native Education (See Rep. of the Bloemfontein Conference, page 20).

3) The want of the Arithmetical sense.

In the preceding pages, I have dealt with the best means of developing those literary faculties of the mind which are so prominent amongst the Bantu tribes. A system of education ought to foster the natural abilities and gifts of a race. It ought also to remedy its defects, and a thorough teaching of arithmetic must be given in the Native schools precisely because the mathematical sense is feeble in most of the Native pupils. The method generally followed is to teach them European numeration. I think that this is the only reasonable course, as their own system is much too complicated, and no elaborate arithmetical work would be possible if counting were done in the vernacular. The danger which we meet with in this branch of study is once again the tendency to be satisfied with merely mechanical work in which the reasoning faculty plays no part. Do not be content if you find your pupils' eyes shining and their hearts thrilling when they are merely reducing feet into inches, or yards into feet! Complete your teaching by giving them a problem which appeals to their reasoning powers!

4) Seven principles of Native Education.

In conclusion, I would say that Native Education, in order rightly to direct the evolution of the race, must be actuated by the following principles, the first four being a résumé of the foregoing considerations, whilst the last three are also of great importance.

1) The teaching of vernacular reading and writing is the foundation of the whole.

2) The teaching of the European languages must be given at first orally and never allowed to become a merely mechanical effort of memory.

3) Arithmetic must play a considerable part in the programme, and be taught as a means of developing the still dormant reasoning faculty.

4) The study of the vernacular Grammar is a first-rate means of developing the sense of classification amongst young pupils.

5) The Native curriculum must try in addition to meet other wants peculiar to the Natives. They have not been taught a number of common scientific facts which White children naturally learn through their environment, so they ought to be given an elementary course of science in order to check notions of witchcraft and other superstitions.

6) Industrial Training is of the first necessity to a race which, though highly gifted in this domain, has still to be civilised and can aspire to something better than mere unskilled labour. Agriculture ought to be

taught by preference, and, where possible each school should have its experimental garden subsidised by the State.

7) Last but not least, Native Education ought to give a prominent place to the religious and moral element, these being of the utmost importance in the uplifting of a race in which character is weak and whose religion is still unrelated to morality.

I do not attempt to deal here with the problem of Higher, Normal and University education for the Natives. These also ought not to be mere servile imitations of White methods, but so organised as to answer to the special requirements of the Natives, and I would refer the reader to the Report of the Bloemfontein Conference on this point ; all those who have taken the trouble to study this question will agree that such higher education ought to be liberally offered to the Black race. The more qualified physicians, advocates, or ministers can be trained, the more numerous will be the élite which, sooner or later, must take the lead in the development of the race. Is it not in the interest of all that superstition should disappear, that hygiene should be taught, that justice should be administered irrespective of colour, and that Christian morality should be preached ? Natives are ready to pay for these higher qualifications. I do not see any reason why they should be prevented from acquiring them, if their intellect be equal to the task.

Since this book was first published, all the African Colonies have been visited by a Commission of educational experts under the auspices of the Phelps-Stokes Fund and the Foreign Missionary Societies of America and Europe, and the results of this inquiry have been published in the two epoch-making reports of Dr. Th. Jesse Jones on *Education in Africa.* It is unnecessary to state how entirely the author of these lines agrees with the spirit which animates these reports and with the recommendations they contain. The British Government has also issued a memorandum on its educational policy which is inspired by the same conviction that Native Education must adapt itself entirely to Native life, and which recommends the use of the vernaculars as of the highest importance. A new era seems to have set in, in which the problem of Native Education is being faced more seriously than ever before, and an attempt is being made to solve it according to the best interests of the Africans. Let us hope that the Africans themselves will understand that the kind of mental development at which such a course of instruction aims, in accordance with their character, their traditions and their actual wants, is infinitely preferable for them to that servile imitation of the Whites which is still the aspiration of some amongst them.

CONCLUSION

I have reached the end of my study of the Life of a South African tribe in its principal manifestations, social, mental and spiritual. In order to write a complete anthropological monograph, I ought to have also dealt at length with the physical features of the Thongas. This would have led me too far. However I have taken a few anthropometric measurements, which have been published in the *Bulletin de la Société neuchâteloise de Géographie* of 1917, together with an explanation kindly written by Dr. E. Pittard of Geneva, whose competency in this domain is well-known. I now come to my conclusion. The aim of this book being twofold, scientific and practical, I shall try in these final pages to answer two great questions, one appertaining to Science : How far can the present-day South Africans be described as Primitives? the other, of greater practical importance : How far can the South African tribe withstand the new condition of things brought about by twentieth-century civilisation?

CONCLUSION

I. *How far can the present-day South African Bantus be described as Primitives ?*

One often hears of Primitive Humanity. Do the South African tribes belong to it? This is a very difficult question to answer, as we do not know exactly what Primitive Humanity was and what the evolution of these tribes has been. In the absence of any ancient written record, of any remains of an ancient stone civilisation, we can only make conjectures. But these are based on three sets of facts : Native traditions (to which, however, we must always apply severe criticism), traces of an old and obsolete past actually found in the language or in the rites, and comparison with early civilisations now discovered in palaeolithic settlements, or apparent on the ancient Egyptian monuments, etc. I do not claim to have obtained positive evidence on all points, and I shall leave a good number of interrogation marks in the course of this attempt. We know, however, that Science proceeds by successive approximations. I submit my table of the development of civilisation in the South African tribe as a hypothesis, open to any amendment which further discoveries may suggest.

I hesitated before writing anything about the *first period*. A number of Native traditions declare that, at a remote period, their forefathers had no knowledge of *fire*, (I. p. 24, II. p. 33). According to some of my Pedi informants, fire would be of relatively recent origin in certain clans. We cannot, however, believe that fire was ever absolutely absent, seeing that the cave dwellers of the Mousterian age, at the end of the glacial period, knew of it, as is attested by the fire-places found everywhere in the Mousterian deposits. It is probable that the first ancestors of the Thongas lived on roots and fruits, having but very simple weapons, and scarcely any clothing. This condition of things may have prevailed long before the Bantu stock was formed. The race perhaps passed through the totemic phase, which is still to be found amongst more primitive races (I. p. 335), and has left some traces amongst the Thongas up to this day. Mother-right, the traces of which are so clear, was probably the family system of those times, of which we know nothing definite. What was this system? It is impossible to say, and the only feature of which we are sure is that female descent prevailed during that period. Funeral rites probably existed, as they are met with in Mousterian burial-places, and they imply, as previously shown, a belief in

Ancestrolatry. Who knows if the idea of an All-Father, which is almost universal in primitive humanity, was not already in existence? The idea of the divine, in one form or another, would seem to have been one of the earliest conceptions of the human mind. Its appearance in the dim consciousness of this ancient being from whom we are descended was perhaps the signal of his attainment of a true humanity. But this is speculation, and I do not wish here to leave the solid ground of Science.

In a *second period*, the beginning of which it is impossible to fix and which I consequently separate from the first by dots, in the table, animals are domesticated, the goat probably first. Agriculture sets in. The soil is tilled with wooden hoes. Male descent supplants female descent and the patriarchate becomes the family system ; its further development leads to the formation of the clan, an enlarged patriarchal family. I conjecture that it is at this stage that the Bantu stock was founded (1). The language was probably the Ur-Bantu, and it is very interesting to reconstitute its main elements, grammatical features, and vocabulary, by a comparison with the present Bantu dialects. Things called by the same word in all existing dialects were probably in existence at that period (2). I imagine that the physiological taboos were already

(1) As regards the origin of the great Bantu family, I will only briefly mention the very interesting *theory of the cycles of civilisation*, advanced by some modern anthropologists. According to some scientists, there have been ten successive cycles in the evolution of mankind. First, the Tasmanian cycle, now extinct ; secondly, the cycle of the Boomerang, still existing in Southern Australia; third, the cycle of Totem, and fourth, the cycle of the Masks, both of which are met with to-day in North-Western Australia and in New Guinea. The fifth cycle is the cycle of the Bow, which succeeded to III and IV all over Melanesia and was superseded later by cycle VI, called Maleo-Polynesian. The latter forms the transition between the primitive cycles, I—VI and those of the semi-civilised and civilised peoples, i. e. the Hindu, the Chinese, the Semitico-musulman, and the European. According to this theory, Africa was invaded first by populations belonging to the three first cycles, which have been preserved down to the present day in the tribes of the Bushmen and Pigmees. A second invasion, composed of representatives of cycles IV and V, and called the Nigritian invasion, later on overran the greater part of the Continent, from Madagascar up to the Senegal. The Sudanese Negroes are the remnants of these Nigritians. Later still a third invasion, called Protohamitic, brought to Africa elements belonging to cycle III, which had undergone a considerable evolution, and to cycle VI. These have mixed with the Nigritians and this fusion has given birth to the Bantus. Opinions vary as regards the origin of the Bantu language, some believing that these Protohamitic invaders brought it with them, whilst others think that the Ur-Bantu resulted from the fusion of the Nigritian language with the language of the Protohamics. These theories are the result of a minute comparative study of the customs, languages, implements and beliefs of all fractions of primitive humanity ; they do not pretend to be more than a hypothesis, but they will undoubtedly be useful to Science as such, and further study will show how far they can be adopted.

(2) This argument ought not, however, to be pushed too far. I have been able to ascertain that the fowl was unknown amongst the Pedi clans of the Northern

624

then in force, as they are found almost identical amongst Semitic peoples, as shown in Leviticus. The hierarchy must have soon followed the institution of patriarchism, and of the clan. Witchcraft probably existed ; it must have been a belief of primitive humanity, as it is still present in a very similar form amongst peasants and uncultured people in civilised lands. We have the right to suppose also that astragalomancy was practised. Some features of the Thonga language show that mythological conceptions then prevailed which seem to have almost entirely disappeared at the present time (I. p. 36, II. p. 306). This period must have lasted for tens, perhaps hundreds of centuries, until the South African tribes, after endless migrations, reached their present abode, probably pushing the early occupants towards the South ; at the end of the XVth century we find the Thonga tribe located near Delagoa Bay (1).

The third period is inaugurated by the invasion by the clans mentioned in our Introduction. White men appear, trade begins, stuffs are adopted by women, the men retaining their mbaya. Iron is introduced both by these invaders and by the White whale-fishers and traders. Agriculture undergoes a new development ; so also do military tactics,

---

Transvaal, in the beginning of the XVIIIth century, having been introduced by the Ma-Lemba about 1750. In spite of this, the Pedis call it *khuɡu*, the same word as *ḷuku* in Thonga, Ur-Bantu *ku ṭu*. The name of the thing may have been introduced at the same time as the thing itself, and incorporated by undergoing the phonetic permutations required by the dialect (Compare *Folklore*, Sept. 1908, The Balemba).

(1) The *Lourenço Marques Guardian*, in a very favourable review of Vol. I (Oct. 7, 1912), expresses the regret that I have not dwelt at greater length on the first origin and migrations of the Thonga tribe. The writer thinks that this was formerly a much larger tribe "the basic element in the Hamitic invasion of the coastal region." As far as I know, no document exists on which evidence on such questions could be based. The Portuguese chronicles of the XVIth and XVIIth centuries describe a state of things which is quite modern compared with the first Bantu invasion of South Africa, that of the *Zindj*, to which Masoudi's "Golden Meadows" makes an allusion, A. D. 943. When the Portuguese travellers reached the shore of Delagoa Bay, the stream of migration had already taken an Eastern or North-Eastern direction (I. p. 23). — As regards inferences drawn from the wide-spread term *Thonga* (Ronga, Tonga), I think they have very little value ; this word probably means "people of the East," as *Kalanga* means people of the North. It is applied by Natives to those tribes which dwell eastwards of them, whatever their origin may be. It is a geographical designation, like the term Orientals, and discloses nothing as regards the ethnological features of the tribes to which it is applied. In fact, as regards language, customs, folklore, there is much less affinity between our Thongas, the Tongas of Inhambane, and the Tongas of Zambesi than between them and the Zulus.

We must be content to remain ignorant of facts as to which there exists no reliable record.

THE EVOLUTION OF

	Costume	Implements Weapons	Food	Trade	State	Family system
1st Period (Pre-Bantu)	*Men.* Mbaya? *Women.* Skins?	Wooden clubs?	Fruits and roots.	?	Nomadic.	Female descent.
2d Period Ur-Bantu till 1500	id.	Pottery. Basket work. Wooden hoes? Bows? Wooden pillow.	Goat. Millet, Pumpkins. Game caught in traps.	Exchange of wares for produce.	Agricultural.	Male descent.
3d Period 1500 -1820	*Men :* Mbaya. *Women :* Skirts of cloth.	Pottery. Basket work. Iron hoes and assagais. Bows.	Goat. Sheep? Ox? Millet. Sorghum? Beans?	Godji (p. 142). *Sales :* Amber, Ivory, Skins, etc. *Purchases :* Stuff, Beads, Copper, Iron.	id.	Patriarchate. Lobolo. Polygamy.
4th Period 1820-1910	*Men :* Zulu belt. *Women :* Skirts. Keimao.	id. Guns. Bows disappear.	id. Maize, Peas, Bananas, Mangoes, etc.	*S.* Mafureira, India-rubber, Skins. Commercial expeditions. Introduction of European money.	Agricultural. Yearly military expeditions in Gaza.	id. Decrease of Polygamy.
1910	Increase of European dress.	Increase of European implements. Decrease in Native arts and crafts.	id. European food. Alcohol.	Decrease of Native trade.	Work in towns.	id. Family life injured by the long absence of men.

the Natives now possessing better weapons. Decided progress has certainly taken place all round, the invading population being superior in civilisation to the old one. The Thonga language is definitely formed with its six dialects. Folklore is enriched by the contributions of all the various clans. Ancestrolatry still reigns in the religious beliefs, with a relatively clear notion of Heaven and of an All-Father. This change was gradual until 1820.

THE THONGA TRIBE

Tribal system	Military system	Language	Folklore	Religion	Taboo	Magic
Totemism ?	?	?	?	Ancestrolatry. All-Father ?	Sympath-etic.	?
Clan.	?	Ur-Bantu ? Sex-denoting suffixes. 11 Classes of Nouns. Formation of Thonga.	Mythological conceptions. Tales.	Ancestrolatry. All-Father.	Physiolog-ical. Hierarchic. Agri-cultural.	Witchcraft. Astragalo-mancy.
Invasion of neighbouring clans.	Lineal formation. Skirmishes.	Thonga. 8 Classes of Nouns. Six dialects.	Decrease of Mythology. Rich folklore.	Ancestrolatry. Clearer notion. of Tilo, All-Father.	id.	id.
Formation and disappear-ance of military kingdoms. Dual Control. (I. p. 542).	Zulu circular formation. Cruel wars.	Progress of Ronga dialect. Adoption of European expressions (Portuguese Dutch and English).	Addition of Asiatic and Portuguese elements.	Ancestrolatry. Tilo concep-tion less clear. Christianity. Islam. Possessions.	id. Military.	id. Possessions.
Authority of chiefs decreases. Increase of the number of detribalised Natives.	Decrease of military and political spirit.	id.	id.	id. Progress of Christianity.	Severity. of taboos decreases.	id.

Fourth period. At this time a new period begins, owing to the profound disturbance caused by the invasion of the Ngoni army under Manukosi. The men's costume changes. The clans are amalgamated under the Zulu conqueror. The military spirit increases. War, accompanied by bloodshed and all the Zulu war-panoply, replaces the skirmishes of former times. In Gazaland the year is divided into two halves, one for agricultural labour, the other for the military plundering

627

expeditions organised by the Ngoni kings. Foreign elements increase in number and power. Asiatic and Portuguese influences begin to be felt. A considerable Native trade develops in Lourenço Marques. The Ronga clans dwelling near the town acquire more influence. This brings us up to the present time, which I need not describe more fully.

In 1920, we see European civilisation invading the whole territory of the tribe, by leaps and bounds, and the changes, which in previous decades had been slow, becoming rapid and profound. The tribe loses its coherence more and more ; the authority of the chief decreases and that of the White Commissioner increases. Taboos and ancestor-gods no longer receive much credence ; Islam makes some recruits, owing to intermarriage, and Christianity pushes forward its Missions. The few indications given in this part of the table show the trend of evolution at the present time.

This outline of the development of the tribe — an outline which is submitted, I repeat, with the utmost reserve, — does not confirm the opinion generally held in former times regarding Black tribes, i. e., that they are in a state of utter degeneracy. On the contrary, *a slow progress* may be observed, generally due to outside influences, notwithstanding the fact of long industrial stagnation ; this progress has been so marked in agriculture, in the family and in the social system, that it is no longer possible to describe the Bantus as absolute Primitives. They would be more fittingly spoken of as Semi-Primitives. On the other hand, there seems to have been almost complete *immobility* in the religious domain, even a process of degeneration, if the old monotheistic idea has really become less clearly defined in the last century. Folklore has been enriched, but, as a whole, the mental and spiritual life has evolved very little. Of course I do not mention the quite modern changes brought about by missionary enterprise and Islam propaganda.

II. *How far can the South African Tribe withstand the new condition of things brought about by Twentieth-Century Civilisation ?*

There have been more changes in the South African tribe during the last fifty years than during the fifty or five hundred preceding centuries, and this process of transformation is bound to continue at a geometrical rate of progression during the fifty years to come. Taking into consideration for a moment the real and permanent interests of the Native, let us ask to what probable goal this transformation is leading him. I leave on one side for the present the influence of missionary enterprise.

Civilisation has certainly brought some *blessings* to the tribe, and I have carefully and impartially noted these ; the disappearance of deadly famines, owing to the development of trade ; better clothing (this is a mixed blessing) ; better seeds and agricultural implements (plough) ; the possibility of earning money ; the incentive to work in order to pay taxes, (Natives would certainly not call this a blessing!) ; the decrease of polygamy ; and the broadening of ideas, consequent on travelling and work in towns.

But the *curses* of civilisation far exceed its blessings for the South African Native : he has lost more through it than he has gained. Amongst them are the loss of political interest and responsibility (I. p. 543) ; the loss of hierarchic respect for the chiefs and elder brothers; the loss of personal dignity ; in addition may be noticed a decrease of religious faith and respect for taboos.

Further, the vices of Civilisation have found a lamentably ready welcome on the part of these Primitives : alcoholism of a degraded type (on the Coast), onanism, sodomy (in the Compounds), looseness of morals, — and these have caused new and very dangerous diseases which are now quickly spreading amongst them : alcoholic cachexy, syphilis, a great increase of consumption, due to the work in towns, not to speak of the criminal instincts which have developed under these influences (II. p. 610), murder, and rape (hence the Black peril, unknown in the primitive state). The tribe has lost its standards and traditions and moral and physical results have quickly followed.

To help it in the fight against these new and terrible foes, the Black race fortunately possesses considerable physical strength and great fertility. But these may not necessarily last for ever. They are capable of being lost. We find the Mpongwe tribe, in French Congo, fast disappearing as a result of a longer contact with the debasing influence of the Whites; the birth-rate is reduced to almost nothing and this formerly large tribe will probably die out in the course of one or two generations.

I cannot conceal the fact that I consider the situation of the South African tribe, under present conditions, as very serious. If these influences are not checked, I believe that the extinction of the race is possible in the long run, and I think every thoughtful observer will come to the same conclusion (1). Ought not steps to be taken by the Government to check the progress of the evil? Would not a policy of segregation for instance, be desirable ? Or, would it not be in the interest of the Natives to remove them to tropical Africa, leaving South Africa to the White man? These questions have been discussed at length in South African papers, and I have nothing to say about them except that such steps seem to be absolutely impracticable. I am convinced that the only remedy for these deadly perils is the formation, in the Black tribe, of a strong moral character, accompanied by sufficient enlightment of mind to enable the Native himself to perceive the danger, and to overcome it.

*

* *

Various ways have been suggested to attain this goal. Leaving aside the eugenic effort suggested by D. Kidd, in his Kafir Socialism, we may mention what is called the *Gospel of Work* which some people have recommended. Let the Natives be forced to work with their hands, and their character will soon improve! There is much truth in this theory, and I believe regular manual work is a blessing for the Blacks as it is for any other race. Let us remark however that this "Gospel" is not always preached with the sole idea of benefiting the Black race. Moreover, even if it were possible to enforce labour on the South African Bantus, in this age of liberty, what would be the ultimate result? Would it really transform them? As soon as they could rid themselves of the obligation, they would run away and become worse than before. Labour is a great educator, provided the worker is in agreement with the law of labour, and this agreement can only be obtained when the heart of the savage is changed by a power of another kind.

*

* *

In the conclusion to Volume I, I have myself advocated the grant to the Native of certain political rights which were after all very modest ;

(1) These remarks apply especially to the Thonga tribe. The situation of the Zulu and Sutho tribes is better, in as much as the sale of intoxicants is prohibited amongst them. However, many of the dangers here described threaten those tribes also.

this proposal was not made with the intention of taking part in South African politics (which I am quite willing to leave to those whose duty it is to attend to them), but as a means of protecting the Native mind against degeneration, and I believe such an enactment might help to mould the character of the race, as no human being can make any true moral progress if he has no responsibility. This would not, however, be sufficient in itself, and the lowering of character, produced by present-day influences, would even render the enfranchisement of the Natives dangerous.

*

*   *

My conclusion is that the only means of salvation for the South African tribe is to be found in a regeneration achieved by Christianity, while education should, at the same time, provide the enlightenment of mind which is also a primary necessity. My readers will do me the justice to acknowledge that I have not often alluded to the great work of Christianisation in which I am engaged. I am however a missionary, and as such, I have a faith and I entertain a hope. May I be allowed to express it in a few words at the close of this study?

I am convinced that Christianity is the only true solution of the problem ; not merely a new set of rites which should take the place of the old animistic rites, but a *spiritual Christianity*, combining in perfect harmony religious belief and moral duty, accepted by the Bantu soul, — that soul which is eminently religious, — and leading the weak and carnal Bantu savage to the heights of the Christian ideal, thus victoriously replacing the non-moral religion and the non-religious morality of the Native.

Christianity, *the Religion of sanctity*, affords the only true satisfaction to that aspiration for purity so conspicuous in Bantu rites. Science will soon dispel all the superstitious dread of taboos. Let these imaginary fears be replaced by the fear of moral wrong, let sin become for the Christianised Native the real, the true, taboo, and a sound life will then be possible.

Christianity, the Religion of conversion, *regeneration*, supernatural transformation, will bring within the reach of the Native a power from above to deliver him and save him. Magical conceptions are doomed to die before long in the light of Science ; the absurdity of the axioms of primitive humanity will soon be perceived. But the faith in an all

631

powerful Father will free the savage from the fear of spirits and open his heart to the holy influence of the teachings of Christ.

Christianity, *the Religion of love*, love between individuals, and love between the races, will regulate the relations between Whites and Blacks, who are both indispensable to the cultivation and full utilisation of the marvellous riches of South Africa, will dispel race hatred, and promote the helpful collaboration of Africanders and Africans.

*

* *

But are the Bantus capable of accepting such a lofty and spiritual religion? I would answer : "Yes." Their intellect can understand the Gospel of "the Father who is in Heaven," as they already possess the rudiments of this central teaching of Christianity in the beliefs of Ancestrolatry, and in their conceptions of Heaven. That their heart is able to grasp it by faith — the only condition of entrance into the kingdom of God — is proved by a thousand instances. I fully recognise that many, perhaps most of the Christianised Natives, have not attained to the heights of moral and religious life, that their conduct is often in strange contrast with their profession. "Mission Kafirs" are not in very good repute. But I have seen many, in the humble circumstances of kraal life, who have been thoroughly transformed, women who have displayed wonderful qualities of sweetness and perseverance, and men whose character has become firm and strong, full of love and disinterestedness ; I know self-denying, consecrated, even pastoral souls amongst them, who are by no means inferior to European Christians, and I have sometimes had a vision of the South African tribe, less hampered by social and worldly circumstances than ourselves, transformed by the powerful spiritual influence of the Gospel of Jesus Christ, approaching the Christian ideal as nearly, and perhaps more nearly than we do! This was a dream ; but the reality remains, the Bantu soul is capable of regeneration as well as the European.

*

* *

Therefore let all the friends of the South African tribe work for its salvation. This is a sacred duty ; according to a great law of the moral world, if the superior race does not work for the moral betterment of the inferior, the inferior causes the superior to degenerate.

So let the Christian Church increase its Missions, let the Government multiply the schools. Let the Native Commissioner, the mistress of the house, the storekeeper, the Compound Manager, instead of treating the Black man with contempt, remember that he is a moral being, and must become more and more so through their influence. Let the educated Natives also be aware of their immense responsibility towards their tribe in this respect. Native industry may disappear, the tribal life come to an end, the old restraints fall away ; something better will take their places. Bantu collectivism is dying out. In its stead Christianity will promote a healthy and progressive individualism and, under the new regime, the race will take its proper place in the South African Commonwealth. I see no other way in which it can escape destruction.

*

* *

The Africander population, formed by the amalgamation of some of the best stocks of the Aryan race, has certainly a great future in store for it. May it be blessed on the sunny shores and on the high lands of South Africa. May it enrich itself, and humanity, by bringing to light the marvellous mineral wealth hidden in the rocks of this ancient land. But if the expansion of the Africander race were obtained at the cost of the ruin of the former occupants of the country, it would be an immense pity and an undeniable blemish. For, however bright the future of the Africanders may be, Africa would no longer be Africa if there were no more Africans!

*

* *

May God preserve the Life of the South African Tribe!

633

POST SCRIPTUM.

Before laying down my pen, I have one more duty, a very agreeable duty, to perform. I would express my thankfulness to all those who kindly helped me in this work, to my colleagues, some of whom have given me valuable information, to the Council of the Swiss Romande Mission, which has always encouraged me in my study of Native life, and to the English friends who have kindly revised my manuscript. In this connection, I wish particularly to mention Miss G. Quin, co-editor of the *Student World*, who has taken great trouble to make it more adequate to the requirements of the English language. If the second edition shows any improvement over the first in this respect, it is entirely due to her. I wish also to thank Mr Clement Heaton, who designed the Thonga warrior on the cover, and Mr. P. Wavre, who drew the plans. I must not forget Professors H. Borle, J. Lecoultre and G. Attinger, who kindly translated the Latin notes.

I am grateful also to the professional anthropologists who have shown a kind appreciation of the first edition, and hope that the new material added in the second will prove equally useful to the cause of Science. But my greatest wish is that many South African citizens, by a perusal of these pages, may acquire a more exact knowledge of the Natives, that some prejudices may thus be destroyed, and some interest and sympathy aroused, and that in this way my book may ultimately help to create a better understanding between Whites and Blacks.

TABLE OF CONTENTS

OF VOLUME II

FOURTH PART

AGRICULTURAL AND INDUSTRIAL LIFE.

635

TABLE OF CONTENTS

SIXTH PART

RELIGIOUS LIFE AND SUPERSTITIONS.

TABLE OF CONTENTS

639

Table of Contents

LIST OF ILLUSTRATIONS

List of Illustrations

GENERAL ALPHABETICAL INDEX

and

Glossary of the Native terms most frequently used

in Vol. I & II

Library of the Mystic Arts

A LIBRARY OF ANCIENT AND MODERN CLASSICS

BARTON, R. F. Autobiographies of Three Pagans in the Philippines. intro. by Dr. Nancy Oestreich Lurie. ill. index bibliog. 320 pp. 5½″ x 8¼″ 62-19195. $7.50 ANTHROP
"It is difficult to realize that the people in these autobiographies, two men and a woman live on the same planet that we do. Head-hunting and spearing your enemy are everyday occurrences. Anyone who knows your kin is an enemy, unless he is your kin. It is the savage eye for an eye and tooth for a tooth of Biblical times, even though coming of the Americans has discouraged some of the practices. R. F. Barton was among the Ifugaos long enough to select three representatives of the tribe. In the autobiographies he gives their life history before marriage, including many of their ceremonies and customs. It is an interesting and informative anthropological study." — WICHITA EAGLE & BEACON

BERNHEIM, H. Hypnosis and Suggestion in Psychotherapy: The Nature and Uses of Hypnotism. intro. by Ernest R. Hilgard. index. 428 pp. 6⅛″ x 9¼″ 63-22664. $10.00 PSYCH
Hypnosis has had a checkered career over a period of centuries, going through cycle after cycle of general approval and total eclipse. The fate of this book indicates how fragile the reputation of hypnosis has been; written almost eighty years ago, and translated into English a few years later, it has always been acknowledged as a great classic. Yet it has been out of print for some seventy years. It was not obsolete; nor was it suppressed. It has simply been neglected — as has hypnotism itself. It was the Second World War that reintroduced hypnosis in psychotherapy, and the widespread contemporary interest dates from that time. Today its potential is recognized by practically all medical societies over the world, and courses in hypnotism are appearing in medical school curricula and in training programs for psychiatric residents. Numerous psychologists are also turning to hypnosis as a fertile field for research and therapy.

BULLOUGH, Vern L. The History of Prostitution. index. 320 pp. 6⅛″ x 9¼″ 64-16619. $7.50 HIST
Prostitution, like the weather, has often been talked about, but very rarely has any scholar bothered to do any research on the topic. Few serious studies on prostitution have been undertaken by social scientists over the past fifty years. Although an occasional sociologist, psychologist, psychiatrist, or anthropologist has concerned himself, the historian has totally neglected the subject. As a result this book is the first attempt at a serious history of prostitution in English in this century.
The author, Dr. Vern L. Bullough, is a historian who has specialized in the history of medicine and science. He has published numerous articles, primarily on medical history, in various learned journals. He was assisted in his researches by his wife, Bonnie L. Bullough.

COOMARASWAMY, Ananda Kentish. Buddha and the Gospel of Buddhism. intro. by John C. Wilson. ill. index. bibliog. glossary. 370 pp. 6⅛″ x 9¼″ 64-16160. $10.00 REL
A classic introduction to Buddhism, Coomaraswamy's book was originally published in England in 1916. It was reprinted without change in 1927, and it is now finally available in its original form in an American edition. The author was revered both in the East and the West for his unique contributions to art

and philosophy as well as religion. An ardent Indian nationalist, his life work became the preservation of India's heritage and the monumental task of teaching the West to respect and revere the great civilization of India.

When Coomaraswamy died, Aldous Huxley spoke of his "unique importance as a mediator between East and West."

The author was fond of calling himself a traditionalist and often emphasized the virtues of orthodoxy. He was always suspicious of the Western fashionable interest in Buddhism and frequently spoke with considerable irony of the contemporary offbeat Zen enthusiasts. "The suspicious popularity of 'Buddhism' in Europe," he wrote in 1938, "has rested upon a very thorough misunderstanding of what Buddhism really means. The essential doctrines of Buddhism, like those of all orthodox relgions, are in radical opposition to our modern individualism."

The book continues to be a solid exposition of Buddhistic thought and its reissue should be timely in view of current rapprochment between the West and Eastern religious systems. Some twenty plates add interest and value.—VIRGINIA KIRKUS SERVICE.

FEILDING, Everard. Sittings with Eusapia Palladino and other Studies. intro. by E. J. Dingwall. 324 pp. 6⅛″ x 9¼″ 63-18682. $10.00 PARAPSYCH

"The author, well known as an objective observer of psychical phenomena, presents primarily a detailed report of 13 seances with the noted Italian medium of the 20th Century. There are included accounts of other mediums and of the stigmata of a French abbe. Facts are given; conclusions are left for the reader." — JOURNAL OF THE AMERICAN MEDICAL ASSOCIATION

"William James deplored the cheating and the vulgarity connected with the mediumship of Eusapia Palladino, but he believed that there was a residuum of phenomena in her performances which could not be explained. So did Everard Feilding of the Society for Psychic Research. He put her through the most rigid tests possible early in this century and concluded that she possessed some inexplicable power which caused tables to levitate, bells to ring, and lights to flash. In this most interesting collection of Feilding's writings we find that although he was a serious researcher, he always retained a sense of humor and a healthy skepticism. Eric Dingwall, who was his friend, has contributed a witty and appreciative introduction which reinforces the impression one gets from these papers that Feilding was a "most acute and well-balanced investigator" of ESP. Recommended for all libraries interested in this field of research." — LIBRARY JOURNAL

GUIGNEBERT, Charles. Jesus fwd. by Joel Carmichael. index. bibliog. xv + 560 pp. 6⅛″ x 9¼″ 56-7837. $10.00 REL

This historical study of the life of Jesus and the origins of Christianity has received the highest possible praise from biblical scholars of the status of Niebuhr, Barth and Pfeiffer. Its author, Charles Guignebert, is generally considered one of the finest examples of European scholarship. He spent a lifetime of research into the genesis of all forms of religious belief; toward the end of his life he held the chair of the History of Christianity at the Sorbonne.

REINHOLD NIEBUHR: "The virtue of Professor Guignebert's venture lies in his comprehensive analysis of the scholarship of the past decades in this field. The specialists are acquainted with all the evidence which he analyzes. But there is no book of recent years which will give the interested layman a more comprehensive account of what has been written and said about the life of Jesus and a fairer estimate of conflicting evidence. Naturally the author has a position of his own to maintain, but the reader is permitted to see how he arrived at it, and with what cogency and plausibility he defends it against contrasting views."

ROBERT H. PFEIFFER: "Aside from Guignebert's JESUS, only Goguel's LIFE may be regarded as a serious attempt to write a critical and objective historical work.

Guignebert furnishes an excellent introduction to the subject, a reliable guide to beginners, and an informing manual for scholars. We need to be reminded again by Guignebert of the strict and sober discipline required of the true historian."

JAFFE, Aniela. Apparitions and Precognitions: A study from the Point of View of C. G. Jung's Analytical Psychology. intro. by C. G. Jung. index. 224 pp. 6⅛″ x 9¼″. 63-19744. $7.50   PSYCH
The author, well known for her valuable contributions to the literature of analytical psychology, was specifically selected by Dr. Jung to write this book. The book represents a psychological evaluation of more than 1500 personal accounts elicited in response to a series of articles by Dr. Jung, dealing with prophetic dreams, coincidences, premonitions, apparitions. The articles appeared in the popular Swiss magazine, *Schweizerische Beobachter,* and the astonishing response to it came from all social classes — farmers, workmen, tradesmen, office employees and various professions.
One of the notable things to come to light in Dr. Jaffe's book is the fact that among the Swiss, who are commonly regarded as stolid, unimaginative, rationalistic and materialistic, there are just as many ghost stories and strange tales as is likely to be found in any other land; bewitching, sorcery, magic spells, as practiced in the Middle Ages and remoter times have by no means died out, but presently flourish among the Swiss as rampantly as they did centuries ago.
The author leaves aside the questioner of ultimate truth; instead she tries to inquire into the psychological questions: Exactly who is it that sees a ghost? Under what psychic conditions does he see it? What does a ghost signify when examined for its content as a symbol?

KING, C. Daly. The States of Human Consciousness. fwd. by Roy Finch. index. v-xiii + 176 pp. 6⅛″ x 9¼″ 63-10385. $7.50   PSYCH
The crucial thesis of this book is that in addition to the forms of consciousness known to all human beings (Sleep and Waking) there exist two further forms not yet widely known (Awakeness and Objective Consciousness).
What led such an extremely skeptical man as Dr. King to accept the unorthodox idea that additional states of human consciousness are possible? There were four main lines of evidence which convinced him: These were: 1) the neurological and physiological teachings of the Guardjieff Institute; 2) his personal psychological experiments and experiences; 3) his historical studies of ancient civilizations; 4) his studies in behavioral patterns.

LEARY, Timothy; ALPERT, Richard; Metzner, Ralph. A Guide to Psychedelic Experience. 150 pp. 8″ x 9″ 64-19705. $5.00   PSYCH
During the past few years newspapers and magazines have poured out unrestrained criticism on the subject of psychedelic drugs. Meanwhile certain technical journals have simultaneously dealt out unrestrained praise. Whom are we to believe?
Perhaps the most objective evidence available on these important new drugs comes from recent studies made by four scientific research groups, which administered LSD and psilocybin to 462 persons — among them physicians, lawyers, writers, ministers, psychologists, artists, musicians, engineers and housewives. The percentage of these persons reporting it was a pleasant experience was 73%; the percentage reporting they wished to try it again was 82%; a total of 67% reported the experience brought them greater regard for other human beings; 67% felt a sense of relaxation and freedom from anxiety and tension; 65% felt it was of lasting benefit; 38% said it increased their interest in nature, art, music; and 64% felt the experience had changed their lives.
Drs. Leary, Alpert and Metzner have for years been among the most prominent names in the research of psychedelics. They were engaged in a program of experiments with the drugs at Harvard University, until sensational national

publicity, unfairly concentrating on student interest in the drugs, led to the suspension of the experiments. Since then, the authors have continued their work without academic auspices.

Like other scientists involved with psychedelic research. the authors maintain that the drug is only one component of the psychedelic session. Equally important is the mental and spiritual preparation, both before and in the course of taking the drug. The authors find no need to invent new mental and spiritual materials for this purpose. The great literature of meditation lends itself very well to this use. This particular guide uses preparation material from THE TIBETAN BOOK OF THE DEAD.

LEGMAN, G. The Horn Book; Studies in Erotic Folklore and Bibliography. index. bibliog. 565 pp. 6⅛" x 9¼" 63-19743. $12.50   REF

The author is probably the most learned and most controversial figure in the field of American folklore. He is also the principal living specialist in erotic folklore. A former bibliographer for the Kinsey Institute, he enjoys repute as a lecturer and as the editor of *Neurotica* magazine. He is also the author of *Love and Death: A Study in Censorship,* now in its second edition. In his present work, the author's intention is to give the real facts about erotic literature and folklore. Eloquently, he attacks the substitution of fakelore for folklore in the mass communications media of America today. After establishing the value of unfettered folk-art, Mr. Legman analyzes with penetrating psychological discernment the displacement of sexual symbolism in our society and makes a strong case for authentic, unexpurgated collections. He attacks the patently illogical and insensible idea that sex must be expunged — while allowing the sadistic programs, books and plays an uncriticized place in our society. Murder, torture, cannibalism freely appear in our mass media, while the healthy normality of sexual intercourse between man and woman is deprecated or silently omitted. And the author points a serious warning: "The substitution of allowed sadism for prohibited sexuality in folk literature and mass communications can only result in the most sinister abnormalization of the whole psychic structure of future generations."

The book's table of contents follows:

MARTIN, Eva. Reincarnation: The Ring of Return. index. bibliog. v-xi + 306 pp. 5½" x 8¼" 63-18492. $5.00   REL

The idea of reincarnation has always appealed powerfully to man's innate sense of justice, to his yearning for eternal progress. Yet, strangely enough, there are not many books to be found in English on the subject. Nor are any of them likely to be, as the present volume is, an anthology of the great writings on reincarnation.

"This first American edition of what is regarded as a standard work in its field, is comprehensive in that it covers the pre-Christian era, the early Christian era and other writings of the first five centuries. Miscellaneous sources are drawn upon and material from the first three decades of the Twentieth Century is also included. Almost exclusively, the author in her quotations, turns to the poets. Such a book as this, as the publisher remarks, 'whatever its shortcomings is not likely to become dull reading.' " — CHRISTIAN HERALD

PODMORE, Frank. From Mesmer to Christian Science: A Short History of Mental Healing; intro. By E. J. Dingwall. index. xxi + 306 pp. 6⅛" x 9¼" 63-21599. $10.00   PSYCH
"This short history of mental healing covers broadly and impressively just about everything from Mesmer to Christian Science. Certainly, spiritual healing has become an important part of our everyday life. In medicine there are psycho-analysts and an entire new school of therapy along with the use of hypnosis as an anesthesia; and in religion, not only Christian Science and New Thought, but many movements within the established churches and synagogues. More and more it brings into sharp focus the 'miraculous therapy' of Jesus. In these pages one follows the steady march of mental healing from quackery and chicanery to respectability, with something added." — *Dr. Daniel A. Poling,* CHRISTIAN HERALD

"Since the first appearance of this book in 1909, no publication has superseded Podmore's critical and detailed study. An outstanding member of the British Society for Psychical Research, he traced the subject from the hectic days of pre-Revolutionary Paris to the beginning of the 20th Century. Obsessed with the idea of fraud, the medical profession obstinately rejected all evidence of the validity of these investigations, abandoning the field to amateurs and fanatics. Eventually the phenomena which Mesmer attributed solely to a material fluid came to be explained as a purely spiritual process. The progeny of Mesmerism therefore include not only hypnotism and aspects of experimental psychology, but also Spiritualism, New Thought, and Mental Healing, of which Christian Science is most prominent. Recommended for most psychology collections." — LIBRARY JOURNAL

PRINCE, Walter Franklin. The Case of Patience Worth. intro. by John C. Wilson. 509 pp. 6⅛" x 9¼" 63-23268. $10.00   PARAPSYCH
The author, a renowned psychologist and a pioneer in scientific psychic research, regards the case of Patience Worth as one of the most fascinating and enigmatic psychic manifestations of all time. In the conclusion of his book, Dr. Prince states that he could offer no rational explanation to the riddle of Patience Worth, despite years of impartial scientific investigation.
Patience Worth identified herself as a spirit from 17th Century England and she communicated through a medium, Mrs. Pearl Curran, an unlettered Missouri housewife. Over a period of five years, Patience created and communicated through Mrs. Curran an enormous quantity of poetry and prose of astonishing quality. Her literary creations displayed original genius, enormous erudition, familiarity with classic literature and history, piercing wit and penetrating wisdom; in brief, creations which could not conceivably have come from the simple, unlettered Mrs. Curran, who had never been out of the Mid-West and who had managed to complete a grammar school education only after considerable difficulty.

ROSSMAN, Joseph. Industrial Creativity: The Psychology of the Inventor. intro. by Gardner Murphy. index. bibliog. 288 pp. 6⅛" x 9¼" 64-16161. $7.50   PSYCH
In this scholarly and painstaking study of the mental processes of creativity, Dr. Rossman, long associated with the U.S. Patent Office, presents many startling conclusions developed after a long and careful analysis of source material obtained from 700 active and important inventors. Dr. Rossman, a chemical engineer, a member of the bar practicing before both the U.S. Supreme Court and the Court of Customs and Patent Appeals, a famous patent attorney, and a doctor of psychology, is perhaps the only man who could have undertaken such a study.

Popular fantasy pictures the inventor as a wild-eyed, impractical dreamer. But the cumulative portrait that emerges in this book reveals an ability for keen analysis, a mind strikingly original and observant, an astonishing perseverance in the face of apparently insurmountable obstacles.

Dr. Rossman's book was first published primarily to help inventors understand all the implications of the inventive process. That was thirty years ago. Today it is published anew, with new material by Dr. Rossman. This time he addresses his book to all those interested in the nature of creativity. For those more specifically interested in scientific invention, there is a considerable body of original information.

SMITH, Susy. The Mediumship of Mrs. Leonard, photographs. bibliog. 256 pp. 6⅛" x 9¼" 64-17317. $7.50
PARAPSYCH

This is the first comprehensive study taking in the entire life work of Mrs. Leonard, the last of the great trance mediums of the golden age. She is now well into her eighties. This important new work is destined to endure as a classic in the search for psychic truth; it presents the strongest evidence ever obtained of the survival of the human spirit — of earthly memories abiding beyond the grave.

The scientific evidence in the case of Mrs. Leonard is the most documented in psychic history. No trance medium has ever been more thoroughly investigated and researched. Most of her career was spent not as a private medium but under the exclusive control of the Society of Psychical Research. The Society established a framework of painstaking supervision and kept exact records of everything said at Mrs. Leonard's sittings.

This book continues the series from University Books dealing with the great mediums. The two outstanding physical mediums, D. D. Home and Eusapia Palladino, are already represented. Of the three great trance mediums, Mrs. Piper was introduced in *William James On Psychic Research* and Helene Smith in Flournoy's *From India To The Planet Mars.* The third trance medium is Gladys Osborne Leonard.

APOCRYPHA. Introduction by Morton Enslin, Professor of Biblical Languages and Literature, St. Lawrence University. Bound in white and gold, 3-color slipcase. xv + 239 pp. 7¼" x 11" 62-12335. $15.00
REL

"In 1924 the Nonesuch edition of the Apocrypha appeared, limited to 1325 copies. This new edition is an almost exact facsimile of that very beautiful work, bound in a most attractive cover with stamped gilt design, and boxed. Most marked of its changes from the original, and one that enhances the value of the work considerably, is an Introduction by the editor of this Journal, Dr. Morton S. Enslin, who in brief, concise paragraphs provides excellent prefaces to the work as a whole and to each of the books individually. He places the Apocrypha in its proper context in biblical literature, indicates the inappropriateness of the name when applied to the books as a whole, and shows how it was that Luther split off these writings and placed them 'in the limbo between the Old Testament and the New.' The individual introductions serve to provide the backgrounds, probable datings, and general contents of each of the fourteen pieces. This is a valuable work for both the biblical scholar and the lover of fine books." — *J. Calvin Keene,* JOURNAL OF BIBLICAL LITERATURE

BIRREN, Faber. Color: A Survey in Words and Pictures: From Ancient Mysticism to Modern Science. ill. index. 250 pp. 7⅜" x 10½" 62-18889. $15.00
PSYCH

"This book is a compilation of information concerning color, from the physiology of the eye and theories of color vision to the ancients' belief in magical qualities of color, and even current theories of color and personality. The author has written several books on color and color psychology, particularly relating color to commercial purposes." — LIBRARY JOURNAL

"An introduction to the history of color, both ancient and modern, and to its

various uses. This book is highly recommended." — PSYCHIATRIC QUARTERLY
"All in all, an absorbing book in an uncrowded field, and one which does credit
to the author's erudition and intuition." — ST. LOUIS POST-DISPATCH

BIRREN, Faber. Color Psychology and Color Therapy: A Factual Study of the Influence of Color on
Human Life. intro. by Felix Morrow. ill. photogs. index. biblio. xv + 302 pp. 6⅛" x 9¼" 61-14266.
$7.50
PSYCH
"Faber Birren is a consultant on the use of color in industrial and other applications, and perhaps without peer in this field. The book, however, goes much
farther than the mere applications and their psychology. There is fascinating
detail from historical, medical, occult, physiological sources as well — fascinating
and documented... Recommended." — LIBRARY JOURNAL

THE BOOK OF THE DEAD: the Hieroglyphic Transcript of the Papyrus of ANI. tr. and intro. by
E. A. Wallis Budge. ill. index. appendixes. xiv + 704 pp. 6⅛" x 9¼" 60-12165. $12.50   REL
This is the collection of texts which the ancient Egyptian scribes composed for
the benefit of the dead. A book-length introduction by Sir Wallis Budge, late
Keeper of the Egyptian and Assyrian Antiquities in the British Museum, gives
us its history and theology. This is an exact reproduction of the famous Medici
Society edition of 1911 except that the original two volumes are here bound
as one.

BUCKE, Richard Maurice, M.D. Cosmic Consciousness; A Study in the Evolution of the Human Mind.
bibliog. xvii + 326 pp. 7¼" x 9¾" 61-11100. $5.95   PSYCH
One of the great classics of mystical experience, this work was first published in
1901. The author saw the emergence of a new faculty, the natural outgrowth of
our present level of consciousness to a level as far above it as it is above the
simple consciousness of animals. William James read the work when it appeared
and wrote to the author: "I believe that you have brought this kind of consciousness 'home' to the attention of students of human nature in a way so
definite and inescapable that it will be impossible henceforward to overlook it
or ignore it... But my total reaction on your book, my dear Sir, is that it is an
addition to psychology of first rate importance, and that you are a benefactor of
us all."

BUDGE, E. A. Wallis. Amulets and Talismans. ill. b/w 22 plates, 300 ill. index. xxxix + 543 pp.
6⅛" x 9¼" 61-7163. $10.00
REL/ARCHEOL
"This encyclopedic volume represents years of research and an extensive knowledge of ancient civilizations. The author, as teacher at Cambridge University
and curator of the British Museum, has accumulated a wealth of data dealing
with demonology, divination, astrology, numerology and the belief in the
prophylactic properties of the gems prevalent among the people of the ancient
civilizations of Sumer, Babylon, Persia, Egypt and others. The author throws
new light on many passages in early biblical writings which will give the student
of the Old Testament often a clearer meaning of the archaic sense of the text.
'Amulets and Talismans' is a reliable reference book of lasting value." — THE
LUTHERAN

BUDGE, E. A. Wallis. Osiris; the Egyptian Religion of Resurrection; 2 vs. bound in one; intro. by
Jane Harrison. ill. 14 b/w plates, 212 line cuts. index. appendix. xliii + 440 pp. 6⅛" x 9¼"
61-10531. $15.00
REL
"In this full-length study, Dr. Wallis Budge, the late Keeper of the Egyptian
and Assyrian Antiquities in the British Museum, interprets Osiris as a year-god
who dies and lives again. In contradistinction to Frazer, he dwells on the native
African origins of this ancient Egyptian cult and avoids the obvious parallels
with the Mid-Eastern gods Attis and Adonis... His work will be read with profit
and enjoyment by all students of comparative religion." — LIBRARY JOURNAL

CHANG, Garma C. C. The Teachings of Tibetan Yoga. intro. by John C. Wilson. 128 pp. 6⅛" x 9¼"
62-22082. $5.00   YOGA
"One has always to be careful with books claiming to bring to light the occult
tradition or the Tantric practices of the yogis in Tibet. Mostly they are based on
second-hand information embellished with a liberal coating of fancy and fiction.
But the works of Garma Chang are clearly not of this dubious variety. A scholar
in Chinese, he has practised the Tibetan Yoga under traditional Gurus in that
land of the Lamas and whatever he writes he does with a high sense of responsibility and imparts a genuine touch which only a person with direct acquaintance with the subject could give... A profound work to be read and re-read by
all serious students of Yoga." — *M. P. Pandit*, THE VEDANTA KESARI

DAVID-NEEL, Alexandra. Magic and Mystery in Tibet. intro. by Aaron Sussman. photogs. xiv + 320 pp.
6⅛" x 9¼" 56-13013. $7.50   OCCULT
"Precisely the person to explore Tibet... absolutely fearless. Her accounts of
Tibetan religious ceremonies and beliefs are the fullest and best we have." —
THE NEW YORKER

DINGWALL, Eric J. Some Human Oddities: Studies in the Queer, the Uncanny and the Fanatical.
ill. bibliog. appendixes. 198 pp. 6⅛" x 9¼" 62-14948. $6.00   PSYCH
DINGWALL, Eric J. Very Peculiar People: Portrait Studies in the Queer, the Abnormal, and the
Uncanny. ill. index. bibliog. appendixes. 224 pp. 6⅛" x 9¼" 62-14949. $6.00   PSYCH
"These reissues of two fascinating books, originally written in 1946 and 1951
respectively, will be welcomed by all lovers of true tales of the weird, strange
and abnormal. Here are stories, scholarly written and scientifically analyzed, of
visionary mystics like Emanuel Swedenborg, masochistic saints like St. Mary
Magdalene de Pazzi, flying friars like Joseph of Copertino, mediums
extraordinaires like D. D. Home and Eusapia Palladino, pornographers de luxe
like Hadrian Beverland, transvestites like James Allen, and many others."—M. D.
PUBLICATIONS
"Dr. Dingwall recounts some real-life stories that rival fiction for strangeness.
He views and interprets the lives of these queer folk through the eyes of a
psychic researcher — one of great note, indeed, and one with a sound academic
background. The author has combined his talents as historian, psychologist and
psychic researcher to produce a work for the scholarly with a taste for the
macabre." — MEDICAL JOURNAL OF AUSTRALIA

FLOURNOY, Theodore. From India to the Planet Mars. intro. and final chap. by C. T. K. Chari.
xxxvi + 469 pp. 5½" x 8½" 63-16228. $10.00   PARAPSYCH
Recent research into extra-sensory perception and the problems of survival and
reincarnation has given a new and decisive importance to this classic. The author,
who was professor of psychology at the University of Geneva, has consistently
received the highest praise for his critical and objective study of that remarkable medium, Helene Smith. Eulogistic estimates of his work have been
made even by such eminent scientists as F. W. H. Myers, William McDougall
and William James.

FOX, Oliver. Astral Projection: A Record of Out-of-the-Body Experiences. fwd. by John C. Wilson.
xiii + 160 pp. 5½" x 8½" 62-19195. $5.00   OCCULT
The noted psychic researcher, Dr. Hereward Carrington, reports in one of his
works: "The only detailed, scientific and first-hand account of a series of
conscious and voluntarily controlled astral projections which I have ever come
across is that by Mr. Oliver Fox, published in the *Occult Review* for 1920."
The articles were expanded into a book. This is its first publication in the
United States.

DATE DUE

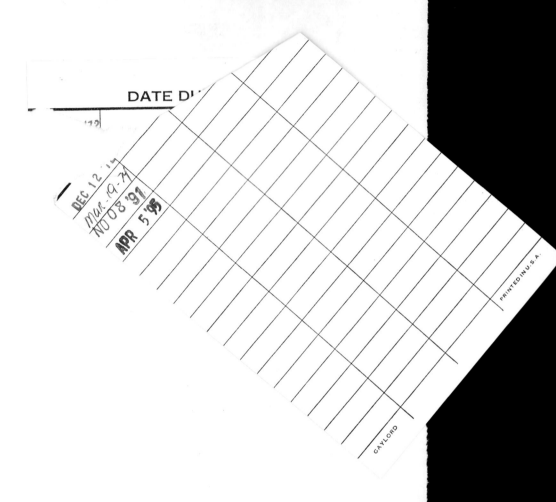